INTERIOR DESIGN

Handbook of Professional Practice

INTERIOR DESIGN®

Handbook of Professional Practice

CINDY COLEMAN, EDITOR-IN-CHIEF

McGraw-Hill

New York Chicago San Francisco Lisbon London

Madrid Mexico City Milan New Delhi San Juan

Seoul Singapore Sydney Toronto

Cataloging-in-Publication Data is on file with the Library of Congress

1234567890 CCW/CCW 0987654321

ISBN 0-07-136163-4

The sponsoring editor for this book was Scott Grillo, the editing
supervisor was Steven Melvin, and the production supervisor was
Sherri Souffrance.

The project consultant and packager was Judith R. Joseph,
Joseph Publishing Services, LLC.

The art director was Jospeh A. Guglietti, Joseph Guglietti Design.

It was set in Monotype Baskerville and Franklin Gothic by
Northeastern Graphic Services, Inc.

It was printed and bound by Courier/Westford.

McGraw-Hill books are available at special quantity discounts to use
as premiums and sales promotions, or for use in corporate training
programs. For more information, please write to the Director of
Special Sales, McGraw-Hill, 2 Penn Plaza, New York, NY 10121-2298.
Or contact your local bookstore.

This book is printed on recycled, acid-free paper containing a minimum
of 50% recycled, de-inked fiber.

"The future belongs to those who believe
in the beauty of their dreams."

–Eleanor Roosevelt

CONTENTS

PREFACE

Mark Strauss, Publisher, *Interior Design* Magazine

"This is the era of design."

The mass media proclaimed the above as the new millennium began. Academics and professionals have been holding conferences about it for a while now. Designers themselves have insisted on it all along. But what, exactly, does that statement mean? A proliferation of hip hotels and award-winning potato peelers do not an era make.

Because those of us who are part of the design profession are optimists, always on the lookout for how we can make our environment better, we're eager to claim that the twenty-first century is, at last, the era of design, the time when design—and designers—have come into their own and taken power as a cultural force. But do we agree about what design is? To be sure, each designer has a unique vision and works in a unique way. Yet, we're all part of one profession, and being a professional of any kind acknowledges that there is a common ground shared by its practitioners. Do designers know the coordinates and parameters of their profession? Do they realize what they must *learn* if they are to be successful designers in the twenty-first century? More important still, as professionals, do designers know what it means to *do* design?

"The New American Professional: Distinctive (towering) competence."

In *The Circle of Innovation*, Tom Peters refers to the New American Professional (NAP) as a "white collar professional . . . whose creativity/organization effectiveness is barely mentioned in the pages of business and management books." For designers, that phrase should strike a responsive chord. Pick up a best-selling business book and if it does, in fact, contain a reference to the work of designers, the reference is peripheral at best. This, in part, is why this book needed to be written. Whatever specialty designers work in, whether they're seasoned professionals or relatively new to their careers, they need a single written source of best practices and benchmarks for excellence. The identification of this need was the impetus behind the *Interior Design Handbook of Professional Practice*, a joint venture between McGraw-Hill and *Interior Design* magazine.

Traditionally, the question at the forefront of designers' minds has been "What do clients want?" The *Interior Design Handbook of Professional Practice* asks—and answers—another question altogether: "What do designers need?" This is a book not only for the present, but also for the future. It is prospective. It assumes that, yes, this *is* the era of design. And it becomes a tool for designers to be better prepared to sustain the profession of design and carry it forward.

"Work is not where you are. It's what you do."

These words, from the manager of the real estate program at a global consulting and technology firm, sum up how business leaders perceive the workplace as the twenty-first century begins. They apply to the designer's workplace as well. Although the client may be in Copenhagen and the designer in Maine, communication happens, design is implemented, work gets done. Once-narrow professional boundaries have stretched to span the circumference of the globe. In design, as in all slices of life, the globe—and, at the same time, the individual—is the place to be. It's where things are and where they'll stay for the foreseeable future.

Globalization is only one of the challenges grappling the design profession. It is wise to expect and prepare for challenges from all directions, including the economy, the physical and social environment, and academia. Today, design transcends aesthetics. Through access alone, designers are in a position to provide leadership in the realization of the New World.

Our daily life reflects an unsettled time. Groups of people, as well as organizations and nations, seek new leaders, with new definitions of leadership. Designers must step up and take their places in the front ranks. Individuals and organizations everywhere are in transition, adapting to an economy that looks much different than it did even a decade ago. In the old economy, products were, for the most part, tangible. Now, expectations shift continually. The new economy values new information and new perspectives, an intangible product, that seem and feel very different to us, that require us to experience new levels of perception, that put demands on our sensibilities. Now, and apparently forever, individuals and businesses want higher quality and better, faster performance from their environments, from service providers, from their tools and toys, from anyone, anyplace, or anything that affects the individual. On this competitive stage, high quality is still the goal but speed is gaining on it for first place.

"All depends on the quality of the conversations."

In the 1990s, the design profession became capital- rather than labor-intensive. A design project required plenty of tasks, to be sure, but many of them could be relegated to machines rather than delegated to people. To rationalize the expense of bringing new technology into their organizations, design firms expanded the scope of their services. Because technology abhors stasis, new business opportunities continued to appear. However, as services expanded, capital expenditures expanded as well. The pressure on design firms intensified.

Design firms that are successful and that will remain so have an inherent understanding of the way people actually live and work. These firms are committed to intellectual as well as socioeconomic diversity and inclusion. They collaborate with, or sometimes employ, psychologists, sociologists, anthropologists, management experts, and financial analysts in order to better serve their client's aims. This change is profound and represents a new view of the profession, one that is multidisciplinary and user-centered. Above all, this view acknowledges that design, and designers, have a social responsibility. This improved value system for the design industry insists that design projects create a problem-specific solution and at the same time balance all of the client's goals—financial, organizational, functional, cultural, and environmental.

Successful firms are also taking a nonlinear approach to the process of design. Effective design is measured by the final product, to be sure, but also by the degree to which the process of design encourages everyone it affects to collaborate and to share and integrate ideas. In an organization, this brings together people at all levels, with all types of responsibilities. In a family, it means all generations, with all types of needs. This new inclusiveness understands the rigors of the design process and the complications of daily life. It anticipates new demands and continual change inside and outside the organization, the family or the group.

"You do not merely want to be considered just the best of the best. You want to be considered the only ones who do what you do."

Evolution is swift. Designers must not simply change but maneuver to a position ahead of the field. To stay there, to keep moving toward the ever-shifting finish line, they need support, information, and new knowledge. The *Interior*

Design Handbook of Professional Practice describes the changes currently occurring in the design profession and industry. It suggests new, unique ways of thinking and working. Ideally, this book will become a catalyst for all designers who seek excellence in interior design practice. It will be an essential tool for those who have made a commitment to sustained excellence and continually move the profession forward.

Interior Design magazine is proud to bring together the best writers and thinkers in the field today whose mission, under editor-in-chief Cindy Coleman, was to define design for the new millennium in terms that will help professionals, academics, and students of interior design realize their commitment to professional excellence. The *Handbook* is designed, itself, to be used flexibly and repeatedly by professionals in search of new definitions, new strategies, and new benchmarks by which to measure success.

INTRODUCTION

Cindy Coleman, Editor-in-Chief

THIS BOOK HAS THE ANSWER. WHAT IS THE QUESTION?

Designers know how to give advice. They are also skilled at asking questions. According to our training and the tradition of our profession, our questions focus on our clients: Who is the client? What does the client want? Toward the end of the twentieth century, as information technology insinuated itself into the office, the home, and the space and time between the two, interior designers began to appreciate the importance of framing the question another way: What does the client need? No one argues that interior designers are skilled at asking the right questions and producing effective answers. But that's only half of the story, and it's the end of the story. The first half of the story, the point where it should begin, is with interior designers themselves. What do interior designers need? That is the question this book was designed to answer.

WHAT DO DESIGNERS NEED? KNOWLEDGE.

The next iterations of that question move the discussion in three principal directions. What kinds of knowledge do interior designers need to do their work? What knowledge does the interior design profession require to remain viable now and not merely relevant in the future, but a powerful force for social change? Ultimately, how can design practitioners and educators create a body of knowledge that is unique to interior design? How can this body of knowledge put us on a level playing field with other professions, sustain our profession over the long term, and give designers opportunities to influence new thinking in our industry, the academy, and society?

WHAT IS THE PROOF THAT IGNORANCE IS BLISS?

The impetus for this book comes from designers themselves. Many have come to realize, through powerful anecdotal and first- or second-hand experience, that the interior design profession as we have traditionally known it is at a crossroads. Crossroads, in fact, may be too mild a term for our situation. Some go so far as to compare the interior design profession to the population of spotted owls—beautiful and useful contributors who have come perilously close to extinction. Cultural and economic circumstances have helped bring us to this point, to be sure. But do we know how, and to what extent, we ourselves are responsible for our situation?

It is time, now, to stop and step back, take the long view of the present and make intelligent decisions about our future. What future is there for interior designers? What is the future of our profession? If we want to create our own future, on our own terms, we must be willing to take the steps necessary to make sure that we do, in fact, have a future.

How often, in the context of a design assignment, have we felt it our responsibility to say to the client, "If you don't take the time and resources to do it right, when will you take the time and resources to do it over?" But now we're not asking the question of a client. We're asking the question of our profession and ourselves.

WHY THIS QUESTION AND THIS ANSWER, AND WHY NOW?

This book was developed as if it were a design assignment. First, we defined our mission: To give interior designers the knowledge and tools they need to shape and sustain our profession and the environment where human beings live and work.

Having chosen to accept this ambitious assignment, we gathered a team of six advisors: Frank Duffy, Neil Frankel, Ed Friedrichs, Linda Keane, Eva Maddox, and Mayer Rus. The insights of this group give the book a perspective that is as broad as it is deep, encompassing design theory and education, global professional practice and the experiences of design firms large and small. The group's members are professionals whose work includes seminal accomplishments in the recent history of design. Who better than they to show us our way to the future? These respected experts led us to others—the authors whose contributions make up this book.

WHERE DO WE BEGIN?

Just as we all periodically take an inventory of our work, living spaces, and lives, this book begins with a look at designers themselves. We assess who we are as a group and where we are in the history of our profession, which is roughly 100 years old. We also compare interior designers with other professionals. Do designers have an education that matches their ambition? Do they have the legal and regulatory support they require to do their work? Do the quality of their work and the ethical standards of their profession give them that coveted intangible that can drive a career—respect?

During the last decade of the twentieth century, social and economic changes were swift, profound, and permanent. Many designers succumbed to the tyranny of speed, only to discover that, in their haste, they had spent time and resources and progressed nowhere. Others battled to protect the designer's turf, only to find that management consultants and other business professionals had co-opted design principles for themselves, combined them with twenty-first-century management strategies, and are using them to win the war. In the second part of this book, best-practice examples show designers how to be more strategic in their methods, using information technology, financial management, marketing and human resources skills, and team dynamics to power the practice of interior design.

WHERE IS THE HEART OF IT?

The heart of this book is interior design itself. In Part Three, the authors show strategy in action, presenting works that have become benchmarks of interior design for the ways in which they address design strategy and research, sustainability, and global and specialty practices. This part also describes the legal environment and legislation that affect interior designers in the United States. Following the dictum that power isn't something that's conferred, it's something that's taken, American designers who choose to become involved in legislative affairs will grant themselves the power to affect the profession of interior design for decades to come.

Part Four focuses on the designer's scope of services. Narratives from a varied group of designers describe their individual methods of approaching the process of design. These descriptions address prelease services, positioning and programming, schematic design, design development, and contract documentation and administration. Part Five focuses on the management process and delineates the criteria for a successful design project, showing designers effective ways to manage relationships with the in-house design team, consultants, and clients.

WHAT IS AT RISK?

During the French Revolution executions were popular public affairs, and all of Paris was agog over the mind-numbing, heart-stopping efficiency of a new and improved model of the guillotine, a beheading device that consisted of two 14-foot posts from which an 88-pound diagonal metal blade, when its support mechanism was released by the executioner, dropped at the rate of 21 feet per second.

From the aristocrats' point of view, one of the heroes of the Revolution was the Scarlet Pimpernel, who formed a secret society dedicated to rescuing their class from the guillotine.

One of the Pimpernel's henchmen, a doctor, was led to the guillotine nevertheless. He valiantly placed his head in the notch above the basket and waited for the blade to fall. The executioner lifted the lever of the support mechanism but the blade stayed in place. "It is a sign!" the public shouted. "The doctor has done no harm. He is meant to be free!" The doctor raised his head, was whisked onto a waiting horse by the Pimpernel and sped to safety.

Another Pimpernel henchman, a lawyer, was next in line for the blade. He lowered his head. The executioner raised the mechanism. Again the same thing happened. Nothing. "There is nothing to negotiate," cried the populace. "The malfunctioning blade has cast doubt on his guilt!" The lawyer, too, was whisked to safety.

Next in line was Marie Antoinette, Queen of France, wife of King Louis XVI and a well-known designer in the land. One of her famous works was a farmhouse in the gardens of Versailles, where she liked to dress up as a milkmaid and pretend that she was a simple peasant. Marie ascended to the guillotine and put her head in position for its destiny. Again the executioner raised the lever and again nothing happened. Marie, willing to atone for an offhand remark about cake and, because she was a designer, in possession of a naturally contributive temperament, turned her head upward toward the blade and said to the executioner, "Perhaps if you'd toggle the mechanism ever-so-slightly to the left . . ." At which point the blade achieved its mission even more efficiently than its usual 70th of a second, and Marie's head fell into the waiting basket and the designer was no more.

THE MORAL OF THE STORY?

It's in the designer's nature to solve problems. But now, it's time for interior designers to solve problems and design solutions for their own profession. Our profession must become a group of people who speak with one voice on matters of regulation, legislation, ethics, and excellence. We must coalesce as an assembly of well-educated minds that, focused on a research question or a matter of social policy, can create, hold, and perpetuate new knowledge that will contribute to the universal intellectual enterprise. Because it's time for us to use every tool we can get our hands on, it's time for this book.

What do designers need? Knowledge. If that's a simple answer, it's as simple as a good design. There's more to it than we, or anyone, can anticipate. But, it is not more than we can—and should—handle.

INTERIOR DESIGN®

Handbook of Professional Practice

ONE

Back

ground

Growing a Profession

EDWARD C. FRIEDRICHS, FAIA, FIIDA

Some historians of interior design believe that the profession really started in 1965, when Cornell University-educated architect Art Gensler opened a small firm in San Francisco that focused on corporate office design. An entrepreneur by nature, Gensler saw that the demand for interior design services among corporate clients (and those catering to them, such as the owners of office buildings) vastly outstripped the supply of firms prepared to provide these services competently. Although others, such as Skidmore, Owings & Merrill's Davis Allen, did specialize in corporate office interiors, Gensler went beyond them in organizing his small architecture and design firm around this market.

In doing so, he helped to separate interior design from architecture and interior decoration–and to establish its identity among the design professions. As this new handbook on interior design practice demonstrates, the process that Art Gensler helped set in motion succeeded in creating a new profession. Even now, however, interior designers are struggling to gain official sanction for its title and practice and to define their boundaries. This struggle often pits them against architects and residential interior decorators, both of whom claim–with some legitimacy–to practice interior design.

To put the situation in perspective, consider that it took centuries for the architecture profession to define itself, secure its boundaries, and finally obtain public sanction for its title and practice. Even today, the American Institute of Architects and its state and local offshoots battle with building designers, contractors, engineers, interior designers, and others over the question of "who is entitled to design what" in the built environment.

One reason for the struggle is that interior design is a hybrid profession whose roots trace back to architecture, the fine and decorative arts, graphic design, and even home economics. Especially at a larger scale, designing building interiors is a collaborative process, too. Interior designers are routinely part of teams that include architects, engineers, and other professionals and specialists. In this context, these "border wars" are meaningless: the interior designer's specific contributions are what matter.

INTERIOR DESIGN AS A PROFESSION

Until recently, interior design has been a self-certifying profession, similar to urban and regional planning (with its professional appellation, "certified planner"). In many states, individuals are still free to call themselves interior designers, regardless of their qualifications, and to offer interior design services. Only a business license is required.

This is beginning to change. Regional chapters of both the American Society of Interior Designers (ASID) and the International Interior Design Association (IIDA) are pushing hard to secure for interior designers the same protections—of title and practice—that architects now enjoy in the United States. Architects are licensed on a state-by-state-basis, and their activities are overseen by registration boards that administer licensing examinations, issue licenses, and discipline their licensees for malpractice and other practice-act infractions. To advocate change in the interest of the profession and their clients, design professionals should understand the nature of the arguments currently being made for and against such professional protections, and the factors that justify guarding interior design as a profession.

Arguments and Counter-arguments

Historically, both professions and trades have sought to limit entry to their ranks and to guard their traditional privileges by eliminating potential competitors. When possible, they have used the law to support this gatekeeping. California Governor Jerry Brown, in the late 1970s, proposed to "sunset" the practice and title acts of a wide range of trades and professions, including architecture and landscape architecture. The trades and professions resisted, arguing that public health, safety, and welfare would suffer if registration ended. That was their only possible argument: in America, anything else would be restraint of trade.

In seeking to license the title and practice of interior design, the ASID and IIDA are also making a public health, safety, and welfare argument. Opposing them, understandably, are architects and interior decorators, their main competitors among design professionals, who question whether such public health and safety considerations apply. Some architects question the need for state sanction of interior design practice, given its focus on non-load-bearing structures. Some interior decorators and residential interior designers argue that the requirements put forward by the proponents of interior designer licensing go beyond what is actually needed to protect public health, safety, and welfare. That would make those requirements exclusionary and therefore in restraint of trade.

The arguments for and against licensure have a political component as well. A dispute in the early 1980s in California pitted licensed architects against registered building designers—a category created as a compromise to preserve the traditional rights of draftsmen, carpenters, and others to design houses and small buildings. Similarly, the AIA and its civil, professional, and structural engineering counterparts regularly bicker over what their respective practice acts allow them to design or engineer. Similar compromises can be expected for interior design in relation to architecture, interior decoration, and residential interior design.

The legal and political possibilities available to both sides in arguments for professional protections will continue to cloud rather than resolve the issue of what constitutes a profession, so let us consider other factors that justify interior design as a profession.

Professionalism

Traditionally, professionals have pointed to credentials as evidence of their professionalism. This is what separates them from lay people, para-professionals, and "mere technicians." However, David Maister—a well-known consultant to professional service firms—argues that while these things may point to competence, true professionalism depends on attitude. A professional, in Maister's view, is a "technician who cares"—and that entails caring about the client.

The real subject of interior design is enclosed space—that is, the settings within buildings that house human activity. First and foremost, interior designers are concerned with how people experience these settings . . .

In trying to define professionalism, Maister lists the following distinguishing traits:

- *Taking pride in your work (and being committed to its quality)*

- *Taking responsibility and showing initiative*

- *Being eager to learn*

- *Listening to and anticipating the needs of others*

- *Being a team player*

- *Being trustworthy, honest, loyal*

- *Welcoming constructive criticism*[2]

His point is that professionalism is not just education, training, a certificate or license, and other credentials. In saying that these things are *not* the *sine qua non* of professionalism, Maister is really arguing for a *client-responsive* professionalism—as opposed to one that uses its credentials and presumed expertise as an excuse for ignoring or even bullying the client.

Arrogance is an issue in the design professions. Too many designers regard their clients as patrons, not partners. Design commissions become opportunities to further personal ambition rather than meet the client's goals and needs. The implication is that design is self-expression, that the creative process is largely if not exclusively the province of the designer alone.

Although there is inevitably an aspect of self-expression in the design process, its creative power is enhanced, not diminished, by collaboration. In collaboration, we become partners in a larger enterprise, and that gives our work its energy and spark. In arguing for "professionals who care," Maister is drawing attention to the collaborative nature of their relationships with their clients. It is a partnership to which both parties contribute their expertise. Formally, professionals act as the agents of their clients. As professionals, they have other obligations that affect this relationship— obligations that are intended, among other things, to protect clients from themselves. However, designers who assume they "know better" than their clients miss the opportunity to get into their clients' heads and understand their world. They need that knowledge to connect their work to their clients' larger goals and strategies, the real starting points of innovation in the design process.

What Makes Interior Design a Profession?

Interior design is a profession in part because of designers' special skills and education, but also because of designers' special relationships with their clients. According to *Webster's New Collegiate Dictionary,* a profession is "a calling requiring specialized knowledge and often long and intensive academic preparation."[4] An art is a "skill acquired by experience, study, or observation, an occupation requiring knowledge and skill, and the conscious use of skill and creative imagination especially in the production of aesthetic objects."[5] A craft is "an occupation or trade requiring manual dexterity or artistic skill."[6] These definitions stress a difference in training, suggesting that only professions require university study. That difference does not precisely hold anymore, since both arts and crafts are taught at the university level. Recalling David Maister's definition of a professional as a "technician who cares," we might ask, "Who benefits from the care that interior designers exercise in the course of their practice?" Clearly, the beneficiaries are those who use the settings that they design.

In defining the professional practice of interior design, the Foundation for Interior Design Education and Research (FIDER) provides the following outline of its scope:

- *Analyzing client needs, goals, and life safety requirements*

- *Integrating findings with a knowledge of interior design*

- *Formulating preliminary design concepts that are aesthetic, appropriate, and functional, and in accordance with codes and standards*

- *Developing and presenting final design recommendations through appropriate presentation media*

- *Preparing working drawings and specifications for non-load-bearing interior construction, reflected ceiling plans, lighting, interior detailing, materials, finishes, space planning, furnishings, fixtures, and equipment in compliance with universal accessibility guidelines and all applicable codes*

- *Collaborating with professional services of other licensed practitioners in the technical areas of mechanical, electrical, and load-bearing design as required for regulatory approval*

- *Preparing and administering bids and contract documents as the client's agent*

- *Reviewing and evaluating design solutions during implementation and upon completion[7]*

While it is accurate as far as it goes, this definition misses the heart of the matter. The real subject of interior design is *enclosed space*—that is, the *settings* within buildings that house human activity. First and foremost, interior designers are concerned with how people *experience* these settings and how their design *supports* their different activities. These concerns form the core of the interior design profession's specialized knowledge.

EDUCATING INTERIOR DESIGNERS

Like architecture, interior design is taught through a combination of studio work and coursework—the former a remnant of the old apprenticeship system that once characterized both architecture and the arts and crafts. In addition to studio training in design and visualization, professional interior design programs typically provide a foundation in:

- *Human factors*

- *Materials and systems*

- *Codes and regulations*

- *Contracts and business practices*

Unlike architecture, most interior design programs do not address the engineering side of building construction—e.g., coursework in the static and dynamic analysis of structure. Interior design also differs from architecture (and interior decoration) in its concern for every aspect of the interior environments that people use every day.

The human experience in these settings is a broad topic that includes history and culture, psychology and physiology, organization theory, and benchmark data drawn from practice—together with lighting, color theory, acoustics, and ergonomics. These subjects need to be part of the professional interior designer's education and training.

How do interior designers gain an understanding of client and user needs? "By asking them" is a reasonable answer for smaller projects, but larger ones make use of social science research methods such as participant observation, network analysis, and surveys. Exposure to these methods through coursework in anthropology and sociology is helpful, especially as strategic consulting emerges as a specialty within the profession. (Strategic consulting seeks to align a client's real estate and facilities strategies with its business plan. Typically, it helps the client define its real estate and facilities program and establish the quantitative and qualitative measures of its performance.) Business clients expect their design teams to understand the strategic context of their projects. Coursework in business and economics can begin that process; immersion in the industry, by reading its journals and participating in its organizations, is the next step. Once designers reach a certain level of responsibility, management becomes part of their job description. Coursework in business and management can make this transition easier.

A Knowledge of Sustainable Design Principles

"Building ecology," as the Europeans call it, needs to be part of interior designers' knowledge. They should know how to design to conserve nonrenewable resources, minimize waste, reduce CO_2 and SO_2 levels, and support human health and performance.[8,9]

INTERIOR DESIGNERS AND SUSTAINABLE DESIGN

In tackling the problem of indoor air pollution in the 1980s, the interior design profession led the way in raising public awareness of the value of sustainable design. As advocates for the user, interior designers have a special responsibility to understand sustainable design principles and evaluate their appropriateness for their projects. Sustainability also offers many opportunities to deliver added value for clients. As case studies by the Rocky Mountain Institute[9] have shown, the resulting gains in building and human performance provide a reasonable (and even rapid) payback on the client's investment, especially when these measures are used in combination. Here are some examples.

• *Lockheed Building 157, Sunnyvale, California.* Lockheed spent $2.0 million to add sustainable design features to this 600,000-ft^2 office building that reduced its energy consumption and provided a higher-quality work environment. Control of ambient noise was also achieved. Lower energy costs alone would have repaid Lockheed's investment in four years. Because the improved quality of the workplace reduced absenteeism by 15 percent, the investment was actually repaid in less than a year.

• *West Bend Mutual Insurance Headquarters, West Bend, Wisconsin.* West Bend used a number of sustainable design features, including energy-efficient lighting and HVAC systems, roof, wall, and window insulation, and thermal storage. Utility rebates kept its cost within a "conventional" budget. The building is 40 percent more efficient than the one it replaced. It provides an "energy-responsive workplace" that gives users direct control of thermal comfort at their workstations. A study showed that the building achieved a 16 percent productivity gain over the old one. A productivity gain of 5 percent (worth $650,000 in 1992 dollars) is attributable to the energy-responsive workplace feature alone.

• *NMB Headquarters, Amsterdam, The Netherlands.* This 538,000-ft^2 project exemplifies what Europeans call "integral planning": designing the building and its systems *holistically* to reduce operating costs and increase quality and performance. About $700,000 in extra costs were incurred to optimize the building and its systems, but this provided $2.6 million a year in energy savings—and a payback of only three months. Employee absenteeism is down by 15 percent, too.

Gensler's experience reinforces the Rocky Mountain Institute's findings. On office campus projects, they found that providing under-floor air supply and ambient lighting can reduce the cost of workplace "churn" (the need to shift workstations to accommodate changes in occupancy) from as much as $5.00/ft^2 to less than $1.00/ft^2. For an office campus in Northern California, these same features allowed them to redesign the entire workplace to accommodate a different set of users just six weeks before its opening—with no delays. By avoiding the cost of delay, the client essentially paid for the 10 percent higher cost of these features before the campus had even opened.

THE CULTURAL IMPACT OF INTERIOR DESIGN

Settings, the designed spaces within buildings, are "where the action is."
When human or organizational change occurs, settings are where it takes
place first. As my colleague Antony Harbour points out, the U.S. workplace
has been dramatically transformed over the last 40 years, but U.S. commercial
office buildings still have the same floor plans. The settings have changed
much more than their containers. Although settings are more ephemeral than
buildings, they have equal if not greater *cultural* impact.

Interior Designers and the Workplace Revolution

Because of the economic pressures of recession and globalization and technological developments such as bandwidth (the proliferation of electronic
networks to convey voice and data communications on a global basis), the
workplace has undergone profound change in the last decade. While technology is given credit for the productivity gains that have swept the U.S.
economy in this period, interior designers who specialize in the workplace
have had a major role in helping U.S. companies integrate new technologies
and work processes. Alone among design professionals, they understood that
these settings are the "connective tissue" that could make this happen.

Interior design professionals understand that design fuels organizational
change, regardless of the scale of its application. Think about where we work
today. Behind the modern city, whether London, Tokyo, or New York, are
nineteenth-century assumptions about work—that it occurs at specific times
and in specific places, for example. Now people work "anywhere, anytime,"
and there are compelling reasons, such as the problems of commuting, to distribute work geographically.

Not only the locus of work has changed in our culture; the mode of work has
changed as well. In the last century the workforce moved from Frederick
Taylor's "scientific management" to ways of working that are increasingly
open-ended, democratic, and individual/team-tailored. Along the way, the
workplace changed, too. Taylorism was about efficiency (and uniformity).
What followed shifted the focus to effectiveness (and diversity). What's the
difference? As Peter Drucker explains, "Efficiency is doing things right; effectiveness is doing the right thing."

The Modern movement, aping Taylor, took "Form follows function" as its credo. Today, though, we might amend this to "Form follows strategy." If design firms are now involved in strategic consulting, it is because interior designers paved the way. Their ability to give form to strategy gave them an advantage over competing consultants, because they knew how to make strategy actionable.

Yet this focus on strategy does not entirely explain the impact that interior designers have had on the workplace. More than any other profession involved in the design of these settings, they have been able to use their knowledge of workplace culture to design work settings that genuinely support the people who use them. Interior designers make it their business to know how people actually inhabit and experience the built environment. Their work—certainly the best of it—consistently reflects this understanding. The licensing controversy notwithstanding, interior designers today are valued members of building design teams precisely because they bring this knowledge to the table.

Some of the most valuable research on the workplace in recent years has been done by interior designers who specialize in work settings for corporate, financial, and professional service clients. Gensler's Margo Grant and Chris Murray, for example, have done pioneering work documenting the changing strategic goals of these companies and how they play out in spatial terms. Their benchmarking studies give Gensler and its clients a wealth of comparative data about facilities trends across the developed world's economy. Needless to say, this is a competitive advantage in the global marketplace.

As Peter Drucker points out, it used to be that the skills needed in business changed very slowly:

My ancestors were printers in Amsterdam from 1510 or so until 1750 and during that entire time they didn't have to learn anything new. All of the basic innovations in printing had been done . . . by the early 16th century. Socrates was a stone mason. If he came back to life and went to work in a stone yard, it would take him about six hours to catch on. Neither the tools nor the products have changed.[10]

Today, however, we are in the midst of a period of remarkable technological innovation, equivalent in its impact to the cluster of spectacular breakthroughs that occurred in the last quarter of the nineteenth century. Technological innovation is one reason that professions evolve. Social change, the evolution of "everyday life" and its values, is another. "Faster, cheaper, better!" is the catch phrase of the new economy. Every shaper of the built environment faces these related changes, as clients demand a new responsiveness. Design professionals should rethink linear and segmented processes, reflecting nineteenth-century practices, and begin to envision how everyone engaged in designing and constructing the built environment should approach their practice to achieve the speed, responsiveness, and innovation that clients require.

IMPLICATIONS OF BANDWIDTH: NEW TOOLS, PROCESSES, AND PRACTICES

The bandwidth revolution has given interior designers an entirely new set of tools—not just for design, but also for collaboration. As is true for most innovations, their early applications were focused on existing practices. Today, though, a new generation of designers is at work who grew up with these tools. As they move into the mainstream of practice, they will start to use them to reshape practice.

Bandwidth is transforming the production process: how furniture, furnishings, and equipment get from designer to manufacturer to end-user. It makes it possible both to speed the production process, by tying it more directly to purchasing, and to consolidate orders to secure larger production runs and better prices. And it creates a world market for these products that should increase their variety.

Bandwidth will also make it steadily easier for virtual teams to work collaboratively, to "construct" a virtual setting in three dimensions. This collaboration takes place not just between people, but between computers, too, so that in time fabrication will follow design without the need for detailed working drawings. As the process becomes more seamless (and more common), it will extend to other aspects of construction. At some point, "design/build" may really be a single process. Currently, we are only halfway there. A lot of the infrastructure is in place, but the interface is still maddeningly primitive.

At the same time, we are trying to use the infrastructure to support traditional practice models. It may take a "push" from the outside, such as another oil shock that makes the price of airline tickets less affordable, to force designers to change their ways and embrace virtual collaboration wholeheartedly.

Thanks to bandwidth, manufacturing has gone from Henry Ford's assembly line, with its uniform products, to Dell's (and now Ford's) "mass customization." Service industries have changed similarly. Across the economy, customers want the cost advantages of mass-market mass production, along with the quality and performance of custom design.

DESIGNING IN FOUR DIMENSIONS

At the same time as clients demand an increased level of responsiveness, knowledge workers demand "consonance" in the workplace. They approach potential employers looking for a "fit" with their values and lifestyles. In a buoyant economy, they can afford to be selective—and intolerant of "dissonance." The built environment gives form to consonance and provides its framework. To keep pace with social and technological changes, design professionals must learn to see that framework as one that changes with time—and therefore design in four dimensions.

The current rate of technological change suggests that designers will face considerable pressure to practice with time in mind. Both the container and the contained—"structure and stuff," as Stewart Brand put it in *How Buildings Learn*—change over time, but at different rates of speed.[11] The trends of mass customization and congruence suggest that settings will change frequently, which puts pressure on the rest to facilitate the change. This brings us back to *sustainability*, which also demands of "stuff" that its residual value be salvaged through recycling and reuse.

Designing in four dimensions means rethinking our conceptions of buildings. "There isn't such a thing as a building," Frank Duffy asserts. Buildings are just "layers of longevity of built components"—they exist in time. What matters for their designers is their "use through time." Duffy finds the whole notion of timelessness to be "sterile" because it ignores time as the building's fourth dimension—they exist in time, so they have to evolve to meet its changing demands.[12]

Also working from a "time-layered" perspective, Brand proposes a holistic approach to time-sensitive design.[13] He identifies six components of buildings: site, structure, skin, services, and space plan. While interior designers are focused on the last two, they have good reason to want to influence the rest: they all affect the building's use through time. To exercise this influence effectively, of course, interior designers have to understand the characteristics of these components, and the possibilities of the other elements of the built environment. Interior designers do not have to be engineers, or vice versa, but both need to know enough about the others' business so they can approach the building in a holistic or time-layered way. As Brand says:

Thinking about buildings in this time-laden way is very practical. As a designer you avoid such classic mistakes as solving a five-minute problem with a fifty-year solution. It legitimizes the existence of different design skills, all with their different agendas defined by this time scale.[14]

To be responsive to the user in the building design process, interior designers need to have this broader knowledge of the building and its components. In the end, their ability to sway others in the design and delivery process will rest primarily on issues of use over time—issues that are primarily functional and strategic, and that constantly require new skills.

LOOKING AHEAD

Interior designers face resistance in their quest to be recognized as a separate profession. In 1999, the American Institute of Architects (AIA) put together a task force to review the question of licensing interior designers. As *Architectural Record's* Robert Ivy reported:

They found that interior designers seek to distinguish themselves from less-qualified decorators, protect the right to practice, estab-

lish gender equity in a field dominated by men, and earn the respect of their fellow professionals.[15]

"The designers' viewpoint is consistent," Ivy added, citing his magazine's April 1998 roundtable discussion with interior designers. "Despite their gains in the industry, they feel slighted or disparaged by architects." Yet, he says, "there are unavoidable differences between architects and interior designers":

Architectural education is more rigorously focused on life safety, as well as structure, building science, and codes. By contrast, the AIA task force reported that in the 125 interior design programs currently available, education can vary from two to four years, and current testing for certification focused more on aesthetics than safety. The differences do not stop with pedagogy. Architects tend to engage the entire design problem, considering not only the contents of the interior, but the interior's relation to the exterior envelope, its construction and building systems, and the natural and human-made surroundings. A healthy building—light-filled, safe, and promoting human habitation—should be architects' professional norm. When we are operating at a high level of accomplishment, our work is holistic, integrating complex technical systems and social requirements into structures that engage the landscape, sustain their inhabitants inside and out, and enrich the community.[16]

Should interior designers be licensed? Here is Ivy's answer:

Our own professional status reflects a public trust we have earned at high cost, and it should not be diluted. . . . Practice legislation may not be the panacea that interior designers seek, if it is achieved without commensurate, fundamental changes in [their] education and experience.[17]

However, interior designers can make a strong case that they should be accorded the distinctions and protections that are part of other design professions such as architecture. No less than architects, interior designers are engaged in "the entire design problem." As advocates of the user, and as designers who are "fourth-dimension sensitive," they are often the first ones in the building design process to point out how one or another of the building's components makes it harder for its settings to evolve easily to meet new needs. As designers' interest in indoor air quality demonstrates, they are concerned with quality of life, too—with user performance, not just building performance.

ARCHITECTURE'S STRUGGLE TO BECOME A PROFESSION[1]

Interior designers who anguish about the time it is taking to secure state sanction for their profession's title and practice should bear in mind that it took architects a lot longer. Arguments over who is and is not qualified to design buildings punctuate the history of the profession.

In the Middle Ages in Europe, the master masons were the building architects. During the Renaissance in Italy, artist-architects supplanted them. They were considered to be qualified as architects owing to their training in *design*. Architects such as Brunelleschi and Michelangelo took a strong interest in engineering and technology, too, as they strove to realize their ambitious building projects. With Vitruvius, they believed that architecture was a liberal art that combined theory and practice. Master masons, who apprenticed in the building trades, were disparaged because their training was purely practical.

Yet the Italian Renaissance also saw the emergence of the professional in Europe's first true architect, Antonio Sangallo the Younger. Apprenticed to the artist-architect Bramante, Sangallo helped implement many of Bramante's later buildings. In time, he established a studio that is recognizably the prototype for today's architecture and design firms. The architectural historian James Ackerman has described him as "one of the few architects of his time who never wanted to be anything else."

Four diverging traditions emerge from the Renaissance: artist-architects, trained in design; humanist-architects, trained in theory; architect-architects, focused on buildings and striving for a balance between theory and practice; and builder-architects, focused on construction but still interested in designing buildings.

Artist-architects looked for patrons; architect-architects looked for clients. In the seventeenth and eighteenth centuries, we see this distinction played out between "gentleman" architects and the emerging profession. Thomas Jefferson counted architecture among his gentlemanly pursuits, a trait he shared with others of his class. Lord Burlington, who did much to establish the architectural profession in England, was widely criticized by his peers for his "unwonted" interest in the pragmatics of building construction. When the Institute of British Architects was established in 1834, noblemen could become honorary members for a fee. (Significantly, all connection with the building trades was forbidden.)

In the eighteenth and nineteenth centuries, English architects also faced competition from surveyors. In his *Dictionary* of 1755, Dr. Johnson gave essentially the same definition for the words "surveyor" and "architect." In England, at least, the two professions remained closely aligned through much of the nineteenth century—with both designing buildings. Engineers designed buildings, too. In 1854, one of them even won the Institute of British Architects' Gold Medal.

PROFESSIONAL ETHICS

Like other professionals, interior designers must contend with ethical issues. Indeed, the issues can be quite similar to those of allied and other learned professions. Like architects, lawyers, and doctors, interior designers can also do bodily harm and create financial damage if they practice incompetently or unethically. They can also put people at risk by failing to be effective advocates of their interests. Here are some examples of these issues as they arise in interior design practice.

- *Life safety.* Designers sometimes bemoan codes and regulations, but these rules exist to establish a minimum standard of health and safety. Failure to meet code can delay a project, which damages the owner, and can also cause bodily harm.

- *Confidentiality.* Interior designers often have access to confidential business information—a planned acquisition, for example, or a new business plan or strategy. This knowledge is shared with interior designers only because it has a direct bearing on their work, and it is shared with them in confidence. Ethically, and often by contract, that confidence must be respected.

- *Conflict of interest.* Interior designers are their clients' agents, so they have an obligation to avoid or disclose to them any potential conflicts of interest. (Disclosure means that you are prepared to end the conflict if the client so requests.) The *appearance* of conflict can be as problematic as the reality. Just as voters worry when politicians become too cozy with special interests, clients start to wonder when interior designers accept gifts or junkets from contractors and vendors. The occasional lunch, party, box of candy, or bottle of wine is no problem, but all-expenses-paid vacation trips and other costly "perks" cross the line. They create the appearance if not the reality that design decisions—specifying a product, for example—are being made to repay favors rather than to serve the interests of the client.

- *User advocacy.* Interior designers have a responsibility to users. If, in their judgment, a project's requirements, though legal, compromise user comfort and performance unacceptably, they have an obligation to try to change them, or to resign from the project if the client is unwilling to make changes. Design professionals have a broader obligation to educate their clients on the value of design features that improve user quality of life and performance.

- *Competency.* Professional competence reflects ongoing mastery of the skills and knowledge demanded by professional practice. Professional certification or licensing formally requires a level of mastery that necessarily lags behind what design professionals actually need. For example, FIDER's requirements do not yet specify that interior designers know the principles of sustainable design. That lag does not excuse professional interior designers from mastering these principles, or any new skills that may be necessary to maintain their professional competence.

Interior design came into its own in the 1990s as settings came to be seen as strategic resources. The catch phrase "Place matters!"—so emblematic of the second half of the decade—turned out to be literally true. When people have real choice about when and where they spend their time, the quality of these settings—their ability to support people in their desired activities—becomes crucial, often the deciding point. A "place" can be part of the landscape or cityscape, a building or building complex, or an enclosed indoor or outdoor setting. The word implies a richness and wholeness that mocks the design professions' efforts to carve it into parts.

The built environment today has immense range and diversity. Much development embraces multiple uses. The time dimension of buildings is changing, too, with more components expected (or needed) to be ephemeral rather than "permanent." Already, many projects today feature *hybrid* teams that are organized around each project's particular blend of uses and timeframes. These interdisciplinary teams are the future. They expose each profession to the others and give all of them a shared perspective about "place" that transcends each one's necessarily narrower view.

This shared viewpoint may eventually give rise to entirely new professions, which we may no longer be willing to categorize as "architecture" or "interior design." In time, too, the division between design and construction may prove to be an artificial boundary, no longer justified by practice. Professions are conservative forces in society, constantly resisting pressures to change, yet constantly placed in situations where the need to change is obvious and imperative. New professions arise in part because old ones fail to adapt.

Compared to architecture, interior design is still in its infancy—a profession that is just now marshalling its forces to secure the recognition to which it feels entitled. All this is taking place against the background of our entrepreneurial and bandwidth-driven era. How important is it, in this context, to secure the profession's boundaries or win state sanction for its practice? If it helps strengthen the education and training of interior designers, and encourages them to meet their responsibilities as professionals, then it is probably well worthwhile.

Especially today, it is hard to predict the future of the interior design profession. One clear way to prepare for it, however, is to make the education of interior design professionals much more rigorous. This argues for a more comprehensive curriculum, as I have outlined previously, and for a four-year professional degree program at the undergraduate level.

It also argues for *learning*, as Peter Senge calls it—not just maintaining skills, but actively learning from practice. Senge's point, made admirably in his book, *The Fifth Discipline,*[18] is that work itself is a learning experience of the first order. Our interactions with clients, colleagues, and other collaborators provide constant glimpses into an unfolding future. If we are attentive, we can understand some of what the future demands—and take steps to meet it appropriately. People who care about their careers, and who take their responsibilities as professionals seriously, need to make learning a constant priority.

Notes

1
This brief account is drawn from Spiro Kostof (ed.), *The Architect*, Oxford University Press, New York, 1977, pp. 98–194.

2
Maister, David H., *True Professionalism*, The Free Press, New York, 1997, pp. 15–16.

3
Maister, *True Professionalism*, p. 16.

4
Webster's New Collegiate Dictionary, G. & C. Merriam Co., 1977, p. 919.

5
Webster's, p. 63.

6
Webster's, p. 265.

7
Foundation for Interior Design Education and Research (FIDER), "Definition of Interior Design" (from FIDER's website: http://www.fider.org/definition.htm).

8
A good introduction to this topic is Diana Lopez Barnett and William D. Browning: *A Primer on Sustainable Building*, Rocky Mountain Institute, Snowmass, CO, 1995.

9
Romm, Joseph J., and William D. Browning, *Greening the Building and the Bottom Line*, Rocky Mountain Institute, Snowmass, CO, 1994.

10
Daly, James, "Sage Advice" (interview of Peter Drucker), *Business 2.0*, August 8, 2000.

11
Brand, Stewart, *How Buildings Learn*, Viking, New York, 1994, p. 13.

12

Quoted in Brand, *How Buildings Learn,* pp. 12–13. The quotations are from Francis Duffy, "Measuring Building Performance," *Facilities,* May 1990, p. 17.

13

John Habraken took a similar position, initially in relation to housing, in the 1960s. See, for example, his *Variations: The Systematic Design of Supports,* MIT Press, Cambridge, MA, 1976, and *The Structure of the Ordinary: Form and Control in the Built Environment,* MIT Press, Cambridge, MA, 1998.

14

Brand, *How Buildings Learn,* p. 17.

15

Ivy (FAIA), Robert, "The Keys to the Kingdom," *Architectural Record,* September 2000, p. 17.

16

Ivy, "The Keys to the Kingdom," p. 17.

17

Ivy, "The Keys to the Kingdom," p. 17.

18

Senge, Peter, *The Fifth Discipline,* Currency/Doubleday, New York, 1994.

19

Kostof, *The Architect,* p. 138.

Bibliography

Brand, Stewart. *How Buildings Learn: What Happens After They're Built.* New York: Penguin USA, 1995.

Browning, William D., and Joseph J. Romm. *Greening the Building and the Bottom Line: Increasing Productivity Through Energy-Efficient Design.* Snowmass: Rocky Mountain Institute, 1994.

Cuff, Dana. *Architecture: The Story of Practice.* Cambridge, MA: MIT Press, 1992.

Gutman, Robert. *Architectural Practice: A Critical View.* New York: Princeton Architectural Press, 1988.

Habraken, N. J., and Jonathan Teicher (Editor). *The Structure of the Ordinary: Form and Control in the Built Environment.* Cambridge, MA: MIT Press, 1998.

Habraken, N. John. *Variations: The Systematic Design of Supports.* Cambridge, MA: MIT Press, 1976.

Kostof, Spiro (Editor). *The Architect: Chapters in the History of the Profession.* Berkeley: University of California Press, 2000.

Lopez Barnett, Dianna, and William D. Browning. *A Primer on Sustainable Building.* Snowmass, CO: Rocky Mountain Institute, 1995.

Maister, David H. *True Professionalism: The Courage to Care About Your People, Your Clients, and Your Career.* New York: Free Press, 1997.

Senge, Peter, M. *The Fifth Discipline: The Art and Practice of the Learning Organization.* New York: Currency/Doubleday, 1994.

Webster, Merriam (Editor). *Merriam Webster's Collegiate Dictionary.* Springfield: G. & C. Webster Co., 1977.

2

History of the Profession

CINDY COLEMAN

Interior designers can trace their profession to many who preceded them, from the cave painters at Lascaux to the creators of the frescoed interiors at Pompeii, to the holistic architecture, interiors, and furnishings of Robert Adam and Thomas Jefferson in the eighteenth century, and to Frank Lloyd Wright in the twentieth.

In the mid-nineteenth century, during the Industrial Revolution, the farm economy, though still robust, was gradually supplanted by a new industrial economy centered in or near the great, developing American cities of New York, Boston, and Chicago. The transition from farm to industry allowed Americans to see their houses as more than shelter and a place to sleep when work outdoors was done. Industrial workers' days were not necessarily shorter than those of farmers. However, for industrial workers and city dwellers in particular, home became a refuge that provided physical comfort and even aesthetic pleasure in contrast to the noisy, gritty, and physically exhausting atmosphere of the factory.

As women had more time to spend on the comforts of home, the large department stores of England and America developed and included sections devoted to drapery and upholstery. Specialty retailers included Liberty of London for fabrics and Tiffany and Affiliated Artists in New York, which produced lamps, vases, and other finely crafted decorative items.

At the end of the nineteenth century in England and America, the Arts and Crafts movement developed as a direct response to the Industrial Revolution. Its members, including William Morris, Charles Voysey, and Gustav Stickley, celebrated handcraft and deplored the social conditions, as well as the machine-made designs, the Industrial Revolution had created. The Arts and Crafts movement initiated small workshops devoted to woodworking, pottery, and weaving, and brought together artists and architects to study the interiors as well as the exteriors of buildings. Design integrity within the contemporary cultural and social context was the concern not only of the Arts and Crafts movement, but of other groups including the Wiener Werkstratte and the Bauhaus, which developed and flourished in the twentieth century.

Sensitivity to the role of design in society is as relevant at the beginning of the twenty-first century as it was at the dawn of the twentieth. Some, in fact, have referred to the year 2000 as the beginning of "the design century." Today, design is relevant as never before, particularly to the world of work. Following World War II, business theories and practices began to evolve and proceeded at a manageable pace; with the widespread use of computers in the 1980s, that evolution picked up speed and continues to do so today, when the only organizational constant is change. After World War II, the residential and corporate branches of the interior design profession began to move on separate tracks. Both have traveled rapidly, but in different directions. The interior designer's role as a professional consultant to business and organizations is the focus of this chapter. It is important to emphasize, however, that design is a global language that transcends home and workplace, geography and culture. To be a designer is to understand what all men and women have in common—their humanity.

INTERIOR DESIGN EMERGES AS A PROFESSION: 1900 TO 1930

The formal study of interior design began in the United States at the end of the nineteenth century. Programs and curricula typically developed in art schools; at the great land-grant colleges of the Midwest, which were open to women and also boasted strong programs in home economics; and within academic programs in architecture, primarily at East Coast universities.

When interior design actually became recognized as a profession is a subject for debate. Some scholars believe that interior design was not acknowledged as an independent profession in America until 1897, when Edith Wharton and Ogden Codman, Jr., published *The Decoration of Houses*. The authors are considered the first to define the profession as it is viewed today, by clarifying the difference between interior decoration, which deals with surface treatments, and interior design, which encompasses the design of interior spaces.

Elsie de Wolfe, a contemporary of Mrs. Wharton's and a disciple of her approach, is considered to be one of America's first professional interior designers. Her expertise, however, was on the side of interior decoration, which she used with great skill in the creation of interiors for the industrialist Henry Clay Frick and other wealthy New York families. She also accepted commissions from the prominent Beaux Arts architect Stanford White. Early twentieth-century women who are also considered among the first design professionals are Nancy McClelland, who brought design services to the general public through the decorating department she established at Wanamaker's department store in Manhattan; and Eleanor McMillen, whose McMillen, Inc. is considered to be America's first interior decorating firm.

By the turn of the twentieth century, the Industrial Revolution had reached full maturity. Daily life in the developed world had become increasingly mechanized, and Thomas Edison's electric light bulb was adding time to the work day and changing the nature of work. At the same time, the seeds of the Information Age—a century in the future—were being planted with Bell's telephone in 1876 and Edison's subsequent inventions of the telephone transmitter, the stock ticker, the phonograph, and the movie camera. During the early part of the twentieth century, there was little if any distinction between residential and nonresidential interior design; it was not until after World War II that North Americans became open to the idea of hiring design professionals for both their houses and offices. As the century began, the archetype of the workplace was the assembly line that Henry Ford created to produce the Model T.

An early business theorist, Frederick W. Taylor, extended the assembly line from the product to the worker. Considered to be industry's first efficiency expert, Taylor conducted time-study experiments that he developed into the concept he called *scientific management*. In Taylor's view, human workers could—and should—function as mechanically as machines. If workers were discouraged from thinking creatively and independently and completely removed from decision making, and if work was broken down into its simplest units, with all members of a single group of workers dedicated to identical tasks, efficiency would result. Taylor's methods, developed for the factory, eventually found their way into offices, along with typewriters, calculators, and switchboards and the women and recently arrived European immigrants who were hired to operate them.

Ford's assembly line, and Taylor's translation of it to human activity, next found its way to business and the chart of organization. The hierarchical organization, with its mechanical, organizational, and psychological elements now delineated, was born and grew. Once a suitable interior was designed to contain it, it flourished.

In the corporate hierarchy, order ruled. To stay in control, however, the ruling order needed to keep an eye on the workers. Workplaces were designed for management, who typically constricted a large group of workers in a single, vast space. From the giant panopticon that was the top of the hierarchy, managers looked down over rows of workers at their typewriters or sewing machines or tables where they assembled the typewriters, sewing machines, Victrolas, and other machines that had become part of twentieth-century life.

At the turn of the twentieth century, the hierarchy was the metaphor for society in all its forms; the elevator, invented in 1857, suggested that, in a democratic American society, workers could aspire to access any level they chose. This was the era of the great retailers such as Marshall Field, whose establishments were organized into departments, just like the Ford Motor Company. This was the era that saw the construction of the Eiffel Tower as a brand mark for Paris, along with the great railway hotels, large city apartment buildings, the modern hospital, and the first skyscraper office buildings.

In business, Taylor's scientific management prevailed, but he had his critics, who were concerned about issues that interior designers still find themselves dealing with a hundred years later. They included Mary Parker Follett of the Harvard Business School, whose humanist, behaviorist approach to the management of organizations represented the opposite side of Taylor's machine-tooled coin. In the 1910s she championed such far-sighted approaches to work, and the workplace, as "the law of situation" and cross-functional teams. She also insisted that individual workers, rather than being merely static units of work with a prescribed place on a linear assembly line, as Taylor would have it, contributed to the strength of the organization as a whole. She believed that, within the organizational structure, men and women should be free to experiment until they found ways of working that were effective for the tasks at hand and for themselves as individuals.

In the 1920s, Harvard was also the academic home of Elton Mayo and his colleague Fritz Roethlisberger, who are the acknowledged creators of the human relations movement and whose work also has contemporary implications. They conducted their famous Hawthorne experiments over a period of more than 30 years—from the 1920s to the 1950s—at the Western Electric Hawthorne Works in Cicero, Illinois. Their studies, which anticipated the current interest and advancements in ergonomics, focused on the physiological aspects of work, particularly the impact of various levels of illumination on workers' efficiency and the causes of fatigue. They also studied the psychological aspects of work and looked closely at employees' motivation, satisfaction, and personal well-being, particularly as these abstract states took form in workers' relationships with their supervisors.

The Harvard theorists, along with Chester Barnard at AT&T and other humanists, created a groundswell against scientific management. It was now clear that not all work fit the model of Ford's assembly line. And simply because the assembly line itself depended on human beings but was, in fact, profoundly dehumanizing, it was time to step back and rethink the nature of work—and the workplace. The time had come for a paradigm shift in the way organizations were structured and in the way the physical spaces of organizations were designed. But then came World War II, and the hierarchy not only prevailed, it joined the military.

THE BAUHAUS ARRIVES IN AMERICA: 1940 TO 1950

The end of World War II brought a period of prosperity to the United States that lasted almost 20 years. America had definitively won the war. By putting its own interests aside and contributing its physical and material resources to the war effort, corporate America was in large part responsible for the country's victory. Although American business quickly recovered from the war, the military mindset prevailed during the remainder of the 1940s. At the Ford Motor Company, decision making was based on numbers; numbers and rigid control also defined management. This approach led eventually to systems analysis, a rational, mathematically rigorous method of decision making that was considered to be especially effective in situations of uncertainty.

The war effort had been American through and through, but now that peace had come, corporations wanted to reclaim their unique identities. They wanted new headquarters that would function like the great cathedrals of Europe—buildings that would announce the importance of these corporations to society, reflect their mission, embody their technological expertise,

The time had come for a paradigm shift in the way organizations were structured and in the way the physical spaces of organizations were designed. But then came World War II, and the hierarchy not only prevailed, it joined the military.

advertise their vision and confidence, and share their uniquely American exuberance. Corporate America looked to the architectural and design communities for their new image. It would be architects and designers associated with the Bauhaus in Germany who would make that image reality.

Founded by Walter Gropius at the end of World War I, the Bauhaus, or "building house," was conceived not only as a school but as an artistic utopia that brought together artists, craftspeople, and workers. Its emphasis was on theory as well as application. Its goal, as Gropius stated in his 1919 prospectus, was "to unify all disciplines of practical arts as inseparable components of a new architecture." The Bauhaus, which could trace its roots to the Arts and Crafts movement in England and the Wiener Werkstatte in Austria, sought to humanize technology. Its curriculum taught the spectrum of arts and crafts, including planning and building; weaving; photography; the visual arts, including woodcarving, metalsmithing, and ceramics; and advertising and graphic design.

The members of the Bauhaus included the painters Paul Klee and Wassily Kandinsky; the architect Mies van der Rohe; the designers Josef Albers, Herbert Bayer, Marcel Breuer, and Laszlo Moholy-Nagy; and many others. During little more than a decade, from 1919 to 1933, they produced works that have become icons of modernism. Bauhaus supporters included Albert Einstein, Arnold Schoenberg, and Marc Chagall.

After a post-World War I economic boom, the German economy deteriorated precipitously. One of the goals of the Bauhaus was to create an orderly worldview from the economic, social, and political chaos that prevailed in Germany between the two world wars. The Bauhaus was committed to giving its students "integrated personalities," to educating them in contemporary culture as well as artistic theory and technique. Bauhaus designs combined technological expertise with the school's philosophy of egalitarianism and dynamism.

The Bauhaus, however, existed in a climate of ascendant fascism. First located in Weimar, the school moved from there to Dessau and finally, in 1932, to Berlin, where it stayed for less than a year. The Bauhaus closed voluntarily in 1933, unwilling to accede to the conditions of Hitler's German Reich, now firmly in power. Many of the Bauhaus masters fled to America. In 1937 Walter Gropius took a position at Harvard, where he was later joined by Marcel Breuer. Mies van der Rohe settled in Chicago in 1938 and became the head of architecture at the Illinois Institute of Technology. Other "Bauhauslers" soon joined him, forming the "new" Bauhaus that ultimately led the United States into the forefront of modern design.

Before World War II, the professionals who planned and designed office environments–known today as contract interior designers–were not identified with a discrete area of professional expertise. A doctor, lawyer, or corporation that wanted assistance arranging an office interior space was referred to a furniture dealer, who provided desks, chairs, and credenzas and sources for lighting, floor and wallcoverings, and office equipment. The selection of office furniture was primarily the domain of manufacturers' representatives, who were also responsible for delivery, installation, and customer service. There were exceptions to the rule, however, most notably Frank Lloyd Wright. In his 1937 project for the Johnson Wax Company in Racine, Wisconsin, he designed not only the building but the interiors and furnishings as well.

Beginning in the 1930s, and especially with the prosperity that followed World War II, North Americans became open to hiring professionals to design their residences, especially with the growing celebrity and social cachet of decorators including John Fowler, Terence Herbert Robsjohn-Gibbings, and Billy Baldwin. By definition, these residential interior decorators dealt with surface treatments, and their services were generally understood and valued. Films and popular magazines brought the idea of fine residential interiors to a broad audience. Eventually, women's magazines and particularly shelter magazines showed their audiences that, with the help of a professional, it was possible to turn the idea of a finely decorated residence into reality. Corporate clients, however, saw no need to call in a professional to design an office interior. In the business world, this service simply was not understood or, if it was, it was considered to be the same as serious residential interior decoration–expensive and elitist.

In 1932, in connection with an exhibit at New York's Museum of Modern Art, Philip Johnson and John Russell Hitchcock published *The International Style: Architecture since 1922,* which clearly defined Mies van der Rohe's New Building as a distinctive style. The International style had an immediate influence on corporate buildings, and later influenced residential architecture and interiors as well. Buildings in the International style have steel skeletons and eschew decoration. Their glass skins make them interactive, with the glass mediating between the interior and exterior, between the buildings' users and the world outside.

These sleek new corporate buildings required interiors that were compatible with their exterior architecture. Recognizing the need for an innovative approach to the office environment, Florence and Hans Knoll established Knoll Associates in 1946 to design and manufacture furniture in the Bauhaus style. Florence Knoll, an architect who had trained under Eliel Saarinen and Mies van der Rohe, established the Knoll Planning Unit, a design studio that provided Knoll's furniture clients with interior architectural and planning services. The unit, which became a laboratory for interior spaces, experimented with the design, scale, and configuration of task-related furniture. One of Knoll's hallmarks was to insist on standardization of all of an office's design elements, with everything from furniture to stationery part of a coherent, seamless system. Although some corporate clients and their employees chafed at the Knoll approach and considered it too constricting, its rigor helped American businesses establish their identities firmly in the American mind. The Knoll approach was a precursor to the contemporary concept of branding.

DESIGNERS LEARN TO STUDY HOW ORGANIZATIONS BEHAVE: 1950 TO 1960

In the early 1950s, the New York office of Skidmore, Owings & Merrill (SOM) became one of the first major architecture and engineering firms to offer interior design as a professional service. SOM eventually became established as the world's leader in contract interiors, providing design services for such major corporations as Pepsi Cola, Chase Manhattan Bank, and Union Carbide. Under the direction of architect Davis Allen, SOM established its signature modern style.

By this time, Mies van der Rohe was established in America at the Illinois Institute of Technology (IIT) in Chicago. One of his colleagues at IIT was Herbert A. Simon, professor and head of the Department of Political and Social Sciences and a future Nobel laureate in economics. Simon's academic interest was the nature of organizations, which he viewed as not abstract and one-dimensional but concrete and complex, reflecting the individuals who comprised them. Simon maintained that, to understand how organizations make choices, it was first necessary to understand how people in organizations make decisions.

In the 1950s, academia began again to study human-centered work. At the Harvard Business School, the work of Malcolm P. McNair led to the development of organizational behavior as a new area of study. Conceived as a backlash against prewar concepts of human relations and the rigid systems analysis of the postwar years, organizational behavior was descriptive instead of prescriptive: it studied how organizations and workers actually behave, instead of recommending how they ought to behave.

Late in the decade, following the model of the Knoll Planning Unit, the larger furniture manufacturers established entities devoted to practical research. The Steelcase Corporate Development Center in Grand Rapids, Michigan, became a proving ground for the company's own designs. In 1958, another furniture manufacturer, Herman Miller, Inc., formed a research division to study the workplace. Herman Miller retained artist-designer Robert Probst to direct the division and to convert his findings into design ideas. The result was Herman Miller's "Action Office," a system of free-standing panels, countertops, and file pedestals that were flexible and easy to configure, whatever the constraints or freedom of the interior space. This new "systems furniture" complemented Simon's theories and also echoed those of the prewar humanists who rejected the assembly line in favor of worker autonomy and flexibility. The modular elements of the Action Office could adapt to workers' changing needs and perform independently of a building's architecture.

Also in the late 1940s and 1950s, the husband-and-wife team of Charles and Ray Eames introduced their "recognition of need" philosophy of design, which insisted that interiors should be constructed primarily for the people who inhabited them and using the furniture and tools they needed to do their work effectively and efficiently. The Eameses believed that furniture should be appropriate, informal, egalitarian, ethical, and socially conscious. They used their talents to create furniture that was aesthetically pleasing; and by first studying human beings at work, they created furniture that actually improved the work process.

All of the Eameses' work, from furniture to films, produced a deep, substantive reflection of America's technical ingenuity and particularly its postwar optimism. Their modular shelving and storage units, produced by Herman Miller, were the first products to combine the efficiency of mass production with integrity in design and materials. Previously, if corporate managers wanted custom furniture, the only sources were dealers who specialized in high-end furniture, or the architects of their buildings. The Eameses greatly influenced the product design industry, from furniture to lighting to general office equipment.

The Eameses' work was the genesis of the furniture and product design industry as it is known at the beginning of the twenty-first century. Their example, and their success, encouraged many designers and furniture manufacturers to establish productive, long-standing working relationships. Architects Mies van der Rohe and Eero Saarinen and designers Isamu Noguchi and Harry Bertoia produced chairs, tables, and lamps for Knoll International. In addition to producing work by Charles and Ray Eames, Herman Miller, Inc. produced designs by Isamu Noguchi and Alexander Girard, as well as the Comprehensive Storage System created by its design director, George Nelson.

CORPORATE INTERIOR DESIGN FINDS ITS IDENTITY: 1960 TO 1970

The 1960s in America saw widespread questioning and experimentation at all levels of society, from the personal to the institutional. Student protesters storming a university president's office and putting their feet up on his desk became one of the decade's many indelible visual metaphors. In a time that saw a U.S. President and other political leaders assassinated, civil rights marches proceeding peacefully alongside cities on fire, and the Vietnam war back-to-back with TV commercials for toothpaste, the hierarchy was on shaky ground. Once the dust settled, it was clear that values had shifted and the time had come for the rigid hierarchy to relax and make room for individual talent and entrepreneurship.

The 1960s introduced the contract interior design profession as we know it today. While in the 1950s architecture firms had begun to offer interior design services, the 1960s saw these interiors studios mature and develop into large, independent design firms that offered comprehensive interior design services.

One outstanding example is Gensler, Inc. In 1965, Arthur Gensler began his eponymous company in San Francisco, with $200 and two colleagues. The company initially provided space-planning services to business clients. Since then, Gensler's focus has expanded from space planning and office interior design to comprehensive architectural services; the company has grown from one office to 23 around the world, with more than 2,000 employees. Today, Gensler is acknowledged by its peers as the most respected and best-managed interior architecture firm in the United States.

THE INTERIOR DESIGNER JOINS THE MANAGEMENT TEAM: 1970 TO 1980

The volatile cultural climate of the 1960s and early 1970s may or may not have contributed directly to the ascendancy of the open office. Nevertheless, it was in the 1970s that major American corporations, including General Electric, began looking to Peter Drucker for management consulting expertise. Drucker, who coined the term "management by objectives," was one of the first to see the information economy developing and with it a new type of employee–the "knowledge worker." Drucker also insisted that decentralization should be the model of a company's corporate structure, and many companies took Drucker at his word and extended decentralization to real estate.

Until the 1970s, office buildings and particularly corporate headquarters were located primarily in major cities. The obvious advantages were access to business services and transportation. But high rental costs, combined with the competitive advantage of new and rapidly changing technology, escalated the cost of new construction and maintaining existing structures. It became expensive if not prohibitive for a large company to relocate to another downtown building that offered up-to-date infrastructure, the required technology, and other amenities. Soon, companies began to move their headquarters from the city to the suburbs, with its abundant land and low-cost spaces. The workforce followed, continuing the boom in suburban and exurban housing developments and shopping malls that began after World War II.

These trends, in turn, led to the speculative office building. In response to the exodus of businesses from the city, real estate developers created an entirely new type of office complex. Suburban buildings were no longer created in the image of their corporate tenants, like the Seagram Building or the CBS headquarters in New York City. Instead, developers created anonymous groups of buildings on cheap and vast expanses of land, much of it unused farmland. The model of a low-profile, meticulously maintained corporate campus replaced the intense, vertical office tower. In keeping with its emphasis on cost control, the speculative office building was basically a shell that required the most efficient, most cost-effective use of space. This requirement demanded an entirely new type of professional: the space planner.

In the space-planning process, the first step is programming. The space planner interviews the client and, through questionnaires and face-to-face meetings with workers and their supervisors, determines the amount of space required for various functions. Projected growth or shrinkage are factored in, and the collected data help the planner determine the amount of space needed for each function or employee. The end result establishes the square footage the client requires. Armed with this information, the real estate broker can shop the various spaces or buildings on the market, looking for the most favorable lease option. If the client is considering more than one building, the design firm rejoins the team to organize the program information into a space plan showing locations of partitions, doors, and furnishings. This allows the client to visualize how the organization will fit into space in one or more buildings.

Many large interior design firms were formed during this time, with several created for the sole purpose of offering space-planning services. Between 1974 and 1984, the number of jobs in the United States, many of them occupied for the first time by women, increased by approximately 24 percent. Commercial interior designers became increasingly competitive, positioning real estate brokers as intermediaries between their firms and their clients.

For the industry, this situation was a double-edged sword. Interior design professionals entered the decision-making process earlier than ever before, which gave them an opportunity to expand their role and increase their influence. Many interior design firms became expert at analyzing building options and expanded their services to include a full range of pre-lease services. This ultimately positioned designers as consultants who offered valuable advice that would have a strategic and economic impact on their clients' businesses. The downside, however, was that, as real estate brokers became more involved and aggressive at the planning phase of office design, clients expected to pay lower professional fees for basic design services.

In addition, interior design firms that provided only space-planning services contributed to the confusion about what a professional interior designer actually does. Traditionally, a new tenant's landlord had paid for space planning. The fee for this service was extremely low, averaging five cents per square foot. Full-service interior design fees, meanwhile, averaged three dollars a square foot. Many clients did not understand the differences between space planning and comprehensive interior design services, which include much more than programming alone. A contract interior designer has expertise in conceptual design, design development, contract documentation and administration, and furniture specification. In addition, qualified interior designers have the technical knowledge to integrate architecture and construction and the ability to create interiors that are not only efficient, cost-effective, comfortable, and aesthetically pleasing, but that make workers more productive.

On a parallel track during the 1970s, as large interior design firms grew to accommodate the increasingly specialized needs of their corporate clients, residential interiors were created by practitioners associated with small or frequently solo design firms that offered a much more abstract product—good taste. Beginning in the late 1950s, Mies van der Rohe created landmark apartment buildings in Chicago whose interiors were in spirit if not in fact made for Bauhaus furniture. In the 1970s, European and especially Italian furniture design, notably from the Memphis group, contributed to the creation of innovative residences. For the most part, however, especially in America, homes that were professionally decorated recalled scaled-down versions of traditional British or Continental interiors. Following their training, as well as public perception, residential specialists were recognized experts at furniture, finishings, and overall visual presentation. They were not considered—nor did they consider themselves to be—strategists or planners. The public perception of "interior design" had solidified early in the twentieth century. In the intervening century, particularly in corporate America during the decades following World War II, the definition changed but the perception did not.

The widespread misunderstanding about their expertise put interior designers on the defensive. Since clients who were knowledgeable about design were the exception rather than the rule, designers were forced to explain and justify the value of design. The situation was exacerbated for designers in the late 1970s with the beginning of the country's first post-World War II recession.

The 1970s were a wake-up call for corporate America. Not only was the economy shaky, but "Japan, Inc." offered formidable competition. The corporate hierarchy was by now on the endangered list. W. Edwards Deming, an independent business consultant, had been an advisor to the Japanese after World War II. His concept of the learning organization, which he developed in the 1950s, had helped Japan achieve its own postwar business recovery. Deming believed that insights into the system and useful ideas for changing it should find their way upward from the bottom of the organization, not be handed down from above. He encouraged companies to foster their employees' intrinsic motivation and insisted that no one is better equipped to resolve systemic problems than the people who work with the system daily and who know it best. A true visionary, Deming foresaw the transformation of the American economy from goods to services and steered companies toward an emphasis on quality and customer satisfaction. He is popularly known for his concepts of "total quality management (TQM)" and "quality circles."

Globalization signaled the beginning of the end for the bureaucratic mindset, particularly when it came to corporate design. The days of rigid design standardization were clearly over. As they acknowledged global influence and competition, corporations knew that developing new business approaches was part of the deal.

THE COMPUTER JOINS THE WORKFORCE: 1980 TO 1990

By the early 1980s, global competition had forced America to completely rethink the way it did business; in addition, advances in computer technology had reached critical mass. The resulting profound change for organizations, the workplace, and individual workers created a host of euphemisms for the word *lay-off—reengineer, downsize,* and *rightsize* among them. Just as the early 1980s brought profound change to the structure of business, it also changed the way corporate leaders thought about their companies' real estate holdings, offices, and equipment. The 1980s brought radical change to the profession of interior design as well.

In the 1980s, companies continued the workplace economies that they had introduced during the heyday of reengineering. Because workers spent a greater amount of time at the office, they became attached to their computers and their workspaces. For the first time, interior designers needed to understand the concept of social dislocation as it applied to the workplace. Ergonomic and health issues came up as well. Workers complained that computers produced eye strain. The repetitive keystroking used during word and information processing created something entirely new—carpal tunnel syndrome. Long hours sitting in one place produced back problems and made choosing a well-designed office chair not only a matter of aesthetics but a health and insurance issue as well. Interior designers began to take a holistic approach to their work and explore new areas of knowledge, such as management and the social sciences, that their education may not have included.

The furniture systems that had been designed in the 1960s and 1970s, though an ideal solution for their time, were not able to address the technologically and physiologically based problems of the new workplace. Now, interior designers were called upon to do no less than integrate furniture, technology, ergonomics, building systems, and the environment. Design professionals not only had to expand their skills and knowledge, they needed to change their work style. Specifically, they had to learn to work quickly and collaboratively with their clients and to see office design from the perspective of every position on the organizational chart.

For a time, the speculative office building and its emphasis on first-time costs had relegated interior designers and furniture manufacturers to the periphery of the business decision-making loop. The new client–designer collaboration brought designers and manufacturers together for the first time in decades. Designers had gained a deep, fundamental understanding of workplace issues. Manufacturers realized that they could intensify the partnership if they listened to what designers had to say and learned from it. In addition, they could also add the critical component of research to their knowledge base. Manufacturers began behavioral and observational research to study different solutions to workplace problems; that research continues to the present.

The economy was moving rapidly, too, with the high-risk economic climate creating great fortunes almost overnight. Talented residential designers including Peter Marino, Sister Parish, and Mark Hampton saw their once-small firms burgeon during the 1980s. Their clients became more significant as well. In addition to increasingly high-end residential work in New York and cities around the world, many received commissions to restore landmark residences and public buildings in the United States and abroad; others created and licensed their own lines of furniture or home accessories. At the same time, shelter magazines hit their stride. Computerized printing techniques made color reproduction beautiful but relatively inexpensive, and magazines such as *Architectural Digest* had influence to match their circulation. On the residential side of the street, interior design was becoming big business and remains so as the twenty-first century begins.

Global competition, coupled with a recession in the late 1980s through the early 1990s, lured many American interior design firms—corporate and residential alike—into the global market. These firms, particularly those specializing in corporate interiors, were lauded for their understanding of the building process. Some corporate design professionals, however, were criticized for bringing large but efficient buildings to countries where they were culturally problematic. Many European workers, for example, consider direct sunlight and fresh air to be standard office equipment and found it hard to adjust to permanently closed windows, closed-off interior cubicles, and air conditioning.

Nevertheless, a new breed of interior design professional had emerged. The weak economy of the early 1990s required many design firms that had been successful in the previous two decades to redefine their own businesses. In addition, the design profession became capital-intensive rather than labor-intensive. To rationalize the expense of capital expenditures for new technology, design firms began expanding the scope of services they provided. Many followed corporate America's lead and downsized, reengineered, or even closed their doors. Those left standing were stronger and better qualified to work in partnership with their clients.

THE NEW LIBERAL ART OF TECHNOLOGICAL CULTURE:
1990 TO 2000

Today, interior designers find themselves working quite differently than in the past. Richard Buchanan, head of the department of design at Carnegie Mellon University, goes so far as to suggest that since 1995 the design industry has experienced a revolution. He maintains, in fact, that, like the culture itself, design has evolved to become the "new liberal art of technological culture."

Traditionally, the liberal arts have comprised the humanities, the social and natural sciences, and mathematics. The liberal arts are distinguished by a set of disciplines such as grammar, logic, and rhetoric that have the ability to create bridges to areas of specialization such as the basic sciences and medicine, which have their own, sometimes arcane, vocabularies.

To design spaces well, interior designers, like anthropologists, must continuously cross back and forth among many different corporate cultures and terrains of knowledge. In this sense, design is a liberal art that connects discrete areas of knowledge to all other elements of the culture. This is increasingly evident in design firms that have moved into strategic planning and other highly specialized areas of the design process. These firms are successful because before they even begin to conceive a design, they study workers in the workplace. The designers in these firms are organizational behaviorists whose solutions reflect the way people actually do their work.

CONCLUSION

Since the early twentieth century, American designers have been concerned primarily with visual symbols and artifacts. The current information revolution, however, has shifted the designer's focus away from the exclusively visual and toward the interaction of people with each other and the spaces they jointly occupy. A new definition of symbol and artifact acquires meaning only in the relationships people create with the things and the spaces around them.

The relevance of Frederick Taylor's theories ended with the last century. As the third millennium begins, the machine and the linear assembly line no longer work as metaphors for the organization. The accurate metaphor now—fragile, robust, and continually changing all at once—is the human brain itself.

Today, successful design firms are embracing the brain-as-metaphor and taking a holistic and nonlinear approach to the process of providing design services. Today, effective design demands collaboration, along with the integration of ideas from participants at all levels of an organization. Only the people involved in it are fully able to interpret the rigors of the work process; they are, in fact, part of the design team and play a crucial role in interpreting how best to address the changing requirements of their own workplace.

Recently there has been increased emphasis on an improved value system for the design industry—a system that encourages designers to create problem-specific solutions for each design project. At the same time, interior designers are in a position to help their clients maintain a balance between their business and operational goals, particularly as they relate to an organization's financial, functional, and cultural climate.

Individuals and organizations around the globe are in transition from the traditional economy, based solely on tangible products and assets and the physical constraints of space and time, to a new, knowledge-based economy whose foundation is intellectual capital, including human beings and technologies that are willing and able to work anywhere, "24/7/365," to create a unique body of knowledge for themselves or their organization. This shift is occurring rapidly, and competitive pressure threatens to replace quality with speed. It is imperative, however, that the people who inhabit organizational environments take the time to perform better. Likewise, organizations must build time into the production cycle of knowledge-based products. Only high-quality information will reach the widest possible global audience and, ultimately, have the broadest influence.

Interior designers' professional competence today, and in the future, depends on their full participation in the information revolution. Designers must consider learning a lifelong enterprise and transform what they know into a deep understanding of the role of the designer—the professional who makes it possible for human beings to accomplish their goals individually and as participants in whatever organization or situation they are part of. The journey will no doubt be difficult, but, in undertaking it, designers will continue to enhance their role and their importance to society.

Bibliography

Abercrombie, Stanley. *George Nelson: The Design of Modern Design*. Cambridge, MA: MIT Press, 1995.

Brown, John Seely, and Paul Duguid. *The Social Life of Information*. Boston: Harvard Business School Press, 2000.

Cerver, Francisco Asensio. *Interior Design Atlas*. Cologne: Konemann Verlag, 2000.

Danz, Ernst. *Architecture of Skidmore, Owings & Merrill, 1950–1962*. New York: Frederick A. Praeger, 1963.

Duffy, Francis. *The New Office*. London: Conran Octopus, 1997.

Fiedler, Jeannine, and Peter Feierabend. *Bauhaus*. Cologne: Konemann Verlag, 1999.

Fiell, Charlotte, and Peter Fiell. *Design of the 20th Century*. Cologne: Benedikt Taschen Verlag, 1999.

Gabor, Andrea. *The Capitalist Philosophers: The Geniuses of Modern Business: Their Lives, Times, and Ideas*. New York: Times Business, 2000.

International Interior Design Association Foundation and E-Lab LLC. *A Study of Interior Design: Analysis of the Needs of Practice and Implications for Education*. Chicago: IIDA Foundation, 1999.

Larrabee, Eric, and Massimo Vignelli. *Knoll Design*. New York: Harry N. Abrams, 1990.

Margolin, Victor, and Richard Buchanan. *The Idea of Design: A Design Issues Reader*. Cambridge, MA: MIT Press, 1996.

Massey, Anne. *Interior Design of the 20th Century.* London: Thames and Hudson, 1990.

Neuhart, John, Marilyn Neuhart, and Ray Eames. *Eames Design: The Work of the Office of Charles and Ray Eames.* New York: Harry N. Abrams, 1989.

O'Mara, Martha A. *Strategy and Place: Managing Corporate Real Estate and Facilities for Competitive Advantage.* New York: The Free Press, 1999.

Pye, David. *The Nature of Design.* New York: Reinhold, 1964.

Stern, Robert A. M., Thomas Mellins, and David Fishman. *New York 1960: Architecture and Urbanism between the Second World War and the Bicentennial.* New York: Monacelli Press, 1995.

Wharton, Edith, and Ogden Codman, Jr. *The Decoration of Houses.* New York: W. W. Norton, 1978.

Zelinsky, Marilyn. *New Workplaces for New Workstyles.* New York: McGraw-Hill, 1998.

3

Intelligent Interiors

WILLIAM J. MITCHELL

The focus of interior design has shifted, over the centuries, as successive waves of technological innovation have taken effect. In the preindustrial era buildings consisted essentially of supporting skeletons and enclosing skins; interior design was mostly a matter of structure and spatial organization. With the Industrial Revolution, buildings acquired sophisticated mechanical and electrical systems—in effect, artificial physiologies; interior designers were increasingly concerned with selecting and procuring specialized equipment and with configuring machine-powered systems to support specific activities. The early modernist architect Le Corbusier summarized this new condition, and the attitude he took to it, by describing a house polemically as a "machine for living in."[1] Now, in the twenty-first century, inexpensive microelectronics, software, and increasingly pervasive digital networks are ushering in the age of intelligent interiors.

Twenty-first-century buildings are acquiring artificial nervous systems. Electronics and software are becoming important elements of interior design solutions. And designers can now think of rooms as "robots for interacting with."

PREINDUSTRIAL INTERIORS: STRUCTURE AND SPACE

To put the emerging capabilities of intelligent interiors in perspective, let us begin by considering a typical preindustrial building—the elementary habitation of an agricultural worker shown, in its now ruined and abandoned state, in Figure 3-1. It consists of a single rectangular space with doors at either end and windows on opposite sides. Its basic function was, simply, shelter. The stone walls and the corrugated iron roof provided protection

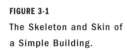

FIGURE 3-1
The Skeleton and Skin of
a Simple Building.

from the wind and the rain, and relief from the heat of the sun. The walls mitigated extremes of heat and cold by supplying insulation, and through their thermal mass, they would heat up in the warmth of the day, then reradiate thermal energy to the interior in the cool evenings. When these passive strategies did not suffice, a fireplace produced additional heat. And, when it got really cold, there were blankets to huddle under.

The door and window openings provided connection to the exterior, together with mechanisms for controlling the character of that connection. They could be opened and closed manually to vary the flow of air. And, through filtering mechanisms such as screens, shutters, blinds, and drapes (probably minimal in this particular case), they provided straightforward ways to manipulate qualities of interior light, view, privacy, and protection from bugs and dust.

The interior was not subdivided, like a modern home, into specialized rooms. Instead, the space was adapted for different purposes at different times, through use of very simple, mostly portable furniture and equipment. There was a bed for sleeping, table and chairs for eating and reading, and a water basin for washing. The fireplace served as an elementary cooking device, and the great outdoors as a privy.

There were no pipes and wires embedded in the walls and beneath the floor, no mechanical or electrical devices, and no demands for the services of plumbers, electricians, or appliance service people. Water was supplied from a rainwater tank fed by runoff from the roof. Firewood was cut from the surrounding scrub and hand-carried to the hearth. There may have been a kerosene lantern filled from a drum outside the door. And perhaps there was an evaporative cooler hanging in the branches of a nearby tree.

MACHINE-AGE INTERIORS: DOMINANCE OF MECHANICAL AND ELECTRICAL SYSTEMS

Now contrast this simple, base-case building with a typical twentieth-century suburban home. The most obvious difference is that the more modern interior is subdivided into numerous specialized rooms for particular purposes—typically several bedrooms for different family members, living room, dining room, kitchen, bathrooms, laundry, and garage. The designer's most fundamental task is to configure these rooms in response to a program—that is, to get their sizes, proportions, interrelationships, and orientations right.

Each of these rooms requires specialized furniture and machinery to support the associated functions. So a second crucial design task is to select, specify, and procure the necessary items. There is bedroom, living room, and dining room furniture, and there are kitchen, bathroom, laundry, and entertainment fixtures and appliances. Natural light from the windows is augmented by a variety of different electric light fixtures—with the specifications of these varying according to location and purpose. And there are heating and mechanical ventilation fixtures to provide active means of climate control.

To keep all these specialized devices running, the house is elaborately networked with supply and removal systems. There are hot and cold water supplies and sewer connections to the kitchen, bathroom, and laundry; the plumbing plan is an important part of the design. There may be gas supply, as well. There are air supply and return ducts to all the rooms; this requires another sheet of construction drawings, and introduces another trade. And there is electrical wiring everywhere—yet another drawing and trade.

All these systems require control devices, so the designer is required to select, specify, and conveniently locate these. They consist mostly of faucets and valves for the plumbing, and switches and dimmers for the electrical system. Perhaps there are some rudimentary automatic controls—thermostats for the air conditioning and timers for the lights.

Finally, the internal networks of the house are connected to large-scale utility networks. There are metered connections to water, gas, and electrical supply networks. Municipal sewer and garbage disposal systems remove waste. The garage would be no use without connection to a street system. Unlike the primitive dwelling considered earlier—which was essentially autonomous in its operation—the modern house is so dependent on its utility connections that it quickly becomes uninhabitable if these are disrupted.

Other modern building types—offices, manufacturing facilities, warehouses, retail facilities, schools, hospitals, laboratories, and so on—can be analyzed in similar ways. All consist of differentiated and specialized interior spaces, with furniture and equipment adapted specifically to the particular functions of those spaces. These spaces are tied together by internal mechanical and electrical networks, and these networks are linked to large-scale utilities. Throughout the nineteenth and twentieth centuries, as the mechanical and electrical systems of buildings became increasingly elaborate and sophisticated, they demanded growing shares of design attention (Figure 3-2). They also accounted for increasing proportions of construction documents, and they began to dominate construction and operating costs.

DIGITALLY NETWORKED INTERIORS

Since the late 1960s, digital networks have emerged as an increasingly important new type of interior system. Their development began with the implementation of elementary computer networks in major business, research, and educational facilities. The adoption of Ethernet and token ring standards, together with the growing popularity of personal computers and engineering workstations, led to the proliferation of local-area networks (LANs) in workplaces during the 1980s and the 1990s. As the twenty-first century dawned, digital network connections were becoming commonplace in almost all types of interiors, and as ubiquitous as electrical outlets.

In their physical characteristics and space requirements, these networks are highly varied. Optical fiber may be used for the highest-speed links; this is bulky, cannot be bent around sharp corners, and—though fairly easily accommodated in special chases and trays in new construction—can be very difficult to retrofit gracefully into existing interiors. Coaxial and twisted-pair copper

FIGURE 3-2
Mechanical and
electrical networks
have become increas-
ingly elaborate and
sophisticated in
modern buildings.

wiring serves for lower-speed links; this is less demanding in its requirements than fiber, but the sheer number of cables may add up to a significant space demand. Wireless networks reduce the need to run cables everywhere, but they have other limitations: they still require transceivers at closely spaced intervals, they are generally slower than the wired alternatives, and they are subject to interference problems.

Networking also creates a significant demand for space—particularly accessible closets—to accommodate switching equipment. These closets are now an increasingly important element of interior space programs.

The growing need to provide network connection anywhere, and to power digital electronic devices, creates some particular interior design challenges. In some cases it suffices to provide power supply and network access around the perimeter of spaces, and perhaps on columns. Where a higher density of access points is required it may be necessary to introduce floor or ceiling grids. Cabling can also be run through demountable partition and furniture systems, but this increases their complexity and cost, and makes them harder to take apart and reconfigure.

Throughout the nineteenth and twentieth centuries, as the mechanical and electrical systems of buildings became increasingly elaborate and sophisticated, they demanded growing shares of design attention.

INTELLIGENT INTERIORS

The activity that converts a merely *networked* building into an *intelligent* building is the integration of electronic sensors, robotic effectors, and control intelligence into the network so that the building can respond more effectively to changing interior requirements and external conditions. This is becoming increasingly feasible as the cost of microelectronics drops, as electronic intelligence is embedded in a widening array of devices, and as these devices are networked.

Electronic sensors correspond to the eyes, ears, and other sensory organs of living organisms. Computer-connected microphones and digital cameras (particularly in the form of increasingly ubiquitous Webcams) are the most obvious. Pressure sensors not only make keyboards possible, they can also be embedded in flooring and furniture to track locations of furniture and inhabitants. Position sensors range from the mechanical and optical sensors of the PC mouse to ultrasonic and electromagnetic sensors that precisely track coordinates of objects in three-dimensional space, to Global Positioning System (GPS)-based sensors that track automobiles, boats, and airplanes. Motion sensors tell whether there is activity within a space. Electronic and optical tags and badges, together with special readers, allow objects to be identified. Climatic sensors can keep track of temperature, humidity, and air movement. Specialized chemical sensors exist in vast variety. And medical sensors—implants, bedside devices, and noninvasive sensors in the surrounding environment—can monitor your bodily condition.

Robotic effectors are machines that have been networked and brought under computer control; they correspond to the hands, feet, and other organisms that living organisms employ to accomplish their goals. Computer-controlled displays, printers, and audio output devices have, of course, become very familiar. Less obviously, any household device may now be thought of as a potential robotic effector. Lighting, heating and ventilating, water and sewage, cleaning, and security and safety systems of buildings may also be integrated with networks. So may actuators that operate doors, windows, and blinds or other privacy and sun-control devices. And there are innumerable specialized devices such as computer-aided design and manufacturing (CAD/CAM) production machines and surgical robots.

Control software relates the input from electronic sensors to the output from robotic effectors. In its simplest and most familiar form it specifies a fixed sequence of operations—the cycle of a dishwasher or microwave oven, for example. More advanced control software applies decision rules in order to determine appropriate responses to current conditions. Thus an air-conditioning system may respond to temperature variations by varying its cooling output, a houseplant irrigation system may respond to soil moisture content by increasing or decreasing water supply, a clothes washer may respond to the particular fabric and cleaning problem by adjusting its chemical mix and cycle, and so on.

The most sophisticated control software has the capacity to observe and learn. For example, an advanced climate-control system might observe patterns of variation in external climatic conditions and internal user behavior, develop predictive models based on these observations, and thus anticipate needs. Instead of merely *reacting* to a drop in temperature, as a simple thermostat-controlled system would, it might *anticipate* the drop and prepare for it efficiently by adjusting heat production. Even more ambitiously, advanced control software might coordinate the actions of multiple devices and systems; on a snowy winter morning it might wake up a household by turning up the heat at the usual time, making wake-up calls at appropriate moments, switching on the lights, setting appliances to work to prepare breakfast, piping in personalized versions of the day's news, and starting the car.

Control software need not be fixed for the life of a device. Software-controlled devices may be reprogrammed as necessary—thus providing far greater flexibility than was possible with the hard-wired devices common in the past. And, where a device is networked, reprogramming may be accomplished by downloading the new software from the Internet.

These new capabilities fundamentally change the way in which buildings respond to the requirements of their inhabitants. Preindustrial buildings, as we have seen, relied mostly on passive strategies for responding to environmental variation and meeting user needs. Buildings of the industrial era made much more use of active, electrical and mechanical devices to perform these tasks, but depended on manual and simple automatic control systems. The intelligent interiors of the twenty-first century will increasingly integrate diverse electronic sensors, robotic effectors, embedded intelligence, networking, and control software to create distributed systems that respond in far more sophisticated and efficient fashion (Figure 3-3).

FIGURE 3-3
Buildings of the 21st century are acquiring electronic nervous systems. (House_n project, MIT, 2001. (Courtesy of Kent Larson)

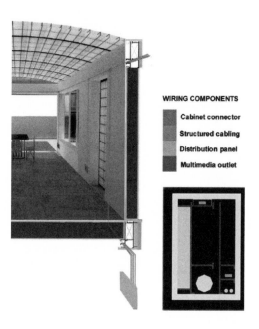

CONNECTION TO GLOBAL NETWORKS

Just as a building's internal plumbing is connected to the external water-supply network, and its electrical wiring to the electrical grid, so its internal network (the nervous system of its smart interior) is normally connected to an external information utility—the Internet.

The Internet had its origins in the 1960s, with the invention of packet-switching for digital telecommunications and implementation of the Arpanet —a network that initially connected a few large computers at universities and research centers. Later, development of the TCP/IP protocol allowed packet-switching networks to be readily interconnected, the proliferation of personal computers and engineering workstations increased the demand for interconnection, and the Internet emerged. Growth accelerated with the superimposition of the World Wide Web, the development of graphic browsers to facilitate surfing the Web, and the dot.com investment boom of the late

1990s. By the dawn of the new century, the Internet was functioning as a true global utility—though still very uneven in its geographic and socioeconomic penetration.

Physically, the Internet consists of servers (computers that store and pump out digital information), clients (intelligent devices that consume information), telecommunication links, and switches that route packets of digital information from their sources to their intended destinations. The long-distance and building-to-building links that hold it together are extraordinarily heterogeneous; they may be formed from any mixture of high-speed fiber backbones, repurposed telephone or cable television copper wiring, terrestrial wireless links, geosynchronous satellite links, and low-earth-orbit satellite links. From an interior designer's perspective, the most critical link is that linking a building's internal network to a point-of-presence (POP) on a high-speed backbone; this will largely determine the speed and reliability of the building's linkage to the external digital world, and hence the functions that can effectively be supported. Telephone dial-up access is slow and discontinuous but the only thing available in many contexts, cable modem access makes use of the cable television system to provide faster, continuous access, DSL does the same with telephone wiring, and dedicated lines or satellite links provide very high-quality service at commensurate cost.

In general, it is useful to think of our burgeoning digital environment as a large collection of nested networks linked to each other, at well-defined points, by electronic "bridges." At the lowest level are the very fast, miniaturized circuits of digital electronic devices. These are connected to the somewhat slower networks that integrate the smart elements of our immediate surroundings—perhaps bodynets linking implanted, wearable, and handheld devices, plus the internal networks of automobiles, and the local-area networks of buildings. These, in turn, are linked into utilities at neighborhood, city, and regional scale. And finally, the high-speed backbone of the Internet ties everything together at a global scale. To the extent that there are significant differences in speed and reliability between small-scale and large-scale networks, there are clear advantages to storing software and data locally, near to where they will be used. To the extent that these differences are disappearing, though, so are the advantages of this local availability. We are entering an era in which local software and data resources will be far less important factors in the functionality of smart spaces than ready access to the distributed resources of the global network.

INTELLIGENT SUPPLY AND CONSUMPTION

As the utilities that supply a building become smarter in their operation, and as a building's systems and appliances become more intelligent consumers of resources, the relationship of supply and demand becomes more sophisticated. For example, an advanced electrical supply system might vary its prices dynamically according to current demand, and provide for buildings to "run the meter backwards" by pumping electricity from solar collectors or fuel cells back into the grid. In this context, a smart dishwasher might wait until prices were low before switching itself on, or even choose a moment when it could run on locally produced power rather than power supplied by the grid.

Devices that consume information can be programmed to "shop" the Internet automatically for content they require at advantageous prices. Thus Napster, the controversial Internet music distribution system, looks for specified recordings and downloads them from wherever they are most conveniently available. Similar software can be employed to find and download video. If sites charge for downloads, then this sort of software can be set to look for the least expensive sources.

The same principle can be extended to refrigerators, pantries, and household appliances such as clothes washers. In the future, many of these devices will monitor their own contents electronically and automatically order new supplies, as needed, over the Internet.

THE NEW FUNCTIONS OF INTELLIGENT INTERIORS

In general, the effect of embedded digital intelligence, together with Internet connection, will be to make interior spaces more flexible and versatile. In the home, for example, electronic delivery of digital audio and video files can turn any room equipped with suitable displays and digital audio playback devices into a versatile entertainment site—extending a trend that began with radio, the gramophone, and television. The same applies to hotel rooms, dormitory rooms, automobile seats, and airplane seats. Instead of a shelf filled with audio CDs and video DVDs, what is now needed is a fast connection to Napster or some equivalent.

The effect on workplaces will be even more dramatic. Traditionally, workplaces have been located in close proximity to necessary raw materials, machinery, files, and so on, and work has been carried out during well-defined working hours. Today, though, information work—which is an increasingly dominant occupation in advanced economies—can be conducted almost anywhere there is a network connection. Files can be accessed remotely, software tools can be downloaded as necessary, and much (though not all) interaction with customers and co-workers can be accomplished through electronic mail, chat systems, specialized transaction software, telephone, and videoconferencing. This does not mean that everyone will become a full-time telecommuter, but it does provide much greater flexibility in work times and places. In a world of network connections and intelligent interiors there is no clear distinction between work and non-work places; almost any place—an office cubicle, a library desk, a home study, a cafe, an airport lounge, an airline seat—may serve as a workplace when necessary.

Similarly, almost any intelligent interior can function as a study, library, or classroom. Distance-learning technology can deliver educational resources wherever and whenever they are needed. In some contexts this means that online resources substitute for older modes of face-to-face instruction—particularly where the goal is to serve large numbers of students at low cost. In other contexts online resources complement and enhance face-to-face instruction, as when students bring their wireless laptops to a seminar and surf the Web to find material that is relevant to the ongoing discussion, or when the images discussed in an architectural history class are available online for later review.

More surprisingly, perhaps, intelligent interiors have the potential to deliver medical services in radical new ways. Once, before medical treatment depended on highly specialized resources, doctors made house calls. In the industrial era the prevailing pattern was to transport patients to specialized clinics, surgeries, hospitals, and nursing homes, where specialized knowledge and equipment were concentrated. Intelligent interiors now open up the possibility of continuous, unobtrusive, remote medical monitoring, of remote medical examination, and of controlled delivery of medication through smart implants, intelligent pill dispensers and medicine cabinets, and the like. These sorts of capabilities are likely to be increasingly important as aging baby-boomers create unprecedented demand for medical services.

CONCLUSIONS

Today's buildings serve their purposes through complex combinations of the passive capabilities of structure and skin, the dynamic capabilities of mechanical and electrical systems and appliances, and the sensing, processing, and control capabilities of computational devices and networks. The addition of electronic intelligence generally enhances the versatility of interiors, allows them to adapt more effectively to changes in occupant requirements and exterior conditions, and makes them into more efficient consumers of resources. As the necessary technologies continue to develop, and as designers learn to make effective use of them, intelligent systems will become an increasingly crucial concern of interior design, a more and more dominant cost element in construction and fit-out, and a fundamental determinant of client and user satisfaction.

Note

1
Le Corbusier, Charles E. J., *Towards a New Architecture* [trans. Frederick Etchells], The Architectural Press, London, 1927.

Bibliography

Banham, Reyner. *The Architecture of the Well-Tempered Environment.* Chicago: University of Chicago Press, 1969.

Mitchell, William J. *City of Bits: Space, Place, and the Infobahn,* Cambridge MA: MIT Press, 1995.

Mitchell, William J. *E-topia: Urban Life, Jim—But Not as We Know It.* Cambridge MA: MIT Press, 1999.

4

The Professional Association

JAMES P. CRAMER, Hon. AIA, Hon. IIDA

Throughout the history of interior design, sole designers, design studios and firms have been pioneers in leading and nurturing the larger universe of designers toward new levels of achievement and recognition. Much of this activity has also taken place in professional nonprofit associations, which are dedicated to improving professional practice. But why join? Design professionals work hard at a wide range of tasks, all of them necessary for successful results and successful business and professional development. Elsewhere in this handbook, interior design professionals are urged to embrace life-long learning and to develop new skills to keep pace with market trends and technological developments. These development activities and the critical tasks that make up a day's work week after week make time a precious commodity for the serious designer. In a professional life with such demands, it may seem that joining an association is simply too much to ask.

In some cases, that may be so; for a particular designer, a particular professional association may not add enough value to make membership worthwhile in the face of competing demands for the designer's limited time. Yet associations are critical to the advancement of the interior design profession and its affiliates.

Throughout the history of design, leaders of these associations have evaluated, surveyed, and assessed (sometimes intuitively) the interior design profession outside their own studios (not just in terms of their own self-interest), and have established teams and organizations that work together to address issues of common concern. These societies, leagues, and associations have been formed, both informally and formally, to provide extra leverage for the priorities and causes of the design community. Design associations provide enhanced information sharing, legislative initiatives, continuing professional education, and fellowship of like-minded, although diverse, professionals around the world. Today, the interior design associations are continuing to build toward the future of the profession by reinventing themselves, proving their legitimacy, and driving toward new value propositions. Individual designers owe it to themselves to understand the history and value of the professional associations and the factors they should consider when deciding which association is the right one for them.

COLLABORATION IN DESIGN–FROM BUILDING STRUCTURES TO BUILDING A PROFESSION

Professional associations may seem like a modern phenomenon, and a specialized one at that. For centuries, however, design professionals have practiced in close connection with other trades and other design professionals. Historically, "association" in design appears in different modes, involving different degrees of hierarchy and control. "Association" has also been a tool for different purposes, from the creation of buildings to the enhancement of social prestige to the betterment of design as a profession. But across these modes, design practices have three things in common: socialization, cross-disciplinary connections, and professional collaboration.

It is not commonly understood that prior to today's professional interior design associations, there existed near-invisible enclaves of designers within the arts and architecture community who gathered socially and for the purpose of idea sharing. Most of this history is impenetrably difficult to access. However, we are able to pull together threads of early activity at the Architects Club founded in 1791 and the London Architectural Society founded in 1806. These societies included interior design in their discussion programs and often emphasized the importance of interior elements and decoration. The London Architectural Society was a learned society whose members were obliged to read an essay and exhibit an unpublished design each year or pay a forfeit. Some of the records of these early European initiatives are currently housed at The Royal Institute of British Architects (RIBA) in London. After visiting the RIBA Library, one comes away with an awe-inspiring sense of the talent, sensitivity, and power of interior design during the last three centuries in Europe.

ASSOCIATED TALENTS FOR INTEGRATED DESIGN

Throughout the preceding centuries

Throughout the preceding centuries, interior designers were increasingly motivated to come together to discover key issues and understandings of the practices and policies of the day and also to put into place initiatives to enhance and protect their practices and to advocate for good design.

By the middle of the eighteenth century, property owners in Asia, Europe, and America could avail themselves of loosely integrated building and design services, including architecture, interior design, and decoration. At that time, it was quite common for the architects, or master builders as they were also called, not only to decide on the structure of the buildings but also to choose the interior finishes. For instance, in the mid-1700s, one of the exceptionally talented design leaders of the time, Robert Adam, was commissioned to design residences, churches, institutions, and general-use projects, including, in many cases, the furniture for his buildings, which was frequently made by Chippendale. Robert Adam ordered the silk damask for the walls, he designed the furniture, and he designed the floors, whether stone, wood, or fabric. Adam was an interior designer. He was also an architect who was designing, creating furniture and furnishings, and decorating spaces that defined the tastes of the era.

This loose association of services continued throughout the eighteenth and nineteenth centuries. In America, the architect Thomas Jefferson designed both buildings and furnishings. While working as the U.S. Ambassador to France, he was fascinated with interior elements that could be placed in such a manner as to substantially enhance a room's spatial quality. In England in the 1820s, William Porden rebuilt Eaton Hall for Earl Grosvenor, designing the exterior and interior architecture as well as the furniture. Daniel Marot worked in Holland, England, and France, and almost always took responsibility for the architecture, interior design, and decorative detailing and placement. During this period, design professions were loosely defined by their specific functions, but they also commonly embraced all rolls, which provided integrated services and a unified vision for their private and public clients.

Another significant early association model in the history of design evolved from independent project collaboration initiatives into collaboration on the mission and purpose of design. One of the most influential architects of the nineteenth century, A. W. N. Pugin, stood apart from the other major architects and designers of that time in that, while he typically created every detail for a building, he did it without any staff—no draftsmen, designers, or clerks. Even so, a talented alliance of devoted colleagues who appreciated his principles and understood his aims carried out his work in design, metalwork, stained glass, tiles, and ceramics. The noted interior designer John Gregory Crace provided Pugin with interior design expertise from his own office of designers (an early example of what we often refer today as outsourcing). Pugin's extended organization functioned as a de facto professional association that included social and policy initiatives and, through their writing, advocated theoretical viewpoints on ornament, urban design, and social improvement. Pugin's "society" supported its "members" in a meaningful and practical manner in their everyday work and ultimately became much more—an informal social network of like-minded people and an influential information-sharing consortium. This network of designers and craftspeople became a tiny virtual association, one of the thousands of predecessors to today's interior design associations.

ASSOCIATIONS AND THE FUTURE OF DESIGN

From historical documents we learn of many informal alliances that began to emerge to create organic and organizational energy flows to understand and promote the increasing value of interior design and space-planning services. Some embraced a primary interest in promoting the future of interior design as a distinct profession.

This drive to promote interior design was enhanced when its leading proponents connected design with social issues in a variety of ways. While Edith Wharton was bringing attention to this new and distinct profession in the United States, as a result of her famous writings on interior decoration, in Paris, Elsie de Wolfe was making her own contributions as an outspoken advocate of interior design's relevancy. Both Wharton and de Wolfe began to knit together and bring to attention the many diverse design talents. These designers were a high-profile social force, and the newspapers took notice. Wharton and de Wolfe were not only interested in serving a newly rich clientele and upper-class nobility but also were responding, in a creative and meaningful manner, to the extraordinary social and cultural changes of the time. Designers were increasingly called upon to enhance the quality of the human condition in hospitals, schools, hotels, and in the marketplace.

ASSOCIATIONS IN THE TWENTIETH CENTURY: FRAGMENTATION AND INNOVATION

After Wharton and de Wolfe championed the essential social role of this emerging practice, designers began to professionalize as well as specialize, and within the last 70 years, professional associations have become institutions in the design industry. It is now possible to identify the changing roles that these professional institutions have played in dividing responsibilities among design and building professionals and to perceive how professional associations have shaped practices—both for specific groups of design professionals and at the margins of an association's "territory."

Trends in the nineteenth and twentieth centuries reshaped the design, building, and construction industry. There was a movement toward specialization, which divided responsibility for the different areas of practice and led to fragmentation and implementation of a linear, step-by-step approach. Thus, the American Society of Civil Engineers and Architects served only civil engineers, not architects, and the American Institute of Architects (AIA) was formed as a standalone not-for-profit organization in the mid-1850s for the benefit of architects. The AIA and the Associated General Contractors then advanced the idea that separate construction documents and contracts be drawn up between the owner, the contractor, the architect, the engineer, and the interior designer. The long-followed master builder approach, which integrated functions and techniques and utilized design-build as the service delivery method, moved out of favor, largely because of an agreed-upon division of power between contractors—the builders and tradesmen—and the professionals.

It is now possible to identify the changing roles that these professional institutions have played in dividing responsibilities among design and building professionals and to perceive how professional associations have shaped practices . . .

One of the associations' new roles was to make sense of the newfound niche opportunities and higher degrees of challenges as a result of this fragmentation. The American Institute of Architects provided direction by codifying this division between the building and design professions, which they incorporated into their Code of Ethics, by warning of an inherent conflict of interest that existed between these different roles.

Just as separate professional specialties formed new alliances and enclaves of leaders, a few design professions still sought innovation and took initiatives toward the integration of talents and services. One needs to look no further than the cooperative, multitalented design studios at Cranbrook, or the integrated processes at Frank Lloyd Wright's Taliesen Studio, or the total design philosophy and implementation of the work of Charles and Ray Eames. Consider the Bauhaus movement, or the practice of John Portman in Atlanta, who further led the movement toward the integration of services in the later part of the twentieth century by arranging for financing, taking lead responsibility as developer, designing the buildings and furnishings, and arranging for facility management to provide ongoing stewardship for the building. Today, Portman's chairs, tables, and artworks are commonly found in his own office building and hotel projects. He was also one of the architects responsible for reintroducing into the mainstream the integrated design-build method and challenging the American Institute of Architects to rewrite their Code of Ethics to allow architects to once again take on single-source responsibility and answer directly to the owner for design as well as construction services. Portman's own colleagues exemplify how special-interest groups and professional interest areas within an association can challenge and prevail in changing the policies of associations.

Except for those few instances, however, fragmentation in design and construction was common during the first 80 years of the twentieth century. Therefore, while the twentieth century promoted professionalism to new levels, it also was a period characterized by less-than-efficient design and construction. There was more written about risk assessment and defining authority than about efficient practices, and more about power and position than about collaboration.

The trend toward professional and association specialization next gave rise to new associations such as the Institute of Business Designers, the International Society of Interior Designers, the Construction Specifications Institute, the Design-Build Institute of America, and the Urban Land Institute.

MAJOR ASSOCIATIONS AND THEIR GOALS

Today there are interior design associations in almost every country throughout the world. In the United States, the three primary associations are the International Interior Design Association (IIDA), the American Society of Interior Designers (ASID), and the American Institute of Architects' Interiors Professional Interest Area (PIA).

The International Interior Design Association provides a wide variety of services and benefits to over 12,000 members. Its mission is to promote excellence in interior design and to advance the profession through knowledge. The IIDA was formed by three smaller associations: the Institute of Business Designers, the International Society of Interior Design, and the Federal Designers Council. It advocates for design excellence, organizes the interior design community worldwide, maintains educational standards, responds to trends in business and design, and provides information about interior design and related issues. The IIDA has nine international regions with more than 30 chapters and 64 U.S. City centers. It is based in Chicago's Merchandise Mart. Its Internet site is www.iida.org.

The American Society of Interior Designers was formed in 1975 with the consolidation of the American Institute of Designers (AID) and the National Society of Interior Designers (NSID). The ASID serves over 30,000 members, including approximately 7,000 students and 3,500 product representatives. The ASID provides services in government affairs, conferences, publications, online services, and continuing education. Members include both residential and commercial designers. The ASID focuses primarily on U.S. issues, although it has some international members. The ASID's headquarters are in Washington, D.C., just down the street from the east front of the U.S. Capitol. Further information is available at www.asid.org.

The American Institute of Architects has an active interior architecture committee called the Interiors PIA. The AIA was founded in 1857 in New York

City and is the largest design association in the world outside of Asia. The AIA provides education, government advocacy, community redevelopment, and public outreach activities with and for its 63,000 members. With 305 local and state chapters, the institute closely monitors legislative and regulatory actions at all levels of government. It provides professional development opportunities, industry standard contract documents, information services, and a comprehensive awards program. The AIA houses one of the largest professional practice libraries in the world. It has chapters in Europe and Hong Kong but focuses primarily on U.S. issues. The Interiors PIA includes both interior designers and architects. For more information, see the Internet site at www.e-architect.com.

INTERDISCIPLINARY AND INTERASSOCIATION AFFILIATIONS

Often, designers also affiliate with other organizations, including the Urban Land Institute (ULI), the International Facility Management Association (IFMA), the American Design Drafting Association, the National Kitchen and Bath Association (NKBA), the National Trust for Historic Preservation (NTHP), the Institute of Store Planners (ISP), the Business and Industry Furniture Manufacturers Association, the Design Management Institute, and the Industrial Designers Society of America (IDSA), among others.

There is also an organization called the International Federation of Interior Architects/Designers (IFI). The goals of IFI, which serves interior design associations globally, are to promote the interior architecture and design professions, to represent its practitioners, to act as a clearinghouse for professional and cultural information, to encourage international cooperation, and to assist and serve the industry. The IFI engages in a number of activities to further these ends, such as maintaining a public relations program, lobbying for policies benefiting the practice, organizing conferences, and supporting minimum standards of education and a Code of Ethics and Practice. Its membership is composed not of individuals but rather of organizations. It is located in Johannesburg, South Africa. More information is available at www.ifi.co.za.

Today, the leaders of these associations are integral parts of the push toward growth and relevancy. The associations are actively seeking their leaders for the future. They know that the growth of the design associations is directly proportionate to the collective strength …

LEADERSHIP OF ASSOCIATIONS: A KEY TO STRATEGIC CHANGE

What lies ahead for the design associations? Each association is actively interested in the future health and vitality of the interior design profession. Today, the leaders of these associations are integral parts of the push toward growth and relevancy. The associations are actively seeking their leaders for the future. They know that the growth of the design associations is directly proportionate to the collective strength, willingness, and ability of the volunteer leaders who set the wheels of change in motion. Leadership is essential for future success. However, the climate for associations to thrive is much different today than it was even five years ago.

Looking backward and looking around today, it is possible to document the fact that the leaders of the interior design profession have been in the past and will continue to be involved in the association initiatives to advance the design professions. Consider these association leaders of recent history: Florence Knoll, Sir Norman Foster, Frank Duffy, Margo Grant, Neil Frankel, Henry Dreyfuss, Gary Wheeler, Arthur Gensler, Charles Gandy, Cheryl Duvall, and countless others at local, state, regional, national, and international levels.

Globally, taken country by country, and stated in countless but largely repetitive ways, the interior design associations have five common purposes that are most often cited:

1. To improve the reputation and status of the interior design profession.

2. To serve as a learned society and collect a distinct body of knowledge.

3. To represent the interior design profession to the populations of their countries to whom individuals and the governments can refer for opinion on design matters.

4. To work for the cultivation and improvement of interior design and to take responsibility, on behalf of the public, for the highest standards of both design and public protection.

5. To recognize design excellence and celebrate professional achievement.

ACHIEVING EXCELLENCE IN GOVERNANCE

How do professional associations in the design field implement these goals? Each association has a chief elected officer and a chief executive officer. The former is most often referred to as the president and the latter as the executive vice president. The boards of the associations range in size from about a dozen to nearly fifty. An executive committee of officers helps to establish the governance policies and priorities of each association. The executive vice president usually supervises a staff of specialists in areas ranging from communications to government affairs. The staff size varies considerably depending on the association. In addition to the board of directors, each of the associations has committees, councils, task forces, and/or professional interest areas in such categories as:

1. Residential Interior Design

2. Large Firm Roundtables

3. Hotel and Hospitality Interiors

4. Corporate Interiors

5. Health Care Design

6. Store Planning and Merchandising Design

7. Higher Education and Institutional Interiors

8. Religious and Ecclesiastical Interiors

9. Codes and Standards

10. Forms and Documents

11. Education

12. Industrial and Furniture Design

Many of the design associations have city, provincial, and state chapters. Some of these organizations are full of energy and are driving the regional progress of the interior design profession. In New York City, for instance, the initiatives of the IIDA have brought attention to the role that interior design professionals play in the success of the tourist, hospitality, and retail economy. The IIDA Leadership Forum is often sold out weeks in advance, due primarily to the in-depth and relevant subjects that shape the quality of urban life in New York City.

The ASID, AIA, IIDA, and others have monthly chapter meetings in each of the major cities in the United States. Often, these meetings focus on professional issues that qualify for continuing education units. Each of the professional organizations both offers and requires of their members continuing education at set levels annually. The associations' web sites describe qualifications for membership and for maintaining membership, and provide information on each chapter, with phone numbers and key coordinator information.

CHOOSING TO BE INVOLVED

In some countries, only one association is available for a professional to join. Often, however, there are choices. Designers often ask themselves if membership is worth it, and whether they should get involved. According to Greenway Consulting's research in *Design Intelligence*, eight factors are most often cited as reasons why designers choose not to get involved in a design association:

1. Bureaucracy and red tape

2. Lack of vision

3. Not open to innovation and creativity

4. Poor meetings and flat programs

5. Lack of volunteer appreciation

6. Too much politics with a lack of open spirit

7. Poor management

8. A "pay your dues" mentality

Associations admit that they go through patterns, degrees, and cycles of success in serving their membership. Today, there are also generational issues for associations to consider. Sophisticated technology, too, has made for a different membership environment.

Interior designers are seeking greater responsiveness from the associations and their leaders. They are more carefully considering the return on investment that they get for their volunteer involvement, attendance at conferences, and purchase of forms, documents, and resources.

Each association has a governing body usually called a board of directors. These boards meet at state, regional, national, and international levels. They set policies, define the association's vision, determine the measurements of success, and make decisions regarding fiduciary obligations. Most of all, however, the boards of these interior design associations are the champions of their organizations and of the future of the design professions. Board members serve terms ranging from two to five years. During their term, board members debate key issues of the day and deal with questions such as "Should this body be inclusive or exclusive?" "What should our priorities be this year?" "How can we be better managed, better led, and more relevant to our constituencies"? In recent years, the boards of the design associations have been hotbeds of political action and have brought forward broad changes affecting the future of the design professions.

Each association has its own culture and style. And while some of the associations continue to lead in certain areas, others choose to lead in other areas. It is useful to examine characteristics of these associations to ascertain where they "fit" with your own expectations. Keep in mind the following:

1. Are the meetings well attended?

2. Are there frequent communications?

3. Are there regular professional development programs offered for members at all levels?

4. Is the board of directors prepared for their duties? Are they leaders?

5. Do the leaders participate in the meetings?

6. Does the organization encourage a plurality of ideas in their discussions or are issues railroaded through the meetings of members?

7. Are the meetings of the association controlled by a few outspoken members?

8. Are issues resolved or do they carry over from meeting to meeting?

9. Do the leaders take action?

10. Are issues brought to closure?

11. Are the meetings good social experiences–is there camaraderie and meaningful social purpose?

TRUSTING YOUR ASSOCIATION?

While twenty-first-century organizations are formed because of common purposes and goals, not all associations function effectively despite their lofty ambitions. The most critical factor that makes some of these organizations more effective is "trust." Much has been written about trust. It is recommended that a trust assessment be conducted before investing time and money in an association. This is prudent behavior. Look for shared purpose, shared culture, and for confidence in the leadership. Here are some questions to ask of associations before you become involved:

1. How involved are volunteers in the organization? What is the turnover rate? What percentages are involved locally and nationally?

2. How much of my membership dollar goes into administrative overhead? Exactly how is my dollar divided? What are the priorities of the budget for these changing times?

3. Who are the leaders and what are their qualifications? Are these the leaders that peers respect the most?

4. What barriers are associated with involvement in the leadership activities?

5. Does the association board have a strategic plan? Is it available to see? How does the board measure success? How does it communicate that to the membership?

6. What mechanisms does the association have to understand the membership's changing needs? Does it have a way to get timely and meaningful feedback on the services it offers?

7. How does the association explain the value of membership in terms of return on investment?

8. Could I have sample copies of the last three newsletters so that I can determine whether the association's emphasis is relevant to my own professional work situation?

9. How do I qualify for professional status? What credentials does the association offer? How do I maintain my qualifications?

Once design professionals choose to join a professional association, they are likely to continue to retain their membership. About 25 percent of first-year members will choose to drop out, but thereafter membership retention is normally around 92 percent. Still, each design professional retains the choice of whether to continue to be a member of the association. To ensure that the association is accountable to their needs, members should assess the quality of communications from the leadership to members, from the association to the public, and between the staff and the members. Such communication plans, often in place within the association, are crucial because, without them, associations flop around without strategic continuity from year to year. Without continuity, the association creates needless inefficiency, waste, and inconsistent service. Members quickly see the difference.

THE VALUE PROPOSITION

Members of professional associations have a responsibility to assess the value of their associations on an ongoing basis. Continuing assessment not only keeps the organization relevant and accountable to the association but contributes as well to the legacy of the profession.

In general, the interior design associations have played a positive role in the advancement of the profession of interior design and those affiliated with the profession. Still, there are fragmented constituencies, and much progress needs to be made before today's associations reach their potential. There is a trend toward collaboration with other design associations, and this trend should produce a sharper edge—and more relevant services for the future.

Each of the associations in its own style has opened up to candid conversations with both insiders and outsiders about its future vision and viability. The associations understand that it is vital to get outside the charmed circle, which is often to some degree blinded by self-interest. (It is hard for an association to save itself from the inside alone.) Therefore, new and youthful membership, young associate and outside board members, and ongoing perspectives from surveys help to keep the associations fresh, strong, and relevant.

Interior design organizations of the future will develop strengths in both their knowledge capital and their social capital. One without the other will produce an imbalance and a missed opportunity. Each day the associations are moving one way or the other. They are more relevant—or less. They are faster—or slower. They are soulful—or shallow. They are collaborative—or they may seek short-term wins regardless of what is right for the longer term. In sum, they are smart—or they are not. It is the collective wisdom, therefore, of the design associations that provides the fuel for future relevancy, strategic development, and service growth benefiting the profession.

Bibliography

Berger, Lance A., Martin J. Sikora, and Dorothy R. Berger. *The Change Management Handbook: A Road Map to Corporate Transformation.* New York: McGraw-Hill Professional Publishing, 1994.

Cramer, James P. *Design Plus Enterprise: Seeking a New Reality in Architecture.* Washington, DC: AIA Press, 1994.

Cramer, James P. *Almanac of Architecture & Design.* Norcross: The Greenway Group, 2001.

Hesselbein, Francis, Marshall Goldsmith, Richard Beckhard, and Richard F. Schubert. *The Community of the Future.* Drucker Foundation Future Series. New York: Jossey-Bass, 1998.

Mau, Bruce. *Life Style.* London: Phaidon, 2000.

5

The Regulatory Organization

BETH HARMON-VAUGHAN, FIIDA

Modern professions have emerged as occupations that offer a unique value to the society in which they exist. By these definitions, interior design has developed into a true modern profession over the past 30 years. It has experienced growing demand for sophisticated services, which enhance clients' quality of life as well as their bottom line. Through this growth, interior design has defined itself as a true profession, sharing characteristics of most other professions with a unique body of knowledge and theoretical foundation, standards for formal education, testing of candidates for basic knowledge and skills as entrée into the profession, ethical standards, and legal recognition. Professions begin to define themselves through an institutional infrastructure, which develops and monitors standards of practice for the profession.

For interior design, two key aspects of the professional infrastructure are the Foundation for Interior Design Education Research (FIDER) and the National Council for Interior Design Qualifications (NCIDQ). FIDER is a specialized accreditor whose mission is to establish standards for post-secondary education and then evaluate and accredit programs based on those standards. NCIDQ develops and administers an examination for qualified, entry-level designers seeking professional status. The examination tests minimum competence in the theory, knowledge, and skills necessary to enter the professional practice of interior design and to protect the public health, safety, and welfare. The examination is required for professional status in the North American interior design associations as well as license in those American states or Canadian provinces where interior design licensing is available.

Both FIDER and NCIDQ subscribe to the definition of interior design which has been endorsed by the International Interior Design Association, the American Society of Interior Designers, Interior Designers of Canada, and the Interior Design Educators Council. FIDER and NCIDQ consider this definition as they address their missions of accreditation and testing. The definition states that the professional interior designer is qualified by education, experience, and examination to enhance the function and quality of interior spaces for the purpose of improving the quality of life, increasing productivity, and protecting the health, safety, and welfare of the public. The professional interior designer:

- *Analyzes clients' needs, goals, and life safety requirements*

- *Integrates findings with knowledge of interior design*

- *Formulates preliminary design concepts that are aesthetic, appropriate, functional, and in accordance with codes and standards*

- *Develops and presents final design recommendations through appropriate presentation media*

- *Prepares working drawings and specifications for non-load-bearing interior construction, reflected ceiling plans, lighting, interior detailing, materials, finishes, space planning, furnishings, fixtures, and equipment in compliance with universal accessibility guidelines and all applicable codes*

- *Collaborates with professional services of other licensed practitioners in the technical areas of mechanical, electrical, and load-bearing design as required for regulatory approval*

- *Prepares and administers bids and contract documents as the client's agent*

- *Reviews and evaluates design solutions during implementation and upon completion*

FIDER

FIDER is a specialized accrediting agency, accrediting interior design programs at colleges and universities in North America. Its mission is to "lead the interior design profession to excellence by setting standards and accrediting academic programs." FIDER has established standards for postsecondary interior design education, evaluates college and university interior design programs based on the standards, and publishes a list of accredited programs.

Recognized internationally by design professionals, FIDER is acknowledged as an information source for excellence in interior design education. As a specialized accreditor, FIDER is a member of the Association of Specialized and Professional Accreditors (ASPA) and recognized as a reliable authority on interior design education by the Council for Higher Education Accreditation (CHEA). CHEA is an association whose mission is to review processes used by accrediting agencies, assuring good practices in accreditation.

Accreditation is a process unique to the United States and Canada, which replaces government regulation of education as found in most other countries. It is a process of self-evaluation and peer review that promotes achievement of high academic standards, making education more responsive to student and societal needs. Standards developed by interior design practitioners and educators with concern for continued growth and development of the profession are central to effective accreditation. Graduates of FIDER-accredited programs receive an education that is recognized by the interior design profession as meeting requirements for entry into the profession. In the future this factor may affect the right to practice in states with licensing or registration acts.

Though graduation from a FIDER-accredited program is not required to practice interior design, students can be confident that these programs voluntarily placed themselves before the scrutiny of the profession. Accredited programs have invested time, energy, and money to ensure that their graduates receive an education that meets the standards of the profession, which will serve them immediately after graduation and into the future.

History

FIDER was established in 1970 as a specialized accreditor of postsecondary education programs in interior design. The founding organizations were the Interior Design Educators Council (IDEC), the American Institute of Interior Designers (AID), and the National Society of Interior Designers (NSID). The AID and NSID merged in 1975 to form the American Society of Interior Designers (ASID). The intent of the founders was to promote excellence by developing standards for interior design education, acknowledging the increasing demands of an emerging profession.

Graduates of FIDER-accredited programs receive an education recognized by the interior design profession as meeting requirements for entry into the profession. In the future this factor may affect the right to practice in states with licensing or registration acts.

In 1997 the professional societies' leaders joined the FIDER trustees in developing plans to address the future of interior design accreditation. FIDER's governance structure was identified as a significant strategic concern. With the support of the founding organizations, FIDER was restructured in 1999 from a trust into a nonprofit corporation. The new structure was designed to maintain productive connections with all "communities of interest," to assure continued collaboration between interior design educators and practitioners. Today, FIDER maintains strategic relationships with those organizations.

The FIDER board of directors, the governing body of the foundation, is responsible for ensuring that the organization fulfills its mission. The board sets standards, determines the process through which accreditation occurs, maintains relationships with the design community, and secures funds and other resources. The board of directors is responsible for maintaining the legal, fiscal, and ethical integrity of FIDER. Financial support for FIDER comes from fees paid by institutions for accreditation, annual fees paid by programs to maintain their accreditation, and contributions from the profession, industry, and interior design press. There are nine directors on the FIDER board, each serving a maximum of two three-year terms. A director represents each of the five constituent groups. Those five directors appoint four other directors, who represent all other stakeholders in the profession. The executive director is an ex-officio member of the board.

The mission of FIDER is further achieved through the work of additional commissions and committees. The Accreditation Commission and Board of Visitors are hands-on volunteers, trained in the standards and evaluation process, who are responsible for implementing the process of program accreditation. The FIDER Research Council validates the accreditation process through studies and encourages research in interior design. The Standards Council monitors the standards through periodic surveys. Standards are revised when significant or cumulative developments in the interior design profession occur, which must be addressed through education.

Because postsecondary interior design programs exist in different types of institutions, in 1999 FIDER adopted a single set of standards for professional degree programs. These standards were developed through research with practitioners and educators to determine appropriate levels of preparation necessary to enter the practice of interior design. The standards are structured around a series of educational outcomes rather than a prescribed length of time or number of credit hours. The panel of visitors assigned to conduct the on-site program review is responsible for evaluating evidence of these outcomes against the standards. The single set of standards focuses on theory, method, technical foundation and skills necessary to practice interior design, as well as 30 credit-hours of general education.

Beginning January 2000, new programs and programs applying for reaccreditation will be evaluated using the new FIDER 2000 Standards. By 2002 all FIDER-accredited programs must comply with the standards, including those programs currently accredited as preprofessional, two-year programs.

The Accreditation Process

Accreditation is initiated when a program applies to FIDER and meets the minimum standards for application. Once the application is accepted, the program prepares and submits a standardized self-study. When the self-study is received, FIDER assigns an evaluation team comprised of a three-person panel of qualified educators and practitioners, and schedules the site visit. Program evaluation occurs through a site visit conducted by the evaluation team. Site visits are usually three days in length. During this time the panel of visitors evaluates samples of student work and meets with faculty, students, administrators, and advisory board. Specific program outcomes are reviewed against FIDER standards. At the conclusion of the visit, the team prepares a written evaluation. The team report, with comments and recommendations, is sent to the FIDER Evaluation Committee and is then forwarded to the Accreditation Commission for a final accreditation decision. The commission may grant a maximum six-year accreditation, or it may deny accreditation, depending on the program's level of compliance with the standards. The time frame for the initial accrediting process can be 12 to 18 months. Once the term of accreditation has expired, the program must be reevaluated using the same process to make certain it continues to meet standards and remains current with the changing demands of the profession. Volunteer interior design practitioners and educators supported by a professional staff conduct the FIDER accreditation process.

NCIDQ

The primary mission of the National Council for Interior Design Qualification is to develop and administer an examination which tests minimum competency to enter the professional practice of interior design. Through the examination process, it serves to identify to the public those interior designers who have met the minimum standards for professional practice by passing the NCIDQ examination. The council endeavors to maintain the most advanced examining procedures, and continually updates the examination to reflect expanding professional knowledge and skills. It seeks the acceptance of the NCIDQ examination as a universal standard by which to measure the competency of interior designers to practice as professionals. NCIDQ is the only examination acknowledged by the International Interior Design Association, American Society of Interior Designers, Interior Designers of Canada, and the Interior Design Educators Council. In addition to responsibilities for examination, NCIDQ is charged with defining, researching, and updating bodies of knowledge, conducting field surveys, analyzing candidate performance, evaluating subject areas and item validity, developing and pretesting questions and problems, improving scoring, implementing grading and jurying procedures, reviewing education and practice requirements, and identifying public health, safety, and welfare issues.

To sit for the examination, the candidate must apply to NCIDQ and meet education and experience requirements. Once the application is accepted, the candidate is eligible to sit for the next scheduled examination session. The exam is structured as a two-day test. The first day is multiple-choice tests, which examine knowledge of codes, standards, and technical aspects of interior design. The second-day tests are practicum problems in which knowledge is tested through application. The exam is offered twice annually at proctored test sites throughout North America. Completed exams are sent to jury sites and scored by trained review teams. The candidate may retake those sections that were not completed successfully.

History

Established in the late 1960s to issue credentials to qualified professional interior design practitioners, the council has been in effect since 1972. It was formalized as a not-for-profit organization when it was incorporated in 1974. NCIDQ's founders were the American Institute of Interior Designers (AID) and the National Society of Interior Designers (NSID), the two national organizations that were then preparing to merge into what became the American Society of Interior Designers (ASID). All national design organizations whose membership was made up in total or in part of interior designers were asked to join.

The NCIDQ was founded as a separate council to certify, through a qualifying examination, those interior design practitioners competent to practice. It also studies and presents plans, programs, and guidelines for the statutory licensing of interior design practitioners. The incorporation charter of the council provides membership for American state or Canadian provincial regulatory agencies. It does not offer membership to individuals. Representatives from state/provincial regulatory agencies and professional societies are appointed to serve as delegates on the NCIDQ council of delegates for two-year terms. The NCIDQ board of directors with professional staff manages the activities and affairs of the council, which has the right and authority to manage its affairs, property, funds, and policies.

Successful completion of the NCIDQ examination is a prerequisite for professional registration in those American states and Canadian provinces that have enacted licensing or certification statutes to protect the health, safety, and welfare of the public. The NCIDQ examination must also be passed by every interior designer applying for professional membership in NCIDQ's constituent member organizations: the American Society of Interior Designers (ASID), Interior Designers of Canada (IDC), and the International Interior Design Association (IIDA). The NCIDQ is a member of the International Federation of Interior Architects/Interior Designers (IFI), an organization representing many of the interior design associations around the world.

Certification and Licensure

Certification is generally defined as a voluntary form of recognition of an individual, granted by a nongovernmental organization or agency. However, minimum competency in any profession is usually a baseline standard accepted by state and provincial governments for purposes of legal recognition. In addition to the development and administration of the professional competency examination, NCIDQ also administers a certification program for interior designers. Certification is available to those practitioners who meet minimum competency standards for the practice of interior design. This certification includes minimum requirements for education and experience as well as completion of the NCIDQ examination. NCIDQ certification is included among the license eligibility criteria in all American states and Canadian provinces with enacted statutes.

Certification by the NCIDQ gives the interior designer a credential that acknowledges his or her preparation to practice interior design professionally, through education, experience and examination. NCIDQ certification serves as qualification for professional membership within interior design organizations and for nonaffiliates represents a voluntary individual accomplishment. Certified designers receive a certificate that identifies them as qualified practitioners, ensures recognition of expertise, and assists development and self-improvement through the individual's understanding of a body of knowledge to practice interior design competently.

Record Maintenance

As part of the NCIDQ's ongoing effort to provide administrative support to facilitate legal recognition for interior design practitioners, the council's board of directors approved a record management requirement effective in 1990. Individuals pay an annual fee for record maintenance that enables NCIDQ to:

1. Maintain an accurate mailing list of certificate holders for ongoing notifications pertaining to the NCIDQ's certification program

2. Update state and provincial regulatory agencies with current certification data for residents within a given jurisdiction

3. Confirm NCIDQ certification status for initial licensing purposes in states and provinces

4. Act as a clearinghouse for purposes of licensing reciprocity

IDEP Program

The career path of a professional interior designer involves formal education, entry-level work experience, and passing the qualifying examination. Entry-level work experience is required of candidates for the NCIDQ examination, as well as by the major interior design organizations for professional membership. American state and Canadian provincial licensing boards require proof of quality interior design experience for licensure and/or registration. NCIDQ developed the Interior Design Experience Program (IDEP) as a monitored, postgraduate internship program to assure that candidates are prepared and qualified for examination. The program is administered by the NCIDQ for graduates of interior design education programs.

The general purpose of IDEP is to reinforce interior design graduates' education as they enter professional practice and prepare for the NCIDQ examination. The program promotes the acquisition of professional discipline, skills, and knowledge. It also provides structure, direction, resources, and support to the training experience. These contribute to the development of competent interior designers and enhance interior design entry-level work experiences. The IDEP program has been developed using the Definition of an Interior Designer and the Common Body of Knowledge established by the NCIDQ and FIDER.

The IDEP has been developed to assist entry-level interior designers in obtaining a broad range of quality professional experience and to establish performance guidelines for the work experience of new interior designers. The program serves as the transition between formal education and professional practice, recognizing the unique differences between programs of education and diversity of practice. Most important, the IDEP facilitates the development of competent interior designers who can provide professional interior design services and work as team members involved in the design of the built environment. The NCIDQ also produces a number of publications to support the mission of the organization, including study guides, practice exams, jury check sheets, and studies such as *Analysis of the Interior Design Profession.*

In order to ensure the continued acceptance of NCIDQ certification in existing and proposed licensing statutes, the NCIDQ examination continues to evaluate minimum competencies for the profession. However, as minimum competencies in any profession may change or evolve with the development of the profession and with the demands of the public, the examination and other certification standards are continually reviewed and modified accordingly. The NCIDQ encourages current certificate holders to keep current with the profession through periodic reexamination. At the present time, this is a voluntary action, and existing certificates are not jeopardized if a certificate holder elects to take a subsequent examination. The NCIDQ will issue renewal acknowledgments to those individuals, already certified, who are successfully reexamined in 1990 or thereafter. NCIDQ certification provides interior designers with peer recognition, allows reciprocity to practice in licensed jurisdictions, and promotes public acceptance through awareness of a profession with certified practitioners.

Contact Information

NCIDQ
1200 18th Street, NW, Suite 100
Washington, DC 20036-250
Telephone: 202–721–02
Fax: 202–721–022
E-mail: ncidq@ncidq.org
Website: www.nicdq.org

FIDER
60 Monroe Center NW, Suite 300
Grand Rapids, MI 49503-2920
Telephone: 616–458–0400
Fax: 616-458-0460
E-mail: fider@fider.org
Website: www.fider.org

Sources for this section were provided by the FIDER and NCIDQ websites.

Association of Specialized and Professional Accreditors at aspa-use.org

Council for Higher Education Accreditation website at chea@chea.org

Foundation for Interior Design Education Research website at fider@fider.org

National Council for Interior Design Education Qualifications website at ncidq@ncidq.org

6

The Culture of Design Education

LINDA KEANE
MARK KEANE

Productions at the limit of literature, at the limit of music, at the limit of any discipline, often inform us about the state of that discipline, its paradoxes and its contradictions. Questioning limits is a means of determining the nature of the discipline.

Bernard Tschumi, Manhattan Transcripts

At present, interior design education may seem to be bifurcated: designers learn from established methods of design education in school, then learn from their actual practice. One aspect of education emphasizes theory, another practice, technique, and specialization. On a daily basis, it may be difficult to understand how education merges with practice and practice with education. To contemporary design professionals, that bifurcation may be seamless, and their work may change the way designers, and their clients, view interiors and habitation. The practice of interior design involves cultural production of spaces for habitation. Our very definition of habitation, the place where we spend most of our time, is being challenged by the pervasiveness of computers, expanded with global connectivity, and heightened in value by the sense that design is increasingly sophisticated, diversified, and sustainability oriented. Design education, as well, is redefining itself as a liberal arts-grounded, ideological, knowledge-based, innovative education. If design professionals share the trend in design education toward problem seeking (rather than problem solving) and a more fully theorized approach to habitation, they can better assess how their own practices will best mesh with an increasingly complex world, and can better rethink and refresh their approach to the work of design to meet that world's challenges. In looking at the education of the interior designer, it is essential to develop an approach to design education that embraces the changing understanding of both interiority and the practice, theory, and life-long learning of design.

INTERIORITY: DESIGN AND THE ARCHITECTURE OF SPACE

Interiority, or the quality of interior space, is a concept of boundedness and openness, both physically and culturally. Physically, interiority is the product of boundaries; culturally, it implies the presence of the other, or the exterior, to create the conditions that render it inside. The presence of the exterior demands a relationship between that which is outside and that which is inside. On the one hand, design professionals work with interiority as a space created and conditioned by the exterior–by a building's walls, its shape, or its skin. In *Complexity and Contradiction,* Robert Venturi writes that "designing from the outside in, as well as the inside out, creates necessary tensions, which help make architecture. Since the inside is different from the outside, the wall–the point of change–becomes an architectural event."[1] On the other hand, designers work with interiority as a space that itself can condition a building's shape. For interiors, the wall is not only an event; it is the beginning of a double-sided boundary. Martin Heidegger writes, "A boundary is not that at which something stops, but as the Greeks recognized, the boundary is that from which something begins its presencing."[2] For many designers, the inside has been considered integral with the outside. Frank Lloyd Wright considered them to be integrated. "In Organic Architecture, then, it is quite impossible to consider the building as one thing, its furnishings another and its setting and environment still another. The Spirit in which these buildings are conceived sees all these together at work as one thing."[3] Just as an exterior can have an impact upon interiority, interiority can impact exteriority or exist independently. The emergence of interior architecture as a distinct field results in part from the twentieth-century phenomenon of build-outs and renovations, where the design of a building's skin and core is separated from the design of its habitable space. Linda Pollari and Richard Somol write that interior architecture tends to question the limits of space and relates "the vocabulary of the interior–'wallpaper,' 'carpets,' excessive 'material palettes' to inform diverse projects and practices."[4]

The relationship between the exterior and the interior, open to such diverse interpretation as design "from the inside out" or design from the "outside in" is changing the breadth of interior design education and the practice of interiors. Olivier Leblois, architect, furniture designer, and professor at L'Ecole

In architecture, concepts can either precede or follow projects or buildings. In other words, a theoretical concept may be either applied to a project or derived from it.

Bernard Tschumi,
Manhattan Transcripts

Speciale d'Architecture and Camondo in Paris, writes that the main point is that there is no "interior" architecture and no "exterior" architecture; (interior) architecture is a spirit and way of feeling, seeing, living; the question is not the difference between the exterior and the interior, but what resides in all the places that are in between. He cites Foucault, who said that one's identity is not in status, fact, and knowledge, but in prospect, traject, and perspect.[5] Others define interior architecture as the "holistic creation, development, and completion of space for human use or humanistically conceived space following Vitruvius's dicta—firmness, commodity, and delight."[6] Interior architecture is no longer limited in practice by medium or location (the interior), but is now characterized by a more multidisciplinary agenda. John Kurtich and Garret Eakin, in *Interior Architecture,* set forth a threefold definition of the practice of interior architecture: first, integrated finished interiors completed with a building; second, completion of space in an existing enclosure; and third, the preservation, renovation, or adaptive re-use of buildings with an interior focus.[7] This expanded description identifies emerging areas of expertise with requisite professionals. In practice, the arena between the inside and the outside is being shared by capable transdisciplinary architects and interior architects as its very boundaries become permeated.

Culturally, the "limits" of the interior are transforming in definition and in practice as well. The field of interior design is being redefined by the development of cyberspace, with a whole new type of space to be considered. As William J. Mitchell points out, "You can enter and exit virtual places like rooms." Through the computer, endless communities of virtual rooms can be entered, experienced, and moved through without the restraints of gravity. On-line, individuals and groups use virtual space and spatial metaphors such as "chat rooms" to inform and entertain themselves, even though they are removed from each other in proximity. Cyberspace takes shape depending upon how we use it: "Depending on the interactions that interest you—it's the pick-up bar, the seminar room, the mardi-gras, the shopping mall, the library, or the office." We can now access and interact on the trading floor, experience and contribute to the growth and decline of companies on screen, explore the virtual Guggenheim and visit cities long ago lost to the accumulation of civilization.[8]

Both the physical and the virtual bounds of interiority are expanding and opening, as is the understanding of what constitutes design and who is a designer.

DESIGN AS A BASIS FOR LEARNING

Education of the interior designer

Education of the interior designer begins with the premise that, to design space where people live their lives, the designer must learn and reconceptualize the habitable—what people in a time and place accept as space they can live in—with ease, comfort, pleasure, and well-being. In dealing with the habitable, designers attempt to sustain the art of living. To meet these goals, designers must learn how to learn about the habitable, how to continually redesign their education, and how to expand their expertise.

Learning the habitable is a process of gathering and processing all sorts of information about the ways in which people live, interact with each other and with the environment, and change the way they live. It depends not only on something that professors can quantify, scholars can recount historically, researchers can document, scientists can evaluate, and decorators can stylize; to learn the habitable, designers must constantly redefine livability. Inside is where we choose to spend most of our lives. Just as designers must see that the concept of interiority looks outward as well as inward, they must understand that learning the habitable is not simply an inward-looking endeavor. It takes living and studying how we live, where we live, what we want with living, and how our existence defines the world. As part of investigating and inventing the culture of habitability, the designer must exercise awareness, understanding, and acceptance of diversity. If designers are to learn about the habitable in a meaningful way, and thereby reconceive ideas of privacy, shared, and public place, they must understand changing lifestyles, mobility, aging populations, shifts in family constituency, personal, local, and global environmental strategies.

One of the essential requirements of educational endeavors is a commitment to teaching how to learn, and in the design field this commitment suggests that in the undergraduate years design students should be exposed to a broad educational experience inclusive of many design and design-related disciplines. Many design programs begin with a "year of discovery," an approach to awareness that establishes a deeper relationship with the environment, people, things, and space. In this initial year, design students explore the thinking integral to allied disciplines—architecture, landscape architecture, industrial design, product design, graphic design, and environmental design. Unfortunately, during the latter half of the twentieth century, segregation into "allied

Design is a means of sustaining the arts of everyday living in a technological world.

Bill Stumpf, *ACD Newsletter*

fields" after that first year became the norm. Generations of architectural and interior design educators supported this artificial separation by omitting exposure to, understanding of, and collaboration with the other disciplines. By separating academic disciplines that share similar goals of improving human habitation, design educators have failed to fulfill their responsibility as educators. This separation of the disciplines has specialized and vocationalized activities that are by their very nature complex, comprehensive, and collaborative. The "year of discovery" in design education needs to continue throughout the educational experience, mixing disciplines and offering "real-world" exchanges and collaborations.

Undergraduate education needs to have a broad base if design students are to be fully prepared to specialize later in a particular field of knowledge and evaluate how best to design graduate education to meet their goals. The education of the interior designer is an education in sustaining the art of living. Currently, design institutions are facing the challenge of redefining just what constitutes an education in design. As the knowledge base increases and the field of practice expands, design institutions must critically evaluate both the breadth of undergraduate introduction to the field and the expectations of skill development and design experience needed. At the graduate level, design institutions offer theoretical and technological specializations as well as professional and creative coursework. Degrees in Consumer Research, Environment Branding, Edutainment, and the Creative Workplace are appearing and promoting new specialization in culturally developing areas. As the range of interiority is redefined, and its expanded practice recognized, the need for selective learning becomes a necessity as well as an issue. A design student's path may continue beyond the undergraduate introduction to include diverse foci at the graduate and postgraduate levels. Design students must choose carefully not only what to learn, but also from whom to learn it. As much as the reputation and pedagogical affiliation (decoration, design, or architecture) of an institution matter, so do the individuals who are teaching and who envision the future direction of the teaching of interiors. When design students and design institutions accept that there is value in learning from a range of teachers and practitioners, they begin to understand how to learn about a broad-based discipline.

At its best, design education constantly redesigns itself. Through critique and reevaluation of its methods and by imagining the designer of the future, design education is moving from a proscriptive approach to an inscriptive practice. The proscriptive approach to design starts with the functional needs of others. Proscriptive solutions are problem-solving solutions. Inscriptive design methods are problem seeking, and pose questions and probabilities as both process and product. Galen Cranz writes in her book, *The Chair,* "As our ideas change, so do our chairs." Designers should necessarily refer to old ideas, history, and advocacy when they rethink the concept of comfort in ways that will allow them to overturn the artistic approach and allow them to reconceptualize the how, why, and where. The first proscriptive error is to accept an object's form and function as already established. Ms. Cranz calls for a new theoretical model acknowledging the reality that different parts of the body and the mind work together in complex ways. In keeping with an inscriptive approach, she suggests that body-conscious design should integrate critical principles of ergonomics, psycho-social entities of people, and the psychological experience of movement in space.[9] Working similarly within the inscriptive method, Katherine and Michael McCoy, past Directors of Design at Cranbrook and currently at the Illinois Institute of Technology's Institute of Design, teach and practice an *interpretive approach* to design as cultural production; in *interpretive design*, design professionals accept that meaning is partially a negotiation between the viewer/user and objects. They are aware that meaning is embedded in objects symbolically and linguistically, but also phenomenologically, ergonomically, and experientially. In *New Thinking in Design,* Michael McCoy describes how he takes *interpretive design* into practice in product design, furniture, and interiors. McCoy points out that he uses a lot of the same attitudes and methodologies in interiors projects as he uses on electronic projects. "In the case of an interior, one addresses how public space symbolizes or talks about the cultural condition that supported its making–or just how public space indicates its possibilities for use–the way of seeing and the methodology are the same."[10]

DESIGN AS KNOWLEDGE

Design educators have struggled with the relationship between instruction and reflection, production and invention, vocation and critical practice. Design education, inherently linked to practice and industry, is about learning "trust" in a process of discovery, the endpoint of which is not initially known or even predictable. From Vitruvius' *The Ten Books on Architecture,*[11] the oldest extant writing on architecture, we learn that architects need to be equipped with knowledge of many branches of study and varied kinds of learning, and that this knowledge is the child of practice and theory. For the designer of space, both practice and theory are necessary and interrelated components of a complete education.

In interior design education, "practice" is twofold. At the level of instruction, it involves developing technique and skills in a liberal arts setting that fosters thinking and understanding. The designer learns to understand all of the practical aspects of people's intimate connections to the habitable, through material things and behavioral research. Traditionally, interior decoration has dealt with the application of color, texture, and materials, and the knowledgeable and selective collection of furnishings and objects signifying ownership and occupation of space. We collect things. We surround ourselves with objects of necessity, of delight, of use and of memory. Peter Gomes, professor at Harvard University, writes, "I cannot remember a time when I was not interested in things and their arrangement."[12] We embed our homes and work places with things that contribute to the ease and pleasure of our existence and define who we are and sometimes even how we are. When designers question the limits of the inside and accept our natural impulse to fill our spaces with collections, they need to reconceptualize the very idea of habitation. For designers, the study of space is the study over time of human use and experience. With occupation of space comes habitation. With habitation comes complex interaction, associations, activities, and experience. We develop relationships with each other, with the world outside, all through the "designed" world of the artificial.

In an important way, however, in the design studio, practice becomes theoretical. To practice effectively, the design professional must question the parameters of habitation and of design practice, not only through factual research and expertise, but through challenging the philosophy of how we might work to reveal how we might live. The relationship between practice and theory in design is similar to the relationship between science and philosophy, experiment and understanding. In *The Story of Philosophy,* Will and Ariel Durant write of the difference between science and philosophy: "Science is analytical description, philosophy is synthetic interpretation. Science wishes to resolve the whole into parts, the organism into organs, the obscure into the known. It does not inquire into the values and ideal possibilities of things, nor their total and final significance. The philosopher is

Theory, if not received at the door of an empirical discipline, comes in like a ghost and upsets the furniture.

Erwin Panofsky

not content to describe the fact; he wishes to ascertain its relation to experience in general , and thereby get to its meaning and worth."[13] Knowledge comes of science, but wisdom comes with experience. In "The Science of Uncertainty: The Potential Contribution of Design to Knowledge," Clive Dilnot asks, What replaces scientific experiment and prediction? He states that the quick answer to the first part is that propositions replace experiment. The quick answer to the second part is that explanation replaces prediction. Propositions are to design what experiment is to science. What design offers is the capacity to create propositions about things ("this could be that"): if experiment deals with the rule ("if this, then that"), design deals with the possibility ("could this be?").[14]

In this sense of "what could be," practice and theory are essentially intertwined in the development of a knowledge base for the interior designer. As interior design defines itself as a discipline with its own educational standards and curricula, its own professional organizations, publications, and legal recognition, it needs to have as part of its base of knowledge its own philosophy, its own theory. As Stanley Abercrombie wrote in the 1970s, interior design "turns towards architectural writings where philosophical thinking about interiors has long been subsumed."[15] Today's convergence of theory and history as critical studies is essential to the cultural content of design thinking and making, and needs to be integrated within interior design studios. If interior design as a sustainable practice is to concern itself with the understanding of current conditions to propose new forms of practice, it must develop its own critical history, theory, and philosophy based on the nature and quality of human habitation.

Design professionals are beginning to understand the importance of a broad base of knowledge in the community as a whole. At a recent International Interior Design Association Research Summit, the importance of research to a humanistic practice of interior design was discussed. Schools contribute scientific data, gathering information on everything from "what makes a creative environment to the effects of lighting on worker performance." Susan S. Szenasy, editor of *Metropolis* magazine on art, architecture, and design, reports in "The View from La Jolla," on the many active areas of research in the field of interiors. Industry invests in market research, in manufacturing processes, and in how people use products, translating this information into cutting-edge development. Interior design offices keep records of projects, collating client needs, project types, material performance; this knowledge base develops the firm's profile and forms a competitive edge. The interior design community, its schools, offices, and related industries generate a rich body of knowledge about human beings and the environment. This community must begin to share this knowledge and connect the activity in academia with the research of firms and manufacturers. This sharing must also address and reach out to the public to begin to build value in design.[16]

LIFELONG LEARNING: A K–80 APPROACH TO LEARNING

You and I are molded by the land, the trees, the sky and all that surrounds us, the streets, the houses. . . . Our hearts are shaped by the plaster walls that cover us and we reflect plaster wall ideals. . . . When I make a vase, a cup, or a saucer, they will be my expression and they will tell you who I am and what I am.

Bernard Maybeck

The more complex the world becomes, and the more knowledge there is to master, the more a designer's broad-based education and knowledge will increase in value. If design professionals are to analyze and reconfigure the culture of living in the light of diverse lifestyles, new conceptions of work, entertainment, recreation, and communication, they must be aware of and keep abreast of changing perceptions, cultural shifts, use of sustainable materials, and the impact and potential of new technologies. In the light of such a complex task, developing the designer is a life-long educational process, a process that must be emphasized and supported more fully than it is now by the educational system.

If the field of architecture has expanded with respect to what its practitioners need to learn—some 22 years plus for architects, according to Harvard's Joseph Hudnut's list made in the 1940s—so too has the field of interiors expanded. Originally, design involved the practice of the decorator equipped with knowledge of history, styles, textiles, furnishings, and sources, and on the other hand the integrative architect (who included details of lighting, furnishings, form, structure, and environmental issues seamlessly). Now, the field has enlarged to include differentiated practices in the public realm—design of the workplace, commercial spaces, industrial applications, furniture, entertainment environments, and immersive virtual worlds. The expanding field of interiors puts more demands on academia and on the need for establishing a strong commitment to continuing education.

Internationally, interior design practice complements the practice of architecture in the preservation of interiors, renovation of spaces, or completion

The more complex the world becomes, and the more knowledge there is to master, the more a designer's broad-based education and knowledge will increase in value.

of new construction. In the United States, most interior programs begin with interior decoration; an exception is the program at The School of the Art Institute started by Ms. Marya Lilien, a Polish architect and the first woman apprentice to Frank Lloyd Wright. She taught "design from the inside out" prior to World War II. The interiors program at the Rhode Island School of Design was redirected in the late 1940s by Ernst Lichtbau, who desired a more rigorous approach to design. He also emphasized an architectural sensibility heavily influenced by his Austrian education under Otto Wagner and other Viennese designers of the Secession. Following World War II, more schools began offering programs in interior design. The Interior Design Educators Council states that there were 70 four-year degree programs in interiors at mid-century. In 1971, the Foundation for Interior Design Education and Research (FIDER) was formed by the Interior Design Educational Committee (IDEC) and other professional societies. FIDER proposed to establish and administer a voluntary plan for accreditation of interior design education programs. A formal exam, the National Council for Interior Design Qualifications, was created in 1974 by the design societies, including Industrial Design. In 1990, the Coordinators Network of the IDEC surveyed 75 of 213 baccalaureate-degree interior design programs in the United States and Canada. At that time, only a few architecture programs co-listed emphasis or degrees in Interiors. In the year 2000, FIDER listed 130 accredited programs in Interiors, and the *Peterson Guide to Architecture Schools of North America* showed almost one-third of the 130 accredited architecture programs offering degrees in Interior Design or Architecture.[17]

Unfortunately, design is not considered valuable and essential to education. The vocabulary and understanding of design thinking is not presented in the early educational system. Young designers thereby miss an invaluable introduction to this necessary interface with living and learning. Meredith Davis, board member of the American Center for Design, completed a two-year study with the National Endowment for the Arts to see how design was being used in K–12 classrooms. The study, "Design as a Catalyst for Learning," published in 1997, selected 169 teachers from 900 nominees purported to be using design in their classrooms. Of the 169 teachers who were selected on the basis of course outlines and project descriptions, fewer than 5 percent were art teachers. Most of their references were to the "elements and principles of design" (color, line, shape, etc.) rather than to the kind of complex problem solving associated with the design professions. Almost none made the link to the cognitive and conceptual issues embedded in the design process.[18] The building blocks of questioning, creative thinking, insightful research, and problem seeking are not introduced as an essential part of elementary or secondary education. Elementary and secondary teachers are not considering either that there are relationships between how we live and what conditions we live in, or that these relationships are critical for how future generations might perceive, impact, and change our living.

In response to this educational problem, design professionals have begun the task of connecting both architecture and interior design to education in grades K–12. Although architectural organizations such as the American Institute of Architects have several programs nationally, and local chapters in Chicago and Philadelphia have done the same, the essential task must be served jointly from both disciplines. Since the early 1990s, interior design educators have indicated that involvement with the K–12 population is critical to the future of the field. Stephanie Clemons, ASID, IDEC, writes that interior design is a natural field to infuse into elementary education. She offers a comprehensive model with which to introduce interior design through career awareness, career exploration, and work-based experiences in progressive stages throughout elementary and secondary education. To raise teachers' awareness and understanding of the very nature of design, design professionals must intensively involve and reeducate art and design educators.

Design professionals and educators must send the message that interior design education, like other design education, is but an introduction to life-long learning. Two-year certificate programs offer the briefest of introduction to vocabulary and skills, more vocationally specific than culturally connected as "reflective designing"; four-year undergraduate programs combine liberal arts with design studio development, more effectively balancing why with how; emerging three-year master's programs graduate an older, more broadly educated student into the field. Most four-year interior design programs have the studio class at the core of the curriculum. In traditional models, liberal arts, social studies, and art, architecture, and design history and theory courses complement the work in the studio, as does instruction in color, materials, technology, and professional practice. In emerging interior architecture models, critical studies are embedded in the design studio experience as the basis for cultural production. At the end of the twentieth century the Interna-

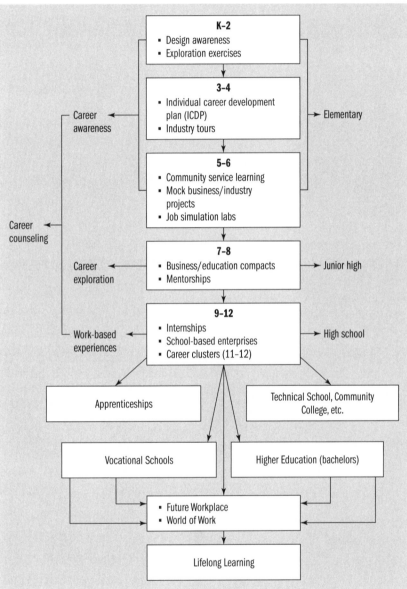

FIGURE 6-1
Model for Interior Design
Involvement in K-12.
(Reprinted with
permission from
Interiors & Sources)

tional Interior Design Association (IIDA) hosted a Large Firm Roundtable on Interior Design Education. The Foundation for Interior Design Education and Research (FIDER) concurrently began conducting surveys for revisions of its Standards. The National Council for Interior Design Qualification (NCIDQ) and other professional bodies, including the Boyer Report for Architecture Education and the National Council for Architectural Registration Board (NCARB) Survey for Professional Aptitude, began self-studies reviewing the education of designers. Many of these surveys acknowledge the understanding that life-long learning is integral to design education. The effort to distinguish between that which needs to be introduced in an academic setting, understood and applied in school, acquired during internship, and testable and applicable during practice, is being questioned, along with definition of the limits of practice.

One way to send this message is to enhance and support continuing education. Continuing education offers opportunities for practitioners to infuse work with new thinking, changing technology, and new methodologies. The IIDA is implementing an initiative to look at the continuing education needs of the profession. Neil Frankel, past president of the IIDA, writes that currently continuing education offerings are random, nonsequential, and inconsistent in quality. Available material needs to be cataloged and enriched with both current expertise in the profession and emerging theoretical content. "The ultimate goal is to create a cogent, systematic educational road map that will lead design professionals to literacy and effectiveness at every point on the learning curve, providing momentum for a lifetime of learning."[19] In addressing a practice that is changing and redefining its range, continuing education becomes essential.

The consciousness-raising efforts outlined so far must not remain static, and must incorporate an understanding that interior design is challenged by new thinking about interiority. Although programs exist which continue to respect the skill of the decorator, emphasizing the world of the artificial, there are other forces at work on both the conception of interiority and design of space. Claudia Dona writes that "Many old distinctions, in short, will have to be abandoned and supplanted by new ways of thinking if we are to respond to the different design needs of the new human reality now emerging."[20] She accepts that this is the attitude of society, which for historical reasons has introduced the necessity of continuously redesigning itself. Karim Rasid, the Cairo-born Canadian industrial designer, says that "Today we are dealing with a society based on experience, so objects need to blur experience with form."[21] Mark Taylor, professor of religion at Williams College, says that "we are undergoing a reconfiguration of the very spatiality of experience."[22] As definition of interiority influences our living on the inside, interior design practice and educational needs of the interior designer expand. From the interiors of homes, to the office, to commercial and institutional space, to riverfronts and streets of the cities, to the World Wide Web, the inside and outside of cultural existence and production are being physically and virtually connected. Divisions between architecture and interiors, objects, space, and our habitation with and in them are sharing meaning and contributing to understanding.

INTERIOR DESIGN EDUCATION TODAY

As designers study not only interior decoration but also interiority, different pedagogical models have developed. When the International Interior Design Association (IIDA), the International Interior Design Association Foundation (IIDAF), and E-Lab (now Sapient) collaborated on a study of education, practice, and the industry, they found two distinct models in education: "simulation" and "safe-haven." Schools that offer "simulation" replicate the office environment and its proceedings. The "safe-haven" model pursues interior design through ideation and invention. Simulation and safe-haven models differ in context of projects, interpretation (evaluation) of the design process, and the nature of collaboration between students and faculty, and they expose students to very different educational experiences.[23] These models are presented within three disciplinary orientations to design education: interior decoration, interior design, and interior architecture.

According to the IIDA/E-Lab Report, "The main goal of a simulation school is to cultivate an environment where students learn sets of skills that can transfer directly to the workplace."[24] Real clients, real programs, real time and budget constraints form the proscriptive approach to interior design education. Boundaries are explicit, and a linear design process is emphasized. The shortcoming of the "simulation" model is that it involves more instruction in the practice of interiors and less ideation and invention in the culture of habitation; collaborative experiences are not modeled, and a theoretical basis for student work is often lacking. The majority of interior programs offer the simulation model and have practitioners as instructors. Graduates become entry-level designers and technicians.

Interior design is a broad-spectrum discipline that thrives in the vitality of energy, intellectual engagement, mutual respect, conflict, and collaboration that flow from contact with other environmental specializations.

The "safe haven" model cultivates a creative, idea-based environment. Inscriptive practice or the rethinking and situation-seeking approach is emphasized. More full-time design educators teach in this model, which fosters creativity and individual voice. Students are challenged and expected to achieve senior designer and high-level critical positions in emerging practices. The industry standard of auto-cad is often omitted or supplemented with exposure to digital modeling, animation, and interactive information architecture. "Safe-haven" model schools are marked by graduating students who lack definitive competency and marketable skills. The IIDA/E-Lab Report concludes that a combined approach offering both "safe haven" and "simulation" experiences best prepares the student for high-level entry into the profession.[25]

The range of instruction, inquiry, implementation, and invention is ongoing in the continual definition of interior design education. Programs are located in various settings—Schools of Architecture, Art and Design, Human Ecology, or Human Economics. In the "design education" mode of instruction exist programs which emphasize Interior Decoration. These curriculums stress historical styles, history and placement of furniture, color, textiles, window treatments, lighting, materials, and selection of complementary objects. Students graduating from decorative programs tend to work in private practice, residential interiors, commercial product, store-home consulting, furniture and material showrooms, antiques, object appraisal, and commissioned art positions. Schools emphasizing inquiry are based in material, environmental, and cultural design research programs. Implementation as a "design education" model exposes students to principles of residential interior decoration and space planning but also promotes specialized training in commercial space planning, contract design, project management, facilities management, and potential specializations in lighting, acoustics, museum curatorial work, or exhibition design. The professionalism of this type of program stresses functional design planning principles equally with aesthetics and performance standards of materials and furnishings. "Invention as Design Education" promotes the emergence of interior architecture, a field practiced and recognized in Europe. This model develops critical thinking and strategic interpretive research skills along different trajectories than either architectural education or design education. Human scale and use are the basis for research and design as culturally connected practice. Studios balance creative exploration of ideas with practical skill development and competency. Study trips, internships, and digital immersion in delineation, modeling, and communication broaden the experience of this educational model. Interior design education ranges in approach from instructional to vocational to educational.

An IDEC study offers a basic interiors curriculum with recommendations for course content in Creative Work, Technical Work, Communication Skills, Professional Procedures, and Academic Studies–Liberal Arts. These recommendations were adapted as the basis for FIDER's standards. The E-Lab/IIDA Report speaks to the present move of both firms and practice toward architecture. In the most positive sense of this direction, theory and research methodology are becoming embedded in the aesthetic and functional expectations of interior designers, resulting in a valued design-as-knowledge form of practice. This move toward architecture currently offers a range of approaches. The E-Lab/IIDA Report concludes that there are currently three types of programs—one in which architecture subsumes interior design, one in which there is an institutional and ideological link with architecture, and, lastly, the program in which the differences between the two are emphasized and in which no true linkage exists. These studies currently accept and encourage diversity and differing emphases within interior design education under the flexible framework of 60–80 percent creative and professional work and 20–40 percent liberal studies. From instruction to invention models, the import of liberal arts in the design education curriculum increases.

Interior design is a broad-spectrum discipline that thrives in the vitality of energy, intellectual engagement, mutual respect, conflict, and collaboration that flow from contact with other environmental specializations. Interior design education needs to strengthen its programs and raise the overall quality of the diverse offerings while emphasizing its expertise in human-scale research and interaction. While celebrating interior decoration, design, and architecture, it needs to balance real-world skills with basic creative education of the designer. Practitioners bring current ideas from the office and industry into the studio, but more full-time academic teachers are needed to contribute to a theoretical and philosophical basis for interior design.

Design education is flexible, vital, and poised to redefine itself in a positive way. Cecil Stewart, past president of the AIA and an educator for over 25 years, says that America is leading the world in design education. He reports that design education is more fluid to change and more connected to the emerging practice and reality of industry. Scott Ageloff of the New York Institute of Interior Design stresses education over vocation. In a school that still respects the importance of the residential market, a broad-based education emphasizing life-long learning—speaking, writing, and thinking—serves a profession that evolves and changes. Sally Levine of the Boston Architectural Center supports a diverse number of entries into the field of interior design. As the profession works toward achieving title and practice acts, she hopes that it will not limit access to the field. Brian Kernaghah of the Rhode Island School of Design writes that, clearly, interior design education is undergoing a period of redefinition. The Royal College of Art in London acknowledges in its catalogue the rapidly changing role of design and emphasizes a multi-disciplinary experience encouraging confident, fluid attitudes and ability to work creatively with other fields. "Quality and courage are pitched equally against issues of probability and possibility." Creative resourcefulness on the part of the designer is identified with inscriptive practice. Architecture studios share space with landscape, interiors, graphic design, object and furniture design, real-world affiliates. Michael Vanderbyl, dean of the School of Design at the California College of Arts and Crafts, expects that students make connections—between culture and design, between themselves and the world.[26]

INTERIOR DESIGN PRACTICE

The IIDA/E-Lab Report

The IIDA/E-Lab Report concludes that "the identity of interior design was not clearly defined," internally or by the public. This is understandable in light of the differing interior design education models—interior decoration, interior design, and interior architecture. The report concludes, "Clients' perception of the skills and scope of interior designers differs drastically from the vision interior design has for itself. Most clients still believe that interior design is about surface decoration."[27] The report defines four types of interior design practice. The cooperative model features architecture firms that have both design and technical teams who work collaboratively on larger corporate projects. The separated model consists of firms that deal in the tenant improvement realm; architects oversee project management, while interior designers contribute color, materials, and treatments. The third model is the interior design firm, which features the "designer as decorator." This work is mostly residential. The fourth firm type is architectural. In this model, architects work as "master builders" and integrate both external and internal space conception, detailing, and completion. In the cooperative and separated models, junior designers from both architecture and interior design programs serve almost identical roles; there is an accepted collaboration and respect for knowledge and area of expertise. In the decorative and architectural models, the report suggests that interior designers and architects fulfill distinct but limiting roles. Respecting decoration and design as necessary but distinct areas of practice, both the profession and the academicians must clarify interior design's contributions. As Pollari and Somol put it, "If one axis of interior architecture agenda is to emphasize section over plan (unlike space planning), another is to orchestrate relations between bodies, space, and events in a dispersed field, rather than promote the selection and placement of objects (. . . as in decoration)."[28]

The profession needs to address this confusion and serve as an educational advocate to the public. To replace client confusion with understanding, the profession must first accept its expanding range of expertise and related educational models. By focusing on "human scale" and human issues in cultural production of environments, the practice of interior design will continue to serve the public creatively as well as responsibly, with a wide range of expertise. From the physical to the virtual, the practice of creating space has a range of expected expertise and application based on human scale and interaction. Strategically, interior design philosophy and principles need to enter more fully into public education, beginning with career awareness in K–12 classes. Public participation by students, teachers, and practitioners in urban projects and diverse community-based projects will begin the process of establishing a working relationship among the schools, the industry, and the populations that they serve.

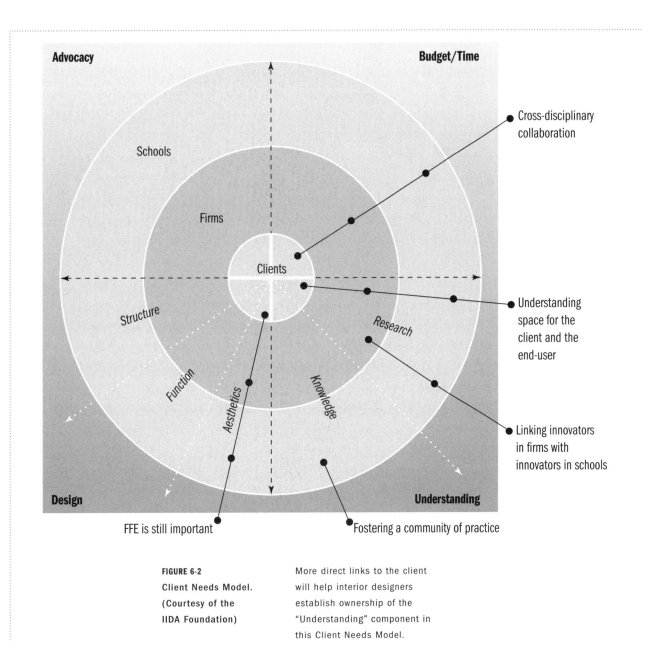

Advocacy

Schools

Firms

Clients

Structure

Function

Aesthetics

Knowledge

Research

Budget/Time

Cross-disciplinary
collaboration

Understanding
space for the
client and the
end-user

Linking innovators
in firms with
innovators in schools

Design

FFE is still important

Understanding

Fostering a community of practice

FIGURE 6-2
Client Needs Model.
(Courtesy of the
IIDA Foundation)

More direct links to the client
will help interior designers
establish ownership of the
"Understanding" component in
this Client Needs Model.

HOW THE STUDENT HAS EVOLVED

As programs in interior design have evolved, students in interior design have
evolved as well. Traditionally, students were trained in color, textiles, materials, furnishing, historic styles, selection, and placement. In most projects,
these students resurfaced and reimagined spaces based on individual client

needs and room-by-room definition. As the speculative office place emerged, students began more and more to reconceptualize the workplace as their predominant space-planning exercise. They evaluated material performance and workstations as kits of interchangeable parts. This exercise developed into corporate contract design. Design students learned about product information from manufacturers, and they studied the history of furniture and styles. As the lighting industry matured and our habitation evolved into a "24/7" existence, the study of general lighting expanded in complexity and specificity to include task lighting, accent lighting, and mood-enhancing lighting. Lighting specialists emerged. As the science of acoustics became more sophisticated, acoustical specialists emerged. As the realm of interior design grew from residential to include commercial and institutional, students found that a subjective response to the individual client became complicated, and that they needed to respond objectively to a more general, anonymous public. Collection of objects for social status began to give way to reimagining broader cultural meanings. "Theming" of interior space (and architecture) became more emotive and experiential. Students found it possible to take a cross-disciplinary approach to branding environments when the rise of marketing eclipsed personal taste in corporate culture. Students are increasingly computer literate, and this literacy is affecting definitions of and behaviors in both physical and virtual space. Many students are "nontraditional"—the average age of entry is often older than 25, and for many, the interior design degree is a second degree. Most students continue to be career oriented, desirous of employment in a design field and committed to making a contribution to the quality of life.

While the student comes to his or her educational experience often older, computer literate, and desirous of design, it does not seem that the student comes more sophisticated nor mature in the realm of design. Students still need awareness raising, instruction in research methodology, and studio experience to transform information into innovation. Students initially seem to need hands-on instruction before gaining the independent resourcefulness necessary to the designer. Even with life experience, students need introduction to the vocabulary of design in order to express their ideas and to collaborate with others. While students need to be opened to new ways of thinking, they also seem to continue to need confidence to address the complexities of most situations.

WHAT STUDENTS EXPECT FROM EDUCATION

Design programs are on point to be state of the art conceptually and technologically. Students want to be up to date with the information they are learning. They also want to be challenged to be innovative. Most of them expect technological training as well as creative work. One students says, "I want to have practical skills when I graduate, but more than that, I want my school to value experimentation, new methods of working and new design ideas."[29] Students seek a demanding arena in which to question, learn, produce work, and discuss ideas.

Many students are looking for a broad exposure to allied design disciplines—industrial design, graphic design, furniture design, fashion design, and architecture, as well as an education in interiors. "As the benefits of a well-designed environment become increasingly apparent, a need for a strong practical and abstract training will surface. I think there will be a move away from strongly 'segmented' professions and many design-related fields will start to overlap. The designer will become increasingly accountable for his/her design decisions—and thus form a new emphasis on social and environmental factors."[30]

Student evaluations commonly review the promptness, professionalism, and depth of knowledge presented by instructors. Students also speak to the inspirational and motivational nature of the teaching. They find encouragement, constructive criticism, and confidence testing to be pedagogical challenges. They also expect that the critique and feedback process will deliver a truthful measure of strengths and weaknesses in the maturation of the designer. Students require that teachers be both educators and practitioners. They thrive on conversations in and out of the classroom. For students, teachers also serve as mentors, and provide portfolio review, recommendations, advise on placement, and in some cases, career counseling.

Students also want to have a clear understanding of the position of the program. They expect an interior design program focusing on residential design to provide grounding in the necessary areas to render them knowledgeable to begin practice. Students in interior design programs expect cooperative experience during their school years to balance the practical with the creative.

Design programs are on point to be state of the art conceptually and technologically. Students want to be up to date with the information they are learning. They also want to be challenged to be innovative.

Students in interior architecture programs expect a broadening relationship with architectural education while they maintain intimate relationships with user-centered design, lighting, details, furnishings, and materials.

WHAT STUDENTS EXPECT FROM THE PROFESSION

Students have high expectations from the profession. For those who truly appreciate the opportunity to work with people, to reimagine new uses and new concepts for habitation, design is a lifestyle. It includes life-long learning from the academies, from the offices, from industry, and from society. Students champion the understanding that good design is integral to our future and undertake jobs in which they can make a difference. "As a professional, I expect to work in a field which is increasingly open to experimentation and which invites the designer to take part in creating real environments, not just shells. I expect color and delight to become more important to interior design. I expect good design to be seen as an important factor in a happy life."[31] Some students continue their education to specialize in their respective fields, interior decoration or interior design. Some continue to focus on furniture, industrial design, lighting, and architecture, taking training in the office. Many continue their education in related fields, combining their educational experience into an innovative marketable network of design abilities. Some choose not to become expert in any one area, but to broaden their understandings so as to work in an expanded arena.

WHAT PARENTS EXPECT

Balancing the intensity of the actual educational experience—the demands of creative thinking and invention, which stress many students—with the reality of the demands placed on the graduate, design education still carries the reputation of salaried art for parents of degree-seeking students. High school art and design teachers report that parents first and foremost want students to get quality job placement from a college education. With expectations of job placement comes job security, and with job security comes reflection on satisfaction and the lifestyle the job will afford. Interior design education must allow students to develop skill and competency that can lead directly to marketability. Parents must be convinced that interior design is not a luxury, but a valued service. Even without an introduction to design in the K–12 years, students' parents expect that design programs will lead to jobs. Interior design programs which require "co-op" experience, some as much as six months, assure parents of their child's future employability. Other programs offer the option of working for credit and experience before entering the work world after graduation. Working and gaining practical experience during school tremendously matures studio skills, assists students in discerning their direction after graduation, and advances their schoolwork so that they can build a better portfolio. Travel programs, an integral component of most architecture programs, are important for interior architecture students as well; as the market expands into the global workplace, parents and students need to understand diversity as integral to the "multiverse" view of the world. More interior design programs are developing study trips to other countries or allying with architecture travel programs; exposure to different cultures broadens designers' understanding and sensibilities about global diversity. Experience with diverse ethnic and cultural communities broadens students' experience with differing rituals, traditions, and points of view. Universal design principles are informed by regional design issues. Parents are often unaware of the full range of possibilities afforded by a degree in interiors. Career options need to be strongly communicated in academic promotional literature, and strong connections need to be established with alumni.

WHAT THE PROFESSION EXPECTS

The IIDA/E-Lab study found that the public had distinct needs but only a "limited perspective" of how an interior designer could answer to the furnishing, finishes, and equipment (FFE) needs of a project, and no real perspective on how the design professional could address the overall scope of a project. The public believes that business aspects of projects–scheduling, time, budget, and trades coordination—belong to architects or construction managers. The public's shallow perception of the skills, abilities, and arena of expertise of the interior designer is not consonant with new definitions of interiority. Design professionals must help the public understand design through education and events, not only through the work of individuals and firms. Collaboration among educational institutions, the profession, and the industry is needed. The business service provided by interiors professionals is of value. If aesthetic improvements alone are deemed a subjective luxury, designers need to implement more critical activities in the business aspects of their practice. Collaborative design methods such as the inscriptive practices, user programming, interactive design, community involvement, and ethnographic research are all methods which embed shared and reconceived knowledge into reconceptualization of activities and answered physicality. The study reports that when interior designers address client needs directly, they will address the problem of limiting perceptions. It follows that interior design needs to be a sustainable practice, one that provides services that are understood as integrally embedded and necessary to the quality of life. A sustainable practice implies a "green practice," but also a deeper relevance and involvement with user needs and human-scale involvement in the built environment. The practice of interior design can answer to these needs.

The public has the perception that firms are emerging that combine programming, design, and user-centered research in the global marketplace. These firms build valued service by continually conducting multiclient research, which results in leading-edge thinking that directly serves design. It also keeps clients informed and challenged. Such firms practice in a broad range of traditional disciplines: graphic design, furniture, interiors, smart building design, and urban design. Such a firm is DEGW International, located in eight different countries. DEGW emphasizes user research parallel with design practice. Frank Duffy, chairman of DEGW, says, "We try to understand why people want things and what they want and what the trends are." Investigations lead to ideation and ideation leads to invention. "Our strength, our reputation, our ideas come from these research projects."[32] DEGW hosts in-house training sessions to connect research ideas with practice, as well as regular multiclient roundtables. This type of firm is sought as a programming interface between clients and other project collaborators by contributing user-centered research as a strength. Such practices seek designers whose experience is cross-disciplinary and who are equipped to bring individual talents and skills to a collaborative team. Interior design education needs to capitalize on its intimate relationship with clients and their needs to define user-centered research as one of the strengths of the discipline.

Doblin Group, a firm that practices "strategic design planning," assists clients in understanding change and utilizes such understandings to transform industries through directed use and application of design knowledge. They believe that designers have "the vision and the values needed to invent holistic, integrated concepts for the future, fixing many parts of everyday life." The firm gives designers the tools needed to be coequal to financiers, marketers, organizational design experts, researchers, engineers, and manufacturing experts. Utilizing innovative user-centered research, the firm surveys human activity and use with commonplace technologies. Disposable cameras, videotapes, and digital tape recordings are analyzed in depth before design concepts are initiated. "The truth is, no designer or engineer, in my judgment, can reinvent something unless and until it's broken down to the point where their common sense, logic, intuition, spirit, and brilliance can wrap around it adequately."[33]

WHAT ARE THE FUTURE IMPLICATIONS FOR DESIGN EDUCATION?

In a critique of design education, John Chris Jones, professor of design at the British Open University, writes that the available design skills are still inadequate to the scale of difficulties that the new technologies are bringing to them. Interior design education will be impacted by a blurring between the traditional allied disciplines of architecture, industrial design, and furniture design. In transitioning from proscriptive to inscriptive approaches, it will graduate designers less and less as technicians than as creative leaders critically and competently able to reconceptualize how we create, renovate, and habitate space. It will accept and design for change. At the same time there must be continued respect for the skills and abilities of all contributors. According to Duffy, "not everyone has all the skills—no one of us has all the abilities."[34] It is important in understanding change to acknowledge that no one discipline will have all the answers.

A recent survey of interior design educators, practitioners, and firms by FIDER published in *Interiors & Sources* (March 1999) identified the need to develop the traits and values of good interior design practice: attributes such as creative and analytical thinking, ability to focus on user needs, ethical practice, global understanding, and appreciation of diversity were sited; embrace technological use as a design, communication, and presentation tool; increase awareness of protection of the client and consumer through understanding and application of codes and regulations. These goals speak to the desire to acknowledge the cultural contribution of the interior designer. This is in keeping with the IIDA/E-Lab Report, which calls for the development of a distinct identity for interior design—an identity that as a practice provides a "human-centered" sensibility to the design of the built environment. This human interaction and emphasis should be the catalyst that unites the various schools, the public, and the industry. From the point of human interaction comes this more expanded definition of interior architecture.

For interior design education, the problem with design suggests that designers and design educators need to redesign the problems they face; they need to accept breakdowns in disciplinary barriers, and collaborate. Interior design education will expand its arena of knowledge and expertise to include the branding of environments based on human need and activity, sustainable practices, user-centered research, interactive information architecture, smart spaces, immersive environments, and design knowledge as value design. Eva Maddox and Associates works with clients holistically reconceptualizing attitude and appearance, redefining image, marketing, and interiors based on the company's history and projected future. The work of Diller and Scofidio employs video surveillance as interaction between users of space both interior and exterior. The Virtual Guggenheim and the New York Stock Exchange "interiors" by Lise Ann Couture and Hani Rashid of Asymptote bring information about stock movement graphically alive and engage the viewer in an interactive on-line tour of galleries and works of art. "Smart spaces" proposed by Richard Rogers and others offer sensible interactions with space serving our comfort, security, and use through sensors and embedded technology. Knowledge of user behavior and interaction with objects and space concepts of habitation are changing as we connect publicly from the privacy of our homes. Interior design education will provide an experience and exposure that prepares students for a future that is constantly changing and evolving. It is in knowing this that design education of interior design education becomes key. Design is always rethinking itself, reflecting on its parameters, questioning existing constraints with its contribution. Design must overcome outdated disciplinary divisions and demonstrate to students and the public the interdisciplinary complexity of the changing charge and organization of its practice. As practices evolve—architectural firms designing interiors, interior firms branding environments, and graduates from both emerging as cross-disciplinary practitioners—it is essential that the relationship between disciplines in academic programs overlap, the relationship between schools and industry open, and the relationship between practice and education become significantly more collaborative.

The development of interior design education as a value-based service will require that schools look for opportunities to expose students to varied experiences beyond the traditional role of furnishings, finishes, and equipment. Opening studios to communities, offering services to individuals and institutions who cannot afford design consultation, will change the misnomer that interior design is mere luxury. Collaborative projects with the public will contribute creative design thinking to the renovation, adaptation, or creation of spaces. Design Response, Inc., based in Campbell, California, offers the services of pro-bono interior designers to local community agencies. Collaborative teams of designers, architects, artists, craftpersons, and interns contribute design services to the local community. The organization, led by volunteer designer Helen Carreker, completed over 100 projects in the 1990s. Carreker says, "It is very gratifying to see these newly emerging designers finish their training, assume career positions in the field and continue to use their talents to give back to the community."[35] Design Build opportunities such as the University of Auburn's Rural Studio, led by MacArthur Foundation Awardee Samuel Mockbee, and the Jersey Devils' community projects, led by Steve Badanes, at the University of Washington, allow hands-on construction experience, introducing students to the logic, problems and physical realities of joining disparate materials in the creation of objects in the public sphere in collaborative community practice.

Interior design education will continue to emphasize consumer and user needs and to develop new methods of research that will structure ways of studying and understanding activities in people's everyday lives, with a focus on learning what people actually do. Designers will amass information in reusable, easily organizable formats for collaborative networking and creative thinking. Interior design education will benefit by research and application of new materials, similar to George Beylerian's "Material Connexion," a digital research library, service, and data bank on green materials via the web. Interior design education will combine the science of research with the wisdom of human experience to contribute to the quality of life.

Interior design education must offer students an integrated approach and an integrative course of study. Design educators can expand design's area of experience, open its traditional boundaries, and allow for comprehensive study and practice if they approach design education more as a liberal arts education with integration of the history of ideas and study of life. This education offers designers the potential to network all of their thinking, research, and creative envisioning to influence our habitation. Interior design education is less about training the designer as technician, and more about developing the designer into a leader in imagining innovations and implementing them.

Notes

1

Venturi, Robert, *Complexity and Contradiction*, Museum of Modern Art Papers on Architecture, New York, 1966, p. 86.

2

Heidegger, Martin, *Poetry, Language, Thought* (trans. Albert Hofstatder), Harper & Row, New York, 1975.

3

Wright, Frank Lloyd, Edgar Kaufmann, and Ben Raeburn, *Frank Lloyd Wright: Writings and Buildings*, Meridian Books, New York, 1960, p. 102.

4

Pollari, Linda and Richard Somol, "Complex Interiority," *LA Architect*, May–June, 2000, p. 14.

5

Leblois, Olivier, private communication.

6

Leblois, Olivier, private communication.

7

Kurtich, John, and Garret Eakin, *Interior Architecture*, Van Nostrand Reinhold, New York, 1993, p. 3.

8

Mitchell, William J., "Who Put the Space in Cyberspace?" in Peter Anders (ed.), *Envisioning Cyberspace*. McGraw-Hill, New York, 1999, p. xi.

9

Cranz, Galen, *The Chair, Rethinking Culture, Body, and Design*, W. W. Norton, New York, 1998, p. 15.

10

McCoy, Michael, "Interpretive Design," in C. Thomas Mitchell (ed.), *New Thinking in Design*, Van Nostrand Reinhold, New York, 1996.

11

Vitruvius, *Ten Books on Architecture*, Dover, New York, 1960, p. 5.

12

Gomes, Peter, "An Unruly Passion for Things," *NEST, A Quarterly of Interiors*, Summer 2000.

13

Durant, Will and Ariel Durant, *The Story of Philosophy*, Simon & Schuster, New York, 1953, p. 2.

14

Dilnot, Clive, "The Science of Uncertainty: The Potential Contribution of Design to Knowledge," presented at "Doctoral Education in Design," Ohio State University, Oct 8–11, 1998.

15

Abercrombie, Stanley, *A Philosophy of Interior Design*, Harper & Row, New York, 1990, p. x.

16

Szenasy, Susan, "The View from La Jolla," *Metropolis*, January 2000, p. 14.

17

Peterson Guide to Architecture Schools, ACSA, Washington, DC, 1998, p. 2.

18

Davis, Meredith, "Design as a Catalyst for Learning," Association for Supervision and Curriculum Development, Alexandria, VA, 1997 (via e-mail, August 31, 2000).

19

"IIDA Notes," *Interiors & Sources*, June 1999, p. 124.

20

Dona, Claudia, "Invisible Design," in John Thackera (ed.), *Design after Modernism*, Thames and Hudson, New York, 1988, p. 152.

21

DaimlerChrysler Awards 2000, DaimlerChrysler Corporation, 2000, p. 14.

22

The Chronicle of Higher Education, August 4, 2000, p. A16.

23

IDA/E-Lab Report, p. 48, http://www.ameritech.net/users/iidafdn/Education_Analysis.pdf

24

"IIDA Notes," *Interiors & Sources*, June 1999, p. 124.

25

IDA/E-Lab Report, pp. 27–28.

26

"CCAC School Catalogue," California College of Arts and Crafts, 2000.

27

IDA/E-Lab Report, p. 13.

28

Pollari and Somol, "Complex Interiority," p. 15.

29

Dow, Russell, student at the School of the Art Institute of Chicago, interview, July 10, 2000.

30

Pike, Lynda, student at the University of Pretoria, South Africa, interview, August 2000.

31

Bisagna, Elisabeth, student at the School of the Art Institute of Chicago, interview, June 2000.

32

Duffy, Frank, "The Choreography of Change," in C. Thomas Mitchell (ed.), *New Thinking in Design*, Van Nostrand Reinhold, New York, 1996, p. 28.

33

Duffy, Frank, "The Choreography of Change," p. 18.

34

Duffy, Frank, "The Choreography of Change," p. 18.

35

Carreker, Helen, *Interiors & Sources*, June/August 2000.

7
Opportunity for Change:
Design in the
New Economy

KAREN STEPHENSON, Ph.D.
with NEIL P. FRANKEL, FAIA, FIIDA

Throughout history, every time a person walked into a newly built environment, he or she walked into a space museum; a museum of inner space, not outer space. Groundbreaking ceremonies and ribbon cutting rituals in praise of new constructions are a testimony to the importance of place, that is, how we live and work in space. This chapter provides a view into the client or sponsor's expanding expectation of the designer's contribution and the profound potential this evolution has to increase the value of design and of the design profession.

A TRANSITION FROM AN OLD TO NEW ECONOMY

Fifteen years ago the intellectual, Michel Foucault, predicted a shift in how people perceive and value place. His philosophical body of work traces this transformation of attitudes from the concept of simple *location* in seventeenth-century physics, to a *fixed location* of a disciplined individual in the eighteenth century, and finally to the *regulated workplace* of the nineteenth century. As any good archaeologist does, Foucault went into the field and pieced together a "site analysis" that included an architectural examination of prisons, factories, asylums, hospitals, and schools.

Each of the institutions Foucault investigated possessed a built reality whereby people were placed in a line of cells or cubicles, side by side, like a suburb. The result was that each individual became fixed in his place, constantly located. We can observe this phenomenon today by simply walking into any corporation or university. Then as now, hidden away from view behind the walled, partitioned offices of what was labeled "universal planning" are the docile Stepford drones disciplined to serve.

Sadly, the recent stakeholders responsible for shaping the built environment have progressed no further than their predecessors have. Unwittingly, we have caged and enraged ourselves with artifacts from this industrial era. Hierarchical planning in the workplace, those Dilbertian cubicles in which we make our nests, results from reducing space to its barest economical essentials just as the factory floor eliminated extraneous human movement to ensure robotic efficiency, accuracy, and the IQ equivalent of a machine. The errors of this old economy are obvious with hindsight: we know now that what we really needed was another head—more knowledge—and not necessarily another pair of hands. And we found out that the deprivation of space can and does sink a human to an existence that is nasty and bureaucratic.

Is it any wonder that the vast savannas of the new economy give us a sense of newfound freedom? Instead of becoming a vanishing point in a warehouse of cubicles, today's knowledge workers become targets of human capital. Pundits have theorized that the vast distance between people would be compensated by the simultaneity of an Internet response, where intimacy would be achieved through immediacy; that theory has been undermined by research that indicates that even those who sit side-by-side in physical proximity continue to communicate through e-mail. Virtual has become the preferred mode. Have we substantively moved away from geography to recapture a sense of the communal, albeit electronic, flow—something we lost somewhere along the way in the fight for the right to be alone in the corner office?

We suggest that the new economy has not replaced our primordial need to be between. Rather, the Information Superhighway has cut a swath through our parochial perceptions and permitted a new view from afar. It has punctuated the evolutionary path we have traveled and let us see how we fit in space and time. Indeed we have met a felt need over the Internet precisely because of the way we live in gated corporate suburbs. But as bland as those corporate suburbs are, we are not likely to abandon physical proximity nor our old institutions because they still meet that primordial need for physical intimacy—that fluid sense of community that comes and goes with belonging and that is inexorably linked to the raw territorialism of our hominid forebears. Virtuality has simply added another dimension to the space-time continuum. It has cast a spotlight on the sterile corporate office where a bureaucrat trumps brain and brawn any day of the week.

If this is so, then the workplace becomes *very* important. In truth, the workplace is the icon of the new millennium. It's the pivotal place for uniting a divided industry around the common cause of design. Never was design more critical in integrating components of the built environment—built environments sprinkled with spaces called "kitchens," "front porches," "courtyards," and "plazas"—points of intersection between public and private,

---

"The present epoch will perhaps be above all the epoch of space. We are in the epoch of simultaneity: We are in the epoch of juxtaposition, the epoch of the near and far, of the side-by-side, of the dispersed. We are at a moment, I believe, when our experience of the world is less that of a long life developing through time than that of a network that connects points and intersections with its own skin."

Michael Foucault, "Of Other Spaces"[1]

opacity and transparency, real and virtual, open and closed, and corporation and family. It has become a new economy hearth, a place of congregation where ideas flow informally among colleagues and are realized in enterprise. It is not that territorial divisions are destined to disappear entirely, but only that they will be reconstituted. Old economy institutions never die without leaving traces of themselves. They persist, not only by sheer force of survival, but because they still answer unmet needs. The material neighborhood will always constitute a bond between men. But it is the redefinition or redistricting of the material neighborhood that catalyzes a unification of an industry now divided by prior conceptions of professional specialization, e.g., territorial divisions, if you will, that are no longer relevant.

Figure 7-1 summarizes some of the more apparent features of each paradigm, comparing recognizable characteristics and hallmarks of the old and new economies.

WHO OWNS THE WORKPLACE?

Owners, those defined as client or sponsor, real estate developers, financial institutions, architects, interior designers, organizational development analysts, as well as contractors and vendors have all staked a claim. Like professional segregationists, they possessed their own tradition of territorialism to own the intellectual property of their domain. And the resulting built environments, like a reflecting pool, mirrored the composition of that knowledge legacy. They created environments and buildings that were works of art, when perhaps what was needed was more listening about what constituted the "art" of work—the serendipitous interactions—that could give meaning and aesthetic from 9 o'clock to 5 o'clock.

The inertial drag of an industry steeped in its own functional silos ultimately led to more litigation, acrimony, and regulation. Any industry will cannibalize itself if it cannot invent. But threaded through the industry is the common language of design.

The role of the designer in the work of the built environment continues to evolve in a track parallel to our society. When the author Sigfried Giedion

Old Economy	New Economy
Theory of limited good	Theory of unlimited good
Propinquity	Synchronicity
Local knowledge	Ubiquity of access
Command and control	Influence and trust
Technology backbone	Appliance peer-to-peer
Centralization	Network
Fixed hard cost	Variable soft cost
Opacity	Transparency
Tangible assets	Intangible assets
Rigid	Flexible
Dedicated use, single task	Multi-use, Multi-task
Long life	Half-life
Bricks and mortar	Clicks and mortar

FIGURE 7-1
Comparative Table of
Old and New Economy
Paradigms.

referred to architecture as the "epoch of our time," he posited a parallel relationship between design and the socioeconomic climate for client services. The extraordinary developments in the world of technology, the evolving changes in the sociology of place, and the increased expectations for the role of the built environment in supporting human activity provided the platform for an expanded role of the designer.

The evolution of the designer's role is critical to understanding the opportunity for increasing the value of design. This evolution, prompted by our increased access to information, an amended list of client priorities, and cross-functional expectations of our physical settings, such as the home office, retail as destination, and hospitality as entertainment, has set a new agenda for the goals, responsibilities, core competencies, work relationships, and public perceptions of the designer.

The designer's role has also been influenced by social changes affecting people's perceptions and attitudes toward time. In the old economy, quality was the measurement for which companies competed. In the new economy, quality has become the norm, and speed has replaced quality as the basis of competitive advantage. This change affects the way design work is implemented, which is more interactive and no longer follows the traditional linear pattern of design process.

In the past, the client or sponsor was responsible for providing the design team with direction and information regarding the project. While user groups were often interviewed about their requirements, the sponsor typically acted as a filter through which all information flowed. Today, the user is the participant, and each user has a distinct and direct relationship with the designer.

This change significantly affects the core competencies of the design professional, who is no longer insulated by the client or sponsor and is required to interpret the user's intent. The designer's new competencies rely on a broader literacy about all subjects concerning the user. In the old economy, the designer's training was geared to issues important to the sponsor: image, function and efficiency. Today, *how* work gets done becomes the basis for design decisions and recommendations. The design professional's training must become more multidisciplinary as the designer travels deeper into the organization.

Figure 7-2 graphically compares the relationship of various stakeholders in the project process. In the old economy the project is approached in a linear,

FIGURE 7-2

The Old Economy Relationship Matrix

	Competencies	Goals	Responsibilities	Public Perception	Work Relationship
Designer	Visualize Technical Problem solve	Function Image Budget	Concept Drawing Overview	Implementation	Client/owner Contractor
Technical Consultants	Specialized	Competitiveness Futurize Enabler	Support	Expertise	Designer
Client	Sponsor Facilitate	Image Function Budget authority	Direct Disburse funds Manage Vision	Ownership	Designer User Finance Real Estate
Contractor	Manage Constructor	Budget implemetation Time/schedule Quality of products Performance	Conformance direction, finance drawing, intent, time	Realization	Architect Owner Vendor
Vendor	Produce	Quality Budget conformance	Support	Support	Contractor
User	Value Receive	Internal Information	Supplier of Information	Compliant	Client
Finance	Enable	Containment	Review Control	Invisible	Client

FIGURE 7-3

The New Economy Relationship Matrix

	Competencies	Goals	Responsibilities	Public Perception	Work Relationship
Designer	Visualize Technical Problem solve Establish goals	Function Image Budget development Interpretation of strategic goals Translation of management objectives Value added	Concept Drawing development Technical consultant	Implementation Implementors	Client/owner Contractor Align goals with physical requirements Program potential
Technical Consultants	Technology forecast Program/Application development	Application alternative State-of-the-art equipment and application	Vendor Financial	Visionary Facilitator	Align technical with physical settings Framework plan for future applications
Client	Sponsor Compose team Establish goals Facilitate	Image Function Budget authority Strategic vision Management objectives	Direction Disbursment of funds Management Vision Technology consultant	Ownership Impliment public policy Legislative influence	Architect User Finance Strategic forecast Market anticipation Alliance
Contractor	Manager "Constructor" Value engineering Platform for future applications	Budget implemetation Time/schedule Quality of products Performance Continuous relationship with client	Conformance direction, finance drawing, intent, time Benchmark performance/ specifications Alternative building strategies design/build	Realization Project responsibilities	Architect Owner Vendor Financial User
Vendor	Produce On-going services Just in time applications	Quality of products Budget conformance Relationship building with client, user contractor	Support design/build Time reduction State-of-the-art recommendation/ application	Support Knowledge	Contractor User
User	Value Receive Mangement Distribution of funds Establishing goals	Internal information Tactical applications of vision Effectiveness	Technical consultant	Compliant Leadership w/client	Client Definition of needs Space ulilization
Finance	Enable Creative alternatives	Containment Identitfy pay-back periods Investment	Review Control Monitor investment	Invisible Monitor	Client Contractor Vendor

hierarchical series of relationships. The new economy (see Figure 7-3) shifts this process, making it more interactive and aligning the designer to the project and the end user of the project.

THE INDUSTRY SHIFT

Historically, the workplace has been at the center of controversy for the last two centuries. At the turn of 1900, Futurism swept the United States and Europe like a force of nature. It permeated work, culture, and art: the immobile strength of steel girders bested only by the flexing of the human minds that gave them grandeur. With the dawn of a new economy, we have a different image. Instead of steel girders writ large, they are writ small, housing a virtual reality that travels at the speed of light as though on the wings of Mercury—all to beat a path to the door of this new millennium.

But this door opened onto a world that was an odd reversal of fortune. Instead of last century's visible and physical "place" that housed and held us in gated office structures hidden to others, today we are invisibly connected via the Internet in ways that make us transparent and our actions traceable. We are becoming digitized, abbreviated, and hurled through glass walls and fiber optics to be connected. In the old economy, the visible made us invisible; in the new economy, the invisible makes us visible.

Is there really something happening in the new economy that has implications for the design industry or is this just so much pointing and clicking? In one of those ironic twists, old economy firms have unwittingly colluded to produce the new economy. For example, in hierarchical management, the lines of command and control are neatly drawn only to be stumbled over as people reach across their discreet bodies of knowledge in search of solutions. This leaves legacy firms squeezed in the middle, providing value at new-economy rates but at an old-economy pace. The agility, speed, and resourcefulness required to meet new-economy needs put old-line firms at risk. Many firms don't know how to undergo the substantive change required for success in the new environment.

The new economy brought forth the alignment of management goals with the performance of the physical facilities. People work for ideas, not money. Even "options" are an idea about money! So when ideas became currency in the new economy, the greatest corporate investment became its people and management leadership shifted its focus from efficiency to effectiveness. Management no longer gauged its corporate health on the bottom line only but looked to strategies of assessment such as "triple bottom line" or the "*balanced* scorecard" (emphasis on balanced). Strategies that developed an equation of organizational health encompassing financial, customer, internal business process, and learning and growth issues became intertwined with design recommendation. No client or owner at the close of the twentieth century failed to identify primary concerns regarding issues such as recruitment, retention, absenteeism, health benefit costs, or employee morale. The designer now meets with a client team much more complex in its composition than that limited to the chairman or CEO. Today's client team is now composed of and represented by diverse areas of specialty, such as human resources, financial, marketing, and risk management. Each area brings a unique perspective to the project. Each defines the project goals from its own perspective. Each has its own expectations of defining project success.

The distinction between old and new economy is less about chronology, twentieth century versus twenty-first century, but more about aspiration: the project goal. In the old economy the designer's focus was centered on real estate issues: image, efficiency, and first time cost. In the new economy the designer concentrates on management issues: performance, effectiveness, attraction and retention. By definition, design in the new economy achieves enhanced results for the project, thereby making design a more valuable enterprise.

It is appropriate at this point to compare the old-economy condition to a current new-economy platform and outline the relationship roles of the stakeholders involved with interior space. This view is formed on two axes, that of the list of participants forming the project 'team' and the relationships surrounding the project. Figure 7-4 delineates additional characteristics to be applied to the designer's attributes in support of the project.

Stakeholder Relationship in the Old Economy

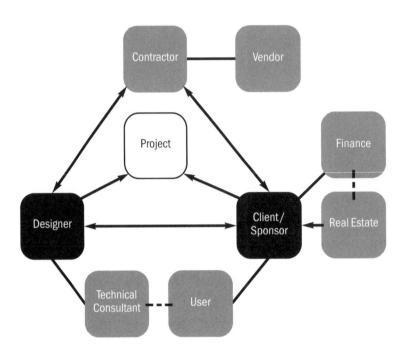

FIGURE 7-4

Stakeholder Relationship in the New Economy

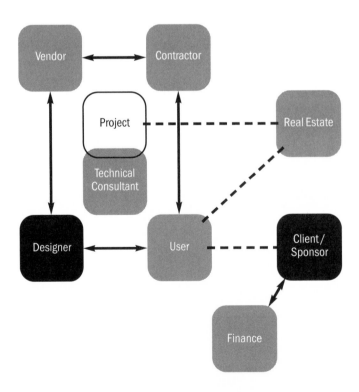

THE GAP BETWEEN PRACTICE AND PROCEDURE

With acceleration of work pace, the workplace needs to have processes in place to ensure task completion and knowledge capture. No sooner is one procedure established than people naturally improvise another as new requests arise. The continual updating or renegotiation of procedural knowledge requires rapid-fire reconciliation. But in old-economy firms, legacy lives long. Consequently, established ways of doing things in the back office often remain untouched, in fact, become fossilized, as the more externally oriented parts of the firm begin to adopt new procedures. Then, one day, the alignment or reconciliation of back-office procedures with front-office practice seems insurmountable and people resort to personal favor for pushing favor, all at a glacial pace. With no immediate solution in sight, the work environment becomes a living museum and the management its custodian. As a consequence, reconciliation of front- and back-office procedures is usually ignored or forgotten in the haste to make profits. Eventually, people don't even recognize the back office, as they become worlds apart. Then one day people can't find the back office anymore because it's buried under a mountain of outdated procedures. It's an arduous task equal to the most skilled archaeologist to interpret history from the stratigraphy of lost processes. Even if one could reconcile procedural records, there is probably nothing written down on paper that even closely resembles what people actually do in the firm today. And therein lies the problem. This misalignment between practice and procedures produces gaps in perception and ultimately expectations around what it is people really do. With no real understanding of how work gets done and how knowledge is transferred, facility managers are coping with artifacts from the past, buried bones, not buried treasures.

And that's the good news. It gets worse. These procedural gaps grow to Grand Canyon proportions and are then appropriated by clever individuals intent on making a business out of arbitraging the gaps (the kings and queens of brokering between things). The early stages of appropriating procedures aren't all bad because in the inefficiencies there are the kernels of new ideas. While these people are cleverly finessing the outdated procedures, the gap between practice and procedure widens within the stratigraphy and, as more and more people get involved over time, this type of tacit knowledge becomes linked, forming a vein of innovation that circumvents the rules—all in the name of progress. This know-how should be shared with those who

In truth, the workplace is the icon of the new millennium. It's the pivotal place for uniting a divided industry around the common cause of design. Never was design more critical in integrating components of the built environment . . .

design environments around work. But the challenge is to find them and mine the vein for its riches before it ossifies. Ossification is the unintended consequence when we leave "well enough alone." Ossification consists of feeding and sheltering these work-arounds, and before long the work-arounds become the real work of the firm. People start to focus their efforts inwardly rather than outwardly on the customer. These work-arounds can become so intricate that eventually its inventors have to create a set of procedures just to manage the catacombs of information paths. All too often, untrained facilities managers must navigate these.

Only experts can steer near great barrier reefs and only experts should treat bureaucracies. Bureaucracies are just like coral reefs. Built on dead or dying procedures, a monstrous structure is created from layer after layer of dead cells of inefficiency until it changes the cultural ecosystem around it. These bureaucracies are an ossified testimony to years of continual misappropriation and misalignment. Over time, these bureaucracies become like barrier reefs—beautiful but dangerous—dangerous because they are hard to change and yet they shape our future. Ironically, solutions are inside a bureaucracy, albeit invisible, intangible, and tacit, residing in the last place someone like Henry Ford may have thought to look—inside people. That's because old-economy firms traditionally define and value capital assets, like elevators as tangible and measurable and workplaces as nothing more than closely packed Dilbertian cubicles carved out of a facilities budget as a hard fixed cost. New-economy firms recognize that their most important asset is not the elevator; rather it's what goes up and down in it and perhaps doesn't even need to be in the elevator at all. If firms can't value their people as assets, then they will never understand how a built environment will retain them.

HUMAN CAPITAL

A multitude of forces have changed this old economy. Industrial-strength economies are geared to capital assets and human costs (bricks and mortar); the new economy is wound around human assets and capital costs (clicks and mortar). However, the greatest capital assets in the world don't mean a thing if you cannot retain the best people. New business models are based on a network value chain that is nonlinear and values the timely and targeted application of intellectual resources when and where they are most needed. Just as the challenge in the new economy is not information but access to that information, so it is for companies that must attract, retain, and marshal intellectual capital, i.e., human resources to provide rapid, customized solutions or services. Mobility is less pressing in a "fast company" than directionality: e.g., the ability to run to, not away from, problems. The knowledge analyst must be behaviorally and technologically enabled to orchestrate input, analyze data, craft a diagnosis, provide prognosis, and solve problems for a client. At any given moment, an individual's intellectual capital is poised to solve and is not unlike a firm's financial capital, stock that goes up and goes down depending on real and perceived value. This is why designers must solve the riddle of the intangible in real space and time. They must understand the nature of work to know how to adapt flexibly between public and private, opacity and transparency.

CONCLUSION

The components of the design industry (client or sponsor, contractor, vendor, finance, user, real estate, technical consultant, designer, and architect) all have a piece of a limited pie in the legacy of their industry. In the old economy, the time to completed outcome was such that each component could execute its own process in its own domain of knowledge. Each part viewed itself as distinct, with a mission that was critical to the positive outcome of the project and was the master of its own universe. With the new economy, changes in technology, demand for shortened time frames, and increased breadth of scope within each component, the industry shifted and began to morph and merge. If the component players continue to protect their domain, border skirmishes will inevitably occur throughout the intellectual domain of the industry.

The industry components must yield and build an integrated process of knowledge hand-shakes rather than default to the emergent processes they now have—vestigial remains of the old economy. Human activity and its segregation into residential and corporate, urban and rural, public and private patterns has converged in mixed-use precincts where people redefine their environments as individuals, groups, communities, neighborhoods, and countries. This redefinition begins and ends with the convergence of work and lifestyles. But a "24/7" orientation does not mean seamless and senseless addiction to work; rather it is a balance and integration of work and life. Continuous activity implies "24/7" sustainability in terms of services. Local services and serendipitous meetings are not bygone memories, but are simply "relocated" to new unprecedented venues that support the nomadic lifestyle. The result is that the raw territorialism of our hominid forebears, punctuated by these disruptive technologies, is evolving and will adapt to new domains and dominions. Who better to meet this new millennium challenge than the design community?

Note

1
Foucault, Michael. "Of Other Spaces," *Diacritics*, vol. 16 (1), 1986, p. 22.

Bibliography

Casey, Edward S. *The Fate of Place: A Philosophical History.* Berkeley: University of California Press, 1998.

Giedion, Sigfried. *Space, Time and Architecture: The Growth of a New Tradition.* Cambridge, MA: Harvard University Press, 1967.

Strat

egy

8

Human Resources

PAUL DOHERTY, AIA

Design firms realize that a highly skilled and motivated workforce is pivotal to success: there is nothing more important to a design firm's health than its human capital. Human capital is managed, measured, and administered through policies and strategies known collectively as human resources (HR). HR sets the tone for how a firm treats, manages, and nurtures its employees and is a major differentiating factor in the marketplace today. When it works correctly, a firm's HR strategy will help recruit and retain valuable employees. Traditionally, only large design firms addressed HR issues with formal processes and benefits.

In today's net economy, however, the importance of HR, or the human side of a firm's business, can no longer be taken for granted and remain stagnant. Firms of all sizes must address HR as a formal, strategic piece of their over-all business strategy if they are to survive "The War for Talent"—a war in which design firms engage in intense competition for talent, and increased client needs are creating a fast-changing environment that does not increase fees. How a design firm navigates through this balance will determine its long-term health. It may seem that the advances that HR software has made in the past few years can help a firm win the war for talent, but these solutions are still falling woefully short.

Technology alone, of course, cannot take the place of a well-thought-out, comprehensive HR strategy that accounts for the "people needs" of design firm employees. For the design firm, effective HR involves striking the right balance over how much responsibility a firm needs to assume with respect to people needs and how much time and money a firm must devote in order to meet these needs. In essence, HR creates the right balance between the strategic needs of the firm and the basic people needs of its employees.

The job market today is scarce in terms of the skills and knowledge that a growing, technology-driven firm requires, which makes the job market highly competitive. Your firm's ability to attract good employees and talent is decided not just by higher wages, but also by the "human" side of your firm, such as its general atmosphere, innovative environment, or creative time schedules that adapt to the changes in workforce needs. The demographics of today's employee market have changed forever as the diversity of society is seen in growing percentages of designers. Included in this are the growing legions of working mothers and/or single mothers and fathers. This has increased the need for day-care facilities or services that firms can help subsidize or pay for as a benefit to talented employees. A new responsibility that is beginning to emerge is the care of elderly parents by firm employees, which has created a new benefit for employees called elder care. As the demographics change, so must the benefits a firm offers.

Six key HR issues have significant effects on a design firm's personnel and are becoming the main differentiators in the marketplace today.

1. *Increasing rules and regulations.* Understanding and setting up policies regarding government-mandated regulations and programs is an important piece of HR and the firm's business. Policies on workplace hazards such as discrimination, sexual harassment, or illegal use of the Internet are no longer considered merely "nice to have"; they are a necessity because of the growing enforcement of laws that carry harsh penalties if the firm does not follow them.

2. *Mobile/temporary workforce.* Because the market cannot provide enough talent, firms are hard pressed to operate in traditional ways, and new ideas of how a firm operates are developing. Alternative, virtual work environments that are created through remote locations and telecommuting are being added to a firm's arsenal of flexibility, which may also offer flex-time schedules. Another increasing area of employment is the temporary or contingent employee. These talented individuals move from project to project and from firm to firm, where they enjoy flexibility, variety, and learning opportunities that make this type of free agent a valuable commodity in the marketplace.

3. *Workforce diversity.* It is no longer a competitive advantage just to adapt to cultural diversity in the design firm; the firm must learn how to capitalize on it. Since the firm is consciously or subconsciously competing on a global scale, having a diverse workforce could be the key to growth that a firm has never had the opportunity to explore before.

4. *Change management.* A proper HR strategy provides vision for how the firm will move strategically through change, and also provides a plan of action that can be implemented. In today's fast-moving, highly connected

work environment, highly touted HR initiatives must be easily implemented. There is nothing worse than a HR change that is announced with great fanfare, only to have nonaction doom the initiative to failure.

5. *Work life.* The design firm of today must be acutely "life friendly," meaning that in order to attract top talent, the design firm's scheduling and general operating policies must take into reasonable account the personal needs of employees outside the work environment.

6. *Technology.* By streamlining the administrative aspects of HR, technology has been a positive development for many tasks, such as resumé screening, posting of jobs, and e-mail communications between personnel. However, many issues that are design specific, such as employee portfolio management, project measurements, and flexible scheduling, are lacking in today's software offerings. The Internet is bringing affordable HR options to our industry as application service providers (ASP) are offering corporate-class solutions as a pay-as-you-go subscription model for our industry's smaller-sized firms. This means that the traditional large expense of implementing corporate-class technology by one entity can be shared by many subscribers, lowering the cost.

For the design firm, then, these six challenges can be met with a HR policy that carefully and comprehensively accounts for getting, keeping, and benefiting from good employees: recruiting, hiring, development, retention, compensation, and communication.

RECRUITING AND HIRING

Profitable and healthy design firm HR practices begin with smart hiring. When design firms recruit, interview, hire, and train people who should not have been hired anyway, they lose time and money and waste effort. No design professionals want to spend the bulk of their time each day putting out fires. Unfortunately, because of bad hiring, many managers and designers spend their time as firefighters rather than as strategic thinkers, planners, and designers. Design firms can avoid hiring the wrong people, but only if the firm follows a strict process that involves identifying needs, allowing flexibility, and requiring technological competence.

Before starting the hiring process, the design firm should ask itself what kind of position it is asking the market to fulfill. This seems simple, but most design firms stick by the traditional methods of hiring by posting a job description that places a person into a supervised routine based on a set of job specs. Because the design office has changed so much over the past few years, this traditional approach misses three main issues of the "new economy" design office.

1. A job description no longer means "one particular set of tasks." Job descriptions that lock people into performing tasks can inhibit speed and agility, both of which are critical in today's workplace. Employees are expected not only to do the job to which they are assigned, but also to "contribute." To contribute, design firm employees must maintain core competencies while learning something new based on high-quality standards, keeping clients happy, and keeping costs under control.

2. What designers considered to be a routine job a few years ago now has to be flexible in its tasks without the support of direct supervision. Some employees do not work well in this type of environment and must be supported in other ways.

3. Although until recently design firms have classed technological skills as "nice to have," now they find them to be imperative. Design firms of all sizes consider basic technology skills to be critical to the decision-making process. Firms can no longer afford to have employees who cannot communicate digitally.

Your firm should ask itself these key questions before making a move to recruit talent:

- *What are the most pressing competitive priorities facing your firm right now?*

- *Will hiring a person help your firm stay competitive?*

- *What are the key trends in the industry, and do your firm's overall business goals match these trends?*

MENTORING

The best way for a design firm to foster professional growth and ensure that its employees learn how the firm operates is to assign a mentor, sometimes called a sponsor. These are employees who act as a new hire's "big brother" or "big sister," sometimes for a period of time, but more likely until a certain professional threshold is reached. The role of a mentor can vary from just being available to answer questions and give support when necessary to having periodic meetings that provide goals and feedback to the employee. Mentors are different from supervisors in that they do not oversee the employee's day-to-day work performance.

The key to a successful mentoring program is to make an educated selection of mentors and prepare the mentors for their role. Here are four criteria that the design firm should use to ensure successful mentoring.

1. *Choose good role models.* Choose employees who possess a good attitude that you would like others to emulate. Mentors do not necessarily need to be your most senior managers, but they should be naturally empathetic and genuinely enjoy helping others.

2. *Get recommendations.* Ask project managers and others in your firm who they think would make a good mentor.

3. *Find common ground.* Finding similarities between the employee and the mentor, such as having attended the same design school or having similar design tastes, is key for good rapport.

4. *Provide training.* Provide expectations to mentors about what is required of them, the role they will be playing, and what they can expect in return (time commitment, extra time off, etc.).

If the mentor and employee are not getting along, it is best to introduce the employee to another mentor quickly. A postmentor interview with both the affected employee and the mentor should take place so that the source of the friction can be isolated and worked out.

Over the past decade, talent has become more important than capital, strategy, or R&D. Think about the sources of competitive advantage that companies have. Capital is accessible today for good ideas and good projects.

RETAINING THE "BEST AND BRIGHTEST"

The most frustrating aspect

The most frustrating aspect of the design business today is recruiting talented individuals, nurturing their growth, and then watching that talent walk out the door. How can the design firm retain its best and brightest talent?

If the firm is people focused, it will do very well in today's high-speed, competitive environment because it will keep its best and brightest. If the firm pays no attention to its employees' needs, it will lose its talent base and may not survive. HR should be focused on creating a people-centric firm that is flexible in its compensation and willing to listen to its employees for its wants and needs. To be people-centric, the design firm should measure its ability to offer:

- *Pay and benefit packages*

- *Opportunities*

- *Job security*

- *Pride in work and firm*

- *Openness and fairness*

- *Camaraderie and friendliness*

In order to attract the best talent, the design firm should provide a message of who they are and what they expect from an employee. The best people respond to four kinds of messages:

1. *Go with a winner.* This message is for people who want a high-performing firm, one where they will have lots of advancement opportunities.

2. *Big risk, big reward.* People who respond to this message want an environment where they will be challenged either to do exceptionally well or to leave—a firm where there is considerable risk but good compensation, and where they can advance their career rapidly.

3. *Save the world.* This message attracts people who want a firm with an inspiring mission and an exciting challenge.

4. *Lifestyles.* People who respond best to this message are seeking a firm that offers more flexibility and better lifestyle benefits, such as a good location.

COMPENSATION

The compensation system adopted by a design firm is one of the main engines driving its business. Compensation is a very expensive engine to maintain and can be the firm's number one expense. Payroll and other compensation issues, such as insurance and other benefits, however, form a major part of how the firm is perceived in the market and how it operates as a business. When a design firm decides how much to pay its employees and establishes pay scales, awards bonuses, and offers other incentives, it can profoundly affect the quality of its designs, its work, and its ability to attract and retain good employees.

It is good practice for a design firm to set a basic wage policy that is based on a strategic system that has a constant eye toward the needs and goals of the firm. Many of the established salary practices of the past, such as automatic pay increases for the amount of time you are at the firm, have given way to new systems such as project-oriented, performance-based pay. An effective compensation system should ensure the following results.

- *The firm's compensation policies are in line with state and federal laws involving minimum wages and job classifications.*

- *The firm's compensation policies are competitive enough to keep pace with the changing climate of today's labor market, particularly in recruiting and retaining top design talent, who are in very strong demand.*

- *The firm's pay scale for the various positions (project manager, lead designer, associate, principal, etc.) reflects the relative importance of the position and the skills that performing those positions require.*

- *The firm's payroll costs are in line with the overall financial health of the company.*

- *The firm's basic philosophy is clearly understood and strongly supported by all employees.*

No matter whether their HR practices are traditional or cutting edge, all design firms must meet basic legal requirements applicable to compensation and benefits. Before the firm sets its salary policies and wage structures, it should be sure to consult with an attorney and get advice on state and federal wage laws and other mandates. Some basic items to remember about state and federal wage laws is that they require that employers pay wages on time and at regular intervals, and there are regulations regarding what can be deducted from an employee's paycheck. Most states permit employers to deduct only withholding taxes, Social Security, unemployment taxes, and state disability payments. All other deductions, such as medical insurance premiums, life insurance premiums, 401(k) contributions, or other employee-paid benefits, require the advance written consent of the employee.

The design firm's compensation policy should take into account the firm's mission and strategic goals. For instance, if the firm's strategic goal is to become the dominant firm in the industry within the next three to five years, it will have to offer attractive wage and benefit packages to attract the right people to fuel its growth. It may also need to pay highly talented people more than their market value today so that it can benefit from their contributions three to five years from now. If the firm's goal is to improve productivity, effectiveness, and efficiency, it will want to tie compensation to performance and productivity metrics that can be measured in a periodic manner.

A design firm's compensation system should preserve the firm's financial health. A good rule of thumb for establishing the firm's compensation system is to determine the firm's cost/revenue ratio. The key feature of this ratio is what profit margin the firm realizes on its services. Although profit margins in some industries are high enough, upwards of 50 percent in some cases, to absorb higher payroll costs, in the design industry, profit margins tend to run in the 12–15 percent range. Consequently, payroll in most design firms runs around 30 percent of total revenues, including benefits and taxes.

Many design firms spend considerable time and effort designing a pay system, then leave it to the paycheck alone to communicate employee value and firm philosophy. To succeed, the firm must not only create a fair system, but also ongoing communication about the firm's financial condition to managers and between principals. This will help to effectively explain, administer, and support firm pay policies to all employees. If there are any changes to your firm's pay system, immediate and open communication can help alleviate unfounded rumors, increase trust, and create a healthy work environment.

BENEFITS

For many potential design employees, the benefits package is as important as the wages. Benefits are any form of compensation that is not part of an employee's basic pay or is not tied directly to either the requirements of a job or performance in a position. Design firms should realize that benefits today are no longer one type of package that everyone in the firm receives. Although all benefits packages contain some benefits in common, today's benefits are highly customizable to meet employees' noncompensation needs.

With the rising costs of health insurance and the increasing trend toward investing in retirement plans beyond Social Security, benefit packages can make or break a prospective employee deal. HR benefits have become a time-consuming business element, not only because the design firm must choose which benefits to offer, but also because it must administer the details, reconcile employee desires, and meet the realities of the firm's financial position.

Exactly which benefits the firm offers and how much of the firm's payroll goes to pay for these benefits depends on the financial health of the firm and whether the benefits meet the firm's strategic business plan goals. As mandated by law, a benefits package consists of three basic elements: Social Security/Medicare, workers' compensation, and unemployment insurance. After these basics, employee benefits are voluntary. Popular offerings include health insurance, dental insurance, life insurance, time off, leaves of absence, sick days, 401(k) investment plans, profit sharing, stock options, tuition reimbursement, child-care assistance, elder-care assistance, and an increasing benefit of an in-house concierge, who can take care of things such as laundry/dry cleaning, car care, post office chores, etc.

The best way to keep design firm employees happy is to listen to their needs and adapt the firm's offered benefits to meet these needs. The firm should conduct an orientation as to what benefits are offered and the processes involved. The orientation will allow the firm to educate new and existing employees. In addition, it will offer the firm insight into what works, what doesn't, and what changes may need to be made.

EMPLOYEE MANUALS

An employee manual keeps the design firm's basic policies and procedures well documented and accessible to all employees. The firm should be careful to separate "firm policies" from "job-specific procedures." If the firm makes the distinction in its employee manual between policies that apply to everyone in the company (general hours, payroll, vacation, etc.) and procedures that relate specifically to how people get their work done (CAD layering guidelines, etc.), it will create less confusion in the firm as a whole. The firm can also create this distinction if it creates procedure manuals for job-specific tasks.

Employee manuals should be simple, clear, and concise. It is important that the policies described are understood and accepted by all affected employees, for two reasons. First, if the employee manual communicates basic issues of being an employee at the firm without overly formal, bureaucratic wording or phrasing, it will go a long way toward building trust within your firm. Second, the employee manual is a legal document and can be used for the firm and against the firm in legal cases. The firm should make sure that an attorney reviews the manual before the firm publishes it. In addition, all employees who receive the hardcopy version should be required to sign a document acknowledging the receipt of the manual and that they understand the contents. This document should be kept in the employee's files. Even though the manual should be maintained in hardcopy form for this legal purpose of acknowledgment, the firm should also produce it in soft copy. The employee manual should be made available through the firm's intranet, or at the very least it should be easily accessible via the firm's computer network. This availability practice allows all employees to have easy access to firm policies at a moment's notice.

Employee manuals should include the following:

- *A Welcome statement from firm leader(s)*

- *An Equal Employment Opportunity (EEO) policy statement (including sexual and other forms of harassment)*

- *The firm history and overview*

- *The Firm Mission Statement and values*

- *Basic firm rules: work hours, business ethics, smoking, drinking, drugs, dress code, sick days, holidays, etc.*

- *Performance appraisal procedures*

- *Disciplinary procedures*

- *Health, safety, and security rules and procedures (fire exit maps, etc.)*

- *Benefit, pension (401k) and/or deferred-income programs*

- *Parking and transportation information*

BEST PRACTICES

"Best practices" are guidelines for how a firm can improve its human capital. The following elements are considered HR best practices in leading design firms today.

- **Aggressive recruiting.** *The traditional laid-back approach to recruiting in the design field is giving way to aggressive tactics that are becoming the norm today. Online recruiting via e-mail and through the firm's Web site are two major, and inexpensive, new ways to get the word out about the firm and to target market-talented individuals quickly and effectively. The Hillier Group (http://www.hillier. com) uses its Website to engage a potential employee through an entertaining yet informative site. The design of the site sets the tone for the culture of the firm.*

- Maintaining a creative, healthy firm culture. *The work style and environment of the design firm has a bigger influence on its bottom line than firm members may think. Stagnant, nonflexible firms will bleed talent, but energetic, forward-looking leadership will provide vision and fuel the growth of successful firms. In essence, although success for the design firm starts at the top, it is enabled by proper HR policies that help nurture the firm's vision. Gensler (http:www. gensler.com) has been recognized by many in the design community as a leader in providing a nurturing, creative culture that is measured in its business success.*

- Communicate regulatory changes. *To maintain a stable work environment, the design firm must communicate changes to regulatory HR procedures and policies between the firm and employees in a timely way. Many successful design firms share the best practice of open communications and education as to what changes mean to employees.*

- Strategic staffing. *One important best practice element is hiring the right people at the right time. The design firm should take the time and effort to make sure that each staffing decision made will meet the goals and operational needs of the firm.*

- Temporary staffing. *Temporary, sometimes called contingent, staffing has become a staple of best practice at leading firms. When it brings in talented individuals from time to time on a per-project basis, the firm gets the value of a fresh viewpoint outside the firm's knowledge base, and the project team members get the introduction of innovative ideas and new ways of working. When managed properly, contingent workers can be a wonderful element of a successful design firm.*

- High-performance work models. *The hierarchal studio model of the 1900s has given way to two basic models that are delivering high-performance measurements for leading firms:*

  - *Autonomy: The firm gives the people who do the work more power to determine how it gets done.*

  - *Teaming: The firm gives a group of employees an assignment, provides resources, and authorizes them to do what's necessary to best get the work accomplished.*

- **Work/life.** *Best practice makes work/life issues a priority of the firm. Human compassion and understanding far outweigh rigid HR policy in certain cases. In some successful firms, selected HR policies are viewed as guidelines with room for interpretation. Flextime, child care, elder care, and telecommuting can produce measurable improvements in employee morale, satisfaction, and productivity, while decreasing turnover and absenteeism.*

FUTURE TRENDS

The design industry is struggling to find and hold onto talent. At times, designers, managers, and production personnel seem to be involved in a perpetual revolving door, and nowhere is this more evident than in the information technology (IT) and design areas of the businesses. How can the design industry justify paying a computer network administrator a fraction of the salary than that person can get in any other industry? Are designers surprised anymore when a talented designer leaves the profession, because she has been offered high wages to work for a computer gaming company or Hollywood? Designers are losing their most valuable people, the people that keep firms operating, due to ignorance, low value perception, and cheapness. Other industries are picking up on the fact that designers pay their people poorly and are raiding firms of all sizes for their personnel.

In the July 1998 issue of *Fast Company* magazine, Charles Fishman interviewed Ed Michaels, a director of McKinsey & Co. in Atlanta, on the recent McKinsey study titled, "The War for Talent." This was a year-long study that involved 77 companies and almost 6000 managers and executives. The study reported that the most important business resource for the next 20 years is talent: smart, sophisticated businesspeople who are technologically literate, globally astute, and operationally agile. The results of this study are ominous, as the search for the best and the brightest will become a constant, costly battle with no finish line.

Historically, design firms have had people lining up at their doors. Now they must compete aggressively for talent. The first step is to find talent. Nontraditional approaches to recruiting are emerging because firms need to convince IT and design talent that they will find challenging and lucrative positions in the design industry. Designers are using incentives unheard of just a few years ago to lure talent—for instance, signing bonuses, expense accounts, travel to conferences, and flextime.

In order to keep the talent already available to designers, design firms must acknowledge that they operate now in a changing landscape. In a way, designers are involved in a silent battlefield in the war for talent. That battlefield involves people who have been at the same firm for 3 to 10 years, people between the ages of 25 and 35. Most firms are losing more people in these ranks than they realize. And those people are often some of their best employees. When asked what they were looking for in deciding where to work, people answered, a great job in a great company, one that is well managed, has terrific values, has a great culture. They also want "headroom"— a job where they can make decisions on their own, without having to go through a bureaucracy.

The stakes are high, and in certain cases talent retention will be the determining factor in success and even business survival. After all is said and done, the design firm's business depends not just on strategies, but on people.

Bibliography

Buckingham, Marcus, and Donald Clifton. *Now, Discover Your Strengths*. New York: The Free Press, 2001.

Fishman, Charles. "The War for Talent." *Fast Company*, Issue # 16, p. 104, http://www.fastcompany.com/online/16/mckinsey.html

9
Financial Management

GARY E. WHEELER, FASID, FIIDA, AIA

The design professions have struggled between the art and business of design for decades. As artists we naturally focus on the aesthetic and design sides of our talent. However, as business people we have the reputation for ignoring the financial management of our firms and that of our clients. In order to do quality work we must have a foundation of good business practices as well as an understanding of what this can offer us.

By definition, financial management is the measure of our success in how well linked all the components of our business are (i.e., what we do, what it costs to do it, and how profitable these actions are). According to *Webster's New World Pocket Dictionary*, the definition of *financial* is "1. money resources, income, etc. 2. the science of managing money," and the definition of *management* is "1. a managing or being managed; control, direction, etc. 2. the persons managing a business, institution, etc." Regardless of whether one works for a large design or architectural organization or in a one-person firm, the same basic practices and principles apply.

First, a business plan—what we are trying to accomplish within a given practice —must be tied to our financial resources and goals. Strategic planning teaches us to review the world around us, to assess our impact on our business environment, and to plan to accomplish our goals and objectives. Therefore, financial management is not just the reporting of results, but rather is integral to practice management and success.

Financial management is necessary for two very simple reasons: first, because we want to do our very best work; and second, because we need to support our practice financially. Responsible financial management will provide and maintain the opportunity to do consistently more challenging work, and it will keep us in business!

FUNDAMENTAL PRINCIPLES OF FINANCIAL MANAGEMENT

Income or "Payment for Services"

To have a clear understanding of the fundamentals of financial management, we need to define the following terms.

- Gross income: *total compensation for all services and products.*

- Sale: *award of a commission upon which income can be earned.*

- Net income: *total compensation less*
    - *Vendors' costs—products and services*
    - *Consultants*
    - *Out-of-pocket nonreimbursed expenses*

- Earned income*: net income recognized as a result of delivering a portion or all of the product or service.*

- Profit: *earned income less all cost of service and expenses.*

The fundamentals for management and profitability are the same for contract or residential design practices. Both need to be based on the value of services and the time it takes to deliver and manage these services. Remember, all you have to "sell" is your talent and time.

Practice Expenses or "Cost of Services"

One of the biggest issues in many design firms is the disconnect between income and expenses. Since time is money, many design firms *give away* the only asset they have—their time. This is an area in which many residential designers underestimate their value. If you are compensated solely through the sale of product (i.e., furniture, accessories, materials), the time you invest in research, selection, acquisition, installation, and handholding is easily lost. If you do not track this time, you will most likely give away more than you receive.

In a contract practice, the tracking of time to deliver a project is easier since it is accomplished mechanically. Getting staff to fill out their time cards accurately and timely is the key to earning revenue, issuing invoices, and speeding payment for services.

Once you understand the various areas of expenses, setting up a tracking system is relatively easy. Your accountant will be able to assist you in establishing these systems. The cost of services can be generally grouped into three categories.

1. **Cost of labor–*generally variable***

   • Direct salaries or hourly wages

   • Customary and statutory benefits such as Social Security, vacation, health benefits, etc.

2. **Cost of operations–*generally fixed***

   • Rent

   • Phone

   • Technology

   • Lights

   • Heating

   • Taxes

3. **Cost of sales and marketing–*generally variable and nonbillable***

   • Staff support

   • Brochures

   • Advertising

Financial management is therefore the balance between income and expenses.

Fixed versus Variable Expenses

The following two areas of expense are the foundation for financial planning. Certain items are nondiscretionary, such as rent, phone, lights, heating, and taxes. You must pay these items to stay in business. Others are discretionary, such as advertising and photography. While advertising may help you position your firm within your target market, it is not required for you to operate your firm.

• ***Fixed expenses*** are long term, slower to change, and less controllable on a day-to-day basis. They include such items as a lease for office space or equipment. Generally, these fixed expenses require a commitment of five to ten years. Taxes on your lease, while generally stable, can change depending on the economic climate of the city and state in which you practice.

- *Variable expenses* are short term and more controllable. They are generally the focus of most financial management approaches and tools, due to this element of control. Items such as advertising, reproduction, photography, and salaries are all items that can be manipulated on a short-term basis.

Financial Management and Control

There are two basic ways of tracking income and expenses, accrual accounting and cash accounting.

1. **Accrual accounting–*net business value.*** This process accounts for all assets and liabilities.

   - **Assets**
     - Fixed assets–furniture, computers, etc.
     - Nonfixed assets–accounts receivable, value of uncompleted contracts
   - **Liabilities**
     - Fixed liabilities–long-term commitments, e.g., bank loans, leases, etc.
     - Nonfixed liabilities–consultant/vendor cost, accounts payable

   The accrual value is the net amount remaining after you have collected everything due you and paid everything you owe.

2. **Cash accounting–*operating worth***

   - Business value excluding fixed assets and liabilities

   The cash accounting process shows you the value of your company at any given snapshot in time. If you have done the work but not been paid, there is no value on the books. Therefore, your bank will look very closely at how you manage your billings.

   It is possible to have a positive accrual value and a negative cash value. For example, the cost of office furniture is accrued by spreading its cost by depreciating its value over time, but you have to have all the cash up front to buy it.

FINANCIAL MANAGEMENT STRUCTURE

The financial management structure of your company will depend on your business philosophy, type and size of practice, and legal description.

Residential

The residential interior design practice is generally composed of single practitioners or firms of 12 or fewer employees. If you are in a primarily residential practice, there are several ways you can receive compensation for your services. The traditional way has been through the sale of furniture and accessories. Usually these items are purchased from a wholesale source and marked up 40 to 50 percent for sale to clients. Depending on the items and their rarity, some items can even be doubled ot tripled in price. However, in the past few years many manufacturers have opened their showrooms to the public or established retail outlets. This was a business decision necessary for them to survive. It has also led the residential design community to rethink their compensation structure. Today we find many firms charging an hourly fee and either arranging the acquisition of product through a third-party supplier (dealer) or selling the product to their clients at a reduced markup. In addition, the retail market has been greatly expanded by savvy marketing and excellent products from such companies as Crate & Barrel and IKEA stores. Although consumers can now buy well-designed products without a designer assisting them, they still need the designer's *talents* to coordinate their home environment into more than pieces of furniture from a sales floor.

The practice of selling furniture and accessories as the key compensation method is under attack by many sources. The design community continues to be featured in everything from *The New York Times* and *The Wall Street Journal* to local newspapers about the duping of the public. These articles almost always focus on the exorbitant prices charged to clients, without regard to budget or our clients' best interests. In addition, as legal recognition of the interior design profession continues to spread, government agencies are taking a strong stand against this method of compensation. The issues of protecting the health, safety, and welfare of the public are in conflict with the segment of the profession that is compensated primarily through the sale of products.

It appears that there is a trend toward an hourly or value-based compensation structure similar to the contract practice. This is an easier way of being

Financial management is necessary for two very simple reasons: first, because we want to do our very best work; and second, because we need to support our practice financially.

compensated for services, but it will require a major shift in residential practice throughout North America. Most of Europe already practices this way. The interior designer or architect designs the space and specifies the furniture; the client then buys these items directly from the manufacturer.

Contract

The other major segment of the design industry is the contract design practice. These practices tend to be larger than the residential practices and are composed of firms that have 20 to 200 employees. Often these firms are divisions within architectural firms or are stand-alone interiors practices that often partner with architectural firms. Much like the residential practice, the stand-alone contract design firm usually has one to three leaders—or principals—within the practice who are the standard bearers for the design direction of the firm. These practices can focus on corporate, institutional, health care, retail, hospitality, and education, just to name a few areas. What is common among all of these practice groups is the way most of them receive compensation through an hourly-based structure.

Generally these practices charge an hourly fee based on a commodity compensation structure of cost per square foot. During the last decade or so contact design services have come under great pressure by the real estate community, resulting in tighter profit margins. At the same time, clients are not only expecting more service but also better quality of services at a faster turnaround time. Increased client expectations, coupled with higher salaries and expanded benefits, have resulted in a reevaluation of the compensation philosophy of the contract practice. As we shift from a "project-based" practice to a "relationship"-based practice, the value of the service is becoming more important than the time it takes to produce it. This strategy is borrowed from the financial consulting firms, which discovered some time ago that the impact one has on a business is more valuable/important than the time it took you to evaluate that business. More and more design firms are "consulting" with their clients long before there is a project. Assisting clients in the evaluation of existing real estate and strategy development to support the client's expansion goals are just two examples of consulting services.

Most contract projects are broken down into several phases, starting with programming and ending with construction administration and client move-in. Executing each of these phases requires certain talents and expertise to execute. Through tracking time and productivity, firms are able to establish benchmarks for developing fees on new projects. By learning from past projects, one can more accurately develop a marketing and fee strategy for new projects.

Many design firms have at least one key leader who is a doer/seller. In other words, the key marketing person is also the one leading the project delivery effort. In a small practice the process of selling and doing can be easier to control. One gets a project, does the project, and then searches for another project. While this process can lead to times of being very busy and others that are slow, the small practice generally can anticipate these shifts in the workload. However, the larger the practice, the more these ups and downs cause problems with cash flow and staff. Today many offices are diversifying into two or more areas to make sure that when one practice area is slow, another is busy. Diversification can even out the ups and downs of the business. Depth of expertise and leadership focus is key to this diversification.

Other practices have full-time dedicated marketing staff who focus solely on developing project leads and client relationships. Others use a combination of business development staff and administrative support staff, working with senior marketing staff (usually principals) who are experts in their given program area, such as interior design. This format usually exists in a large firm where staff resources are sufficient to support such an organizational strategy. A great deal of contract design is based on responding to Requests for Proposals (RFPs), which often requires extensive resources of time and documentation to prepare properly. The proposal can often be the first and only opportunity one has to get in front of prospective clients. Without focused and appropriate proposals, your one chance to make an impact can be lost before you are even in the game.

Your marketing approach should be developed based on your target market and the maturity of your service offerings. Generally, marketing costs range between 8 and 10 percent of your overall budget. If you are entering a new market area where you have little or no reputation or experience, marketing cost can be considerably higher. Your approach to entering a new market can vary depending on your reputation and knowledge. By using research, writing papers, speaking at public forums where potential clients or partners may be in attendance, and publishing your findings, you can build a strong professional reputation which will enable you to broaden your product offerings.

Whether you are compensated by a markup on product, an hourly rate, or one based on a cost per square foot, the bottom line is that your talent and the time you take to develop your ideas are the key to your success. For sound financial planning it is necessary to track accurately the time you spend to service your clients. Without this data you cannot manage the resources necessary to run your business successfully.

FINANCIAL MANAGEMENT TOOLS

Alice:

Would you tell me please, which way to go from here?

Cheshire Cat:

That depends a good deal on where you want to go.

Alice:

I don't much care where.

Cheshire Cat:

Then it doesn't matter which way to go.

Lewis Carroll, *Through the Looking-Glass,* 1872

If you do not know where you want to go, how can you possibly get there? We all struggle with this issue. In today's fast-changing business environment, not only are we under pressure to change, but also our clients are constantly reevaluating their lives, both professional and personal. To help us try to get a handle on where we are going, there are some tools such as strategic planning we can use to guide us.

Strategic planning is the lead effort in business organization planning and growth. It sets the stage for change, provides a framework for everyday decision making, and guides an organization into the future. It helps an organization decide which fork in the road to take. The strategic planning process was used by many of the nation's top corporations in the past, but it has gained new status through the use of scenario building. Strategic planning enables us to look at multiple options for the future and therefore be prepared to react proactively to the world around us.

In its most basic form, strategic planning is a process that involves analysis of the world around us—not just the design world—through investigating the current trends. What is happening now—and what will happen later?

- *Economically*

- *Technologically*

- *Politically*

- *Culturally—socially and demographically*

- *Environmentally*

By taking this global view we can focus on how these areas may affect the design profession. An example is the government and private-sector initiatives undertaken by the U.S. Green Buildings Council (USGBC). The USGBCs initiatives have a direct impact on the products and services we can provide our clients.

Strategic planning *is "the process by which the guiding members of an organization envision its future and develop the necessary procedures and operations to achieve that future . . . the plan that helps an organization create its future"* (L. Goodstein, T. Nolan, J. W. Pfeiffer).

Once the environmental scan is complete, we can focus on "where are we?" Through an internal evaluation process known as a SWOT (Strengths, Weaknesses, Opportunities, and Threats) analysis, we can evaluate the impact of our clients' changing needs. First we focus on the strengths and weaknesses of our firms. What differentiates us from our competitors? In which fundamental areas are we strong or weak? This requires the leadership to be open and honest in their internal evaluation of current staff, financial standing, design abilities, personality issues, etc. This first analysis focuses on what is generally under our control.

When you come to a fork in the road, take it.

Yogi Berra

Next we look at opportunities and threats for the future. These items are often not under our control. Issues such as legislation, the global economy, and political change are not under our personal control. However, we must be prepared to react to both the positive and negative aspects of changes in these areas. Quite often an opportunity can also be a threat, and vice versa. If there is an opportunity we do not address, it may come back to haunt us.

When the external and internal analysis is complete, you can develop a strategy for "where do you want to go?" By establishing goals (broad description of a nonmeasurable or time-sensitive aim) and objectives (measurable outcome derived from a goal), we can set the course for our business and financial planning. Strategic plans are generally a rolling three-to-five-year look at where we want to go, with detailed plans for the current year outlining what needs to be done to achieve the plan.

- **Develop alternatives–scenario planning.** *Creatively develop and explore alternatives that move the organization toward achieving its vision and mission. This is the fun part—it's essentially brainstorming.*

- **Decide on the goals and objectives.** *Goals and objectives are intended accomplishments, designed to resolve a critical issue and/or improve the execution of key operations or responsibilities.*

- **Decide on the strategies.** *A strategy is a statement of how an objective will be achieved through the allocation of human and financial resources. It frequently specifies a time frame for accomplishment.*

- **Decide on the performance indicators.** *A performance indicator is an observable measure or attribute, which reflects how well an organization is implementing or accomplishing its strategies in support of an objective. How well have we succeeded?*

Upon completion of your strategic plan, the year's *business plan* can be developed. Resources, both human and financial, are assigned based on the priorities established in the strategic plan. Therefore, the combination of strategic planning and the development of the business plan become the road map for meeting your company's long-term goals. The fundamental principles of financial management all come into play during this process. The foundation for a successful practice has now been established. Implement the plan. Make it happen!

Financial management requires sound business planning. By knowing where you want to go, understanding the business climate that affects your area of expertise, and developing sound management tools, one is able to properly plan and manage the *business of design*.

Bibliography

Goodstein, Leonard D., Timothy M. Nolan, and William J. Pfeiffer. *Applied Strategic Planning: A Comprehensive Guide.* New York: McGraw-Hill, 1993.

Lipnack, Jessica, and Jeffrey Stamps. *Virtual Teams People Working Across Boundaries with Technology* (Second Edition). New York: John Wiley & Sons, Inc., 2000.

Schwartz, Peter. *The Art of the Long View.* New York: Doubleday, 1991.

10

Marketing: Position and Identity

LISBETH QUEBE, FSMPS

In the beginning, interior designers, architects, and engineers would never have used the words "marketing" or "sales." The words had an unsavory connotation, calling up images of used-car salesmen in checkered coats or encyclopedia peddlers in scuffed shoes rather than urbane design professionals. In fact, until the 1970s, the canon of ethics of the American Institute of Architects (AIA) expressly forbade blatant promotion, and the organizations that preceded the International Interior Design Association, the Institute of Business Designers (IBD) and the American Society of Interior Designers (ASID), were of similar mindsets. So how was work secured? Through connections and visibility—sometimes known as the "old boy network." Talent and a striking portfolio were imperatives, but a design professional's practice expanded based on whom he or she knew. A professional's merits were extolled by friends and colleagues, and for a fortunate few, through news stories and magazine articles written by others. As a professional, your eyes were kept suitably downcast.

Today it's a different story. Of course, the old boy network still plays an important part. Designers must still be both visible and connected. In a profession where commissions are granted based on trust, recommendations and references are forever the gold standard. Yet, over the past three decades, design professionals have accepted professional services marketing as an important part of their business. There is a thriving association, the Society of Marketing Professional Services (SMPS), that comprises individuals whose prime responsibility is marketing and sales. It was founded in 1973 and now has over 5,000 members, including principals and marketers from interior design firms, architectural firms, and other allied professions. Today, there are myriad methods for promoting designers and their firms to potential clients. Designers can choose from elective methods, such as advertising, exhibiting, sponsorship, publishing, speaking, and web page promotion. And they must respond to strict requirements from potential clients for formal qualification packages, proposals, presentations, and project tours.

Fortunately, advances in technology have allowed design professionals to make quantum leaps in both the quality and speed of delivery of marketing submissions and materials.

Even though design professionals are aware of these techniques, there is often hesitancy or even real reluctance to move aggressively into a proactive marketing program. Such a program takes work and resources. Marketing, business development, and public relations do cost money, in the form of time and actual dollars. Lots of heated debates occur about marketing expenses, and what "industry average" is or ought to be. In truth, there is no pat answer. But if marketing is thought of as an investment, the picture will become clearer. Just as individuals pick the amount of money they want to invest, and just as they pick the stocks or bonds they wish to use to reach their financial goals, design professionals must determine how to invest in building their practices. They must decide what they want to do and how much they want to spend. If they are smart, they will keep track of what they invest, and what they get in return, in the form of new fees. Periodically, they should compare the two. In a new effort, one dollar may be spent to make five. But in two to four years (depending on the sector being entered), tangible results should be seen. Marketing efforts should yield a return on investment that allows a practice to flourish.

WHAT IS MARKETING?

So what is this thing called marketing? "Marketing" is used as an all-encompassing word, but it can be really broken up into three components. *Marketing* generally refers to all of the activities that prepare us to approach a prospective client sector. *Business Development* refers to the activities in which we interact directly with these prospects, which leads to sales, those activities that actually close the deal. *Communications,* of which public relations is a major part, refer to those activities that garner visibility in the clients' worlds.

Business development and sales activities are activities that we will examine in Part Four. Briefly, business development begins with identification of a potential client, qualification of the lead (is it viable, and is it right for the firm?), and continues through a period of "courtship" until the time comes for a sales pitch. Networking–keeping in touch with friends in the industry–is another important activity that falls within business development.

In this chapter, we will examine the aspects of marketing related to developing and maintaining a company identity and making plans. These components of marketing include determination of company position, preparation of a strategic plan (which generally looks forward some three to five years), a marketing plan (which is prepared annually), and a marketing budget (which supports the marketing plan). Market research is also included, which may be associated with exploring a new type of client, a new location, a new service, or the firm's current image. Finally, to market effectively, designers need to develop and maintain certain systems. These may include lead-tracking systems, project/personnel databases, visual resources (photographs, slides, and/or digital imagery), and brochures.

This chapter will also address marketing communications. The part of communications called branding affects both how the work is done and how the work (and the firm) is perceived. The part of communications that is more outwardly focused is called public relations. The goal of public relations is to garner visibility in a positive way and, to the largest extent possible, control the content. Such control is not particularly easy when an editor or critic writes about us or one of our projects. But we can create our own advertisements, news releases, articles, exhibits, and speeches, and with some effort, get our story out in the way we want it to be heard.

SELF-DEFINITION

Identify the Firm's Practice Models

The first step in marketing

The first step in marketing is to have a clear sense of the company's identity. The design firm should evaluate just what type of company it is—what kind of work it values, the degree of specialization, the practice model, and what differentiates it from other design firms. Only when the firm has identified its position within the industry can it develop a brand identity for the firm.

Design firms are like snowflakes: no two are exactly alike. Yet it is possible to place firms in broad categories. In 1987, Weld Coxe, founder of The Coxe Group (consultants to the design industry), and David Maister, a Harvard professor, did just that. They postulated that most firms were driven by one of three values: ideas, service, or product. All were perfectly proper, and none was superior to the others. They also recommended operational and marketing approaches suited to these different values. The design profession has evolved significantly since then, but there is still much validity in their thesis.

In Coxe and Maister's model, a firm driven by ideas tends to do projects that are unique. This type of firm is hired to create a specific solution to a specific problem. There will be no other like it—one Hayden Planetarium, one Guggenheim Bilbao. Idea-driven firms get much of their work through the notoriety they gain through publication. A service-driven firm generally works on complicated projects for clients who need a lot of attention. These firms often work for large corporations, hospitals, universities, or government entities. Service firms sell most effectively through the person(s) who will do the work, often supported by business development representatives. A product-driven firm knows how to do a particular type of project extremely well. It has the systems and processes in place to pump out a perfect Wal-Mart or Bank One every couple of days. To sell this process, it relies on a sales staff that can bring in signed contracts. Every firm may not be described perfectly by any of these models, and most firms are hybrids of a sort. But it is still worthwhile to examine the firm's staff, projects, and style of service when fashioning a marketing approach, and thus Coxe and Maister's model remains a useful tool.

Identify the Firm's Degree of Specialization/Globalization

Besides a firm's values, there are other important areas of practice to examine. One of the most important is specialization. Although designers like to think of themselves as Renaissance men or women, that goal is hard to achieve in today's world. Things have gotten a bit more complicated; there's a lot to know about just one subject, let alone five or six. Clients are less apt to hire a generalist, with just two or three of a project type on his resume, than they are a specialist, who can show a long history with a type of facility or client. There is a rationale for this. When designers are retained, clients put their trust in them. Clients want designers to understand their industry—its protocol, its processes, its language, its technology, and its competitive environment. They want to be assured that the designers know what they are doing. After all, their jobs, or businesses, are on the line.

It is wise and quite necessary to have a specialty, but it is a little scary—and perhaps foolish—to have all your eggs in one basket. Keeping a firm healthy and protected is always a balancing act, driven by the design professional's vision of its size and breadth of practice. What if a specialty area experiences a recession or even disappears? So does the practice, if it has only one specialty. The safest position is to have a limited number of specialties, and to have no more than 50 percent of the practice in any one area. That way, if the hospitality sector experiences a downturn, a firm still has corporate or health-care clients to feed the business.

Even though the world is getting more complex, it seems to be getting smaller. Today, a U.S.-based firm is as likely to be doing work in Barcelona or Beijing as it is in Baltimore. The normal course of practice is to develop a specialty that is first local, then regional, then national, and finally international. As the portfolio deepens and recognition as an expert is gained, the breadth of practice will expand. A firm may then export its knowledge in ever-broadening circles. Technological advances are making it easier for more and more firms to work on a global basis.

Differentiating the Firm from the Competition

Being a good—even a great—designer is not enough. A firm's potential client base needs to know it exists. More important, it needs to know why this particular firm is better than its competition. As clients evaluate design firms, they generally go from a long list of candidates to a short list. And whether designers like it or not, it is generally a fact that any of the finalists has the ability to do the job. So why should clients pick any one firm from among the competition? The successful firm will be the one that can articulate why it is better—what sets it apart. That is the differentiation message.

A design firm must develop a message that differentiates it from the competition for a marketing communications campaign or for a specific client pursuit. Without such a message, the campaign or presentation will lack direction and punch. A message may center on a distinctive process, a certain area of expertise, or an especially talented individual. To be most effective, it must be something no one else can claim. Because process is easiest to duplicate, messages built on process are harder to sell. Many firms talk about "the charette process," or their "unique" programming methodology (in truth, rarely unique). A message about expertise is effective, given the facts to back it up, but others can make similar claims. After all, there *are* ten firms in a Top Ten ranking. A message about the firm or its people ensures uniqueness. No two people have worked on the exact same projects, in the exact same role, or have the same degree of recognition.

A message may have several levels, but it must have one clear theme. That theme must resonate throughout the presentation, starting it and summing it up. That theme must carry consistently throughout an advertising campaign —a series of ads building on one strong idea. That theme must repeat throughout a comprehensive marketing communications campaign, so exhibits, advertisements, talks, and even nametags deliver a consistent image and idea.

Before Marketing: Developing a Brand and a Strategic Plan

The theme a firm chooses to carry in all its marketing messages is a key component of the concept known as *branding*. In recent years, the idea of branding has intrigued the design industry. Long associated with product marketing, branding is now moving into the service realm, led by the major consulting firms and real estate organizations. So just what is the concept of branding, and can it work for a design firm?

Simply stated, a product or a service is transformed into a brand when there is an emotional connection with the customer. A brand creates a strong product/service personality, one that transcends the product or service itself. Swatch isn't about keeping time; it's about fashion. McDonald's isn't about hamburgers; it's about family experience. Nike isn't about gym shoes; it's about lifestyle. Brands can be applied to companies, products, and even people (such as Michael Graves or Martha Stewart). A brand is a promise. A brand implies both authenticity and differentiation. A brand is about trust; it makes a continuous promise of future satisfaction.

Positioning is an important first step to the branding aspect of marketing, because developing a brand requires a clearly articulated vision of the company or service, and an absolute commitment to long-term execution. A brand does not happen overnight, simply because someone develops a clever advertising slogan or eye-catching logo. The product or service itself creates the brand, and design professionals are more likely to understand the implications of their brand by talking to their customers than by debating the subject internally. To develop a brand, designers must understand what their clients expect and deliver on it, continually and consistently. They must keep the promise implied by the brand.

Maintaining a brand takes continuous attention and constant improvement. Companies that manage their brands successfully change their corporate culture to support the brand, infusing enthusiasm for the brand in every employee. They make their product different, not just their advertising. Public relations and advertising are used to support their product or their actions.

The most important aspect of branding is third-party endorsement. How people feel about a brand is more important than what they actually know about it. Branding exemplifies loyalty at the gut level. It is a concept well worth implementing, with clarity and perseverance.

MAKING PLANS

Strategic Planning

A wise design professional will recognize that having a well-defined company identity is not enough. Designers must make careful, thoughtful short-term and long-term plans for their companies. In business school lingo, they must make "strategic plans" and "business plans." Just the words "strategic planning" can strike fear into the most stalwart of hearts. It implies exhaustive market research, a maze of calculations, hours spent in dimly lit conference rooms arguing with colleagues over wordy mission statements that end up so generic as to be meaningless. In truth, strategic planning can be a simple process that brings designers back to the fundamentals of their practices.

A strategic plan is a broad vision. It looks out over the next three, five, or ten years. Given the rate of change in the design industry, three to five years is the more sensible option. A strategic plan is a positioning exercise, establishing the long-range goals of the firm. It addresses the desired culture of the organization; its position in the industry; its project delivery processes; issues related to people; and perhaps financial performance objectives. It is largely the product of the leaders of the firm, with input from selected senior staff. It can be one page or ten. Ideally, the strategic plan is part of a planning continuum, preceding and lending direction to the annual business and marketing plans.

Marketing Planning and Budgeting

A marketing plan is a written document that outlines specific performance goals related to marketing for a specific period of time, and which establishes a plan to meet those goals. You can write a marketing plan for the firm as a whole, for a specialty sector within the firm, for a service, or for a specific location. A marketing plan is a valuable communications tool, as it puts in writing the expectations and the rules for the marketing effort. It serves as a common road map, by assigning responsibilities in an understandable way. It makes people accountable, and enables designers to measure their marketing performance.

Marketing plans are doomed to fail unless the people who are responsible for their implementation are involved in creating them, and that means principals as well as marketing and business development staff. When designers participate in the planning, they feel a sense of ownership. It is important to include the firm's principal officers (who have access to financial data) in market planning so the marketing plan will make business sense. The plan must generate enough revenue from new sales to make good business sense, and the marketing budget must be affordable. A marketing plan should be written annually, and tied to the firm's fiscal year.

BASIC COMPONENTS OF A GOOD MARKETING PLAN:

1. *Audit:* "Where do you stand? What are you good at?"

2. *Outlook:* "What's out there? Where can you be effective?"

3. *Goals/objectives:* "What do you want to achieve?"

4. *Strategies:* "How are you going to do that?"

5. *Tools/resources:* "What do you need to do that?"

6. *Budget:* "What will it cost? Can you afford it?"

7. *Implementation:* "Who's actually doing what, and when?"

The Audit

In the audit, you assess your current situation. You can't figure out where you're going if you don't know where you stand. First, take a look at the sectors you serve. To protect yourself from a downturn in any one market, give some consideration to maintaining at least two (and preferably three) strong "core" sectors. Each core sector should generate at least 20 percent of your sales, but it should be no larger than 50 percent. If one market gets too big, you don't work to make it smaller, but you do invest more in some of the others to get back in balance. Examine your services. Evaluate the effectiveness of the ones you are currently providing, and determine if there are others you should add. Look to see where your projects are located, geographically. Look at the profitability of your sectors. Try to identify project types on which you consistently perform well. Examine your technical strengths and weaknesses. Strengths can include such things as innovative planning, specialty knowledge, award-winning design, and a strong record of repeat commissions. Examples of weaknesses include an inability to meet budgets or schedules, lousy references, overextended staff, and no depth of experience. Look at your competition, to ascertain what they are doing and how it could affect you.

In this phase, you can also analyze your marketing effectiveness. First, examine your sales in terms of fees. Look at what you sold this year and in previous years. Compare this to your goals. Look at your "hit rate." Note how many times your proposals got you to the interview, and how many times your interviews got you the job. This tells you where you have to improve. Look at what you spent on marketing. Compare it to what you sold, to see if you received good value.

The Outlook

In developing the outlook, try to determine what markets offer the best opportunities. This can be a project type, a geography, or a service. When you think you know where the opportunities lie, try to determine the best opportunities for you. Just because an area is strong does not mean you should be in it. You may not be capable of—or interested in—serving it.

To define the outlook properly, it may be necessary to do a little market research. Market research involves determining what kind of work you want to do (a task made easier after the self-definition exercises mentioned earlier) and finding where to get it. What do you focus on? It may be a new client type (such as Fortune 500 companies); a new project type (such as law offices); a new service type (such as facility management); or a new geography (such as the Southeast). What do you consider? You consider forces and trends that drive the market. You evaluate the size of the market, and its maturity. You investigate funding. There can be great need and no money. You look at the competition. You examine the cost to enter the market.

There are several ways to conduct market research. There are "direct" methods, which can be as simple as a literature search or a questionnaire. There are "indirect" methods, which can be via telephone or person to person. You don't have to talk to 300 people either. If you get consistent answers from a half-dozen knowledgeable people, you probably have the answers you need.

Setting Goals

The third component, goal setting, forms the basis of the marketing plan. Goals must be specific, realistic, measurable, and limited. "Do good design" is not specific—who decides what is "good" anyway? Goals must be realistic, meaning they must be attainable within reason. There is no faster way to get discouraged than by setting goals so grandiose that they cannot possibly be achieved. Your goals must be measurable—not "Make a profit," but "Make a 15 percent profit." Goals must be limited. Prioritize. Don't try to do everything at once. It's a short twelve months. Last, goals must be collective. Acceptance by the people responsible for implementation is absolutely critical.

Goals may touch on many things. You may target the amount of net fee to be generated. You may describe the types of clients you would prefer to secure. You may delineate types of projects you would like to add to your portfolio. You may define geographic areas for penetration. You may allude to your desired reputation or level of recognition. You may enumerate a desired size in staffing or position in a ranking.

The strategic section of a marketing plan details the means by which you reach your goals and objectives. In developing your strategies, you should take advantage of your strengths, offset your weaknesses, and respond to marketing opportunities. Strategies define action. They may address any number of things: your activities with past or current clients; contact campaigns; networking activities; participation in client organizations; involvement in community activities; and public relations activities, including advertising, announcements, articles, award submissions, direct-mail campaigns, special events, exhibits, news releases, speeches, and seminars.

Determining Tools/Resources

In the tools/resources portion of the marketing plan, you determine the resources and tools necessary to carry out your strategies. Your resources are your people. Look at your strategies and try to determine if the proper people are in place (at the principal, technical, and marketing levels) both to get the job and do the job. Your tools are your collateral materials. Look at the things you need to implement the strategies—such as project photography, brochures, direct-mail pieces, a web page overhaul, or even a database.

The Marketing Budget

The marketing budget prices your strategies. It tells you if you can afford the time and money allocation required to meet your firm's marketing goals. It ultimately tells you if your goals are realistic. The first time you prepare a budget, it seems a daunting task. Over time, as you get to know the marketing habits of your particular cast of characters, and the costs to accomplish certain tasks, it gets easier. First, you choose your approach. There are three basic methodologies for creating a marketing budget: the projection method, the percentage method, and the goal-based method.

The projection method, also referred to as the comparison method, relies on using prior year costs for development of the upcoming year's budget. You must determine what has been spent year-to-date on marketing labor and expenses and project the final year-end costs. The challenge is to decide if that line item will stay the same, increase, or decrease in the upcoming year. Add the line items, and you have your budget.

The percentage method, also called the top-down method, simply allocates a set percentage of the firm's total operating revenues to marketing. That percentage will generally range between 5 and 15 percent, although some firms report costs as low as 3 percent and as high as 18 percent. The accepted average, in the year 2000, is probably between 7 and 9 percent, but then, what firm is average?

The most accurate method, goal-based budgeting, is a "bottom-up" method that assigns costs to each item in your marketing plan. Although more time consuming to set up initially, it is by far the most accurate and manageable budgeting methodology. With a detailed marketing plan, you will be able to estimate the funding required to complete any identified task. Once you have priced what you want to accomplish, you can test this number against available dollars. If you cannot afford the marketing program identified in your plan, you can cut specific items intelligently. Thus, planning continues throughout the budgeting process.

Implementing the Marketing Plan

The final step of the marketing plan is implementation. Smart firms complete an "action plan," which can be a simple matrix or calendar that covers three things. It defines specific tasks (" What is to be done?"). It assigns responsibility ("Who is to do it?"). It sets a time frame ("When will it be done?").

MEASURING RESULTS

Too many firms go to all the trouble of creating a marketing plan, file it neatly away, and go about business as usual. Smart firms monitor the plan or, as so eloquently put by Society for Marketing Professional Services (SMPS) past president Thomas Stokes Page, "determine the degree of plan disintegration." A good marketing planning process requires a systematic method of evaluation. Did you do what you said you would do? Did you get the results you wanted?

There are a number of methods for monitoring and evaluating the entire marketing effort. Keep a sales report that tells you the amount of fees you sell each month. Track your marketing costs and compare them to your budget. Use your sales report to identify the new commissions brought in and compare those fees to what you spent on marketing in the same time period. These exercises allow you to evaluate your return on investment. Create a "hit rate" report that tracks your success from proposal to interview, and from interview to commission. Use your firm's financial statements to determine what percentage of your net revenues is being expended on marketing

So is all this planning and measurement really necessary? There are certainly many firms with no organized marketing plans or tracking systems. You *can* survive in a wholly reactive stance (for a while, anyway). But consider this. A marketing plan provides direction. It instills accountability. It builds teamwork. There is simply no more effective means of getting everyone moving in the same direction, and it allows measurement of progress from year to year.

MARKETING COMMUNICATIONS

Once you have developed a clear sense of your firm's identity, crafted a strategic plan, and written a marketing plan, it is crucial to work on how your company's image is conveyed to the world beyond your office doors. You must work to manage the representation of your firm through use of the media and effective public relations, activities that are often grouped under the umbrella of marketing communications.

Your Audience

As a design professional, you have a number of audiences—your professional peers, associated members of the design industry, your community. No audience is more important than your current and prospective client base. In Part Four we will discuss client interaction from a business development standpoint. However, there are "softer" ways of influencing existing and potential clients, and that is through various media.

Your next most important audience is your network, and here too, media can be influential. Clients look to your network—which should include brokers, architects, engineers, contractors, program managers, and specialty consultants—for information about you. What your network sees, reads, hears, and conveys about you is critical in the marketplace.

The community at large is also your audience. You have an opportunity to be known by people who are not part of the design and construction industry, or who may not even be potential clients. But if "six degrees of separation" has any validity, many people can affect your business, through introductions, recommendations, or recognition.

Internally Produced Material

Historically, design firms use printed brochures as a means of communicating their experience and expertise. Volumes can be printed on this subject, but suffice to say that the best brochures express the firm's work by showing how it addresses specific client needs. The preprinted portfolio of images that was used predominantly in the past is being supplanted by just-in-time electronic project pages, combining the requisite photographs with text that can be customized for any given situation. These types of pages can be reconfigured and recombined, creating a brochure system that is flexible and responsive to customer issues. A base brochure system like this can be supplemented with smaller custom pieces that apply to a specific market sector, project type, or service offering.

With the advent of the Internet, electronic media have made rapid gains in acceptance and importance. A web page offers the opportunity for unlimited worldwide access to your people, portfolio, and "pitch." A web page is a dynamic tool, but it takes a skilled writer, a superb designer, and a technology guru to help get the message across. And unlike a brochure, it is never done. It must be changed, updated, and periodically reinvented in order to draw people back for multiple visits.

Exhibits are another great way to be seen. Some sectors, albeit not all, offer great opportunities to promote your projects and your people. Both "unmanned" exhibits and exhibit booths are accepted tools for marketing professional services. Opportunities to exhibit include gatherings of European real estate entities; annual conventions of the American Society of Hospital Engineers; various meetings of the Urban Land Institute; and the annual convention of the International Council of Shopping Centers.

Advertising is gaining more acceptance in the design industry. To be most effective, an ad campaign must be coordinated and repetitive. For the majority of firms, this is just not financially feasible. A full-page four-color ad may cost between $4,000 and $15,000 in our world (and that does not include the national business magazines, where a page may run upwards of $30,000), so a few a year is a major investment, especially for a return that is difficult to measure. Still, some firms are making the foray into building their brand through advertising.

Externally Produced Material—Getting the Press to Cover You

You work hard to secure new projects. You should work almost as hard at getting them written about. As design professionals, we struggle mightily to get the eye of our own industry publications. And while it is a definite coup to be featured in *Interior Design*, *Interiors*, or *Architectural Digest*, it is just as useful to be featured in your client's trade press. An article in *Modern Healthcare* or *Facilities Design and Management* can be very influential, and more likely to be seen by those who can hire you. It is also beneficial to land in the local newspaper, not to mention *The New York Times*. You must court editors and writers as you court clients. Get copies of their publication calendars, and see if they are contemplating any articles that might logically include one of your projects or a sage quote. Let them know about work in progress. Think about story lines that would garner interest. Send press releases about new projects, at selection and at completion. Send press releases about promotions and awards, too.

Print media—magazines, newspapers, or trade journals—are a potent means of conveying information about you and your firm. The fact that someone would write about you or your projects is a powerful endorsement, worth many times what you can say about yourself. Enclosing reprints from recognized trade publications (both design and client-focused) lends credibility and caché to qualification packages and proposals. A monograph or book on the firm, published by a third party, is an unparalleled marketing tool.

Be an Expert

If a client is to entrust you with his project, he must feel you are an expert. It won't do just to tell him; you have to provide evidence of it. A stellar list of projects is the best way, but that is icing on the cake if your *curriculum vita* includes a nice list of publications and speaking engagements. Authoring an article, either on your own or with a colleague or client, gives instant credibility. If you are taking the time to research and write an article, find the opportunity to speak about it, too. Professional organizations (preferably your clients') are constantly seeking speakers for their conventions and meetings. Get on their agenda. Why not present as an authority to 30 potential clients rather than grovel for admittance to the office of a single one?

Teaching is another way to add to your credibility. If Harvard University puts you on the roster, that says something. It is equally true of any credible university or technical college. Teaching has a bonus. It not only helps in marketing, it helps in recruiting the stars of tomorrow.

SUSTAINING CLIENT RELATIONSHIPS

You can hire the best marketer in the universe, create the most brilliant of ad campaigns, deliver the most compelling of interviews, and not get work. Why? Bad references. There are no marketing tricks that can overcome poor performance. Your past and current clients, and their references, are your most effective allies in bringing in new work. Your clients must be willing to speak to others about your performance. They must be willing to tour your prospective clients through their space. Your articles and speeches will be doubly effective if delivered in collaboration with your client. All this takes their time and energy, so they have to be enthused about helping you. You have to have made them your trusted friend.

Marketing is not cheap. It can consume anywhere from 5 to 15 percent of your revenue. The best way to reduce marketing costs is by keeping the clients you have and securing more work from them, without an onerous marketing process. If you don't have to market and sell every project, your marketing costs will naturally be less. That doesn't mean you don't "market" your existing clients. You must nurture existing relationships with the same level of energy and focus as you do new ones. Take the opportunity to socialize with your clients. Get to know them on a less formal basis. You are likely to find the relationship rewarding on a personal as well as financial level.

The more you can learn about your clients' world, the more you can help them succeed in their business, the more valuable you will be. Expand your vision to include theirs. You will not only design a better facility; you will help them reach their goals. And in doing so, reach yours.

Bibliography

Coxe, Weld, Nina F. Hartung, Hugh Hochberg, Brian J. Lewis, David H. Maister, Robert F. Mattox, and Peter A. Piven. *Success Strategies for Design Professionals*. New York: R. R. Donnelly and Sons, 1987.

Coxe, Weld. *Marketing Architectural and Engineering Services*. New York: Van Nostrand Rheinhold, 1983.

Quebe, Lisbeth. *The Marketing Budget*. SMPS Core Series of Marketing Information Reports, 1992.

Society for Marketing Professional Services. *Marketing Handbook for the Design and Construction Professional*. BNi Publications, 2000.

Spaulding, Margaret, and William D'Elia. *Advanced Marketing Techniques for Architectural and Engineering Firms*. New York: McGraw-Hill, 1989.

II

Team Dynamics

JON R. KATZENBACH
TRACI A. ENTEL
KAREN MAHONY

Both the sole designer and the design team are legendary parts of the professional landscape of design. However, there is a theory in design that the best and most truly creative work can come only from one person's mind. It is this theory that often makes team performance more difficult in design than in other professions. Yet, while the designer as sole creator may be a strong factor working against the establishment or prevalence of teams in design, incredibly difficult demands on designers that have led them to rely on collaborative work and experience has shown that teams work. For example, architect William F. Lamb faced many challenges and set difficult goals for his most famous building, the Empire State Building. The architectural atmosphere of the 1920s encouraged him to build the tallest and most famous building in the world. In addition, he needed to meet the new zoning restrictions of 1916 while still achieving architectural excellence. Facing these tough external pressures, Lamb also set high expectations for his design team—to complete the tallest building in the world within 18 months of the initial sketch. It is now well known that the design and execution of the Empire State Building was so well married that the supplies appeared like magic and stories rose higher each day. And so, "with perfect *teamwork*, Empire State was built."[1]

With perfect teamwork, Empire State was built.

Rem Koolhaas,
Delirious New York

In design, as in most professions, there is work for the single ego and there is work best suited to teams. In this chapter we explore the meaning of teams within the design field. Designers express the need for teams and collaboration, and often credit teamwork for the success of their projects, and yet the design industry is famed most for individualists. Both Frank Lloyd Wright and Howard Roark, the fictional architect in *The Fountainhead,* by Ayn Rand, were constantly victims of their unwavering ego. Our theory encourages designers to identify and distinguish between when the single ego should control a design project and when a team model should be used: this distinction is the key to success in using teams in design.

EVERYONE KNOWS ABOUT TEAMS—RIGHT?

Many management books have been written stressing the need for teams and providing advice on team building. Much of the teams theory that is discussed in this chapter comes from *The Wisdom of Teams,* by Jon R. Katzenbach and Doug K. Smith.[2] This book has since become a best-selling classic in modern business literature, with close to 500,000 copies distributed globally across many countries in over 15 different languages. Katzenbach is generally regarded as the leading expert on team performance in large organizations, particularly with respect to leadership teams.* *The Wisdom of Teams*, like other texts, champions the virtues and benefits of teams; however, it approaches the theory of teams by focusing on the lessons learned by *real teams* and *nonteams* and applying these learnings to other groups struggling with their performance. Research for *The Wisdom of Teams* expanded to hundreds of people in dozens of professions and organizations. Many of the real-life examples confirmed ingoing hypotheses, but many additional insights were developed as well, and the subject of team performance was much less well understood than initially suspected. This chapter discusses what Katzenbach and Smith learned from a wide range of real-life situations in many industries, and applies that to what we learned about team performance in the design profession.

Many of Katzenbach and Smith's basic team findings may be considered as common sense by team practitioners; however, many groups striving to implement team performance do not apply their existing knowledge and miss the opportunity for a real team effort. The inability of teams to succeed without a shared purpose is common sense to most people, and yet many teams are not clear *as a team* about what they want to accomplish and why. People may have attended team-building training sessions and then struggled to translate the teachings to their work environment. In contrast, they may have been fortunate to be part of a situation where a demanding performance challenge resulted in the group becoming a team, almost without really thinking about it. One designer recalled a team experience when a project fell into disarray due to a delayed carpet delivery. The carpet was a floor finishing for an office in a skyscraper. The delay from the factory resulted in a delivery to the skyscraper after the crane was due to leave and work permits would have expired. Together the affected parties solved the problem, which at the outset had seemed insurmountable. Yet they never thought consciously about "becoming a team"; their entire focus was on finding the best way to solve the carpet problem. That turned out to be a team.

Team performance opportunities occur at all levels and situations in organizations, e.g., teams that recommend, teams that produce, and teams that manage. Unfortunately, such opportunities are not always recognized, leaving a great deal of team performance potential untapped. Each group will encounter various challenges, but similarities are more important than differences when striving for team performance. Our traditional workplace metrics are usually not in line with promoting team performance. Job descriptions, compensation, and career paths are focused mainly on individual performance, with teams considered only as an afterthought. As a result, real teams need to establish very clear group goals, working approaches, and metrics that can offset the natural tendency to focus only on individual performance and accountability. For example, as long as Michael Jordan was concerned primarily about his own individual scoring, the Chicago Bulls did not win a championship. After Jordan elevated the importance of helping others to score, the collective score reflected the accomplishments of one of the best teams in National Basketball Association history. It is difficult for us to trust our career aspirations to outcomes that depend on the performance of others, whereas delegating or assigning accountability to one person rather than a group is our preferred method of management.

UNDERSTANDING TEAMS

Many of us may have experienced teams, but some of these experiences may have been rewarding whereas other experiences were a waste of time. The potential impact of teams is widely underexploited despite the rapidly growing recognition of the need for teams. People simply do not apply what they already know about teams in a *disciplined* manner. As a result, they miss out on performance potential, become discouraged, and fail to seek out new team opportunities. One designer described being involved with a long-term hospital design project and discovering that she was the only person in the group who had read the project strategy brief which described the design objectives and goals. The brief had been prepared at the start of the project with a great deal of input from the client management group, but the vital information had not been passed to new group members as they joined the project. This was an impediment to potential creation of a team. The challenge to understanding and building teams is more demanding than simply making team implementers understand the compelling arguments of why teams make a difference or even producing a clearer distinction between a team and a nonteam. Team performance requires mastery of a simple discipline that differs from normal group and managerial behaviors.

Real teams, not just groups of people labeled teams, are a basic unit of performance. In any situation that requires the real-time combination of multiple skills, experiences, and judgments, a disciplined team will invariably achieve better results than a collection of individuals operating in confined job roles and responsibilities. Teams can be quickly assembled, deployed, refocused, and disbanded and are more productive than groups with no clear performance objectives, as members are committed to deliver tangible, agreed upon results. At the same time, teams are not the only way for a small group to function as a performance unit. The single-leader unit or working group is an equally useful performance unit when "the leader really knows best," and most of the work is best accomplished by individuals rather than groups.

Performance Challenges Are Essential

Significant performance challenges energize teams. A team will face an uphill struggle to develop without a performance challenge that is meaningful to all involved. Companies with strong performance standards spawn more "real teams" than companies that simply encourage "more teams and teamwork" through company-wide initiatives that often lead only to frustration. Personal chemistry and a desire to become a team may lead to teamwork values; however, it is critical to understand that *teamwork is not the same thing as a team*. Colleagues can exhibit teamwork by looking out for one another and being considerate in the workplace, but this does not enable them to perform as a team. A common set of performance goals that the group recognizes as important, and holds one another mutually accountable for, is what leads to a real team effort. The differentiating factor is that collective performance is the primary objective, not "becoming (or behaving as) a team." Promoting teams for the sake of teams will seldom lead to team performance. Real teams are much more likely to flourish if leaders aim their sights on group performance results that balance the needs of customers or clients, employees, and shareholders. Clarity of purpose and goals has tremendous impact in our rapidly changing world. For example, one architect expressed the importance of understanding early on the growth intentions in a specific client situation. The client, a management consulting firm, required a new office design. At the start of the design phase the client employed only 12 people but wanted the design to reflect a working space for 20—exploiting the luxury of working space rather than the maximum capacity for the office. However, an important part of creating the design was understanding that the client had plans to grow quickly to 30-plus employees, and that therefore, after a period of time, constant change to accommodate each additional employee would be required. The architect and the client worked as a team in making these accommodations.

Individualism Need Not Impede Teams

Throughout our development, we are instilled with a strong sense of individual responsibility through our parents, teachers, and coaches. It is therefore not surprising that these values follow through in our working lives, where all advancement and reward are based on individual evaluations. Left unattended, self-preservation and individual accountability will hinder potential teams, and this often happens in design. Frank Lloyd Wright was an American individualist who did not use his ego for the advancement of teams. The motto, "Truth against the world," was carved into the wall of his childhood home and became a symbol of his resistance to compromise. When the Chicago school of architecture developed the steel frame to generate space previously unimaginable, Wright, as an accomplished architect, refused to embrace the innovation, preferring to continue using his own techniques. To Wright, architecture was not a collective effort; it was a highly individual artistic form of expression, and he took much pride in the finished product. Wright worked with only a few contractors, and most relationships were difficult. Wright did not even collaborate well with clients. After inviting Wright to spend the night in houses he designed, hosts would awake to

Throughout our development, we are instilled with a strong sense of individual responsibility through our parents, teachers, and coaches. It is therefore not surprising that these values follow through in our working lives . . .

discover their living room furniture completely rearranged, or even discarded, to match his own vision of the room.[3]

This individualistic nonteam behavior exhibited by Wright is mimicked in fiction. In Ayn Rand's *The Fountainhead*, Howard Roark is the prototypical individualist designer. Roark refuses to see his personal vision compromised in the slightest. In a characteristic example, Roark receives a commission to ghost-design a public housing project, and agrees on the condition that the buildings not be altered in any way from his designs. When it becomes clear that the plans have been altered mid-project, Roark blows up the unfinished building. Roark's condition to undertake the work, and his later behavior, are the antithesis of team design. The result of his project, one intended for the good of the public, is lost in a battle against his ego and stubborn philosophy.

However, if recognized and addressed, particularly with reference to how to meet a performance challenge, individual concerns and differences become a source of strength. Real teams do present ways for each individual to contribute and thereby gain distinction in three ways: (1) team members recognize the contributions of one another in ways that are truly meaningful; (2) teams take great pride in their joint accomplishments, and when those are recognized, every member of the team feels rewarded; (3) enlightened organizations take account of the team contributions of individuals when they are evaluating and advancing individuals. Indeed, when tied to a common team purpose and goals, our need to distinguish ourselves as individuals in design can become an energy source for team performance.

Teams Facilitate Problem Solving

Through jointly developing clear goals and approaches, teams establish communications that support real-time problem solving and initiative. The flexibility and responsiveness of a team allow approaches to be realigned as new information and challenges come to light. Teams also provide a unique social dimension. Real teams do not emerge unless the people in them work hard to overcome barriers blocking collective performance. By tackling these obstacles together, people on teams build trust and confidence in each other's capabilities. This collective commitment causes teams not to feel as threatened by change as an individual, and to enlarge their solution space. An added bonus is the discovery that teams seem to have more fun! Team members will often talk about the fun aspects of working together, and a highly developed sense of humor is often seen in top-performing teams as it helped them to deal with the pressures and intensity of high performance.

A Few Words of Caution

Teams are not the solution to everyone's needs. They will not solve every problem, enhance every group's results, nor address every performance challenge. When misapplied, team efforts can be excessively wasteful, if not disruptive. However, when teams work well, and are focused on legitimate team tasks, they invariably outperform other groups and individuals. Appropriately focused, they represent the best proven way to convert visions and values into consistent action, and to energize processes across organizational boundaries, bringing multiple skills together to solve a difficult problem. The good news is that there is a *team discipline* that, if rigorously followed, can transform the typical resistance to teams, such as beliefs that teams waste time in meetings, squander resources, and impede decisions, into team performance. While some elements of this discipline must be learned, most center on common-sense ideas. Unfortunately, like all disciplines, the price of success is strict adherence and practice.

TEAM BASICS: A WORKING DEFINITION AND DISCIPLINE

To apply what we learned from our "Wisdom of Teams" research as a practical discipline in the design context, it is essential to define a team. At the heart of this definition lies the fundamental premise that teams and performance are inextricably linked. Through listening to people who are or have been members of teams and potential teams, the following definition has been developed to distinguish a team from a mere group of people with a common assignment:

A team is a small number of people with complementary skills who are committed to a common purpose, performance goals, and approach for which they hold themselves mutually accountable.[4]

Teams do not happen by magic, but persistent application of the definition (or discipline, which Katzenbach calls team basics) will enhance most people's team performance. Focusing on performance rather than personal chemistry or togetherness will shape teams more than any other factor. The team cannot apply the basics selectively; each one must be adhered to—you must "get an A on all of the basics."

Small Number

Rather than being a formulaic rule, the notion of "small number" is more of a guide. While groups of 30 or 40 people can theoretically become a team, the strong tendency is for such groups to break into subteams, due to the problems associated with larger groups interacting constructively as a group. Large groups may exhibit herding behaviors and as a result tend to settle on less clear statements of purpose, which will ultimately be detrimental to the team. Virtually all the teams encountered in the research ranged between 2 and 25 people, with the majority numbering less than 10. Several years ago, a research group at du Pont concluded after extensive study that groups with more than 12 members usually became increasingly dysfunctional as size increased.[5]

Complementary Skills

Teams must possess or develop the right mix of skills necessary to do the job at hand. These complementary skills fall into three categories: technical or functional expertise, problem-solving and decision-making skills, and interpersonal skills. A team cannot hope to succeed without a mix of skills and talents that matches what the performance task requires. Of particular importance are the technical, functional, and problem-solving skills imposed by the project's purpose and goals. No team can achieve its purpose without the requisite skills. It is rare for a team to include every single skill required at the outset, but teams are powerful vehicles for driving personal learning and development. As long as the skill potential exists, the dynamics of a team cause that skill to develop. Indeed, teams naturally integrate performance and learning and achieve the balance of short-term performance with longer-term institution building which has been an ongoing challenge of the popular learning organization theory.

In design, the existence of complementary skills is often the strongest building block for a team. The process of design typically involves a group of people, with varied skills and experience, playing critical roles at different phases of the work. Recognizing the importance of the roles of each party is the primary enabler for a real team opportunity. Hugh Ferriss, inspired as a child to become an architect by a photograph of the Parthenon, recognized that the Parthenon was built in a "fortunate" period when engineers and artists worked together and the public valued and rewarded their cooperation.[6]

Committed to a Common Purpose and Performance Goals

Purpose and performance goals go hand in hand; teams do not exist without both. Most teams shape their purposes in response to a demand or opportunity put in their path. The best-performing teams invest a tremendous amount of time and effort exploring, shaping, and agreeing on a purpose that belongs to them both collectively and individually. Groups that fail to become teams rarely develop a common purpose that they own and can translate into specific actionable goals. The power of a purpose lies in the fact that it is a joint creation that exists only as a result of the team's collaborative efforts and therefore inspires pride and responsibility. The purpose gives the team an identity and keeps conflict constructive by providing a meaningful standard by which to resolve clashes between individual interests and team interests.

To establish a common purpose in a design project, it is important to choose and mobilize the entire project team at project inception. During the first phase of design work, involving all identified parties in setting strategic objectives enables a project to be built on a common purpose to which the entire group has contributed. However, bringing together experts including the client, architect, engineer, designer, other specialists, and in some situations even financiers or lawmakers is often a challenge. Often constraints such as financial goals set by senior project management or clients less informed of the process of design prevent such early involvement of these parties. Architect Renzo Piano understands the importance of early involvement by the entire project team; he is known for working collaboratively with designers of varying specialties. Piano has alleviated the problem of early mobilization of a project team by creating roles for engineers and other critical contributors within his studio, therefore ensuring involvement from project inception. Piano's spirit of collaboration is noted in talking about the process of design, when he speaks of "we," even chastising one writer for attributing buildings specifically to him rather than to the firm.[7]

The surest first step for a team trying to shape a common purpose meaningful to its members is to transform broad directives into specific and measurable performance goals, e.g., coming in under the design budget, responding to all customers within 24 hours. The successful design team defines clear goals that will focus team discussions. When goals are ambiguous, discussions on pursuing them are much more difficult to have. Clear goals aid the formation of *team work-products* that will tend to differ from both organization-wide missions and the sum of individual objectives. The work-product definition will require roughly equivalent contributions from most team members, must be acceptable to all parties, and add real value.

An important enabler of real team development and project success is working with the client to understand and set performance goals for the design project team. While often in a design project a single mission or desired end-state might be clear to different members of a project team, most likely the members will have individual project performance goals. The client-side project manager may be most concerned with keeping on budget and with end-user satisfaction, while the lighting expert is most concerned with achieving the optimal balance of natural and artificial light. The lighting balance goal must be compatible with the constraints of the realistic budget goal. Both parties' performance goals are important to the success of the project, but in order to be truly committed to a common purpose, these goals must be open and understood by all.

Committed to a Common Approach

Teams also need to develop a common approach to working together. The approach must include an economic and administrative aspect as well as a social aspect. To meet the economic and administrative aspect, every member of a team must do an appropriate amount of "real work" together. This "real work" reaches beyond reviewing, commenting, and deciding and involves subsets of the team "rolling up their sleeves" and interacting closely with each other to produce collective work-products. Team members must agree on who will do particular jobs, how schedules will be set and adhered to, what skills need to be developed, how continuing membership is to be earned, and how the group will make and modify decisions. Agreeing on the specifics of work and how it fits to integrate individual skills and advance team performance lies at the heart of shaping a common approach. Effective teams always have members who assume important social roles such as challenging, interpreting, supporting, and summarizing. These roles help to promote the mutual trust and constructive conflict necessary to the team's success and tend to evolve over time.

Mutual Accountability

No group can ever become a team until it can hold itself accountable as a team. By committing to hold themselves accountable to the team's goals, each individual earns the right to express his or her own views about all aspects of the team's effort and to have these views receive a fair and constructive hearing. Mutual accountability cannot be coerced any more than people can be forced to trust one another; however, mutual accountability does tend to grow as a counterpart to the development of team purpose, performance goals, and approach. Accountability arises from and reinforces the time, energy, and action invested in figuring out what the team is trying to accomplish and how to get it done. When people do real work together toward a common objective, trust and commitment follow. Teams that outperform other similar teams and exceed their own performance goals are rare—we call these teams *high-performing or extraordinary teams*. Such teams are differentiated by a high degree of personal commitment from all team members. This level of commitment is almost impossible to generate on purpose without high risk, because it is invariably a function of overcoming an "impossible obstacle."

Design team members should be aware that others may feel accountable to different parties—the lighting specialist to the general contractor, the general contractor to the architect, the architect to the client-side manager, the client-side manager to the client sponsor. Only by understanding and recognizing these sometimes conflicting accountabilities can mutual accountability be achieved.

BECOMING A TEAM

In many instances the choice to become a team is neither recognized nor consciously made. Often a structured *single-leader working group* will make more sense for the performance goal and situation at hand. A working group relies on its formal leader for direction, and on the individual contributions of its members—working largely on their own—for performance results. This is in marked contrast to a team, which strives for magnified impact that is greater than the sum of each individual's role. The choice between a team and a working group depends largely on whether the individual achievements can deliver the group's performance aspirations, or whether *shifting (multiple) leadership, collective work-products*, complementary skills, and mutual accountability are needed. By knowing the strengths and weaknesses of both teams and working groups, we are in a better position to choose which model to apply to a situation. Applying a rigorous discipline can enhance both real team and working group success.

Working Groups

Working groups thrive in hierarchical structures where individual accountability counts the most. The best working groups tend to come together to share information, perspectives, and best practices, to make decisions that help each person carry out his or her job better, and to reinforce each other's individual performance standards. The focus of a working group is always on single leadership control, individual performance goals, and individual accountabilities. As with a team, the working group will obviously benefit from a clear purpose and a common understanding of how performance will be evaluated. But unlike teams, the single-leader unit (or working group) uses its purpose only to delineate individual roles, tasks, and responsibilities. The working group roles will typically match formal organizational positions. Often, to get their work done, a senior team member will delegate to a junior colleague outside the group. Members may compete constructively with one another as they pursue individual performance targets and may also provide support and counsel to a member having difficulties. However, members do not take responsibility for results other than their own and will not try to develop additional, incremental performance requiring the combined, real work of two or more group members.

Although a team promises greater performance than a working group, there is considerably more risk involved with teams. To begin with, achieving team performance is just plain hard work. Moreover, a leap of faith is required to overcome values of individualism and the reluctance to trust one's fate to others. "Faking" this leap of faith will lead to a failing team, which will divert members from their individual goals and result in a group performance less than the sum of individual performances. Working groups are less risky and do not need to invest time shaping their purpose, objectives, and approach,

An important enabler of real team development and project success is working with the client to understand and set performance goals for the design project team.

since a leader usually establishes them for the group. Like all interactions involving a group of people, both teams and working groups will benefit from obvious good management practices—meetings with agendas, good communication, and time-efficient processes. The working group is efficient in the use of members' time and its formation and success will benefit from applying the following discipline:

- *Working-group members work mostly on individual tasks that match their skills and experience.*

- *The work-products of the group are largely individual.*

- *The group leader drives a rigorous working approach.*

- *Each member has strong individual accountability to his or her task.*

Most of the time, if performance aspirations can be met through individuals doing their jobs well, then a working-group approach is more comfortable, less risky, and less disruptive than trying to achieve the more elusive team performance levels. If the situation does not demand increased performance, then investing time to improve the effectiveness of the working group will be more worthwhile than the group floundering as the members try to become a team. As people are more familiar with the working group, this tends to be the model that achieves performance results faster. The group does not have to spend time figuring out how it will work together, and the leader can rapidly assign tasks to individuals with the appropriate skills.

While setting project objectives and establishing a working approach both lend themselves to working as a team and enabling teams, designers find the creative design stages more difficult for team efforts to succeed. After the project objectives are set and the client's needs are clear, what is needed is a design. It is at this stage of the work that the "design ego" is most prevalent. The lead designer will propose a design to the client and to the other design specialists, but the lead designer functions as the work group leader. For this stage of the work it is difficult to use a real team, because it is said that the camel is a racehorse designed by a committee. However, this is not always the case. Rockefeller Center, conceived in the 1920s, was the product of not one designer but many, including architects, builders, engineers, and also real estate specialists, financiers, and lawyers. Each contributed experience and imagination to solve the complex design challenge. A photograph taken during the planning stages of Rockefeller Center can be interpreted as a real team at work. Nine men involved in creating the specifications of the project crowd around the plan and two miniature models of the three-block site. The photo captures two men adjusting the model, while the others look on with enthusiasm, as if any of them could reach down and adjust the model themselves.

One global design firm recognizes the innate difficulty of forming a real team during design development, but acknowledges there are opportunities for "real team moments." Internally the firm uses a process for discussion called "discourse on design." Here a project team explains unresolved design issues to a group of peers. While this group of peers does not join the project team permanently, during the session, problems are solved with complementary skills, mutual respect, shifting leadership, and the common purpose of achieving the most appropriate design for the client. Often the "discourse on design" is viewed as a turning point or guiding light for a project.

Potential Teams

On the path to becoming a real team may lie what is termed a *potential team*. This is a group that has a significant need for incremental performance and is trying hard to improve its performance impact. Typically, the potential team is lacking clarity around purpose, goals, or work-products and discipline in developing a common working approach. Mutual accountability between members tends not to have been established.

Perhaps the greatest performance gain comes from successfully making the step from a potential team to a real team. There is no best answer as to how to make this transition; however, an underlying pattern is that real teams do not emerge unless the individual members take risks involving conflict, trust, and interdependence, and together complete hard work and learn to shift the leadership role. The most formidable risk involves building the trust and interdependence necessary to move from individual accountability to mutual accountability—and from single to shifting (multiple) leadership roles. This usually requires an adjustment of attitudes that must come primarily through action, not words. Not every potential team becomes a real team. Individual differences, threats of being personally disadvantaged, actions that destroy instead of build mutual respect and interdependence, and unconstructive conflict are among some of the forces that can block team performance and produce a performance level less than that of a working group.

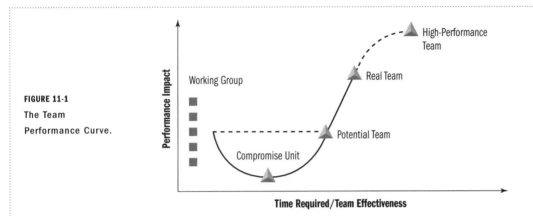

FIGURE 11-1
The Team
Performance Curve.

Everyone who worked hard to invest in the team will suffer lost time and disappointment and will be more reluctant to try teams in the future.

Moving from Potential to Real Teams

There is no guaranteed way to build team performance; however, a variety of common approaches can help potential teams take the necessary risks to move toward becoming a real team.[8]

1. *Establish urgency and direction.* All team members need to believe the team has urgent and worthwhile performance purposes, and they want to know what the expectations are. Indeed, the more urgent and meaningful the rationale, the more likely it is that a real team will emerge.

2. *Select members based on skills and skill potential, not personalities.* Teams must have the complementary skills to do their job or the ability to develop the necessary skills. With the exception of certain advanced functional or technical skills, most people can develop the needed skills after joining a team. All of us have the capacity for personal growth and need only be challenged in a performance-focused way. The question instead may become whether the team is willing to invest the time and effort to help potential team members grow. Training tends to work best when it is supplied "just in time" and is customized to meet the group's specific performance needs.

3. *Pay particular attention to first meetings and actions.* In everyday life, initial impressions mean a great deal, and this holds true for teams. When a potential team first meets, everyone watches one another to confirm or dispel preconceived assumptions and concerns. Close attention in particular is

paid to the team leader. How the leader handles this initial interaction is critical to the team's success in moving forward, and a poor start may never be recovered. Meetings away from the work site may promote less inhibited interactions, which will help to get the team off to a good start. Interruptions will be fewer and no party will have the advantage of "home turf." The financial and time investment in an off-site meeting may help to convince more skeptical members of the importance of the project.

4. ***Set some clear rules of behavior.*** The most critical early rules pertain to attendance, not limiting discussion topics, confidentiality, fact-based analytical approach, end-product orientation, constructive confrontation, and everyone doing real work. Working with these rules may seem a little odd at the outset, but their conception and adherence to them test the group's credibility.

5. ***Set and seize upon a few immediate performance-oriented tasks and goals.*** Most teams, as they reflect on their success, can trace their advancement to key performance-oriented events that molded them together. Potential teams can set such events in motion by immediately establishing a few challenging and yet achievable goals that can be reached early on. Some early wins in the design project will give the team a boost and help to build confidence as it tackles more challenging problems.

6. ***Challenge the group regularly with fresh facts and information.*** New information causes the potential team to redefine and enrich its understanding of the performance challenge, thereby helping the team shape its common purpose, set goals, and define a common approach. Potential teams err when they assume that all the information needed exists in the collective experience and knowledge of the group. It is hard to imagine a design project without regularly changing facts—delivery times, availability, and regulations.

7. ***Spend lots of time together.*** This seems like common sense, but it is often not the case. Time spent together must be both scheduled and unscheduled. Creative insights as well as personal bonding require impromptu and casual interactions. Fortunately for design teams, this time spent together need not all be face to face and teams can take advantage of technological advances in telecommunications to bring them together "virtually." However, even the most "technologically advanced" virtual teams require face-to-face (synchronous) time together at critical points throughout the process. You cannot do it entirely "virtually"!

8. *Exploit the power of positive feedback, recognition, and reward.* Positive reinforcement works as well in a team context as elsewhere. When someone risks bringing up a sensitive issue, perhaps challenging design individualism, other team members can use positive reinforcement to signal openness to similar challenges. This positive reinforcement will have more bearing if the leader shows his or her receptiveness to open discussion.

With these approaches in mind, consider this real team example in California. A home furnishings company abandoned its plans to move into a San Francisco office building, and a rising Internet company wanted to acquire the space. The building developer, who had planned to house the home furnishings company and had financing based on this plan, gave the prospective client a small window of opportunity—the Internet company could occupy the building, but it had only one month to make changes to the current plan. Clearly, the Internet company had very different design requirements from the intended user. As a result, there was much work to be done, and the client hired a global design firm. That firm quickly mobilized a highly qualified team consisting of architects, engineers, the building developer, property owner, other design specialists—plus the client. The assembled team was briefed on the task and spent the next month working closely together toward a solution that would meet this demanding performance challenge. Each member of the team provided valuable input and solved important parts of the problem. The project required mutual accountability and shared work-products building on the complementary skills of each team member. Hence, it is highly unlikely that the incremental performance required could have been met through the working group model.

THE ROLE OF A LEADER

Real Team Leaders

While leaders are essential to both working groups and real teams, the leader's role clearly differs between the two models. In a real team the leadership role will *shift to different members* of the team depending on the situation faced by the team at a particular time. The good news is that most people can learn the skills required to be an effective team leader. Getting people to work as a team depends more on the leader's attitudes than the individual's personality, reputation, or rank. The attitudes of real team leaders reflect the following beliefs: (1) they do not have all the answers and therefore will not insist on providing them; (2) they do not need to make all the key decisions and do not attempt to do so; and (3) they cannot proceed without the combined contributions of all the other team members and so avoid actions that might limit members' inputs or intimidate them in any way. Ego is not a principal concern of real team leaders.

The viewpoint that "only the team can fail" begins with the leaders. Leaders act to clarify purpose and goal, build commitment and self-confidence, strengthen the team's collective skills and approach, remove externally imposed obstacles, and create opportunities for others. Most important, the leaders *do real work themselves*. At the same time, a critical balance must be struck between doing and controlling everything themselves and letting other people do work that matches their talents and skills. When observing the best real teams in action it is often difficult to pick out the nominated leader, as each member will be doing real work, making decisions, and taking on the leadership role throughout the various stages of the project.

One architect interviewed felt he had been part of a real team based on this shifting leadership pattern. The team was designing a new headquarters for a top U.S. automotive company. The team had no previous experience working together, and none of the members was on his "home turf." This leveled the playing field and avoided any preset hierarchy—a familiar hurdle to achieving real team levels of performance. The team had a clear mission and understood the implications of their designs on the working environment from the beginning. With an optimistic set of attitudes and a difficult performance challenge, the team spent "24-hours a day working and living all together in the war office." Within a few months, an interesting leadership pattern had emerged and continued throughout the effort. A project leader in week one was a follower in week three and then a leader again later on in the project. Thus, by applying the disciplines of team basics and shifting leadership roles, the project not only achieved its purpose and goals, but was also a very moving experience for all involved. Friendships were generated and nicknames were formed for team members.

Real team leader behaviors are not difficult to learn or practice. However, we are ingrained with the thinking that authority or leadership is to command and control subordinates and to make all the tough decisions ourselves. While these attitudes may succeed in a working group, they will ruin a potential team. Team performance requires the team to be decisive, the team to be in control, and the team to be a hero—not the leader or any single person. Taking risks, interdependence, constructive conflict, and trust will not occur if the leader calls every shot and always has the final say. A real team leader has to take risks by giving up some of the command and control. However, the leader suddenly stepping back and giving up all control rarely works either. He or she must relinquish decision space only when and as much as the group is ready to accept and use. The leader must show in everything he or she does, or does not do, a belief in the team's purpose and in the people who make up the team. It is essential that the team leader strike the right balance between providing guidance and giving up control, between making tough decisions and letting others make them, and between doing difficult things alone and letting others learn how to do them. In a very real sense, the best team leaders are essentially "gap fillers"—stepping in only when and where needed.

Working-Group Leaders

In contrast, with working groups it is always obvious who is leading the group because the leadership role will always be fulfilled by the same person. When time is of the essence, and the leader really does "know best," this model can be fast and efficient. The leader will have been through a similar situation previously and therefore has the most experience in the group at handling the particular challenge. Although the individual inputs of other group members are important, the leader functions as the ultimate decision maker. Members are accountable *to the leader* for their individual work-products, and it is the leader who is responsible for overall group performance. The role of the group leader is more of delegation, motivation, and integration rather than actually being involved with other members doing real work. Conflicts, issues, and differences of opinion are resolved by the leader, and the goals and working approach of the group are established by the leader. As with teams, the group will benefit from the leader exhibiting good management practices.

Working-group leaders simply follow a different discipline than team leaders. That discipline contrasts with the discipline of teams as follows.

1. The size of the group can be much larger than for teams, because there is much less need for the group to do real work together. There are few "collective work-products," since most of the work can be assigned to individuals to accomplish effectively and efficiently.

2. The performance purpose of the group is usually established by the leader. Often, in fact, it has been assigned to the leader by upper-level managers. It is, however, a powerful performance purpose—and it is that purpose that differentiates the single-leader "performance unit" from the less disciplined "effective group."

3. The specific objectives of the group are determined by the leader, since she is held accountable for its performance by those above her. The majority of these objectives, of course, break into individual assignments or goals for each of the members. While the leader may interact with each member in translating group objectives into individual assignments, the leader remains the final determiner of what goals and time frames will be set and met.

4. The group's working approach is designed by the leader. Again, while the leader may interact with individual members in shaping the individual roles, the leader has the experience and know-how to determine who should be given what assignments.

5. The leader holds each member individually accountable for tasks assigned and agreed upon. Individuals feel a much stronger responsibility to the leader to deliver as promised, and do not worry much about what others are doing.

Thus the single-leader unit is fast, efficient, and effective—when tasks can be easily assigned to individual members, and when the joint work-products of the group are much less important than the individual work-products. Single-leader units, however, do not rise above the level of "effective groups" to become performance units without a strong, clear performance purpose and a leader who enforces consequence management.

MAKING A CHOICE FOR TEAMS IN DESIGN

Those leading design groups must look to the particular performance challenge at hand to help them decide how best to lead, and which discipline to apply (real team or single-leader working group). If the performance challenge can be met through maximizing each individual's contribution, then the leader can rely on the normal decision-making and delegation processes found in a working group. However, if the challenge cannot be met by traditional good management practices, if collective work and end products are more important than individual results, and if different people need to lead, then a real team approach should be seriously—and consciously—considered.

The team approach is becoming more applicable to design today, due to technological and cultural changes. The technological changes that have affected design require greater participation from multiple experts and therefore create more opportunity for real teams. For example, buildings like the Empire State were designed in part based on the availability of natural light and ventilation. Advances in technology have eliminated this design constraint, but have increased the need for cooperation from various technical specialists. Artificial lighting, cooling and heating systems, and more recently, complex phone and computer networks, are standard in workplaces today and require technical experts to work closely together. Additionally, as the variety of structural and decorative options available to clients increases with innovation, so does the number of potential vendors involved in a project.

A major cultural change that has affected the opportunity for real teams in design is the effort to create environmentally responsible designs. Whether "green" movements are introduced by regulatory or ethical guidelines or by the good intentions of curious and innovative designers and clients, the green movement is a way to get the project team motivated around a single "collective" goal. Green architecture is concerned with delivering an improved quality of life to the end-user. One aspect of this movement is that the architecture creates a sense of communication with nature, which is recognized as a stimulant to a healthy work environment and possibly encouraging social interaction. This is part of a project's goal and increases the emotional intelligence and joint commitment required by the team, which can be a strong driver of the common purpose aspect of a real team.

Performance goals within green architecture are often quantifiable and now public. With the introduction of the *Leadership in Energy and Environmental Design* (LEED) rating system, architects and designers are working together to meet formal and public performance goals, recognizing them for contributing to a "healthy and prosperous planet."[9] Additionally, not unlike the technical advances discussed above, producing green designs requires expertise and cooperation along lines perhaps not considered in the past. For example, buildings such as the Jubilee Campus at the University of Nottingham, England, and the Commerzbank Headquarters in Germany (featured in an exhibit organized by the Architectural League of New York) function on leading engineering designs.[10] Therefore they need to be far more precisely engineered than conventional buildings, and as a result, engineers are integral leaders from the earliest moments of the design process.

If considering a team approach to design, it is important to know that real teams have a finite life. Operating as a team is often an intense experience, which cannot be maintained for a long period of time. As the team progressively meets its design challenges, the purpose of the team may become less clear and strong. At this point it is acceptable team behavior to hand off the task to another team or move into another phase of the project where the working-group model is more appropriate. This next group or phase may contain several members from the original design team, but their roles may be modified, for example, to implement recommendations made by the initial team. Taking a specific stage in the design process, the client is often the leader in the postimplementation phase. In design today, however, change is endemic—designs must be built for ongoing flexibility and mobility without compromising the design intent—and the ongoing involvement of the designer is common. While the design teams may morph, the initial trust and accountability between, and development of the designer–client relationship must be recognized as the critical component to all high performance in design.

CONCLUSION

This theory of teams presents two models for design groups to work effectively together, real teams and single-leader working groups. Both models are valid, and by making the conscious choice of which to adopt up front, design groups may benefit and achieve greater success. The approach to take will depend largely on the performance challenge faced by the group, the amount of investment the group is willing to make in shaping its purpose and goals, and the group's ability to develop mutual respect among all members with respect to what is required to ensure the success of the project. Traditionally, design may have leaned toward the working-group approach, with a visionary leader calling all the shots. However, the rapidly changing design environment is presenting many opportunities where a real team can achieve greater performance.

Acknowledgments

Special thanks to Ate Atema, Atema Scheuer Design, New York, NY; Roz Cama, Cama Inc., New Haven, CT; Carol Jones, City Interiors, Vancouver, BC; Gervais Tompkin, Gensler, San Francisco, CA.

Notes

1

Empire State: A History, Empire State, Inc., New York, 1931, as cited in Rem Koolhaas, *Delirious New York,* Monacelli Press, New York, 1994.

2

Katzenbach, John R., and Douglas K. Smith, *The Wisdom of Teams,* Harvard Business School Press, Boston, 1993.

3

Zevi, Bruno, *Frank Lloyd Wright,* Burkhauser, Boston, 1999.

4

Katzenbach and Smith, *The Wisdom of Teams,* p. 45.

5

John R. Katzenbach, personal communication.

6

Koolhaas, *Delirious New York.*

7

Buchanan, Peter, *Renzo Piano Building Workshop: Complete Works,* Vol II & III, Phaidon Press, London, 1993. Massimo Dini, *Renzo Piano: Projects and Buildings*, Electa/Rizzoli, New York, 1984.

8

Katzenbach and Smith, *The Wisdom of Teams,* pp. 119–127.

9

"LEED: A Look at the Rating System That's Changing the Way America Builds, " *Environmental Building News,* June 2000.

10

Ten Shades of Green, The Architectural League of New York, New York, 2000.

12

Virtual Teams

JESSICA LIPNACK
JEFFREY STAMPS, Ph.D.

Using today's technology to work across company boundaries and in partnership with vendors and customers is quickly becoming the preferred working method of many industries. The design industry, to continue to do "smart work," will also benefit from becoming more aware of how much more productive and cost-effective it can be to work in virtual teams rather than only face to face.

For companies as traditionally grounded as architecture and design firms, this is, for many, a real eye-opener. "I can't think of any project that we do on our own," says Gary Wheeler, past president of the American Society of Interior Design (ASID), who leads the Chicago office of Perkins & Will, the architectural, engineering, and interior design firm. "There is just too much to know and there are too many specialties in the built environment." Wheeler's office is just completing a project for ADC, the Minneapolis-based broadband company. "We did all the program interviews over their intranet site allowing up to 5,000 people the opportunity to give input. We got 30–40 percent response, where normally we get 10–20 percent. We're involving people from HR, IT, facilities, and management on the core team. We validated our findings with them then shared them with leadership. A great deal was done via the net."

This chapter will tackle the major questions: What are virtual teams? Why should design firms think seriously about using them? And finally, what have others learned about the challenges facing virtual teams that make a designer's success more likely?

VIRTUAL TEAMS: WHAT ARE THEY?

A virtual team, like any working team, gathers expert people together to solve a particular problem or create a particular product. Working in teams, face to face, is a well-recognized organizational concept. But what if the virtual team is able to do its work across geographic and internal barriers by using electronic technology, thus enabling the team to work together in totally new ways. People are now able to work interdependently across space, time, and organization boundaries.

Our electronic technology together with strong trust are what links virtual teams and makes them function well. This element of trust is so important it deserves its own section later on in this chapter. But for now, let's look briefly at what we mean by this new electronic technology linking virtual teams.

NEW TECHNOLOGIES

Digital communication may be real-time or time-disconnected, and it is effectively unlimited in terms of the number of people it can reach. Today's almost miraculous interactions are not only fast, but thanks to increased memory capabilities, we are able to recall, reprocess, and link to other information in ways we only imagined a few years ago.

Now we can interact with people in entirely new ways. We can have online conversations, meetings, and conferences—in real (synchronous) or "disconnected" (asynchronous) time—using various interactive media. We are now privileged to be able to choose our methods of communication. We know that face-to-face meetings help build trust. Real-time media keep people in synch. And asynchronous media create the ability to link over time and across boundaries.

GENSLER REDEFINES PLACE

The move to virtual teaming is happening in all industries; with it comes a rethinking of the meaning of physical space. The architecture, design, and consulting firm, Gensler, responded to a client's question: "Can we sustain growth and performance as a purely virtual network?" The client, Paragon

Biomedical, runs clinical trials for major pharmaceutical companies, with 150 people working mainly from home offices. But Paragon was concerned with creating more collaboration and connectivity than T1 lines, state-of-the-art laptops, and DSL lines had to offer.

In a February, 2000 interview with us, Loree Goffigon, VP and director of Gensler Consulting, said that Paragon wanted new real estate featuring "corporate hearths"—ideal settings for face-to-face interactions. They wanted new places where Paragon people could meet, train, and find workspace on demand in key locations including Irvine, California, the company's original home.

"Philosophically, the creation of these places is about learning, access, and building community," says Goffigon. Her firm finds itself working with "a greater number of providers, including technology consultants, ad agencies, and graphic design firms. Our work is happening much more collaboratively and across a broader spectrum of organizational areas because the questions our clients are asking are more comprehensive and systemic."

We use the word "sites" today to mean much more than physical space. Sites are the on-line "corporate hearths"—places people visit digitally. Sites may range from little on-line rooms to sprawling corporate campuses like Microsoft's in Redmond, Washington, to vast cyber-facilities like America OnLine.

People create on-line places from the ground up. To do so, they use virtual analogs of desktops, rooms, offices, factories, malls, and communities. These and other familiar "place" metaphors serve as the building blocks for local cyberspace. We anticipate that these metaphors will rapidly evolve from cartoon-like storefronts and graphical menus to increasingly sophisticated three-dimensional virtual realities that members will walk into and around. As the early computer game-playing generations of kids grow up, they are incorporating the representational features of game technology into virtual team interfaces.

To operate effectively across boundaries, virtual teams become masters of media in preparing and delivering results as well as in running their own organizations.

We like to encourage people to imagine having "process rooms" on the web where you can grow the intelligence of the team as people collaborate over time. Process rooms are really backstage interactions that can occur in safe places to share private information for the team. These on-line rooms can be used for both real-time meetings as well as ongoing asynchronous storage, recall, and reuse of shared information. The room grows from an empty space at the start of a team's life to become progressively more organized and customized by the actions of the team itself as it molds the space to its particular needs. Teams typically spend time in places structured by length, width, and depth. Virtual teams spend "time" or disconnected time in cyberspaces structured by people, purpose, and links.

DOES PROXIMITY DETERMINE COLLABORATION?

What comes to mind first when you think of a team? A group of people working side by side, in close proximity to one another—a basketball or soccer team, perhaps? From a personal perspective, the important distances are the very short ones. How close people prefer to be for interpersonal interactions varies by culture—from inches to feet.

How far away do people have to be before they need to worry about compensating for distance? Or, put another way: How close do you have to be to get the advantage of being in the same place? That is, what is the "radius of collaborative co-location?" In the world before the web, collaboration falls apart at a fairly short distance.

MIT Professor Tom Allen tells us that, based on his research, people are not likely to collaborate very often if they are more than 50 feet apart.[1] The probability of communicating or collaborating more than once a week drops off dramatically if people are more than the width of a basketball court apart. To get the benefit of working in the same place, people need to be quite close together.

Globally, the farther apart people are physically, the more time zones they must cross to communicate. Thus, time becomes a problem when people who are not in the same place need some of their activities to be in sync. The window for routine same-time (synchronous) work shrinks as more time zones are crossed, closing to effectively zero when people are on oppo-

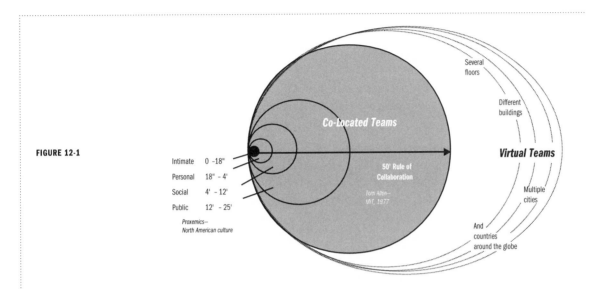

FIGURE 12-1

site sides of the globe. But even people who work together in the same place can have problems being in the same place at the same time, such as those in sales or consulting who rarely occupy their offices at the same time. Even apparently co-located teams often cross time boundaries and need to think virtually.

WHY SHOULD DESIGN FIRMS USE VIRTUAL TEAMS?

As Gary Wheeler mentioned earlier, the design industry is extraordinarily collaborative. It can be no other way, given the degrees of sophistication and complexity that surround it and influence it. Gathering needed experts into "process rooms" on-line is not only time-efficient, but significantly reduces travel and meeting time costs.

Although Shell Oil Company, a leader in virtual teaming efforts, is not a design firm, their virtual team benefits may be applicable to any industry, including the interior design fields:

- **Reduce costs** *by cutting travel costs and time, creating new "e-economies" of scale, and designing better, digitally enhanced processes.*

- Shorten cycle time *by moving from serial to parallel processes, establishing better communications, and generating more widespread trust.*

- Increase innovation *by permitting more diverse participation, stimulating product and process creativity, and encouraging new business development synergies.*

- Leverage learning *by capturing knowledge in the natural course of doing the work, gaining wider access to expertise, and sharing best practices.*

Design teams that work virtually will find they can do together what they cannot do alone. And most amazing, their whole will be more than the sum of their parts. And, as Hank McKinnell, president and COO of Pfizer, the pharmaceutical company, says, "No matter how effective any one person is, all of us are smarter than any of us."[2]

Most of the virtual teams we have interviewed for the book we authored, *Virtual Teams* (Wiley, New York, 2000) use telephone conference calls to provide real-time meetings; many also rely on videoconferencing. People at Buckman Labs, for instance, found that a very active on-line conversation through their intranets can be fast-paced enough to seem almost real-time. Many find that asynchronous communications, like threaded conversations resembling verbal exchanges, are effective ways to communicate. These "virtual water coolers" offer entirely new options for shaping meaningful aggregations in virtual teams while supporting their dispersion.

Time can be stretched. This is an obvious benefit to design teams. Virtual teams began viewing time as representing the results of human choice and design—why, when, and how we will meet; why, when and how we will divide and do the work. Co-located teams can quickly share these ideas, correct misunderstandings, and work through problems. Virtual teams need to be more explicit in their planning. Clarifying goals, tracking tasks, and accounting for results are all part of the elaborating process in a manner visible to all members of the team. This really does work if—*if*—all members of the team have a very clear shared purpose. And if they are based on trust, one of virtual teams' greatest challenges.

VIRTUAL TEAM CHALLENGES

Some virtual teams fail. One of the reasons is that there are obvious differences in working environments. If people do not make accommodation for how different it really is when they and their colleagues no longer work face to face, teams can fall apart.

Everything that can go wrong with in-the-same-space teams can also plague virtual teams. Only worse, because it can go wrong faster and less gracefully. Going virtual is for most people a wrenching experience, both in adapting to new technologies and in adopting new behaviors and working relationships.

Egos, power plays, backstabbing, hurt feelings, low confidence, poor self-esteem, leaderlessness, and lack of trust all harass virtual teams. When communication breaks down, people must take measures to repair it. It is just that much more difficult to communicate across distance and organizations using tenuous electronic links.

TRUST: THE KEY TO VIRTUAL RELATIONSHIPS

People work together because they trust one another. They make deals, undertake projects, set goals, and lend one another resources. Teams with trust converge more easily, organize their work more quickly, and manage themselves better. Less trust makes it much more difficult to generate and sustain successful virtual teams.

Without daily face-to-face cues, trust is at once both harder to attain and easier to lose. Mistrust slips in between the slender lines of long-distance communication stripped of the nuances of in-person interaction. Business can grind to a halt when trust breaks down.

Successful virtual teams pay special attention to building trust at each stage of their development. Trust originates in small groups—families, friendships, and myriad formal and information associations based on shared inter-

Design teams that work virtually will find they can do together what they cannot do alone . . . their whole will be more than the sum of their parts. And, as Hank McKinnell says, ". . . all of us are smarter than any of us."

ests and common concerns. People fundamentally trust others—or not. Trust enables people to establish purposes and construct links. The greater the trust, the lower the cost of communication and relationship building. The more extensive the network, the greater the opportunities arising from commonly held goals.

There are challenges facing virtual teams, no doubt about it. But the benefits far outweigh the potential bumps in the road. As we climb the learning curve of distributed work, great teams will become the design industry's norm, just as it is fast becoming the way other industries work together in new ways.

Notes

1

Allen, Thomas J., *Managing the Flow of Technology: Technology Transfer and the Dissemination of Technological Information within the R&D Organization,* MIT Press, Cambridge, MA, 1977, p. 47.

2

Dr. Henry McKinnell, interview, January 19, 2000.

Bibliography

Beckhard, Richard, and Reuben T. Harris. *Organizational Transitions: Managing Complex Change* (Addison-Wesley Series on Organization Development). Reading, PA: Addison-Wesley, 1987.

Berners-Lee, Tim, Mark Fischetti (contributor), and Michael L. Dertouzos. *Weaving the Web: The Original Design and Ultimate Destiny of the World Wide Web.* New York: HarperBusiness, 2000.

Lama, Dalai, Howard C. Cutler, and Dalai Lama Bstan-dzin-rgya-mtsho. *The Art of Happiness: A Handbook for Living.* New York: Riverhead Books, 1998.

Miles, Raymond E., and Charles C. Snow. *Fit, Failure, and the Hall of Fame: How Companies Succeed or Fail.* New York: Free Press, 1994.

Rheingold, Howard. *The Virtual Community: Homesteading on the Electronic Frontier* (Revised Edition). Cambridge, MA: MIT Press, 2000.

13

Investment in Knowledge: Commitment to Learning/ Applying/ Creating

JAN JOHNSON, IIDA

Many designers share a common frustration: they feel undervalued by their clients and marginalized by other professionals. This perception (and probable reality) stems from designers' failure to recognize the importance of knowledge in design practice. This knowledge is two-fold: (1) knowledge about the process and possibilities of design—not simply the output, but the outcome—and (2) knowledge about the client and the context of any design project. With this knowledge, designers can demonstrate that their services are more than a commodity and genuinely *add value*. They will also be better able to set, manage, and meet the expectations of clients and peer professionals.

The acquisition of knowledge, in and of itself, is not the answer, but a commitment to life-long learning may be. The "magic" is not in information itself, but rather in knowing what to do with it. Learning is a way of approaching problems and projects that improves both the process and the outcome. Learning can prepare designers to better understand the conflicts clients face in providing a more effective place to work or a satisfying place to live within constraints related to the project. Through increased awareness and knowledge of the client's world, designers are better prepared to identify their client's motivations and needs and thereby develop effective solutions.

THE PRACTICE

Design is a process of applying a body of knowledge and the ability to create toward the realization of an outcome. Interior design, more specifically, occurs in the arena of the interior environment. Examining each of these elements—"a process," "a body of knowledge," "the ability to create," and "the realization of an outcome"—in the context of interior environments places the challenges and opportunities facing the profession into sharp focus.

The design education system and design firms succeed in properly preparing and mentoring future professionals when they fully address *each* of these elements, beginning with "process." This process of design–concept, design, development, testing, and deployment–is generic enough to describe virtually every design activity, from software to soft drinks, and yet fluid enough to change with every project and each client's needs. The concept of "fluidity" is critical. Without it, control of knowledge in design, as in any other profession, can mean "telling" a designer who is not capable of interacting fluidly with a client may take up a preset solution and go in search of a problem to which to apply it. For interior designers, process is neither "asking" nor "telling"; rather, it is all the parts in between, and their *integration*. Much like the players in a jazz ensemble, who can't improvise well without having mastered the basics and agreed to a structure of rhythm and chord changes, the most innovative interior designers rely on the basic structure of the design process. Just as jazz technique should provide the means and process to resolve any musical question, design should provide the mindset, the means, and the process to address *any* problem.

Design practitioners contribute to and strengthen the profession when they expand the body of knowledge that defines interior design. These knowledge areas can include such "soft" areas as human behavior or ethnography, or "hard" sciences, such as financial analysis or the management of information technology. The "softer" subjects provide insights into the needs of the users of environments in all their complexities, while the "hard" topics provide parameters and metrics to evaluate the merits of any given solution.

An understanding of creative abilities–how we acquire and enhance creativity–is also crucial to the design process. These abilities are vital not only to design practices, but to the outcomes provided to clients. This is especially true in the corporate and health-care arenas, where the environment can positively (or negatively) influence the performance and satisfaction of its occupants, or the level of patient care. As designers expand their understanding of the creative process and those environmental conditions that support creativity and effective problem solving, they can place this knowledge in the service of their clients.

- **output:** *n.* 1 the product of a process, esp. of manufacture, or of mental or artistic work. 2 the quantity or amount of this. 3 the printout, results, etc., supplied by a computer.[1]

- **outcome: *n*.** a result; a visible effect. Result, consequence, end, aftereffect, upshot, development, outgrowth, aftermath, follow-up.[1]

The last key element of the design process is the realization of an *outcome*. When the goal of designers is to realize particular outcomes for their clients, they harness the possibilities of design and demonstrate its benefits. This is particularly important today, given that designers are often engaged in turf battles with factions of the architectural community. Designers struggle to demonstrate the relevance and value of interior design to those that they would serve, and to improve the educational preparation for those entering the profession. A focus on outcome reminds clients and other design professionals of the value and scope of interior designers' services.

Outcome and output differ in important ways. When designers provide mere output, their services are a commodity; when they achieve beneficial outcomes, their services add value to the project—and become more valuable to the clients. Outcome means translating vision into strategy and strategy into delivery. To provide outcome, designers have to discover, interpret, and document the links between the client's intents and their materialization. The pursuit of outcome fosters dynamism and organizational learning among design professionals and their client participants.

THE NEW CONTEXT OF THE DESIGN PRACTICE

It is hard to know whether life is getting more complex or we are just getting better at seeing the complexities that were always there. Either way, much has been written in the popular press about the way we each experience life's complexity. On a personal level, we lament high levels of stress and the increased pace of life. Some celebrate the dismantling of the old loyalties between employer and employee, while others feel betrayed. We decry the erosion of the nuclear family even though statistics confirm that the "normal" two parents-with-children household actually has long been the exception rather than the rule. We struggle to balance work and our personal lives.

Design practitioners contribute to and strengthen the profession when they expand the body of knowledge that defines interior design. These knowledge areas can include such "soft" areas as human behavior or ethnography …

We debate the appropriate balance between personal responsibility and government intervention and support.

On the level of commerce, every enterprise, from health care to retail to corporate America, is grappling with the e-phenomenon and the uneasy feeling that the rules have changed in ways we do not yet understand. New businesses are springing up to combine commodity purchases across multiple corporations and capitalize on massive buying power, while other companies are replacing the intermediary with direct channels of access. In the field of interior design, clients are seemingly at once both more knowledgeable and less well equipped to address their own issues. And they expect designers to deliver solutions that are more dynamic, contextual, and intelligent than ever before.

Coping with these phenomena (let alone contending with them successfully) requires that designers respond at three interrelated levels—personally, in their business decisions, and with societal interests in mind. If the design profession employs the design process in the service of effective environments (or experiences) at all three of these levels, it can truly be part of the solution to the problems clients are beginning to sense they now face. Getting there requires understanding the ideas described above—the process of the activity, creative ability, the application and integration of knowledge, and the goal of an outcome. Understanding in all of these areas is strengthened and nourished by learning.

THE VALUE OF LEARNING

Peter Senge's *The Fifth Discipline* is the classic business text for advocating the value and characteristics of learning organizations. This book is extremely valuable for a number of reasons: it serves as a wonderful example of valuable knowledge outside of the design profession; it clearly demonstrates the benefit of an attitude or practice of life-long learning for the individual, the practitioner or member of an enterprise, and the profession; and it provides a practical road map for developing such a practice.

Senge lists five new "component technologies" or disciplines that "provide vital dimensions in building organizations (or professionals or professions) that can truly 'learn,' that can continually enhance their capacity to realize their highest aspirations":

- **Systems thinking** *(a conceptual framework to make the full patterns clearer, and help see how to change them effectively)*

- **Personal mastery** *(achieving a special level of proficiency—the discipline of continually clarifying and deepening our personal vision, of focusing our energies, of developing patience, and of seeing reality objectively; or to use another writer's phrase—"the marriage of sense and science")*

- **Mental models** *(deeply ingrained assumptions, generalizations, or even pictures or images that influence how we understand the world and how we take action)*

- **Building shared vision** *(the practice of unearthing shared "pictures of the future" that foster genuine commitment and enrollment rather than mere compliance)*

- **Team learning** *(developing extraordinary capacities for coordinated action, producing extraordinary results and growing individual members more rapidly than could have occurred otherwise)*[2]

All of these skills, and systems thinking in particular—which combines elements of the other four—are not only critical to a designer's development and "personal mastery" of the profession, but are also at the heart of designers' ability to understand, interpret, and develop solutions to clients' dilemmas. Taking each of these disciplines in turn, designers can begin to see their relevance as individual practitioners, as members of firms, and as members of the profession.

PERSONAL MASTERY

Senge describes personal mastery as "the discipline of personal growth and learning." He explains, "People with high levels of personal mastery are continually expanding their ability to create the results in life they truly seek." He adds that "'Learning' in this context does not mean acquiring more information, but expanding the ability to produce the results we truly want in life. It is lifelong generative learning—[and] suggests a special level of proficiency in every aspect of life—personal and professional."[2]

Bill O'Brien, president of Hanover Insurance, explains why this personally motivated growth and learning is important in the professional context: it is an important precondition for realizing full potential and becoming successful. He says, "Whatever the reasons, we do not pursue emotional development with the same intensity with which we pursue physical and intellectual development. This is all the more unfortunate because full emotional development offers the greatest degree of leverage in attaining our full potential. We believe there is no fundamental tradeoff between the higher virtues in life and economic success. We believe we can have both. In fact, we believe that, over the long term, the more we practice the higher virtues of life, the more economic success we will have."[3]

Designers who seek personal mastery seize every opportunity to add to their understanding of their profession, their clients' circumstances, and the world at large. They nurture passion—their own, their staff's and their clients'. They encourage their team to look beyond the obvious and the expected and to develop a shared vision of what is possible.

Firms promote personal mastery when they nurture the development of the person as a professional and encourage designers' contributions to each other and to their communities. Some have even offered sabbaticals to their staff to pursue subjects that not only challenge them personally but also add balance to their lives. At minimum, many firms encourage their staff to attend the programs offered by professional associations, industry partners, or outside educational providers; some even offer their own internally developed coursework. Others support personal mastery by encouraging their staff to do what they do best. The most supportive employers try to spot the particular core competency or personal passion of an employee and encourage the employee to take on roles and responsibilities that apply that expertise or passion. Rather than pigeonholing their staff into narrow, prescribed roles, they encourage staff to cross traditional role boundaries or pursue a skill or area that expands their practice and breathes new life into their work. Designers nurtured in this way evidence the difference in their lives, their work, and their ability to address their clients' challenges.

In some cases, particular management practices will emphasize that employees should gain personal mastery of skills beyond the process of design—skills critical to being an active participant in business and society. One management style, precipitated by the trend toward flattened organization structures (and practiced by at least one major firm), drives a great deal of responsibility to the lowest possible level. As a result, inexperienced staff members are accountable for client interactions and project delivery. To make this work, the recruiting process seeks to identify general communication skills, the ability to think in common-sense terms, and recognition of when experienced assistance is required. And with this experience, staff members are expected to hone these social and business skills.

MENTAL MODELS

Design relies heavily on mental models—the images, pictures, assumptions, or stories we carry around to describe or explain the way the world works. The way designers treat volume, arrangement, materials, or lighting is highly dependent on the response these things engender in the occupants of the space. A designer will try to use mental models to create a particular reaction or evoke a particular feeling.

Senge explains that mental models affect what we do because they affect what we see. He points out that the challenges we face because we all operate from our own mental models "lie not in whether they are right or wrong—by definition all models are simplifications. The problems with mental models arise when the models are tacit—when they exist below the level of awareness. When [we] remain unaware of our mental models, they remain unexamined. Because they remain unexamined, they remain unchanged."[2] In other words, in order to think outside the box, you have to recognize what box you are in. Senge describes the Detroit automakers as an example of this phenomenon, saying, "As the world changed, a gap widened between Detroit's mental models and reality, leading to increasingly counterproductive actions."[2] He goes on to point out that "entire industries can develop chronic misfits between mental models and reality. *In some ways, close-knit industries are especially vulnerable because all the member companies look to each other for standards of best practice.*"

How can the design profession prevent this counterproductive myopia? How can designers improve their awareness of their own mental models and that of their clients and become more open to change? Senge advocates two "learning skills": skills of reflection and skills of inquiry. He says, "Skills of reflection concern slowing down our own thinking processes so that we can become more aware of how we form our mental models and the ways they influence our actions. Inquiry skills concern how we operate in face-to-face interactions with others, especially in dealing with complex and [conflicting] issues." Senge refers to the work of David Schon of MIT in showing the "importance of reflection on learning in professions including medicine, architecture and management. While many professionals seem to stop learning as soon as they leave graduate school, those who become lifelong learners practice what he calls 'reflection in action.'" For Schon, this ability distinguishes the truly outstanding professionals: Phrases like "thinking on your feet," "keeping your wits about you," and "learning by doing" suggest not only that we can think about *doing* but that we can think about doing something *while doing it.*[4]

So much of what designers do is match cues in the environment with the meanings that designers or their clients attribute to those cues. For instance, *wood connotes richness and prestige; the generosity of space is directly correlated to one's status; and asking people what they want should make them more accepting of the outcome even if they don't get what they asked for.* Continuing education courses on the way people respond to color, or what distance from our bodies we consider our personal space, for example, are great ways to challenge assumptions and add to an understanding of the mental models people share. Through such courses, designers will learn that some models are universally applicable, while others depend on culture, geography, societal norms, religious beliefs, or other manifestations of our diversity.

By constantly practicing these skills of reflection and inquiry, designers improve their practice and better understand and interpret the intentions and goals of their clients.

SHARED VISION

Building a shared vision means providing a common focus and impetus for the accumulation of new knowledge. Senge explains, "Shared vision is vital for the learning organization because it provides the focus and energy for learning. While adaptive learning is possible without vision, generative learning occurs only when people are striving to accomplish something that matters deeply to them. In fact, the whole idea of generative learning–'expanding your ability to create'–will seem abstract and meaningless *until* people become excited about some vision of what they want to accomplish. . . . A shared vision is a vision that many people are truly committed to, because it reflects their own personal vision."[2]

This notion of shared vision applies to projects, teams, firms, and professions. For teams, shared vision creates alignment and motivates team members to exceed expectations. (It also helps get people to *just stick around*–which is important nowadays, when attraction and retention are hot issues.) An employer, a team leader, or a client can create shared vision by making the time to develop this mutually held possibility with integrity and convincing his or her colleagues to buy in. Designers who approach their projects with the goal of first establishing shared vision find that it engenders commitment and creates alignment, facilitates decision making, and seems to bring out everyone's best thinking and creativity. Developing a shared vision also provides the opportunity for the client to expand upon ideas and ambitions for the project and see the links between decisions and their outcomes.

So how is shared vision established? Some firms hold "vision" sessions with their clients and invite as broad a cross section of representation as can be persuaded to participate. They begin by bringing the client's goals to the surface–not only for the project, but for themselves or their organization. They then get the group to imagine what needs to happen or what activities should occur for those goals to be realized. Then they discuss what qualities or attributes of the environment would support those activities. A part of this session is also to have everyone either determine or articulate (in the case of business) what their corporate culture or brand is about, and what constraints or parameters must be respected. This understanding provides another level of context for the project.

Sessions like these also go a long way toward engaging the participants in the process and getting them to support the outcome—they now understand and agree with the context in which decisions or recommendations are made. Also, they more thoroughly understand what contribution the design firm made to ensuring a successful and relevant outcome.

Developing shared vision is particularly challenging in geographically dispersed businesses. One approach used by several of the "giants of the industry" gathers the senior management together on a regular basis to exchange successes and failures and otherwise reinforce the values and goals of the organization. Here, shared values begin with establishing a concise vision that permeates the entire organization and is then reinforced on a consistent and continuous basis.

One large, U.S.-based architectural and interior design firm describes itself this way:

As a means of bridging the diversity of interests in a profit-centered and highly entrepreneurial organization such as ours, it is our desire to build consensus and engender support for the way we see ourselves in the market and recognize the values under which we behave.

There are two components to the Vision:

- *The core purpose—we have a core purpose that defines our strategic goal. It is the "near sighted" portion of our vision. It is strategic in the sense that from time to time, our interpretation of the market will require redefining the core purpose to properly respond to market opportunity.*

- *The core values—the "far sighted" portion of our vision is represented by those standards of conviction and behavior that are so central to the beliefs of the company that they will not change even though the market may urge a redefinition.*

- *Our Core Purpose: To be the "Corporate Occupancy Resource." Whatever the occupancy need of our corporate client, be prepared to enable them to satisfy those needs. Help our clients become more successful through improved performance of the space they occupy yielding increased productivity of their human resources.*

- *Our Core Values:*

  1. *Always do what is right for the client. Recognize success from our client's perspective and do what is best to enable that success.*

  2. *"Don't mess with our people." Recognize the dedication, commitment and value of our staff. Defend their integrity and achievements and stand behind them in their faults. Assure our clients of service—not servitude.*

  3. *Cling to integrity, responsibility and accountability. In whatever we do, always be prepared for the bright light of scrutiny. Always perform with integrity, take responsibility and be accountable.*

Don't be afraid of making a profit. Profits allow us to live a little better, to continue to provide and perpetuate the value we create, and build a platform for others to join us.

TEAM LEARNING

Team learning combines aspects of personal mastery and shared vision, but further emphasizes the need to apply these elements on a larger scale. According to Senge, team learning is a discipline, one in which members align and develop the team's capacity to create the results its members truly desire. Team learning builds on the discipline of developing a shared vision, but goes beyond it. According to Senge, team learning "also builds on personal mastery, for talented teams are made up of talented individuals. But shared vision and talent are not enough." He refers to a common problem among teams: they may be made up of talented individuals, and they may share a vision for a while, yet they fail to learn. He compares these failed teams to a great jazz ensemble; it "has talent and a shared vision (even if they don't discuss it), but what really matters is that the musicians know how to *play* together." Senge goes on, "There has never been a greater need for mastering team learning in organizations than there is today. Individual learning, at some level, is irrelevant for organizational learning. Individuals learn all the time and yet there is no organizational learning. But if teams learn, they become a microcosm for learning throughout the organization."[2]

Senge then goes on to describe the three critical dimensions of team learning. The first dimension is the need to think insightfully about complex issues. According to Senge, "Here, the team must learn how to tap the potential for many minds to be more intelligent than one mind." The second dimension is the need for innovative, coordinated action. As Senge puts it, "Outstanding teams . . . develop . . . 'operational trust,' where each member remains conscious of other team members and can be counted on to act in ways that complement each other's actions." The third dimension of team learning is the role of team members on other teams. Senge provides the example of the actions of senior teams, most of which are actually carried out through other teams. To Senge, this "connectedness" of learning teams continually fosters other learning teams by spreading the practices and skills of team learning more broadly.[2]

To develop in all three dimensions of team learning, a team must master the practices of dialogue and discussion, the two distinct ways that teams converse. Senge explains that in dialogue, the participants freely and creatively explore complex and subtle issues. This exploration involves "a deep 'listening' to one another and suspending of one's own views." By contrast, in discussion, the participants present and defend different views, and search for the best view to support decisions that must be made at the time. No matter what mode the participants adopt, Senge says, "the discipline of team learning, like any other discipline, requires practice."[2]

Designers have always worked in teams—cross-functional groups with particular expertise (project management, design, technical coordination, or consultation)—who come together to apply their skills and knowledge to achieve their clients' desired outcomes. This time-honored process also fosters learning among colleagues and junior members of the teams. This interaction and on-the-job-learning is a major element of designers' professional development. When designers interact with and learn from each other, when they mentor junior staff and encourage their curiosity and exploration, they do the profession the biggest service they can offer.

One of the greatest challenges designers face right now is to foster this process of mentoring and team learning in the face of the pressures of tight fees and light-speed schedules. Practicing team learning, however, provides part of the solution—effective teams are more efficient and deliver more relevant, more comprehensive, more beneficial outcomes. Firms that have broken the cycle of lower fees and less time for investigation or mentoring have found that they can charge higher fees and enjoy greater profitability because they are working "smarter" and more effectively and at the same time delivering more value to their clients.

SYSTEMS THINKING

In summarizing the five component technologies of team learning, Senge notes that systems thinking integrates the other four, "fusing them into a coherent body of theory and practice." It keeps the other disciplines from being "separate gimmicks" or "the latest . . . fad(s)." Systems thinking "needs the disciplines of building shared vision, mental models, team learning, and personal mastery to realize its potential. Building shared vision fosters a commitment to the long term. Mental models focus on the openness needed to unearth shortcomings in our present ways of seeing the world. Team learning develops the skills of groups of people to look for the larger picture that lies beyond individual perspectives. And personal mastery fosters the personal motivation to continually learn how our actions affect our world. Lastly, systems thinking makes understandable the subtlest aspect of the learning organization—the new way individuals perceive themselves and their world."[2] In other words, systems thinking allows us to see the connections between things—to understand the larger context in which people must make choices. It lets us see what any given decision is related to and what it will affect.

Understanding how economic conditions, culture, business intents, personal preferences and beliefs, current and future technologies, and societal trends may all play a part (and come together) in the development of an interior environment may be the most important ability designers can have. By applying all these learning skills and, in particular, systems thinking, designers can identify and communicate "the value proposition"—the particular assembly of decisions, approaches, and solutions that truly responds to the client's needs and adds value to their lives or organizations.

THE VALUE OF THE WHOLE PICTURE

Systems thinking implies integration—that we put together the whole picture. "From an early age," Senge cautions, "we are taught to break apart problems, to fragment the world. This apparently makes complex tasks and subjects more manageable, but we pay a hidden, enormous price. We can no longer see the consequences of our actions; we lose our intrinsic sense of connection to a larger whole." We lose the ability to address and balance all the elements of a given situation, and instead find ourselves optimizing one part and in the process, suboptimizing the whole.[2]

In many cultures, the traditional role of the "architect as master builder" is still in practice. It provides a single point of responsibility and accountability wherein the designer has a mission to design and provide a solution developed with creativity but delivered to support the goals and objectives of the client. Unfortunately, pressures on fees and the threats of litigation have fostered an attitude in U.S. practices of risk avoidance. This does not excuse the design profession from the requirement to take a holistic approach to solutions—one that embraces the interests of all constitutive parties and beneficiaries.

Taking on the role of "integrator" presents a wonderful opportunity to create value. When done well, one creates results that are greater than the sum of the parts. This role does not presently exist in any formal way in the design industry—but no one else is as well positioned to provide it as the interior design profession. Even our metaphoric jazz band has a leader. The goal of the design profession should be to assume that leader's role.

If designers do not take on that leadership role, they give away an incredibly valuable opportunity to play the most important role there is—to be the

If designers do not take on that leadership role, they give away an incredibly valuable opportunity to play the most important role there is—to be the one who "owns" the vision, who identifies those skills and expertise needed and nurtures the relationships . . .

one who "owns" the vision, who identifies those skills and expertise needed and nurtures the relationships between the elements (so as to acknowledge and leverage the linkages between these elements), the one who monitors the process and the outcome for its adherence to the vision. It is in this leadership role that a designer's knowledge and understanding of the myriad of interrelated topics that must be integrated is most needed. It is in this role that an ability to create a shared vision and an effective team will ensure a valuable outcome. And the responsible assumption of this role is the one thing that most clients want and cannot provide themselves.

THE IMPORTANCE OF DEPTH

Learning has also been described as having three levels: *understanding, application*, and *integration/creation*. Understanding usually involves familiarization with a given subject. Application requires the ability to apply information in appropriate (and often predictable, repeatable) ways—in short, to do something with it. The third level, integration/creation, requires one to apply information in new, previously undiscovered ways; to use information and an understanding of its predictable application to bring into being something that did not exist before. Knowledge acquired and applied through each of these three levels of learning is needed to create and to innovate; every question posed should be seen as an opportunity to provide more than what was requested.

THE IMPORTANCE OF BREADTH

To adopt Senge's notion of systems thinking is to focus on both the elements that would make up a whole system (of something) and the relationships between these elements. For example, designers who apply systems thinking to the development of an effective corporate work environment need to understand and apply knowledge about space, technology tools, the organization's culture and practices, all of which help define the environment. Designers must understand and apply knowledge about people: how they react and respond to spatial cues; how they use tools in their activities; what behaviors are deemed acceptable or not. Designers also need to understand and apply knowledge about the organization: their goals and strategies for achieving those goals; how work gets done and the nature of teams; the financial impacts of our recommendations in the context of that corporation's structure and economic situation. And the industry itself, its relative maturity and health, must also be understood systemically. Lastly, designers must consider the capabilities of those who would change and manage any program that is developed.

Systems thinking requires understanding the relationship between all these elements and how a decision in one area will affect another. If the designer encourages customization in individual work environments, will it create an unmanageable inventory of space and furniture components? If the designer discourages personal choice and control in the physical environment, will management's initiatives to empower (and even retain) their workforce be undermined?

IMPLICATIONS FOR THE INTERIOR DESIGN PROFESSION

If we accept the premise that designers use their skills and knowledge as designers to produce "outcomes" for their clients, then we can conclude that designers are in the service business. The designer's job is not to produce drawings, or oversee construction sites (although these are often necessary parts of the process); nor is it to get published, or enjoy the envy of colleagues. Designers' "shared vision" should be to bring about the result that serves the client best.

The trick for designers is to *manage* the client relationship and experience—to bring to bear their personal mastery, compare and clarify their own and their client's mental models, create a shared vision of what this project might or should accomplish, form and nourish an integrated team to achieve the vision.

The challenge is to embrace these principles and develop these disciplines. The result will be better, more satisfied individuals, designers and professionals. Professions and professionals are defined in part by the unique body of knowledge which informs them, which they apply, and to which they add. Interior design is no different. And, like other professions, interior design can only be improved by both expanding the boundaries of knowledge and committing to its life-long acquisition. Doctors are better healers when they integrate humanity with science, mind with body. Lawyers bring not only other legal precedent but also subject expertise to bear to argue a point of law successfully. Interior designers serve their clients best (and therefore increase their perceived value) when they master the theoretical and practical body of knowledge that defines interior design, and effectively integrate information, facts, and intelligence about the related topics that form the context of a given assignment.

Design professionals must expand their ambitions and commit to acquiring knowledge and understanding throughout their careers—so that they can integrate and apply what they learn to the act of designing, with the goal of improving the other three components of design: to hone their personal skills and become more facile in the entire process of design; to inspire and nurture the creative act; to increase their ability not only to satisfy the expectations of their clients, but to exceed them—and do so repeatedly and profitably.

Notes

1

The Oxford Dictionary and Thesaurus, American Edition, Oxford University Press, New York, 1996.

2

Senge, Peter M., *The Fifth Discipline*, Currency Doubleday, New York, 1990, pp. 3, 6–10, 12, 176, 191–192, 206, 236–237.

3

O'Brien, Bill, *Advanced Maturity*, Hanover Insurance, Worcester, MA.

4

Schon, Donald, *The Reflective Practitioner: How Professionals Think in Action*, Basic Books, New York, 1983.

14

Information Technology in Interior Design

WILLIAM J. MITCHELL

Traditionally, interior designers have employed two-dimensional drawings and three-dimensional scale models to represent design proposals. These representations continually evolve, and they serve multiple purposes (Figure 14-1). At early stages in the design process they support the rapid exploration of design ideas; designers think with their pencils in their hands, or by manipulating rough models. As ideas develop, visual and tactile representations are increasingly used to focus discussion among designers, clients, consultants, contractors, and other members of the design and construction team. They also serve to formalize the division of responsibilities among members of the team, and to coordinate and integrate the work of different team members.

At later stages, representations become more precise and formal. They are used less as exploratory tools and more as careful records of decisions that have already been made. They become the basis for area calculations and material quantity measurements, for cost analyses, and for various analyses of technical performance—structural, lighting, thermal, acoustic, and so on, as necessary. At the construction stage they serve as contract documents, and as the basis for necessary approvals by government agencies. Finally, at the postconstruction stage, as-built representations may become the foundation for ongoing facility management operations.

Since the late 1960s a third form of representation—the digital model—has become increasingly popular in architectural and interior design. The interface to the digital model is provided by computer-aided design (CAD) software—just as the interface to a digital text file is provided by word-processing software, and the interface to a digital image file by image-processing and digital paint software. Contrary to much popular belief, CAD systems do not replace traditional drawings and scale models; the paperless design process turns out to be as mythical as the paperless office. Instead, the three forms of representation complement one another in a way that allows design and construction processes to become far more efficient, and that allows previously inaccessible design possibilities to be explored.

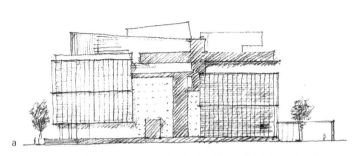

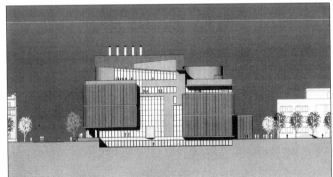

FIGURE 14-1
Different representations
used at different stages,
and for different
purposes, in Fumihiko
Maki's development of
the design for a new
Media Laboratory
building at MIT.

a. Early sketch.
b. Physical model.
c. Developed technical drawing.
d. CAD perspective of an interior space.

TRANSLATING AMONG REPRESENTATIONS

Each of the three basic forms of representation has its particular technical
advantages and disadvantages and associated costs. Each is well suited to
particular stages and purposes within a design and construction process, and
less well suited to use in other contexts. A typical design process, therefore,
involves translation back and forth among two-dimensional drawings, three-
dimensional scale models, and digital models. Sometimes these translation

steps are mechanical, but sometimes they are used as opportunities to make decisions and add information.

For example, two-dimensional drawings—particularly plans and sections—are cogent abstractions that represent fundamental properties of a design in a particularly powerful and useful way. However, they are not the most vivid and accessible way to describe qualities of three-dimensional space and light. And, when they are in paper format, they are difficult and expensive to modify and to keep consistent as modifications are made. (If you change the plan, you have to be sure to make the corresponding changes to the elevations and sections, and maybe plans on other floors.)

Three-dimensional models are typically more time-consuming and expensive to produce, but they provide a better way to understand the complexities of space and light. They are an excellent means of focusing a discussion, and (within limits) they support rapid exploration of options simply by moving pieces around.

Digital models are extremely versatile and flexible, they support automatic measurement, analysis, and simulation through application of software, and they can be transmitted rapidly and inexpensively through computer networks. However, they are not directly visible; they must be translated into other formats—displays, printouts, or physical models—before they can be inspected and discussed.

Translation paths among these three types of representations, and between representations and the three-dimensional reality of a constructed building, are shown in Figure 14-2. Some have long been familiar to designers; it is standard, for example, to translate sketches into working models during the exploration of design ideas, and equally common to move from models to drawings. The process of construction translates working drawings into full-scale physical reality, while the inverse process of measured drawing (often a crucial early step in interior renovation projects) produces drawings that correspond to the built reality. Historically, though less so today, it has also been common to construct directly from three-dimensional scale models, and to produce miniature model versions of existing buildings.

Some newer translation processes have also become familiar with the growing popularity of CAD. Printing and plotting processes translate digital models into two-dimensional drawings on paper, while digitizers and scanners

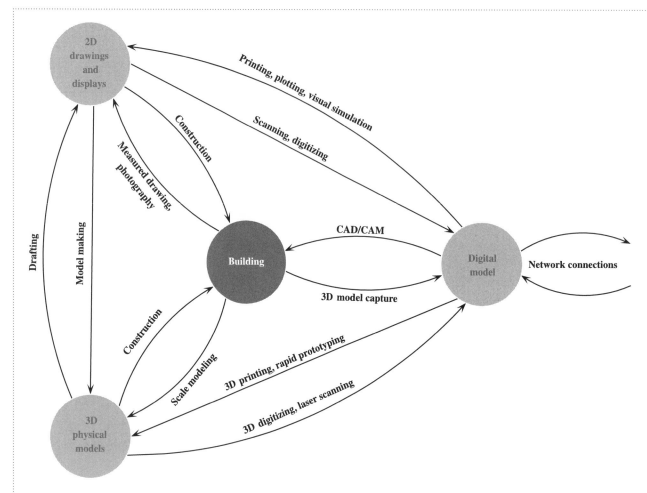

FIGURE 14-2
Different types of
representations of a
building and translation
paths among them.

allow designers to go in the opposite direction. Since the development of relatively inexpensive, high-quality, large-format color printers, production of prints from digital files has become the standard means of preparing architectural and interior design presentation materials.

On-screen displays are also, of course, visual renditions of information contained in a stored digital model and provide a way to edit that model; unlike printing, plotting, and scanning, which are batch processes, they establish a highly interactive relationship between digital and graphic representations. As CAD technology has developed, and as more computer power has become available to support sophisticated interfaces, graphical interaction with CAD systems has gradually become smoother and more fluid.

The translation paths between digital and physical models are a newer development, and as yet, much less familiar to most designers. Various types of three-dimensional digitizers and scanners can now be used to convert the geometric information represented by a physical model into digital form (Figure 14-3). And rapid-prototyping machines—in essence, the three-dimensional equivalents of laser printers—can be used to "build back" physical models from digital ones (Figure 14-4). Many rapid-prototyping technologies are currently in use: laser-cutters quickly and accurately produce cardboard, wood, or plastic cutouts that can later be assembled by hand; deposition printers deposit small particles of plastic or ceramic in layers; stereolithography machines employ computer-controlled laser beams to selectively solidify polymer solution; multi-axis milling machines carve three-dimensional forms out of solid blocks; and yet other types of devices produce layered models by utilizing lasers to cut and fuse sheets of resin-impregnated paper. The more advanced three-dimensional digitizing, scanning, and rapid-prototyping devices are still scarce and expensive, but their availability will grow and their costs will drop over time.

In principle, it is possible to make these translations as highly interactive as those between a digital model and screen display in a typical CAD system. The necessary technology is still mostly at the research stage, but it will eventually become commonplace in design studios. One approach is represented

FIGURE 14-3
3-D Laser Scanner.

FIGURE 14-4
Physical Model produced
by a 3-D printer.

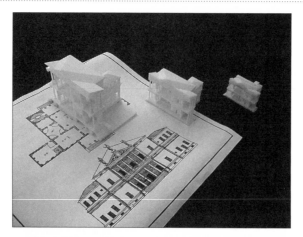

FIGURE 14-5
Luminous Table
developed by John
Underkoffler and Hiroshi
Ishii, in use in the
design studios at MIT.

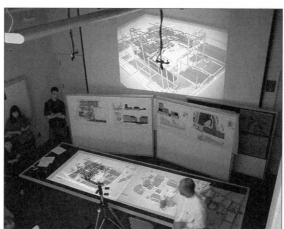

by the Luminous Table, developed at MIT's Media Laboratory by John Underkoffler and Hiroshi Ishii (Figure 14-5). Users of the Luminous Table directly manipulate physical model elements such as wooden blocks. Video cameras and computer-vision software are used to construct, in real time, a corresponding three-dimensional digital model. Computations are instantaneously performed on the digital model, then the results are video-projected back onto the physical model. Dimensions, areas, and volumes can be calculated and displayed, accurate shadows can be cast, airflows and pedestrian flows can be simulated, and so on.

An alternative approach is to employ some combination of immersive, stereoscopic displays and tactile feedback devices. In the future, we can anticipate "smart clay" and other means of accomplishing the close, interactive coupling of physical and digital models. Figure 14-6 illustrates potential future interrelationships of graphical interaction with two-dimensional displays, tactile interaction with smart clay and the like, and the digital model.

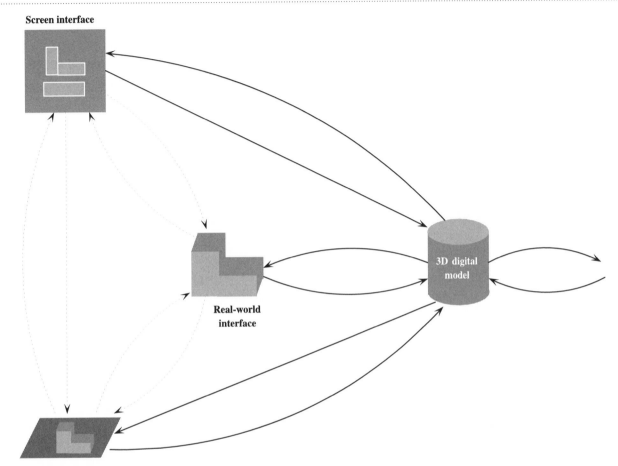

Screen interface

Real-world interface

3D digital model

Tactile interface

FIGURE 14-6
Relationship of a 3-D
digital model of a
building to different
types of interfaces:
traditional, 2-D
on-screen interface,
3-D tactile interface,
and the constructed
building itself as a real-
world interface. Heavy
lines show actual
connections and lighter
lines show implicit
connections.

EMERGENCE OF CAD/CAM CONSTRUCTION

Most early CAD systems were intended for use as drafting systems. Their primary purpose was to speed the process of creating traditional construction documents, to reduce the cost, and to reduce errors. They represented designs as sets of two-dimensional drawings—floor plans, elevations, sections, details, and perspectives—often organized in "layers" that explicitly recalled the drawing layers that had been drafted on translucent sheets of paper or Mylar. To facilitate construction of drawings, they provided layout grids, snap operations, geometric construction operations (such as insertion of an arc through three points), and copy-and-repeat operations. These early systems proved particularly effective in large-scale commercial, industrial, and institutional interior projects that involved extensive repetition of bays, columns, standard floor plates, and standard items of furniture and equipment. In projects with less repetition, their benefits were less substantial.

An obvious extension of CAD drafting technology is to provide facilities for associating nongeometric properties with graphic elements. This soon became a standard software feature of more advanced CAD systems. Thus, for example, a designer might associate vendor's name, product serial number, and various items of technical data with the graphic symbol for a chair. The data could then be retrieved interactively by pointing at a display, and it could be used to compile sorted and tabulated reports, such as furniture and equipment schedules. These features greatly enhanced the usefulness of CAD software at the construction documentation and postoccupancy facility management phases of architectural and interiors projects.

A less obvious, and technically more difficult, move of CAD software designers was to begin building CAD systems around three-dimensional digital models rather than sets of two-dimensional, digitally encoded drawings. To succeed, this strategy depended on the availability of far more powerful computers, the emergence of software technologies such as three-dimensional surface and solid modeling, and the development of more complex and sophisticated graphic interfaces. Gradually the technological pieces fell into place, and three-dimensional CAD modelers had become commonplace in architectural and interiors practice by the 1990s.

One advantage of a three-dimensional model is that it can be used, in conjunction with rapid-prototyping devices, to produce three-dimensional physical models as well as two-dimensional prints and plots. An even more important advantage is that it can be used to drive computer-aided design/computer-aided manufacturing (CAD/CAM) machinery and on-site positioning machinery. This establishes a new type of linkage between the digital model and the constructed building, as was shown in Figure 14-2. CAD/CAM technology translates the digital model directly into full-scale physical reality, thus *eliminating* rather than automating the production of traditional construction documents. Conversely, new three-dimensional imaging and electronic surveying technologies facilitate construction of three-dimensional CAD models of existing buildings.

CAD/CAM technology first developed in the manufacturing industry—particularly in the automobile, ship-building, and aerospace areas—and has only more recently moved into architectural and interior design and construction. The variety of CAD/CAM machinery now available is immense. There are digitally controlled machines for cutting and bending steelwork, for cutting sheet materials such as glass, plywood, and sheet metal into complex shapes, for milling wood and stone, and many more. They will play an increasingly important role in fabrication of components for architectural and interior construction.

MULTIMEDIA DESIGN AND CONSTRUCTION PROCESSES

Today, an architectural or interior design and construction process is likely to involve most or all of the types of representations shown in Figure 14-3, together with most or all of the translation paths among them. Designing and building have become truly multimedia activities.

The process that has been pioneered by Frank Gehry and his partners and collaborators, and that has enabled the efficient design and construction of such innovative projects as the Bilbao Guggenheim Museum (Figure 14-7) and the Conde-Nast cafeteria interior (Figure 14-8), strikingly illustrates this. The exploration of design ideas begins with the production of quick sketches and three-dimensional physical models. As the design converges, physical models are digitized to create corresponding digital models—particularly of

FIGURE 14-7
Frank Gehry's Bilbao
Guggenheim Museum.

the complex curved surfaces that have come to characterize Gehry's work. Design development is then based on the three-dimensional models, and takes place largely in a CAD environment. Physical models are repeatedly "built back" from the digital models, through rapid-prototyping, to provide a check that the visual and spatial qualities are developing appropriately and to provide compelling presentation materials. Eventually, the developed CAD model serves as the basis for a CAD/CAM fabrication and erection process.

This type of multimedia process opens up design territory that had hitherto been imaginable, but inaccessible as a practical matter. The complex curved

FIGURE 14-8
Frank Gehry, curved
glass interior of the
Conde-Nast cafeteria,
New York.

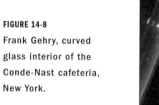

forms of the Conde-Nast interior would have been extremely difficult to represent using conventional drafting and physical modeling techniques, for example. Even more important, it would have been impossible to build on an acceptable budget and schedule. But CAD/CAM techniques allowed the efficient production of the complex, nonrepeating curved glass shapes. This and similar projects illustrate that designers are now finding ways to break free from machine-age assumptions about mass production, repetition of parts, and economies of scale, and are beginning to explore the exciting new potentials of digitally enabled mass customization.

MEASUREMENT, ANALYSIS, AND SIMULATION

In addition to supporting rapid-prototyping and CAD/CAM, three-dimensional digital models facilitate the use of measurement, analysis, and simulation software. This software extracts the input data needed from the CAD model, processes them, then displays the required results for consideration by designers, consultants, and clients.

Visual simulation software is the most familiar tool of this type in interior design. In essence, this software computes the spatial and spectral distribution across the surfaces of an interior that is illuminated in a specified way, then displays the result as a shaded perspective image. The amount of computation required to produce an accurate result is immense, but that is rarely much of a problem today. When properly set up and calibrated, advanced rendering algorithms (in particular, radiosity and raytracing) can now produce scientifically accurate, photorealistic results (Figure 14-9).

The most advanced acoustic simulation software is equally impressive. In one of its forms, this software accepts a three-dimensional CAD model of an interior (such as a concert hall) as input, and asks the user which seat she would like to occupy. It also requires input of a musical performance recorded in an acoustically "dead" chamber—that is, with no sound reflections and reverberations. It then calculates the auditorium's acoustic effects, and replays the performance exactly as it would sound at the specified seat.

Interior airflow is another area in which computer simulation has made impressive advances. Techniques of computational fluid dynamics now allow

FIGURE 14-9
Visual simulations of
unbuilt architectural
projects, produced by
Takehiko Nagakura and
his students at MIT.

a. Le Corbusier's Palace of the Soviets
b. Terragni's Danteum

precise simulation and visualization of both natural and artificial airflows within spaces, and hence more effective design for human comfort and safety. These techniques are particularly effective for tasks such as the design of complex atrium spaces, where airflows may be complex and difficult to predict by conventional means, where comfort conditions are difficult to control, and where safety issues such as smoke propagation are of crucial importance.

The possibilities for computer measurement, analysis, and simulation of designs are almost endless. As the necessary research is done, and as software vendors make increasingly comprehensive and sophisticated software toolkits available to interior designers, the capacity to produce accurate and compelling predictions of an interior's performance in all its important dimensions will become an increasingly important competitive factor. Clients and regulating authorities will know that this is possible, and they will demand it.

As three-dimensional digital models increasingly support visual simulation, other forms of analysis and simulation, rapid-prototyping, and CAD/CAM, the benefits resulting from construction and use of these models will increase. At the same time, better interfaces, more powerful computational facilities, and more sophisticated software will drive down the costs of constructing, editing, and maintaining these models. As a result, they will increasingly displace two-dimensional "drafting system" digital models in everyday practice.

Where plans, sections, and elevations are needed, these two-dimensional representations will automatically be produced as specialized graphic reports from the three-dimensional model.

INTEGRATION OF CAD, INFORMATION MANAGEMENT, AND ELECTRONIC COMMERCE

As CAD data become increasingly crucial in design and construction, efficient management of CAD project and library databases is becoming a critical practice task. Approaches to this task have evolved a great deal over the years.

In the early days of CAD in architecture and interiors, the idea was to maintain a definitive, centralized project database on a mainframe or a minicomputer. Members of the design and construction team accessed that database whenever they needed information about the current state of the project, and they entered the results of their work back into that database. The idea was simple and elegant, but its comprehensive and effective implementation proved very difficult—particularly on the relatively puny computers of the time.

With the personal computer and engineering workstation revolution of the 1980s, CAD users began to work with locally resident software rather than by logging into a central machine, and they tended to manage their own files on their own PCs. This was effective for small projects, but it created a management nightmare on large-scale, long-running projects involving many designers and consultants. It was difficult to keep versions straight, to keep multiple representations of a project consistent, to ensure that everyone had the most current information, and so on. Strong standards and conventions and strict management controls were needed to prevent chaos.

Now, in the network era, with increasing use of local-area networks within organizations and the Internet for long-distance linkage, members of a design team can be electronically interconnected. Design databases can be maintained on servers, and can be managed—with appropriate access controls— with the aid of sophisticated software. Some design and construction management organizations have implemented such systems on their own, and dot.com startups have emerged to offer comprehensive, on-line management and distribution of design and construction data. Whether traditional design and construction organizations end up controlling this business, or whether the task of on-line design and construction data management is taken over by the new, specialist players with large amounts of venture capital behind them, it seems clear that the future belongs to electronically interconnected, geographically distributed design and construction teams. Increasingly, designers, consultants, clients, fabricators, general contractors, construction managers, and regulatory authorities will be tightly interlinked through the Internet and the web. Rapid digital transfer of CAD and other data, and use of specialized software for managing, safeguarding, and distribution information, will become the norm.

One of the most dramatic consequences of this development will be the growing integration of CAD and electronic commerce capabilities. Instead of selecting materials and products by flipping through printed catalogs and consulting sales staff, designers will increasingly resort to on-line catalogs. Choices will be recorded by linking CAD databases to product catalog data. Prices will be quoted, and negotiation and bidding processes will efficiently be carried out in on-line environments, making use of electronic procurement technologies that are already employed extensively in other fields. Increasingly, CAD systems will look like specialized browsers that provide access, as needed, to information and resources residing on servers scattered throughout the web.

VIRTUAL STUDIOS AND CONFERENCE ROOMS

The combination of CAD capabilities with extensive web resources and on-line data management tools can be regarded as a virtual design studio—an electronic facility for supporting the work of a design team that is wholly or partially geographically distributed. Use of such a capability has many potential advantages: it facilitates the export of design services, it allows the aggregation of the best expertise for a project on a global scale, it keeps traveling participants in close touch, it provides the possibility of tapping into inexpensive labor markets for routine aspects of the process, and it can even support 24-hour operation by taking advantage of time differences between widely separated locations such as Los Angeles, London, and Hong Kong. It also, of course, removes many geographic constraints on competition among design firms.

Within such an environment, digital telecommunication adds the possibility of *remote* interaction to that of local, face-to-face interaction. Similarly, digital storage adds the possibility of *asynchronous* communication to that of synchronous. (In asynchronous communication the parties make use of recorded messages of some kind to remove the necessity of being available at the same time.) The combinations of these possibilities are illustrated in Figure 14-10.

The various options do not substitute directly for one another, since they have different strengths, weaknesses, and associated costs. Local synchronous interaction—for example, by meeting around a table in a conference room—is most intense, effective, and satisfying for many purposes, but it is also the most expensive and difficult to arrange. Remote synchronous interaction, through on-line chat, teleconferencing, or videoconferencing, removes the element of travel time and cost but limits the possibilities for effective communication. Local asynchronous interaction, for example by inspecting a large collection of drawings stored in a flat file, can provide enormous bandwidth for information transmission but lacks human directness. Remote

FIGURE 14-10
Modes of Design Interaction.

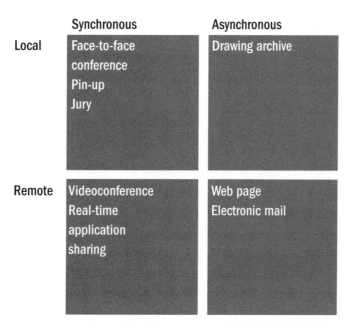

asynchronous interaction, through e-mail, voice-mail, and the web, is the most inexpensive and convenient but the least direct. Thus a major task of office and project management, today, is to choose and provide the most effective and economical combination of these capabilities.

As the effective bandwidth of everyday digital telecommunication grows, the balance among these capabilities will shift. Remote, synchronous communication will become better and cheaper. In particular, Webcasting and video-conferencing will become increasingly commonplace, and it will migrate from specialized conferencing facilities to individual laptop and desktop devices. "Virtual conference rooms," which combine good, inexpensive videoconferencing with concurrent, remote access to CAD files, etc., will become an increasingly crucial part of everyday design practice and teaching.

CONCLUSION

In general, the closely interrelated fields of architecture, landscape architecture, urban design, and interior design were fairly slow to move from paper-based to computer-based techniques for recording, editing, managing, and distributing information. This was largely a consequence of the fragmented, labor-intensive character of the industry, which made it difficult to invest in new technology on the necessary scale.

The personal computer revolution of the 1980s dramatically changed the conditions of practice, however. CAD and visual simulation systems became everyday practice tools. Design firms quickly found that they could not compete without them, and students began to realize that fluency with CAD was now an essential career skill.

Now, the Internet revolution has irreversibly and dramatically altered the conditions of design practice once again. In the twenty-first century, interior design firms will find themselves increasingly reliant upon three-dimensional digital modeling, rapid-prototyping, CAD/CAM construction, advanced analysis and simulation techniques, on-line management of design data, electronic commerce techniques for product selection and procurement, and 24-hour, globally distributed work processes.

Bibliography

Mitchell, William J., and Malcolm McCullough. *Digital Design Media* (Second Edition). New York: Van Nostrand Reinhold, 1995.

Mitchell, William J. *Roll Over Euclid: How Frank Gehry Designs and Builds.* Frank Gehry, Architect. Editor, J. Fiona Ragheb, Published by the Solomon R. Guggenheim Museum, distributed by Harry N. Abrams, Inc., 2001.

Mitchell, William J. *Vitruvius Redux, Formal Engineering Design Synthesis.* Editors, E. K. Antonsson and J. Cagan. Cambridge, UK: Cambridge University Press (2001, in press).

Pinto Duarte, José, João Bento, and William J. Mitchell. *The Lisbon Charrette: Remote Collaborative Design.* Lisbon, Portugal: IST Press, 1999.

THREE

Pract

ice

15

Strategic Practices

Dr. FRANCIS DUFFY, RIBA

Sometimes an outsider can see things that are invisible to those who live and work closer to home.

The conventional office buildings and interiors to which North Americans are so accustomed, in both their high- and low-rise manifestations, are not the only kinds of office environments that are conceivable. Nor are they immutable. They are the direct consequence of the culture, the work practices, and the economy of a very particular nation in a remarkable period of its history. Many features of the conventional office that everyone seems to take for granted—for example, the cubicles satirized by Scott Adams via his hapless cartoon characters, Dilbert and his colleagues—are by no means inevitable. Nor are they entirely an accident. History and ideology made them. They are very much the product of the century that has been called "the American Century." The dominance, the persistence, and the global diffusion of the American model of the office is the direct consequence of the triumphant international success of the American economy in the last hundred years.

We have entered a new century and have begun to experience what it is like to work in a very different kind of economy. Many observers believe that this new economy, because it is based on the exchange of knowledge rather than trading in goods, is tending to become more open ended, participative, and interactive. The old economy was characterized by bureaucracy, i.e., by the hierarchies of impersonal control needed to extract greater and greater efficiency within the closed systems appropriate to manufacturing. The depersonalized culture of command and control and of divide and rule—so strongly advocated by Frederick Taylor and so energetically exploited by Henry Ford—permeates the physical fabric of the conventional North American, twentieth-century office.

Culture becomes implicit in physical artifacts and, once we have become accustomed to it, we find it easy to underestimate its strength. However, the cultural significance of the office environment becomes very clear when the late twentieth-century North American office is compared with its contemporary Northern European equivalent. The physical consequences of the prevailing social democratic culture on the offices of Northern Europe—particularly Germany, Scandinavia, and the Netherlands—are strikingly different. Individual office rooms, all exactly the same size, are provided for everyone without regard to hierarchy. Everyone enjoys direct access to daylight. Everyone expects to be able to open his or her own window and control his or her own environment. The design of office buildings and office furniture reflects a huge respect for the rights, the individual comfort, and the well-being of every office worker. Ergonomics is elevated to a very high level of respect and influence. Adjustability for each and every individual is taken for granted. Statutory negotiations in Workers Councils about the quality of working life have resulted in low, narrow, highly cellular, naturally ventilated office buildings equipped with many individually operable windows, personally adjustable furniture, and superb staff amenities. Of course, the typical environment of the conventional corporate North American office is very different.

Speaking globally, however, it is the highly corporate and conventional North American model of the office, rather than its much less widely diffused social democratic, Northern European counterpart, which has become dominant. Cities all around the world do not consider themselves proper cities unless they build high office buildings in the manner of Chicago or Dallas or Atlanta. Business parks, worldwide, are based on North American prototypes. Big, deep, simple, American-style office floor plates are what most global corporations still want, wherever they happen to be. Construction practices invented in Chicago are everywhere. American furniture manufacturers have become world leaders in a globalizing industry—hence the ubiquity of American space planning techniques, space standards, and floor layouts. In fact, so deeply rooted has the conventional, late-twentieth-century North American office become in the practice not only of architects and interior designers but of the entire property and construction industries, including that relatively new but highly conservative profession, facilities management, that change has become almost unthinkable.

This observation would be a matter of academic interest were it not for an acute sense of a growing contradiction between what the conventional office has so long represented in terms of business values and the very different kind of work culture of the emerging economy of e-commerce. This is not simply to argue that the conventional North American model of the office is inferior or that the Northern European model is superior. Both have been created, entirely legitimately, in different economic and cultural environments. The point is that neither is absolute, neither is permanent, neither is the perfect solution. It no longer makes sense to choose between them. *Both* are likely to become obsolescent for exactly the same basic reasons—irresistible technological, social, and cultural change.

This chapter is about the architectural and design implications of these changes. Our first premise is that all office buildings everywhere must reflect and also support—and certainly not contradict—the spirit of their age and of their place. Our second premise is that, because of the impact of information technology on society, work cultures, in different ways in different places, are all about to change to a degree not experienced since the end of the nineteenth century. New ways of working, unprecedented networks, and completely novel work cultures are beginning to be realized. Change can be expected everywhere. The purpose of this chapter is to explore the likely manifestations of technological, social, and cultural change and to make some practical predictions about the consequences of such changes on the office environments that will be necessary to support the emerging knowledge-based economy.

THE DRIVERS OF CHANGE

Information technology makes innovation in workplace design entirely possible. Economic drivers make change in workplace design absolutely necessary. These drivers operate at three very different levels—the business imperative to increase efficiency in space use, the business potential to use space to enhance organizational effectiveness, and the business advantage inherent in using space as a powerful medium of communication that can stimulate and accelerate organizational change. To take advantage of all three drivers in the design of offices demands a very different design process from that to which we have become accustomed in North America—and everywhere else.

Conventional North American offices have always been used to increase business efficiency. There has been constant pressure from occupiers—especially in recent years from newly professionalized and frequently outsourced facilities managers—to drive down occupancy costs by reducing the amount of space allocated to each office worker. Workplace standards have been ruthlessly rationalized and simplified. Space planners are always attempting to tackle the intractable problems of paper handling. However, until very recently, there has been much less interest in the potentially much more rewarding but much more difficult challenge of managing the use of space *through time* more efficiently. Today both home working and workplace sharing are becoming much more attractive because of the technically exciting and mobility-encouraging potential of wireless telephony.

However, the bitter experience of some unsuccessful experiments to intensify space use is teaching occupiers that cost cutting is not enough. Too urgent an emphasis on saving money, by driving space use harder and harder, has always been the curse of conventional office planning and paradoxically runs counter to innovation because it can stir up so much end-user reaction.

Far more cogent as an agent of change is the use of innovative design to add value to businesses by stimulating more effective ways of working. Effectiveness goes well beyond cost-cutting efficiency. The economic driver for effectiveness is not just to save money but to add value to businesses by using space to create the potential for open-ended improvement in the quality of work done. Architectural devices, such as internal streets and carefully designed and located social spaces, can be powerful ways of enhancing serendipity and maximizing the potential for interaction among the diverse departments of large organizations. Nonhierarchical, interconnecting, transparent, open plan spaces can be used to encourage communication among disciplines, levels, and departments in businesses that must bring together creative knowledge workers from many disciplines. Bright colors, stimulating environments, rich amenities, and diverse settings can be used to attract and retain staff in the highly competitive commercial environment created by very low levels of unemployment. Imaginatively designed, the working environment can provide an infrastructure that stimulates creative people to even greater efforts.

The third economic driver for change in office design is the use of physical environment to express corporate intentions and business strategy in ways that are more powerful and more sustainable than any other medium of communication. Many businesses are learning to use design to express and promulgate the social values that underpin the empowerment of staff, the encouragement of creativity and innovation, and the generation and sharing of knowledge. Office space can be designed in ways that cry out loud that interaction is more attractive than isolation, that openness and transparency are preferable to separation and opacity, openness to enclosure, networks to hierarchy, that negotiation is more effective than command and control.

THE NEW IMPORTANCE OF TIME

Perhaps the most far-reaching consequence the of change is that powerful, ubiquitous, reliable information technology is leading to the development of new processes and new ways of working. These in turn have made it obvious that new conventions in the use of time are even more inevitable than new conventions in the design of office space.

Things that have been taken for granted for a hundred years—such as the eight-hour working day and the five-day working week, such as the need for a vast infrastructure of roads and railways designed to get hundreds of thousands of commuters to their desks every day at the stroke of nine—are hangovers from our industrial past. Why was synchrony so important? Where did the idea of mass commuting come from? Both came from the time when the only way to get work done was to assemble workers all together in one place, at their lathes, or their spinning jennies, or their typewriters, so that when the bell rang, and the power surged, everybody would begin to work all at once, under close supervision, in complete unison. Needless to say, the technological necessity for such feats of synchrony no longer exists. In the age of the Internet, most of us are free to work not just whenever but wherever we like.

This is not to say that a civilized society does not need conventions in the use of time and space to keep things in place, to keep us all sane. The simple reality is that the temporal and spatial conventions that we have inherited from the industrial societies of the nineteenth century no longer have the functional logic underpinning them that once made them impossible to ignore. That we are in urgent need of new conventions becomes abundantly clear when the printouts of time utilization surveys—a technique of recording observations of when people are in the office and of what they are doing—are examined. It is not true, as is often observed, that the office seems half-empty even at the busiest times of day. Observations of hundreds of cases show that the truth is that office workplaces are rarely occupied for more than one-third of the time that they are available, even during the core 8-hour working day. Even today, with our still relatively undeveloped use of information technology, office workers are much more mobile both within and outside the office than is assumed in conventional space standards and design practice.

It seems obvious that the trend toward even greater mobility will continue. Home working will be an experience that most of us will share to some extent. Daily schedules will become more ragged and more complex. Office buildings will become more sociable and more permeable, less impersonal and hermetic. Patterns of commuting will become more diffuse. The function of the city, and of the office within the city, will be to attract and support mobile, demanding, and highly interactive people rather than simply to accommodate a static, docile, silent workforce at the lowest price.

CHANGES IN DESIGN

Against this background the conventional North American working environment, however efficient it may be—and even that is highly questionable given observed patterns of how space is actually used over time—is failing to stimulate a changing, increasingly knowledge-based workforce to greater productivity because it is broadcasting the wrong messages.

A recent book by Jeremy Myerson and Philip Ross, *The Creative Office,* provides an interesting measure of the impact of some of the changes that are taking place in office design as a result of the three drivers outlined above. The book, typical of a burgeoning genre of semi-design, semi-business publications, illustrates 43 international case studies of innovative office design. The lively running commentary reflects general user satisfaction. The case studies are grouped thematically—new offices that exemplify teamwork, innovative environments that facilitate the exchange of ideas, novel workplaces that have been designed to encourage community, and, finally, fresh interiors where information technology has been used to facilitate mobility both within and outside the office.

This is just the kind of data that conventional developers and real estate brokers still seem to find very easy to dismiss. In the conservative property industry, change is resisted. This may be because many of the cases are examples of the new economy—particularly media and information technology. Another possible reason is that by no means all the cases are North American—only 13, in fact; while 13 are from Continental Europe (including one from Turkey); another 13 are British, and four are from Asia/Pacific.

However, neither international experience nor creative enterprise should be treated lightly at this point in the development of a new global economy based increasingly on creativity and knowledge. Most of the cases are new economy businesses but, interestingly, the old economy is heavily represented too. Myerson and Ross's case studies include such mainstream heavy hitters as Boeing, Owens Corning, and McDonalds, as well as six major banks and insurance companies, not to mention IBM, Nokia, and Andersen Consulting (with two case studies). All this provides a useful insight into how new business trends are affecting some relatively advanced users of office space.

This book raises one question rather sharply for those who provide, design, or deliver corporate real estate. The 43 case studies are all examples of users who have succeeded, by extraordinary effort, for one business purpose or another, in achieving something radically new and different from office design. Whether reinventing or simply inventing themselves, what choices have they made regarding their office buildings and design of spaces?

Eighteen of the businesses (42 percent) have gone to the trouble of building new, purpose-designed offices for themselves. In all of these, in North America as well as in Northern Europe, care has been taken to invent novel, highly unconventional—not necessarily the most efficient—architectural forms to create places where ideas can be more easily exchanged or a sense of com-

Things that have been taken for granted for a hundred years . . . such as the need for a vast infrastructure of roads and railways designed to get . . . commuters to their desks every day at the stroke of nine—are hangovers from our industrial past.

munity generated. Seventeen of the cases (40 percent) are examples of adaptive reuse of structures originally designed for entirely different purposes, such as warehouses, industrial sheds, and old houses. These buildings have obviously been chosen because they have what might be called "character"—big volumes, striking roofs, interesting detailing which creative tenants have enjoyed converting to bring them into business use. Strong architectural features, so often lacking in developers' conventional high-rise rent slabs or low-rise tilt-ups, seem to be attractive because they make good team spaces or can be used to enhance staff mobility.

Only five of the cases (11 percent) are fit-outs in what are clearly older but more or less conventional rented office buildings. The least number of cases (three, a mere 7 percent of the sample) are fit-outs in the newer kinds of speculative offices that the property market finds it convenient to supply today.

There is a message here for the property industry. This exercise could indicate that supply-side inertia, not lack of user demand, is responsible for the industry's failure to anticipate what seems to be a radically different pattern of demand. Developers, real estate brokers, architects and designers, as well as building systems and building product manufacturers, and last but not least furniture manufacturers, have an urgent incentive to reexamine what may be in danger of becoming an obsolescent range of products.

Three additional British case studies, drawn directly from recent experience, illustrate in a little more detail what changing user demands means for the design of the office. The circumstances of the three projects are quite different. The new head office of a retail pharmaceutical firm, Boots the Chemists—the British equivalent of Walgreens—is the largest. The client's objective project was to create a unified corporate center. About 2,800 people from five different sites have been brought together in an entirely new office building linked by a major internal street to a totally refurbished Skidmore, Owings & Merrill building dating from the 1960s. The Grosvenor Estate example is much smaller. Grosvenor is a major London-based developer and landowner with its origins in the eighteenth century. In this case a mere 200 people moved to a new office in the West End of London. Their journey, in another sense, was somewhat longer: from offices which would not have been out of place in the nineteenth century to the twenty-first century, from a picturesque warren of more or less disconnected, eighteenth-century houses into a single, brand-new office building. Egg, an entirely new

Internet bank set up by the British insurance company, the Prudential—no relation to the U.S. firm of the same name—did not even need to move. Its converted high-volume industrial shed in Derby accommodates the 1,000-member staff of an entirely new call center for an e-commerce bank that, typically, did not even exist three years earlier.

Only one of the three examples, Grosvenor's own speculative building, is remotely like a conventional North American office building. Of course, UK developer standards are higher—for example, the building is equipped with a full access floor of the kind that has been standard in the UK for 20 years but, for some reason, is still rare in the United States. Good as the building is, it was extensively modified during construction for Grosvenor's own use.

All three new offices have been specifically designed to increase business efficiency by driving down occupancy costs. Workplace standards, in each case, have been simplified. The waste inherent in paper storage has been attacked. Cableless phone systems make it possible to intensify space use. In two of the cases (not in the call center, where the operational needs are different), the information technology infrastructure that makes it possible to share workplaces, although not yet fully exploited, is already in place.

More important is the way in which the three businesses have used design to add value by stimulating more effective ways of doing business. Improvements in effectiveness have been achieved in various ways. In the Boots the Chemists project, a long continuous, multilevel street runs from end to end of the complex, linking a chain of immediately adjacent social and service spaces. These have been designed specifically to enhance serendipity and to maximize the potential for interaction among thousands of people in the diverse parts of what is by any standard a very large organization. Grosvenor's nonhierarchical, open plan, so very different from the offices the company inhabited before, is an architectural way of encouraging communication across disciplines and between levels. In a completely different business culture, the cheerful colors and the stimulating environment of Egg is an obvious architectural means of attracting and retaining staff in a particularly competitive business. All three examples clearly demonstrate the trend toward an increasing proportion of the space budget being taken up by shared, collective activities—project rooms, meeting spaces, rooms for training and meetings, touch-down spaces, social areas, etc.—spaces that are increasingly necessary as settings for complex interactive knowledge work.

The obverse should also be noted: the relative, and indeed frequently absolute, decline of the area devoted to individual workplaces. As mobile working and home working increase, these trends will certainly accelerate.

The messages that design can communicate about business strategy are critically important in all three cases. These three businesses are doing far more than simply accommodating themselves—they are using building projects to accelerate programs of business and cultural change. In Boots the Chemists, every design detail, every step in the design process was used to drive home vitally important messages to every member of staff at every level about the importance of better communications, better team working, better thinking. Grosvenor's design iconography is a carefully judged program to express to staff and visitors the importance, for a highly progressive, international property company, of maintaining continuity with its values and its history. The company is deliberately using its new space to communicate a sophisticated message to the world about its corporate intentions. Egg is using its space not just to attract and retain key staff but to demonstrate to staff and customers what e-commerce is all about.

Common to all three projects, and to the increasing number of similarly innovative office projects round the world, is something quite new: the purposeful and considered use of innovative design to stimulate change. This is a long way from corporate real estate's habitual view of office design as the cheapest way of accommodating as many people as possible in the smallest possible workstations. The big difference is that design is now being used with strategic intent.

CHANGES IN THE DESIGN PROCESS

The chief reason, however, for drawing attention to these three projects is not just that they exemplify how office design is being used to improve business performance, but also to illustrate how the process of office design is changing.

What is essential to understand is that, although the physical design of the new office is critically important, innovation in physical design is literally unthinkable if the process by which physical design is procured and delivered is not reinvented. The process by which successfully innovative offices, such as the three British examples described above—Boots the Chemists, Grosvenor, and Egg—have been designed, is different from conventional design thinking in at least four fundamental ways.

First, these three businesses, and indeed all organizations that want to use design to accelerate cultural change, have learned that they must keep their hands on the tiller. Outsourcing of project management, at least in a strategic sense, is impossible. Design leadership and managerial ownership of innovative office projects, from inception to completion—and thereafter—have become vitally necessary. A clear vision about the purpose of proposed design changes must be articulated and sustained, preferably from the very top of the organization, right through such projects.

Second, these three businesses, and indeed all innovating organizations, have come to understand that data are essential to measure the performance of what is designed against what was intended. Hunches and rules of thumb, old or new, are no longer good enough. Without data, old habits die hard.

Third, the three case study businesses, and again all organizations that know what they are doing with design, have realized that innovative design means that more and more people not only want to but have the right to be involved in the design process. Ordinary people are becoming directly involved in choosing the working environment that seems right for them—not surprisingly, because they know that they *are* the business and they are totally in accord with the discretion they are used to exercising over the domestic and social environment of the rest of their lives. Design is becoming more open and democratic—architects and designers can no longer hope to avoid a genuine creative dialogue with powerful and articulate end users. That will always mean listening, patience, empathy, and, occasionally, confrontation.

Fourth, in a changing and increasingly complex business environment, these three businesses, and indeed any organization that is attempting the same ambitious degree of change, have had to recognize that a systemic approach to design is necessary. In the old economy, when everything was supposedly in its place and when everyone was told exactly what he or she had to do, it was quite possible for the designer of the office environment to work without reference to parallel initiatives in restructuring the organization or installing new information technology. The physical office environment can no longer be designed without reference to the parallel redesign of the two other main dimensions of working life—the design of the social system of the office and the design of the ways in which information technology is used in the office. This means, of course, a total restructuring of the conventional design process.

In effect, these are the four essential conditions for success in designing for new ways of working. Many architects and designers dislike the fourth and last proposition because they fear loss of artistic autonomy. Abandoning the romantic idea of the architect as a totally independent agent does not, however, necessarily mean loss of design influence. In office design the opposite is far more likely to be the case. In an integrating culture, the more architects and designers are involved in the politics of their clients' democratic processes of decision making and the more they are involved in integrated decisions involving the design of their clients' social and technological systems, the more influence they will win.

THE IMPACT OF E-COMMERCE

The three case studies outlined above and the 43 examples of creative design in Myerson and Ross's book are only the beginning of the story. As the wider implications of e-commerce on the property and construction industries become clearer, architects and designers will have even less reason to attempt to isolate themselves from process. The process sketched above means that architects and designers must continually ask themselves what their design is actually *for*. Architects and designers must involve themselves in their clients' business strategies, face up to organizational and technological issues, learn to avoid intermediaries, and work directly and extensively with end users.

The conventional office is the product of a late-nineteenth-century and early-twentieth-century social and technical system, a system that was as mechanical and closed as its makers could devise it to be, a system that divided in order to rule. The office environments that are the consequences of the

*The new office . . .
has to proclaim an
entirely opposite set of
values—networks,
knowledge, interaction,
enjoyment, transparency,
fluidity, life. The
big design question is
what iconography
is appropriate to
express such values.*

values of this older economy have become no more and no less than a metaphor for hierarchy, control, separation, meanness, opacity, dullness, stasis, death. The new office, to be relevant in the new economy, has to proclaim an entirely opposite set of values—networks, knowledge, interaction, enjoyment, transparency, fluidity, life. The big design question is what iconography is appropriate to express such values. To answer this question architects and designers will have to come to terms with yet another level of process—understanding what delivering the new work culture really means in the widest social and economic context.

Disintermediation and the Democratization of Design

The Internet makes possible disintermediation, i.e., stripping away layers of middlemen to give everyone, including all office workers, direct access, for example, to the design process. Disintermediation means the inevitable democratization of the design, procurement, and delivery of every aspect of the office environment. From this perspective, five major disconnects are opening up between what e-commerce offers and how things are done in the conventional way.

The first gap is between the openness, choice, and responsiveness offered by the Internet and conventional real estate procedures based on hierarchy and control. The second gap is between the highly branded, easy-to-access, fun-to-use style of the web and the tired, slow, old economy delivery we know so well in property, construction—and design. The third is between the locational freedom offered by ubiquitous technology and the rigid demarcation of work and life that we have inherited from the mores of the late-nineteenth century. The fourth disconnect is between design that stimulates and attracts people by offering multiple choices and the sterile stereotypes of the conventional office. The fifth is the difference between using change management techniques to accelerate organizational and cultural change and confining such techniques to far less ambitious damage limitation.

Frequently the argument is made that increasing dependence on electronic communications will destroy the need for face-to-face interaction and make places—and hence the physical design of the workplace—redundant. Nothing is less likely. In the world of virtuality, e-commerce will make real materials, real experiences, real places more rather than less significant. To compete with the virtual world, the office has to become more attractive. The more we do not have to go to work, the more design quality will matter.

We have frequently used the somewhat unlikely metaphor of the club to attempt to describe the quality of a social and physical environment that allows people freedom in time and space in an environment that is all the more affordable and all the more attractive because it is based on commonly agreed conventions of the use of space and time. Three things make a club work. The first is an imaginative understanding of how people are prepared, under certain conditions, to share space over time. The second is a statistical understanding of the probable consequences of the aggregated consequences of so much individual discretion and choice. The third is the willing acceptance of conventions of the use and time to support an agreed, common good. Old-fashioned gentlemen's clubs, despite their sexism and elitism, had all these features. Two thousand people literally clubbed together to time-share a palace that provided a richness, a range of settings, an array of options that none of them could afford individually.

The metaphor of the club helps to articulate three paradoxes that encapsulate both the potential and the challenges of inventing the new office. First, the more mobile people are, the more enjoyment of the qualities of place will matter to them. Second, the more we are prepared to share and manipulate the resources of space and time, the more physical design choices we shall have to enjoy. Third, as we argued earlier, the more the architects and designers are prepared to involve themselves with those who design the nonphysical systems that complete the world of work—process and people—the more freedom they will have to invent innovative and interesting physical design solutions.

Designing for the Knowledge Economy

Architects and designers will have to fight both to get things right and to do the right thing—Peter Drucker's famous distinction between efficiency and effectiveness. The conventional North American office with its strong roots in the old economy of Frederick Taylor and Henry Ford is a powerful reminder of how design, of a very different sort, was very often used, in a less fortunate age, to exploit and manipulate people. The persistence of outmoded—not to say, contaminated—design conventions, at least by contemporary standards, particularly in North America, tells us how strong the Taylorist value system remains in our culture—otherwise its growing incongruity would long ago have become intolerable. But the persistence of outmoded managerial ideologies embedded in the physical fabric of the conventional office is largely explained by a conservative delivery system, obsessed partly by efficiency but even more by its own short-term interests. The big danger, at this crucial moment in the development of the knowledge economy, is that office buildings and office interiors that speak far more eloquently about the past than about the future will drag us all, despite our highest aspirations, downward and backward.

The landscape of e-commerce is certain to be very different from that of the conventional office. Change management has become an essential part of the design process. Conventional ways of designing are no longer good enough—because they are as divisive, fragmentary, and unchanging as the physical environments they produced.

Bibliography

Clements-Croome, Derek, Editor. *Creating the Productive Workplace*. London: E&FN Spon, 2000.

DEGW. *Design for Change—The Architecture of DEGW*. Basle: Birkhauser, 1998.

Duffy, Francis. *The New Office*. London: Conran Octopus, 1997.

Mitchell, William J. *e-topia*. Cambridge: MIT Press, 1998.

Mitchell, William J. *City of Bits: Space, Place and the Infobahn*. Cambridge, MA: MIT Press, 1995.

Santa, Raymond, and Roger Cunliffe. *Tomorrow's Office*. London: E&FN Spon, 1996.

Turner, Gavin, and Jeremy Myerson. *New Workplace, New Office*. London: Gower, 1998.

16

Sustainable Design

WILLIAM ODELL, AIA

"Green" design, "environmental" design, and "sustainable" design all refer to the same topic often discussed today within the design community: how can we think of design as *environmentally responsible design*?

Designers may wonder what the issue is; after all, many aspects of environmentally responsible design are already common practice. Improved indoor air quality is becoming an important goal for most professionals, and many methods for achieving it are being incorporated into the general practice. Products that emit substantially fewer volatile organic compounds and materials that have substantial recycled content are common. Our buildings are far more efficient than they were just 20 years ago. Many of these elements have found their way into the regulatory framework that shapes the design and construction industry. Some of this change has come about because society has mandated it through legislation. Other aspects have come about simply because designers and owners have discovered better and more effective ways to design buildings.

Yet for many and perhaps most of the designers who think about sustainable design, these topics are considered design options at best. Environmentally responsible design, or *sustainable* design, as we will call it in this chapter, is not standard practice now because most of the profession remains to a large extent uninformed about the issues involved or the options before them. And if that attitude persists, the design profession will be unable to cope with clients' needs. The design profession has a real stake in becoming educated about sustainable design. In a few short years, sustainable design will be standard practice. Society simply has no other option. We live in a world with growing concerns about the quality of the environment that surrounds and supports us, that supports human life. Environmental threats are real and appear to be growing. The issue is not whether the earth will continue to be able to support life, but whether the earth will continue to be able to support human life. The earth has proven over many millions of years to be quite capable of supporting a myriad of life forms, which have adapted to many changes in the condition of the globe, from the ice age to the impact of asteroids. The question is whether the earth can support the impact of people on its air, water, and soil. While there remain many controversies about the relative cause and effect of human interactions on the environment and even more controversy about the timing of specific effects, there is a growing consensus within the overall scientific community as to the overall trends. Those trends indicate that the health of the environment is deteriorating, at an accelerating pace, because of the impact of humans.

It is, in many ways, a revolutionary time in design. Significant environmental concerns mean that the very definition of good design is being redefined. Sustainable design, green design, and environmental design will be common practice in the future. Soon, the central practical issue for designers will change from one of education to one of ethics. In the near future, a design will be considered good only if it is healthy for its users and for the earth's environment. Building designers are primarily responsible for the decisions that affect our built environment. They have a unique opportunity. For every material, system, or product decision that they make, there is a significant range of choices. Some are toxic to users and the earth. Others are far less so and in some cases approach sustainability and even a degree of healing. The choices are for design professionals to make. If they choose conscientiously and wisely, they have the opportunity not only to improve individual buildings, but also to help build a healthier environment for all. If, collectively, design professionals can improve the environmental performance of the built environment, they can have a tremendous impact in reducing the overall environmental problem on earth. That impact is not only significant but also within the profession's reach, within the bounds of existing market forces.

Even though growing numbers of clients are asking about sustainable design issues, it will remain the responsibility of designers to bring their full knowledge of environmental issues to each project. In what follows, we will develop the range of issues facing design professionals, and indicate the knowledge they must master, using buildings as a central example.

ENVIRONMENTAL CONCERNS

The modern environmental movement generally originated in the 1960s. There was growing concern about the use of pesticides and the quality of air and water. Lake Erie was dying, as were many of the acid rain-plagued forests of the Northeast. Waste was a growing problem and recycling was virtually unknown. The first of a series of what became known as "Superfund" sites, where extensive pollution was identified, became important local and national issues. Efforts to deal with these issues received widespread public support. The Nixon administration addressed environmental concerns with the first broad environmental legislation and the creation of the Environmental Protection Agency. The concerns were heightened in the 1970s by the energy crisis and later by the concern over the discovery of a hole in the ozone layer. During the 1980s, many people began to realize that it was necessary not only to clean up environmental problems but also to find innovative ways to avoid the pollution problem in the first place. Today, we are increasingly finding that not only are there many ways to avoid pollution but also that in doing so we can produce buildings that are more attractive, productive, and economical to build and operate than "typical" buildings.

In the last three decades we have made a great deal of progress in dealing with many environmental issues. The air is substantially cleaner in most of our major urban areas. The water quality in many rivers and streams is also much higher. Most of our industrial processes are cleaner than they were just a decade ago. Our buildings are far more energy efficient than they were in the 1960s. The industrial nations of the world worked together to eliminate the use of chlorofluorocarbons (CFCs), one of the gases most damaging to the ozone layer, and are working on other issues. Lake Erie has come back.

THE SITUATION TODAY

The problems that we face today are of a substantially different kind than those we faced 30 years ago. Many of the problems of that time were highly visible—dirty lakes and streams, smog, and dying forests. That public visibility had a great deal to do with the widespread public support for dealing with the problems. Many of today's problems are much less visible. The problems are less obvious but no less critical. While progress has been made in lowering the release of CFCs into the atmosphere in the industrial world, CFCs continue to be produced in the emerging nations of the world, with production accelerating. Other damaging gases continue to be released by all nations. Toxic emissions, while lowered, continue to be released into the air and water by industrial and other processes. Recycling has become an industry in many areas but is still in its infancy. In general, while we have done much to reduce the rate of environmental degradation in many areas, the general trend is that of degradation of the environment.

SEEING BUILDINGS AS DESIGN PROBLEMS: COSTS AND BENEFITS FOR USERS AND THE ENVIRONMENT

Sustainability is generally defined as an ability to meet today's needs without compromising the ability of future generations to meet their own needs. As simple as this definition may be, its application to the work of designers can be challenging. There are many unanswered questions, little understanding of most issues, and, frequently, less than ideal choices. This is particularly true in the building industry. On the other hand, there are many ways to improve the environmental performance of our building designs today within common construction budgets, time constraints and programmatic needs. The challenge is to focus on the problems and issues involved and begin to address them systematically in the design and delivery of facilities. One can start by understanding the specific impact of buildings.

The Impact of Buildings

The impact of buildings is a significant part of the overall problem of environmental degradation. Buildings use a significant portion of the earth's resources and produce an even larger proportion of the pollution released into the air, water, and soil. According to the World Resources Institute,[1] buildings use 17 percent of fresh water flows and 25 percent of harvested wood. Buildings are responsible for 50 percent of the production of CFCs. They use 40 percent of energy flows, generate 33 percent of CO_2 emissions, and produce 40 percent of the landfill material from construction and demolition waste. The Environmental Protection Agency estimates that one-third of all buildings suffer from "sick building" syndrome.

We have these problems with the design of most buildings in part because decisions made by one party are paid for by others. Moreover, building owners simply never see the full costs of many of these decisions. Pollution created in the manufacturing of a given building material, for example, is a cost paid for not by the building owner but, generally, by the public at large, when the toxins eventually have to be cleaned up. The true cost of a building includes not only the cost of the "bricks and mortar" that go into its construction but also the cost of the people who use it. The construction costs of buildings are small compared to the costs to the people who occupy them. This is true of all building types. In the typical $100/\text{ft}^2$ office building, for example, the costs of its occupants may range from $200 to $500 per square foot *annually*, depending on the occupant. Clearly, it makes more economic sense to make sure that design decisions promote the health and productivity of the people using the building.

Benefits

Sustainable design is clearly important to help solve our increasingly urgent environmental concerns. It also can improve overall building performance and makes sense economically. Ironically, the extremely poor performance of a typical building today, in terms of energy efficiency, air quality, and other measures of environmental performance, often is paralleled by the building's equally poor performance as a productive place to be and work.

Buildings that make better use of energy and other resources save money. Lower operation costs lead directly to a higher building values, by raising the net operating revenue. There is increasing evidence beyond common sense telling us that healthy buildings are more productive. There is also evidence that healthy buildings lease or sell faster than ones that are less so.

FIGURE 16-1

High performance glass products are now quite common. Their thermal performance is far superior to the glass of just a few years ago and is improving every day. This triple-glazed system at the Federal Reserve Bank of Minneapolis helps to keep valuable heat inside the building during winter months.

PRACTICAL PROBLEMS IN SUSTAINABLE DESIGN

The challenge for designers is to understand the overall impact of their individual design decisions on human health and the health of the world around us. This issue must become as important and intuitively understood as cost and schedule decisions are today. As daunting as this sounds, the good news is that today there is a growing list of better choices and resources to help us make those choices. The key is to understand the central goals of sustainable design, the obstacles facing designers, and the life "history" and life cycle of a given material or product.

Environmental Goals

After they take account of the true costs of a building and the benefits of sustainable design, how can designers define the overall environmental goals that the society as a whole and the design industry should seek? The following are key goals for the interior design profession.

- *To promote the efficient use of resources, including materials, water, and energy*

- *To understand the life cycle of all the materials we use in order to understand the overall environmental impact of our decisions*

- *To create healthy indoor environments for building users*

- *To protect ecosystems in the selection of the materials that go into a project*

- *To move toward eliminating waste in the production, transport, installation, and use of materials*

- *To help users move toward eliminating waste by making recycling easy*

- *To move away from the use of fossil fuels and toward the use of sustainable energy resources*

- *To find ways to let building users know why the building has been designed the way it has, to help raise the general awareness of the issues and opportunities*

Obstacles

There is no shortage of obstacles to achieving the goals of sustainable design applied to buildings. For one thing, there are many unanswered questions. While there is generally widespread agreement within the scientific community that the environment has been degraded, there is disagreement as to particular causes, effects, and timing in many areas. Many manufacturers literally cannot tell us exactly what goes into a given product. In many areas, it may seem at first that the design industry has limited choices available for environmentally responsible products. While the design industry is, generally, more and more aware that environmental issues are part of the professional equation, it is also to a great extent ignorant of the specific issues involved and how they should be addressed. Moreover, there is vocal resistance in many areas of society and within the profession concerning environmental issues. Some designers mistakenly fear that considering environmental issues will challenge their "artistic expression." Others think of the topic as a confusing addition to an already crowded design agenda. Unlike the largely nonpartisan approach to these issues earlier, the issue has become "political" for some. Finally, for many, there is a perception that "green" either costs more, is impractical, looks "odd," or inhibits freedom of expression.

The Present Situation

Despite these many real and perceived obstacles, there is reason to be hopeful. There is a growing list of resources and examples from which to learn. While the industry has a long way to go before all building will truly be sustainable, there have been many successes. Many material manufacturers are researching and redesigning their products. With a little research, you will find that for nearly every building product there are many environmentally superior options to choose from. More owners, suppliers, and contractors are becoming sensitive to the issue and trying to improve their own performance. Enough "green" buildings have been built for us to know that they need not cost more and may frequently cost less. Finally, some of the best designs and designers of recent years have embraced these issues in innovative and imaginative ways, giving young design professionals worthy examples to learn from.

Many of the issues that were considered environmental options just a few years ago–clean air, clear water, limited energy conservation–are today required, have widespread support, and are standard practice. Many of the environmental issues that we face today will be addressed by "standard practice" for the interior design industry in a very short time. Part of this change will happen because society has no other choice–it will be required. There is only a limited amount of water available in central and west Texas, for example, and controls become tighter every year. Part of this will come about because of public consensus that will demand healthy buildings. The nearly total ban on smoking within buildings, for example, has been followed by other expectations of the basic health requirements of building on the part of the general public. Part of the initiative will come from clients who see the benefits or want to reduce risk. The large number of "sick" buildings of the late 1980s received wide attention by major building owners.

A large part of the change, however, will come about simply because it makes more sense in all of these aspects–the health of the occupants, economy, and flexibility for all concerned. Why would we continue to produce buildings that are unhealthy and inefficient when we know they do not have to be?

FIGURE 16-2
Many options for ceiling
tiles are now available
with high post-consumer
recycled content, for
either cellulose com-
position or mineral
composition tiles.

Building Codes

The building codes that govern the design and construction of buildings are
a product of the late nineteenth century. They came about because of many
problems that came with the Industrial Revolution. When society began to
deal with the fires, building collapses, and other problems associated with
industrialization, there was a long period of trial and error as problems were
discovered and solutions tried. The trial-and-error method of defining issues
of fire safety and structural integrity continued for nearly a hundred years.
We live and practice today with the greatly expanded and refined product
of those early efforts. These various standards are widely understood and
accepted, and are clearly part of "common practice." Sustainable design/envi-
ronmental issues are, more or less, where building and life safety codes were
in the early part of the nineteenth century. We are just beginning to understand the basic issues and just beginning to explore the solutions.

Material and Waste: The Life-Cycle Issue

The "life history" of most building materials is one of waste. Ninety-four percent of the material that contributes to productivity of the average product in the United States has already become a waste by-product by the time the product gets to the end user. This includes building products. If packaging is accounted for, the percentage is higher. Waste in this regard is defined as materials released into the air, water, or soil that are not usable by any other life form on earth. Nature, for the most part, knows no waste. Each organism's "waste" is "food" for another life form. Man is the only life form that systematically produces waste in the true sense, i.e., material that is no longer useful by any other organism on earth. The toxins, heavy metals, and other materials that we regularly produce as by-products of our complex manufacturing processes are truly waste. Once released into the biosphere, these materials accumulate and can enter the food chain. These materials can bio-accumulate in organisms. There is growing evidence of a cumulative impact on the lives of many organisms. Amphibians, for example, are particularly susceptible to these impacts. Lower in the food chain, with shorter gestation periods and skins that absorb materials directly, they tend to be more immediately affected by toxins within their environment. A Missouri botanical research organization, for example, has predicted that the world population of frogs will be reduced by 50 percent within 10 years.[2] There are increasing concerns within the scientific community that the accumulation of toxins is having a detrimental effect on life at many levels.

The solution to this problem is not to find better ways to deal with pollution once it is made. The solution is rather to redesign the things that we make to eliminate the toxins in the first place. What is not acceptable in the end is "down-cycling." Down-cycling is the recycling of materials—plastics for example—into a lesser product. Recovering mixed plastics to use in lumber is a short-term solution, for example. While this extends the life of the materials involved—the plastics—it only delays the eventual disposal of the material in a landfill with the toxins involved. Such recycling is a short-term solution at best.

The objective is to recycle into products in such a way that material is never lost to the overall system—it simply evolves into another form. The model for this is nature itself. In doing so, there are two ways we can emulate nature. The first way is to make products that include only compounds that are biodegradable, i.e., they are part of nature. The second way is to design products so that they can eventually be recycled. Recycling in this case means producing materials that can be recycled into another product. Many carpets are now designed and manufactured so that they can be eventually remanufactured into more carpet. Furniture manufacturers, equipment suppliers, and others are also beginning to redesign their products in a similar fashion.

THE LIFE CYCLE OF A CHAIR

For most of the history of the design profession, the knowledge of materials and products has been limited largely to short-term knowledge that extends from the showroom through installation. This knowledge represents only a small part of the history of these materials and products. For example, consider a simple desk chair. The chair may consist of several dozen materials, including the metals, paints, fabrics, plastics, foams, glues, and lubricants that go into the final product. Each of these components in turn is made of a set of materials that have gone into producing that component. The paint will be the end product of the interactions of dozens of different chemicals and processes. Each of those chemicals has a history going back to the original raw material sources. The aluminum fittings have previously traveled over many continents as the raw material was processed. The steel has a similar story.

For most products today, the history of production is one of pollutants at every step released in one way or the other into the air, water, and soil. Those emissions represent a large percentage of the overall waste that results from the production of the chair. Each step also uses energy in various forms with its resulting pollution. Each material that goes into the final chair has a similar history. Each material or subcomponent is delivered to the manufacturer's assembly plant. Those materials will generally have been transported from some distance. They will generally have come from plants that use great quantities of energy and other resources. The plants, primarily those located outside the United States, will frequently be unsafe and unhealthy for the workers. The waste generated will be great. The chair is finally delivered to the building site from a distant factory by transportation that is itself inefficient. It will be delivered to the job site with packaging material that will have been used once and will end up in a landfill.

While the chair is in use, there is a good chance that it will give off gases that are evaporating from the glues, foams, and other material that went into its

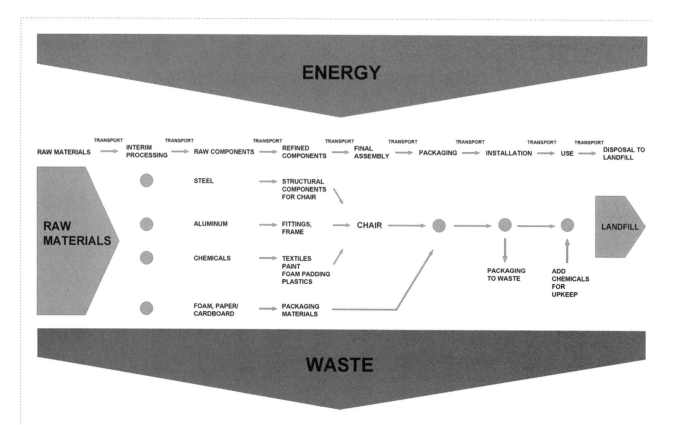

FIGURE 16-3
Life Cycle Diagram of
Typical Commercial
Chair.

creation. Those gases, once released in a confined space, will have an imme-diately negative effect on people who are chemically sensitive, as well as unknown longer-term effects on everyone else. If the chair breaks in use, there is a better than even chance that its useful life will end at that point. No matter how long it lasts, it will eventually end up as waste buried in a landfill, because there are no other options for disposing of it. When it goes to the landfill, no one will know exactly what went into the product or what chemicals are being released into the soil, water, and air.

Even a modest building design will have hundreds of products that go into the final project. Each of those products has a similar story. In selecting fin-ish materials, furniture, lighting products, systems, or equipment for a proj-ect, it is important to understand as much as possible about the complete life cycle of each item. Many of the concerns about this simple chair are not easily answered—even, surprisingly, by manufacturers who are deeply committed to improving the environmental performance of their products and their manufacturing operations. Many questions, however, are answerable.

There are many greatly improved products. While we have a long way to go in truly understanding the environmental implications of many of the materials and products that we use, more and more information is becoming available concerning the life cycle of projects and their overall impact on the health of users and on the health of the environment. At the same time, while there are many unsatisfactory products and materials, there are also an increasing number of manufacturers producing environmentally superior products. The key to deciding between competing products is to understand the life cycle of each.

LIFE-CYCLE ISSUES CHECKLIST

- **Raw materials.** *Design professionals should consider the raw materials that go into the product. Where do the raw materials come from? Is the material safe and nontoxic? Can it be produced or harvested without polluting the surrounding area? How much energy is used to produce the material? How many other material resources are depleted in producing the material? Does its production help the surrounding community? Is the raw material a renewable resource, or does it come from a recycled material? Is the raw material a salvaged material (wood flooring), or is it a recycled product (ground-up rubber)? Is it an agricultural or industrial by-product?*

FIGURE 16-4
Compressed fiber panels for interior wall construction are made of an agricultural waste product—straw that is normally burned. It also replaces gypsum wall board, eliminating the pollution stream wall board fabrication produces.

- Transportation. *Designers should evaluate the amount of transportation involved at all points, from raw material production through final product delivery. Each mile of transportation requires more energy consumption and produces greater levels of pollution. Are there locally produced products that will serve the need just as well?*

- Production. *It is important that the design professional understand the various production steps that take the raw materials through to a finished product. How much pollution is released into the air, water, and soil in these processes? How much waste is produced in these processes? How much energy is used? How much water and other resources were required in the processes? What other resources are depleted in the production process? Is the process safe and healthy for the workers?*

- Packaging. *Designers should not forget that packaging alone can represent a large percentage of the total waste stream for a given product and looms large in the total waste stream of society. While construction waste recycling is important, avoiding packaging waste in the first place is the most efficient strategy. Is the packaging necessary? How little is necessary? Is the packaging material reusable? If not, can it be recycled in other ways? Many innovations are made possible by using local materials and working with manufacturers. As an example, consider that 50 percent of all hardwood is used for pallets; 95 percent of these pallets are used only one time.*[3]

- Installation. *As designers know, many products, which are otherwise environmentally benign, can fall into disfavor simply because of the installation procedures required by the manufacturers. Is the installation safe for workers? Does it introduce volatile organic compounds (VOCs) into the building? Will the warranty be voided if a more environmentally friendly mastic or finish is used? Are the mastics, finishes, or other required installation materials safe and environmentally friendly?*

- Use. *The design firm should ask whether the material will serve for a long time with a minimum of upkeep. Is it safe for users? Are the maintenance procedures safe? Is it free of VOCs and other toxic compounds?*

FIGURE 16-5

Paint is the most common finish material. Until recent years, most paints off-gassed high quantities of VOCs during and after installation. The paint industry, however, has made great strides in improving the environmental performance of the product. As with all other materials, it is still extremely important to read the label carefully.

While the chair is in use, there is a good chance that it will give off gases that are evaporating from the glues, foams, and other material that went into its creation. Those gases ... will have an immediately negative effect on people who are chemically sensitive ...

- Maintenance. *Design professionals should not overlook maintenance issues. What is required to maintain the product? Are the maintenance materials safe for the maintenance workers and for the users? Are these materials free of toxic materials? What was the life cycle of the maintenance materials?*

- Recovery. *It is also important that designers understand what happens at the end of the useful life of a given building material or product. Each building component will have a different useful life. Carpeting, for example, will generally need to be replaced far more often than ceiling tile. Ceiling tiles will be replaced more often than restroom counter tops or other major fixed elements. At the moment, the overwhelming majority of building products end up in a landfill when they are no longer useful. Can the product be reused? Is the material recyclable into a material resource for another product? Can the product be easily removed? If it is not reusable or recyclable, is the product biodegradable?*

FIGURE 16-6
Linoleum is an old product now being rediscovered in part because of its substantial environmental benefits throughout its life cycle, from raw material sources through maintenance and recycling.

Standardized Labeling

Eventually, designers will be able to answer questions such as these by referring to some form of standard labeling for materials used in the products they choose. Such labels will likely be required by law, much as they are now required for food. A number of such systems are now in use in Europe. In this country, however, standard labeling is in its infancy. Material data sheets are only partly useful. Small amounts of materials are not required to be reported, nor are compounds used in the production process itself. In the meantime, designers will have to ask these questions themselves. Researching the life history of each material and product in a project generally is not possible within the normal pressures of schedule and fees. Fortunately, there are growing lists of resources that can help designers understand these issues and assist them in making timely decisions.

FIGURE 16-7
Common Substances to Avoid when Selecting Materials.

VOLATILE ORGANIC COMPOUNDS (VOCS)		HEAVY METALS (AND THEIR COMPOUNDS)
○ Formaldehyde	○ Isophorone	○ Lead
○ Vinyl chloride	○ Methylene chloride	○ Mercury
○ 4-phenylcyclohexene (4-PC)	○ Ethylbenzene	○ Cadmium
○ Styrene	○ Naphthalene	○ Chromium
○ Benzene	○ Phthalate esters	○ Antimony
○ Methyl ethyl ketone	○ Acrolein	○ Nickel
○ Methyl isobutyl ketone	○ Acrylonitrile	
○ Toluene	○ 1,2-dichlorobenzene	
○ Xylenes	○ Acetone	
○ 1,1,1-trichloroethane	○ Carbon tetrachloride	
○ Trichloroethylene	○ Tetrachloroethane	

INDOOR ENVIRONMENTAL QUALITY AND THE DESIGN PROCESS

Designers need to consider numerous factors when they set out to create an indoor environment. Important factors include the quality of the air, lighting, acoustics, thermal comfort, and visual and actual access to the outside. In designing a new or renovated facility, design professionals should understand not only the individual environmental impacts of each material deci-

FIGURE 16-8
In this laboratory, daylight is the main source of light for most of the day.

sion but also the total impact of these decisions in creating environments that support the building's users.

The design of systems to increase natural light is a good example of how designers can satisfy the user's interior environmental needs and exterior environmental needs at the same time. In the United States, cheap energy after World War II allowed the creation of large hermetically sealed buildings which cut most occupants off from the outside world. Windows no longer opened, and fewer and fewer people ever saw outside. Fresh air was limited in the name of "energy conservation." Increasingly, these kinds of buildings have been questioned from a humanistic as well as an environmental and health viewpoint. In Europe, for example, basic access to daylight is commonly required in many building codes. Many require all building occupants to be within a maximum distance (25 ft) from an outside window. Operable windows are common and also frequently required. In addition to being more pleasant places in which to work, these buildings typically use substantially less energy than does the average U.S. building. Daylighting of interior spaces not only creates more attractive places to work but also can help reduce energy consumption in a building. If a building uses daylight, it will need less energy for installed lighting. In addition, because lights are a significant heat source in most buildings, using less artificial lighting will also reduce the cooling load in the building. If strategies such as this are designed in from the beginning, they can help reduce the first cost as well as the operational cost of the building, and lower its overall environmental impact.

The Environmentally Self-Conscious Design Process

It is not realistic to think that it will generally be possible to design buildings that perform significantly better environmentally within the traditional design process. The traditional process is generally linear in nature, with each discipline adding its part to the project, and it allows designers little opportunity or incentive to rethink basic issues and work toward more integrated design solutions. In addition, designers have many unanswered questions; they are overwhelmed with the many new products coming onto the market every week, all of which prompt new questions; and in many cases, they do not understand the basic science. The issues, problems, and solutions are far from intuitive. To produce high-performance buildings requires a different approach to design—a self-conscious approach. The sustainable design process outlined below is by its very nature rigorous and deliberate in producing a more efficient design. It provides many more opportunities for synergies for first cost and operational savings within a more collaborative team.

THE TEAM

It is always important that designers select the right team for a project. The design professional should select a team with prior experience with environmental issues even though for a time it will be hard to find such experience. What is perhaps most important is that the design team members share a common understanding that it is important to improve the environmental performance of the design, and are willing to work together for better solutions.

The team will include the owner's representative. Every effort should also be made to include those who will ultimately be responsible for operating and maintaining the final facility for the owner. A knowledgeable building manager can greatly help the overall performance of a building. This performance includes energy conservation, building maintenance, and other operational issues. It is important that the manager and his or her team have a clear understanding of the overall and specific goals and objectives for the project design as well as detailed knowledge of how particular systems are designed to be operated.

For larger projects, many different organizations may be involved, e.g., the base building architect, mechanical engineers, the construction firm or manager, and telecommunications consultants. For these projects, it will be helpful to identify one person in each firm to be the "green" shepherd, to make sure environmental information and issues within each firm are passed on to and addressed by the team.

To move toward sustainable buildings, it may be helpful for the design team to include additional team members depending on the size of the project and its resources. In larger projects, energy modeling, indoor air quality (IAQ) and maintenance advisors are frequently part of the team. If at all possible, the construction professional responsible for the project should be included from the beginning. If it is a straight bid project, consider having information sessions for interested contractors prior to the official pre-bid meeting, to explain the project and the overall environmental issues and goals that shaped the design. If appropriate, consider including selected building material suppliers and subcontractors as part of the team. If some product suppliers already have preexisting agreements with the client—for furniture systems, for example—they also should be included from the beginning. The more inclusive the team can be made, the better. The entire team should be part of the initial education sessions.

EDUCATION AND SETTING GOALS

Once the team is in place, it will be extremely helpful to start the project with an education and goal-setting session. While this process is increasingly common in projects, environmental issues deserve their own focus. The issues are new to many people, and it is helpful to start with a common understanding of the issues and see what others are doing to create better-performing buildings. The design team should consider holding an environmental charrette or work session for the entire team to learn together and to begin to outline the environmental goals for the project. Such a session is one of the best ways to get people involved.

FIGURE 16-9
As with other aspects of the design, sharing information with the entire team early in the process will make it much easier to meet environmental goals.

The next step is to define environmental goals for the project. The design team should define these as specifically as possible for each area of the project. For example, energy consumption, water use, and waste are easily quantified. The Leadership in Energy and Environmental Design (LEED) Green Building Rating System (discussed below) can be very helpful in this regard in organizing the various issues and helping the team to set specific standards and goals. Part of the initial session's goal should be devoted to developing a methodology for making decisions and balancing resources.

Some teams have developed large-scale versions of LEED "scorecards," have them laminated for ease of using erasable markers, and use these as one tool for keeping up to date on various issues and the overall progress during the project.

The importance of setting goals cannot be overstressed. Unlike building budgets and schedules, environmental issues are not intuitively understood by most people. It is important that the design team set environmental goals and issues early and then revisit them at each project meeting.

GATHERING RESOURCES AND INFORMATION

Once the design team has set initial goals, its next task will be to gather information about program needs and to explore all options for solving the basic needs with minimal resources. The team should identify specific needs for ventilation, humidification, and filtration, all of which will have an impact on indoor environmental quality and cost—and, if possible, identify local sources

FIGURE 16-10
Selecting environmentally benign materials does not inhibit design quality and, in most cases, does not impact the budget.

of materials. The team should look for opportunities for partnerships with suppliers, local utility companies, and others. It should identify possible sources for salvaged building materials that might be used in a project. If demolition is required, the team should consider what materials might be saved for reuse in the new project. It should also identify sources for building construction waste recycling and locate sources of information to help in the selection of materials. For example, wood paneling and structural members can frequently be reused. Carpet tiles can be renewed. Ceiling tiles can frequently be reused in back-of-the-house areas.

Once the team is in place, it will be extremely helpful to start the project with an education and goal-setting session. While this process is increasingly common in projects, environmental issues deserve their own focus.

DESIGN REFINEMENT AND OPTIMIZATION

Optimization is simply the ongoing review of each design decision or material selection to ensure that it is indeed the best possible selection for the task and goals at hand. For instance, the design team can use an energy model to evaluate energy consumption by load component (lighting, ventilation, plug loads, etc.). The DOE-2 energy modeling system is the best. This modeling system was funded by the U.S. Department of Energy and administered by the Ernest Orlando Lawrence Berkeley National Laboratory. It can work systematically to reduce each load. The most significant benefits will come from the synergy that can be found between systems. Maximizing daylight and minimizing electric lighting, for example, will also reduce the overall cooling load of an office building. If daylight can be used for significant portions of the lighting needs, the overall mechanical system can be smaller.

While they work with the mechanical engineers and lighting designers to minimize energy consumptions designers should also keep in mind the other things that produce high-quality spaces. They should account, for example, for whether there are views to the exterior. Similarly, they should isolate pollution-generating equipment including copiers, fax machines, and printers, to make it easier to exhaust the pollutants involved. And they should make sure there is easy access for maintenance.

As the project progresses, the designers should ask the following questions. Is the design flexible for long-term use? If demolition is to take place prior to construction, are these materials being recycled? Can any of these materials be reused in the new construction? Are there local salvaged materials that can be used? What are the best materials that can be afforded to meet the needs of the project while protecting the environment and health of the building's users? How little is it possible to get by with in terms of resources while still meeting the needs of the client?

FIGURE 16-11
In this demolition of an old hospital, the rigid insulation was salvaged and used in the new facility.

Every aspect of the design should be reevaluated systematically to achieve a better design. Materials should be dimensioned to minimize waste using standard material sizes wherever possible. Minimize on-site finishing of materials to make it easier to keep the building free of off-gassing from these operations. It is generally easier to control these finishing processes in a factory setting. Be clear about environmental requirements expected in the specification, including VOCs, recycled content, and avoidance of materials that have been banned by regulatory agencies. Design for flexibility and adaptability wherever possible, to allow the building to serve for a longer time without additional work. Provide for recycling at each work area and at the loading dock. Experience has shown that recycling is more likely to happen when it has been made convenient to do so.

FIGURE 16-12
Sometimes simply using fewer materials is a way to control environmental impact. In this case, a simple sealed concrete floor eliminates the need for more toxic finishing processes.

SPECIFICATIONS AND CONSTRUCTION DOCUMENTS

Specifications and construction documents require special attention. The industry typically relies on "standard" specifications. However, many of the materials or requirements for environmentally superior buildings may be new. New specifications will have to be crafted that carefully outline the expected environmental performance requirements. Develop a construction waste specification based on research of the local community. If demolition is to occur prior to construction, clearly define what is expected to be done with the materials to be removed. Clearly define those materials that will be salvaged for later reuse.

FIGURE 16-13
Cargill Dow LLC has developed a fiber made from polylactic acid, a corn byproduct. Interface Inc. has designed carpet tiles, shown here, and fabrics made of this breakthrough material.

The pre-bid conference should clearly outline the environmental goals and any unique features or requirements. The design team should encourage all contributors to the project to seek new ways to minimize construction waste and to be open to suggestions, beyond the ones already incorporated into the project, for using salvaged materials.

BIDDING AND CONSTRUCTION

If the construction team was not involved in the project from the beginning, the design team should pay special attention to identifying the overall environmental goals for new members of the team. The team might consider an environmental education session similar to those at the beginning of the design phase. It should pay particular attention to construction waste materials, and any special construction sequencing required. If a construction manager has been involved from the beginning, this educational effort should be directed to the subcontractors' bidding on the project.

Once contracts have been let and construction is about to begin, the design team should prepare a team overview of the project and its environmental goals. Most of these issues, materials, and systems will be new to most of those who will construct the project. If the design team makes clear the issues involved and the goals for the project, the construction team has the best chance of meeting the objectives of the project. As with the design team, it is frequently helpful to identify one person within each subcontractor's crew to be the environmental shepherd to ensure a smooth flow of information and to provide a daily reminder of the specifics of the mission. Many contractors have found it useful to cover a week's outstanding environmental

FIGURE 16-14 and 16-15
In most areas of the country, minimizing construction waste is simply a matter of making it convenient for the subcontractors to separate materials, such as wood, metal, drywall, etc.

issues at the weekly site superintendent meetings, much as they do for job site safety. This practice puts environmental issues squarely into the mainstream of job site activity and helps ensure that nothing is missed.

POST-OCCUPANCY

Once the project is complete, it is important that the design team stay in contact with the building's users and operators to ensure that the building is functioning correctly. Designers should consider creating an operations manual to explain to initial and later operators why particular material and system decisions were made, how they are to operate, and how they are to be maintained. Many materials and maintenance procedures may be new to people. If problems arise, they can be corrected or at least serve as a basis for better decisions in the future.

Ten Simple Things

An environmentally responsible building need not look different from one that is not. To help extend the knowledge of the issues, find innovative ways to explain to users why the design decisions were made as they were. Simple displays can be very effective in raising the overall level of awareness of environmental solutions. The self-conscious sustainable design process takes account of ten factors:

1. **Reduce energy use**. Work with the overall building designer to maximize the use of daylight, reduce the use of electric lighting and reduce overall energy consumption. Consider the use of operable windows.

2. **Use environmentally friendly building materials**. Select building materials based on their entire life cycle, to minimize waste and pollution at all stages while also protecting the health of the building users.

3. **Plan for user recycling**. Make it easy for the building's users to recycle by providing appropriate space and casework to sort and store recyclable materials both at the point of use—e.g., the coffee station—and at the receiving area of the building.

4. **Construction waste**. Provide for construction waste minimization in the specifications for each material as well as a recycling requirement in the general conditions of the specification.

5. **Promote indoor air quality**. Insure that the materials selected promote health with a minimum of off-gassing, that the building is well ventilated before occupancy and during use, and that microbial contamination is avoided. Ensure that the design limits opportunities for mold buildup in ductwork and elsewhere in the building.

6. **Program carefully**. Ensure that the overall program is necessary and minimized to reduce the overall use of resources.

7. **Long-term flexibility**. Design for flexibility in every way possible for the long-term use of the initial and subsequent users.

8. **Maintenance**. Ensure that the building is easy to clean and maintain.

9. **Learn systematically**. Work toward raising the overall environmental performance of not just a single project but all projects. Do this by learning from each to systematically improve your standard specifications, details, and other aspects of design. Use the LEED rating system (to follow) on all of your projects.

10. ***Share and demonstrate sustainability***. If we are to improve the environment for all, the knowledge of how to do so cannot be proprietary information. Share the knowledge gained with your colleagues and competitors as well as your clients.

11. ***Long-term value***. In all ways, think of the design in terms of creating an environment of long-term value.

Rating Systems

Over the last several decades, a number of different rating systems have been developed to evaluate the environmental performance of many things, including building materials. Several systems have been developed that specifically rate the overall environmental performance of buildings. The most widely known and complete systems include the BREEM system, developed in Great Britain in the 1980s and the BEPAC system, created in Canada in the early 1990s. Both of these systems attempt to model every material, system, and operational decision that goes into a building to arrive at a total impact of the building on the health of the earth. Both are computer models of great thoroughness and complexity. In the mid-1990s, both were considered by the new U.S. Green Building Council (USGBC) for a building rating system for the United States. However, the complexity of both systems limits their widespread use. The council decided to create a new building rating system intended specifically to be used as a design tool. That system, the LEED Green Building Rating System (see Table 16-1), under development for five years, was officially released in the spring of 2000.

LEED GREEN BUILDING RATING SYSTEM

The USGBC was formed in 1993. It is a consortium of building owners; material suppliers, contractors; architects, engineers; governmental agencies; and others involved in the design, construction, ownership, and operations of buildings. It is a mainstream organization dedicated to significantly improving the environmental performance of the built environment. The council is a consensus-driven organization.

The LEED Green Building Rating System was initially developed for commercial buildings. Other sections are now under development, including

TABLE 16-1

LEED Green Building Rating System, Developed by the U.S. Green Building Council

SUSTAINABLE SITES

Prereq 1 Erosion & Sedimentation Control

Credit 1 Site Selection

Credit 2 Urban

Credit 3 Brownfield Redevelopment

Credit 4 Alternative Transportation

Credit 5 Reduced Site Disturbance

Credit 6 Stormwater Management

Credit 7 Landscape & Exterior Design to Reduce Heat Islands

Credit 8 Light Pollution Reduction

SAFEGUARDING WATER

Credit 1 Water Efficient Landscaping

Credit 2 Innovative Wastewater Technologies

Credit 3 Water Use Reduction

ENERGY AND ATMOSPHERE PROTECTION

Prereq 1 Fundamental Building Systems Commissioning

Prereq 2 Minimum Energy Performance

Prereq 3 CFC Reduction in HVAC&R Equipment

Credit 1 Optimize Energy Performance

Credit 2 Renewable Energy

Credit 3 Best Practice Commissioning

Credit 4 Ozone Depletion

Credit 5 Measurement and Verification

Credit 6 Green Power

CONSERVING MATERIALS AND RESOURCES

Prereq 1 Storage & Collection of Recyclables

Credit 1 Building Reuse

Credit 2 Construction Waste Management

Credit 3 Resource Reuse

Credit 4 Recycled Content

Credit 5 Local/Regional Materials

Credit 6 Rapidly Renewable Materials

Credit 7 Certified Wood

ENHANCING INDOOR ENVIRONMENTAL QUALITY

Prereq 1 Minimum Indoor Air Quality (IAQ) Performance

Prereq 2 Environmental Tobacco Smoke (ETS) Control

Credit 1 Carbon Dioxide (CO_2) Monitoring

Credit 2 Increase Ventilation Effectiveness

Credit 3 Construction IAQ Management Plan

Credit 4 Low-Emitting Materials

Credit 5 Indoor Chemical & Pollutant Source Control

Credit 6 Controllability of Systems

Credit 7 Thermal Comfort

Credit 8 Daylight & Views

LEED Residential and LEED Interior Construction, which will more specifically address the needs of these industry sectors. Other sections will follow. In the meantime, the LEED Commercial Buildings system will serve well as a tool to help design teams make decisions.

The LEED Building Rating System is based on a series of prerequisites and criteria for various areas of the design. For criteria met, points are awarded reflecting the overall environmental impact of the various components of the building. Various levels of certification are awarded by the USGBC for point levels achieved. A fairly straightforward and user-friendly system to use, it has been designed specifically to help a team organize its decision-making process toward the goal of minimizing the overall environmental impact of a given building design. While LEED is probably not quite as accurate as the BEPAC and BREEM systems, it is likely to have a far greater impact on the environmental performance of buildings simply because it will be widely used. Moreover, it is a tool intended to be used in the design phase, helping to shape decisions, rather than just rating them after the fact.

FIGURE 16-16
In the Nidus Center for Scientific Enterprise, not only are the materials environmentally superior, but they are also on display for users and visitors. The Nidus Center was one of ten buildings to be awarded a LEED Rating during the USGBC's pilot program.

The rating system is generally performance-based rather than proscriptive. It encourages innovation and exploration of new ideas and solutions rather than relying on code minimums. A copy of the complete LEED Rating System as well as information about other resources can be found at http://www.usgbc.org.

Product Resources

Designers have available a growing list of resources for material information, systems and technologies and other aspects affecting the interior design of buildings. Some of the best of these include the following:

Environmental Building News:
http://ebn@www.buildinggreen.com.

- *Environmental Building News* is a very well researched and well written monthly newsletter concerning all aspects of building design. In addition, this organization produces a materials resource database and other educational materials. These include E Build and Green Spec. For the best use of this resource, subscribe to their services.

United States Green Building Council (USGBC):
http://www.usgbc.org.

- The USGBC is a consensus-driven membership organization formed to promote environmentally responsible building. The organization is responsible for creating the LEED rating system. They have a growing list of educational resources as well as the LEED Green Building Rating System. Designers should seriously consider joining the USGBC.

Green Building Resource Center: http://www.geonetwork.org.

- This is a web-based service with a wide variety of resources and links to other resources.

Environmental Protection Agency: http://www.epa.gov.

- This website offers a great deal of information on indoor air quality, emissions, and other topics. Links are provided to many other additional resources.

AIA Environmental Resource Guide

- A materials resource guide.

Environmental Design and Construction

- A bimonthly journal reviewing the latest in sustainable design and construction.

Sustainable Buildings Technical Manual: Green Building Design, Construction and Operations

- Published by the Public Technology and the USGBC.

Two excellent texts on sustainability in general are:

- *The Ecology of Commerce: A Declaration of Sustainability*, by Paul Hawken, New York, Harperbusiness, 1994.

- *Natural Capitalism: Creating the Next Industrial Revolution*, by Paul Hawken, Amory B. Lovins, and L. Hunter Lovins, New York, Little Brown and Company, 1999.

SUMMARY

We face serious threats to the environment and human health. Buildings are a significant part of that problem. They pose a particular challenge to the design industry. However, they also offer the design community an opportunity to improve the performance of our habitable environments, and at the same to have a significant overall impact on the world's environmental problem. The biggest single challenge, however, is for the design community to make sustainable design not only an option, but a requirement.

Notes

1

World Resources Institute.

2

Peter Raven, personal communication.

3

Mendler, Sandra, and William Odell, *The HOK Guidebook to Sustainable Design.*

Sustainable Design Resources in Print

A select list of resources we have found to be especially helpful . . .

GENERAL

Anderson, Ray. *Mid-Course Correction: Toward a Sustainable Enterprise: The Interface Model.* White River Junction, VT: Chelsea Green Publishing Company, 1999.

Hawken, Paul, Amory B. Lovins, and L. Hunter Lovins. *Natural Capitalism: Creating the Next Industrial Revolution.* Boston: Little, Brown and Company, 1999.

Lopez Barnett, Dianna, with William D. Browning. *A Primer on Sustainable Building.* Snowmass, CO: Rocky Mountain Institute, Green Development Services, 1995.

Public Technology and U.S. Green Building Council. *Sustainable Building Technical Manual: Green Building Design, Construction, and Operations.* Washington, DC: Public Technology, Inc., 1996.

ENERGY

Humm, Othmar, and Peter Toggweiler. *Photovoltaics in Architecture: The Integration of Photovoltaic Cells in Building Envelop.* Basel: Birkhäuser Verlag, 1993.

Illumination Engineering Society of North America. *Illumination Engineering Society of North America (IESNA) Lighting Handbook.* 8th ed. New York: IESNA, 1993.

Passive Solar Industry Council, National Renewable Energy Laboratory, Lawrence Berkeley National Laboratory, Berkeley Solar Group. *Designing Low Energy Buildings.* Washington, DC: Passive Solar Industry Council, 1997.

Watson, Donald, Editor. *The Energy Design Handbook.* Washington, DC: AIA Press, 1993.

MATERIAL RESOURCES

American Institute of Architects. *Environmental Resource Guide.* New York: John Wiley & Sons, 1997.

Good Wood Alliance. *Good Wood Directory*. Burlington, VT: Good Wood Alliance, 1996.

E Build. GreenSpec. *The Environmental Building New Product Directory and Guideline Specifications*. Brattleboro, VT: E Build, Inc., 1999.

Kalin and Associates, Inc. *Greenspec*. Newton Centre, MA: Kalin and Associates, Inc., 1996.

Leclair, Kim, and David Rousseau. *Environmental by Design: A Sourcebook of Environmentally Aware Material Choices*. Vancouver, BC: Hartley & Marks, 1992.

Mumma, Tracey, ed. *Guide to Resource-Efficient Building Elements*. 6th ed. Missoula, MT: Center for Resourceful Building Technology, 1997.

Small, Sally, Editor. *Sustainable Design and Construction Database*. Denver, CO: National Park Service, 1995.

Tree Talk, Inc. *Woods of the World*. Burlington, VT: Tree Talk, 1996.

Triangle J Council of Governments, Design Harmony Architects, and Abacot Architecture. *WasteSpec: Model Specifications for Construction Waste Reduction, Reuse and Recycling*. Research Triangle Park, NC: Triangle J Council of Governments, 1995.

INDOOR ENVIRONMENT

Sheet Metal and Air Conditioning Contractors' National Association (SMACNA). *Indoor Air Quality Guidelines for Occupied Buildings under Construction*. Chantilly, VA: SMACNA, 1995.

U.S. Environmental Protection Agency, Office of Air and Radiation. *Building Air Quality: A Guide for Building Owners and Facility Managers*. Washington, DC: EPA, 1991.

ECONOMICS

Dell'Isola, Alphonse J., and Kirk J. Stephen. *Life Cycle Costing for Design Professionals*. New York: McGraw-Hill, 1981.

CASE STUDIES

Rocky Mountain Institute. *Green Development: Integrating Ecology and Real Estate*. New York: John Wiley & Sons, Inc., 1997.

Vale, Brenda, and Robert Vale. *Green Architecture: Design for an Energy-Conscious Future.* Boston: Little, Brown and Company, 1991.

PERIODICALS

Environmental Building News. Brattleboro, VT: E Build, Inc.

Environmental Design and Construction: The Magazine for Successful Building—Economically and Environmentally. Troy, MI: New Business Publishing Company.

Indoor Air Bulletin. Santa Cruz, CA: Hal Levin/Indoor Air Information Service, Inc.

Interiors and Sources. North Palm Beach, FL: L.C. Clark Publishing Company.

The Green Business Letter: The Hands-On Journal for Environmentally Conscious Companies. Washington, DC: Tilden Press, Inc.

17

Design Research and Methodology

JUDITH HEERWAGEN, Ph.D.

The practice of interior design is like the practice of medicine in two important ways: first, design begins with problem identification and diagnosis; and second, it develops a solution (in medicine, a "treatment") derived from an understanding of the specific context and needs. However, interior design departs from medicine in one crucial way: it rarely conducts research to find out whether its "treatments" work. That is, does the design solve the identified problem? (In medical terms, is the diagnosis accurate?) Does the design result in improved comfort, performance, and pleasure of the occupants? Does it support the client's business strategy and needs? Present indicators of design "success"—costs per square foot or square feet per person—do not address these kinds of questions.

A skeptic might argue that interior design has functioned for a long time without a research base. Why is it important now? Several emerging trends are shifting the landscape for interior design, thereby increasing the importance of developing a strong research component at both the educational and professional levels.

- First, *more clients are developing a "show me" attitude. They are increasingly demanding justification for design decisions. When a designer claims that a new interior will increase productivity, clients are asking for evidence. When a designer claims that his or her firm's solutions are successful, clients are beginning to ask how they measure success. The firms who have the best answers to these questions are more likely to get the job.*

- *A second reason for developing a stronger research component in interior design is the emergence of performance-based contracting. While performance-based contracting has not yet become a big issue in interior design, it is increasingly being used in architecture, especially in energy-efficient design. Under this contracting system, the architect is not paid the full fee when construction is complete. Rather, a component of the fee is paid after the building has been operating for a predetermined time period. If the building performs as expected, the architect is paid the remainder of the fee plus a bonus. As we learn more about the relationship between health and interior environmental quality (especially materials selection and HVAC design), clients are going to be looking for designers who have a strong knowledge base in green design and who have some background in research methodologies for testing design outcomes.*

- *A third compelling argument for research is the growing interest in "learning organizations." A learning organization cannot exist without a strong research foundation. Learning is built upon deliberate and systematic inquiry: gathering information, assessing it, relating it to what is already known, testing predictions, and ultimately changing perspectives and practice on the basis of evidence.*

- *A fourth reason is to demonstrate a link between design and the goals and strategic interests of organizations. As facilities become more closely linked to business issues, there will be increasing demand for designers to show that a design is successful, not only from a comfort and aesthetic dimension, but also from a strategic perspective.*

Every design is a hypothesis. However, unlike hypotheses in scientific research, design hypotheses are rarely made explicit in projects. Instead, they remain nebulous constructs in the designer's mind. This chapter builds on the assumption that design hypotheses should be made more explicit and amenable to systematic evaluation.

DESIGN EVALUATION AND THEORY DEVELOPMENT

Research in interior design can take one of two routes. The first is design evaluation and the second is theory development. Design evaluation research is oriented toward real settings, especially assessing what works and what does not in a particular design. Theory development, on the other hand, focuses on understanding basic relationships and concepts. Whereas design evaluation is more likely to be done by design firms, theory development is more likely to be pursued in academic settings or research institutes. This chapter focuses on research tools and techniques that are most useful for design professionals.

Research is relevant to the whole design process and can contribute to design in many ways, including the following:

Programming

- Research can be used to identify problems, needs, and issues that are not immediately evident. Research processes in this context include surveys, structured interviews, behavioral observation, and ethnographic analyses. Although many firms engage in these data-gathering techniques, they are often not applied consistently across times, settings, and populations.

Design concept development

- Reviews of scholarly research can be used to generate new ideas and approaches to interior design problems. However, the design researcher needs to know where to look, what questions to ask, and how to interpret data from other fields in light of a particular design context. For instance, an extensive body of research on teams and teamwork exists in both psychology and organizational behavior, yet designers seldom use this literature to help them understand teamwork. Given the immense interest in creativity and innovation, research on these topics could also prove useful in developing new ideas and relationships for the physical setting.

Design evaluation

- Numerous techniques for post-occupancy evaluations have been developed in the past couple of decades, ranging from very sophisticated methodologies to simulations that provide feedback throughout the design process and implementation. Many of these techniques are already used in design, yet others are overlooked because they are presumed to be too difficult or costly to apply.

A couple of examples may help to illustrate the way research can contribute more fully to design. One highly relevant and timely issue concerns the link between communications processes and organizational innovation. It is often assumed that increased communication leads to innovation. However, scholarly research on innovation shows that increased communication is a

Research in interior design can take one of two routes. The first is design evaluation ... oriented toward real settings, especially assessing what works and what does not ... Theory development ... focuses on understanding basic relationships and concepts.

necessary, but not sufficient, condition for innovation. Other factors also matter, such as the nature of the work and how the organizational culture and policies affect workers' willingness and motivation to share information and work collaboratively.[1]

A recent study of a high-tech firm in Silicon Valley shows that many of the informal team spaces located in easily accessible locations throughout the building were seldom used. The designers had assumed that the technical staff worked in teams and that they needed to get together frequently and spontaneously. However, a post-occupancy evaluation showed that many of the engineers worked primarily alone, not in teams. Furthermore, when the engineers wanted to meet as a group, many found that the informal meeting spaces did not have the kinds of tools, equipment, and furniture they needed. The openness also made it easier for noise to spill into the private work areas bordering the group spaces. Similar results were found in numerous studies described by Sims et al.[2] This does not mean that informal team spaces should be abandoned. Rather, it means that their design should be linked more carefully to the nature of the work and the organizational context. In both the Silicon Valley study and in studies described by Sims et al. some groups found the informal spaces to be very useful and supportive of their needs. When this kind of variability exists (and this is almost always true in design evaluation), it is very important to understand what is producing the variability. For instance, were the teams or their projects different in some fundamental way? Did the spaces have different features and attributes that made some more useful than others?

Without a deeper understanding of these kinds of issues, design can go astray not only in small ways, but also in major ways. Brown and Duguid call this "design that bites back."[3] The example they cite is the decision by the advertising firm Chiat/Day to implement nonterritorial workspaces in its New York and Los Angeles offices several years ago. According to a case study presented by Sims et al., the objectives of the Chiat/Day workspace redesign were to reduce status distinctions, increase collaboration, build collective intelligence, improve quality of work, produce better/quicker products, raise the technology competence of employees, and give employees the freedom to work wherever they wanted. Employees were encouraged to store all information on their computers. If they had hard files they needed to be returned to hall lockers each night and checked out again the following morning. People moved files in portable holders and red wagons to the space where they wanted to work that day. There were team rooms, private spaces, club houses and coffee nooks.

What were the results of this experiment? On the positive side, Sims et al. identified increases in communication, better coordination within groups, a sense of team spirit, and increased access to employees at all levels in the organization. However, serious problems identified by Brown and Duguid led to the demise of the experiment and a return to a more traditional office design.[4] The problems identified by Brown and Duguid included the following.

- *Employees did not want to move around as much as the organization wanted them to. In the New York office, "peer policing" prevented people from "nesting"—e.g., using the same place every day.*

- *Because the spaces varied in their desirability, many employees arrived at work very early to stake out the best locations and thereby prevent others from using these desirable spaces.*

- *Employees, as well as managers, had difficulty locating one another, because everyone was always in a different place. Thus people spent a lot of time roaming around searching for colleagues.*

How could the Chiat/Day problems have been avoided? There are a number of points in the design process when research interventions could have been useful. First, the project would have benefited from a review of alternative workspaces in other organizations, to identify what worked and what didn't. Second, a more thorough understanding of work processes at Chiat/Day might have led the proponents of the nonterritorial office to question some of their basic assumptions. Third, when such a radical departure from current practice is suggested, it is always a good idea to do pilot tests using segments of the organization for experimental intervention before moving forward with the full design program. This enables designers and the organization leadership to identify behaviors and tasks that are most resistant to or amenable to change.

INTEGRATING RESEARCH INTO THE PRACTICE OF INTERIOR DESIGN

If research became an integral part of the practice of interior design, the benefits would be far reaching, including:

- *Increased ability to diagnose client context and needs*

- *Improved design solutions*

- *Development of an internal knowledge base as a foundation for design decision making*

- *Ability to provide clients with valid data from previous projects*

- *Development of metrics that measure the cultural, organizational, and human values of interior design—not just costs per square foot or square feet per person, or other commonly used data*

In today's demanding marketplace, each of these benefits could increase the competitive value of firms that make research an integral part of their practice. Many designers shy away from research out of fear that it is too difficult, too time consuming, and too expensive. Yet it may be more expensive in the long run to ignore research and the potential benefits it affords to those who embrace its potential. This chapter provides an overview of basic research concepts and methodologies relevant to interior design.

BASIC HUMAN-ENVIRONMENT RELATIONSHIPS

Human sensory systems evolved to aid adaptive information processing. Our sensory systems perceive colors, patterns, textures, views, sounds, aromas, light, and artifacts as information that enable us to determine whether a place is habitable and therefore likely to support our functional, social, and psychological needs.

The world that is presented to our senses would be overwhelming if it were not filtered through numerous psychological mechanisms that determine what's out there, what it means, and how we should respond, given our current situation. For instance, if you are alone in the office, the sound of a door opening and footsteps approaching you may mean something quite different if you are alone late at night than if it is early in the morning. In the morning you expect others to arrive, whereas at night you do not. The same information and environmental conditions can trigger very different responses. Because human response to the environment is so variable and influenced by so many factors, many people believe that valid and reliable relationships are impossible to identify. However, good design research and well thought-out hypotheses can go a long way toward overcoming these difficulties.

Human behavior in a given setting depends on the specific features and attributes of the design, the overall purpose of the space, the functions to be performed, and the capabilities and characteristics of the persons who will occupy the space. The implications for design are substantial and include the following points.

- *Environments, except in extreme cases, do not yield "main effects"— that is, they will not affect everyone in the same way.*

- *To design in a truly effective way, much more emphasis should be placed on understanding the variability in human perceptions, sensitivities, goals, work tasks, and work styles.*

- *Greater emphasis should also be given to developing ways to increase choice, flexibility, and variability so that people can select what works best for them under different circumstances.*

The goal of design research is to test these relationships and to build a more credible basis for design decisions. This by no means denies the importance of intuition and new concepts in design. Intuition and imaginative leaps will always be present in good design—just as they are in good science. However, research will help to separate intuition that works from that which falls short of reaching design goals and objectives.

OVERVIEW OF RESEARCH PROCESS AND METHODS

The following sections focus on a variety of research methods and techniques that can be used in design evaluation, with examples of specific applications and research studies. The section starts with general measurement issues, then discusses the most frequently used methodologies, and explore other techniques that are not as widely used, but that could prove to be very useful for designers.

Getting Started

Every design, as noted earlier, is a hypothesis and a practical experiment. By its very nature, design aims to solve problems by intervening in the environment in particular ways. However, both the design hypotheses and the design interventions need to be articulated. These are the foundation for research.

The following questions should be addressed before setting up a research project. Many designers may find it difficult to verbalize design in this way, because much of the design process is intuitive and nonconscious, relying on images, metaphors, and tacit knowledge rather than explicit knowledge and logical thinking. However, these steps are essential to research.

State the design hypotheses (these are derived from the goals and objectives of the design project).
- If you do X (go to a totally open space, reduce the size of offices), what will happen? What behavior change do you expect to see?
- On what basis do you make this claim? What is the logic behind it?

Identify relevant features and attributes of the environment.
- What do you need to manipulate to have this result (e.g., reduced partition heights, smaller footprint furnishings, more visual and aural access to others)?
- Why do you think this will happen?

Expected outcomes.
- What behaviors or other outcomes would tell you that your hypothesis has been supported?
- Why did you select these indicators?

An example may help. As noted earlier, organizations are very concerned with innovation, idea generation, and internal communications. In response to this, many designers are suggesting spaces to enhance informal interactions. Placed in the terms stated above, the hypothesis might look like this:

Design hypothesis.
- Informal meeting areas scattered throughout the workspace will lead to more interactions among workers, which, in turn, will generate more conversations and ideas of value to work. The underlying logic and basis for this hypothesis comes from numerous sources, many of which are intuitive rather than based on previous research. Reasons given for the value of informal areas include: people are more likely to join in a conversation if it is nearby, workers like to take a break from their work and need a different kind of place, informal spaces aid teamwork and spontaneous brainstorming and problem solving.

Relevant features and attributes of the environment.
- Informal meeting spaces in many organizations include the following features and their intended purpose: comfortable seating to encourage lingering, location in open areas adjacent to private workspaces to encourage casual teaming, white boards for discussions, good visual access into the spaces so others can see and hear what is going on and can spontaneously join in.

Expected outcomes.
- This component of design is usually not well articulated. However, to assess the impact of a design, the expected outcomes need to be clearly stated because these serve as measures of success. For instance, potential indicators of successful outcomes of informal team spaces might be increased use of the spaces, increases in the perceived value of the space by users, more frequent interactions among workers, greater generation and flow of ideas, increased knowledge of what is going on in the office, and an increased sense of belonging.

Setting performance goals.
- The design team and the organization need to decide together what degree of improvement they are working toward. Does even the slightest increase in the expected outcomes matter? Or should you aim for a 10 percent improvement, a 25 percent improvement? Setting performance guidelines will help in the evaluation of the research data. Scientific research uses statistical significance as proof of success. However, this may not be as useful to an organ-

ization. The degree and direction of change over time may be more relevant to organizational performance. Very few performance metrics yield statistical analyses to judge whether organizational changes are "working." Instead, managers look at the overall profile of outcomes and make a decision about new policies or procedures based on this.

Once these steps have been accomplished, it is much easier to identify the specific measures and methods to use in gathering data to test the design hypothesis.

Measurement Issues

Key measurement issues are criteria for selecting metrics, the use of control groups, the timing of the measurement process, and deciding how data will be used. Each of these topics is discussed below. The specific measures chosen should meet the following criteria:

- *Relevancy:* addresses the mission, goals, and objectives of the business unit and can be used in strategic planning.

- *Reliability:* produces consistent results when applied again.

- *Validity:* a good indicator of the outcome of interest (it measures what it purports to measure).

- *Efficiency:* using the minimal set of measures needed to do the job; enables conclusions to be drawn from the entire data set.

- *Discriminating:* small changes will be noticed and are meaningful (many workplace effects are likely to be subtle and may show small changes over time).

- *Balanced:* the metrics will include both quantitative and qualitative measures; direct and indirect measures. *Quantitative* data can be translated into numbers and used for statistical analyses. *Qualitative* data, on the other hand, often include interviews and results from focus groups that are more difficult to translate into numeric scales. Nonetheless, such data provide a rich understanding of the context and processes that make it easier to interpret quantitative results. Further, qualitative approaches are often used as a means to develop items for surveys and structured interviews or other data gathering mechanisms. The second aspect of a balanced family of measures is direct versus indirect measures of performance. *Direct* measures include outputs such as sales volume. *Indirect* measures are often correlated with performance or are the building blocks of performance rather than actual performance output. Examples are frequency of use, occupant satisfaction, or absenteeism.

CONTROL GROUPS

Because so many other factors can influence the outcomes you are studying, it is difficult to know whether performance changes are due to the workplace itself or to other factors that may change simultaneously. This is especially true when the design is part of an organizational change effort, which is often the case. Confounding factors may be internal to the organization (changes in policies or markets), or they may be external to the organization but nonetheless can affect business performance (such as economic conditions). The best way to avoid problems of interpreting the success of a design is to use control groups along with pre- and post-studies. An appropriate control group would be a business unit in the same building that does a similar kind of work, but is not going through a workplace change. The control group should be as similar to the design change group as possible.

The control group is studied at the same time as the group experiencing the design changes, with both groups studied during the "pre" and "post" design phases. Although the control group does not experience the design change, they get the same surveys or other measures at the same time. If the design has an impact independent of organizational issues, then the "pre" and "post" responses for those in the design change condition should show greater differences across time than those of the control group. Figure 17-1 illustrates this issue.

FIGURE 17-1
Degree of Change in
Communications after
Redesign.

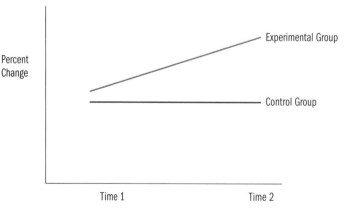

TIMING OF MEASUREMENT

The measurements should be applied before the change and after. The "post" measures should be done six to nine months after project completion, to enable workers to adapt to the new setting. The delay will help to diminish the "settling-in" phase, when problems may be most obvious and the workplace needs to be fine-tuned. It will also reduce the impact of a "halo" effect associated with being in a new or renovated space. After three months the sense of newness usually wears off.

PLANNING AHEAD: HOW WILL MEASURES BE USED?

From a strategic perspective, measurement is a tool to stimulate improvement. Thus, a critical part of the research process is to consider from the outset how the results will be used:

- *Who will receive the results and in what format?*

- *How will the results feed into future workplace projects?*

- *Will there be a central database on design research? If so, who will maintain and update it?*

- *How will information be captured and shared in the most useful way?*

- *How will the outcomes be integrated into a coherent whole?*

Specific Methods and Techniques

SOME KEY TERMS

Several terms used in research present a great deal of confusion. These are subjective versus objective measures, and qualitative versus quantitative measures.

Subjective assessment techniques, such as questionnaires, interviews, and focus groups, are used widely in the design profession during the programming phase and after occupancy to assess occupant response to the new environment. These are called "subjective" rather than "objective" techniques because they assess feelings, thoughts, perceptions, and attitudes that exist in the mind of the person. Objective techniques, in contrast, study things that exist independently of the mind—that is, the features and characteristics of objects. For example, a person's feelings about the amount of privacy experienced in a particular place is a *subjective* measure. The physical measurement of enclosure (e.g., height of partitions, presence of a door) and acoustics, all of which affect the perception of privacy, are *objective* measures. Subjective assessments use techniques such as rating scales, while objective assessments use physical measures that are translated into numbers (square feet, decibels, etc).

The differences between qualitative and quantitative methods are similar. *Qualitative* methods are used to assess subjective qualities of experience. Qualitative techniques include interviews and participant observation. The output of qualitative research is usually a verbal analysis such as identification of themes, concepts, and issues. *Quantitative* techniques, on the other hand, assign numbers to something being measured. Thus, survey data are quantitative because they use rating scales or categories that provide numerical outputs (e.g, average scores, numbers of people in different categories). Quantitative data also include measures of noise volumes, room area, width of corridors, work surface area, lighting levels. Thus, quantitative data can include both subjective and objective measures. Qualitative data, on the other hand, are subjective because the purpose is to identify aspects of experience and perceptions that are inherently subjective. An example may help. Open-ended interviews about people's perceptions of environmental quality are likely to elicit a wide range of concepts, perceptions, and experiences. Research using this technique would analyze the interviews and discuss key concepts and ideas. Future research might take some of these concepts and develop them into a survey instrument that could be used to quantify the perceptions—e.g., how many people share perceptions, what kinds of environmental conditions elicit particular perceptions, etc. If the scale is tested with large numbers of people and is shown to be a reliable and valid measure, it becomes a tool for quantifying environmental perceptions. The field of psychometrics has developed out of the belief that subjective impressions and feelings can be quantified.

SURVEYS

Surveys are used primarily in post-occupancy evaluation to assess occupants' overall satisfaction with the new space. Some key issues to consider in developing surveys are the following:

- *Identify what you want to find out and why.*

- *Develop questions only after you have outlined the information you need.*

- *Make sure to include questions that are of most value and that are related to your design hypothesis. (Many surveys totally forget this component and instead use a boilerplate survey for all projects.)*

- *Eliminate any questions for which data can be easily obtained in other ways (through surveys or administrative records).*

- *Word the questions in such a way that they do not suggest a right or wrong answer.*

- *Keep the survey to ten minutes or less.*

- *Allow for open-ended comments.*

- *Pilot-test all surveys and revise the questions based on feedback from these initial tests.*

- *Use the pilot test to check timing as well as understanding of questions.*

- *Keep survey results confidential, to assure that people will respond with their true feelings.*

Many design evaluation surveys ask respondents to rate both their overall satisfaction with specific environmental features as well as its degree of importance to them.

INTERVIEWS

Interviews are used when more in-depth information is desired than is possible to obtain with surveys, especially at the beginning of a project when little is known about the organization, its culture, or its ways of working. Interviews are more flexible than surveys and allow for follow-up questions. Individual interviews also enable employees to express their concerns and fears more freely—in contrast to focus-group discussions.

Interviews are often used to identify work processes and tasks, amount of time spent on different kinds of tasks, frequency of working in different locations, use of technology, organizational culture, and so forth. Programming

The authors hypothesized that people in windowless offices would use more photos and posters of nature objects or scenes as a way to compensate for the loss of contact with the outdoors.

surveys provide an overall snapshot of organizational life from the employee perspective.

The key drawback in conducting interviews is the length of time they take, both in doing the interview and in distilling the key insights and issues relevant to design decisions. This is especially difficult when there are opposing points of view that could lead to very different design outcomes.

Some suggestions for conducting interviews are

- *Do not ask questions that can be answered with a yes or a no, unless you intend to follow up with a probe (e.g., could you please explain why you feel that way?).*

- *Pilot-test the interview questions to test the length of the interview session and to make sure people understand what you are asking.*

- *When you set up times for interviews, tell the person how long the interview will last, what kinds of questions you will be asking, and what you intend to do with the information.*

- *Unless there is a specific reason not to do so, keep all interviews confidential so people will feel free to express their opinions and fears.*

Interviews are frequently used at the beginning of a project to gather information on work patterns. Questions typically focus on what people do, where they work most frequently, what kinds of technologies they use regularly, the importance of privacy and concentration to their work, and how frequently they work alone or with others. This information is generally used to develop individual and group workspaces.

FOCUS GROUPS

Focus groups consist of people who have some aspect of their life in common (researchers refer to focus-group members as "familiar strangers"). In an organization, focus groups frequently consist of those in similar job categories (same-level managers, clerical staff, administrators, scientists, and technical staff), those from the same administrative unit, or those who share similar environments.

Focus groups are especially useful in understanding different perspectives and for identifying the reasons behind people's opinions and perceptions.

They can be used throughout the design phase and as a post-occupancy evaluation technique. At the beginning of a project, focus groups are useful for identifying work patterns and existing problems, gaining a better understanding of the reasons problems exist, and identifying potential solutions. Focus groups can also be used later in the project to test worker responses to potential designs and to identify potential difficulties that may have been overlooked by the design team. As a post-occupancy technique, focus groups can be used to supplement surveys.

A key drawback of focus groups is that they do not provide information on how many people hold particular perspectives. For instance, if a problem is identified, the focus group will not be able to say how many people experience the problem or how serious it is overall.

Some key issues to consider in conducting focus groups are:

- *Limit the number of questions so that everyone will have a chance to talk.*

- *Aim to have about eight to twelve participants; larger groups make it difficult for all to be heard, and smaller groups limit the range of discussion.*

- *Involve all who will be affected by the design.*

- *In order to facilitate the free flow of ideas and concerns in organizational settings, hold separate focus groups for people at different job levels.*

- *Explain how information from the discussion will be used.*

The specific questions used to elicit discussion will depend on the purpose of the focus group. For instance, questions for groups formed to provide information during programming might include:

- *How do you work now with other members of your group or other groups in the organization?*

- *What types of work go smoothly, and when are there problems?*

- *What factors, either in the organization or the environment, facilitate or inhibit your ability to do your work?*

- *What could be done better, and why?*

PHYSICAL TRACES

Physical trace analysis looks for evidence of how people use a space. It includes assessment of accumulation of material (litter, dust, footprints), selective wearing down of materials associated with use (carpet wear, pathways through a lawn), and the artifacts that people use to personalize an environment. This technique is not often used in evaluating designs, but it could be a valuable addition to subjective measures.

For instance, personal artifacts provide clues about people's personality, interests, and lifestyles. Differential dust accumulation on books in a library suggests that some books are more popular and well used than others. However, physical traces research is often difficult to interpret because other variables that are not studied may be affecting the outcome. For instance, if dust accumulates more readily on books located on the top shelf, this may be due to differences in the difficulty of reaching the higher space for cleaning purposes, rather than to differential use of the books. This type of research is most useful when it is carried out in conjunction with other techniques.

Heerwagen and Orians used a physical trace approach in a study of how workers decorated their offices in windowed and windowless spaces.[5] The authors hypothesized that people in windowless offices would use more photos and posters of nature objects or scenes as a way to compensate for the loss of contact with the outdoors. They performed a content analysis of all non-work-related items displayed on office and cubicle walls for clerical and administrative staff at a large university. They found that workers in windowless spaces, as hypothesized, used significantly more décor with nature themes and surrogate views than similar workers in offices with windows. A majority of the images were positioned in the major field of view, suggesting that they are actually looked at, not just used as decoration. The research provides insights into the value of personalization and the inclusion of natural décor in the workplace.

ARCHIVAL DATA

Archival data are stored in records, either electronically or in hard-copy files. The current interests in productivity, absenteeism, and turnover rates make this kind of data highly valuable to researchers. The data are often used to assess the impact of a design, using a pre–post design analysis. In the pre–post design, data from a selected time period prior to the design change are compared with data from a similar time period after the change is imple-

They found that workers in windowless spaces, as hypothesized, used significantly more décor with nature themes and surrogate views than similar workers in offices with windows.

mented. Archival data can also be used to assess the impact of two different design treatments. In this circumstance, time-related effects that could influence outcomes are controlled. For instance, if absenteeism is assessed for different times of the year in a pre–post study, the differences in illness could be due to seasonal incidence of flu or colds and not to design features. For this reason, most studies using archival turnover or absenteeism data usually assess data for a full year pre and post.

Ulrich used hospital archival data to assess the impact of window views on patients' recovery from surgery.[6] All patients were in the same wing of the hospital, but half of them had views of a small cluster of trees (the "tree" group) and the other half had a view of a brown brick wall (the "wall" group). Ulrich hypothesized that views of nature would have a positive impact on patients' well-being in the hospital. The hypothesis was based on previous research showing that exposure to natural environments, especially trees and water, is associated with positive feelings, heightened interest in the external environment, and reduced stress. The study relied totally on archival data stored in patient records. Data analysis showed that patients who had the natural view stayed significantly fewer days in the hospital, took more mild analgesics, and had more positive recovery processes than the matched group of patients whose view consisted of the building façade.

Archival techniques have also been used by researchers to assess the relationship between productivity and design. In one frequently cited study of personal controls in individual workstations, Walter Kroner and his colleagues studied clerical workers in an insurance company.[7] The company automatically recorded the number of forms processed by each worker on a daily basis. The researchers used these data to assess the impact of personal ambient controls on work performance, using a pre–post study design with workers tested in both the old and new workstations. Unfortunately, the switch to the high-control workstations occurred at the same time as a move to a new office building that differed in fundamental ways from the space in which the baseline data were gathered. The new building was located in a natural prairie setting with trees and a small pond; the old building was in a suburban setting. The new building also had more windows and more open space. As a consequence, most workers in the new building had a view to the outdoors, compared with only a small percentage in the old building. These differences between the buildings made it more difficult for the researchers to determine the extent to which the increases in work performance were due to the general features of the building or to the specific workstations.

These complications are frequent in office design. New designs often are accompanied by new organizational policies and staffing changes. This makes it much more difficult to assess the impact of the design independent of the other factors. The next section deals more closely with these issues and discusses several methods for increasing the validity of design research.

Some key issues to consider in using archival data are

- *Data should be assessed to assure that recording is performed in a consistent manner over the time period of interest. If recording policies have changed during the time period of the study, the data are no longer comparable.*

- *In order to assure confidentiality of records, names should be deleted and a subject number assigned in place of an individual's name.*

- *Understand what the data do and do not represent. For instance, some firms do not distinguish between absenteeism due to personal illness and time taken off to care for sick family members. Thus, if the intent is to look at the impact of the design on illness, it cannot be validly assessed through such absenteeism records. Illness would need to be assessed in a different way.*

BEHAVIORAL OBSERVATION

Behavioral observation is used to identify what kinds of activities occur where, how often, by whom, and for what purpose. The observer uses a layout of the space or a recording sheet that lists the spaces. Behaviors are identified through pilot testing and are coded for ease in transmitting to paper. Although the technique can be time consuming, it is useful when little is known about how a facility is used or when specific behavioral changes are sought. Although it is possible to ask workers what spaces they use and how frequently, these data tend to be unreliable because memory for spatial experiences is not accurate, especially if the behavior is habitual. Also, much behavior is unconscious, and people are not always aware of how they are reacting to a space–especially when their focus may be on a task or on other people. The steps involved in doing a behavioral analysis include the following:

1. ***Conduct preliminary observations to develop behavioral categories.*** This step involves spending time in the existing environment, observing the general flow of activities and behaviors. The outcome of this initial stage is referred to as an "ethogram"—an overview of the general activities and behavioral modes in a specific setting.

2. ***Conduct pretests to assure consistency among observers.*** Behaviors of interest to the research project should be identified and discussed with the researchers who will be doing observations in a pretest situation. Each person should record data independently. After the test period is completed, the group reconvenes to assess the degree of agreement among the data collectors. This process is continued until sufficiently high agreement is obtained to assure that individual observers are rating behaviors in the same way. Agreement of 80 percent or higher is desirable.

3. ***Gather data in existing space.*** The data should be gathered at a variety of times and days of the week over the course of two to three weeks. Periods of intense activity as well as low activity levels should both be included, in order to capture the overall use patterns of a space.

4. ***Gather data in new space.*** The same process and time schedule should be used in the new space to enhance the validity of comparisons. Additional behaviors and categories may be added if the observational period shows that different activities occur in the new space.

5. ***Analyze and compare the two spaces.*** This phase produces the final data output for the behavioral analyses. Primary focus is on changes in frequencies of behaviors, with special attention given to the kinds of activities the new space is designed to promote.

Data Analysis

For design evaluation purposes, data analysis should be kept simple and easy to understand. This section is broken down by data analysis appropriate for specific kinds of methodologies.

SURVEY DATA

Frequency data and mean scores can be used to assess survey data and to compare the old and new spaces. A couple of examples follow. Figure 17-2

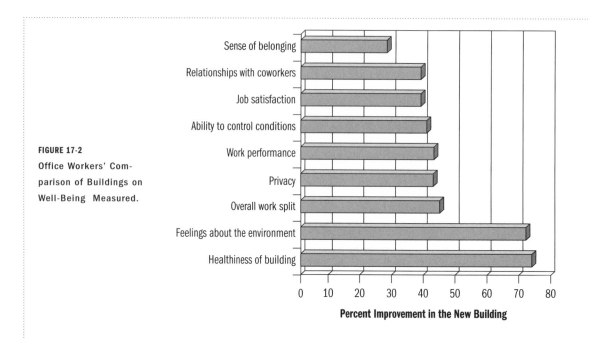

FIGURE 17-2
Office Workers' Comparison of Buildings on Well-Being Measured.

shows data from a study of a new green building in Holland, Michigan, the Herman Miller Green House.[8] The study from which the graph is taken was a pre–post analysis of occupant comfort, satisfaction, and well-being in the old and new buildings. The graph shows the percentage of occupants who experienced positive changes in well-being measures between the old, standard building and the new green building.

Mean scores are frequently used to develop "profiles," as in Figure 17-3.

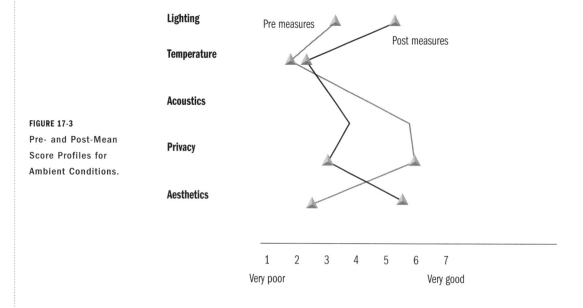

FIGURE 17-3
Pre- and Post-Mean Score Profiles for Ambient Conditions.

BEHAVIORAL MAP DATA

Analysis of behavioral data is frequently displayed on floor plans that show the spatial distribution and frequency of behaviors in different locations.

PHYSICAL TRACES

The study described above by Heerwagen and Orians used content analysis to describe the features of items used to decorate walls in windowed and windowless offices.[9] The content categories were summarized in a simple 2×2 format as shown in Figure 17-4.

FIGURE 17-4

	Windowless Offices	Windowed Offices
Surrogate Views	96	32
Non-views	99	50
	195	82

FOCUS-GROUP AND INTERVIEW DATA

Data from focus groups and interviews must be analyzed qualitatively rather than quantitatively. This means that extensive notes or transcripts need to be made during the sessions. These are read numerous times to identify key themes and issues, especially differences and commonalities among groups.

For example, a series of focus groups conducted by the author for a large financial firm assessed how well a new office design was meeting the project goals. Separate focus groups were held for each of the office units, with managers meeting separately to encourage free and open discussion by their staffs. The groups were asked to rate their perceptions of the degree of progress toward four design goals (all of which were oriented around collaboration, information sharing, and sense of community). After the ratings, each of the goals was discussed and participants were asked for specific examples to explain their rating. The group was also asked to identify environmental and organizational factors that enhanced or inhibited progress toward goals. The data analysis compared perceived inhibitors and enhancers across units as well as differences in perceptions between managers and staff. For instance, one of the goals was to increase cross-unit collaboration, yet very few examples of increased collaboration were mentioned. In fact, most staff felt that there was no inherent reason for them to work across units. In this case, an organizational solution was needed to develop cross-unit projects that would provide a need for collaboration. The environment alone cannot produce collaborative behaviors.

Data Interpretation

When data analysis is complete, the project reconsiders the design hypotheses and asks: Do the data show support for the hypotheses? Very few scientific research studies show complete support for all hypotheses and predictions. Thus, we would not expect to find perfect alignment in design research. Where misalignments occur, it is important to try to understand why this happened. Data analysis could show one of several patterns:

- *The hypothesized results occur.*

- *There is no change pre and post.*

- *The outcomes are affected, but in the opposite way.*

- *Mixed results—some support the hypothesis, others do not.*

This stage is one of the more difficult research processes, particularly when some results are positive and others are negative. We want to focus on the positive and ignore the results that don't turn out the way we expect. However, it is often more valuable to understand why things went wrong. First, you don't want to repeat the mistakes. A second value in understanding negative results is that you often learn more because it forces a rethinking of basic assumptions and a search for further links between the environment and the behavioral outcomes.

For instance, the study on team spaces for the Silicon Valley firm, discussed previously, found that many informal spaces located in hallways were not used. The reasoning behind the design was very logical: because people use corridors frequently and because these are often the location for brief greetings and conversations, people who meet by chance should have the opportunity to sit down and talk further, and others passing by or in adjacent offices should be able to join in. Hence, the design included comfortable chairs, visual openness, and white boards for spontaneous work. The spaces, however, were seldom used, and many of those who did use them found the spaces unsatisfactory. A post-occupancy survey revealed these reasons for the low usage and dissatisfaction: the vast majority of work done by the software engineers in this building was individual effort rather than team work, thus they had little reason to meet spontaneously and frequently in groups in the informal spaces. Meetings were held in conference rooms with appropriate technology. Many also complained about the openness because it created noise that was bothersome to people in nearby offices and because it lacked privacy for group discussions, particularly those requiring security. A third reason for the low ratings was the lack of functionality. Chairs were difficult to move and could not be usefully arranged to allow all to have good views of one another and of the white boards. Thus, the spaces were difficult to use for meetings. And they were seldom used for casual relaxation because the intense work pace of the firm left little room for casual social interactions. The research in this case provided important insights that are now being used to redesign group workspaces that are more appropriate to the nature of work in the company.

A couple more examples of negative results show different lessons learned. In the focus groups discussed earlier that were conducted with the financial organization, one of the stated design goals (e.g., hypotheses) was that collaboration between units of the organization would increase if more interaction spaces were provided. The design included a central commons, numerous small and medium-sized conference rooms, and open workspaces with tables and white boards. Members of the focus groups pointed out that while collaboration *within* units had greatly increased, collaboration *between* units had not. The reason was simple: there was no reason for the units to work together. They did not share clients, tasks, work products, or anything else that would naturally bring them together. The head of the center had made cross-unit collaboration an important goal, but no one had thought about how to accomplish this organizationally.

Another example comes from the Herman Miller Green House study mentioned earlier. In addition to assessing the occupant responses in an extensive pre–post survey, the study also assessed organizational-level success measures using the Total Quality Metrics (TQM) data gathered by Herman Miller for its manufacturing plant. The study had hypothesized that the new green design would improve overall productivity and success because of the enhanced interior environmental quality. Unfortunately, the data analysis showed only modest improvements of less than 2 percent across all TQM measures. However, when data were analyzed relative to the baseline, it was obvious that there was actually little room for improvement. The organization was already operating at such a high level of effectiveness (98.7 percent on-time delivery) that big improvements were not possible. This suggests that other measures of organizational success should have been used instead.

INTEGRATING RESEARCH FINDINGS INTO THE ORGANIZATION

The point of doing research is to improve design by learning more about the effects of the designed environment: what works, what doesn't, and why in a particular context?

The frenetic pace of design work today doesn't often leave time for this kind of reflection, but efforts should be made. When research is done, it often is relayed only to the client and not to the rest of the firm. Internal lectures, seminars, and discussion groups can be used effectively to internalize the lessons learned so that future designs can build upon the successes and avoid the failures of past design projects. Many design firms have recently implemented internal learning components, primarily for continuing education purposes but also for generating an internal design knowledge base. These structures should be exploited and expanded to include Internet-based, enterprise-wide databases and examples. In addition to serving as an internal learning mechanism, such tools would also be useful in marketing and proposal development. Showing data along with photos of spaces in use (rather than the typical design photo devoid of people) would show a knowledge and concern out of the ordinary and would give added value to the firm's talk about fulfilling the goals and needs of clients.

Notes

1

Allen, T. J., *Managing the Flow of Technology: Technology Transfer and the Dissemination of Technical Information within the R&D Organization*, MIT Press, Cambridge, MA, 1977; and T. Amabile, "A Model of Creativity and Innovation in Organizations," in B. M. Staw and L. L. Cummings (Eds.), *Research in Organizational Behavior,* Vol. 10, JAI Press, Greenwich, CT, 1988.

2

Sims, W. R., M. Joroff, and F. Becker. *Teamspace Strategies: Creating and Managing Environments to Support High Performance Teamwork*, IDRC Foundation, Atlanta, 1998.

3

Brown, J. S., and P. Duguid, *The Social Life of Information,* Harvard Business School Press, Cambridge, MA, 1999.

4

Brown and Duguid, *The Social Life of Information.*

5

Heerwagen, J., and G. Orians, "Adaptations to Windowlessness: a Study of the Use of Visual Décor in Windowed and Windowless Offices," *Environment and Behavior*, vol. 18, no. 5, pp. 623–630, 1986.

6

Ulrich, R., "View through a Window May Influence Recovery from Surgery," *Science,* vol. 224, pp. 420–421, 1984.

7

Kroner, W., J. A. Stark-Martin, and T. Willemain, *Using Advanced Office Technology to Increase Productivity,* Rensselaer Polytechnic Institute: Center for Architectural Research, Troy, NY, 1992.

8

Heerwagen, J., "Do Green Buildings Enhance the Well-being of Workers?" *Environmental Design + Construction Magazine,* July/August 2000, pp. 24–29.

9

Heerwagen and Orians, "Adaptations to Windowlessness."

Suggested Further Reading

Aranoff, S., and A. Kaplan. *Total Workplace Performance: Rethinking the Office Environment.* Ottawa: WDL Publications, 1995.

Becker, F., M. Joroff, and K. L. Quinn. *Toolkit: Reinventing the Workplace.* Atlanta: IDRC Foundation, 1995.

Horgen, T. H., M. L. Joroff, W. L. Porter, and D. A. Schon. *Excellence by Design: Transforming Workplace and Work Practice.* New York: John Wiley & Sons, 1999.

Sundstrom, E. *Work Places.* New York: Cambridge University Press, 1985.

18

Global Practice

Dr. FRANCIS DUFFY, RIBA

Design quickly follows money and money always follows power. Baroque architecture was the international language of the Counter-Reformation and is found everywhere from Poland to Brazil. Lutyens and Baker, and their lesser followers, rolled out the iconography of the British Empire throughout India and Africa and Palestine. In the great post–World War II period of American economic imperialism, Skidmore, Owings & Merrill performed a similar service worldwide for corporate giants. Arguably, in the 1980s, following the deregulation and globalization of the banking industry, London only just managed to survive as one of the three great international financial services centers, by rapidly importing great chunks of U.S. know-how in office design. Each of these episodes marked a change in the international scope and the ambition of the design professions.

However, architectural and design projects are inevitably site specific. Most are tiny. This is why the vast majority of design and architectural practices operate on a highly local basis. Robert Gutman, one of the very few sociologists who have taken a serious interest in the architectural profession, tells us in his book, *Architectural Practice: A Critical View* (Princeton Architectural Press, New York, 1988), how few large practices there are, and how very many small ones. In the late 1970s—there is no reason to believe that the overall shape of the figures is substantially different today—there were 25,000 architectural offices in the United States, of which half were one-person offices doing minor jobs. One-half of the remaining 12,500 had fewer than five employees, including technicians and support staff. Only 10 percent of these practices employed more than 20 employees. Two percent of the total 250 firms had more than 50 employees, and these firms collected 30 percent of all fees for architectural services. More up-to-date information from *World Architecture*'s October 2000 survey of the world's largest interior design practices reveals a huge range from the largest practice to the smallest, even in the already highly selected group of the top 100 firms. The biggest Top-100 interior design practice, Gensler, employs 980 interior design staff and has a fee income of over $150 million. At the bottom of the list are 17 firms that employ no more than 10 interior designers and whose annual income is mostly less than $5 million. U.S. firms take the top seven rankings worldwide. There are 55 U.S. firms in the top-100 list and 25 UK firms. No other country can boast more than 3.

Unlike accountants and management consultants—the top firms in these professions are household names, notorious for their ubiquity—and unlike even advertising agencies and product designers, the vast majority of interior designers and architects really do still seem to prefer to work locally. Perhaps they find it difficult to transcend the tight boundaries of national contractual and regulatory frameworks, of local building practices and materials, in order to deliver architectural and design services intercontinentally to clients, many of whom in this era of mergers and acquisitions, are rapidly globalizing. It takes a very particular kind of design practice to succeed internationally and an even more particular kind of practice to combine international reach with substantial, in-depth, local capability.

This chapter addresses the changes that must be made in the delivery of architectural and interior design if the emerging demands of international clients are to be met. The experience described in this chapter is entirely of office design, but the same conclusions apply, *mutatis mutandis*—with the suitable or necessary changes—to other great areas of potential growth for international design, such as retail and sports facilities.

HOW INTERNATIONAL CORPORATE REAL ESTATE HAS DEVELOPED

In the 1950s, office architecture was already being used by certain globalizing businesses to establish their brands internationally. Interior design was being used, even more frequently, for the same purpose. International organizations also frequently used design standards for internal reasons—e.g., to reinforce corporate values in order to buttress corporate discipline. These were the two commercial motives that, from the 1950s right through the 1970s, shaped the classic design programs of such exemplary commissioners of international design services as IBM and Olivetti. Corporate real estate centers imposed the highest design standards on acquiescent, international branch offices, standards that were vetted by designers of the caliber of Eliot Noyes and Ettore Sottsas, and maintained by elite teams of highly skilled, in-house project managers.

Such enlightened design programs, of course, were always exceptional in office design. Cost control and variety reduction, following a logistical, quasi-military model, were much more frequent determinants of the quality of international corporate real estate. The chief instrument by which these more humdrum objectives of international corporate control were achieved was by imposing so-called corporate standards, volumes of rules, specifications and procedures, written, as it were, randomly in diverse locals and rolled out, it has to be said, without much discrimination or local sensitivity, everywhere from China to Peru. Since the beginning of the 1980s, corporate standards have tended to become ever more functional and cost driven. The growing bias toward distancing corporate real estate from strategic business considerations has been encouraged over the last two decades by the increasing professionalization of facilities management and, even more recently, by the ever more popular corporate habit of outsourcing all noncore service functions, including real estate and facilities management. This is the entirely logical, and probably inevitable, consequence of stripping property assets off company balance sheets in order to concentrate capital on what were thought to be essential business objectives.

The Linkage Between Design and Corporate Strategy

Design is likely to become more rather than less important to international business. Today, at the beginning of the knowledge-based economy, real estate, buildings and interiors, can be used more powerfully than ever before as instruments of technological and cultural change. Office design is becoming, at least in a growing number of leading businesses, intimately related to corporate strategy. The paradox is that, as the working environment becomes potentially more and more useful and central to business at the highest level, the operational day-to-day practice of corporate management of real estate has become ever more detached from strategic intent. In many organizations the use of design for strategic business purposes has effectively been ruled out by formulaic cost-cutting procedures. For example, outsourcing corporate real estate, however attractive for short-term financial and administrative reasons, more or less completely divorces it from direct managerial control—and sometimes blots it totally out of managerial awareness, let alone sensitivity or concern. If this is true, as it seems to be in Silicon Valley, where no one has time any more to think creatively about real estate, it is even more likely to be the case in the far-flung, complex, and expensive-to-manage networks of international offices.

Meanwhile, the attitudes of ordinary international corporate real estate executives are changing. Centralized control, on the military model, is certainly on its way out—probably because it is an inherently labor-intensive and expensive way of doing things, whatever triumphs of penny-pinching have been achieved along the way. Under current circumstances everyone on the international circuit in corporate real estate seems to be overstretched, even more starved of time and resources than their colleagues in the United States. Where once hundreds of project managers serviced a large corporation's properties spread across, let's say, the whole of Europe, today the same workload is handled by half a dozen overworked people, always buttonholed, constantly on the move. In these circumstances, and especially given spectacularly rapid growth in certain sectors, attempts to control corporate real estate centrally are liable to be easily ambushed by local practices in brokering, design, and construction.

A related but even more important crisis is the increasing tension between corporate real estate and user interests. Real estate management structures, under the severe pressures described above to cut costs and to outsource wherever possible, are finding it extremely difficult to cope with increasingly empowered users. The French are no easier to deal with than the Germans, and why should the Japanese be any easier than their colleagues in Hong Kong? Economic, demographic, and technological changes are all converging to create a new kind of office workforce, with an entirely different profile, whose expectations of the working environment are increasing and whose potential to create trouble, if not always to effect change, is very much on the increase.

It is interesting to compare European international real estate practice with North American procedures: European businesses operating in the United States have been generally reluctant to import their own standards and procedures and are far more likely to adopt local customs than their U.S. counterparts operating in Europe. This may be partly because of a longer tradition of corporate real estate practice on that side of the Atlantic. It also has to be said that it has been noticed that North American office users are prepared to accept environmental conditions that are much poorer than those to which ordinary office workers have become accustomed in the last two or three decades in Scandinavia, Germany, and the Netherlands (but not, incidentally, for different reasons, in the UK, France, and Italy). American readers may not be aware of how homogenous American corporate culture appears from the European perspective. Despite the federal system and a vast geography, 200 years of a common culture and 100 years of Taylorism have made all U.S. offices—not to mention much of the rest of the paraphernalia of American life—look very much the same wherever they happen to be. Americans, perhaps without realizing it, tend to assume that uniform office design standards *ought* to prevail everywhere in the world, just as they do at home. If they don't find consistency, they impose it. Europeans, from long experience of big cultural and linguistic differences, are much more tolerant of diversity.

CHALLENGES FOR INTERNATIONAL CORPORATE REAL ESTATE

Two fundamental problems facing corporate real estate in the international context remain intractable. These are, first, how to deal with potentially ballooning user demand for better-quality working environments that are strategically related to business purpose, and, second, how to reinvent corporate real estate delivery so that it can keep up with the accelerating rate of change.

The same fundamental economic and technological pressures are working everywhere, although at different rates and on different time scales, depending on relative national wealth and faster and slower rates of technological development. What makes a controlled international design response difficult is that these economic and technological pressures are overlaid by three further levels of complexity—international differences in wage levels and occupancy costs, differences in culture, and differences in the organization of professional services. Architects and designers who wish to work internationally must be prepared to respond to wildly different wage and cost structures, to very different national—and indeed regional—cultures, and to different, and sometimes illogical and contradictory, regulatory systems and modes of practice.

There are five different ways in which international corporate real estate can currently respond to these challenges. The first is to ignore the problem, simply adopting local working practices, more or less in the European way

Americans, perhaps without realizing it, tend to assume that uniform office design standards ought to prevail everywhere in the world, just as they do at home. If they don't find consistency, they impose it.

mentioned above. The second is to throw large project management resources at the problem in an attempt to impose an external order, in the old-fashioned American corporate way. The third is to outsource, which means, in practice, running faster and faster, attempting to deal with problems as they arise. The fourth is to explore ways of providing seamless international delivery packages through unions of developers, realtors, designers, furniture manufacturers, and construction companies. The fifth is to go even further in the direction of outsourcing, relying on specialist providers like Regus and HQ that treat office space as if it were a hotel accommodation in which services are paid for by the minute instead of the real estate way of paying for square feet by the year.

None of these possible responses is likely to be good enough for emerging, knowledge-based businesses, especially given the pressures that are already building up today at the crucial interface between real estate providers, whose power is weakening, and end users, whose power is tending to increase. Designers and architects are accustomed to working at the interface between the supply-side industries—property, construction, and furniture—and the demand side, that is, the people who have to put up with office space every day of their lives. Too often people responsible in house for corporate real estate, and indeed facilities managers as well, are being forced to resist, even to deny, user pressure as if they are now merely a powerless extension of the supply chain. In this situation the designers in the middle, mediating between the suppliers and the customers, have the opportunity to become much more inventive—provided they are prepared to understand, and to become involved with intricate, sometimes passionate, and always risky organizational politics.

Within international corporate real estate departments the pressure toward central control, standardization, and variety reduction are stronger than ever before, largely because of diminishing resources. However, the administrative imperative to control and to simplify is being resisted by even stronger user pressures toward cultural and operational diversity. Everyone who has worked internationally for corporate clients will be very well aware of the classic and ongoing conflict between corporate headquarters and national and regional offices. "I'm from HQ and here to help," is an ancient joke. This ancient managerial turf war is currently being exacerbated by the major structural changes, already mentioned above, in the profile of employee expectations. As all organizations move, in some sectors and in some countries, perhaps more rapidly than others, to shedding low-level clerical staff, increasing dependence on attracting and retaining more and more empowered office workers becomes an increasingly strong imperative. People who are free to make their own choices in the disposition of their space and time also expect to be much more closely involved in the design process. Such people will want at least as much discretion at their workplaces as they enjoy at home and in every other department of their increasingly complex lifestyles. Even more important, ambitious senior managers in advanced and rapidly changing businesses are showing increasing impatience with conventional real estate procedures and standards. They don't like the standard of service that is on offer today. They want to get their own hands on the tiller. They want to shape office space themselves to accelerate and sustain organizational and cultural change.

GENUINE DIVERSITY AND PSEUDO-DIVERSITY

Office users, however intelligent, do not always know the right questions. Nor do office suppliers know all the answers.

One of the difficulties that designers face when designing offices for global businesses is to distinguish between how much diversity is desirable and how much is necessary. Sometimes genuine reasons for regional and operational differences exist. Sometimes pseudo-justifications are invented to buttress convenient cultural differences or to disguise functional similarities. National predilections are often cited as self-evidently sufficient reasons for justifying particular ways of using office space, such as the French preference for enclosed, hierarchical, cellular office rooms, or the German enthusiasm for the super-democratic combi-office, both contrasted with the passive American tolerance of the cubicle and of the deep, more or less windowless open plan. What might work in Dallas or Palo Alto cannot possibly, given such nationalistic formulas, ever work in Dusseldorf or Paris. Such allegedly fundamental differences in space use are, more often than not, simply ploys in the corporate turf wars mentioned above—especially when it is claimed that the same simple preferences should apply indiscriminately across entire countries. In office design, all-encompassing generalizations should always be regarded with suspicion. In fact, in the design of corporate offices, it is always differences within nations, sectors, and organizations that are more interesting than similarities.

Sectoral differences, e.g., between the way the electronics industry and the legal profession use space, are usually much more powerful predictors for design solutions than supposedly monolithic national cultures. Sectoral differences tend to be grounded in process—which is more accessible to observation and to testing than folkloric opinion. The varying culture of organizations themselves is often strong enough to override national stereotypes. Moreover, on closer examination, different subcultures often coexist totally legitimately within the same organization. Such intraorganizational differences are likely to multiply as increasingly diverse cultural and technological structures develop parallel with the knowledge economy.

International Differences in Use of Space

Generalizations about national patterns of space use can be as misleading to designers working internationally as corporate real estate's longstanding centralizing tendency to ignore or iron out inconvenient cultural and geographical differences. There are indeed many genuine factors that should be used with total justice to differentiate North American office design culture from Northern European, from Pacific Rim, or from Latin American. Oddly enough, business-driven, international corporate real estate people have long often ignored two financial differences to which one would have expected them to be very sensitive: staff income and real estate costs. Conventional international corporate space standards are not usually designed to be sensitive to variations in staff salaries and office rents from city to city. It seems very perverse that the same amount of space should be allocated per person in Houston, London, Tokyo, Santiago, and Cape Town, when the differential between earnings in these cities is a factor of five, and between costs of office space is even more.

Air-brushing out meteorological, cultural, and technological differences is equally common. In environmental matters, air conditioning is certainly not required everywhere in the world. In social and cultural affairs, attitudes toward time, gender, and health vary widely. In relation to work processes, there is still a two- or even three-year gap between the take-up of information technology in Europe compared to the United States, and an even wider gap between Europe and other parts of the world.

It will be hard, however, for corporate real estate to ignore a relatively new factor that is introducing a new dimension of diversity into international office design. This is the changing patterns in the use of space over time–daily, weekly, yearly–that are the consequence of ubiquitous networks of robust information technology that allow people, in effect, to invent their own timetables, wherever they happen to be. One practical consequence will be space use intensification in the office, as businesses realize how mobile people are becoming both inside and outside the office. Another practical consequence will be the renaissance of city life, as the importance of unscheduled social and intellectual contact is realized in an increasingly virtual world. Exactly what the new conventions in the use of time and space should be, we don't yet know. But we do know that they won't be as simple as the five-day week and the eight-hour day.

Three plausible, if somewhat cynical, conclusions may be drawn from all these observations. The first is that for corporate real estate purposes, what has mattered most is making the lives of those who deliver and manage corporate real estate internationally as easy as possible. The second is that, from a national point of view, what has mattered most in relation to international corporate real estate norms has been protectionism, i.e., manipulating the market to protect local suppliers. The third is that neither of these considerations should be allowed to have anything to do with designing the kinds of office accommodation that twenty-first-century businesses really do need today as they struggle to develop their international competencies in a period of very rapid change of every kind.

CULTURAL FLUENCY AND ORGANIZATIONAL PLURALITY

Recognizing that some similarities and differences in international real estate are legitimate while others are mere fabrications (smoke screens invented for selfish national or corporate reasons) is an essential step forward for designers who genuinely want to understand how they should best service such a complex market. There is absolutely no doubt that many design opportunities do exist internationally and that design imagination of the highest order will be necessary to satisfy what will certainly be a rapid increase in demand for innovative design by expanding global organizations and business networks.

Cultural Fluency and Design Sophistication

What North American designers particularly need to realize is that they have become accustomed to what has become a dangerously self-sufficient, inward- and backward-looking, conservative office design culture. The convenience of suppliers has been allowed to bear far more weight in office design than the needs of the users. The almost universal success of the homogeneous North American office model in the twentieth century has now turned into a serious problem for internationalizing design practices. Conventional off-the-shelf design solutions, weighed down with Taylorist iconography, are certain to be increasingly challenged in the twenty-first century. The challenge is likely to be felt with particular acuteness by practices hoping to operate overseas where the supply chain is under most strain and where the need for design invention to achieve strenuous corporate objectives is greatest. In existing international design practices, diverse forms of practice and alternative ways of doing things already provide a relativistic stimulus: differences *can* be legitimate; innovation *is* possible. New ways of working are likely to lead to further disintermediation of the supply chain and to yet more democratization of the design process. Neither the cookie-cutter approach of old-fashioned corporate design delivery nor the nationalistic shortcuts of prefabricated design solutions will continue to be tolerated. Users will demand more design imagination and more specialized design services. Hence the need in international practice for greater design sophistication and for far more cultural fluency.

Feedback is an essential component of success for both designers and user clients. Feedback implies infinite possibility for change and improvement. More measures of how well buildings perform in relation to business strategy will become critically important. And, important as measures of how well buildings have been delivered and maintained undoubtedly are, measures of how buildings can be used are even more important.

Standardization Versus Diversity

Given the choice in office design between standardization and diversity, there is no doubt that we now live in a more complex commercial world where greater diversity has now become very much more preferable—and is perhaps even the key to business survival. Standardization of components, layouts, and design elements is only a very primitive way of simplifying delivery, which, of course, is only a small part of the users' problem. Knowledge-based clients, equipped with the most powerful information technology, no longer want to be limited by routine ways of doing things, however efficient. To be more effective they need to reinvent themselves continually. The people who work for them are already highly mobile. They are more and more willing to choose when and where to work.

The choice for design firms is not simply between working abroad and staying at home in the comfort zone of the familiar, American market for office design. The choice is more and more between two sharply contrasted models of design practice, which have big international—and North American—implications. The first is what might be called the imperialist model—even though it has long been familiar even within the democratic United States: a few very large firms rolling out low-cost, standard solutions, offering minimum content and expecting even less feedback, with zero responsiveness to local conditions. The second is the developmental model: many smaller but more intellectually acute, more mobile practices offering open-ended, thoughtful, imaginative responses both to particular and to changing conditions; capable of learning from different physical and commercial environments; enjoying maximum invention through maximum feedback. The first model was the only way in which the earlier part of the twentieth century, with all its intellectual and logistical limitations, could attempt to solve its clients' global office design problems. The second model was made possible by new technology and is obviously better suited to the far more challenging, but much better networked, conditions of the new century.

CONCLUSIONS

International design practice is demanding. However, this is the moment to try it out, because it is the new frontier where innovation is most likely to occur. The users need us. The old corporate real estate structures have become overstretched and dysfunctional. In the globalizing world of commerce, there is everything for designers and architects to play for. It is a world where small practices, well networked, can operate more nimbly than the dinosaur imperialist design practices of the past. New alliances with suppliers–developers, real estate brokers, contractors, furniture manufacturers, information technology suppliers–will be possible because none of the old logistical procedures is working properly any more. But what will keep these new alliances straight, unlike the old ones, is the ethical pressure of designers constantly having to fight for and articulate emerging client and end-user interests. It is this innovating attitude that will give designers and architects the power to change the world.

This is the most challenging field of design practice and the one in which the new rules for user-based design will be invented–rules which eventually may even find their way home.

Bibliography

Duffy, Francis. *Architectural Knowledge*. London: E&FN: Spon, 1998.

Duffy, Francis. *The New Office*. London: Conran Octopus, 1997.

Duffy, Francis. "Forty Years of Office Design." *Architect's Journal*, 2 November 2000.

Gutman, Robert. *The Architectural Profession: A Critical View*. New York: Princeton Architectural Press, 1988.

King, Anthony, Editor. *Buildings and Society*. Routledge, 1981.

Moore, K. Diaz, Editor. *Culture–Meaning–Architecture: Critical Reflections on the Work of Amos Rapoport*. Ashgate: Aldershot and Burlington, 2000.

van Meel, Juriaan. *The European Office: Office Design and National Context*. 010 Rotterdam: Publications, 2000.

Royal Institute of British Architects (RIBA). *Strategic Study of the Profession*. London: RIBA, 1991–1995.

Yeang, Ken. *The Green Skyscraper*. Munich: Prestel, 1999.

19

Specialty
Practices

CHERYL DUVALL, FIIDA

As a profession matures and evolves, it is inevitable that certain practice areas begin to emerge as specialties, requiring specific expertise to address their individual complexities. Interior design is no exception. Just as one may seek the services of a "family doctor" in the medical profession, but later need to visit a dermatologist for a specific need, so might a corporate client encounter similar circumstances in requiring interior design services.

Generally, the core services provided by interior designers follow the six basic phases of design: programming, schematic design, design development, contract documents, bidding and negotiation, and contract administration. Yet these core services may not meet all of a corporate client's needs. As a result, design professionals have developed specialty practices to add supplemental services to their professional repertoires. These ancillary services are related directly to the core services but address the client's needs with more depth and breadth than a general practitioner would. This attention to detail generally requires more time from the designer and thus generates more fees. Even though the cost to the client rises, if the designer executes these ancillary services well, the client enjoys a valuable return on his investment.

Some design professionals may seek a career path focused on one or more specialty services because these services make the best use of a particular set of skills they have already identified. Some may feel most comfortable working in the six basic phases of design, as generalists. Some may simply fall into a specialty as a matter of chance. And for many designers, an initial choice or chance may seem to have set a course that would be difficult to alter. Yet whatever their initial professional choices, all designers should be aware of the directions in which specialty practices take the profession of design. Without this awareness, a designer can fall behind in a competitive market for the best projects, lose a chance to strengthen a client relationship, make a misjudgment about building a design team, or miss an opportunity to develop professionally in the most productive and personally satisfying way possible.

Specialty practices related to the interior design profession are numerous, and new practice areas are developing each year. Designers have traveled widely divergent career paths as they seek, or perhaps stumble upon, their optimum professional role in one or more specialty practice areas. To that end, each category below will highlight real-life examples of interior design professionals who have enjoyed professional growth and experiences in providing specialty practices, outside the core services of interior design, to identify not only what sort of work specialty practices entail, but also the types of personal characteristics that make specialty practitioners successful. For the purposes of this chapter, three broad categories of specialty practices will be addressed: facility management, workplace consulting, and short-term design. Within each of these broad headings, the most prevalent specialty areas will be addressed. Additionally, because the interior design professionals providing these services often work on-site with the client, or may be hired on a contractual basis, a focus on outsourcing will be included in this chapter.

FACILITY MANAGEMENT

Facility management, as defined by the International Facility Management Association (IFMA), is "the practice of coordinating the physical workplace with the people and work of the organization. It integrates the principles of business administration, architecture and the behavioral and engineering sciences." Because many clients of interior designers are facility managers, it is only natural that designers have developed specialty practices in interior design in response to the needs of the facility management profession. As interior designers observe, study, and listen to their clients who are facility managers, they have identified particular needs that require special attention and focus. For some designers, such as those who provide computer-aided facility management (CAFM), specific training is required. Often, the facility manager does not have the time, resources (whether staff, equipment, or funding), expertise, or desire to provide the necessary services in-house. Thus, several specialty practice areas related to facility management have emerged that logically may be provided by interior designers. The four most prevalent areas are churn work, relocation services, CAFM, and owner's representation.

Churn Work

"Churn" in the workplace is simply defined as the movement of workers. Churn is inevitable, and is regarded as a necessary characteristic of a growing and dynamic business. Typically, churn occurs as a department increases or decreases its staff as a natural course of business. For example, a facility manager may receive a call from a department requesting additional workstations or offices to accommodate five additional staff members. Sometimes such a request is easily accommodated—for example, if the neighboring department happens to have five vacant workplaces. More often than not, however, even such a small request can result in a domino effect, requiring that the facility manager not only move people but also reconfigure systems furniture (workstations), demolish full-height partitions, and construct new ones. This "churn work" becomes a subset of interior design, requiring space-planning skills as well as furniture inventory, specification, and construction documentation services.

A facility manager often has in-house staff that is responsible for answering the churn requests in the company. However, he or she may also contract these services on the outside, usually with an "on-call" arrangement, by which an interiors firm may have an agreement to provide churn work as needed, based on an hourly rate or otherwise negotiated fee. Churn requests can be so common in a corporation that it can easily keep one or more persons busy on a full-time basis.

Corporate decisions cause churn to occur. Corporations are constantly adding people, rightsizing, downsizing, reorganizing, merging, acquiring, selling off divisions, creating new divisions, or changing for the sake of change. Elizabeth Seidel, an in-house interior designer and facilities services specialist with the Black & Decker Corporation, defines churn as "the constant movement of people." She cites many reasons why churn occurs, including the obvious, such as hiring people or moving a department. Yet any change at all to an employee's status often involves churn, such as a promotion, which may involve moving to another location in the company or to a private office, or an internal job transfer.

Naoto Oka, a design manager with the World Bank, is involved with churn on a daily basis. He says, "Churn work is like washing clothes in a washer. The size of the container remains the same but what is inside changes locations. If you use the right detergent, it gets cleaner. If you don't, things just get more entangled." He identifies the churn work process as a simple and logical progression:

- *Identify the client's needs.*

- *Establish a game plan.*

- *Sell the plan to the clients.*

- *Prepare drawings.*

- *Implement the plan.*

Elizabeth Seidel has also observed that churn work involves the same activities as an overall new design project. In her opinion, "You can apply the same general design principles to churn work. You need to resolve how your client is going to function. Will the design be functional as well as aesthetically pleasing? Is the cabling and telecommunications supportive? The whole scope of work that a designer would address in an overall large design project is also addressed in churn work, just often on a smaller scale." She describes the following typical activities:

- *Meet with clients to gather and assess needs.*

- *Interact with clients on ongoing basis (hand-hold through the process).*

- *Create the move team that will disconnect and reconnect.*

- *Be sensitive to both end-user requests and corporate mission.*

- *Assist in political negotiations.*

- *Be conscious of cost as though money is your own.*

- *Be concerned for life safety and building code issues.*

- *Coordinate and work cooperatively with a team of people.*

- *Interact with vendors (furniture installers, electricians, data technicians, etc.).*

Seidel lists six personal traits that are important for any interior designer to possess when involved with churn work as a specialty practice area of inte-

rior design: the designer must be flexible, passionate, politically savvy, coura-
geous (ability to do the hard things), desirous to please, and supportive of
corporate policy. She notes that she has performed churn design services in
virtually every job position she has held in her 14 years of professional experience. Those positions have included work as a staff interior designer at
furniture dealerships, private interiors firms, and in-house facilities departments. In each case, the steps were basically the same and required a mastery of personal communication and management skills.

Interior designers play a vital role in assisting companies to understand
churn, plan for it, and strategize the means and methods of managing churn
for future opportunities. Seidel has worked in companies where churn was as
high as 63 percent annually, where she moved 750 people of a total workforce
of 1,200 in one year. The typical percentage of employees moved is somewhat
lower. The International Facility Management Association (IFMA) typically
reports on the average rate of churn in their Benchmark Reports, which in
1997 published an average rate of churn of 44 percent among their respondents. Wise companies will track their rate of churn in order to determine its
overall cost to their organization and consider ways to reduce those costs as
appropriate with corporate objectives.

Churn will always exist. In its simplest form, it is a box move, where people and their boxed possessions move while furniture, fixtures, and equipment remain. But many companies have not invested the money or effort to
achieve these simple box moves, or believe that "box move churn" does not
agree with corporate goals. To reduce the cost of churn through "box moves,"
designers must be flexible in planning, adhere to corporate standards, and
adopt universal approaches to individual needs. Some companies embrace
this approach. For others, the higher cost of churn is acceptable in light of
other corporate objectives. Whatever the corporate policy, churn will always
be present, and interior designers who focus on churn as a specialty will
always find a demand for their services.

Relocation Services

Design professionals provide relocation services as a specialty practice for
those clients who require assistance in managing the physical move of the
relocation process. These services may include any or all of the following relocation components: security coordination, coordination of telephone and

data equipment relocation, furniture management, employee assistance (pre-move consultation, training, and post-move orientation to new space) and the screening, hiring, and overseeing of vendors who actually implement the physical move.

By retaining a relocation specialist, a facility manager is assured that all aspects of the move process are adequately addressed and that the physical move will occur in a safe, efficient, and cost-effective manner. This is especially important in situations where the facilities staff is not able to devote the appropriate time and effort to overseeing all the aspects of a move. A relocation specialist will be concerned with all the major components of the client's relocation impacting both scheduling and costs of each move project. These components include:

1. Lease termination

2. Key business periods

3. Security issues

4. Communication requirements

5. Specialty equipment

6. Food service needs

7. Records storage

8. New and/or reused furniture

9. Construction schedule

10. Building logistics

Although many companies are able to provide these services in-house, it has become increasingly common for a facility manager to subcontract this service. Denise Wesen, manager of plan design and project management for the St. Paul Companies, explains: "We want to keep our internal workforce stable. Since work comes in cycles, we want our staff to be consistently busy. Outsourced consultants fill in for us during the busy periods, enabling us to reserve the lulls exclusively for our internal staff." She believes that relocation services is one of the services under her umbrella that she can outsource effectively, to the right service provider.

RELOCATION CONSULTING CHECKLIST

The following is a comprehensive list of services available for (CLIENT) to comprise a customized Relocation Services package.

PROJECT START DATE   PROPOSED MOVE DATE   PROPOSED COMPLETION DATE

PRE-MOVE COORDINATION

○ Project Initiation Meeting
○ Prepare & Maintain Master Project Schedule
○ Project Meetings
○ Programming
○ Client Meetings
○ Meeting Minutes
○ Space Planning ○ Develop ○ Review
○ Progress Reports
○ Tagging Existing Furniture
○ Tagging Equipment
○ Site Visits
○ Mover Walk Through
○ Prepare Move List
○ Color Coded Move Plans
○ Temporary Signage
○ Room Number Floor Plan
○ Arrangement for Box Delivery
○ Coordinate with Tel/Data
○ Coordinate with General Contractor
○ Interim Moves
○ Other:

FURNITURE COORDINATION

○ Inventory Existing Furniture
○ Determine Furniture for Re-Use
○ Verify New Furniture Counts
○ Furniture Selection
○ Furniture Specification
○ Track New Furniture Orders
○ Schedule Installation
○ Schedule Elevators & Loading Docks
○ Punchlist New Furniture
○ Arrange for Existing Furniture Touch Up
○ Arrange for the Liquidation of Existing Furniture
○ Other:

VENDOR COORDINATION

○ Prepare RFP's for Vendors
○ Copy Machines
○ Plants
○ Artwork
○ Vending Machines
○ Coffee & Supplies
○ Paper Supplies
○ Cleaning
○ Movers
○ Signage
○ Stationary/Change of Address
○ Other Equipment:
○ Other:

EMPLOYEE PREPARATION

○ Write and Distribute Move Guidelines
○ Pre-Move Meetings with Entire Staff
○ Pre-Move Meetings with Client Representatives
○ Move "Event" Planning
○ Other:

MOVE COORDINATION

○ Supervise Moves from "To" Locations
○ Supervise Moves from "From" Locations
○ Verify Receipt of All Items
○ Interim Moves, Existing Site
○ Other:

POST-OCCUPANCY EVALUATION

○ Coordinate the Removal of All Boxes
○ Punchlist Move
○ Post Occupancy Adjustments
○ Furniture & Ergonomic Evaluation
○ Wrap Up Meeting by Phase
○ Wrap Up Meeting Upon Final Completion
○ Project Closeout
○ Other:

OTHER

○ Phased Move(s)
○ Professional Staff Services On-Site

FIGURE 19-1

Interior designers are well suited to provide this service. Interior designers have been trained to pay attention to details, and to care about all aspects of the interior, especially the satisfaction of the occupants upon move-in. Yolanda Mazzoni is an interior designer who often has the project assignment role of relocation specialist. She says, "My role as a relocation specialist allows me to use my expertise with design, furniture, construction, and management and apply it to a role that provides clients with a well-rounded individual that is able to lead, plan, and manage minute detail. The strategic aspect of the planning involved in large complex scenarios is challenging. It is very similar in nature to master planning. The results are black and white. It can be either successful or it fails. When the proper planning is in place, it is always successful and rewarding." Tom Bay, an interior designer who is working as a project manager at the Pentagon, agrees that interior designers are well suited for this specialty practice area. According to Bay, "Usually architectural firms are hands off as far as relocation services are concerned. Even interior design firms were not interested in performing these services after the early 1990s recession. The younger designers are not familiar with the tasks that are required, nor do they understand the furniture aspects that comprise much of the relocation services. This can be viewed as a good thing. Interior designers and architects have refocused on their original goals and calling. This refocus has left a void. And voids result in opportunities for others. For those interior designers who are "old geezers," relocation services represent something we always did. For me, I fell into relocation consultation by accident. Water seeks a void in a downhill struggle. It's a natural flow. There will always be a need for these services, and my background offers the experience that many younger designers just don't have or want to have."

The relocation specialist works with key members of the client's staff and assumes primary responsibility for the relocation process. He or she offers guidance to the client regarding the preparation of the facilities and the communication to the employees affected by the move. The specialist works closely with the client in developing requests for proposal (RFPs) to forward to potential vendors and identifies any outside consultants and/or vendors that may be needed. (See Figure 19-2.) A relocation specialist may perform any or all of the following tasks:

- *Establish a realistic budget and schedule.*

- *Assign responsibilities.*

- *Coordinate vendors and contractors.*

- *Qualify and select move vendors.*

- *Provide furniture management.*

- *Coordinate specialty areas.*

- *Prepare employees.*

- *Provide on-site coordination.*

- *Perform post-move evaluation (see Figure 19-3.)*

Yolanda Mazzoni's services are designed to take companies through a step-by-step process of decision making during the entire relocation process. She describes the process as a team process: "The process begins with the formation of internal and external project teams who set goals and objectives for the move; continues with monthly target dates for meeting set goals and objectives, and ends with a post-move-in evaluation. Generally, the most complex relocation tasks are those involved in the phased relocation and reuse of existing furniture and equipment for the new facility. There is serious work involved in organizing the relocation process that could be overwhelming to an inexperienced team. Creative use of tools and carefully defined procedures minimizes employee downtime, equipment downtime, lost production, and interruptions to customer service."

The typical candidate profile of a relocation specialist reflects a very organized and detail-oriented individual. He/she must be able to interact with all types and levels of individuals from the temporary "move vendor" employees to the client's CEO. The most effective individual is one who is very familiar with furniture systems, electrical/data coordination, and general construction practices. Marci Porritt, an interior designer, was introduced to relocation consulting as an outsourced provider, planning and supervising a series of small moves for an insurance company. She then provided outsourced relocation management at the World Bank, with two other interior designers, moving 4,300 bank employees over an 18-month period: "We handled all of the pre-move activity and vendor coordination. From Thursday through Sunday we would supervise the actual move activity, and on Monday morning we would handle the post-move adjustments." Naoto Oka, a design manager at the World Bank, simply defines such relocation services

(Mr., Ms.)
(Title)
(Company)
(Street)
(City, State, Zip)

RE: Request for Proposal
       Moving Services
       (Project)

Dear (Name)

(Corporation) will be moving into new facilities in (address). The site will consist of buildings; a (#) square foot office building. The employees and equipment will be coming from (#) facilities located in (City) (refer to Exhibit A).

At this time, we are planning a (#) phase move between (dates/dates). Please note that moves will be conducted during regular working hours, overtime hours, weekends and holidays.

Please furnish me with your proposal in accordance with the enclosed Moving Specifications and Proposal Data Sheet. Any proposal, which does not follow this format, will be rejected. In addition, we ask that you complete the enclosed Vendor Qualification Sheet for those vendors whose information is currently not on file with the (Corporation) Purchasing Department.

We are arraigning pre-bid meeting to familiarize you with all the facilities and their contents. It will be held on (date). Please plan on meeting at (time) at (location).

Sealed bids are due on (date/time). Please send an original and three (3) copies to:

(Company)
(Street)
(City, State, Zip)
(Individual)

(Corporation) reserves the right for final vendor selection. Any and all proposals may be rejected at the discretion of (Corporation) may terminate the contract for Moving Services at any time.

If you have any questions regarding this Request for Proposal, please contact me at (#)

Very truly yours,

(Individual)
(Company)

FIGURE 19-2
Standard Request for Proposal (RFP)
for Professional Moving Services.

I. PROPOSAL DATA SHEET

A. PRICING	RATES: UNION		NON-UNION	
STRAIGHT TIME/HOUR				
○ Helper:	$	/Hr.	$	/Hr.
○ Driver & Truck	$	/Hr.	$	/Hr.
○ Supervisor:	$	/Hr.	$	/Hr.
○ Foreman:	$	/Hr.	$	/Hr.
SATURDAY				
○ Helper:	$	/Hr.	$	/Hr.
○ Driver & Truck	$	/Hr.	$	/Hr.
○ Supervisor	$	/Hr.	$	/Hr.
○ Foreman:	$	/Hr.	$	/Hr.
SUNDAY				
○ Helper:	$	/Hr.	$	/Hr.
○ Driver & Truck	$	/Hr.	$	/Hr.
○ Supervisor	$	/Hr.	$	/Hr.
○ Foreman:	$	/Hr.	$	/Hr.
HOLIDAYS				
○ Helper:	$	/Hr.	$	/Hr.
○ Driver & Truck	$	/Hr.	$	/Hr.
○ Supervisor	$	/Hr.	$	/Hr.
○ Foreman:	$	/Hr.	$	/Hr.

B. Please price the individual moves per exhibit (#)

II. FEE'S QUESTIONNAIRE

○ Are your rates portal to portal?	○ Yes ○ No
○ Or, do you charge mileage?	○ Yes ○ No
○ If yes, what is your charge/mile?	$ /mile
○ What is considered overtime?	Before a.m. After p.m.
○ What is your minimum billing charges?	$
○ Tote Size (s)	$ /ea.
○ What would you charge to distribute the totes?	$ /hr.
○ Labels	$ /roll

III. EQUIPMENT QUESTIONNAIRE

List the type of trucks you have available.

....

....

....

....

Do you own the trucks or are they leased?   ○ Own   ○ Lease

Do your men have radios and beepers?   ○ Yes   ○ No

Please furnish the types and quantities of equipment you have available to move computer hardware.

....

....

....

....

How many dollies do you own?

....

Are the wheels made of rubber?

....

IV. The moving company will be responsible for protecting the facility during the move (i.e., masonite laid on all pathways from elevator or port of entry to office area, chipboards, corner protectors, etc.)
Please describe the method you use to protect the building and floor from damage.

....

....

....

....

V. Please state the name if the rigging company you will be using, if applicable.

....

VI. Terms of Payment:

....

VII. (Corporation) insurance requirements are specified in Exhibit (#). Please acknowledge your concurrence with these limits.

....

....

....

VIII. Do you agree with (Corporation) Specifications for moving services listed on the previous page?

○ Yes   ○ No

FIGURE 19-2 (Continued)

POST-MOVE REQUEST

Please complete this form and return it to your Department's facilities contact after moving into your new work space

NAME

DATE

LOCATION

EXTENSION

URGENT!

DESCRIPTION OF PROBLEM

○ Telephone – not functioning

○ Voice Mail – not functioning

○ Terminal/Computer– not functioning

○ Electrical – no power

○ Missing Items (please check Lost & Found)

○ Network Connection

○ Security Badge – not working

○ Other (please describe)

NOT URGENT

DESCRIPTION OF PROBLEM

○ Telephone – training, cords, setup

○ Furniture – repairs, adjustments, missing pieces

○ Keys – missing or broken

○ Other (please describe)

REPORT OF DAMAGE DURING MOVE

DESCRIPTION OF PROBLEM

○ Damaged furniture workstation, office,

○ Damaged equipment – computer, printer

○ Damaged walls, floors, etc.

○ Other (please describe)

Please note that all requests will be prioritized and responded to in order received.

FOR FACILITIES/TELECOMM USE ONLY

DATE & TIME RECEIVED   BY

DATE & TIME REFERRED   BY

REFERRED TO: NAME

RESOLVED: NAME

○ Facilities   ○ Property Mngmt

○ Yes/Date

○ Security   ○ Tel/Data

○ No/Reason

○ Other

FIGURE 19-3

A Post-Move Evaluation Form benchmarks
client's assessment of the move process.

as "you move things which belong to somebody else to a new location using your common sense."

Tom Bay states that the personal characteristics he finds most important in a good relocation specialist include: good listening skills, good problem-solving skills, proactive initiative, ability to think on feet, excellent follow-through, and ability to anticipate unknown challenges. Denise Wesen agrees and adds that it is extremely important to have "a very thick skin. The relocation specialist needs to recognize when he or she has done a good job even if the end user is exhibiting stress. Let it be water off a duck's back. This is especially important if a group has been through a reorganization and people are nervous." Marci Porritt adds that "a positive attitude and lots of energy" are two personal traits that seem vital to the success of a relocation effort.

As with most projects, the key to success is good communication among all parties. Because the move team is comprised of varied individuals with diverse backgrounds, it is especially important that the relocation specialist identify and involve key individuals in all aspects of the planning as early as possible. The remainder of the team may grow or shrink depending on the phase of the relocation and the current tasks to be accomplished, but a core group of key individuals should be consistent throughout the project. The relocation specialist defines the communication and approval processes, and identifies on the schedule and task lists the party responsible and their progress. Wesen notes that the end-user contacts are always involved as a member of the team, yet "it is important for the professional to be in control. We recognize their concerns, and work cooperatively, but we must uphold the fact that we are the professionals in this particular field. It is our primary responsibility to foster good communication that will set realistic expectations." The expertise of each vendor is considered an integral part of the process and a valuable addition to the team. Mazzoni reflects that "the common mistake that many relocation specialists make is when they believe that their way is the best and only way to accomplish the task. There is always a better way to complete a task. Listen, assess, and lead."

Computer-Aided Facility Management

Computer-aided facility management (CAFM) provides organizations a full range of comprehensive facilities-related information that is linked to computer-aided drawings (CAD). The database and linked drawings can easily provide significant facilities-related tools such as up-to-date as-built plans, rent chargeback information in square feet, and accurate inventories of furniture, fixtures, and equipment (FF&E) items. CAFM systems provide facility managers with easy access to information that assists them in determining and tracking the most cost-effective use of the company's real estate and facilities assets. With this information, they are able to plan for future space needs, demonstrate how business units grow and change, understand the impact of new technologies on space use, streamline costs and processes related to managing churn, and provide hard data to substantiate facilities strategies. Often, other internal departments become involved or contribute to the need for this centralized information, such as real estate, human resources, information systems, records management, and telecommunications. The CAFM specialist may be called upon to help in the programming phase of the full-service, six-phase design project, or to track the evolving needs of an entire organization—to the benefit of the company's overall health as it grows.

Interior designers utilize CAFM capabilities to provide accurate and valuable data to assist their clients in important decision making that is related to the planning and design of their facilities. Adriana Stanescu, an architect from Rumania, has been immersed in CAFM for many years. She describes CAFM as "a software platform, a visual information manager that ties maps, floor plans, organization charts, pictures, and diagrams to numeric and textual information. So, CAFM is the tool that enables corporations to manage a large group of assets quickly yet effectively." (See Figure 19-4.) Laurie Gathwright, an interior designer real estate analyst with the Corporate Real Estate Department of T. Rowe Price Associates, describes CAFM as encompassing "a broad range of services, from simply managing space information and drawings within a software package to creation of a 'visual resource manager' in which assets from multiple departments are tracked. I define CAFM as the utilization of electronic tools to aid in the management and planning of real estate and its related resources. The related resources may be any asset that exists within or around a real estate facility, and the associated lease information. CAFM can also be described as an information warehouse in which data that is utilized by many different departments can be stored."

A facility manager may retain these CAFM services as a specialty practice provided by the interiors firm, or he may assign internal staff to provide these services. Before designers can exercise fully the benefits of CAFM,

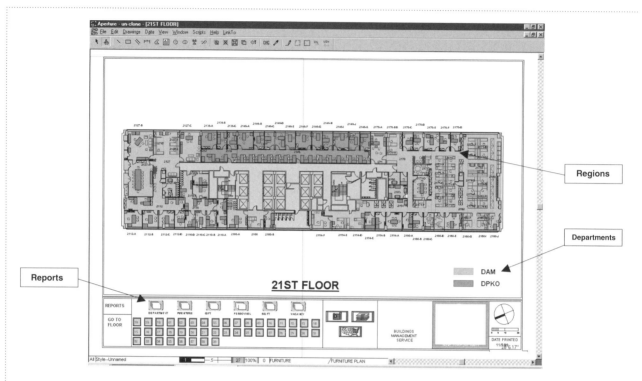

Floor Plan

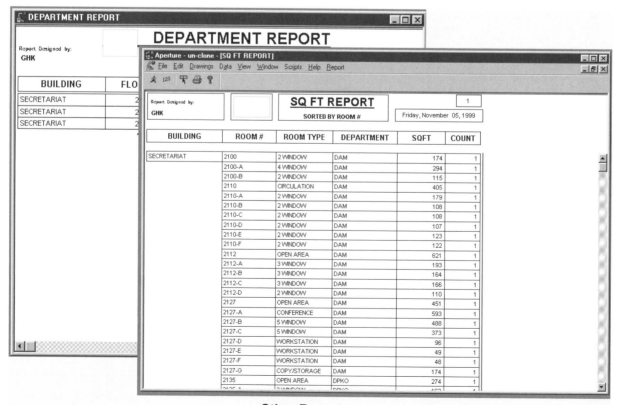

Other Reports

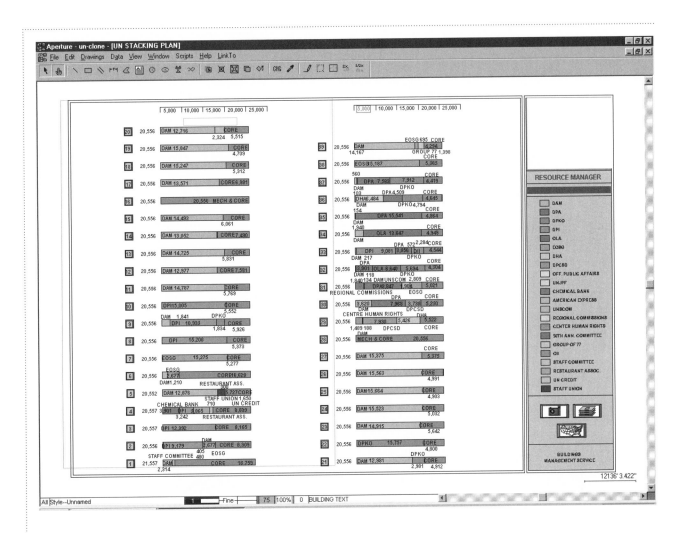

Stacking Diagram

FIGURE 19-4
CAFM, a "software platform," enables corporations to manage their facilities.

they need special training and continuing education. Stanescu, who provides outsourced CAFM consulting to the United Nations, believes that "consultants working in this particular field need first to become fully knowledgeable of the capabilities of the system that they are going to employ. There is no way to interact with clients without mastering the system first. Also there is a need for flexibility and silent acceptance of redundancy on the part of the consultant. That is because the clients rarely have in mind a clear picture of the final product when retaining a consultant."

Each client has its own set of unique needs. However, there are some common activities that relate to interior design and the use of CAFM as a specialty practice. For example, an interior designer could work with the facility manager to establish priorities and determine appropriate tracking and reporting protocols. The designer would then customize a CAFM database to incorporate the company's facilities terminology, reporting protocols, and data management processes. Using CAFM software, such as Aperture, Archibus, or FM/Space, the interior designer would input and maintain project data for facility management purposes, regularly updating and reporting information as required. Stanescu adds, "The area of services enabled by the use of CAFM encompasses a large array of management issues, such as facilities management (space planning, space allocation, personnel, equipment/ furniture, maintenance); property management (leases, vacancy, occupancy issues); and technology management (network documentation, connectivity issues). The structure of CAFM as thus conceived gives consultants the possibility to employ this tool, when a client expresses the need of optimizing the management of a large group of assets. It is my opinion that the key in being successful with CAFM in the future lies with the consultant's ability to find and define those large group of assets for corporate clients and then introduce the clients to the system and its capabilities."

There are many reasons why companies may want to use CAFM and retain a design consultant to minimally help set it up and perhaps ultimately provide comprehensive services. Stanescu offers the following reasons.

- *All organizations face the major problems of managing space, people, and assets.*

- *Facility management (FM) is critical to the success of any fast-growing, highly competitive organization. The top management team views the facility department as a key player in achieving the business mission.*

- *FM encompasses a wide variety of application areas—from space planning and asset tracking to reallocation of resources and compliance reporting.*

- *FM must keep the information up to date and provide it quickly to the management in a form that they can understand.*

- *Existing FM processes may not be working as well as they should, requiring examination and reengineering of the FM processes.*

- *CAFM is a visual information system that can dramatically improve the facility management organization to better serve the business mission.*

- *CAFM gives the ability to provide clear, accurate, and timely information to the rest of the organization.*

- *CAFM views the space needs as a raw material that must be delivered just in time to match the changing needs of the business.*

- *CAFM offers information that will help make the decision easier and more accurate.*

It should be noted, however, that designers and their clients can benefit when CAFM is used in the more typical full-service, six-phase project, especially in the initial programming phase. The interior design professional would document program requirements that have been obtained, through interviewing or questionnaire, into an alphanumeric database as part of the CAFM software package. As the design progresses, the professional adds graphic information to the database. Laurie Gathwright's introduction to CAFM as an interior designer was through a similar process: "I first became involved with CAFM while working on a master plan for an insurance company's corporate campus. I began to manage the software that was used as a programming tool for the project. I became involved in programming for the project, because the data stored in FMS [a specific CAFM product] was so closely linked to the program and master plan. I found that I enjoyed extracting data from FMS and utilizing it to revise the master plan."

Ultimately, a designer can use CAFM to track an entire organization, department by department, maintaining records that provide a basis for budget preparations, rent chargebacks, proactive facility management, and strategic facility planning. Gathwright describes the rationale behind T. Rowe Price's (TRPA) decision to invest in CAFM: "The driving force behind the CAFM implementation at TRPA was the company's growing real estate portfolio. Ten years ago, the company employed 800 people in two locations. At the time of implementation, the company was nearing 3,000 employees in 11 facilities, with plans for three additional sites to open within 18 months. The company now manages close to 1.5 million square feet in 20 facilities, with over 4,000 employees using Aperture [a specific CAFM product]. The resources associated with TRPA's real estate portfolio include personnel, equipment, furniture, and lease information. Multiple departments were accessing data relating to these resources on a constant basis. The CAFM system allowed TRPA to store this information in a single location. The CAFM system is now the most reliable source of information relating to these resources."

Gathwright describes typical responsibilities and activities that an interior designer using CAFM may perform:

- *Interface and coordinate with administrators of systems that relate to the CAFM system. In many companies, personnel information is recorded and tracked in PeopleSoft by the human resources department. It is necessary to coordinate with the PeopleSoft administrator to ensure that the personnel data within the CAFM system are correct and can be updated in a timely manner.*

- *Provide training and general support to all system users.*

- *Coordinate data input. There can be an infinite number of data sources for CAFM systems; it is necessary to ensure that information contributing to the CAFM system is "good" data and is being updated on a regular basis.*

- *Conduct ongoing needs analysis necessary to improve the system.*

- *Perform related responsibilities, such as maintaining lease chargeback reports and providing strategic planning and programming.*

The desired personal traits and capabilities of interior designers performing CAFM consultation or services include: a thorough understanding of facilities management, some exposure to strategic planning and programming, the ability and desire to be detail-oriented, and a combination of technical expertise and the ubiquitous "people" skills. Gathwright feels that the latter "is a strength that I have not seen in many of the consultants that I have worked with through the CAFM implementation process. It is very important, not only to be able to understand and operate the system, but to be able to communicate technical issues to people with limited technical knowledge."

Over time, CAFM provides a historical database that is a valuable tool for assessing cost benefits, determining the viability of alternative approaches, and evaluating facilities options. Stanescu summarizes its benefits:

- *CAFM responds quickly and accurately to all FM requests that come along.*

- *It improves the organization's productivity by using standard templates, symbols, data, and reports.*

- *Its easy-to-understand graphics enable management to make decisions easily.*

- *It makes strategic planning more effective because of the comprehensive understanding of facility assets and how they are used.*

- *It ensures the consistency and accuracy of asset inventories, personnel location, and space information.*

- *It involves less disruption, fewer mistakes, and reduced cost.*

CAFM allows management to develop knowledge related to facilities issues more easily, quickly, and reliably through access to accurate, dynamic, real-time graphic and statistical information. Overall, CAFM provides a company with both detailed and overview information that is readily available and provides the basis for well-informed decision making over the life span of a facility or group of facilities. Interior designers who provide these services are important participants in the overall health and growth of a company.

Owner's Representation

Owner's representation is the specialty practice of acting as the client's advocate in communicating to all parties involved in a project. As the client's advocate, the designer makes decisions and addresses problems in a manner that truly represents the best interest of the client as well as the project. The owner's representative provides a single point of contact for multiple disciplines, and ensures strict adherence to budget and schedule. The owner's representative also assures that all parties are providing quality work and are complying with corporate standards.

Yet whatever their initial professional choices, all designers should be aware of the directions in which specialty practices take the profession of design. Without this awareness, a designer can fall behind in a competitive market for the best projects . . .

It is commonplace that a company, upon embarking on an interiors project, requires someone to represent them and their interests to all constituents involved in the project. When the client retains an interior designer to perform in the role of owner's representative, the client is able to concentrate on his core responsibilities with the knowledge that facilities-related issues will be competently addressed by his advocate. In some cases, interior designers are more experienced than a client's own representative, especially if the client's representative is an office manager or firm partner rather than a facilities professional.

Marilyn Farrow, FIIDA, is an interior designer who has performed the role of owner's representative for several large corporations. She defines this service as "adopting the relationship of 'agency,' that is, putting the best interests of the owner first. When a designer assumes the role of owner's representative, she performs as though a member of the owner's organization, fully accountable and responsible for the business initiative in your care." A few common activities in this role include: soliciting vendors' and consultants' proposals, negotiating fees, negotiating conflicts with departmental end users to uphold corporate standards, analyzing data to achieve cost savings in furniture and construction, recommending new standards to reduce cost of churn, assisting in lease negotiations to achieve project savings, and documenting project activity.

In the early 1990s, Farrow was an independent consultant and project coordinator for Kraft General Foods, overseeing one-third of their consolidations of sales offices in cities throughout the country. She recognized that in her work for the client, "The goal was to minimize real estate expense and foster communication, collaboration, and cooperation. Consolidation was proposed to bring the various divisions' sales persons into dialogue and cooperation, in order to leverage their activities to build sales and minimize expenses. To do this, co-location of the sales forces was proposed, offering parity of quality of environment. Activities included a process of six meetings which included human resources, information technology, management, and me as the owner's representative, to gain concurrence and buy in, select real estate, and realign sales offices to occupy "flex-tech" type of real estate (high-tech warehouse). Kraft benefited financially from using a contracted owner's representative by leveraging the expertise and resources only so long as they were required (18 months)."

Farrow cites key personal traits and characteristics important to this specialty. The designer must:

- *Find it easy to meet people, talk to them, listen, and care about their issues.*

- *Be able to manage (say "no," prioritize, move initiatives toward the desired goal).*

- *Remain focused on the company's business objectives and not be side-tracked by another agenda.*

- *Be comfortable with corporate hierarchy/politics.*

Farrow adds, "If you care more about the client's issues than your own, or can put aside the 'purity of design,' this can be an extremely exciting and fun thing to do! You're playing the big boys' game in their court, and the stakes are high. The 'forgiveness quotient' is lean. It can be exhilarating! One key to my personal success was the short-term nature of the project, and the visible results that occurred which were directly responsive to personal efforts. However, do know that Corporate America can be a lot more 'black and white' than the average design firm, which may or may not be comfortable. For me, this was a very nifty opportunity! I'm extremely grateful for the fun I had, and the credibility it added to my resume. It can open doors you never imagined. Few designers have this arrow in their quiver."

WORKPLACE CONSULTING

Of those interior designers engaged in the practice of nonresidential design, more than 75 percent are involved in designing the workplace. It is therefore no surprise that a specialty practice area of workplace consulting has emerged as one of the leading specialties in the profession.

Workplace consulting is provided as a specialty practice by interior designers who help clients gather and evaluate workplace-related information in order to make informed decisions that will enhance and improve the work environment. The workplace consultant investigates and recommends ways companies can make their workplaces align better with business goals, become more productive, and address issues that affect employee recruitment and retention. The workplace consultant offers clients a broad view of available workplace options and best practices. Workplace consulting includes a number of different approaches to facilities issues, and may range from developing high-level strategic planning to creating a corporate newsletter for employees about to undergo significant change in their work environment.

Interior designers are naturally skilled, through education and experience, to lead many of the efforts required in providing workplace consulting services. Other chapters in this book address a few of these consulting areas, such as strategic planning and sustainable design. Four other common workplace consulting specialties are innovative officing, benchmarking, change management, and post-occupancy evaluations.

Innovative Officing

Innovative officing is a term that describes the design of office environments that optimally support the people, corporate culture, and work processes housed within. Innovative officing includes many traditional workplace components, as well as the introduction of various "alternative officing" concepts, such as hotelling, activity-based worksettings, telecommuting, and shared work spaces.

The interior design professional is a viable consultant to lead companies as they explore how innovative officing can support corporate objectives. Many companies recognize that their office environments have not kept pace with the change of their business, whether it is a change of vision, leadership, culture, or simply growth. Smart organizations realize that in order to be effective, their work environments must align with their business goals and objectives. This realization often leads to the exploration of ways they should change the work environment in order to support these new changes and evolving work processes.

The interior designer who provides these consulting services is especially attuned to his or her client, and works with the client to evaluate and consider options that are appropriate to its business culture and the needs of the staff. Often, the designer will need to introduce new officing concepts, a process which requires an in-depth study regarding how the staff use space, both presently and with an eye to the future. Often, the first step is for the design professional to train and educate the staff at all levels concerning the many workplace options available, as well as the benefits and the potential modifications of the workspace, technology, and work styles that may result from changes in the work environment. These solutions include a great variety of workplace scenarios such as open work areas, teaming environments, shared work areas, teleworkers, satellite offices, and activity-based worksettings. The designer may recommend a number of different solutions, including a more "traditional" approach based on the goals and requirements of each individual client.

The designer's goal is to create a successful work environment that allows the client to use its space resources more effectively and efficiently, while meeting corporate business objectives. Designers can begin to identify the appropriate officing environment for a given client with the following steps:

- *Assess the particular needs of each group.*

- *Document how the current workplace is actually used, using a variety of methodologies (e.g., bedchecks or in-out studies).*

- *Analyze future trends and effects of changes in the uses of technology.*

- *Consider tools for success in implementation.*

- *Identify measurements for success.*

- *Make recommendations for human resources and organizational development responses to the change.*

- *Assess cost factors inherent in a successful transition.*

Rob Davis, an interior designer and workplace consultant with Griswold, Heckel & Associates Inc. (GHK), describes the typical activities that a workplace consultant performs. "Most of the activities of workplace consulting are atypical. The services need to be tailored to the client organization and its circumstances. But in general, the typical activities include: surveys of a variety of sorts, interviews, review of results of previous studies, projections (financial, business, human resources), understanding the business at hand (including linkages between the business and office needs), analysis, and recommendations."

Rob's co-worker, Robert Heizler, is an architect as well as a NCIDQ certified designer, and has developed an expertise in innovative officing. He defines innovative officing as "responding to the minutia in how people work as well as answering what the client has requested. In performing innovative office consulting, we take the extra time and effort to truly dive in and discover how people work. It takes significant time and effort to get into this. It is not 'designing by rote.' It is the right response that all too often gets rubber-stamped into a design solution. It is not the mundane cookie-cutter approach. Innovative office consulting is customized to each individual client's needs."

Robert Wright, national director of design and construction for Ernst & Young (E&Y), was one of the leading pioneers developing E&Y's Workplace for the Future. Wright distinguishes workplace consultation as the "strategic master planning for real estate needs for the office. Innovative officing considers all aspects of the interior workspace: where we should work, where we operate, where people are, where clients are, where business is accomplished."

Wright describes three typical activities or responsibilities that a workplace consultant would lead. "First, they would understand our culture so that they could provide solutions appropriate to our business. Second, they would develop solutions to meet the functional needs of the office. Third, they would introduce, educate, and sell alternative workplace settings."

Heizler emphatically agrees that the role of the workplace consultant is to educate and to be educated. This education takes many forms and is manifested in various ways during the progress of the innovative officing exploration. He makes it clear that: "It is vitally important to keep up with current business trends and ideologies. A workplace consultant must know and communicate what is going on in the workplace and in the interior design profession. He or she must be an avid publications reader, consuming *Fast Company*, *Wired*, and *Business Week* to keep fingers on the pulse of the real world with its real-world issues."

Other traits that Heizler finds important include "the passion to make every opportunity be an innovative officing consideration. It is simply the practice of good design. Don't box yourself in. People who excel in innovative officing think outside of the box. Additionally, the consultant should be focused and skilled at articulating to the client the potential benefits so that the client can think out of the box also. A workplace consultant cannot work independently. He or she must be able and excited about interacting."

Wright describes desirable personal traits he looks for in his workplace consultants: professional, understanding, knowledgeable, good communicator (verbally as well as written), sympathetic versus empathetic, high integrity, perseverance.

Wright has used innovative officing consultants to provide a good starting point with new concepts. These concepts get modified as they go along. He expects the interior design firms that he retains to implement the concepts to "Make it their own. They need to take ownership. I expect them to modify the concepts to meet the needs." (See Figure 19-5.)

Benchmarking

According to former Xerox CEO David Kearns, the definition of benchmarking is "the continuous process of measuring products, services, and practices against the toughest competitors or those companies recognized as industry leaders." In the facilities world, this can be interpreted as the practice of comparing one's own data and practices against other organizations in order to understand and evaluate facilities and the workplace. By benchmarking we learn by borrowing from the best and adapting their approaches to fit our needs. Benchmarking provides an opportunity to share successes and leverage knowledge and experience between organizations. The interior design professional is well positioned to lead this benchmarking consultation. Often, the design professional is already working in the facility and is aware of many factors which may need to be benchmarked, or could be used in the data-gathering process. Sometimes, the facility department may just need to be "jump started" in the process, and use the services of a benchmarking consultant to lead this first-time effort.

Facility managers as well as corporate executives often seek consultation regarding the performance of their facilities. They list four major rationales for such consultation:

1. The business desires to continually improve the performance of its operation.

2. It needs to analyze the comparative costs of maintaining a facility.

3. It has identified a goal of improving the profitability of the company through direct impact on the bottom line.

4. It needs to present a business case to emphasize the importance of the facility manager's role.

WORKPLACE DESCRIPTION

Ernst & Young LLP
McLean, Virginia

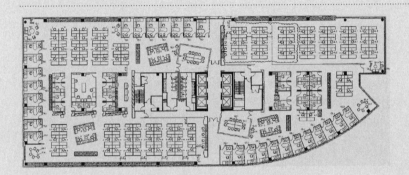

THE CHALLENGE

Recruiting, employee retention and quality of life can have a great affect on an organization's productivity and success. In today's job market, employers scramble for new hires and will do just about anything to keep a good employee. Many organizations are challenged to provide an environment conducive to the employees' productivity and quality of life.

In response to the challenge, Ernst & Young's National Real Estate Group (EYNRE) developed national standards and established a quality benchmark for all locations that address four specific areas;

○ Quality of Life

○ Workplace Standards

○ Workplace Amenities

○ Cost Effectiveness / Timeliness

QUALITY OF LIFE

In an effort to provide both a better quality of life for their employees as well as better service to their clients, Ernst & Young acquired 130,000 rsf of space at Westpark Business Park in McLean, Virginia. The relocation meant a shorter commute for employees to and from work. It also meant less time on the road as most of the firm's high tech and health care clients were headquartered in the area. Creating the new workplace, Ernst & Young implemented the new Workplace of the Future standards to provide consistency and quality that was comparable to recent successful projects recently implemented in California and Texas.

FIGURE 19-5
The design and client team set the goals of
the workplace at the onset of the project.

WORKPLACE STANDARDS

Through the new real estate standards, EYNRE ensured that, regardless of business unit, practice area or location, the workplace maintains a high level of quality and remain consistent with other EY locations. In a profession where the people are as fluid as the projects, the consistency within the workplace can provide a level of familiarity where none might exist.

Each floor of the building is designed with a standard layout so that regardless of seat assignment, employees know where to find team rooms, admin support, copy, coffee and mail areas. This consistency can help both the level of productivity as well as an employee's well being.

WORKPLACE AMENITIES

As a result of hoteling, or workspace sharing, about 40% of the McLean staff do not have a permanent workspace. As a result, a visit to the office does not always require a worksurface as much as it does a familiar face and capable hands. Many of the team members come into the office for either team or client meetings, or to obtain support from the professional service personnel in the central file room, reprographics, word processing or graphics support. The centralized amenities allow for "one stop shopping" to make the most of one's time.

Whether an employee is interviewing new hires in the interview rooms, utilizing the 75 person conference center, or relaxing or working in the lunchroom/café with clients and other EY employees, EY provides a relaxed, yet high quality workplace to support the needs of its professionals.

As a result of buying agreements and standards development, EYNRE has established a cost effective approach to workplace design that is also responsive to the timely requirements for space. Acquisition of new real estate is a serious investment for EY. Timing is critical in getting quality product in a quality space in timely manner. EYNRE's buying agreements and chosen product lines allow for the real estate to be acquired "just in time", saving the firm significant monies.

FIGURE 19-5 (Continued)

Stephen C. Roth is an architect who has been involved in facility planning for over 15 years. He explains the role of benchmarking: "As Director of Real Estate, Planning & Construction for a public utility, I am responsible for the development of service agreements with our customers and business plans for approval by our management. Cost and service quality measures are an integral part of both activities. Benchmarking helps determine our level of competitiveness and (hopefully) our degree of improvement with respect to the providing of services and, therefore, the performance of our jobs, both of which contribute heavily towards a confidence in our ability to provide the best possible service at the lowest possible cost."

In general, facilities benchmarking efforts fall into four broad categories: resource utilization, space management, space assignment, and real estate. Each facilities organization needs to determine what it wants to measure and why, starting small and expanding each year if necessary. Some typical facility factors include density, churn rates, cost per square foot, private office-to-workstation ratios, cost per move, vacancy rates, and resource utilization. Such factors are measured against companies in a client's own industry or against companies of similar structure in different industries. Benchmarking provides the opportunity to evaluate current facilities and set a baseline for analyzing future performance.

James E. Loesch, CFM, is a founding member of the benchmarking and research committees of the International Facility Management Association (IFMA). He points out that benchmarking can fail without clear goals and a complete understanding of its possible consequences for the organization. Every three years, the IFMA publishes Benchmark Surveys to help its members understand and apply the benefits of benchmarking. But Loesch advises that "data for its own sake is wasted effort. You must have a clear understanding of what you want to get out of it. You must have a clear understanding of what your company values and needs, such as its processes, costs, how it does business, and internal customer expectations. You also must know what are in the numbers, both within your company and among other companies against whom you may be benchmarking. Numbers can lie. You must compare apples to apples." Loesch also cautions that all the participants need to think through the implications of benchmarking. Some results could affect change—i.e., the decision to downsize some positions. Some decisions are political, some are union driven, some are culture driven. He advises, "Know

Benchmarking helps determine our level of competitiveness and (hopefully) our degree of improvement with respect to the providing of services and, therefore, the performance of our jobs . . .

your organization, its leadership, its sensitivities and yourself. Benchmarking is not for the weak of heart."

Benchmarking is based on the continuous practice of measuring a number of key indicators of efficiency and effectiveness. The evaluation includes a study of the client's needs, the collection of specific data, and then the analysis of that data in comparison to others in similar industries. Some activities include:

- *Reviewing current facilities data and client information*

- *Touring key facilities, documenting observations, and identifying areas of focus*

- *Reviewing benchmark data in general and specific to the client industry*

- *Identifying other sources of information on facility management in like industries or among similar-sized companies*

- *Comparing and contrasting the data, analyzing and testing reasons for differences*

- *Developing and creating buy-in for a suitable baseline for evaluation and comparison with future performance*

Roth describes the process that his organization uses: "For us, benchmarking a service is a three-step process with the critical intent for the end result being a credible end product. This means that the benchmarked information must be easily understood and useful, which, in turn, means that the benchmarked information must clearly tie back to each group's budget and performance responsibilities."

Many organizations measure the use of their facilities by square footage analyses and comparisons. One of Roth's key activities is "the understanding of the square footage each [internal] customer directly occupies, as well as indirectly uses/benefits from. Given the complex nature of this exercise, the use of a computer-aided facilities information management system (CAFIMS) is required. We track everything in rentable square feet for external comparison purposes and use Aperture as our CAFIMS. The data is exported into an Excel spreadsheet and combined with our cost of service data taken from our company's accounting system to determine both the costs of our services for each of our customers, as well as the per square foot information we use for performance measures and benchmarks."

The interior designer, as benchmarking consultant, gathers and documents the data, and works with the client to set a baseline, develop an action plan, and determine the schedule for monitoring progress against the baseline. This effort can provide answers to key questions, including:

- *How well the space compares with others*

- *Suggestions for changes that would improve the bottom line or improve performance, and justify the expenses of the changes*

- *How well positioned the facilities are to accommodate future developments in technology, workstyles, and evolving needs*

Roth reports on how his company as a public utility uses its benchmarking results. "We trend and benchmark a series of costs, by service. We then identify where our cost improvement efforts are needed and tie those efforts back to our business plan for the coming year. Our customers, our management, and each of our functional groups are then presented with information that clearly identifies the cost of our services, how we compare to others, and where we intend to focus our cost improvement initiatives."

James Loesch is chief facilities engineer for an applied physics laboratory. His organization uses its facilities benchmarking effort to determine "a sense of where his organization is in general. Where is our biggest deviation in a negative area? Are we in the pack? If yes, then I may look for areas in which to improve. If we really stand out as odd in one area, then it may be worth some time and effort to drill down." (See Figure 19-6.) What Loesch finds especially helpful is to identify several benchmark partners to compare "apples to apples," compare raw data, and share. He advises that it often takes a personal relationship with other organizations to accomplish such an intimate activity, especially if salary data are involved.

Rob Davis is an interior designer who is experienced in facilities benchmarking. He appreciates the opportunity to measure how design actually shapes users' reactions and productivity. He says, "I came to be interested in

FIGURE 19-6A
Client Benchmarking Study.

Square footage comparisons with same class and best in class companies.

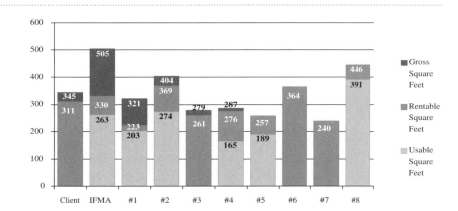

FIGURE 19-6B
Client Conference Room Survey Comparative Analysis.

Ratio of conference room usable square footage to workplace usable square footage.

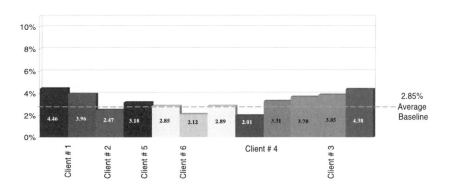

the qualitative aspects of interior design after years of practice. My association with a variety of Fortune 500 companies, and understanding a bit about the internal considerations, politics, and funding issues, intrigued me. In fact, I was always interested in knowing about client businesses. Over time I became interested in being able to help *quantify* the relationship, if any, between design considerations and potential effects on productivity, satisfaction, well-being, etc. Dieter Rams and Stephen Bayley both make the case for 'design' being more than shape or appearance, as does the German philosopher Max Bense in his writings on semiotics."

Davis has worked with a variety of customers, assisting them in obtaining data that could be benchmarked and analyzed to improve performance of the company's facilities and assets. (See Figures 19-7 and 19-8.) He describes the successful benchmarking consultant as a dedicated investigator. He finds that "the most important trait for doing this type of work is curiosity about how things work, followed by an interest in problem solving, followed by the ability to grasp a situation and to devise a means of investigating it in a fairly rigorous and exhaustive manner. This must be combined with the ability to

BENCHMARK DATA

	Owned Sq. Ft.	Leased Sq. Ft.	# of FTE	Gross Sq. Ft.	GSF per FTE	Rentable Sq. Ft.	RSF per FTE	Usable Sq. Ft.	USF per FTE	Sq. Ft. Vacant	Vacancy Rate	Building Efficiency Rate	O&M Cost	OC per FTE	Fixed Asset Cost	FA per FTE	Occupancy Cost per FTE	Lease Costs	Project Costs	Annual Facility Cost
BUILDING A																				
Floor Number 1																				
Department #1																				
Department #2																				
Department #3																				
Department #4																				
Department #5																				
Floor Number 2																				
Department #1																				
Department #2																				
Department #3																				
Floor Number 3																				
Department #1																				
Department #2																				
Department #3																				
Department #4																				
Department #5																				
BUILDING B																				
Floor Number 1																				
Department #1																				
Department #2																				
Department #3																				
Department #4																				
Department #5																				

	# of Moves Annually	# of FTEs Moved	Sq. Ft. Moved	Churn Rate	Floor Churn Rate	Total Cost of Moves	Cost per Move	Total Cost of Box Moves	Cost per Move	Total Cost of Furniture Moves	Cost per Move	Total Cost of Construction	Cost per Move	WORKSTATION STANDARDS									
														A	B	C	D	E	F	G	H	I	Total
BUILDING A																							
Floor Number 1																							
• Department #1																							
• Department #2																							
• Department #3																							
• Department #4																							
• Department #5																							
Floor Number 2																							
• Department #1																							
• Department #2																							
• Department #3																							
Floor Number 3																							
• Department #1																							
• Department #2																							
• Department #3																							
• Department #4																							
• Department #5																							
BUILDING B																							
Floor Number 1																							
• Department #1																							
• Department #2																							
• Department #3																							
• Department #4																							
• Department #5																							

EXHIBIT 19-7

GHK has developed this sample form of information to be collected to provide benchmark data.

Project Summary Data

Date: _____

Job Number: _____

Department Name: _____

Department Number: _____

Contact Person: _____

Phone: _____

Current Location

Building: _____

Floor: _____

Gross sq. ft.: _____   Rentable sq. ft.: _____   Useable sq. ft.: _____

New Location

Building: _____

Floor: _____

Gross sq. ft.: _____   Rentable sq. ft.: _____   Useable sq. ft.: _____

Staff

Previous # of staff: _____   New # of staff: _____

Previous # of offices/workstations: _____

A: ___ B: ___ C: ___ D: ___ E: ___ F: ___ G: ___ H: ___ I: ___

New # of offices/workstations: _____

A: ___ B: ___ C: ___ D: ___ E: ___ F: ___ G: ___ H: ___ I: ___

Gross sq. ft.: _____   Rentable sq. ft.: _____

Costs

Box Move: _____   # of staff moved: _____   per sq.ft.: _____

Furniture Move: _____   # of staff moved: _____   per sq.ft.: _____

Construction: _____   # of staff moved: _____   per sq.ft.: _____

Design/Management: _____   # of staff moved: _____   per sq.ft.: _____

Schedule

PLANNED

planning time: _____   constr. time: _____   move date: _____

ACTUAL

planning time: _____   constr. time: _____   move date: _____

FIGURE 19-8
GHK developed this sample form of information to be collected at the close of a project to update benchmarking data.

understand linkages between seemingly unrelated aspects of the situation. This work is partly deductive and partly intuitive, with neither being good on its own."

Davis believes that interior design professionals who want to pursue this consulting practice must be resourceful, not only for their own work, but also in extracting the information from the client they are serving. To lead a benchmarking effort, the designer needs to have the following personal traits and characteristics. The designer must:

- *Have a broad perspective of narrow specialty service (it's not enough to be a number cruncher)*

- *Possess excellent planning and organizational skills*

- *Be able to analyze data in meaningful way*

- *Have excellent communications skills (listen actively and explain clearly)*

- *Be able to forge relationships, internally and externally*

- *Be detail oriented*

- *Be naturally inquisitive*

- *Be politically savvy*

- *Know about the organization to be benchmarked*

To build the knowledge base they need to benchmark, designers can turn to many excellent external sources, such as web research, conferences, and publications. Davis adds, "Information is widely available to anyone who chooses to look for it. For instance, the definitive statement on occupancy cost comes from The Association of Management Accountants. How do I know that? Well, I needed to know it and took it from there. I made some inquiries, in person and on the web, and ordered their publications. The thing to remember is that there is a professional association for every known activity. Beyond that, there are good books on every subject, but I resist the temptation to read the business 'best sellers,' which dish up the buzzwords *du jour* in such a general manner as not to be really useful."

In addition, designers can easily find information necessary to project plans and make benchmarking evaluations. Davis says, "Fortunately, many complex statistical and forecasting methods have been incorporated into everyday computer programs like Excel, Definitive Scenario, and others. Knowledge of basic business principles is essential. Terms like present value, net present value, rolling averages, and standard deviation should not only be part of the problem solver's lexicon but a part of his or her working knowledge. We've all seen those Texas Instruments pocket calculators that our MBA friends carry. Well, it wouldn't hurt to know what one of those devices does."

Roth identifies the key to successful benchmarking as a mixture of focus and precision. He says, "Whether cost or service quality, the person or organization providing benchmarking services must ultimately tailor the information to its intended audience(s) so that the information is useful and of value. That not only means having the ability to develop an action plan from the information, but also a plan that is aligned with corporate/customer goals and objectives. Without such an outcome, both the corporation and the customer will not have confidence in your ability to deliver the facilities and related services they need at the cost and quality levels they desire."

Change Management

Change is the only constant in today's business world. Whether it is change in one's customer base, technological advances, or the economy, organizations that do not embrace change will not survive. As corporate mission statements and cultures change, changes in the work environment must occur as well in order to support the business goals and objectives of the changed organization. Interior designers are often called upon to develop a methodology for helping clients manage transitions related to change in the work environment. These changes are often needed to reinforce the major organizational changes, such as changes in leadership, purpose, and structure. Appropriate internal resources within the client organization are needed to work hand in hand with the change management consultant to manage the transition successfully. Change management consultation services are individualized to the specific needs of each client and employee user group. The most successful change management efforts foster ownership of the upcoming change among employees by involving them in the process, which also provides valuable input to the interior design process.

Melodee Wagen, a change management consultant, defines change management as "listening, responding appropriately, and communicating. It is the process of helping people manage through the human reactions to effectively and productively function under new circumstances. Change management is the process of informing, pulling, pushing, listening, and helping people through both the change and then the transition to the new reality. Change management is patience."

Diane Schroeder, an interior designer who has led many corporations through the change process, emphasizes that change requires a clear plan and a motivation for staff to follow the plan. She says, "In order for change to occur and perpetuate, there must be an intended result and an envisioned path through the transition. People cannot successfully shift from one set of behavioral protocols to another without a step-by-step transition plan. A new environment cannot force change any more than introducing new relationships or new tools, putting them in a room together and walking away, expecting them to 'figure it out.' Human behavior typically relaxes into routine and familiar surroundings. When an outside element imposes change, it is natural to resist. The key to successful change is to invite the 'people' to become engaged in the change; to create the value of the change to them personally, and to become involved in the physical surroundings that reinforce the ultimate desire. In order to transition to a new way of thinking and behaving, we must borrow elements from the present, put those elements into a new context, and create models to demonstrate the desirable future."

This work involves a change management consultant, often an interior designer trained in change management processes, who typically consults separately with four groups: a steering committee made up of management decision makers, a facilitation team that oversees communication, a focus group composed of representatives of the organization at large, and an implementation team. The change management consultant provides material and guidance to the four groups, and manages the process from the initial discussions through design input and transition management. He or she develops tools to help employees understand and adapt to the changes in their workplace and often works with their corporate communications department to prepare appropriate internal communications materials.

Melodee Wagen has identified three critical activities in leading the change management process. The first critical activity for designers who practice change management is to help senior management understand why they should include change management thinking and behavior from the very beginning of every major undertaking. She says, "It is important to approach the change from the point of view of the individual whose life will be affected by what is happening, or rather effectively happening *to* them. All employees need information, as specific and detailed as possible, but they also need the understanding that change is disruptive, frightening, sometimes personally affecting people's lives, and that business *isn't* 'as usual.' The human response of stress, resistance, and 'mourning the old' does not differ if the change is viewed as positive or negative."

The second critical activity is to assure that the company either fulfills its promises or addresses these promises. Wagen says, "They cannot leave people wondering. Humans will make up their own version of events, speculation will run rampant, and productivity will suffer. It is important that the company understand that although change is a time that offers opportunity for creativity, it is distracting, and is not a good time to increase performance goals unless it is done very carefully."

The third critical activity is to communicate. Wagen says that in benchmarking, the design professional must "communicate, communicate, and communicate again. Repeat the story; remind everyone again and again why we are doing this, why it is important, and what the goals are for the change. Communicate in different media, such as town hall meetings, letters, on the web, through e-mail, and through special project newsletters."

The training that is needed by an interior designer interested in expanding his or her role to include change management is a widely varied path. Wagen found it helpful to pursue postgraduate work, which resulted in a Certificate in Management Studies. Her professional background includes 14 years of work in administration and strategic planning and analysis at Harvard University. She has also served as an on-site service provider at a major high-technology provider, doing strategic planning, master planning, alternative officing studies and implementation, and occupancy planning.

On the other hand, Diane Schroeder has evolved through three decades of interior architecture, always with a focus on communication and human behavior. With her Bachelor of Fine Arts degree from the University of Nebraska, during the first years of her career, Schroeder was assigned to work with teams that developed facilities in Middle Eastern cultures including Jordan and Saudi Arabia. Vast differences in cultures, behaviors, and protocols awakened the realization that the dramas of life and the environments in which they take place are connected and interactive. Asking questions and inviting response in pursuit of a vision toward the way people feel and interact with their environment is the continuity of evolution through generations, business strategies, economic impact, technological influences, and variations in priorities.

Traits and characteristics that are helpful to an interior designer considering this specialty service include: patience, forward-thinking ability, understanding of human and organizational dynamics, ability to persuade as well as collaborate, ability to anticipate and put oneself in another's shoes. Wagen's best advice is to be able to "Tell the truth. Tell why something is happening. If it must be addressed but is still confidential–say so. Be very careful to say what you really believe. Don't promise what you might not be able to deliver." Perhaps the most important trait of a change management consultant is the capacity to see the common elements that can make up a path that staff can actually follow. Schroeder advises that "common denominators will cause bonding and balance. Simplicity evolves out of the interacting complexities. Instead of independent, isolated work environments, many companies are looking for the collective mentality of collaborative teaming to leverage the total knowledge of the workforce." The effect that this change can have on an organization is powerful. Interior designers who are skilled in change management processes provide vital consulting services.

A CASE STUDY: BLUE CROSS AND BLUE SHIELD ASSOCIATION

The Blue Cross and Blue Shield Association (BCBSA), located in Illinois, is a good example of a company that is sincerely interested in supporting and managing change. Diane Schroeder worked with them to implement real change within their work environment to reflect changed organizational philosophies. The BCBSA adopted "change philosophies" to encourage interactive work and team work. The compelling philosophy, "Collectively, we can gain nearly 100 percent knowledge," drove the stated goals:

1. Cultural transformation and the pursuit of excellence, focused on the customer, can be achieved through value added teamwork and shared vision.

2. A teamwork environment is really critical to achieve invention.

3. Teamwork, collaboration, and personal performance go hand in hand in creating a strategic framework.

4. Workplaces designed in parallel with cultural and work process shifts allow people to work smarter for better productivity. The workplace fosters creativity.

5. Function and flexibility are imperative. Workplace factors such as ergonomics, noise level, lighting, HVAC must support worker.

The Blue Cross and Blue Shield Association, upon recommendation by the interior design professionals, retained a professional production company that specializes in corporate communications. Schroeder describes the process: "The production company was to produce a video tape that would run on a continuous basis during the work week throughout the duration of the construction period of the new headquarters facility. The video appeared in an auxiliary area of the existing facility as an abbreviated explanation of the corporate goals, values, relationships, and processes delivered by corporate management. The message was directly aligned with how the workplace would be a tool to break down the barriers and allow 'team collaboration' and 'collective knowledge.' The six-person workplace mock-up adjacent to the video monitor was featured and described by the facilities leader and design team. It was available for all BCBSA employees to visit, try on, and visualize their new work environment. The vision, the plan, the reality was set for change success."

It is important to note that departmental representatives were chosen to participate in a liaison group, and this group was charged with facilitating interactive communication to reinforce the transition toward the new BCBSA culture. One way that group "buy-in" was fostered was achieved through voting by the staff regarding their preference of individual workplaces or open spaces enabling teamwork. As often happens, "the natural human response to resist change" became the overriding opinion, and they elected to continue with a configuration that was similar to their existing environment. The BCBSA traditional work environment was 60 percent enclosed workplaces and 40 percent open workplaces with stand-up privacy. The proposed new environment included a move to 10 percent enclosed workplaces and 90 percent open workplaces. The envisioned spontaneous teaming environment emerged as those involving teaming in scheduled meeting places, returning to individual workplaces with stand-up privacy. However, 10 percent of the open workplaces were housed in a configuration of continual, spontaneous collaboration. A radical transition from a culture of low interaction and high autonomy to a culture of high interaction and impromptu teaming would have required continuous training and modeling of new processes and behavior protocols. As it was, behavior protocols and processes were evolving and not fully identified. Therefore, the results of the voting for "buy-in" became a *transition stage* toward the ultimate vision.

A CASE STUDY: A FINANCIAL COMPANY

In a different example with a slightly different result, a financial company embarked upon a change management process with one of their divisions, Business Credit (BC). They felt it was critical to the success of the space planning and design process that a consistent understanding among all participants was needed. All needed to understand the principles to be employed, and possess a clear sense of their relative priority. BC's senior managers spent considerable time discussing the alternatives, and developing a list of space-planning design principles, ranked in order of importance.

BC was to be a prototype for future planning and cultural change. It needed to implement organizational changes to achieve its goal to become the pre-eminent U.S. asset-based lender. To meet its strategic intent, BC needed to centralize its key operations on one floor (of nine) within the headquarters of the parent financial company. The primary purpose of the BC work environment was to develop a physical space that enabled employees to attain the corporate vision, mission, and goals. The approach considered the relationship of space to strategy, business process, technology, culture, and the activities of work.

Its parent company traditionally experienced an environment with a high degree of individual work and low amounts of collaboration. This was clearly reflected in the typical space standards adopted long ago. However, senior management's view of the new BC was high interaction and high autonomy. They also envisioned high-performance teams with higher levels of interaction, collaboration, and autonomy. (See Figure 19-9.)

The initial facility vision (a collaboration between Steelcase Envisioning™ and the interior design consultant) was that this group's work processes and relationships would be best supported with task-based work settings. Forty-

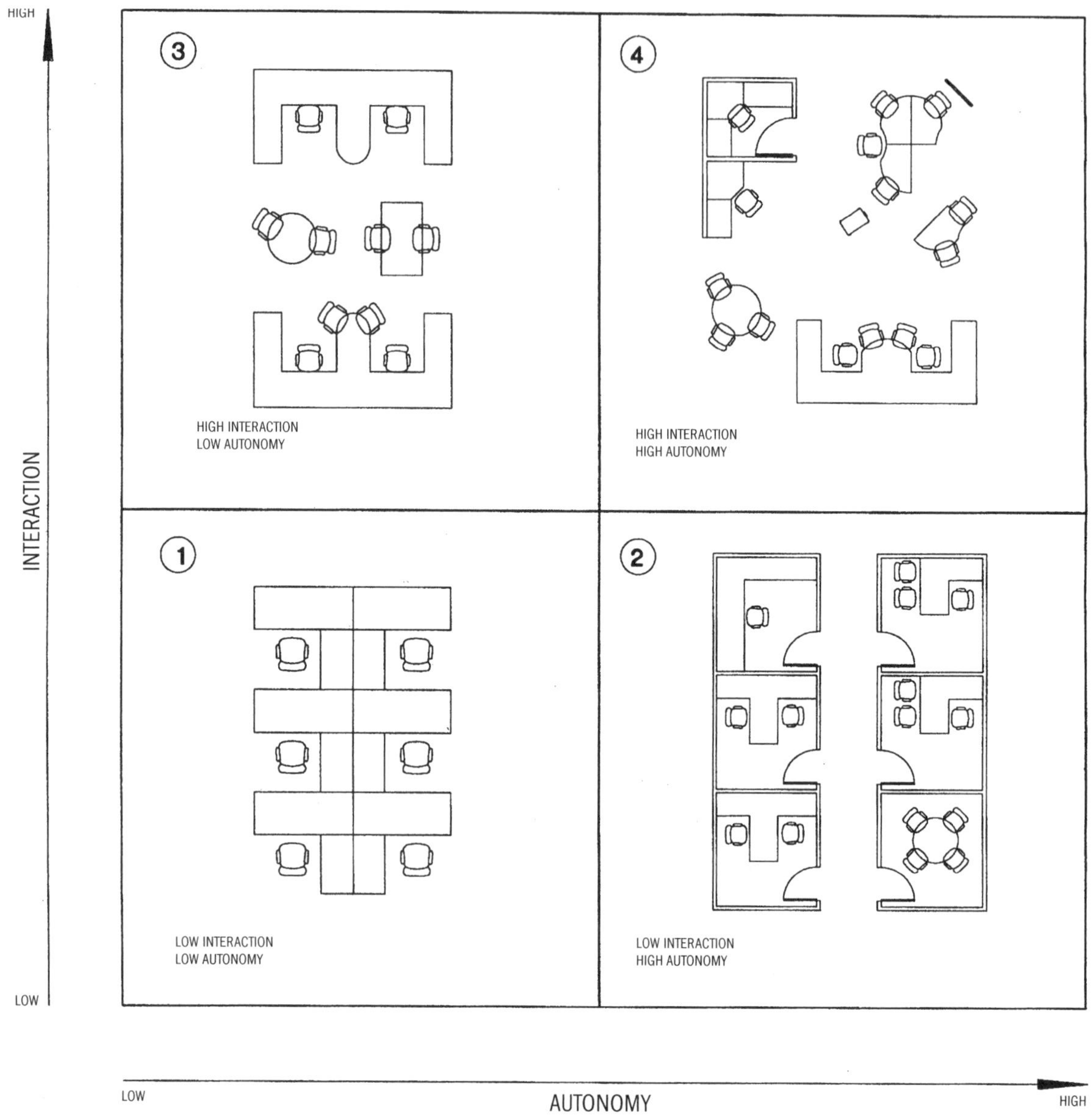

③

HIGH INTERACTION
LOW AUTONOMY

④

HIGH INTERACTION
HIGH AUTONOMY

①

LOW INTERACTION
LOW AUTONOMY

②

LOW INTERACTION
HIGH AUTONOMY

HIGH

LOW

INTERACTION

LOW

AUTONOMY

HIGH

FIGURE 19-9

Each quadrant
describes a working
"neighborhood" that
varies between high and
low autonomy and high
and low interaction.

seven BC employees would be in 16 different work settings, comprised of seven dedicated individual settings and nine shared settings, ranging from technology based, to collaborative, to presentation. Additionally, each employee would be assigned a dedicated individual setting.

However, Schroeder paints the reality picture, once the participants really faced what changes were being considered. She explains, "While the criteria was in place and the vision toward an open, collaborative environment was clearly defined, the employee liaisons were promised by senior management that they would be involved in the formation of the physical environment. The liaisons presented a case to senior management, insisting that if they were to buy into the success of the newly formed BC, they needed to work the way they knew how to work—which was to be in an assigned multitasking enclosed workplace. Team collaboration would be scheduled occasions, reinforcing a common direction with the vast majority of work accruing in the assigned workplace, private to confidential negotiations, allowing meeting space for one or two additional associates. Individual competition, instead of measuring team successes, was clearly a part of the incentive compensation, reinforcing an autonomous culture. Ultimately, a high percentage of private offices was implemented and a culture similar to the traditionally known culture was perpetuated."

Change management is a challenging consulting practice, and one that requires continual education and training. Interior designers who rise to meet this challenge will enjoy high-level discussions and powerful interactions with the top leadership of Fortune 1000 companies. Schroeder is one of these designers. Her work has led her to the conclusion that "there is a gap as wide as the Grand Canyon between a philosophy of 'management' versus 'leadership.' Leadership by example is the most powerful transition methodology. When led to their own intelligence, people will be more inspired, enthusiastic, and creative. They will rise to the occasion of leadership, even at young, inexperienced levels." Melodee Wagen also has gleaned a gem from her many consultations in change management. She notes that "one of the things that usually surprises senior management is how much everyone in the company already knows. If something is going on, word gets out. It is up to the leadership to craft the story, and to provide the facts and rationale, *proactively*. Waiting until all the information is available simply means that you'll be fighting fires of rumors, speculation, and fear. The best habit is to develop a policy and attitude of listening, responding, and then communicating often."

Post-Occupancy Evaluations

It has become increasingly necessary for the interior design profession to demonstrate its ability to positively affect the bottom line of corporations and businesses. Much has been theorized and written about the positive effects of good design on worker productivity, effectiveness, employee recruitment and retention, and employee health. However, it has only been in the last decade or so that post-occupancy evaluations (POE) have become an additional service provided by designers, whether paid for by the client organization or considered by the design firm itself as a research and development endeavor.

Part of the difficulty in pursuing workplace evaluations in a pre-move and post-move analysis is the need for objectivity in what is often a subjective field. The academic world speaks of the need for control groups and scientific measuring devices, but these practices are rarely performed in the measurement of interior design effectiveness and do not reach the designer "in the trenches." Therefore, interested members of the interior design industry have created powerful POE questionnaires and methodologies to analyze the impact of their design solutions, without the use of laboratory-perfect research practices. These methods of research and analysis may be conducted without great expense, often using a standard format of ranking to gather data based on the client's perception of a number of criteria, including functionality, effectiveness, adaptability, aesthetics, privacy, environmental conditions, and safety.

Kathryn Klass, a facility management consultant who specializes in POE, describes the need for workplace evaluations. "Often described as pre- or post-occupancy evaluations, workplace evaluations are the systematic study of facilities from the perspective of the occupants. They help real estate groups understand and respond to the issues in their facilities, develop Best Practices, and build positive relationships with employees."

Interior design professionals who specialize in POE have their own individual approaches to conducting workplace evaluations. While specific methods vary, there are some similarities. Most POE specialists agree that both pre- and post-occupancy evaluations are important. The designer should conduct the first evaluation prior to the client's move or renovation, in order to gain an understanding of the users' current built environment. If the designer will gather data with a questionnaire, the same questionnaire should be used for the post evaluation(s). The post evaluations should take place approximately two to three months following the move, and facilitate feedback concerning the users' initial interaction with their new work space or environments. Ideally, the designer would schedule a third evaluation, occurring 12 to 18 months following occupancy, to potentially identify a previous "halo effect." This third evaluation would offer more in-depth feedback concerning use of common areas, adjacencies of work groups/persons, ability of design to adapt to changes, and the overall functional effectiveness of the design.

Other similarities in approach include: defining the areas the study is intended to address; developing a comprehensive yet easy to answer questionnaire; selecting a standard format of ranking methodology (i.e., a scale of 1–6, with clearly defined response levels); identifying, with the client's participation, a statistically significant pool of potential respondents; communicating the reason for the study with support from top management; and communicating the results of the study in an appropriate manner to senior management as well as to the participants.

Klass shares her experience with POE. In her practice, "pre-occupancy evaluations are performed prior to a major change in the real estate direction or as a result of significant change in the business model. The current situation is analyzed and understood in terms of its positives and negatives, and possibilities for change and improvement are identified. These evaluations establish baselines, identify priorities and specific needs of business units, and highlight issues that require addressing. It is important that such an evaluation occur prior to the planning process so that the information isn't influenced by employee feelings about potential changes." She adds that "Post-occupancy evaluations generally occur four to twelve months after a major renovation or move. Post-occupancy evaluations should not be confused with post-move surveys, which are done immediately after a relocation project, and are specific to the move process. A post-occupancy evaluation provides a measure to determine the effectiveness of space utilization and how it addresses user requirements. (Such items can range widely, i.e., personal workstation surface area, chair comfort, and file storage to building image questions, air quality, and building signage effectiveness.) It provides guidance for future planning, determines the success factors of the renovations, identifies adjustments that are desired or required, and allows a real estate group to incorporate improvements into future projects (or phases of the same project)." (See Figure 19-10.)

POST-OCCUPANCY EVALUATION

Please rate each of the following features of your individual and departmental space according to the rating system below.

Rating System	Not Applicable to me	Very Unsatisfied	Unsatisfied	Satisfied	Moderately Satisfied	Highly Satisfied
	0	1	2	3	4	5

Individual Space
(Cubicle/Office)

Departmental Space
(Common Work Areas)

Individual Space		Departmental Space
_____	Overall amount of space allocated	_____
_____	Space layout meets functional work requirements	_____
_____	Amount of storage	_____
_____	Ease of circulation	_____
_____	Amount of work surface	_____
_____	Adequate space for equipment/shared equipment	_____
_____	Flexibility for change/growth/reconfiguration	_____
_____	Adequate teaming areas	_____
_____	Adequate conferencing/huddle areas	_____
_____	Space appropriate for private meetings	_____
_____	Overall noise level	_____
_____	Departmental and team proximities/adjacencies	_____
_____	Overall comfort (in workstation/conference areas)	_____
_____	Overall rating of the new environment	_____

Please use this space and the back of this page for additional comments:

Personnel Information: The questions below have been designed to help us put your responses to these questions in perspective.

How long have you been with the company?   _____ Year(s)

What is your title/function within your department?   _____

What percentage of your typical work time is spent?

                                                            _____ In your individual work space
                                                            _____ In conference or huddle rooms
                                                            _____ In other departments
                                                            _____ Outside the facility

Thank you for taking the time to assist us in evaluating your office space. This information will be used to improve our office environments.

FIGURE 19-10

A Post-Occupancy Revaluation provides a measure to determine the effectiveness of the space and user satisfaction.

The steps performed by a POE specialist include:

1. Planning and preparation

2. Data collection

3. Data analysis

4. Data reporting and documentation

5. Development of an action plan based on the POE results

There are many reasons for a designer to conduct a POE. Perhaps the best reason for implementing a POE program is that it allows the designer and the client to learn from the past in order to improve on future projects. This is especially beneficial when a client is involved in a long-term, multiphased project, where the results of the initial POE can be utilized to fine-tune and improve future phases before they come on-line. Klass agrees: "Workplace evaluations can enable enhanced communications between a real estate group and the facility users. If the evaluation responses are treated with respect, improved communication and trust will result, even if the specific problems can't be solved. From the perspective of the facilities or real estate group, such an evaluation shows a commitment toward the opinions and concerns of the staff. It increases the profile of the facilities group with the users of the space, and shows their commitment to funding continuous improvement activities. In addition, involving the end-users in the process will increase their understanding of any changes that result."

Many interior designers and their facility management clients are passionate about the need for metrics and the ability to measure the success of an interiors project, especially in the office environment.

The personal traits and characteristics that are found in successful POE specialists include excellent listening and communication skills, ability to sell new ideas, open-minded analytical thinking abilities, excellent follow-through, and passion for the cause. Interior design and facilities professionals who possess these traits are well suited to provide POE consultation services.

CASE STUDY: AN INSURANCE COMPANY

Klass knows first hand of the benefit that POE can have when performed during a long-term, multi-phased project. Her client, an insurance company, had been faced with tremendous change in the last few years and was working to provide world-class services in the insurance industry. To them, this meant excelling in an environment of increasing competition and global reach. Against this background, their Facilities and Space Planning Department (FSPD) began the strategic process of evaluating officing standards in their facilities. It was decided to adopt an open office standard for approximately 95 percent of the office space. In an effort to measure the success of this type of transition, the FSPD began a workplace evaluation to determine how the existing space was being used, evaluate its effectiveness, and help in developing the new standards. Once the shift to open offices was underway, the FSPD completed the second half of this assessment, which was a post-occupancy evaluation to determine if the changes were effective, well received, and met the original objectives. The results informed the next stages of the construction project and provided direction on a much-needed change management program. (See Figure 19-11.)

SHORT-TERM DESIGN

During the second half of the twentieth century, interior design emerged and flourished as a viable profession that delivered needed services to office environments evolving after the Industrial Revolution and the first appearances of the mechanical office. The once-radical office landscapes introduced by the Quickborner Team in the 1960s gave birth to the open plan environment that the comic strip character Dilbert has immortalized today. During these several decades of discovery, trials, and maturation, interior designers developed a well-defined process, with a logical progression of phases that comprised planning, design, and implementation. Although sizes of projects varied, as did their complexities and characteristics, most interiors projects were implemented in about a year's time, give or take a couple of months,

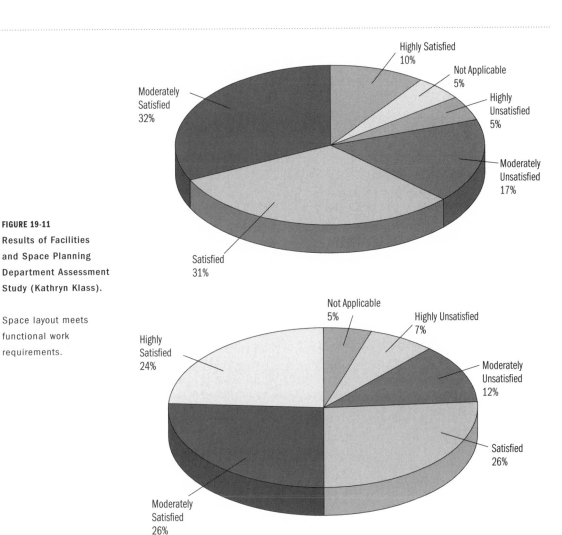

FIGURE 19-11
Results of Facilities and Space Planning Department Assessment Study (Kathryn Klass).

Space layout meets functional work requirements.

with major headquarters' campuses requiring a longer time frame. It was not uncommon in the 1980s to describe a 100,000-ft^2 interiors project with a schedule of ten months from programming to occupancy as a "fast-track project."

However, the escalating advances of technology coupled with the booming economy of the late 1990s have profoundly redefined the term "fast track." New entrepreneurial companies are springing up in unprecedented numbers, many with financing from venture capitalists who are anxious for quick gains and focused progress. These companies and their supporters don't have time to wait. They want everything right now, and this mandate holds true for their interior office environments as well. An emerging specialty practice involves planning and implementing start-up or "incubator" space, for the emerging technology and biotechnology industries.

Incubator Spaces

As defined by Webster, *to incubate* is "to maintain at a favorable temperature and in other conditions promoting development." Thus, a new type of office and lab space called the "incubator" has been introduced in the business community to attract, develop, and promote start-up companies that meet certain profiles for success. These businesses typically receive subsidized or drastically reduced rents for well-equipped office and lab spaces provided by local governments in the hopes that the start-up will meet tremendous success and remain in the region to grow, hire, contribute to the tax base and become a local leader. Interior designers who want to be introduced to both the incubated companies as well as their supporters have found this "short-term design" opportunity to be an emerging specialty practice.

Griswold, Heckel & Kelly Associates Inc. (GHK) has designed a technology incubator in Howard County, Maryland, called "The Center for Business and Technology Development." This 20,000-ft^2 facility hosts about 20 office suites, ranging in size from 120 to 1,000 ft^2, in addition to shared common areas. The Howard County Economic Development Authority (HCEDA) was the champion that secured State of Maryland funding as well as financial backing and support from Howard County government and local private-sector businesses to launch this incubator. Two of the marketing pioneers for HCEDA are Michael Haines and Carol Morrison. Morrison defines incubators as providing "space for a start-up which offers all support services, both physical and educational." Their center furnishes the office suite, and then offers conference, training, and board rooms at no additional charge. Other common spaces and equipment are provided, such as lobby and receptionist, administrative services, copying facilities, facsimile machines, shredders, postage meters and scales, and binding equipment. "Because we provide these common facilities, our start-up companies do not require large suites with underused square footage, which would be more common if they were to locate their new business elsewhere," shares Morrison.

The key to successfully designing an incubator is flexibility. Haines describes their incubator as "a large space divided into a number of different work spaces. Companies can expand or contract in this environment. The sharing of common areas is another example of the importance of flexibility. This incubator is a work in progress."

When asked what start-up companies look for when locating with an incubator, Haines and Morrison list the three top ingredients:

- *Flexibility of the space*

- *Networking through the incubator's contacts*

- *Exposure to the media and public relations opportunities*

Once they are in and established, their next priority is money: they are looking for investors and partners.

Both Haines and Morrison have been surprised at the instant success of their high-tech incubator. It is a magnet attracting volunteers, media, visiting countries, legislators, investors, job candidates, and the public. In the first four months of operation, 750 visitors toured the incubator, including 34 from Japan. The suites are 100 percent occupied, and are looking hopefully to Phase II, which will increase their overall square footage by 50 percent.

Haines and Morrison have visited more than seven incubators in the Mid-Atlantic region and feel that their center's focus on technology and their overall approach is unique in the region. By recognizing that wet laboratories (a type of laboratory facility for wet processes, requiring water and drains) for biotechnology companies can be a limiting factor, the focus of this incubator on technology versus biotechnology has enabled them to remain more flexible in the design of their facility. They also have observed that "there is a trade off between fixed drywall partitions and demountable walls. The demountable partitions may sound attractive, yet they are cost prohibitive and the lack of acoustical privacy is a big issue with start-up companies. Our tenants want privacy."

Current discussions between Haines and Morrison "are focused on the graduation process. Other incubators haven't solved what happens when the start-up is launched away from the facility. Strategic planning is needed to assure that there are appropriate options or facilities for these start-ups to go to when they graduate." Again, for the interior planning consultant, the opportunities are numerous for these companies in need of short-term design solutions with long-term continuous benefits.

Emerging E-business Companies

Emerging e-businesses are reshaping the landscape of traditional business and investment practices, by challenging "conventional wisdom" and are rewriting the scripts of interior design. "*Speed to market*" has been expanded to include *speed to hire, speed to partner, speed to advertise,* and *speed to secure venture capital funding.* Nowhere does the mantra mention *speed to establish an aesthetically pleasing and functional office space.* Implied in the "new world" belief structure is the understanding that the proper office environment will support their objectives. In reality, however, interior design tends not to appear on the immediate radar screen. There are bigger priorities with which to be concerned, yet although space is a minor issue in the eyes of the executives, it is still an issue.

So what is the role of the interior design professional when meeting and working with these "new world" entrepreneurs? It is one that promotes comprehensive flexibility, not only in the design of the space but in the trial of concepts, meeting times, on-the-fly programming and data-gathering activities, and gut-feel recommendations. Perhaps more than ever before, interior design professionals are being consulted to simply make recommendations based on our vast experiences, because there is no time to discuss or history to review that will shed light on the future of this start-up company. It is a new frontier, with few rules and exponential potential for growth.

Keith Hammonds, a *Fast Company* senior editor, described a typical scene in his August 2000 article, "Character Test." He says, "Since January 1999, [Troy] Tyler [35] and his two partners, Andrew Playford, 33, and David S. Kidder, 27, have been forging a company from the ground up. SmartRay now has 25 employees; two rounds of angel financing; four beanbag chairs; and a bare-bones, exposed-duct, one-room office overlooking 23rd Street in New York's Chelsea neighborhood. The corporate dining room is a bistro around the corner. When the three principals want to meet in private, they crush into their building's elevator. Up and down they go, plotting the future." Later in the article we learn more about the early priorities of these dot.com entrepreneurs. When the three partners began to shop for money in the early months of their venture, Hammonds writes, "Almost immediately they found the going rough. 'We had a demo and a business plan,' Playford recalls. 'But that's all we had, really. We didn't have a company. We didn't have an infrastructure. We didn't have space or chairs or employees.'" Once again, the interior design community is made of aware of their position in the food chain of the dot.com client. In fact, designers can achieve greater understanding of the needs of dot.com companies if they compare "old world" and "new world" realities in the dot.com business community.

Old World	*New World*
Currency is cash.	*Currency is stock options.*
Market value is based on doing the right thing.	*Market value is based on doing the instantaneous thing.*
Stock prices increase with the announcement of a new partnership.	*Stock prices increase with the announcement of a big sale.*
There are established rules of hierarchy.	*There are few rules and flatter organizations.*

Some of the "old world" executives are being chosen to lead these "new world" companies. Rick Inatome, CEO of an Internet education company, ZapMe Corporation, felt like a stranger in a foreign land when he left the glamorous trappings of a Fortune 500 business at the age of 46. D. M. Osborne, a senior writer at *Inc.*, interviewed Inatome for the March 2000 cover story, "Getting It." He described Inatome's first days: "Instead of working in an executive suite with a private washroom, Inatome spent his first weeks at ZapMe, based in San Ramon, California, perched on a box in a six-by-six foot cubicle. One day a boisterous young Web designer thrust out his hand and casually inquired of the CEO, 'So, what do you do here?'"

The implications of these scenarios are significant to the interior designer. With the old rules becoming outdated, and new ones being introduced, dismissed, and reintroduced with a different twist, it is imperative that design professionals stay current. It is no longer enough to attend the design industry conferences, but it is increasingly important to attend the many conferences that are targeted to the new economy companies. Similarly, it is commonplace for one to find *Fast Company, Wired*, and *Red Herring* publications on the desks of interior designers working for dot.com clients.

Diane Schroeder, Design Director at GHK, has worked with several emerging e-business companies, leading the design of their spaces to reflect their culture and new identity. She summarizes the differences: "These companies represent an emerging culture of high technology, young candidates in high demand, and high risk with high incentive . . . Business strategies include workplaces that attract and retain the best and the brightest candidates. Leadership toward success is the focus, not an attempt to change the individuals or teams. Traditional office space is not a consideration. E-commerce envisioning hypothesizes workplace tools, including social settings, sleeping and showering areas, lighting drama, and the idea that *work is social*. We are, however, acquiescing to the educational environment with the transition into the creative business environment. The question arises: What happens after dot.com?"

OUTSOURCING RELATIONSHIPS

During the recession years of the early 1990s, many corporations took a hard look at their financial statements and decided to focus only on their core businesses. These decisions usually triggered the outsourcing of all ancillary functions, including facility management and interior design. For some corporations, a skeleton staff remained to direct and oversee the work of outsourced service providers. For other companies, entire divisions were outsourced, requiring the outsourced service providers to answer directly to a vice president of administration or sometimes the chief financial officer. In the IFMA's Research Report #16, *Facility Management Practices*, published in 1996, the data suggested "a shift toward doing more with fewer internal FM staff and/or perhaps a greater use of outsourcing." This recent shift has created a greater demand for outsourced facility management and interior design service providers and their specialty practices, in both the traditional temporary consultant mode and an on-site mode.

The main reason to outsource is typically financially based. Lynda Grasser-Ross, with significant experience and training in real estate and operations-oriented development leasing, has observed that "the main driver to outsource is the corporate decision to disengage from non-core services, with a clear expectation of cost savings." Now with the Fireman's Fund in Novato, California, Grasser-Ross continues to outsource facility planning and design services, citing other drivers that include the need for consistency and best practices. She profoundly believes that best practices are realized when working with outsourced providers who keep abreast of emerging trends in the marketplace, and offer their industry expertise from working with a variety of companies addressing a diverse platform of issues. She feels that best practices is a compelling reason in itself in support of outsourcing.

Baxter Healthcare has long believed in the benefits of outsourcing. It and its sister company, Allegiance Healthcare, created outsourced relationships in order to focus on their core business and let others do what they do best. They wanted to be a low-cost provider with the best value. These outsourced relationships range from clerical services and travel support to real estate management and facility planning.

While much of the recent outsourcing trend did not alter the traditional design services offered by interior design firms (delivering conventional renovation or new construction projects), it did increase the need for specific ancillary services, such as churn work, relocation management, and CAFM services. These services had traditionally been provided by internal staff and now needed to be outsourced. However, the significant shift which affected interior design firms was the desire and expectation by the corporation to outsource their facility planning and design services to a service provider who would actually "sit on-site" with them, the customer. This resulted in a dedicated staff, who resembled in every way corporate employees, complete with security badges, access to computer systems, assigned parking spaces, and regular hours. Naoto Oka, design manager with the Facilities Management Division of the World Bank, describes it simply as "you provide services to clients on-site, but your paycheck comes from your company." Some interiors firms reject this idea, and do not participate in providing on-site services. Other firms embrace it as an opportunity to get close to their customer and become in many ways their strategic partner.

On-Site Provider

Providing on-site facility planning and design as an outsourced service can be a tremendous win–win opportunity for both the client and the service provider. Howard Baskin, an architect with GHK, lived on-site with Bank of America for six years as an outsourced provider in a consultative role. Previously he was an in-house facilities staff member for American Hospital, and knows firsthand what occurs on either side of the fence. He believes that the most important aspect of being an outsourced on-site provider is "the ability to become part of the culture of the company, of your customer. To move from 'vendor status' to full-fledged team member is very rewarding as well as challenging. Sometimes, I needed to keep corporate secrets from the GHK organization. I needed the ability to be a chameleon at times." Baskin delights in the opportunity to "go beyond the traditional architect's role to become a full-fledged business partner with the customer."

Of Baskin's 27 years of professional experience, half were spent in the corporate environment, and half in a consultative role (including his six years on-site with Bank of America). He first joined the corporate ranks because he recognized there was a void in the architectural profession. He did not feel that architects and interior designers knew how to relate to corporate clients. By working for "Corporate America," he began to understand the client, and enjoyed planning and designing, from start to finish. When he was "rightsized" out in 1990, he had a unique perspective and skill set that others in his profession lacked. That void became his opportunity to move into a consulting role.

Similar experiences have been shared by co-worker Kristen Drewke, an interior designer and project manager, who has spent more than ten years on-site with Baxter Healthcare in Deerfield, Illinois. Drewke defines an on-site provider as one who "lives with the client in their house. You are a guest. You learn and live their business and culture. You learn their politics. You feel and are sensitive to their business ups and downs. You feel and are sensitive to their emotional ups and downs. You become business associates and friends. You walk a fine line between your business and theirs. You must always try to balance the two. You require your management's understanding and support of the effort. You should be empowered to make decisions. You must be flexible in thought and process." She believes that on-site providers have an advantage if they have experienced both sides of the industry, with a facilities background as well as a design firm background.

Drewke finds that the work is highly stimulating, and covers a broad area of expertise. She says, "You name it, we've done it. Soup to nuts. I have found that if there are boundaries or guidelines, they move. We have done everything from providing graphics for Earth Day and golf outings, to high-level strategic meetings with upper management. Being on-site has both its ups and downs. But the opportunities are there, if you seek them out and development them."

Mitchell Cohen, president of GHK, pioneered an approach in providing on-site facility planning and design services. When Baxter Healthcare mandated the outsourcing of all non-core businesses in 1990, Cohen led the on-site team which included Drewke. They ultimately retained members of the Baxter facilities staff who were being "rightsized out." Their responsibilities included master planning, strategic facilities planning, standards development, feasibility studies, and churn/move management. Drewke's on-site team continues these and other services, 10 years later.

Cohen emphasizes the need for outsourced on-site providers to be responsive and flexible. He says, "Every service provider has faced a situation in which, temporarily at least, the workload for a client exceeds the capabilities of the dedicated on-site staff. Whether the spike occurs because deadlines are moved up, more work is required or existing staff become unavailable, the response must be the same: to provide staff in a timely fashion at service levels that meet or exceed the client's expectations."

Both Baskin and Drewke cite the following personal traits and characteristics of successful on-site providers: ability to multitask, to focus, and to think on your feet; willingness to address problems as business issues not design/architectural issues; political astuteness; ability to be passionate and take ownership of customer's issues; charm; honesty and a strong sense of ethics; self-esteem and confidence to gain the respect of customers and peers; and courage to push back and challenge.

Sally Jensen, also an interior designer with GHK, is a member of a multi-supplier on-site team, with Johnson Controls, at Sun Microsystems on the West Coast. She describes the philosophy of her on-site team: "We need to be the kind of individuals who *can* and *will* do whatever is required to get the job done, and done well. We must be willing to not only meet the customer's expectations, but to exceed them. It really is important to be friendly and easy, while still maintaining control of the workload. We should be likable to most personality types, and be inquisitive and energized enough to enjoy the diversity of the environment which changes daily. We are in the customer's space, and must respect that fact. We are there for them, not for our own egos."

Jay Erbe was vice president of administrative services for a major insurance company. He maintained a small staff of facilities personnel but supplemented their needs with an outsourced service provider, GHK. Initially, GHK provided an on-site team of three, which grew to a maximum of twelve to correspond to the size of the demand and workload. In addition, staff from GHK's regional offices provided move management and churn management services. Erbe shares "four key considerations when selecting an outsourced provider. (1) *Chemistry*. First and foremost. The in-house manager must not feel threatened by the outsourced provider. We look for complementary and overlapping skills. This becomes a necessary and healthy interdependence. Chemistry builds. (2) *Humility*. The most important quality of an outsourced consultant is to be humble. He should not be out to wave a flag 'this is what I bring to the table.' (3) *Creativity and Options*. The outsourced consultant should bring leading-edge ideologies and alternatives to the table, whether a chair selection, an innovative design detail, or a creative approach to phasing. (4) *Sales and Marketing*. The consultant must be able to sell his ideas to the internal staff and in-house management. Having great ideas is one thing, but selling them and inspiring confidence is a whole other ballgame that must be achieved. Sales and marketing is an art and a science."

Baskin agrees with these four points, and offers two immediate benefits that are realized once an on-site team is in place. First, he believes that the learning curve is reduced as much as half if an outsourced provider sits on-site with the customer. (See Figure 19-12.) Second, Baskin firmly believes that most clients who retain the services of an off-site outsourced provider (one that does not sit on-site) truly do not understand what an interior design and

FIGURE 19-12
The learning curve is reduced with on-site consultants.

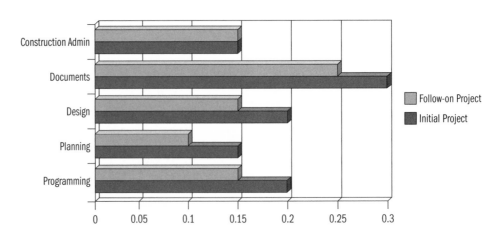

facility planning consultant does. He says, "They don't see the intensity and amount of labor. If the client's project managers could see this, it would greatly increase the amount of professional respect. We seldom experience serious issues when the client literally works alongside the outsourced team."

Lessons learned by Cohen during the past decade with Baxter, as well as from other on-site relationships, are shared with GHK's on-site teams. Cohen is a big proponent of metrics, or the measurement of performance. Annual examinations and reporting typify the "best practices" measurements that have been performed by GHK and other service providers at Baxter. This regular evaluation has enabled Baxter and its outsourced providers to benchmark their own performance as well as compare their results to others in same class or best of class companies. (See Figure 19-13.)

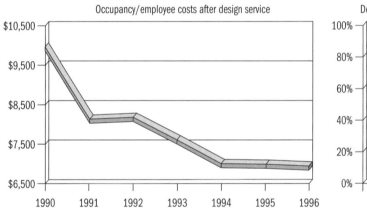

FIGURE 19-13
Examples of Metrics
Reported Annually.

One publication that highlights the successes and challenges of the outsourced relationship *is The Outsource Report*, sponsored by *Facilities Design & Management* and Brown Raysman Millstein Felder & Steiner LLP. Editor Kenneth M. Block, Esq., summarizes in the June 2000 e-Letter issue, "The key to a successful alliance is relationship management. . . . In order for a true alliance to prosper, there must be an understanding of the mutual risks and rewards. Objectives must be discussed and understood and become part of the base of the alliance. Additionally, various types of a risk/reward sharing can be agreed upon, such as cost savings and financial gain. The establishment of joint performance goals and measures using benchmarking techniques is also helpful to measure the performance of both the provider and customer. Measurement of the performance of both parties is the ultimate key to a successful true alliance."

For the interior designer and facility planner, an on-site outsourced service delivery is often a means by which to find career satisfaction and ultimate customer satisfaction.

Temporary Workers and Contractors

Also a significant contender in the outsourced provider pool is the designer who is a temporary worker or independent contractor. These workers seek and enjoy the freedom and variety in contracting their services for a specific assignment, for a specific duration of time. They can work for virtually any organization that wishes to retain their services, whether it be through an agency, interior design firm, or directly with a facility management organization or company.

The distinguishing characteristic of an independent contractor revolves around how he or she is paid. The independent contractor designer assumes all responsibility for the payment of taxes, insurances, healthcare coverage, and other benefits. (See Figure 19-14.) This can be beneficial if the designer wishes to deduct home office expenses, or has other sources of benefits, i.e., a spouse with benefits provided by his or her employer. However, the designer who chooses this mode of work must consider some risk factors, such as errors and omissions, liability, interpretations of IRS regulations, and lack of long-term contracts or commitments.

Marilyn Farrow, FIIDA, has been an independent contractor on several occasions. She describes a few typical activities.

- *Activities can and may be same as any other professional practice. The contractual arrangement under which you provide services and are paid is the only difference.*

- *Care must be taken to be properly indemnified by employers against malpractice, errors and omissions, and liability claims, when electing this form of business relationship.*

- *Must be responsible in filing quarterly "estimated tax" forms, paying all state and federal obligations.*

A COMPARATIVE ANALYSIS OF REPRESENTATIVE EXPENDITURES

BASED ON SALARY @ $75,000

		EMPLOYER'S PAYMENT	CONTRACT EMPLOYEE OBLIGATION
○ SOCIAL SECURITY	Company @ 6.2%	4,687.50	9,300.00
	Individual @ 12.4% on *net* earnings		(8,705 on net)
○ MEDICARE	Company @ 1.45%	1,087.50	2,175.00
	Individual @ 2.9% on net earnings		(2,036 on net)
○ STATE UNEMPLOYMENT	Company @ .7%	525.00	
	No Individual Obligation		0
○ FEDERAL UNEMPLOYMENT	Company @ .8%	600.00	
			0
○ GROUP/LIFE INSURANCE	Company @ $315/mo	3,780.00	
	No Individual Obligation		0
○ DISABILITY INSURANCE	Company @ $28.75/mo	345.00	
	No Individual Obligation		0
		11,025.00	11,475.00
			(10,741 on net)

ESTIMATED ANNUAL EXPENSES:	ANNUAL COSTS
Phone service, 2 lines	1,000.00
Equipment, supplies	1,000.00
Conferences, books, education	1,000.00
Software	300.00
Professional licenses, registrations, memberships	1,000.00
Travel expenses not reimbursed	500.00
▬ Net earnings of $70,200	4,800.00

FIGURE 19-14
Comparative Analysis of expenditures for an independent contractor.

Farrow also cites a few key considerations particular to this specialty.

- *The relationship of "contractor" should be transparent to the customer.*

- *Identifying an alternative source of health insurance is a contributing factor in evaluating the financial viability of this kind of business relationship.*

- *The independent contractor is able to secure retention of "intellectual property" by the individual, a benefit not present when working for a salary.*

Farrow concludes that "the measurements of success must rely on other than 'time clock' perspectives. Contributions must reside in value-add, not time applied."

CONCLUSION

Design professionals began to develop specialty practices when clients began to need supplemental services, beyond those provided in the six basic phases of conventional design services. Designers who offer these ancillary services address the customer's needs with more depth and breadth than would a general practitioner. Because specialists trained and experienced in these specialty areas are prepared to attend to critical details, the client enjoys a valuable return on his investment.

Interior designers have followed widely divergent career paths in the pursuit of expertise in specialty practice areas. Whether these professionals sought out or stumbled upon their optimum professional role pays tribute to the value of the more unconventional practice of interior design in these specialty practice areas.

Bibliography

Becker, Franklin. *The Total Workplace: Facilities Management and the Elastic Organization*. New York: Van Nostrand Reinhold, 1990.

Becker, Franklin, and Fritz Steele. *Workplace by Design: Mapping the High-Performance Workscape*. San Francisco: Jossey-Bass Management, 1995.

Cotts, David G. *The Facility Management Handbook*. New York: AMACOM, 1998.

Duffy, Francis. *The New Office: With 20 International Case Studies*. London: Conrad Octopus, 1997.

Facilities Design & Management in partnership with various sponsors, *The Outsource Report*. New York: Bill Communications.

Friday, Stormy, and David G. Cotts. *Quality Facility Management: A Marketing and Customer Service Approach*. New York: John Wiley & Sons, 1994.

Rondeau, Edmond P., Robert Kevin Brown, and Paul D. Lapides. *Facility Management*. New York: John Wiley & Sons, 1995.

Sims, William, Michael Joroff, and Franklin Becker. *Managing the Reinvented Workplace*. Norcross, GA: International Development Research Foundation, 1996.

Zelinsky, Marilyn. *New Workplaces for New Workstyles*. New York: McGraw-Hill, 1998.

CHAPTER

20

The Legal Environment

BARRY B. LEPATNER, Esq.
DAVID J. PFEFFER, Esq.

Over the past 20 years, design professionals have increasingly encountered challenges from new and varied areas of legal complexity and exposure. In recent years, the design world has been forced to address liability for claims ranging from sick-building-related illness to Americans with Disabilities Act (ADA) violations, to the more common equivocal billings and delay claims brought by owners and contractors. In addition, interior designers and other design professionals in many states have been exposed to increased civil and even criminal liability for practicing in jurisdictions without a license as well as charges for unauthorized practice as a professional. While most designers do not set out to break the law, uncertainty about legal issues may be their undoing.

It is troubling enough for designers to consider the personal and professional losses they might incur if they must defend a legal claim. But legal exposure presents a concrete financial risk, too, even when a designer is covered by insurance. At the same time that legal claims against designers have increased in frequency and complexity, the costs of defending designers against these claims have skyrocketed. The cost of defending a claim too often exceeds the potential liability of the claim itself. Even when the designer has liability insurance to cover a claim, the diminishing coverage, exhausted by the costs of one's defense, may not leave enough insurance left over to pay the claim. In the face of a diminishing liability policy—which is what most design professionals have—a designer can be personally liable for a large portion of the costs of a claim even if the settlement or judgment amount is originally within policy limits.

Even though the risk and costs of liability may seem overwhelming, designers can protect themselves if they are aware of the types of liability they face and what they can do to avoid becoming involved in legal action. This chapter focuses on those areas of the law that pose increased liability to practicing interior designers and other design professionals. Included in this discussion are practical steps for interior designers to take in order to avoid liability. As a related matter, this chapter also sets out a discussion addressing certain business and legal complexities facing the design world. Though this is not intended to be a summary of every area of liability faced by an interior designer, it is the intention of the authors to sensitize practitioners to the need to take appropriate steps, from a business and contractual standpoint, that can limit or eliminate such liability. Because it is not practical to discuss the law and practices of every jurisdiction, design professionals are advised to obtain the assistance of experienced legal counsel.

LICENSING

During the recession of the early 1990s, many architects began to complain that interior designers were usurping the licensed field of architecture, i.e., practicing a profession for which they were not authorized by strict professional training. In order to avoid legal exposure because of licensing issues, interior designers must not only become familiar with the licensing laws and rules in the state where a project is located, but must also be able to distinguish the difference between the services they can legally perform and those services they cannot perform.

Licensing issues can have serious consequences for designers, financially as well as personally. In recent years, the number of complaints filed against designers for practicing without a license has increased dramatically. Interior designers could be prosecuted in criminal court under penal statutes for unauthorized practice, and in addition they now face the possibility that a client will add monetary damages to their claim about the unlicensed practice of interior design, architecture, and engineering. Even if they are not sued, designers are likely to find that a court will refuse to enforce a designer's claim for the payment of fees, if the court finds that the designer performed professional services without the required license.

Perhaps the most important step designers can take is to understand what services they can legally perform in a particular state. The distinction between permissible and impermissible services is not always as clear as it seems. Licensing laws concerning interior designers commonly stress the difference between interior design and the practice of architecture and engineering.

These laws place responsibility for the building systems, i.e., mechanical, electrical, plumbing, life safety, with the architect and engineer who are licensed by state law to seal and stamp drawings for this portion of a project. In New York, for example, the law emphasizes the difference between interior construction "not materially affecting the building systems" and design services that affect building systems. The clear intent is that the latter shall fall within the practice of architecture and engineering. Elements such as cabinets, lighting, and shelving usually fall within the ambit of the interior designer's permissible scope of work. Where an interior design firm's services included designs for floor elevations, changes in walls and openings, and supervision of the general contractor, a New York court found that the interior designer engaged in the unlicensed practice of architecture and noted that "there is a thin—but plain—line between 'interior design' and 'architecture' services."[1] The court held that "the preparation of plans and supervision of construction work are the usual functions of an architect."

In comparison, Florida focuses on the difference between structural elements and nonstructural interior elements of a building. The Florida Board of Architecture & Interior Design defines "Interior Design" as:

Designs, consultations, studies, drawings, specifications, and the administration of design construction contracts relating to nonstructural interior elements of a building or structure. . . . Interior design specifically excludes the design of or responsibility for architectural and engineering work except for specification of fixtures and their location within interior spaces.[2]

The Florida board defines "Architecture" as:

The rendering or offering to render services in connection with the design and construction of a structure or group of structures which have as their principal purpose human habitation or use, and the utilization of space within and surrounding such structures.[3]

When interior design documents are prepared by a registered interior designer in Florida, the Florida board requires the interior designer to include a statement on the plans that "the document is not an architectural or engineering study, drawing, specification, or design and is not to be used for construction of any load bearing framing or walls of structures, or issuance of any building permit, except as otherwise provided by law."[4]

Designers who practice beyond the scope of a license often incur serious civil and criminal consequences. Not only do these designers lose the opportunity to make a valid defense to an owner's malpractice claim, but in states such as California, Illinois, and New York, those who practice without a license commit a crime that subjects them to penalties such as imprisonment, fines, and the revocation of their properly obtained license. Likewise, a designer who unlawfully uses another's title or stamps a drawing could also be subject to penalties. Most states, and the rules promulgated by the American Institute of Architects (AIA), require a design professional to report any instance of licensing law violations to the appropriate regulatory bodies.

Interior designers must be careful not to mistakenly represent themselves to the public as being able to practice beyond the scope of their license. Most states not only prohibit the unauthorized practice of the professions but also proscribe a nonlicensed individual from holding himself or herself out as a licensed person. In California, New York, and other states, an interior designer or interior decorating firm cannot include the term "architect" or similar word in its name or on its advertising material, including business cards or other material which may indicate to the public that the firm is qualified to practice architecture or engineering. Care must also be taken to avoid using terms such as "architectural," "construction supervision," and similar expressions.

To avoid liability for unlawful practice, designers should inform their clients of the services their firm will be performing and explicitly exclude all architectural or engineering services. When drafting an interior design agreement, careful attention must be paid to ensure that the interior designer's services do not go beyond the allowable definition of interior design. This information should be included in the written agreement with the client so there will be no misunderstanding concerning the services to be performed.

PREPARING PROPOSALS

For interior designers, preparing and submitting proposals is a traditional approach to securing new business. The skillful preparation of a Request for Proposal (RFP) can position a firm on a project's short list or, in the best of circumstances, reflect qualifications that distinguish one firm over those without similar qualifications or terms of service. The fundamentals of the proposal process are simple enough: identify prospective clients and projects; clarify the prospect's need to determine your marketing approach; transmit the written proposal; and, hopefully, learn that one's proposal has received the client's approval. Seems easy enough. Or is it? Unfortunately for designers, under certain circumstances the proposal can bind the designer contractually to terms that may be unreasonable. In order to avoid being bound by unreasonable contract terms, interior designers should understand the legal ramifications of preparing a proposal for a project.

What happens if a proposal is answered by a simple client reply stating across the bottom page: "Accepted, please commence services immediately as set forth above." Is there an enforceable contract? Are you responsible for commencing your services immediately? Can you be sued if you do not perform the precise services outlined in your proposal? The legal answers to these questions are frequently "yes." Although RFPs often do not create an offer that the prospective client can turn into a binding contract merely by writing "Accepted" on its face, a proposal can sometimes be interpreted by courts as an invitation or "offer" to enter into a binding contract for the described services. Generally, whether at an auction in a gallery or on an Internet site, when a potential buyer makes a bid and the seller subsequently accepts it, a contract exists because the parties have mutually assented to be bound. It does not matter that the parties may not have worked out every one of the contract terms or that the agreement is not in writing. And the mere fact that the parties intend to reduce their agreement to a writing in the future does not make their "agreement" nonbinding. For this reason, designers should see the process of responding to a potential client's RFP as serious business.

Protecting the Designer from Lawsuit

Design professionals can avoid being unwittingly bound to contract terms if they follow some steps designed to make their proposals precise and to make their intent clear. Under the law of contracts, parties are free, with certain limitations, to decide under what circumstances their assents will become binding. It is also fundamental that contract formation is governed by the intent of the parties. In evaluating the parties' intent, courts look to their expressed words and actions. Two legal rules are well established on this point: (1) if parties manifest an intent not to be bound unless they have executed a formal agreement, then they will not be bound until such time; and (2) the mere fact

Generally, whether at an auction in a gallery or on an Internet site, when a potential buyer makes a bid and the seller subsequently accepts it, a contract exists because the parties have mutually assented to be bound . . .

that the parties intend to memorialize the agreement in a formal document does not prevent the informal agreement from taking effect prior to that event. Consequently, in order to avoid becoming bound by a reply containing unreasonable contract terms, the astute interior designer should follow these four rules for submitting proposals:

1. Review the terms and conditions contained in an RFP carefully.

2. Thoroughly think through fee and schedule terms with an emphasis on staffing availability. Unexpected fees and schedule delays are the main cause of owner dissatisfaction.

3. Qualify proposals to conform to or address special concerns as to how and when your firm will perform its work. Exceptions should be made based on ambiguous and incomplete information contained in the RFP. If your proposal is accepted, these qualifications and exceptions may make the difference between a profitable and unprofitable project.

4. Attach a copy of your firm's standard agreement for services. If your proposal is accepted, you will ensure a full negotiation on all contract terms after your firm has been selected.

LIABILITY AND CONTRACTUAL PROTECTIONS

As team members, interior designers are subject to real and imagined claims from a number of directions; many of them will stem from actions undertaken (or omitted) by another team member. This liability is of two types. The first type of claim, contractual liability claims, arise when designers fail to perform any promise which formed a part of their contract. Contractual liability is usually measured in terms of assumed or due care in the performance of a designer's contractual obligations. The second type of claim involves malpractice or professional negligence, in which clients allege that designers committed professional misconduct, provided services that fall below an acceptable local standard of care, or engaged in other improper conduct relating to their services. Like contract claims, professional negligence claims are usually measured in terms of whether the interior designer's performance fell short of applicable professional standards usually exercised by a member of the profession in the locale where the services were performed.

The law does not expect or require absolute perfection from an interior designer. Unless the parties have contractually agreed to a higher standard, the law tests the efficiency of the interior designer by the rule of ordinary and reasonable skill usually exercised by one of that profession. To prove malpractice, the claimant must almost always present evidence of the standard of care by which the designer's competence may be judged and show that the designer did something, or failed to do something, that violated accepted professional standards.

Design professionals commonly face exposure to liability related to the design, scheduling, construction cost estimating, supervision and inspection, certification of payments due a contractor, and resolution of disputes. We focus below on several of these areas and address specific steps that an interior designer can take to minimize risk of exposure in these areas.

LIABILITY FOR SCHEDULING

If a designer fails to achieve established project deadlines, the owner can sustain substantial damages. A design professional may be liable to the owner if the project is not completed on time as a result of his or her acts or omissions. Because of the increasing number of claims for damages due to delay, designers should include in their contracts specific provisions to minimize liability for this type of claim.

Although a sophisticated owner will want the designer to assist in preparing a project schedule and be responsible for meeting all agreed-upon schedule deadlines, the designer's contract should expressly exclude liability for delays caused by other project team members. Such contractual language could read as follows:

The Designer, in collaboration with the Owner [and the Architect of Record], shall establish a mutually acceptable schedule for the design development and contract documents phases. The schedule shall include commencement and completion dates for such phases in accordance with the Owner's established date for issuance of drawings for bidding. Should there be any deviation from this schedule due to the Owner's programming changes or other causes outside the Designer's control, the completion dates for such phase shall be modified accordingly. As appropriate, the Designer shall assist the Owner [and the Architect of Record] in coordinating the schedules for installation of the work, but shall not be responsible for any malfeasance, neglect, or failure of any contractor or supplier to meet their schedules for completion or to perform their respective duties and responsibilities.

Should the project be delayed through no fault of the designer, the designer should be entitled to an adjustment in the project schedule and compensated for the extra time spent and services rendered on the project past the agreed-upon completion date. The following provision will ensure that the designer is entitled to the schedule adjustment and is properly compensated for the extended time and services rendered on a project as a result of an owner- or contractor-caused delay:

Notwithstanding any other provision contained in this Agreement, if the services covered by this Agreement have not been completed within _____ (_____) months of the date hereof, through no fault of the Designer, the Designer shall be compensated for all services rendered after _____ (_____) months on an hourly basis in accordance with the Designer's Hourly Rate Schedule which is then in effect. The Designer shall be entitled to an adjustment to the project schedule for the number of days the completion of services was delayed.

Finally, designers should take the following general precautions to avoid exposure for scheduling claims: (1) be insistent that all project schedule milestone dates and turn-around times are realistic; (2) ensure that reasonableness standards for time extensions are built into your agreements and that a *force majeure*, i.e., Act of God, clause is included; and (3) immediately inform your client in writing of all delays caused by contractors, consultants, or other parties.

As team members, interior designers are subject to real and imagined claims from a number of directions; many . . . from actions undertaken (or omitted) by another team member.

LIABILITY FOR COST ESTIMATES

Often, clients claim that designers failed to prepare a design within the owner's budget. If a design professional miscalculates the anticipated costs of a project, he may face liability to the owner. In determining whether the designer is liable for cost-estimating claims, courts will seek to assess whether the designer lived up to the reasonable standard of professional skill. If the court finds that the designer did not live up to the reasonable standard, it may hold the designer responsible for damages to the client, and in addition it may deny the designer compensation for services rendered. However, the court will not usually infer liability simply because the cost discrepancy is greater than usual.

Design professionals should think carefully about employing a common protection against such claims: incorporating a clause in one's agreement which limits liability for cost estimates. Such a limitation of liability shifts the responsibility for estimating costs away from the designer. The AIA has sought to insulate architects from providing cost estimates for projects by placing responsibility for cost estimating with the owner. This position, however, will often backfire, and cause an owner, especially a sophisticated one, to lose faith in the designer. Historically, design professionals gained stature in the eyes of their clients by delivering designs that matched project budgets established by the client. By retreating from this standard, designers have painted themselves into a corner. They provide design services with only limited construction involvement and thereby lose control over the contractor and the project costs. In such circumstances, designers are often unable to protect the client from overcharges by contractors. In the end the client loses confidence in the entire process.

The other approach to cost estimates is to work more closely with the owner and other members of the team involved in the project. By agreeing to work closely with the owner, a cost estimation consultant, or with a construction manager, designers can play a more significant role in a project without increasing liability. Those concerned about risk can minimize exposure with a specific contract provision that recognizes the designer's responsibility to make design changes to meet the project budget, at no cost through the design development phase. Once the owner approves the design development documents as consistent with the project budget—based on confirmation from an outside cost consultant—there can be little or no liability to the designer if subsequent bids come in higher.

Design professionals should incorporate provisions into their agreements which reflect their commitment to work with the owner to adopt realistic project costs, while including protective language to minimize their own exposure. Designers should explain to clients that as the result of fluctuating labor costs and the variable prices of materials and equipment, they cannot be reasonably expected to take on the risk of guaranteeing project cost estimates, within certain parameters. Such a provision can take the following form:

Any evaluations by the Designer of the Owner's project budget or statements of probable construction cost, represent the Designer's best judgment as a design professional familiar with the construction industry. It is recognized, however, that neither the Designer nor the Owner has control over the cost of labor, materials or equipment, over the Contractor's methods of determining bid prices, or over competitive bidding, market or negotiating conditions. Accordingly, the Designer cannot and does not warrant or represent that bids or negotiated prices will not vary from the project budget proposed, established, or approved by the Owner, if any, or from any statement of probable construction cost or other cost estimate or evaluation prepared by the Designer.

In order to avoid exposure for excessive cost claims, the designer should explain the cost-estimating process to the client. Before finalizing a contract for the project, designers can explain how project costs are developed and how many variable cost factors affect price predictions. During design and construction, designers should inform clients about how project scope or other significant changes may affect previous cost estimates; in addition, increases in fees may eventuate from design changes at late stages of design development. Designers should be particularly cautious when an owner emphasizes that project costs must be guaranteed. This is a red-flag for design exposure in what may be an unfair and even frivolous legal action.

OWNERSHIP OF DOCUMENTS

Who owns, and has the right to future use of, the written design documents created by a design professional? Do clients who pay for the production of drawings and specifications own the documents? Are design professionals merely selling their ideas to clients, whereby they retain exclusive use to and ownership of their documents? If another designer subsequently completes the project, can the original designer be liable for errors or omissions contained in the design documents?

Absent an agreement assigning their rights, designers generally have ownership rights to the plans and specifications they create. However, contract terms, such as those contained in standardized AIA or ASID agreements, customarily grant the owner a license or permission to copy the designer's documents and use them for particular purposes. Additionally, when a contract does not contain any terms about whether the client can reuse drawings and documents, the client generally has a right to use the documents prepared by the design professional.

Agreements with Clients

Design professionals can protect themselves from exposure should the owner reuse design documents, and from the possibility that the owner might unlawfully use or copy them, if their agreements contain language that states that the design professional is the author and owner of the design work and retains possession to and ownership in the work. Such a provision can be worded as follows:

The drawings, specifications, and other documents (including but not limited to all documents related to interior construction, custom furniture, lighting, fabrics, and carpet [add additional items here]) prepared by the Designer for this Project are instruments of service and shall remain the property of the Designer whether the Project for which they are made is executed or not. As the author of these documents, the Designer shall retain all statutory and other reserved rights, including but not limited to copyright and patent rights. The Owner shall advise its agents, employees, contractors, vendors, and manufacturers who are provided copies of these documents of the Designer's proprietary interest in such documents.

In order to reflect the owner's limited need to be able to use the designer's documents for information and reference purposes after the project is completed, the following language should be added:

The Owner shall be permitted to retain copies, including reproducible copies, of drawings and specifications for information and reference in connection with the Owner's use and occupancy of the project provided the Designer is not in default under this Agreement, except as provided herein or by agreement in writing and with appropriate compensation to the Designer. The drawings and specifications shall not be used by the Owner or others on other projects, for additions to this project, or for completion of this project by others.

Design professionals should negotiate for additional fees with any owner who seeks to utilize the design documents for any future project. If such negotiation is not possible, the design professional needs protection for claims arising out of such future use. An owner should agree to indemnify, i.e., restore any loss to, the design professional for any future loss associated with the owner's subsequent use of the drawings and specifications. The following provision will operate to reduce exposure in the event of the owner's subsequent use of the designer's documents:

In the event the Designer is not retained for subsequent adaptation(s) and the use of the design prepared by him/her for this project, the Owner shall defend, indemnify, and hold the Designer harmless from and against all claims, demands, liabilities, causes of actions, lawsuits, damages, judgments, costs, and expenses, including reasonable attorneys' fees, the Designer may sustain or incur, in connection with, arising out of, as a consequence of, or by reason of the use of the Designer's design on such subsequent adaptation(s) and new project(s).

By including such provisions in agreements with clients, designers will protect their property interests in the tangible manifestations of their work at the same time that they also recognize the owner's need to have some control over the documents concerning the project.

Copyright Laws

U.S. and many international copyright laws protect original works of authorship fixed in any unique and tangible medium of expression. The copyright laws apply to the expression of an idea, but not to the idea itself. In other words, ideas may not be copyrighted, but their "tangible expression" may be. Under Section 102 of the Copyright Act, 17 U.S.C., as amended on December 1, 1990, an original design of a building, embodied in any tangible medium of expression, including a building, design plans, or drawings, is subject to copyright protection as an "architectural work."

Designers should be aware that Section 102 of the U.S. Copyright Act is limited to certain structures. The use of the term "building" excludes many types of three-dimensional works worthy of copyright protection, such as bridges, walkways, recreational vehicles, mobile homes, boats, and gardens. However, the term "building" includes not only structures inhabited by humans, but also those merely used by humans, such as churches, pergolas, gazebos, and garden pavilions. These are limited examples of many other forms which may be copyright-protected.

COPYRIGHT VS. PATENT PROTECTIONS

It should also be noted that a copyright is distinct from a patent. There are three basic differences between the two: first, the subject matter differs because patents are directed at physical, scientific, and technological items, whereas copyrights encompass artistic and intellectual works. In general, copyrightable works are nonfunctional; examples include writing, painting, or a piece of sculpture. Second, patents offer considerably more protection. A patent is a 17-year monopoly granted to the inventor by the federal government in exchange for a complete and thorough description of his or her invention. A copyright is a right granted to the author of literary or artistic productions, whereby he is invested with the sole and exclusive privilege of ownership of a work, including the right to license publishing and distribution rights. Protection under the U.S. Copyright Act is secure for 50 years, after which it may be renewed. Third, unlike the patent process, it is a relatively simple matter to obtain copyright registration. An application is submitted, together with a filing fee and one original copy of the unpublished work to be copyrighted.

Copyright grants four rights exclusively to the author or owner of the architectural work: the right to transform or adapt the work into another form;

the right to make copies; the right to distribute copies; and the exclusive right to display the work publicly. Anyone who violates any of these rights provided to the author or owner of the copyright is committing an illegal act, i.e., an infringement of the copyright.

All authors and owners are advised to have their designs and technical drawings registered with the Copyright Office in Washington, D.C. While registration with the Copyright Office is not essential for the creation of a copyright, the copyright holder is certainly not without incentives to register. First and foremost, a completed registration is an indispensable prerequisite to filing an action for infringement. Once the material has been registered, it is immaterial whether the infringement that leads to the lawsuit occurred before or after the effective date of registration. Additionally, the copyright holder can use a certificate that shows that the work was copyrighted before or within five years after its first publication to provide *prima facie* evidence of the validity both of the copyright and the facts stated in the certificate. A court may not award statutory damages or attorneys' fees for any infringement of an unpublished work occurring before registration or for any infringement of a published work not registered within three months of publication. Other notable benefits of registration include preservation of the copyright, at least in certain circumstances, even when the work as published bears no notice of copyright whatsoever, and protection of the actual owner's interest when the notice erroneously names another as the proprietor of the copyright.

Because of existing copyright laws, even if developer-owners own the drawings, they do not have a free hand to clone a design or one of its elements unless they receive an assignment of the design copyright or unless design is created by an employee. If the developers do not own drawings and do not have a legitimate interest in the work by way of an assignment, they may be required to defend against an infringement action brought by the original creator. Especially if developers intend to use a design at a different location, they might consider acquiring the copyright, which is assignable, along with the drawings, and an agreement allowing them unfettered use of the design plans.

HEALTH AND SAFETY ISSUES

Health studies over the past 25 years have found that increasing numbers of people contract severe respiratory and skin diseases as well as fatigue and headaches resulting from unacceptable levels of gases, bacteria, fungi, molds, and other harmful chemicals in the air circulating throughout enclosed buildings. These symptoms, referred to in the aggregate as "sick-building-related" symptoms, are on the rise. Across the country, physicians report that sick-building-related illnesses increased by as much as 40 percent in the 1990s alone. With the increase in awareness of indoor pollution comes the rise in litigation against owners and design professionals for building-related illness and sick-building syndrome. Both new construction as well as renovation projects are prone to these claims. Substantial lawsuits have been filed by sick tenants, occupants, and visitors against owners and designers. Even when the plaintiffs do not name the design team as defendants in such lawsuits, they are often brought into the litigation by owners who seek to be indemnified by design professionals for the sick-building-related claims.

Illnesses caused by harmful chemicals that are found in buildings fall into one of two categories. The first illness is known as building-related illness, which occurs when readily identifiable fungi or other airborne matter causes actual disease. The second is sick-building syndrome, which occurs when people report symptoms that cannot be traced to one particular cause.

Building-related illness and sick-building syndrome can be caused by a number of different factors, including poor air distribution; inadequate air intakes; sealed windows; contaminated HVAC systems; faulty air filters that fail to filter out noxious impurities; recycled air containing second-hand smoke; construction dust and paint fumes; accumulation of standing water in HVAC condensate trays; and dangerous construction materials such as textile trimmings, dyes and sealants in furniture, and other materials containing heavy metals.

Additionally, the presence of asbestos in commercial and residential buildings has taken on ominous proportions for the real estate industry. The presence of asbestos in buildings has resulted in federal, state, and local legislation to limit the exposure to and handling of asbestos. On the federal level, the

Copyright grants four rights exclusively to the author or owner of the architectural work: the right to transform or adapt the work into another form; the right to make copies; the right to distribute copies; and the exclusive right to display the work publicly.

Environmental Protection Agency (EPA) and the Occupational Safety and Health Administration (OSHA) have promulgated exposure limits to asbestos measured over time periods. There are also special requirements for renovation, removal, and demolition, including negative pressure enclosures, supervisory personnel, worker decontamination areas, clean rooms, and equipment rooms. State and local legislatures and agencies have also enacted legislation concerning asbestos. For example, the New York State Department of Law, which oversees cooperative and condominium offerings, has enacted regulations requiring sponsors to inspect for asbestos and disclose its presence, if any, in the cooperative offering plan. In addition, the New York State legislature amended the statute of limitations for toxic tort lawsuits. Victims in New York may commence an action within three years from the date the injury was discovered, as opposed to when the victim was actually exposed to the toxic material. Other states have enacted similar rules.

An interior design firm can avoid or minimize its liability by incorporating certain exculpatory provisions in its agreements. First, the designer–owner agreement should place all responsibility for air quality with the owner. Since many owners will not accept the additional costs relating to improving air quality without evidence of a real need, in projects where air quality may pose a particular problem, the designer–owner agreement should also provide that the owner retain, at its expense, an air quality consultant.

Second, the agreement should specifically exclude the designer from responsibility for all work related to toxic and hazardous material. The design firm should advise the owner before commencing services on the project that it does not have the expertise to deal with toxic materials and a consultant should be hired for this purpose. The essence of this wording might read as follows:

The Project may uncover hazardous or toxic materials or pollutants including, but not limited to asbestos, asbestos-related materials and PCBs. Notwithstanding any provisions in this Agreement to the contrary, the Interior Designer and its consultants are not responsible for the performance of any services in connection with or related to such materials and the Owner hereby agrees to retain an expert or experts to arrange for the prompt identifications of and/or removal or treatment of such materials identified during the course of

*the Project and to indemnify and hold harmless the Interior De-
signer and its principals, employees, agents, and consultants from
any claims, damages, losses, demands, lawsuits, causes of action,
injuries, or expenses, including reasonable counsel fees, incurred by
the Interior Designer arising out of, as a consequence of, or in any
way related to the existence of such material on the Project.*

Finally, on certain projects where existing air quality issues may pose heightened concerns, designers should request that the owner indemnify them and
hold them harmless from liability related to the existence of toxic materials.
This is especially important where there are known toxic airborne particles
such as asbestos and lead-based paint present on the site.

Realizing that the integrity of a building's health is important, certain practical considerations should be addressed to limit liability for building-related
illness and sick-building syndrome. Designers should pay close attention to
the specification of materials to be used in the building. Although designers
will not usually be responsible for conducting their own testing of materials
used on their projects, designers should not specify materials for which the
side effects may be unknown. They should also hesitate to use newly developed materials before an established testing program has ensured that there
are no health-related effects. When an owner demands a substitution of
materials and the designer believes it could potentially cause pollution problems, the designer should require the owner to indemnify it against any
claims arising out of such substitution.

AMERICANS WITH DISABILITIES ACT—HOW THE ADA AFFECTS INTERIOR DESIGN PROFESSIONALS

Overview of the ADA

The passage of the Americans with Disabilities Act (ADA) has and will continue to have a significant effect on the design community. The act sets
forth requirements with respect to new construction and obligates property
owners to modify existing structures to accommodate the disabled. Interior
designers performing services on commercial projects will find that their
clients will expect assistance in interpreting the provisions of the act which

relate to accessability of places of public accommodation and commercial facilities.

The ADA is the most comprehensive civil rights legislation enacted since Title VII of the Civil Rights Act of 1964. It was designed to protect disabled individuals from discrimination in employment (Title I), public services (Title II), public accommodations (Title III), and telecommunication relay services (Title IV).

Title III of the ADA took effect on January 26, 1992. Despite its many benefits, Title III places serious financial burdens on developers, owners, landlords, and tenants of real property. Many of the requirements under Title III remain unclear, and confusion still exists as to how to comply with these requirements. What is clear, however, is that compliance with the ADA requirements is mandatory and persons with disabilities cannot be charged for the costs incurred in complying with the ADA. It should be noted that construction standards in local jurisdictions are often more rigorous than those in Title III and, therefore, take precedence over ADA requirements. However, where Title III requirements go beyond those contained in the local law, Title III must be complied with.

Title III divides buildings and facilities into two categories: public accommodations and commercial facilities. The Title III requirements apply only to public accommodations. Public accommodations generally fall within one of the following twelve categories:

1. Places of lodging

2. Establishments serving food or drink

3. Places of exhibition or entertainment

4. Places of public gathering

5. Sales or rental establishments

6. Service establishments

7. Stations used for specified public transportation

8. Places of public display or collection

9. Places of recreation

10. Places of education

11. Social service establishments

12. Places of exercise or recreation

Commercial facilities are usually defined as nonresidential facilities used by private entities with commercial operations, such as office buildings, warehouses, and factories.

The following discussion is intended to provide the reader with a general overview of the major ADA requirements and suggestions for avoiding common pitfalls associated with ADA compliance. This section is not intended to provide a comprehensive review of all ADA requirements. The act should be examined whenever a question of compliance arises.

Architectural Barriers

Architectural barriers are physical objects that obstruct a disabled individual's access to, or use of, a facility. An example would be a narrow doorway as the only entrance to a room. To the extent that it is readily achievable, the law requires the removal of all architectural barriers in existing facilities. If it is determined that barrier removal is not readily achievable, there is still a requirement for the public accommodation to make its services, facilities, or privileges available to the disabled in a way that is readily achievable.

The term "readily achievable" means "easily accomplishable and able to be carried out without much difficulty or expense." Because there are no predetermined formulas, the issue of whether a removal is readily achievable is to be determined on a case-by-case basis. However, the following five factors are to be considered in determining whether a change is readily achievable:

1. The nature and cost of the required action

2. The overall financial resources available at the site, the number of employees at the site, safety requirements, and the impact of the proposed action on the operation of the site

3. The geographic separation and the administrative or fiscal relationship between the site and parent entity

4. If applicable, the overall financial resources of the parent entity including the number of employees and the number, type, and location of its facilities

5. If applicable, the type of business of the parent entity

Some examples of types of alternatives are providing a "talking directory" in building lobbies, valet parking for the disabled, providing home delivery, and relocating activities to accessible locations. A person with a disability cannot be charged for the costs of providing alternative approaches.

Title III recommends that barrier removal take place in the following order of priority:

I. The highest priority affords physical access from parking lots, public transportation, and sidewalks. This includes installing ramps, accessible parking spaces, and widening doors.

II. Access to areas where goods and services are available to the public. This includes the installation of ramps, providing Braille signage, and adjusting display racks and cases.

III. Access to rest rooms, which includes the installation of full-length mirrors and wide toilets.

IV. Assume other measures necessary in order to remove other barriers.

Removal of a barrier will be mandated by the courts in all cases where discrimination has been proven. However, if the Justice Department has reasonable cause to believe that a practice or pattern of discrimination exists, it can file a civil suit which can result in ordering barrier removal together with a fine. The best way to avoid such lawsuits is by making good-faith efforts to comply with the ADA before problems arise. Additionally, it is advisable to keep a list of existing barriers that are not removed, together with the specific reasons for not removing them, and to seek the advice of local organizations as to the needs of the disabled persons they represent.

The development of a plan to remove barriers to the disabled could be sufficient to prove such a good-faith effort. In fact, the Justice Department recommends this course in addition to consulting with local organizations representing the disabled. While the "good-faith standard" requires positive compliance efforts, no business is exempt from compliance because of a failure to understand or receive technical assistance in implementing removal of barriers.

New Construction/Alterations

Since January 26, 1993, the law provides that all new commercial facilities and places of public accommodation must be fully accessible to the disabled. If a building permit for a commercial building is approved after January 26, 1992, and receives its first certification of occupancy after January 26, 1993, it must be fully usable by individuals with disabilities. If the permit was approved prior to January 26, 1992, the building is not subject to Title III rules pertaining to new construction even if first occupancy occurs after January 26, 1993. However, the building must still meet the barrier-removal requirements discussed above.

When there are alterations to a commercial facility or place of public accommodation, the altered areas of the facility must be fully accessible to the disabled. Alterations are defined as remodeling, renovation, or reconstruction that affect the use of the building. Alterations do not include usual maintenance such as painting, reroofing, asbestos removal, and most changes to the electrical and mechanical systems except for switches and controls. If the structural conditions of an existing building or facility make it impossible to fulfill the Title III accessibility requirements, those accessibility requirements shall be deemed "technically infeasible."

With respect to an alteration of a building or a facility, "technically infeasible" means that it has little likelihood of being accomplished because existing structural conditions would require removing or altering a load-bearing member which is an essential part of the structural frame; or because other existing physical or site constraints prohibit modification or addition of elements, spaces, or features which are in full and strict compliance with the minimum requirements for new construction and which are necessary to provide accessibility. Where required alterations are technically infeasible, the owner will not have to comply with the alteration requirements of the ADA. It should be noted, however, that if compliance is technically infeasible, the alteration shall provide accessibility to the maximum extent feasible. Any elements or features of the building or facility that are being altered and can be made accessible shall be made accessible within the scope of the alteration.

Penalties for Noncompliance with the ADA

Design professionals face considerable risk under the ADA. As a civil rights law, the ADA specifies that either a private individual or the U.S. Attorney's office can bring a suit against a public accommodation that violates the ADA. It is not necessary to allege discrimination "after the fact." A lawsuit can be filed if the petitioner has reasonable grounds to believe that discrimination is "about to occur" in either a new construction project or an alteration.

One particular case against an architectural firm deserves mentioning. In *United States v. Ellerbe Becket, Inc.*,[5] the United States filed an action against Ellerbe Becket, Inc., an architectural firm, for violations of the ADA. The complaint alleged that Ellerbe had engaged in a pattern or practice of designing new sports arenas across the United States that failed to comply with the ADA and its implementing regulation regarding lines of sight for disabled patrons.

Ellerbe maintained that the ADA was not clear and was open to interpretation as to precisely what was required. Although the government settled with Ellerbe in 1998 for an agreement by Ellerbe to design new stadiums so spectators in wheelchairs still have a full view when other fans stand up, the case presents an example of how easy it is for a designer to incur liability for ADA violations. In order to avoid liability where ADA provisions are unclear and open to interpretation, designers should inform their clients in writing of the ADA issues and require the owner to make the final determination concerning how far they should go in ensuring ADA compliance.

CONCLUSION

There is more to the art of negotiating contracts than limiting liability or deciding how to protect your intellectual property. It is widely recognized that even today's seemingly simple construction projects are far more complex than those built even ten years ago. Owners and designers alike are facing increasing choices in the means and methods of design and construction. It has therefore become more important than ever to integrate business and legal protections into each agreement with the client as well as to coordinate the interior design agreement with those of the other members of the project team.

This change has occurred because owners now recognize that each project is unique, in that to properly ascribe to each of the team members the appropriate responsibilities and liabilities, it is necessary to accurately define all of the variables—the special features needed to match the scope with the project delivery system, and the combination of consultants to be integrated and coordinated to the phased completion dates for separate stages of many projects.

At the outset of each project, the design team must meet with the client and survey what is most critical to them, what factors they most need to see to call the project successful. Even for small and simple projects, the complete investigation calls upon the designer to work with the owner and other project team members to address goal-oriented questions before the design process can effectively begin. If designers identify clients' design and business goals, they can ensure that their agreements with owners contain the requisite legal protections as well as provisions that will coordinate work with other members of the project team. If they adopt a more businesslike approach to the drafting and negotiation of agreements, designers will limit their exposure to liability, be in a better position to meet and exceed their clients' goals, and see more of their projects successfully completed.

Notes

1

Marshall-Schule Associates, Inc. v. Goldman, 137 Misc.2d 1024, 523 N.Y.S.2d 16 (Civ. NY 1987).

2

Florida Administrative Code, Chapter 481, Part I, § 481.203(8).

3

Florida Administrative Code, Chapter 481, Part I, § 481.203(6).

4

Florida Administrative Code, Chapter 481, Part I, § 481.2131.

5

United States v. Ellerbe Bechet, Inc., 976 F. Suppl. 1262 (Dist. Minn. 1997).

Bibliography

Board of Architecture & Interior Design, Laws and Rules, Division of Professions, Chapter 481, Part I, Florida Statutes.

Cushman, Robert F., and Stephen D. Butler. *Construction Change Order Claims*. New York: John Wiley & Sons, Inc., 1994.

LePatner, Barry B., and Sidney M. Johnson. *Structural & Foundation Failures, A Case Book for Architects, Engineers, and Lawyers*. New York: McGraw-Hill, 1997.

New York State Education Law, McKinney's, 2001

Turner, Scott C. *Insurance Coverage of Construction Disputes*. West Group, 1999.

Walker, Stephen G., Richard A. Holderness, and Stephen D. Butler. *State by State Guide to Architect, Engineer, and Contractor Licensing*. Aspen Law & Business, 1999.

21

Legislation

DERRELL PARKER, IIDA

The history of legislation regulating interior design in America began with the attempt to pass the first interior design regulation legislation in California in 1951. This attempt was not successful in creating new ground-breaking legislation; as a matter of fact, it failed in its attempt. It was successful in bringing to the profession a perceived idea that the profession was changing and becoming more complex. It also fore-warned practitioners of the need for legislation that would not only protect the health and safety of the public utilizing interior design ser-vices, but would also protect the practice of interior design.

Since that time, the face of interior design has changed dramatically, and through this evolution the responsibilities of design professionals have become more complex. Today interior designers are responsible for a variety of life safety issues that have, in the past, been in the purview of other design professionals, such as architects and engineers. In many states and jurisdic-tions today, the designer is responsible for planning ingress and egress from interior spaces, many of them in large, complex high-rise projects. In many cases, the interior designer serves as the project programmer, planner, and lead design professional. Because of this evolution of responsibilities, one of the most important factors facing interior design practitioners today is their right to practice the profession for which they are educated, experienced, and examined to practice.

Designers may wonder why they should know the history of legislation in their field. They may believe that professional self-regulation is sufficient to ensure that the design profession fulfills its responsibilities. Like other pro-fessions that affect public welfare, there is a strong case for legal regulation of interior design. The professional interior design community, bolstered by advances in education and experience, has taken custodial responsibility for interior design in today's society. It has developed and promoted a scientific core of knowledge, formal education requirements, including a college-level accreditation system, and a professional examination to focus specifically on interior design. With this professionalization comes regulation: not only title acts (allowing designers to call themselves interior designers) but also practice acts (establishing standards for professional conduct), and through ethical codes as well.

Conceived in the late 1960s and incorporated in 1974, the National Council for Interior Design Qualification (NCIDQ) was established. The council, through its examination, seeks to create a universal standard by which to measure the competency of interior designers to practice as professionals. The birth of this examination came as a result of the growing complexity of the interior design profession, and serves to identify to the public those interior designers who have met the minimum standards for professional practice. The NCIDQ has become the hallmark examination for interior design legislation. In all states with interior design legislation, the NCIDQ is a requirement.

In 1982, Alabama became the first state to enact legislation for the regulation of interior design. This enactment became the catalyst for other states to pursue legislative actions. Interior design professional organizations began to establish state-to-state coalitions for the sole purpose of gaining interior design legislation. Today there are 19 states with interior design regulation: Alabama, Arkansas, California, Connecticut, Florida, Georgia, Illinois, Louisiana, Maine, Maryland, Minnesota, Missouri, Nevada, New Mexico, New York, Tennessee, Texas, Virginia, and Wisconsin, and also the District of Columbia and Puerto Rico. While regulation in some of the states is only for title, in others it regulates both title and practice.

In 1989, the National Legislative Coalition of Interior Design (NLCID) was formed. This coalition was established to aid those state coalitions by becoming a clearinghouse for information about local and national legislative activities. In 1989, the AIA/Interior Design Accord was signed. This accord was an agreement entered into by several design organizations, namely, the American Institute of Architects (AIA), the American Society of Interior Designers (ASID), the Institute of Business Designers (IBD), and the International Society of Interior Designers (ISID). The purpose of the accord was to establish guidelines for states seeking interior design legislation. The general intent of this accord was that the AIA would not oppose attempts by interior designers to gain legislation at state levels so long as those attempts were only for title acts; it did not include any regulations which pertained to definition of scope of practice, sealing of construction documentation, or performance of any design that affected health or life safety.

While the accord was looked on by some to be an instrument to aid interior designers in obtaining title act legislation for their states, many people on both sides of the accord perceived the document to be nothing more than a way for the AIA to control how, and if, interior designers would gain legislation. The accord was abandoned by the interior design participants in the spring of 2000. The accord was abandoned primarily because of a lack of participation by both interior designers and architects. What had been written as a living, evolving document had been allowed to wither and was no longer viable.

Today there are 19 states, as well as the territory of Puerto Rico and the District of Columbia, with varying forms of interior design legislation. There are now active coalitions in all 50 states, of which some are seeking to enact legislation acknowledging interior design as a profession, while others are actively pursuing modifications of existing legislation.

PRACTICE ACTS VERSUS TITLE ACTS

In some states, interior designers may not be able to practice until they meet the requirements of a title act, which establishes the qualifications they must meet before they can practice. Once they qualify to practice, they may be subject to legal requirements that limit the scope and set the standard of professional conduct for their practice. The differences between the two types of legislation deserve some elaboration.

Practice acts define a particular scope of practice as well as regulate the actual performance of such practice by any individual registered to perform those services. Persons wishing to engage in the practice must demonstrate their ability to meet certain standards as set forth by practice legislation. These acts usually require levels of education, experience, and examination. Practice acts are usually reserved for those professions dealing with health, safety, and welfare issues, such as architecture, engineering, and medicine. Professions are regulated by the state. This regulation is usually done by a state board made up of a group of peers appointed by the state's governor.

In states where interior design is legislated, government regulators have concluded that interior designers, especially those working in the commercial or contract arena, do, in fact, have a great deal of influence over the health, safety, and welfare of the public. Therefore, lawmakers have insisted, in some cases, on practice legislation for their interior design laws. All practice acts require that the professional register with a state regulatory board. In most cases where practice legislation is enacted, professionals are also usually restricted from using a particular title until they have met specific qualifications outlined in the law.

Title acts are less restrictive than practice acts, because practice acts are based on the performance and ability of the registrant. Title acts define what professionals may call themselves. The most important reason for title acts is to enable the public to more readily identify those individuals who are qualified by law to use a certain title. This qualification ensures that the person has met the minimum standards required to provide competent services. These standards may or may not be set by education, experience, and examination. In states with title legislation, it is unlawful to use a title without first having met the qualifications as outlined in the state's laws. Title acts do not necessarily regulate who may partake or act in said profession; rather, they limit what practitioners may call themselves and how professional services are offered to the public. Any person who has not met the requirements for title registration set by the state may not represent or identify himself by title. Title acts require registration with the appropriate state regulatory board.

ADVOCACY

The interior design profession is represented by a number of professional organizations. This discussion will be limited to those that are the most actively involved in the legislative arena: the American Society of Interior Design (ASID) and the International Interior Design Association (IIDA). These organizations have played major roles in state-to-state coalitions seeking legislation for interior design. Both organizations have government and regulatory affairs departments that dispense information to their members. Legislative activities in state-to-state and national legislation may affect the associations' membership and the way they practice and pursue legislative agendas.

It is the mission of professional organizations, not only in interior design but also in architecture, engineering, etc., to assure that their members retain the right to practice and receive their fair share of the marketplace. Even so, both the ASID and the IIDA support legislative regulation of the interior design profession, not solely because of market share, but more importantly, to protect health and safety. Both the ASID and the IIDA have assisted state coalitions in establishing the interior designer's effect on such major concerns.

Along with the professional organizations, other collateral organizations contribute to the efforts of interior designers to shape legislation to regulate the profession. These organizations do not operate in such a direct manner, but certainly their efforts are of no less importance. One such organization is the Foundation for Interior Design Education and Research (FIDER). The FIDER accredits undergraduate programs in interior design, for the sole purpose of ensuring the highest quality of interior design education. A FIDER-accredited degree is not a requirement for registration in all states regulating the practice of interior design; however, it is recognized as the definitive accreditation in many states with regulatory legislation.

Another collateral organization that is not involved in the actual legislative process is the National Council for Interior Design Qualification (NCIDQ). The NCIDQ is involved in the examination process. Its membership is comprised of the state and provincial agencies which regulate interior design. In all of the states and jurisdictions with legislation, interior designers must successfully pass the NCIDQ examination if they are to be registered as interior designers by the state. The NCIDQ is also responsible for, and maintains, the Model Language available for states to use when they draft new legislation.

MODEL LANGUAGE FOR LEGISLATION REGULATING THE INTERIOR DESIGN PROFESSION

Model Language for Interior Designers is, as the title indicates, a model that states may or may not choose to follow when they decide to draft legislation regulating the interior design profession. The Model Language is a living document, meaning that it is constantly changing and evolving along with the profession itself. The Model Language is domiciled at the headquarters of the NCIDQ in Washington, D.C., and pertains only to the registration of interior designers. The Model Language is helpful in the effort to create a more uniform profession nationwide, and can be used as a guideline to develop more standard and consistent laws from state to state. This standardization would allow for reciprocity between states that recognize interior design as a profession, and would make it easier for design professionals to receive certification as interior designers in more than one state.

The Model Language, like that of other professions, outlines a definition of the profession of interior design and describes services that may be offered by the registrant. In addition, it outlines the education interior designers must achieve, the examination they must pass, and the experience they must accumulate before they can perform the tasks specified in the legislative definition of services. Model Language for Interior Designers requires that interior designers use a seal and obtain sealing powers to certify technical documentation. Without those powers, interior designers would not be able to submit their documents to building authorities or other governmental agencies for issuance of building permits. The Model Language also addresses the structure and duties of a state regulatory board. In the case of Model Language for Interior Designers, where health, life, and safety concerns are paramount, the regulatory board must address registrants who may cause harm to the public through neglect or error. Therefore, the Model Language contains provisions giving the state regulatory board enforcement and disciplinary powers. As in most laws, the Model Language offers an exemption clause. Exemptions are usually offered to members of other professions who, by virtue of their education, examination, and experience, are also deemed qualified to practice in the interior design profession.

COALITIONS

There are now interior design coalitions in nearly all states, working to enact legislation or revise existing legislation. These coalitions are supported by both the ASID and IIDA through their government and regulatory affairs departments. Each coalition focuses on its state and works to establish grassroots connections in that state. Who better than residents of a state should talk to legislators about why their home state needs legislation? State coalitions were originally formed so that legislation could be approached on a local level to give state lawmakers and local constituencies a face and a name.

Coalitions have been very successful in attaining their legislative goals. They have helped to establish legislation regulating interior design in the 19 states named earlier, Washington, D.C., and Puerto Rico. Coalitions afford all designers the opportunity to partake in the legislative process. Among their membership they include members of interior design professional organizations, nonaffiliated interior designers, architects, and other design professionals who believe that there is a need to regulate interior design. They also believe that interior designers have a definite impact on the health and life safety of their state's citizenry.

EDUCATION

At this time, states that regulate the interior design profession require varying amounts of education for design professionals. One state has no educational requirement, while others require four- or five-year degrees. Most states, however, require at least a two-year degree. Since 1998, the NCIDQ has required that interior designers have at least a two-year degree to be eligible to sit for the examination. While some states recognize other examinations, the NCIDQ examination is the only one that has been adopted by all states and jurisdictions that have interior design legislation.

In 1968, the Interior Design Educators Council (IDEC) was founded with the primary purpose of advancing the needs of educators of interior design professionals. In 1973, FIDER was established. FIDER's primary purpose is to review and evaluate accreditation programs of interior design. FIDER accredits only undergraduate programs of interior design education. The accreditation is based on FIDER'S 12 Standards of Excellence for the Interior Design profession, as follows.

Standard 1.

- Curriculum Structure (The curriculum is structured to facilitate and advance student learning.)

Standard 2.

- Design Fundamentals (Students have a foundation in the fundamentals of art and design, theories of design and human behavior, and discipline-related history.)

Standard 3.

• Interior Design (Students understand and apply the knowledge, skills, processes, and theories of interior design.)

Standard 4.

• Communication (Students communicate effectively.)

Standard 5.

• Building Systems and Interior Materials (Students design within the context of building systems. Students use appropriate materials and products.)

Standard 6.

• Regulations (Students apply the laws, codes, regulations, standards, and practices that protect the health, safety, and welfare of the public.)

Standard 7.

• Business and Professional Practice (Students have a foundation in business and professional practice.)

Standard 8.

• Professional Values (The program leads students to develop the attitudes, traits, and values of professional responsibility, accountability, and effectiveness.)

Standard 9.

• Faculty (Faculty members and other instructional personnel are qualified and adequate in number to implement program objectives.)

Standard 10.

• Facilities (Program facilities and resources provide an environment to stimulate thought, motivate students, and promote the exchange of ideas.)

Standard 11.

• Administration (The administration of the program is clearly defined, provides appropriate program leadership, and supports the program. The program demonstrates accountability to the public through its published documents.)

Standard 12.

• Assessment (Systematic and comprehensive assessment methods contribute to the program's ongoing development and improvement.)

EXPERIENCE

For many years, in interior design as in many other professions, practical experience has been an important item for a professional's résumé. And indeed most designers considered the value of experience only when they were trying to secure employment. Today, now that more states regulate design, design professionals are learning that the length and nature of their experience matters for obtaining certification to practice.

In many areas, interior designers are realizing the value not only of the length of their employment-related experience in the design field, but also of the diversity in the type and quality of that experience. Because of the rapid changes in the field, it is of great importance that today's interior designer acquire broad-based experience in the profession. This experience becomes crucial when interior designers are required to meet demands for technical accuracy in documentation, in planning and programming, and in health and life safety issues. Just as the profession is evolving and responsibilities are becoming more complex, the value of diverse experience is increasing.

NCIDQ and IDEP

Along with the need for diverse experience, design professionals also need a monitored process to document that experience accurately. Until 1999, interior design had no program that monitored interior design experience. Now, however, the NCIDQ is tracking experience for those persons who wish to take the NCIDQ examination, through the Interior Design Experience Program (IDEP). The IDEP is a monitored experience program which ensures that a design professional is exposed to and gains the appropriate experience in all areas of interior design, including those which will be a part of the examination. Up to the present time, the NCIDQ has measured experience for those candidates who wish to sit for the exam based on the candidate's merit and letters of recommendation. When the new IDEP experience program goes into effect, all experience will be tracked and verified by the NCIDQ. This is especially important in states that rely heavily on experience as well as education and examination as evaluative criteria for certification and where this verification element becomes a very important component of a candidate's application for state registration.

EXAMINATION

In 1974, the NCIDQ was founded with the goal of protecting the public by identifying interior design practitioners competent to practice by administering a minimum competency examination for interior designers. It is the major credentialing agency for the interior design profession in the United States and Canada. The NCIDQ offers a comprehensive examination that states use for licensure and professional certification of interior designers.

The NCIDQ requires that candidates who sit for their examination meet an education requirement of at least two years in a formal interior design program of study and that they have at least four years of full-time work experience in the field of interior design practice. The NCIDQ examination measures minimum competency in the practice of interior design. It is the only interior design examination developed and administered in the United States and Canada by an agency that is independent of other interior design organizations. Since this examination is used by regulatory boards as a criteria for registration, and since regulation is based on protection of health, safety, and welfare, it is vital that this examination not be influenced by organizations within the profession, whose primary agendas focus on practice and market share for members, not safety and welfare issues for the public. Without outside voices, the examination might become biased. The NCIDQ continually changes and updates its examination and its procedure for administering the examination.

REGULATORY BOARDS

Another goal of the NCIDQ has been to establish a council of regulatory boards of interior design. This council is known as the *Council of Delegates* and, today, there are 16 regulatory boards represented on the council. Whenever state legislatures pass legislation that regulates a profession, there must be a state regulatory board to oversee the profession. In some states where interior design regulations are in effect, there are independent regulatory boards to oversee interior designers; in other states, the regulatory board may be comprised of many design disciplines, such as architects, engineers, and interior designers. Regardless of the structure, the duties and responsibilities of regulatory boards are much the same.

According to state statute, boards register, license, or certify interior designers, and they maintain rosters of those persons who are registered, licensed, or certified for the purpose of identifying them. Regulatory boards have the power to discipline those registrants, licensees, or certified professionals who do not protect the health and safety of the public or who fail to adhere to the performance standards required of their profession. Regulatory boards may set and adopt Rules of Conduct for practitioners. Most regulatory boards are composed of practitioners of the represented profession or professions and one or more public members. The regulatory board is the venue through which the public can register complaints that a registrant, licensee, or certified professional has harmed someone's health and safety. The members of a state regulatory board are responsible for upholding the statutes governing the profession for which the board is formed.

REGULATION IN LIGHT OF THE WAY DESIGN PROFESSIONALS PRACTICE

In 1904, Elsie de Wolfe began a career in what we now refer to as interior design in America. Nearly a century later, it is doubtful Ms. de Wolfe would recognize the profession that she created. It was not until after World War II that the face of the building landscape began to change dramatically in the United States. The changes occurred with the onset of curtain-wall construction, suspended ceilings, and central building systems, which allowed for environmental control, and changes in construction methods. The changes to construction methods led to larger contiguous areas of interior real estate and the introduction of open office planning concepts. These events, along with the formation of large-scale corporations brought on by the postwar boom, all laid the groundwork for the interior design field and its responsibilities.

Today, interior designers are hired to complete tasks as varied as programming new or reused facilities and planning spatial layouts for large and small interior spaces. Interior designers develop programs for clients based on the varied needs of the end user. Design professionals provide project management and execute technical documents for construction, such as drawings and specifications. The interior designers of today must be able to perform multiple tasks in which they exercise a high level of independent judgment and know local, state, and national codes. They must be able to negotiate contracts, schedule projects, budget projects, and coordinate work in progress. No matter what the project, they must be capable of identifying problems, analyzing requirements, and making realistic assessments, all within the confines of code, budget, and time constraints. Interior designers may work as independent consultants or as a part of a design team with other design professionals.

Health and Safety in the Design Context

Whatever the role of the interior designer today, it is paramount to the profession that the health and safety of the public be protected at all times. Interior designers protect the health and safety of the public by being aware of the consequences of each of their choices and by maintaining a direct knowledge of local, state, and national codes. For instance, when interior designers plan an exit route from an interior core space to a building exit system and design it in compliance with code, they are protecting the health and safety of the public who occupy or use the space. When interior designers demonstrate their ability to know where and how to place grab bars in handicap toilet rooms, or design an accessible counter where reach and approach are correct, they are protecting the health and safety of the public who use those facilities. These are not design elements that the designer can guess about or leave to chance. Before designers can approach them properly, they must possess a base of knowledge that they can access and apply.

In the last *Analysis for the Interior Design Profession* (1998) conducted for the NCIDQ, commercial designers expressed their opinion that some of the most important health and safety issues facing interior designers in the commercial field today were field survey skills, specification writing skills, knowledge of building codes, the Americans with Disabilities Act, and flammability and testing standards. When asked how interior designers create a safe and effective design solution, they responded that design professionals needed to have a knowledge base in the following areas.

NCIDQ LIST OF KEY KNOWLEDGE AREAS
FOR INTERIOR DESIGNERS

- Verbal communication and basic language skills

- Working drawings

- Space-planning principles

- Human factors (ergonomics)

- Professional ethics

- Barrier-free design

- Building codes

- Project management

- Interior construction

- Contract specifications

SELF-REGULATION: ETHICS

The profession of interior design is like any other. No matter how much legislation regulates the field, a profession must still police its own practitioners. Most interior design professional associations have codes of ethics. Most regulatory boards have adopted these or their own codes of ethics for their registrants. While these codes of ethics are different for each group or organization, they are usually written to protect the welfare of the public the profession serves. Codes of ethics may deal with disclosure to a client; for instance, a code of ethics may require that the interior designer disclose a financial interest in a company that may be bidding on the client's project. Codes of ethics may cover truth in advertising. For example, a code of ethics may provide that interior designers are subject to sanctions when they tell a client that they are capable of working on projects that require special knowledge, even though they have never done work in that particular area.

Codes of ethics adopted by the design profession play a key role in ensuring the honesty or integrity of the marketplace. In addition, regulatory boards use them as an additional method of protecting the public from unscrupulous practitioners, those who live up to the letter of the law as set out in the

To date, interior design has not been adequately acknowledged as a profession that requires a distinct set of core competencies that extend well beyond simple decoration; nor has the broad social and economic impact of the profession been recognized.

statutory regulatory scheme, but who may otherwise, through dishonest activities, put the welfare of the public in jeopardy. And while ethics are important to any profession, they cannot be legislated. Although regulatory boards may adopt a profession's ethics code, or establish a code of its own, it is the responsibility of the profession to establish and maintain its own standards of ethical conduct.

TEAM ASSEMBLY

Interior designers work with a variety of different professionals, from architects and engineers to contractors and art consultants. In the built environment, interior designers most likely deal with the largest amount of differing consultants. For instance, on a large architectural project, an architect's team may consist of the architect, structural, civil, electrical and mechanical engineers, interior designer, and landscape architect. Similarly, depending on the size and complexity of the project, an interior designer's team may be comprised of the interior designer and lighting, acoustical, furniture, art, interior plantscaping, window covering, and furniture consultants. Regardless of the numbers or types of professionals on a project team, the interior designer must possess the ability to communicate with each one on a knowledgeable level and guide the project to conclusion. With the complexity of interior design today, no designer can effectively be a one-person show. Design professionals must rely on the expertise of other professionals, yet all of them must function as integral parts of the team.

Due to the onset of interior design legislation, it has become even more critical that interior designers are aware of how best to assemble a project team. Interior designers are now called upon more and more not only to participate in the design team but also to convene, control, and lead the team. In states with interior design legislation that allows for collaboration with other design professionals, the interior designer may serve as lead professional or professional of record. In some instances, the interior designer may be the lead, with the architect as consultant.

UNDERSTANDING THE DESIGNER'S INFLUENCE IN A REGULATED FIELD

Today's interior designer is a blend of technician, artist, sociologist, and psychologist. Interior designers must master the ability to bring facets of all of these elements to their work. They must have detailed technical knowledge of construction and codes, as well as a thorough understanding of health and safety issues, as they pertain to the built environment. In addition, the interior designer must be capable of recognizing cultural changes and how they relate to the welfare of society.

To date, interior design has not been adequately acknowledged as a profession that requires a distinct set of core competencies that extend well beyond simple decoration; nor has the broad social and economic impact of the profession been recognized. Yet the increase in product testing, codes, ergonomics issues, environmental issues, civil rights legislation, and other government mandates testify to the increased level of knowledge and implementation skill required of the interior design professional. The prominence of these issues in laws, regulations, and among the public underscores the need for legal regulation of the interior design profession.

Driven by cultural and societal changes, economic developments, and technological advances, the practice of interior design has become more cognizant of, and responsible for, public health, safety, and welfare. Even the most fundamental design service, such as space planning, which requires attention to corridor and aisle width, in addition to reach dimensions, is critically concerned with the health and safety of the public

Consumer Demands and the Need for Designer Education

Today, we are living longer, and enjoying better health, than at any other time in history. Along with this longer life comes the need for more specialized interior environments. The graying Baby Boomers of today are more demanding and expectant of interior environments that not only provide for their health-care services but also fulfill their cultural and social needs. To provide a viable professional service to these clients, today's interior designer must specialize, diversify, and develop more breadth in both education and experience.

Now that workers use the computer more and more, they perform more and more work tasks in office environments. Those office interiors create very specialized environments. The interior designer must be aware of the nature of these environments, and have a familiar working knowledge of such things as illumination, acoustics, ergonomics, and indoor air quality, along with the ability to properly plan space, interpret codes, and plan for barrier-free design.

Design professionals can address these tasks only by developing knowledge bases through education, examination, and experience. And they must address these tasks, for their application is paramount to the protection of the health and safety of the public, and to the successful completion of all design projects.

Bibliography

Foundation for Interior Design Education and Research (FIDER). *Standards of Excellence in the Interior Design Profession.* January 2000.

Ketter, Kerwin. White Paper.—*The Case for Interior Design as a Separate Core Profession.* Spring 1997.

National Council of Interior Design Qualification (NICDQ). *Analysis of the Interior Design Profession.* 1998.

National Council of Interior Design Qualification (NICDQ). *Report of the Job Analysis of Interior Design.* 1988.

Piotrowski, Christine M. *Professional Practice for Interior Design*, 2nd Edition. New York: Van Nostrand Reinhold, 1994.

Proce

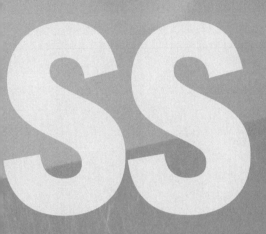

22

Scope of Service Chart

EVA MADDOX, FIIDA

Design firms each have a unique way of approaching the design of a project. The following chapters in this part of the book focus on the designer's scope of services. These chapters are presented as narratives from a varied group of designers each describing their individual methods of approaching the process of design. While these approaches vary due to the size of a project, project type and the design firm's philosophy and resources, the basic scope of services is generally consistent from project to project and firm to firm.

The Chicago-based design firm Eva Maddox & Associates designs a broad range of project type; from residential, healthcare, education, commercial and corporate projects. The firm has combined the best-practice knowledge they derive from their diverse practice to construct the following Scope of Service Chart. The chart is a "snapshot" in time, describing today's key activities generally performed during the course of a project from marketing to project closeout.

The key actions include:

- *Coordinating the project*
- *Developing and monitoring the contract*
- *Fee monitoring*
- *Scheduling*
- *Defining ojectives*
- *Gathering information*
- *Establishing the "Big Idea"*
- *Patterning (when applicable)*
- *Formatting the presentation*
- *Budgeting*
- *Designing*
- *Graphic design*
- *Documenting*

Scope of Service Chart

KEY ACTIONS	PROPOSAL TO CONTRACT	PROJECT INITIATION	SCHEMATIC DESIGN DEVELOPMENT
Project Coordination	• Review marketing information • Review scope • Identify deliverables • Identify client deliverables • Develop task plan • Identify % profit • Review w/ marketing • Review w/ design	• Conduct team kick-off meeting • Establish client communication • Develop client "directory" • Team meeting, post-client meeting • Team meeting, summary report/ review program • Issue report/program to client for approval	• Conduct team kick-off meeting • Maintain client communication • Conduct in-house presentation, 2 days prior to client meeting • Issue meeting minutes
Contract	• Finalize scope of work • Establish fee payment schedule • Finalize contract • Schedule contract presentation • Obtain client authorization • Obtain initial payment	• Scope review • Review deliverables • Review client deliverables	• Monitor work against contract • Monitor need for additional services • Obtain client deliverables
Fee Monitoring	• Confirm fee to work scope	• Review fee & project work against budget • Review task plan • Review profitability goals • Monitor	• Monitor profitability

DESIGN DEVELOPMENT	DOCUMENTATION	BIDS	SITE MONITORING	PROJECT CLOSEOUT
○ Conduct team kick-off meeting ○ Maintain client communication ○ Conduct in-house presentation, 2 days prior to client meeting ○ Issue meeting minutes	○ Conduct team turn-over meeting ○ Maintain client communication ○ Conduct in-house document-review meeting(s) ○ Conduct client-review meeting ○ Obtain client approval ○ Issue meeting minutes	○ Prepare list of qualified bidders; review w/ client & obtain approval ○ Stamp appropriate documents ○ Issue documents for bid ○ Receive & review bids ○ Prepare bid summary & recommendations ○ Review bids w/ client ○ Obtain bid authorization	○ Conduct kick-off job-site meeting w/ all contractors/ vendors ○ Attend job-site review meeting ○ Issue field reports, field conditions, change orders, punch lists to appropriate parties ○ Conduct client walk-throughs ○ Conduct team walk-through for "lessons learned" evaluation	○ Conduct project close-out meeting ○ Distribute close-out reports to: marketing coordinator, senior vice president, project manager, finance manager ○ Close out all project files ○ Distribute materials to marketing as required
○ Monitor work against contract ○ Monitor need for additional services ○ Obtain client deliverables	○ Monitor work against contract ○ Monitor need for additional services ○ Obtain client deliverables	○ Issue authorized bids to successful bidders ○ Monitor work against contract ○ Monitor need for additional services ○ Obtain any client deliverables	○ Monitor work against contract ○ Monitor need for additional services ○ Obtain any client deliverables	○ Obtain copy of final contract ○ Obtain copy of all additional services
○ Monitor profitability	○ Monitor profitability	○ Monitor profitability	○ Monitor profitability	○ Obtain copy of final project progress reports

Scope of Service Chart (Continued)

KEY ACTIONS	PROPOSAL TO CONTRACT	PROJECT INITIATION	SCHEMATIC DESIGN DEVELOPMENT
Schedule	○ Establish project schedule	○ Review project schedule ○ Establish critical internal meeting dates and deliverables ○ Revise/issue client schedule ○ Schedule client kick-off meeting and/or programming	○ Review project schedule ○ Establish critical internal meeting dates and deliverables ○ Revise/issue client schedule ○ Schedule SDD presentation meeting
Schedule	○ Identify team ○ Identify consultants	○ Assign team ○ Assign project responsibilities ○ Establish client contact ○ Monitor	○ Monitor staffing against role assignments ○ Monitor consultants
Objectives	○ Identify internal objectives ○ Establish project objectives	○ Define/establish project objectives ○ Monitor	○ Monitor SDD solutions against objectives

DESIGN DEVELOPMENT	DOCUMENTATION	BIDS	SITE MONITORING	PROJECT CLOSEOUT
○ Review project schedule ○ Establish critical internal meeting dates and deliverables ○ Revise/issue client schedule ○ Schedule DD meeting	○ Review project schedule ○ Establish critical internal meeting dates and deliverables ○ Monitor completion against schedule ○ Revise/issue client schedule ○ Schedule client document-review meeting	○ Review project schedule ○ Establish critical response dates from contractors (bid timeframe) ○ Revise/issue client schedule ○ Schedule client bid-review meeting	○ Review project schedule ○ Coordinate schedules w/ all contractors/vendors ○ Establish critical job-site review dates ○ Monitor contractor/ vendor schedules against work progress ○ Monitor completion against schedule ○ Schedule client walk-through/ review meeting ○ Schedule project team walk-throughs	○ Schedule close-out meeting w/ marketing coordinator & project team
○ Monitor staffing against role assignments ○ Monitor consultants	○ Monitor staffing against roles, assign-ments, profitability ○ Monitor consultants ○ Adjust staffing if required	○ Monitor staffing against roles, assignments, profitability ○ Define responsible party to answer bid questions ○ Monitor consultants ○ Adjust staffing if required	○ Monitor staffing against roles, assign-ments, profitability ○ Define key field coordinator ○ Monitor consultants ○ Adjust staffing if required	○ Evaluate success of team members ○ Evaluate success of consultants
○ Monitor design solutions against objectives	○ Monitor technical solutions against objectives	○ Monitor bids against budget objectives	○ Monitor build-out against design, budget, and schedule objectives	○ Obtain copy of client objectives ○ Obtain copy of objectives

Scope of Service Chart (Continued)

KEY ACTIONS	PROPOSAL TO CONTRACT	PROJECT INITIATION	SCHEMATIC DESIGN DEVELOPMENT
Information Gathering	◦ Gather client background/ information ◦ Identify client vendor alliances	◦ Develop list of questions/interview forms ◦ Conduct client kick-off/programming meeting ◦ Gather client background information ◦ Define areas of research ◦ Define client profile	◦ Conduct project research ◦ Report on findings ◦ Analyze information ◦ Chart results ◦ Identify appropriate product resources ◦ Obtain required "product" samples ◦ Identify code requirements & conformance
Big Idea		◦ Identify Big Idea	◦ Begin conceptual development of Big Idea
Patterning	◦ Determine if applicable	◦ Identify opportunities	◦ Develop conceptual patterning ◦ Apply to preliminary design components
Presentation Formats	◦ Identify contract format	◦ Establish formats for project ◦ Define quality levels	◦ Outline cartoon set of presentation ◦ Develop communication matrix ◦ Outline meeting agenda ◦ Outline presentation booklets ◦ Outline board layout
Budget	◦ Identify client's build-out budget	◦ Obtain client's build-out budget	◦ Prepare preliminary budget

DESIGN DEVELOPMENT	DOCUMENTATION	BIDS	SITE MONITORING	PROJECT CLOSEOUT
○ Monitor against matrix ○ Obtain required "product" samples ○ Confirm "product" availability ○ Confirm code requirements & conformance ○ Finalize research	○ Obtain all design background from team ○ Outline questions/ concerns for design-team review ○ Identify missing information ○ Obtain required technical products, samples, and cut sheets ○ Confirm long-lead items ○ Confirm code requirements & conformance	○ Research qualified bidders for project scope ○ Clarify information for bidders ○ Obtain necessary information to respond to bidders ○ Receive all bids	○ Clarify information for contractors/vendors ○ Monitor substitutions/replacements for discontinued items ○ Prepare addendum(s) as required	○ Gather all data for close-out meeting from team
○ Monitor design solutions against Big Idea ○ Integrate Big Idea	○ Monitor technical solutions against Big Idea ○ Integrate into technical approach	○ Monitor bid pricing/ bid alternatives against Big Idea	○ Monitor build-out for quality control of Big Idea	○ Document the Big Idea
○ Apply patterning to design components	○ Integrate patterning components into documentation approach	○ Identify value of patterning components	○ Monitor execution of patterning components	○ Identify impact of patterning on project
○ Outline cartoon set of presentation boards ○ Develop communication matrix ○ Outline presentation booklets & meeting agenda	○ Outline cartoon set of documents ○ Outline cartoon set of specs ○ Outline meeting agenda & booklet	○ Develop bid-summary format ○ Develop budget-prioritization format	○ Outline presentation of job site to customer: path, clean site, issues	○ Identify information format required for marketing: presentation booklets, color print-outs, plans, presentation boards
○ Meet w/ appropriate vendors ○ Update budget estimate	○ Monitor technical/ design solutions against budget	○ Monitor bids against budget ○ Prioritize budget expenditures against bids	○ Monitor cost of field conditions against bid & budget	○ Obtain copies of all vendor costs

Scope of Service Chart (Continued)

KEY ACTIONS	PROPOSAL TO CONTRACT	PROJECT INITIATION	SCHEMATIC DESIGN DEVELOPMENT
Design	○ Define scope of work	○ Identify key areas of focus	○ Establish design strategy ○ Develop conceptual design components
Graphics	○ Define scope of work	○ Identify areas of application ○ Define methods of output ○ Establish vendor alliances	○ Establish graphic strategy ○ Develop conceptual graphic components
Documentation	○ Define scope of work	○ Establish formats for project ○ Define quality levels ○ Prepare summary report/program	○ Prepare all presentation materials

DESIGN DEVELOPMENT	DOCUMENTATION	BIDS	SITE MONITORING	PROJECT CLOSEOUT
∘ Maintain design strategy ∘ Develop final design components	∘ Develop design/ construction details	∘ Monitor bids to maintain design integrity	∘ Monitor execution to maintain design integrity	∘ Identify measurable results
∘ Maintain graphic strategy ∘ Develop final design components ∘ Refine methods of output ∘ Maintain vendor alliances	∘ Develop graphic/ technical details	∘ Monitor bids to maintain graphic integrity	∘ Monitor execution to maintain graphic integrity	∘ Identify measurable results
∘ Prepare all presentation materials ∘ Mark up all DD information for technical turnover ∘ Develop critical details	∘ Prepare all document sheets as required: engineering, permit, bid, construction ∘ Prepare all specs ∘ Prepare all finish sample sheets ∘ Develop all critical details	∘ Outline & develop bid forms & procedures ∘ Prepare bid packages for: construction items, exhibit components, signage/graphics, furniture ∘ Establish bid authorization log	∘ Prepare job-site observation reports ∘ Prepare field-condition clarification ∘ Prepare change order(s) as required ∘ Prepare punch lists ∘ Prepare/maintain shop-drawing log	∘ Prepare project close-out form

Bibliography

Coates, Joseph E., John B Mahaffie, and Andy Hines. *2025 Scenarios of US and Global Society Reshaped by Science and Technology.* Winchester: Oakhill Press, 1997.

Putnam, Robert D. *Bowling Alone.* New York: Simon and Schuster, 2000.

Senge, Peter M. *The Fifth Discipline: The Art and Practice of the Learning Organization.* New York: Curreny and Doubleday, 1990.

Wacker, Watts, and Jim Taylor with Howard Means. *The 500-Year Delta, What Happens After What Comes Next?* New York: HarperBusiness, 1997.

23

Positioning: Seeking and Securing Work

LISBETH QUEBE, FSMPS

No design professional would disagree with the advice of the wise soul who pointed out that the most important part of any project is getting the job: Without the job, there isn't much to fuss about. When designers set out to get the job, the work of business development can seem to involve a lot of fuss: identifying a market with growth potential; identifying a prospect within that market; getting on that prospect's long list; submitting qualifications; presenting your team in a formal interview; touring projects; proposing a scope of services and fees; negotiating the terms of the contract; and exploring why you did or did not get the commission. That's an exhaustive amount of work before the design firm even starts the project, and it may seem to a busy designer to be a huge investment of resources for an uncertain return. But designers who think of business development solely in terms of the single project miss real opportunities. Getting one job done *well* is a key to starting a good and ideally lasting association.

The design professional's goal should be not simply getting the project, but establishing a long-term relationship. This relationship is created not through marketing the project, but through marketing the client. Maybe only one project will result—some clients build only one house, one school, or one office—but the reference is forever. If the project is an award winner but the client is disgruntled with the process, you have only half-succeeded.

Marketing and business development activities are exercises in building trust. It is only when designers earn the trust of the client that they receive the project. Designers can earn the client's trust by demonstrating that they have current, relevant experience, talent, strong processes, and the ability to listen to and interpret the client's goals. And to prove that they have these assets, designers must understand and use the business development process. This chapter describes the process of developing clients, selling your services, and preparing proposals. At the core of all of these activities is a focus on a rewarding and enduring relationship with the client.

BUSINESS DEVELOPMENT

The primary theme of this chapter is business development, which is an "external" activity in that the design professional interacts with potential clients. Yet designers should start the business development process with some internal activity—market research. Before a member of the firm picks up the phone, gets in the car, or boards the airplane to get in front of a potential customer, it behooves the firm to do its homework.

MARKET RESEARCH

Market research involves determining what kind of work a design firm wants to do and finding where to get it. Design professionals might undertake market research for any number of reasons. They may want to explore a new client sector, such as health care or public work. They may want to explore a new project type within an existing sector, such as alternative officing within the corporate sector. They may want to explore a new office location. They may want to see if adding a new service would be attractive to clients and prospects. No matter what the motivation to do market research, designers should take four steps to do the research well. First, determine what the firm wants to know. Second, determine the ideal source of the information. Third, determine the method by which the firm will gather the information; and last, decide who will do it.

To determine what they want to know about a market, design professionals should write out their questions. These questions can deal with any number of issues: trends in the market; current projects; anticipated projects; desired services; performance criteria; competition; and even favorite periodicals (the firm's future PR focus). Next, the firm should develop a list of people who can provide this information. This list can contain three to 300 people, depending on the purpose of the research. Three savvy observations from well-placed observers can be just as valuable as the thoughts of the 5 to 20 percent who may respond to a larger survey.

Once the issues are identified and potential respondents identified, the firm must decide upon a methodology. It can do a literature search (a smart preparatory move, even if the firm plans to employ other methods). Literature, however, tends to look backward and is therefore in danger of being dated. In comparison, the Internet is a marvelous research tool. It gives design professionals access to corporations, hospitals, public entities, and associations—instantly. Using this current information, they can then prepare a questionnaire and mail it out with a prepaid return envelope. The questionnaire should be simple. If essays are required, people are likely to throw the questions away; if only yes/no answers are required, people are likely to respond. The design firm may also use the telephone, either by enlisting an employee or by hiring a market research firm. The in-house route uses valuable resources but puts the most knowledgeable person on the phone with the prospect. It affords the chance to start building a relationship, but it may stifle the prospect's candor. The consultant route provides anonymity, but designers need to be assured that a professional and knowledgeable person will conduct the interview.

When have the interviews produced enough information? When they have given the firm the input of enough decision makers to indicate a fact or a trend. Only when design professionals have identified a trend can they talk knowledgeably about the situation in the market and use their precious resources in the smartest fashion.

FINDING THE PROSPECT

To get work, designers must know that an opportunity exists, and the more they know about the opportunity (including the client and the potential project), the better their chances of being short-listed and of winning the project. Any useful information about a potential client or project can serve as a lead. Lead finding begins by talking to the right people. Two valid ways to obtain good leads are networking and cold calling.

Networking

To most savvy marketers, the most important element in their lead-finding efforts is an effective network. A network can provide information about markets, potential projects, competition, and just about anything else design professionals want to know. A well-constructed and actively used network can significantly improve a firm's efforts to get additional projects.

Networking usually comes to mind as a means of obtaining leads, but it can be used for much more. Networking allows design professionals to

- *Trade reliable information on new projects.*

- *Generate project teams or partnerships.*

- *Implement market research.*

- *Get information about competitors.*

- *Confirm or discount rumors.*

- *Uncover hidden relationships, or real decision makers.*

- *Alert others to changes within your firm.*

- *Obtain postinterview feedback.*

- *Save a lot of time (and a lot of money) because the firm won't be chasing jobs that are not real or for which the firm is not qualified.*

Every design professional already has a network. The "law of 250" says that everyone interacts with at least 250 people on a relatively constant basis. Part of this network is friends, family, and fellow employees. Part is a professional network of brokers, consultants, contractors, and professional peers. In this professional context, associations and societies can be very useful, and the most useful are those made up of potential clients, such as the International Facility Management Association (IFMA), the International Association of Corporate Real Estate Executives (NACORE), the National Association of Industrial and Office Properties (NAIOP), the Urban Land Institute (ULI), and the American Society of Hospital Engineers (ASHE). Other helpful associations are professional societies such as the American Society of Interior Design (ASID), the International Interior Design Association (IIDA), and the American Institute of Architects (AIA). Designers can also network productively with civic and government groups such as boards of major institutions and chambers of commerce, as well as suppliers of products.

The design professional's goal should be not simply getting the project, but establishing a long-term relationship. This relationship is created not through marketing the project, but through marketing the client.

In order to make the most of networks, designers should follow a set of simple rules. To network well, design professionals must be good listeners, aware not only of the words being spoken but of the atmosphere in which the words are uttered. They must seek to build trust; networking is focused as much on helping others as on helping yourself. Designers who constantly take information, but who do not return anything helpful, will find that their networks will cease to exist. And networking *is* work, work that requires persistence. But compared to "cold" calling, networking is also the quickest source of warm or hot leads. And it pays off. One well-known architect kept meticulous lists of contacts in every city. To him, his greatest asset was not pictures of his work, but the names in his network.

Cold Calling

The design industry develops many of its leads over the telephone. When the contact involves someone the designer does not know, the contact is referred to as a "cold" call. Design professionals make cold calls to do research on a given market and to uncover leads. The goal of a cold call is not to make a sale, but to make a friend. No one buys professional services based on a brief telephone call. The specific goals of cold calling are to establish a relationship and a dialogue, to get enough information to make it possible to decide whether or not to pursue the project, and to set up an appointment.

The first step in cold calling is to target. Decide on the type of client to be reached and the geography to be covered. Next, before the call is made, use association guides and the Internet to conduct a minimum amount of advanced research on the prospect. Identify the best person to speak with, and don't hesitate to go right to the top. Develop a list of questions to be asked. Finally, make the call.

The goal of cold calling is to make the person want to help. Callers should identify themselves by name, company, and a short tag line that identifies what they do. They then have approximately 20 seconds to establish rapport. They should express the need for help in a friendly, courteous manner, and set the stage for asking questions. Rather than simply reading off their list of questions, they should branch off and have a natural conversation, and return to the list to make sure everything has been covered. The conclusion of a cold call may be a simple agreement just to keep in touch, or it may seem reasonable to ask for an appointment, where face-to-face selling can begin.

Cold calling is not finished when the call is complete. It may be a good idea to send something: a note of thanks, a brochure, or a reprint. The goal of the cold call is to make the prospect open a file on the caller's firm. The designer who calls must also make a record of the call. If a contact record form is filled out (manually or electronically), it will help the designer remember the call when it is time to make a follow-up call, allow the firm to track the caller's activity, and make others in the firm aware of the calling activity so that the firm's efforts are coordinated. Design professionals should set aside a regular time for cold calling. Firms should set objectives—five calls a day, five calls a week, or five calls a month—and urge staff to keep at it; their comfort level will grow with experience.

QUALIFYING THE PROSPECT

Through networking or cold calling efforts, a design professional has uncovered a lead. It's a highly desirable commission: the design of a new museum wing. But this designer has spent a career designing patient rooms in hospitals. Should this designer pursue the lead anyway? An important part of the business development process in design firms is making go/no-go decisions. Not every client is right for every designer or every firm. The design professional who has spotted the lead on the museum project could spend a lot of money to get to the interview, working connections and writing convincing qualifications, but 99.9 percent of the time, the designer will be bested by a competitor with a half-dozen museum projects to his credit. If by some miracle the designer is selected (perhaps the designer's Uncle William is the curator), the hospital design firm will probably lose a bundle of money learning on the job, and irritate the museum client in the process.

Design professionals should understand that it is smart to walk away from a project opportunity when

* *The designer or the firm does not have the right kind of experience.*

* *The firm cannot put the right staff on the project.*

* *The client is notoriously difficult.*

* *The designer knows that no profit can be made.*

> - *The designer is sure that the job will go to a favored firm.*
>
> - *The prospective client won't permit contact before the interview, and the designer knows nothing about them.*
>
> - *The designer enters the hunt much too late.*

However, there are instances when it is a good marketing decision to go after a project that the firm is likely to lose. When a design professional has targeted a desirable client, and wants to make a good impression, the firm may decide to go after a project even though its chances are slim. That is, design professionals may make a conscious decision to gain visibility and credibility through a well-crafted proposal and interview process. This exercise is very different from chasing something the design professional has no business chasing at all.

COURTSHIP/RELATIONSHIP BUILDING

When design professionals market clients as opposed to projects, it may take some time before an appropriate project presents itself. Rather than bemoaning this situation, designers should consider it an advantage. The "market clients" approach gives design professionals plenty of time to learn the culture of the organization and establish a relationship. It is much easier to do this now than in the frantic week before the interview.

When it finally comes time for the prospect to make up a list of firms, a design firm that markets clients will be one of the names that comes to mind first if it

- *Works diligently at the relationship.*

- *Telephones on a periodic basis.*

- *Better yet, visits.*

- *Sends interesting articles that pertain to the client or project type, or even to personal interests.*

QUALIFICATION PACKAGES

As a result of a long courtship, a referral from a broker, or a stellar reputation, a design professional is asked to submit qualifications for a particular project. The client issues a Request for Information (RFI), Request for Qualifications (RFQ), or Request for Proposal (RFP). The industry uses these terms interchangeably, although the latter (RFP) is more likely to request a scope of services and fee, addressed later in this section.

In an RFQ, the potential client poses specific questions that the design professional answers in a qualification statement, a written exhibit of experience. Always customized, the qualification statement is a sales tool that can put a firm ahead of the competition. The main objectives of a qualification statement are to communicate how well design professionals understand the client's concerns and to show how they will address those concerns. The client determines the elements of qualification statements and proposals. Design professionals should follow the order in which the questions are asked, and answer the questions directly and as briefly as possible. They should adhere to the client's format because clients often compare submissions side by side. If clients cannot find designers' responses easily, those designers will be eliminated.

Even though every RFQ is different, designers are likely to be asked for certain components. One extremely important component of the qualification statement is the cover letter that accompanies the qualification package. The letter may be the only thing a client reads, and it certainly can serve as a refresher after he has waded through a dozen or so weighty submissions. The designer should make the letter a concise summary of key selling points, and make it engaging.

In the first part of the submission, the design professional will introduce your firm. This introduction should be brief, one page at the most. It should be relevant to the project, and emphasize the project type for which the RFQ was issued. Next, the submission should present the project team—the individuals who will work on the project. The designer may want to precede this section with an organization chart or a written preface that clearly states names and project roles, and follow with the individual résumés of the team. Résumés should be kept to one or two pages. The designer should use project roles, not corporate titles, and tailor the individual's project experience so that it is related to the proposed project.

The design professional will definitely be asked to present relevant experience. The submission should include only the most relevant examples, and it should explain why each example demonstrates the design professional's capability to do the client's job. The client may ask how the designer will approach the project. This question affords designers the opportunity to tell how they will address (and solve) the client's concerns. They may wish to briefly restate the problem, so it is clear that they understand the issues involved. They may want to state a planning or design philosophy, relating it directly to the particular situation. The client may even require that designers develop a preliminary work plan that identifies specific tasks, responsibilities, and timeframes. They may also ask designers to provide references. Designers will find it well worth the time to call every reference they list, tell them to expect the call, educate them about the potential project, and cue them about important points of emphasis. These calls to references also give design professionals an opportunity to touch base with their references.

What should the design professional do with all that marketing material in the submittal? Use a "Supplemental Information" section for preprinted project pages, reprints, project lists, and award lists. The client may choose to look at it or not, but he will not have to wade through volumes to get to the information he really seeks.

A good submission produces results. The client

- *Knows that the designer understands his concerns.*

- *Knows that the designer has the team, the experience and the approach that can address those concerns.*

- *Looks forward to meeting the designer in person.*

SELLING YOUR SERVICES

Presentations depend less on technical expertise or experience and more on personalities and planning. Presentations can be in many different formats, from simple meetings to multimedia events. Regardless of format, there are two major objectives. The first objective is to deliver a clear message. Design professionals do that by developing a theme based on their firm's strengths, making the theme seem beneficial to the audience, and focusing on what the client wants and needs to know. The second objective is to establish team chemistry. A team's selection is based on trust. The design professional should strive to make the clients think they would be comfortable working with the design professional, and that the firm is eager to solve their problems.

Understanding Your Audience

Design professionals must develop a presentation that resonates with the audience, and to do that, they must understand that audience. Of course, designers have a tremendous advantage if a client has hired them previously, or if they have been courting the client for a period prior to the selection process. In such a case, the designers seeking the project will have a sense of the personalities, preferences, and dynamics of the selection committee. In other cases, designers need to know everything there is to know about the project. But it is not enough to know about the proposed project. It is also necessary to understand the concerns of each member of the committee, and these concerns may differ from individual to individual. Ideally, designers should understand every angle, and play to each concern. They should also consider the style of the client, so that they may mirror that style to a certain extent. A bunch of suits pitching to some dot.com executives in jeans does not telegraph chemistry. On the other hand, the presentation will not work if the professionals giving it come across as blatantly phony. Presenters will be most comfortable (and persuasive) just being themselves.

Preparing for the Presentation

To get ready for a presentation, it is good practice to invite all who can contribute—even if they may not actually attend the presentation—to a strategy

Presentations depend less on technical expertise or experience and more on personalities and planning. Presentations can be in many different formats, from simple meetings to multimedia events.

session. The session should start with a data dump—everything everyone knows about this client and this project. Next, the session should devote time to determining the overall message of the presentation. The team should worry about delivery style and visuals *only* after it has decided on the message. The advertising firm of Hill and Knowlton used to call this message the SOCO—the *single overriding communications objective*. What is the *one* thing that the presentation team wants the client to remember about the designer and the firm? Everything the presenters say must support this overall message. The team must figure out what the client does not need to be told. Remember, no one can retain more than three or four key ideas. Some presentations (lectures, for instance) are informational, and happen in a logical and sequential order. Sales presentations are motivational, intended to persuade the audience. The order of topics and time allocated to each are determined by the issues of the audience.

In determining the media and tools, the presenters must consider the message, the audience, the room, and the cost (versus the resulting commission). Experts say that visual aids can raise the effectiveness of a speech some 40 percent. Visual aids must support your message; they will *never* take its place. Presenters may choose to use presentation boards, slides or photographs, electronic media such as PowerPoint, videos (on their own or embedded in a PowerPoint show), or models. Less is more, so presenters should not feel compelled to use visuals all the time. These aids should be used only when they add value to the message or to the designer's and the firm's image.

The presenters should consider the quality of their visuals. They should be sure that their visuals remain uncluttered. If they use only bulleted topics and simple graphics, they allow the audience to concentrate on them and their topic. If they use graphics and color, they can draw the audience's eyes to their most important points. Bigger is definitely better. If the audience can't see it, the point will be lost.

For all presenters, rehearsals are *mandatory*. Preparing for presentations involves three key elements: coaching, team building, and motivation. Rehearsals are to benefit the entire team, so individuals should allow enough time for the entire group to rehearse and receive coaching. The first go-around is strategic, as each presenter determines what he or she will say and receives the concurrence of the group. In the next round, the presenters should determine time frames for their portion of the presentation, and do one or more timed rehearsals, offering comments at the end. These comments should be in the form of constructive, not destructive, criticism. And the presenters should not forget to rehearse questions and answers. If presenters have the answers to the toughest questions worked out, they will enter the presentation with more confidence.

Delivering the Presentation

Style alone never sells a job. However, presenters' physical skills do have a profound effect on their message. Presenters communicate a great deal about themselves and their abilities with verbal skills and physical skills (including body language), and your interactions with tools and visuals communicates a great deal about you and your abilities.

Presenters can benefit from close attention to verbalization. Speakers must be seen as experts; they should avoid words like "I think," "perhaps," or "maybe." If they sound insecure or unsure, why should clients believe them? They should also be conversational, and should avoid talking like an interior designer or architect, in technical terms and flowery descriptions. They should also be candid, to demonstrate that they are aware of the client's concerns and conflicts. Actual delivery is important as well. Presenters should speak slowly—much more slowly than their normal rate of speech. They should talk loudly enough so the people in the back of the room can hear them. (Speakers always sound louder to themselves than they do to their audience.) If they increase volume their inflection and energy will increase too. Voice, pacing, tone, and volume should generally match the words presenters are speaking. Presenters should *not* rely on notes; notes serve only to diminish the design professional's aura of expertise.

Body language can provide additional—potentially negative—information. Speakers should not fold their arms—that is considered a hostile and aggressive move. Similarly, they should not put their hands in their pockets—that telegraphs nervousness and distracts the audience, especially if the speakers have change in their pockets. Clasping the hands is another way of saying "What shall I do now?" and presenters should avoid that gesture and other types of fidgeting.

Presenters can also use their bodies to create an immediate, positive impression. They should move quickly and with enthusiasm as they approach the stage/lectern/front of the room. Their gestures should be about the same as their gestures when they are having a normal conversation with friends. If their gestures feel fake, they will look fake. Presenters should alternate between body movement and no movement at all, and underscore their words with their facial expressions. For the best effect on the audience, body positioning is important. Presenters should always face the audience; they should never turn their back or talk to the projection screen. Normally, presenters (and their shoulders) should be at a 45° angle to the room. This positioning establishes a nonthreatening stance and opens the presenter's body to the screen when it is necessary to gesture or move.

To get the message across, presenters need to make visual connections with the audience. They should establish eye contact with one person for the duration of a sentence, or while they explain a concept. Presenters should not feel that they have to look at every audience member at any given moment; if they try to maintain too much eye contact around the room, their eyes will be all over the place, and they will look frantic. They should simply look at one person at a time. This "connected" approach will allow speakers to really see someone, and to get some visual feedback. When presenters are not speaking, they should pay attention to the speaker, in order to focus the attention of the audience.

Presenters can work not only with their physical cues but also with their dress to make clients feel comfortable. They should dress appropriately, considering the client. Presenters will benefit if they find out what the majority of the audience is likely to wear, and dress just a bit nicer. By all means, presenters should wear comfortable clothes. If speakers are pulling at their drawers or wincing because their shoes are too tight, they will be distracted (as will their audience). Designers should not hesitate to use "color psychology" to their advantage. Dark colors project authority, power, and control. Bright colors get attention.

To make these physical considerations work in the context of the whole presentation, the presenters should set the room up in advance. They can mark the light switches they intend to use. They should know the location of electrical outlets. If possible, presenters can arrange the seating in a semicircle to focus and contain the energy of the audience. Throughout the presentation, the presenters should keep the lights on. Bright lights increase the energy in the room and make the audience and the speakers more alert.

If the speakers plan to use a computer during the presentation, they should master it in advance. The intense pressure of an interview is an incredibly poor time to try out any new technology. Speakers should make sure that they do not waste time serving the technology; the technology they use must serve them and their audience. Above all, presenters should remember that they themselves are the most powerful visuals.

Speakers send the strongest message when their words, body language, and tools all support each other. Ultimately it is up to the presenters to make clients feel comfortable with their team's material and style. As presenters, their main task is to engage their audience's attention and keep it focused on their message. The audience will forgive a stumble or two, but it will not forgive a boring performance.

After the presentation, presenters should always get a debriefing, win or lose. They will benefit if they learn why they succeeded or what were their mistakes. Presenters should think of debriefing as research. They will get the most out of the process if they use open-ended (but not leading) questions. Presenters should develop a format for sharing what they have learned with the team, and debrief humanely.

PROPOSAL PREPARATION

Usually, design professionals will be asked to make a proposal in conjunction with their presentation, or shortly thereafter. The primary purpose of the proposal is to delineate the designer's services and present the proposed fee for these services. A proposal may become the basis of a formal agreement (contract), or it may serve as the agreement itself. Firms sometimes specify that fees that are over a certain amount require a formal agreement rather than a proposal form of agreement.

Designers should keep in mind that the proposal is distinct from the process leading up to it. The qualifications and presentation were persuasive, promotional exercises, while the proposal is a legal document. While designers are still in a selling mode, they should be fully prepared to actually do everything they say they will do. There are three basic parts of a proposal: the scope of the project, the scope of services, and professional fees. A proposal may also contain sections relating to schedule, team, and work plan. It is a smart move to initiate this document, rather than to respond to an owner's contract, so that the designer can establish the framework for negotiation.

Identifying Scope of Services

The *scope of services* is the defining element of the proposal, and should be written with great care. It should be preceded by text that clearly describes the scope of the project, so there is a common understanding between owner and designer. The scope of services is usually divided into *basic services,* which are covered under the designer's base fee, and a*dditional services,* which the client may add as options. If designers are working with an owner's agreement as a base document, they should make sure that the client has not shifted services that they normally consider "additional" into basic services. Sometimes it is advisable to list items that are not covered in the usual scope of services, to reduce the possibility of future misunderstandings, but for the most part, the proposal should be a positive document.

Identifying Compensation

Professional fees are the second key part of the proposal, and perhaps the most agonizing part of its preparation. Designers can make use of definite strategies for presenting their fee. If the owner is considering several firms, the designer will want to present the fee so that the owner can make an apples-to-apples comparison. This comparison is usually easiest when designers keep the basic services simple and in conformance with industry standards. If designers include in their basic services certain services that most other firms do not, their fee is likely to be higher. Fees can be presented on a square-foot or other unit basis, on an hourly basis, as a single lump sum, or as a percentage of the construction cost (although this is more common in architectural proposals). The proposal should clarify the terms of payment, by time period or phase. It should protect the design firm against unreasonable withholding of fees, and give the firm recourse when payment is delayed. Later, in an attachment or in the formal agreement, designers can cover more negative provisions, such as limiting the time to contest invoices, the amount of interest charged on late payments, and adjustments to the fee if the project is delayed or put on hold.

NEGOTIATING THE TERMS

Once the client has selected the designer, client and design firm are in a mutual love-fest. Neither wants to destroy that harmony with a nasty negotiation process. However, the negotiation of satisfactory terms is crucial to the success of the project and, ultimately, to the financial health of the design firm. Ideally, if the designer's (or the client's) proposal is fairly reasonable and the fee acceptable, there will be no confrontation. But if there are issues to be addressed, designers have an opportunity to use the negotiation as a forum to communicate the project process. An experienced client already knows that the project process is not a straight path, but the inexperienced client needs to be educated about potential risks in the process. Most owners expect designers to approach negotiations with the same level of professionalism and analysis that they will exhibit on their project. Like the presentation, the negotiation is another demonstration of how the design professional will work. The designer's goal in negotiations is mutual understanding and an equitable agreement. To get there, designers should prioritize issues and get help when they need it, from their attorney or their insurance carrier.

FORMALIZING THE AGREEMENT

Once signed and dated, the proposal may serve as the agreement, often augmented with additional terms. It may serve as the basis for a formal agreement, customized by the firm, by the client, or as offered by a professional organization. The American Institute of Architects' B-141 form can be used for interiors as well as architecture, and AIA B-171 is written specifically for interiors projects. Whatever the form, it formalizes the project terms and the relationship. It should be a celebratory occasion, launching a new collaboration or continuing an existing one. Design professionals are advised to take the time to acknowledge it with their clients, as a key step in building a solid platform for the creative process.

Bibliography

Coxe, Weld. *Marketing Architectural and Engineering Services*. New York: Van Nostrand Rheinhold Company, 1983.

Coxe, Weld, Nina F. Hartung, Hugh Hochberg, Brian J. Lewis, David H. Maister, Robert F. Mattox, and Peter A. Piven. *Success Strategies for Design Professionals*. New York: R. R. Donnelly and Sons, 1987

Quebe, Lisbeth. *The Marketing Budget*. SMPS Core Series of Marketing Information Reports, 1992.

Society for Marketing Professional Services. *Marketing Handbook for the Design and Construction Professional*. BNi Publications, Inc., 2000.

Spaulding, Margaret, and William D'Elia. *Advanced Marketing Techniques for Architectural and Engineering Firms*. New York: McGraw-Hill, 1989.

24

Predesign Services

SHARON TURNER

The value of predesign services should not be underestimated—this is where a project begins its life, and a good start sets the standard for the quality of service and delivery for the project as a whole. Put simply, whatever the extent of the commission, this is where the goals of the project are clearly identified and understood by the project team.

Predesign involves primarily establishing the necessary information to design and administer the project and determines how the design firm will relate professionally to the client and the wider project team. The opportunity for developing trust and strong collaborative working relationships in this phase will go a long way toward achieving a successful outcome for the overall commission.

PREDESIGN PROJECT METHODOLOGIES

Broadly speaking, interior design firms are involved in predesign services in three ways. The first is the project initiation phase of a standard interior design commission, when the space to be designed has already been identified and the scope of work has been predetermined by the client. The second is when the design firm is part of a wider project team charged with identifying space requirements and assisting in the selection of the most suitable space or building, or evaluating the extent of work required in an existing building or property portfolio. This is also known as prelease service. The third is when a client organization is undergoing some form of major change, e.g., corporate relocation, merger, acquisition, or a radical rethinking of workplace needs and so employs a design firm in a consulting role for the change process.

Typically, these three types of commission take one of three approaches: a conventional project initiation approach, a pre-release team approach, or a consulting approach.

The Conventional Approach–Project Initiation

In this scenario the project is typically in an existing space already under the control of the client, or the space has been negotiated for prior to the appointment of the interior design firm. Predesign services in this scenario usually involve no more than initial meetings with the client team to establish the project reporting and administration structure and to set the work plan and schedule for the future phases. This is typically undertaken by either the principal-in-charge of the project or the project manager of the design firm. In addition, from the client side, attendance should include the client or client representative, a client information technology representative or consultant, and from the consultant side the mechanical, electrical, or plumbing (MEP) engineer where applicable.

From the interior designers perspective, a typical project initiation meeting should cover the following topics:

- *Project and team organization structure*

- *Reporting and approval procedures*

- *Budget and cost-control procedures*

- *Identification of project or building constraints*

- *Client corporate guidelines, space standards, and business plan documentation*

- *Headcount, organization structure, adjacency requirements*

- *Summary of existing client programming data*

- *Identification of programming methodologies and components*

- *Distribution of "as built" drawings, computer disks*

- *Identification of field survey requirements*

- *Development of the work plan and schedule*

- *Review of fee invoicing and payment procedures*

A word of caution, however: when the interior designer has come late to the table there have been many instances of clients underestimating their space requirements, particularly as headcount growth is so difficult for many organizations to predict. I remember a case in point where a client and his broker had been searching and negotiating for a 75,000-ft² space requirement for four months. Three buildings had been short-listed prior to the appointment of the interior design firm, which subsequently discovered that the real space requirement was 110,000 ft². A sobering thought economically and potentially disastrous in a tight property market.

These initial meetings are then followed by the detailed programming phase and the project proceeds in a traditional phased way. Fees for the project initiation phase usually form part of the overall interior design fee for the project, which is most commonly stated as dollars per square foot.

The Prelease Team Approach

The recession of the early 1990s resulted in clients taking a very cautious approach to acquiring real estate and looking for better value for money in the buildings they occupied. As a result, both end-user clients and the brokerage community are now retaining the services of interior design firms earlier in the project process than in the past. This type of predesign service is more common to larger commissions involving corporate relocations and consolidations. However, recently the dot.coms and new media firms are also using interior designers in prelease building evaluation and negotiations, as they are having to move quickly in a tight real estate market. A standard prelease team consists of the client representative, the real estate advisor or broker, legal representation, the architect/designer, and engineers (as necessary).

Many large occupiers are finding that the large blocks of space they require are not readily available for lease in most locations, and given the tight restrictions being placed on obtaining finances by lending institutions, more developers are replacing speculative office developments with design-to-suit projects or pre-let projects. Developers are seeking large corporate users to come into their projects as the major tenant and quite often to take an equity position in the project. Several developers since the recession have become development managers for large corporate clients who own land and want to develop buildings to suit their requirements. This is a return to the strong commercial markets in many of our city centers during the 1960s and 1970s, which were responsible for the formation of city business districts in the United States. This has also been the case in Europe more recently, e.g., La Defense in Paris, Frankfurt, and Canary Wharf in London, to name a few.

In this scenario the interior designer, as a part of the wider professional team, establishes the clients' "big picture" space requirements in the form of a strategic program and develops the ideal building footprint arrangement. With the assistance of professional engineers, the interior design "pro forma" for a new location/building and the infrastructure needed to support the environment is established. Once signed off by the clients' senior management, the "pro forma" is used to begin the property search.

In the case of a build-to-suit requirement, the information will be used to solicit responses for developer's proposals.

This very often results in suggested modifications to the base building design offer, to better suit the client's needs and assists the team in making its final recommendations.

A typical site/developer appraisal checklist would include:

- *Location, access, and transportation links*

- *Size, massing, and core provision*

- *Planning authority consent status*

- *Ownership scenarios (freehold site purchase/developer leaseback)*

- *Construction challenges*

- *Costs (property, relocation, business, and construction)*

- *Building footprint and loss factor efficiency checks*

- *Stacking diagrams and test fits*

- *Rating how well the building meets the ideal space strategy*

The true value to the client of this type of collaborative predesign service is the development of a clear space strategy and the criteria for a space search, analysis of short-listed sites or buildings, and professional advice in supporting negotiations and decision making. The value to the interior design firm is that this type of commission, when executed properly, often leads to a full-service interior design commission following the leasing or building acquisition.

Because the time span of this sort of commission can often be a year from the start of the process to making a final decision on a building, this predesign service is offered as a stand-alone commission based on either a fixed or not-to-exceed fee.

The Consulting Role

The third type of predesign service involves understanding how design and environment can affect the alignment of business goals, corporate culture, and real estate needs. It rarely takes the form of a traditional design project in a predetermined location. These projects are more likely to be predesign feasibility studies involving the recommendation of future space strategies, relocation scenarios, or exploration of alternatives with a view to implementing major space use changes in a client organization.

Existing real estate portfolio consolidations consist of reviewing and analyzing existing conditions, space efficiency, and effectiveness. The analysis would attempt to answer the questions of what is working, what isn't, and why not?

The review of existing conditions, especially environmental conditions, requires measuring existing performance against preset guidelines or "best practice" criteria. Obtaining these data requires the services of engineers; almost always MEP and fire protection (FP) and sometimes structural. The data are presented in report format, with recommendations for upgrades, costing information, and implementation logistics.

This type of due-diligence study is best reported in the form of a spreadsheet, so that comparisons between building and/or locations can be easily understood. The report would also contain "big picture" stacking scenarios and test fits of typical building floors to establish efficiency and loss factors. For an example of a building evaluation checklist, see Figure 24-1.

Predesign feasibility studies are projects that exist outside a "live" interior design project and involve the design firm providing knowledge-based advice to set new goals/guidelines for workplace design and occupancy targets. These projects are nearly always driven by the need to occupy less space, use existing space more efficiently, or provide a better-quality environment for staff and customers.

These projects are invariably for large-scale corporate clients. Virtually all large relocation projects involve a predesign feasibility study prior to the real estate decisions being made or the appointment of the interior designer to

QUALITATIVE SCORING MATRIX

After reviewing the shortlisted properties, each criteria has been scored on a scale of 1–3
(3-Meets the Requirement, 1-Does Not Meet Requirement).

SHORTLISTED PROPERTIES			BUILDING NO. 1		BUILDING NO. 2	
Element	Weighting	Criteria	0.00%	Score	0.00%	Score
1 LOCATION	20%	Within designated area of search				
		Road Access				
		Access to Public Transport				
		Access to Airport				
		Proximity to Customers				
		Proximity to Competitors				
		Proximity to Major Highways				
		Proximity to Local Amenities				
		Average Score				
		Average Score × Weighting (%)				
2 BUILDING	10%	Image				
		Surrounding Areas				
		Self Contained Building				
		Signage/Prominence				
		Expansion Option				
		Average Score				
		Average Score × Weighting (%)				
3 BUILDING AMENITIES/ SERVICES	5%	Reception Space				
		24 Hour Access				
		Building Security				
		Age of Plant				
		Uninterrupted Power Supply (UPS)				
		Average Score				
		Average Score × Weighting (%)				
4 AVAILABLE SPACE	15%	Configuration				
		Flexibility				
		Independent Access				
		Floor Plate Size				
		Efficiency Factor				
		Existing Condition				
		Average Score				
		Average Score × Weighting (%)				

FIGURE 24-1

Building Evaluation Checklist.

SHORTLISTED PROPERTIES			BUILDING NO. 1		BUILDING NO. 2	
Element	Weighting	Criteria	0.00%	Score	0.00%	Score
5 SPECIFICATION	15%	Air Conditioning				
		Suspended Ceilings				
		Raised Floors				
		Core Configuration				
		Elevators				
		Average Score				
		Average Score × Weighting (%)				
6 PARKING	5%	Designated Parking				
		Free Parking Closeby				
		Average Score				
		Average Score × Weighting (%)				
7 LEASE TERMS	5%	Length of Lease Commitment				
		Break Clause				
		Expansion Option				
		Average Score				
		Average Score × Weighting (%)				
8 TIMING	10%	Optional date for relocation				
		Deadline date for relocation				
		Average Score				
		Average Score × Weighting (%)				
9 LANDLORD CONTRIBUTION	15%	Significant contribution to fit out				
		Average Score				
		Average Score × Weighting (%)				
AVERAGE RATING						
TOTAL RATING/100%	100%					

design a given space. These studies are usually carried out with the client's facilities management team, the interior design consulting team, and frequently with the input of business or management consultants who report on improving business processes and operational criteria. Many large corporate clients are amending their design services criteria to exclude those design firms that cannot offer this type of consulting service.

The fees for these projects are usually on a fixed-fee or not-to-exceed basis.

WHO IS INVOLVED WITH THE PROCESS?

All three types of predesign services are influenced by the tangible project parameters of schedule and budget, with key issues such as "We will pay double rent if we are not relocated by _____. "There can be no down-time for our operation." These can be understood and planned for by the project team.

Less tangible, yet critical to success, is the definition and understanding of what the true goals and objectives of the project are, and—importantly—what the measures of success are for the project in the eyes of the board and/or the employees. The design professional needs to understand how the client views the situation—the history, the boardroom politics, the perception of themselves in their marketplace, and the degree of potential change to be planned for from the outset.

The predesign phase reports and recommendations must come to clear and impartial conclusions to be credible with the direct client and senior management, and to be responsive to the needs of the business. The methodology for gathering this information, the analysis, and presentation of recommendations is extremely important to establish early on the points of consensus on what the project is about. Quite a tall order for an outsider to come in to a client organization and accomplish. But it is exactly the reason why the design professional can see, without bias, the issues surrounding the client's existing situation and/or proposed project. Because we are not from "in-house," our opinions are often more readily accepted as being impartial and therefore more credible.

ESTABLISHING A PROJECT STRATEGY DEVELOPMENT TEAM

In the second and third types of predesign services the interior designer forms part of a wider strategy development team. Ideally this should consist of the client's corporate real estate team, facilities management, information technology, human resources, and the interior designer, with input from engineers, a real estate professional, and other consultants on an as-needed basis. The strategy development process involves the following:

- *Hold strategic planning sessions with the business heads.*

- *Determine the business objectives and change/flexibility targets.*

- *Ask "Where are the opportunities for change in the corporate culture or process?"*

- *Keep space programming macro; detail is not required at this stage— think big picture.*

- *Question the real need for physical proximity between people/ departments/business units.*

- *Establish the information technology and services infrastructure requirements at the earliest opportunity.*

- *Establish the level of amenities to be provided.*

- *Establish existing conditions if appropriate.*

- *Establish the real drivers behind the project.*

Even if the client has chosen to outsource the management of the project to a client representative or project management consultant, it is critical that a strategy development team be set up in this manner. Building credibility with the direct client and senior management is key to a successful project.

The finalized strategic program or real estate strategy report is signed off by the client and the information forms the yardstick to highlight the challenges of the project and sets out the criteria to measure the suitability of various occupancy scenarios and locations that may be considered.

This collaboration ... very often leads to an advantageous negotiating position for the client if the building is spatially inefficient, loss factors are exceptionally high, or specifications fall below those "reasonably" expected.

THE ROLE OF THE REAL ESTATE PROFESSIONAL

Armed with the client's building criteria or space strategy report, the real estate professional, who is representing the client, finds and screens prospective locations/buildings that meet the client's criteria. He or she will liaise with the strategy development team to provide the interior designer with base building information, floor plans, and services provision information. However, being primarily financially driven, he or she brings to the team the market knowledge and negotiating skills to obtain for the client the best lease terms, landlord contributions and incentives, building management, and services provision. We, as the design professionals, are expert witnesses to what is on offer in terms of existing conditions, upgrade requirements, and compliance of the building with the client's pro forma. This collaboration between interior designer and real estate professional very often leads to an advantageous negotiating position for the client if the building is spatially inefficient, loss factors are exceptionally high, or specifications fall below those "reasonably" expected.

WORKING WITH OTHER CONSULTANTS

For most predesign phases or projects, the primary consultants in addition to the interior design firm are the MEP and FP engineers and the structural engineer, who, depending on the requirements of the project, needs to confirm structural loading and provide supplemental design. As a result, the structural engineers play a smaller role than the mechanical engineers.

It is this group of three consultants who provide the primary professional licensed service to the client. They take the legal responsibility for their portions of a project and are held accountable by the state that granted them a license to practice. Quite often, code consultants help expedite the filing of the documents with statutory authorities having jurisdiction over the project while providing expert advice on the design's compliance with city, state, and federal codes.

Whether the client contracts directly with these consultants or they are contracted through the interior design firm on behalf of the client, these consultants should follow the directions of the interior design firm regarding meeting deadlines and coordinating their work.

When specialized interior projects, such as trading floors, present themselves, it is prudent to have the MEP and FP consultants contract directly with the client. As a user group, traders have a heavy reliance on the mechanical systems' design to support the trading floor environment and operations, provide redundancy backup in case of failure, and to build in operational security within the space. Because of these sensitivities, the project is better served if the client has direct control of these services. This is also true in the case of retaining information technology (IT) consultants for all types of clients, not just for heavy IT users such as traders.

If the predesign commission includes a search for new buildings or locations, the engineer provides a scope of services similar to the interior designer's. In most cases this can be summarized as a due-diligence study to investigate whether enough capacity exists in the base building systems to meet the client's systems needs. If the services provision falls short, the engineers need to quantify that shortfall. At a later stage this can support the client's lease negotiations with the building owner.

In a tight property market the client's real estate consultant needs a quick turnaround on confirming the viability of potential locations from both the designer and engineers. The interior design firm needs to respond quickly in providing empirical information that leads to an informed decision about why the prospective location is or is not viable. The key to this process is making an informed decision. To make this process credible, the bases by which one judges a candidate location must be consistently applied by using an "ideal" benchmark. These benchmarks are determined by designer and engineer in the project initiation phase at the outset of the commission.

In projects where the client is considering an equity stake in a building, the number of consultants needs to be expanded to include waterproofing, vertical transportation, structural, curtain wall, and other specialty consultants to ensure that the building complies to the specifications and drawings prepared by the owner's consultants. For projects of this nature it is common for a construction manager to be retained by the client to consult on the owner's contractors means, methods, logistics, and costs. If the client's design team requires building modifications, they need to be properly priced as additions and deductions by the owner for charge-back to the client.

Where any type of property search is involved, the client should have a professional real estate advisor involved as well as legal counsel. With today's reliance on IT, the client's communications and IT advisors (in-house, outside, or both) should be involved in the project from the beginning. How those are managed vary from being completely in-house to completely outsourced, depending on the client's organization and the size of the project.

As you can see, these teams can become quite large. How they are organized, the reporting structure, and approval processes differ greatly among different clients. The Internet and project management software enables us all to communicate more efficiently and deliver information that is readily accessible to all parties.

Regardless of which of the three typical predesign services one may be performing, the common thread through them all is to gather enough information at an early stage to truly understand the challenges of the project. This, in turn, will result in a more informed design process and better design solutions in later phases.

Bibliography

Duffy, Francis. *The New Office*. London: Conran Octopus Limited, 1997.

Hammer, Michael, and James Champy. *Re-engineering the Corporation*. New York: HarperCollins Publishers, 1993.

Myerson, Jeremy, and Philip Ross. *The Creative Office*. Corte Madre, CA: Ginko Press Inc., 1999.

Riewoldt, Otto. *Intelligent Spaces*. London: Calmann & King Ltd., 1997.

25

Programming for Change

PAMELA ANDERSON-BRULÉ, AIA

At the commencement of any project, when the designer begins the process of discovery into a client's needs, wants, and desires, one thing is surely present no matter what the project or client type, and that is *change*. Whether it is a residential client in search of a home, a corporation in search of a headquarters, a government agency in search of a public facility, a new project or a remodel, there will be change.

Change is a powerful occurrence that has notable effects on humans whose lives are wrapped around its events. Change brings with it every spectrum of emotion, from excitement and expectation to fear and apprehension. It is in the presence of the unknown that these emotions can often be magnified and affect the quality of communication and understanding that needs to be present to design a project successfully.

In order to begin to discover the effects of change on the client and therefore on the client's future needs, one must consider the effects of change on the client's entire system. If you are designing for a family, the effects of change will be different for the husband than for the wife or the children. In corporate work, what works well for the finance department might cause conflict with the human resources department. Therefore, we must look at our clients as a whole system and we must also understand their parts, their structures, and their strategic objectives, if we are to assist our clients in making successful decisions about their future.

Programming in a broad sense is the process, methodology, and tool used in the discovery and/or creation of the unknown and the known. Depending on the complexity of the problem, the magnitude of change, and the emotional and factual understanding of the client for its own future desired state, it can be simple and straightforward, or extremely elaborate, with a multitude of interrelated or interconnected parts.

"Traditional" programming records a description of space needs and documents the elements within a project that are necessary to meet the client's requirements. The process used to establish this document is typically an interview, or perhaps a questionnaire, between the client and the designer recording the client's responses. The client is then asked to review the information and confirm the content of the program, which then becomes the guide and checklist for the designer.

This traditional method assumes that clients are capable of understanding their own circumstances, analyzing their effects, replanning and reorganizing for their future, and then clearly communicating this to the designer in terms of building needs. It also assumes that the clients' representatives have a thorough understanding of their entire system and the complexity of their own cultural, technical, financial, and organizational needs. In most cases, certainly, clients do not even completely understand their own current state and are often responding to their existing physical space or cultural archetypes in a way that may no longer be valid.

How, then, do you begin to build common understanding of the "change" that will occur, and how do you assist your clients through the process of discovering the unknowns?

PROCESS AND METHODOLOGY

Process Design and Development

You must begin with a planned process, which is designed around the end results that you and your client seek. Similar to the way you would design a project, you must start with a conceptual idea of the process, you must explore areas for analysis, and you must determine what level of effort and cost the client is willing to invest in development. Once these concepts are outlined and agreed upon, a game plan, with agendas, must be created, which will guide you through the process. It must be facilitated in a way that allows for open exploration, honest feedback, and well thought out direction. The process must address the emotional, cultural, and operational and/or functional needs of the client. It must include the analysis of existing conditions as well as the projection of the client's future needs, which will support the client's strategic objectives.

It is important to understand that the discussions need to be highly interactive, participatory, and open to questioning by all. In *Excellence by Design: Transforming Workplace and Work Practice*, by Turid Horgen, Michael Joroff,

William Porter, and Donald Schön in association with the Space and Organization Research Group (SPORG) of the Massachusetts Institute of Technology's School of Architecture (John Wiley & Sons, New York, 1998), there is a discussion of "process architecture." The book describes the necessary steps to providing process leadership to accomplish the goals of transforming a workplace. "Process architecture requires openness to creative tension between the user and practitioners. This approach is much more demanding than traditional programming. . . . Process architecture demands a tolerance or zeal for open-endedness and persistent uncertainty. For the process architect, the design is never entirely complete . . . However, one characteristic of the design process is that one rips apart what has been, looks at it with different eyes, and puts it together in a way it has not been put together before."

A variety of facilitation methods can be used in an interactive manner for information gathering. They include one-on-one interviews, focus groups (structured discussions, with preselected participants, internal and external to the organization), open forums, workshops (internally focused working sessions), and benchmarking (guided tours, of similar or relative projects, with focused discussions). It can also be appropriate to use questionnaires, surveys, etc., to gather information that can provide valuable data to the project, where an inclusive process does not affect the outcome of the information.

The concept of facilitating a process, rather than just doing one, is fundamental to reaching a superior level of service to clients. It is as important that the building be ready for an organization as it is that an organization be ready for the building. Facilitating clients through this interactive process can often be the catalyst for change to begin and to continue even after they occupy their space.

As an example, for the San José Martin Luther King Jr. Library, a large joint use facility was envisioned, where city and state university libraries would be integrated into a single facility. The vision was to create seamless service, a united culture, and a project unique in the nation, between two distinctly different organizations. A facilitated process allowed for the discovery and acknowledgement of complexity and initiated the necessary steps to cultural and operational development, years before the completion of the facility. In this way the architecture of the organization was developed in unison with the architecture of the facility, and alignment was reached between the organizational objectives and the vision.

Systems Analysis

To begin to truly understand your clients' needs, you must understand their current state or system. In order to accomplish this, you must go through a discovery process, which will allow you to gain enough insight about them to record their current state. This is typically done through an interactive process, involving enough of the individuals within the organization who have accurate data and information.

One example of this might be the programming of a public health clinic. If you were to interview the administrative staff and ask them to map out their current work process, you would probably get a completely different outcome than if you asked the same task of the nurses, and you would get yet another if you asked the doctors. The reason is that each of the participants sees the system from a different perspective and in fact does not understand exactly what actually happens. Through this example, we can see why it is so important to use "cross-functional" teams of individuals when you are working with organizational complexity.

It is also important to talk to each of the department or groups individually, so that you can understand their individual perspectives and needs, in isolation from the whole; otherwise, you may easily miss an important issue. Even in the case of residential design, if you discuss the client's needs with only the couple, you may never discover an unspoken but truly important need of one of the individuals.

Also, through the interactive process of defining the existing conditions, one needs to record what works and what does not work within the system. Often, in a designer's excitement to create a new space, things that worked quite well, and are truly important to the client, can be lost and are not missed until the project is complete. By asking questions about what works and why, the designer can gain a deeper level of insight into a variety of conditions in the client's organization. This will make the designer more astute when the program is finally complete and as the design is being developed.

Work/Life Flow Analysis

Work flow analysis or life flow analysis (for residential projects) is one tool which helps record the day-to-day reality of an organization or group. Every aspect of the organization or group must be discussed as you walk through a typical day, week, month, and year. It is important to capture physical, cultural, emotional, financial, technological, and organizational needs that are attributed to the way one leads one's life and work.

If any one of these aspects is forgotten, the user and the designer will not be fully aware of how change might affect them and will be unable to plan a design that will support them fully. As our lives become more complicated, as change becomes a constant, and as time becomes more demanding, the way we work, live, share knowledge, and survive will become more dependent on the quality of the spaces in which we live. The ability of the design space to nurture our personal and professional needs will better serve our personal responsiblities both within organizations and society as a whole.

External Factors and Drivers

Once this information is captured, the discussions should expand to external factors that will drive the system. Something as mundane as how the garbage is stored and collected, how supplies are delivered, how the children enter the house on a rainy day, can often lead to process discoveries that have real and serious design implications.

Logistical Issues

Another level of analysis that should be performed is the review of logistic issues that will affect the project and the client in the process of completing design and construction. Does the project need to be phased? Will your client occupy the space during a remodel? How will move coordination be handled? What contingencies need to be included in the schedule? All these may seem to be construction-related questions, but in fact they may lead to the discovery of elements that will need to be considered in the program, design, and certainly in the project planning from the very beginning of the project.

Conclusion for Systems Analysis

The concept of doing a full investigation into all of the matters that might affect your client in the process of change leads to the discovery of the unknowns and allows for you to work collaboratively with your client to

In the current state of the world of acquisitions, mergers, blended families, joint-use projects, etc., there is a real need for the development and understanding of a client's culture if a designer is going to have an appropriate level of insight . . .

design the next steps. It should be noted that one should never be married to the end result while proceeding through this process. The real solution to the need for change may in fact not be in a built project, but in organizational change. It is not until we have gone through these interactions with our clients that we can build a new system for them that will support them in the future in every aspect of organizational success. Inevitably, the journey that you will go on with your client through this discovery process will be in and of itself more valuable, to them and to you, than simply the end result. As important as it is to plan out the process, it is equally important to continually monitor your progress and to be completely open to redesigning the process when the need arises.

CULTURAL DEVELOPMENT

In the current state of the world of acquisitions, mergers, blended families, joint-use projects, etc., there is a real need for the development and understanding of a client's culture if a designer is going to have an appropriate level of insight to design the project. Even when working for existing companies, organizations, agencies, and individuals, there is often a "cultural void" in their own understanding of themselves. If there is not alignment on this level, the project is at constant risk of inherent conflicts that can develop from the individual whims of participants.

It is important to make sure that there is the right level of participation in a project by key decision makers. A core team of key representatives and stakeholders who will validate the proposed plan and provide direction and leadership throughout the process should be selected at the very beginning of the project. If an organizational vision exists, it must be reviewed and validated, and if it does not, it must be built. The core values of the client must be articulated and aligned with the stated vision. This provides the framework for decision making and should be constantly present as programming decisions are reached. The success of the programming effort can then be measured by the degree to which the program supports the organization's core values, vision, and objectives.

Ideally, development of the client's new system will include the "right people," at a deep organizational level, at the right times. However, not everyone in an organization will have been involved, and communication is necessary to ensure that nonparticipants will accept and support the proposed changes in their environment. A plan can be developed that will address the needs of the whole organization as it moves toward implementation, and might include ongoing communication, an input and feedback loop, and individual and team training where needed to prepare for future operations.

THE SPACE PROGRAM

The space program document can reflect both the programming process and its outcome. Elements of a comprehensive space program for a complex organization might include all of the following components, whereas a residential space program might contain only a few of them in a reduced format.

1. *Introduction.* Description of how information is organized within the document, a glossary or definition of terms, general assumptions, etc.

2. *Organizational vision, core values, and strategic objectives.* Vision statement, core values, and objectives which provided the framework for the decisions that led to the space program and should guide the designer throughout the project. For a residential project this might be a written "dream" of their future home by the clients.

3. *Process and methodology.* A summary of the process and its participants. Future users of the document will gain an understanding of how and why decisions were made.

4. *Operational plan.* Documentation of future operational and functional scenario(s), developed through systems analysis, which form the basis for the space requirements. An operational plan could also include an implementation strategy (the necessary steps to achieve the future scenario), and address resource allocation (budgeted time and expense for staff, consultants, and any other necessary resources to implement the operational plan).

5. *Critica-issues list.* A description of any issues or elements that are critical to the success of the project, or that must be addressed or resolved in design.

6. *Space program.*

   a. Space allocation standards: Where appropriate, standards for space allocation can be developed based on functional requirements, hierarchy, etc. Especially in large facilities, standardization of the size and technical requirements of conference rooms, workspaces, etc., facilitates the creation of modular spaces that support future reconfiguration or alternative use.

   b. Qualitative spatial requirements: A narrative that describes the vision for the quality of the space, which can include "how the space should look or feel."

   c. Building standard assumptions:

      i. Technical standards: Includes structural, mechanical, electrical, technology, lighting, plumbing, security, communications, audiovisual, and acoustical requirements.

      ii. Departmental grossing factors: A factor applied to the net square footage of each department that accommodates interdepartmental circulation, etc., and creates the total departmental gross square footage.

      iii. Building grossing factors: A factor applied to the sum of the departmental gross square footage that accommodates building systems, building circulation (department to department and vertical, where applicable), wall thickness, etc.

   d. Quantitative spatial requirements:

      i. Quantity, square footage allocation, and function for each type of space: For each type of space, the total quantity, net square footage, functional and use comments, and staff projections.

      ii. Space data sheets for each type of space:
         1. Technical and building systems requirements that reflect conditions atypical to building standards
         2. Projected furniture, fixtures, and equipment

   e. Space layout diagrams: Typical conceptual space diagrams, e.g., conference rooms, training rooms, workspaces, standard office layout, etc.

   f. Functional adjacencies: Describes the primary, secondary, and tertiary adjacency requirements of individual spaces in relation to other spaces.

    g. Functional stacking diagrams: Describes the adjacency requirements of individual departments or subdepartments in relation to other departments, both horizontally and vertically (multiple floors).

    h. Site development criteria: Site requirements developed through the systems analysis, such as accessibility, parking and transportation, and amenities such as proximity to other services, etc.

7. *Appendix.*

    a. Meeting memoranda

    b. Participant listing

TOOLS

The level of information collection that has been outlined can be overwhelming. Yet, if any of the details are forgotten, the outcome can be a missed detail, an inaccurate assumption, a design with flaws, and an unsatisfactory end result. If we accept "that the quality of the project is equal to the quality of the process," and that information management is the key to meeting the functional as well as quality goals of the project, then we must find a way to collect, record, change, track, measure, and learn from information.

The current means available to accomplish this effectively are through a relational database. Development of a relational database, which is designed to support the process and includes the specific types of information required, acts as both a repository and checklist for information. When a database is used, it can be designed and programmed to capture specific information, as well as allow change tracking and program reconciliation to development of the design. The most important aspect of inputting information in a database is to ensure that its integrity is maintained over the life of the project.

Program reconciliation is accomplished by comparing design documentation at periodic intervals (i.e., 50 percent design development, 100 percent construction documents, etc.) to the initial space program. Tracking the initiation and approval of changes to the space program, as reflected in the actual design, are necessary to ensure that the original goals are eventually met at completion of the project, or are revised to accommodate the change.

CONCLUSION

Programming is really the art of knowledge management, which is constantly changing and expanding along with our ability to manage information. We need to creatively collect, record, and manage this information if we are to accomplish the act and art of design. Innovative design must be fundamentally functional and in alignment with the vision, goals, and objectives of our clients and their organizations. In essence, it must not only align to their strategic needs, but also to their cultural and even emotional needs. We can never reach this objective if we are not willing to expand our thinking, invest in our tools, and train ourselves in the art of facilitating the design process. We must be willing to involve ourselves at an emotional level if we are going to achieve meeting the emotional needs of our clients through design.

Bibliography

Fox, Matthew. *The Reinvention of Work*. San Francisco: Harper, 1995.

Churn in the Workplace. Zeeland: Herman Miller, 2001.

Collaborative Settings Fostering Teamwork in the Workplace. Zeeland: Herman Miller, 2001.

Horgen, Turid, Michael Joroff, William Porter, and Donald Schön. *Excellence by Design—Transforming Workplace and Work Practice*. New York: John Wiley & Sons, 1998.

Kelley, Tom, Jonathan Littman (Contributor), and Tom Peters. *The Art of Innovation: Lessons in Creativity from Ideo, America's Leading Design Firm*. New York: Doubleday, 2001.

Propst, Robert. *The Office: A Facility Based on Change*. Seacaucus: Birch Lane Press, 1986.

Reinventing the Corporation: Office Environments: The North American Perspective. Zeeland: Herman Miller, 2001.

Supporting Collaborative Work. Zeeland: Herman Miller, 2001.

26

Programming: Strategic Planning

DEBRA LEHMAN-SMITH, IIDA

The client is the driving force behind every project. And, as everyone already knows, every client has a distinctive set of corporate qualities and project-specific criteria. Thus, it is of utmost importance that the first step in the design process be to gain a thorough understanding of who the client is and what they are all about. This information-gathering phase has traditionally been known simply as the programming phase of a project. Today, this phase needs to include not only programming, but also client insight, workplace analysis, and test fits. Thus, the phase is actually best titled "Strategic Planning." The thoroughness of strategic planning can mean the difference between the success and failure of the project.

The following sections describe the strategic planning components and the significance of each, while periodically using AmSouth Bancorporation as a case study. AmSouth Bancorporation is a financial institution located in the southern United States. A few years ago, AmSouth decided to relocate their offices from eight office buildings scattered throughout Birmingham, Alabama, to one corporate headquarters. AmSouth had many of the typical client goals and project issues and thus will serve as a good example as we begin to understand the strategic planning phase.

CLIENT INSIGHT

Uniqueness. This is what makes each of us individuals. It is essential to recognize this in our clients, as the best interior design comes from an in-depth analysis and understanding of what makes a particular company and its workforce unique. Understanding the company's culture and business goals and the workforce's lifestyles provides direction for the architectural design.

This is your chance to really get to know your client's company, personality, and working style. Since you will be working with this client for a number of months or years, it will help to establish positive relationships early. While working on the AmSouth project, we quickly learned that the client's representatives were true Southerners. And, due to the fact that there was no local metropolis offering a variety of cultural experiences near the project site, our project team members began to acclimate themselves by allowing our hosts to introduce us to a variety of Southern customs, including meals with fried green tomatoes and grits. After spending a few months on the project, some members of the team even began unconsciously to develop their own Southern drawls, thus further relating to the client. Through these bonding experiences, we were able to gain a solid understanding of the personalities of both workforce members and the corporate culture.

This insight into the client is best gained through a combination of your own research about the company and its business industry combined with invaluable information learned during client insight meetings. These meetings should review the client's organization, corporate goals, and objectives for the future. Some of the basic topics that should be discussed include the following:

Corporate business goals and objectives.
- The goals and objectives offer a look into the background of the company. Often, this discussion is associated with a history lesson of who the company is, where it began, and how it got to where it is today.

Corporate mission statement.
- The mission statement will give you insight into the culture and environment of the company. This will aid in determining how best to approach the client while discussing the project.

Project goals.
- The goals of the new office will vary from client to client. It will be important to understand the specific goals and ensure that they are incorporated into the workplace analysis. Some common goals include increased flexibility, cost effectiveness, sustainable design, employee attraction and retention, and incorporation of better high-technology and data systems.

Management strategies.
- The strategies that a company uses to manage its workforce and company are important to note. These will be the strategies that will be used once the new

office is designed, so they must be accommodated within the new design. If the company is a law firm with a one-to-one attorney-to-legal assistant ratio, it may be important to locate that legal assistant directly adjacent to the attorney he or she is working with. However, if a pool of legal assistants works with a number of attorneys, it may be more efficient to designate an area of an office floor to locate all legal assistants together, so that they may better collaborate and save valuable office space at the same time.

Through discussions of these topics, valuable information can be learned that will form a strong foundation of knowledge for the project. For example, if the client states that one corporate goal is to become more efficient and also increase the size of the corporation, it will be necessary to design a flexible office that can accommodate future growth by potentially modifying workstation sizes and/or adding workstations. Thus, this office would not be designed with a large number of enclosed offices. On the contrary, the office design concept should begin with a design structured around standardized, movable office systems, which should be further analyzed during the workplace analysis.

PROGRAMMING

After gaining an understanding of a client's organization, learning how an organization works, communicates, develops, and processes information is crucial in determining the most effective interior plan and design. Groups within the company work, behave, and interact differently, based on their responsibilities and individual needs.

A tour of the client's existing facilities to gain a basic understanding of the overall operations should occur early in the programming phase. Following the tour of the facilities, the next step is to conduct a series of interviews. The process for interviewing representatives for all the divisions of a corporation may take up to several months, but the wealth of data gathered makes it worth the effort and is essential to the project. For the interviews, the client should select the staff members they believe will be most insightful and knowledgeable about the company's programming topics. Thus, it is often helpful to give the client a list of potential interviewing questions or topics a few weeks prior to the scheduled interviews to aid in their determination of the interviewees. The following list of topics should be discussed in these meetings:

- *Current and future staff projections*

- *Current and future departmental responsibilities, work processes, and functional requirements*

- *Critical department adjacency requirements*

- *Individual personnel functional and adjacency requirements*

- *Specific and unique space needs requirements*

- *Support space requirements (workrooms, computer rooms, meeting spaces, etc.)*

- *Office and workstation space standards*

- *Technology issues specific to department functions*

- *Base building requirements (structural, HVAC, plumbing, ceiling height, etc.)*

From this information and the information gained through the client insight investigation discussed earlier, a program can be created to define the basic physical requirements of the workplace. Now, the amenities and infrastructure of that workplace must be determined.

WORKPLACE ANALYSIS

Once the program is complete, the interior project team assesses the further workplace requirements for the project. Beyond the basic square-footage calculations and numbers of workstations, chairs, files, and other office equipment, workplace analysis topics must be incorporated to create a complete project understanding. These topics, listed below, may have been conceptually introduced during the initial client insight process as vague concepts and now become the evaluation criteria for the workplace analysis.

Flexibility.

- Determine how often a company shifts departments and/or changes teams, and how simple this process needs to be. This can lead to discussions regarding movable or fixed partitions and the cost impacts of flexibility.

Uniform office/workstation size.

- The amount of open versus closed office space and the sizes of offices and workstations that are required to support various office functions must be determined. A standard office/workstation size or a limited number of sizes to delineate hierarchy in an office is an important factor in any project. These workstations can be composed of various components, which can become a "kit of parts" to aid in their flexibility, while keeping costs down and providing a module for spatial layouts. At AmSouth Bancorporation, six modular workstation configurations were created to be utilized by all company employees. Since the completion of this project, the flexibility of these workstations has allowed for an incredible cost savings to AmSouth as they periodically reconfigure their departments.

Technology.

- One of the most expensive investments for a corporation and one of the largest components of the construction budget is technology. It is essential that the amount of flexibility, redundancy requirements, needs for multisite operations, reliability of the system, employee accessibility (home or office), and the type of distribution (wireless or broadband) be taken into consideration in evaluating the business strategy for integrating technology into the facility.

Security.

- Visibility of security, how it is best integrated into the building management systems and architecture, is part of the corporation philosophy regarding security. The increased risk of violence in the workplace from employees or the outside has changed how security is viewed.

Acoustics.

- There are fundamental conflicts between productivity and open office designs which provide flexibility. Studies now define high-intensity and low-intensity noise. These help affect decisions about building systems and products that can make open office space more productive.

Uniqueness. This is what makes each of us individuals. It is essential to recognize this in our clients, as the best interior design comes from an in-depth analysis and understanding of what makes a particular company and its workforce unique.

Shared conference facilities.

- The interior designer needs to fully understand how conference rooms are used, what sizes are most functional, and who the users are. Once that is discerned, decisions can be made about whether there should be centralized or decentralized conference rooms or a combination, what services need to be adjacent, and if they are used by the public or not. The amount of real estate required for departmentalized conferencing is greater than for a central conference facility, but if departmentalized conference rooms are not of concern to the corporate culture, the additional cost may be acceptable.

Support spaces.

- These are the spaces that are critical to the operation of the facility and can consist of mailrooms, records storage, stockrooms, and catering kitchens. Again, the amount of real estate dedicated to their use has a cost impact, but their functionality is equally important. The company needs to assess where these spaces should be located and consider alternative solutions such as off-site storage or less costly basement or windowless space.

Communication areas.

- One of the most important programming objectives for today's companies is increasing communication among employees through spontaneous interactions and strategies such as teaming. Companies have found that the faster information is shared, the faster it is processed. The faster ideas are shared, the faster they are improved. Closed-door sessions are now rarely the preferred method of working. Thus, teaming spaces are often incorporated into the office design. These spaces vary in size and design depending on their purpose.

Amenities.

- Additional amenities and services within the workplace are becoming increasingly common. The following amenities may be incorporated into the design to raise worker satisfaction and productivity:

  - *Dry cleaners*

  - *Fitness center*

  - *Child care*

  - *Café*

  - *Cafeteria with take-home meals*

The following services can be provided to improve worker morale by saving them time outside the office:

- *Dog walking*
- *Vacation planning*
- *Flower delivery*
- *Employee-interest courses (non-work-related)*
- *Medical facilities and personnel*

All of these amenities and services are viewed as extremely valuable by employees, as many employees are working extended hours and already have little free time to spend with family and friends. More and more companies are asking for interior areas that encourage creativity. AmSouth incorporated an employee cafeteria, fitness center, and outdoor running trail into the design of the headquarters.

Special equipment.

- Every company has special equipment requirements unique to its culture, business, and work process that directly affect an office building's architecture and systems. Vaults, library shelving, and high-density file storage, for example, require increased structural reinforcement in the floors.

Budget.

- Every project has a budget that must be worked into the design. Regardless of the budget, the architect should strive to accommodate all required project goals. Understanding the budget allows you to help the client to make the most effective choices for their office design.

Obviously, every client will not require the same level of infrastructure and amenities. Some may simply need a few tables and chairs and the basic levels of telecommunications networks, while others want to incorporate every aspect listed above to the highest degree, ensuring that they have the most up-to-date technologies and flexibility to easily modify their office in the future.

TEST FITS

The strategic planning phase can culminate in a series of test fits of potential office locations. Taking all the information gathered in the initial stages of the strategic planning, test fits place the client in any number of potential locations. This allows clients to see how their needs might be met in each location, and which one most effectively meets their needs.

The selection of these sites can be driven by the client's desire for a particular site or building location or type; the financial benefits of a site; market conditions, which often dictate which sites are available at which times; features and existing amenities, such as existing telecom infrastructure, of a site; the potential for growth within the site; or, most likely, a combination of these factors.

Test fits begin with a synthesis of the programming and workplace analysis information into basic spatial requirements for the office. The designer should ensure that the test fits each accommodate the required adjacencies and support requirements in addition to the spatial requirements. Additionally, the following should be incorporated into each test fit:

- *Client-desired traffic patterns*

- *Design feasibility*

- *Cost effectiveness*

During the design for AmSouth Bancorporation's new headquarters facility, a number of test-fit options were discussed. As mentioned earlier in this chapter, AmSouth formerly had 1,200 employees housed in eight different office buildings across Birmingham, Alabama. They decided to create a corporate campus to house all employees at one location, which led to test-fit options ranging from numerous buildings placed within one campus setting to one tall high-rise building to house everyone. It was also very important that the location of the headquarters offer pleasing aesthetics and basic amenities for its employees, who largely live in the suburbs of Birmingham. All of these basic project requirements were discussed and evaluated during the first three stages of the strategic planning phase.

In the end, AmSouth decided to create one campus structure, located in the Birmingham suburbs, which is composed of two long, narrow towers straddling a ravine and connected by an enclosed bridge housing a dining facility. The site and building design work together to deliver AmSouth's project design requirements. Thus, the combination of the client understanding, programming, workplace analysis, and test fits together led to the success of the project.

CONCLUSION

The modern office is a work in progress. The office, work format, and worker are still evolving in the new economy, and values are shifting. Production-based value assessments are on the decline as increasing emphasis is given to the knowledge worker. This fundamental shift, which has seen graphic acceleration due to technological advances such as the Internet, requires the interior designer to invest time at the beginning of each project to understand the true nature of the client.

Often, after completing the strategic planning, the direction of the project and preconceived notions of the design are changed from that of the initial direction. It is important to remember that this is a preliminary phase of the project and can be reevaluated throughout the duration of the project. For example, while working on AmSouth's corporate headquarters facility, the departmental requirements changed dramatically, decreasing their required space allocation from a full four-story building to only half of that building. From the programming and workplace analysis, the designers had already determined that the offices should be designed as movable partitions to provide flexibility in the design. Since the offices were an open office format as opposed to a closed office format, the designer was only required to redesign and relocate the movable partitions and furniture and did not need to redesign the walls, plumbing, HVAC, electrical, or telecommunications systems, which resulted in a cost savings for the rework of $2.5–$3 million.

Thus, we are brought back to the driving force of the design—the client. It is imperative that we, as interior designers, take into account in any design the unique nature of each organization and its precious resources and staff. If the design reflects the corporate culture and creates an energizing workplace environment, it will succeed for its client, even when unforeseen obstacles are encountered at a later stage of the project.

Bibliography

Architectural Record. "The Gap Inc. Business Week Awards Architectural Record." *Architecture Record,* October 1998.

Duffy, Frank. *The New Office.* London: Conran Octopus Ltd, 1997.

Giarrusso, Theresa Walsh. "A Few Good Amenities." *Facilities Design & Management,* September 1998.

Kent, Cheryl. "Owens Corning, Toledo, OH." *Architectural Record,* June 1997.

Nall, Daniel H. "Underfloor Air-Delivery Systems." *The Construction Specifier,* February 1998.

O'Mara, Martha. *Strategy & Place: Managing Corporate Real Estate in a Virtual World.* Boston: The Free Press, 1998.

Wilson, Alex. "Access Floors: A Step Up for Commercial Buildings." *Environmental Building News,* January 1998.

27

Programming: Shared Vision

ANDRE STAFFELBACH, FASID, FIIDA
JO HEINZ, FIIDA

Programming is a process: it is an investigative, research-oriented process that defines the requirements and purpose of the project. The programming process solidifies the relationship between client and designer by ensuring that the participating parties have a shared vision of the project's goals and objectives. It evokes consensus as to the expectations of the design team and assists the designer in performing "due diligence" to define the information essential for the ensuing phases of the design process.

A thorough programming process will assist in ensuring the best possible project outcome. It will reinforce the guidelines for project development and guarantee that problem solving is focused on the critical issues of the project. Good design cannot be incubated without strong investigative programming. For a design to be both pleasing and functional, the designer must share the heart of the client, see the same future, and know from historical experiences where and how to lead the journey. Without ample time spent in developing this common understanding, efforts to solve the problem will have no logical or reasonable basis for being.

Once a program has been defined, documented, and approved, it will serve as a "check and balance" for the evolving solutions and define the boundaries for creativity. Design solutions should be assessed by their ability to achieve the programmatic requirements. This logical basis for analysis adds validity to the design process.

The primary goal of programming is to develop an innovative and measurable tool that will serve as a strategic road map for problem solving. Because each project is unique in its needs, applications, and requirements, programming efforts must be customized to adapt to the individuality of each project.

METHODOLOGY

The methods utilized for effective programming all involve *investigation*. This investigation is achieved through a variety of techniques:

Observation.

- Programming demands on-site observation of operations. It is only through this "hands-on" observation that the programmer can understand the physical complexities of the client's requirements. Through unobtrusive walk-throughs and inconspicuous observation sessions, the programmer will gain valuable insight into the flow of work, the culture of the organization, the type and pace of activities, and the behaviors of those who inhabit the spaces.

Inquiry.

- The quality of the questions asked directly influences the quality of information received. The programmer should avoid questions that can be answered with a "yes" or a "no," as they provide minimal insight. Questions that evoke substantive responses will allow the programmer to gain insight and then follow up with other probing inquiries. It is important for the programmer to focus on collecting data that is relevant to the project. The programmer should take the lead to sort the data gathered and discard information that could potentially blur or cloud the real issues.

Interviews.

- Interviews should be conducted with key individuals or teams of individuals within an organization. These interviews should be organized to capture the broadest spectrum of input possible. It is often helpful to include a variety of individuals so that the discussion is active and encourages differing opinions. The programmer should serve as a facilitator of open and uninhibited discussion. If individuals in the interview group tend to dominate discussion, the programmer must work to gain participation from other, less vocal participants.

It is helpful to schedule interviews with ample time for relaxed inquiry, and to provide participants a safe haven to express their opinions. Interviews should be conducted in a place separate from work activities, and questions should be prepared well in advance in order for the interview sessions to stimulate the group's thinking.

It is beneficial to issue a memorandum about the upcoming programming interviews to the participants. If the memorandum highlights the subject matter of items to be discussed, it will enable individuals to organize their thoughts concerning the upcoming interview.

Focus groups.

- In large organizations, focus groups are beneficial to determine the reactions to impending change or gain opinions on multiple options for the facilities.

  The programmer may wish to use a facilitator for the focus group to elicit maximum responses on the relevant issues. It will be important to determine a reporting mechanism to communicate the issues and concerns that the focus groups uncover. These issues often form the basis for fear and insecurity about impending change. If the design solutions address and conquer these fears, the success of the project will be enhanced.

Benchmarking.

- Benchmarking can be a valuable tool in programming efforts, as it allows an organization to evaluate its position with respect to competitors or leaders in a given industry. Benchmarking statistics are readily attainable through various industry sources and can be utilized in developing questions to utilize in programming or as a tool to assist the organization in formulating project objectives.

DOCUMENTATION

The statistical data gained from programming efforts serves as a reference for project development. The database will depict the physical situation, headcount and headcount projections, and overall spatial statistics, thereby providing a two-dimensional footprint of space requirements. (See Figures 27-1, 27-2, and 27-3.)

With the database documentation in hand, the client can understand the overall programming projections by detail or in summary. This documentation gives the design team and the client an opportunity to reevaluate business strategies, target areas that need more in-depth study, and define expectations.

FIGURE 27-1

ABC COMPANY: Southwest Region
Headcount Summary Report (by Division)
Date of Report: XX

		Year 1	Year 2
Operations			
Operations Administration		9	9
	Total	9	9
Fleet & Commercial			
Fleet & Commercial Administration		1	2
Commercial Accounts		53	54
Special Billing		5	5
	Total	59	61
Product Development			
Prod. Development Administration		1	1
Product Development		3	7
	Total	4	8
Credit & Collection Services			
Credit & Collection Services Administration		1	2
Consumer Accounts		36	61
Prime/Consumer		69	69
Credit Card Control		29	36
Fraud Products		1	1
New Accounts		56	79
Recovery Administration		31	31
	Total	223	279
	Grand Total	295	357

FIGURE 27-2

ABC COMPANY: Southwest Region
Square Footage Summary Report (by Department)
Date of Report: XX

		Year 1 SF	Year 2 SF
Operations			
Operations		782	797
Fleet & Commercial		5,193	4,674
Product Development		482	975
Credit & Collection Services		11,919	15,999
Customer Service		14,569	10,919
Operations		41,998	50,315
Project & Transition Mgmt		2,507	2,857
Administration		1,996	1,989
Common Areas		53,074	53,074
	Total SF	132,520 SF	141,599 SF

It is critical that the programming database information be accurate. All components of an organization must be included to ensure that all personnel types, equipment, specialty needs, workflow, adjacencies, etc., are captured. Miscalculations in a programming database can create profound inefficiencies in the physical workplace once the project moves from database to reality. The programmer should verify that mathematical calculations are checked and tested prior to the publication or release of data.

FIGURE 27-3

ABC COMPANY: Southwest Region
Square Footage Detail Report
Date of Report: XX

Operations

Position	Type	Status	Space Code	Site	Year 1		Year 2	
					Qty	SF	Qty	SF
Equipment Area	N/A	N/A	EQ1	3N	2	133	2	135
Storage	N/A	N/A	ST1	3N	5	239	5	243
				Subtotal	7	372	7	378

Position	Type	Status	Space Code	Site	Year 1		Year 2	
					Qty	SF	Qty	SF
Executive Secretary	Non-Exempt	FTE	A3	3N	1	66	1	68
Sr. Vice President	Exempt	FTE	OF1	3N	2	345	1	351
				Subtotal	3	411	2	419
				Total for Division	10	783	9	797

ORGANIZATION OF DATA

The programming information will consider the following:

People
- Employee profiles and diversity from position to position
- Responsibilities and autonomy

Structure
- Organizational reporting
- Management/hierarchy
- Work group dependencies
- Policies and procedures
- Business operating hours/rotations/shifts
- Physical environment

Process
- Task and cycle time analysis
- Product quality

Where traditional programming provides factual computations of goals, personnel, technology, space needs, and adjacencies, strategic programming/planning focuses on gathering information that is intuitive, anecdotal, and not necessarily measurable . . .

Technology

- System flexibility and growth capabilities
- Compatibility
- Redundancy

Capital

- Current assets life cycle versus new purchase
- Lease-versus-purchase decisions
- Short-term investments versus strategic investments

Future

- Flexibility desired
- Anticipated change

EXPANDED PROGRAMMING TECHNIQUES

To remain competitive, today's organizations are undergoing turbulent, self-generated changes in an effort to streamline productive costs while nurturing a positive and desirable work environment. Decisions made in this tempest carry the promise of great opportunities that can be outweighed by huge risk. Thus, to ameliorate these liabilities, anticipating future gains demands a greater reserve of strategic thinking that extends beyond traditional systematic analysis. In preparation for leveraging these contradictory forces, diverse strategic programming and change management methods add value to programming efforts.

Where traditional programming provides factual computations of goals, personnel, technology, space needs, and adjacencies, strategic programming/planning focuses on gathering information that is intuitive, anecdotal, and not necessarily measurable by mathematical principles. The goal of strategic programming and planning is to provide a plan whereby the client will gain competitive advantage by capitalizing the unique capabilities of the organization. It presents a specific vision of the future and establishes measurable long-term and interim goals.

Along with determining the evolution of the physical environment, cross-functional teams can be engaged to represent human resources, technology, and finance to direct positive thinking and activate powerful changes throughout all aspects of the client's business.

Strategic programming and planning strategies may include occupancy planning and analysis, project cost analysis, real estate acquisition analysis, contingency plans, and "what if" scenarios. Entrusted with the key executives' visions, the strategic programmer behaves more like an investigative reporter, studying the work processes, pinpointing creative and applicable ideas from observations, searching out issues that may directly impact the firm's business applications, and reading between the lines, gleaning truth from interaction.

Scenario planning adds a powerful dimension to planning strategies. This planning tool empowers the client to flesh out strategic issues and render alternative future images rather than relying on conventional planning techniques. By using scenarios, preparing for unexpected shifts in the business or the economy at large, the client may rehearse the future without experiencing associated risks.

Tasks that may be included in scenario planning include:

- *Identify the focal decision.*

- *Identify key forces in the local environment.*

- *Identify driving forces.*

- *Rank forces by importance and uncertainty.*

- *Select scenario logics.*

- *Flesh out scenarios.*

- *Analyze implications.*

- *Select leading indicators.*

The strategic programming/planning process has the potential to define for the client valuable insight as to

- *Decisions to be made.*

- *Driving forces.*

- *Predetermined elements.*

- *Critical uncertainties.*

- *Purpose of the spaces.*

- *How value can be added.*

- *Productivity gain potential.*

- *Risks and opportunities.*

- *Gaps between processes and expectations.*

In summary, programming is essential to an effective design process. It is a skill that will enhance the interior designer's problem-solving ability and focus creativity on the critical elements of a project.

Bibliography

Borja de Mozota, Brigitte, Colin Clipson, and Mark Oakley. *Design Management: A Handbook of Issues and Methods.* Oxford: Blackwell Reference, 1990.

Burstein, David, and Frank Stasiowski. *Project Management for the Design Professional: A Handbook for Architects, Engineers and Interior Designers.* New York: Whitney Library of Design, 1991.

Pena, William, Steven Parshall, and Kevin Kelly. *Problem Seeking: An Architectural Programming Primer.* Washington, DC: AIA/CRESS, 1987.

28

Schematic Design: Communicating the Design Spirit

ORLANDO DIAZ-AZCUY

The schematics are the most inspirational and creative phase of the design process. Schematic design is when you communicate the three-dimensional and decorative ideas about the space to the client. To reach a point where you actually have ideas to communicate, you need to have completed the programming and the planning phases based not only on the quantitative information, but the philosophical as well.

While the entire design process is a collaborative one, schematic design should be the responsibility of a single mind. This phase of the process is the most creative expression of the project: schematics illustrate the spirit of what the space will become, therefore it should express the designer's insights and intuition. In the case of a collaborative or group effort there must be a designer who can synthesize the various points of view. While all the individuals are creators of their own ideas, the master coordinator must synthesize the different ideas. It is not easy to be the single creator of an architectural expression, and it is even more difficult to be the orchestrator of differing opinions.

Programming also includes finding out what the social behavior of the company is and what image the company wants to project to the public. In residential projects, it includes how the clients live now and how the new environment will change them in the future.

The information gathered during the programming phase should also accurately capture the identity of the client. The planning phase of the project should begin to express the potential architectural character. Sometimes, however, the reality of design practice gets in the way, and the individuals who gather and plan the space are not necessarily the persons who develop the schematic design. The designer should be assessing, or participating in the assessment of, the purpose of the project through the programming and planning phases.

Schematics are for expressing to your client what the solutions will look like in a general sense. You need to be able to express your ideas both verbally and visually. Verbalization immediately communicates your expression for the project.

Visually, there are several techniques for presenting schematic designs, including renderings or models or virtual computer realities. My reservation about them is that they make a very detailed perception, especially in the case of computer-generated drawings (they don't call it virtual reality without a reason) where the definitions of the lines create the impression of a finished idea. I prefer to use hand drawings that not only show the reality but also the illusion of the ideas conveyed. The client is going to interpret exactly what he or she sees. With the schematics, you want the client to see a general picture and get a feeling about how the space is going to look. Schematics should illustrate; they shouldn't document. It's important for clients to realize that the specifics of the interior (architectural details, finishes, materials, furniture, fabric, paint color, flooring) have yet to be precisely determined.

The most important factor for the designer is to understand and be emotionally involved in what he or she is about to create. No good solution comes out of dislike (of the project or the client). Empathy with the project is of extraordinary importance.

Great ideas don't execute themselves. A design is what you build, not what you think you wanted to build. The compromises and the limitations are integral parts of the design. The big idea is a reflection of two equally important components: first is how well the designer integrates the desires and requests of the client into the solution, and second is how experienced, talented, and creative the designer is in such interpretations.

Creativity for its own sake doesn't necessarily constitute a viable solution and often it results in ideas that are out of sync with the program. One has to reevaluate the solutions as well as the program. The idea might be so strong and unique that it conflicts with the program, or the idea might be so weak as not to represent the desired goals of the project.

Our programming is always tainted by our own and the client's experiences, and without careful attention, can produce preexisting solutions. The designer should evaluate when the end result for a project may be close to a preexisting solution. The designer's task is not to reinvent the wheel, but it is the designer's obligation to make sure that every effort has been made to ensure that the client's individual characteristics and preferences have been expressed in the program, in the schematics, and, ultimately, in the finished space.

One should always begin programming by asking: "What makes them different than anyone else? What do they tell to their potential clients? What image do they want the public to have of them?" Those questions help us begin to analyze our clients, their perspectives, their philosophies, and their images.

There is the tendency to begin a project with predisposed ideas, for example of open- or closed-plan offices. One must make an effort to integrate those considerations into discussions so that solutions aren't taken for granted.

The most important and eventually most satisfying aspect of the project for any client is creating a building or a space that truly represents them. In order to achieve the desired effect, the designer has to resolve a variety of conflicts even when clients might have a clear vision of who they are, and have strong opinions of what they like. For example, the CEO of the company understands the company's image and the demands of the budget, but someone who is only concerned with the dollars may give the designer instructions based only on financial concerns, which may result in design decisions that don't produce what the company needs. Another type of conflict arises when the business partner of the design company gets information from the client about programming and budget, and then translates that information to the designer in a way that omits the client's philosophical concerns or imposes the business partner's own opinions. The designer has to be involved in the preschematic phases of the project; the designer will hear and discover things about the client that other people won't.

A commercial client (a corporation, a financial firm, a law firm) is much more apt to define its identity. Commercial clients do this all the time because they have to define to their customers what they do and what they make. Hospitality clients have a better perspective because they know who their customers are, who they want to attract, what image they want to portray, and what their economic parameters are.

In residential design, clients, for the most part, are couples with different upbringings who have lived in different environments most of their lives. Aesthetics are one of the last things that any couple ever discusses. They

In residential design, clients, for the most part, are couples with different upbringings who have lived in different environments most of their lives. Aesthetics are one of the last things that any couple ever discusses.

might talk about how nice it would be to have a house in the country, or that they'd like a larger place in the city, but they rarely talk about what kind of house or place they might have. Most residential clients tell you what they want, but not who they are.

Most design programs are concerned with quantity of space and how that space is distributed. A program generally maps out the working relationships among people, but it rarely touches on how people performing any given function interact on a personal basis or the degree of privacy or social interaction they need to have.

We should recognize that economics and time are integral factors that affect the possible solutions. One should not design for solutions that create delays and discomfort for the client unless the client accepts that these solutions are beneficial. Nor should one design beyond the economic parameters established by the client.

When doing schematics, the designer must be responsible for both budget and time. An experienced designer knows when he or she is pushing the boundaries of one or the other. Sometimes he or she knows that the best solution requires extending the time or expanding the budget, or both. It is then the designer's responsibility to present to the client the repercussions of these ideas, and that these changes are being suggested not to fatten the designer's ego or wallet, but because they are actually the best solutions for the client.

It is a designer's responsibility to adjust the designs' creativity to the economic means of the client. A great idea without the money to execute it is not a great idea. In order to know how to budget for the proper expectations, it is imperative that at least general information is obtained before beginning the schematics. There is no truth to the statement: "I don't know." Clients always know, or at least they know what their limitations are. A client who says to you, "Give me ideas and the price and I will tell you if I want it" offers more drawbacks than you might suppose since it can easily result in solutions that lack a cohesive point of view.

The amount of time it takes for a project to become reality is the factor least within the designer's control. While, in general, we know how long the normal design and construction process takes, approvals and construction considerations are outside the designer's control and often create the most undesirable results. The designer's responsibility is to create solutions that can be accomplished within the reasonable and customary time that it takes to execute an idea of similar complexity within standard practice.

Creating things that work is not a real criterion. Functionality is an integral quality of whatever is created. A good idea is only good if it serves the purpose for which it is created. For the client, the most confusing attitude in design is that aesthetics and functionality are forces that work against each other. Aesthetics are the most esoteric quality of a good solution, but they are by far the most easily perceived and appreciated qualities of any project. They are also, in the end, the most emotionally fulfilling. There is no human pleasure deeper than emotional pleasure. Aesthetics are not contradictory to time and money.

Uniqueness is a responsibility of the designer, who takes a vow of creativity just by choosing this profession. The designer does not just issue formulaic solutions; he or she applies his or her mind and experience to the particulars of each specific client and problem. No two people, no two businesses, no two families are alike. Therefore, no two solutions should be alike. Uniqueness does not necessarily entail reinventing the wheel with each and every project. The human mind is the greatest known computer in the universe, with the ability to create infinite combinations of all the available resources. The designer must use his or her mind to the fullest to strive for the best answer. At the same time, uniqueness is the quality the client most frequently inhibits inadvertently. People have a picture in their minds of what they want, and intrinsically it is what they have already seen. In contrast, the designer's ability is to see what has not been seen before. While knowledge of what the client wants provides a great starting point (it can set a general direction) it can also impede creativity. It takes time to explore, converse, and prove to the clients that multiple possibilities exist in addition to those they've seen. It is extremely important that the proper time be allowed for the designer to get to know and prepare the client for all possibilities.

A good idea doesn't build itself. The designer needs to know or understand all of the existing physical conditions, as well as the new conditions to be created. This information is critical to the designer in the course of generating ideas, as well as during the design process itself. Consultants, therefore, are very important because they can analyze the physical limitations as well as the physical possibilities of all components of the solution, both materials and technologies. The proper knowledge of materials old and new and the unlimited ways to use them should be part of the designer's vocabulary while preparing a solution.

Designers need to understand that the original concept might change during the course of the project due to unforeseen circumstances. No one can expect the schematic design to cover all the possible conflicts: Rather it sets the path, a good path, for design development of the project.

29

Schematic Design: Limitless Possibility

MICHAEL BYUN
TRAVIS CLIFTON
DAVID GROUT

In our firm, Gary Lee Partners, we are positioned to offer a full range of professional design services to address our client's workplace, facility and design requirements. Our firm is composed of professionals with extensive talents and experiences in building construction, office technology, furniture design, and strategic planning. This unique makeup of the firm brings a multifaceted and comprehensive problem-solving approach to each project.

Limitless possibility distinguishes our approach to the schematic design phase as distinct from other phases in the design process. Finding the appropriate solution for a client means exploring both potential and possibility within a defined budget and schedule. This process requires a great deal of passion involving listening, architectural analysis, and a keenly developed aesthetic.

Clients who want to effect change not only receive a different "look" to their space, but enhance their culture and performance as well. Our firm's objective is to facilitate an ongoing dialogue about how "space" can best support the goals of the client. Through this dialogue the design team begins behaving as a consultant, helping the client identify its organizational and cultural goals and define its brand or image for its employees, communities, and peers. This communication between client and designer directly informs design solutions.

The primary purpose of the schematic design phase is for the team to develop a preliminary design concept. This concept incorporates three aspects, a working set of guiding principles specific to the client's goals that will act as a touchstone throughout all phases of the project, and function and aesthetics that are manifest in the organizational and visual concepts. Both the organizational and visual concepts stem from the vision set forth by the client team.

METHODOLOGY—BUILDING A DESIGN CONCEPT

Our design firm's key mission is to create innovative spaces. Successful spaces depend on the delicate interplay between several factors: function, aesthetic, and the client's goals. Yet, the critical element is assembling a team of individuals who will listen to the client, analyze the structural and spatial needs, and translate the values into visuals. This is the design team.

THE DESIGN TEAM

From the inception of the project, the principals select the team members whose talents and expertise best fit the project needs. Each project is assigned a project principal, a project manager, technical support, and one or two other team members; these constitute the core design team. This team participates in the design effort through all phases of the project. The additional team members may be needed based on the scope of work, size of the project, and possible schedule requirements.

The project principal is responsible for the overall success of the project from the perspectives of both the client and the firm. The project manager acts as the design lead for the project. This aspect of the project manager's role is unique to our firm. The project manager is also the day-to-day contact for the client and internally manages the project team. A technical support individual is an integral part of the team, providing a code, detail development, engineering coordination, and budget perspective.

These specified roles clarify responsibilities and lines of communication and accountability for the client. Yet, good design comes from strong, well-rounded individuals who understand all aspects of the design process. Thus, our firm's strength comes from the depth of experience and knowledge that renaissance design professionals bring to a team.

GUIDING PRINCIPLES—ESTABLISHING A SET OF CLIENT GOALS

From our first discussions with the client, the design team begins assessing the client's goals for the project. In the programming phase, the design team gathers and documents quantitative or measurable information and qualitative or intangible issues. Personnel quantities, projected growth, departmental or room adjacencies, support functions, furniture requirements, and equipment requirements and storage needs comprise the bulk of the qualitative information. The client's image/brand, culture/personality, and the desired mood and perception of the client by its peers, respective industries, or communities represent the major qualitative issues.

Often the quantitative information is more easily accessible than the qualitative. Many discussions will be needed to draw out the intangible goals of the client. A space that "creates energy," "encourages interaction," or "establishes an egalitarian environment" may be initially unknown to the client, yet exactly what is wanted for the space. Not only is it critical to identify these qualitative issues, the team must also encourage the client to imagine the possibilities that change can effect in their culture. Thus, some goals open more possibilities than others might.

Once these client goals are firmly established, they become guiding principles for both the organizational and visual aspects of the project.

THE ORGANIZATIONAL CONCEPT

After the team has established the client's goals, the next step is to fully analyze the fixed elements unique to that building that affect the space organization within. Development of an organizational concept is critical to the design process as it lays the foundation for on-going decision making. Building orientation, the location of relative building core functions, ceiling height availabilities, and window placement and sill conditions will all determine the building's support of the client's goals. An assessment of the building core functions relative to compliance with local and federal building and life-safety codes may also factor into planning.

Careful study of significant architectural features profoundly affects the development of an organizational concept. Often an outer/inner design strategy is most effective. Window placement and scale, for example, can establish a grid upon which an entire organizational concept can be built. In addition, the design team explores the client's quantitative data through a series of diagrams and studies.

Initial adjacency/bubble diagrams, massing/block and stack diagrams, and diagrammatic studies of specific space flesh out relative scale, key adjacencies, and spatial considerations of the various functional requirements. Bubble (adjacency) diagrams help the project team assess initial departmental or functional requirements and adjacencies. Blocking/stacking diagrams specifically illustrate spatial relationships of various functions in a multifloor configuration and could help a client determine, for example, which floor the main reception area should be located on. Finally, diagrammatic space standards explore room layouts and space sizes by drafting various studies based on proposed equipment and furnishings, relative furniture placement, and desired circulation space.

These initial studies are manifest in a series of studies which, when overlaid, fully illustrate the developing three-dimensional aspects of the organizational concept. The American Guaranty Corporation's organizational concept, illustrated on the following two pages, demonstrates this comprehensive analysis: layer one examines the base building and identifies the parameters of existing core functions; layer two identifies a building organizational system; and layer three's blocking diagrams articulate the allocation of the quantitative requirements. When completed, this organizational concept establishes the parameters within which potential design solutions must comply. This multilayered approach becomes an invaluable communications tool for the client team, internal team members, and outside consultants.

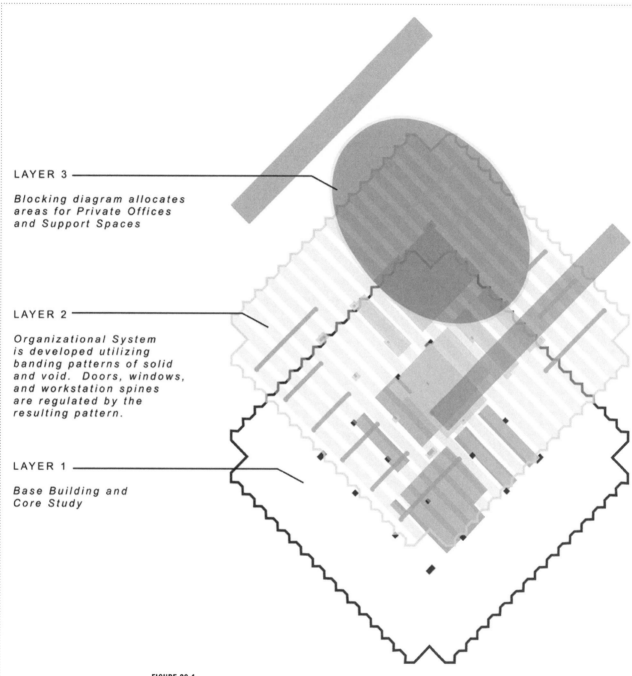

LAYER 3

Blocking diagram allocates
areas for Private Offices
and Support Spaces

LAYER 2

Organizational System
is developed utilizing
banding patterns of solid
and void. Doors, windows,
and workstation spines
are regulated by the
resulting pattern.

LAYER 1

Base Building and
Core Study

FIGURE 29-1
American Guaranty
Corporation's
Organizational Concept.

Extruded Organizational
Concept Plan

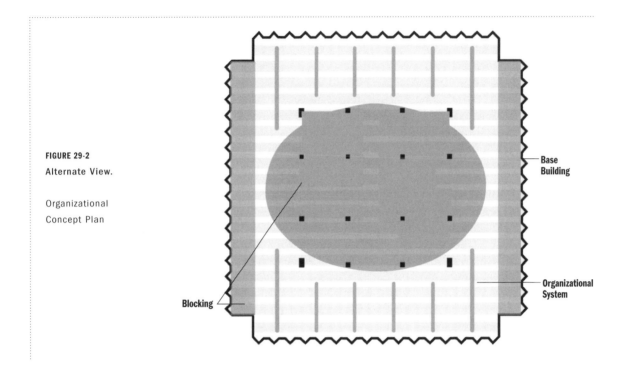

FIGURE 29-2
Alternate View.

Organizational
Concept Plan

Base
Building

Organizational
System

Blocking

THE VISUAL CONCEPT

The visual concept is just as integral to the design as is the organizational concept. The visual concept applies the client's goals to the design. This may translate into the visual and kinesthetic issues of scale, proportion, color, texture, movement, and qualities of light, and specifically into initial color palette, finishes and furnishings. Many of the intangible goals of the client may factor into the visual concept. At this stage of the design process, the visual concept is somewhat preliminary, as many of these details will be more firmly established in the design development phase. Yet, the client must be able to "see" that its goals will be manifested in the visual as well as organizational plans; the design team must show it has heard the client.

To effectively achieve this challenging goal, the design team first establishes a common language with the client. Making the transition from words to images ensures that the client and design teams interpret the issues in the same way. Knowing that "creating energy" can reflect a range of meaning, the design team puts together a series of nonarchitectural images that correspond to the language that it has heard from the client team. An image of grocery store shelving demonstrates flexibility through modularity; an image of a calla lily can represent elegance. Client review of these image boards in the initial schematic design presentation can prevent design from developing in the wrong direction.

The following list details some possible elements or goals included in a visual concept:

- *Dynamic energy within a space*

- *Bright and evenly lit, open, large spaces*

- *Low contrast in materials and monochromatic finishes*

- *More focused light for closed intimate spaces*

- *An expanded palette of finishes*

Perhaps a client wants to create a dynamic energy within the space. The use of a curved wall can act as the central organizational principle encouraging movement throughout the space. This one architectural feature not only creates movement, but also affects the visuals of the space by its scale, proportion, color, texture, how it is lit—and the list goes on. Ultimately, many of our client's goals will be manifested throughout the visual concept. The design team communicates to the client team the initial aspects of the visual concept through a series of image boards at two separate presentation meetings.

COMMUNICATION METHODOLOGY

Communication is a critical element of the entire design process, but particularly in the schematic design phase. The design concept relates to the initial dialogues with the client team, the stated quantitative and qualitative goals, and the established goals. The success of the project relates directly to the design team's ability to listen and respond to these expressed goals.

One of the most significant aspects of this phase of communication happens during the charette, a series of sessions where the core design team sketches, discusses ideas, and shares images. Often, this process opens up to include many members of the firm.

Clearly conveying these goals to outside consultants expands and strengthens the team and its potential to effectively meet the client's needs. Ultimately, the design team must propose the developed design concept to the client team in preliminary and final presentations. Establishing clear project goals not only supports the team in developing the design concept, but also the team's understanding and confidence that the project and process are moving in the right direction.

Communication with the client begins during the programming phase when project team members discuss the client's goals and assess its current culture. Day-to-day dialogues within the entire project team, whether in formal team meetings or impromptu conversations, are on-going throughout the schematic design phase.

One of the most significant aspects of this phase of communication happens during the charette, a series of sessions where the core design team sketches, discusses ideas, and shares images. Often, this process opens up to include many members of the firm. Drawing from this depth of experience and creative problem solving allows our design firm to use all its talent without assigning the entire firm to each project.

To further strengthen the team, we call on outside experts such as consultants, suppliers, furniture manufacturer representatives, general contractor(s), engineer(s), and specialty consultant(s). The design team researches and discusses with suppliers and furniture manufacturers' representatives appropriate material samples, furniture options, pricing, and initial lead-time information before finish, lighting, and furniture recommendations are presented to the client.

Depending on the project schedule, the general contractor may only be needed to confirm preliminary budgetary construction numbers or perhaps brought on as an active team member to facilitate an intense project schedule. Similarly, the design team assesses the need for mechanical, electrical, plumbing, fire protection, or structural engineer(s), as well as specialty consultants. Typical specialty consultants include a lighting consultant, an audio/visual consultant, security consultant, and even a kitchen consultant.

For an effective and dynamic presentation, the design team must select tools that can most succinctly describe the major concepts to the client. Using words and images, the design team "moves" the client through the design process.

PRESENTATIONS

Within the schematic design phase we typically schedule two key meetings between the design team and the client, a preliminary schematic design presentation and a final schematic design presentation. The presentations offer an opportunity to formally present the preliminary design concept and to discuss the path that seems to be most appropriate for the client's own function, vision, and budget. It is therefore critical that the key decision makers on both the client and design teams are present at these meetings.

For an effective and dynamic presentation, the design team must select tools that can most succinctly describe the major concepts to the client. Using words and images, the design team "moves" the client through the design process. This starts with the review of the relationship and massing diagrams, and continues with the space standards and building analysis. "Moving" the client team through all of the analysis helps its members better understand the presentations of the organizational concept plan and visual concept boards, which in turn lay the groundwork for more specific plans to follow. These specific plans include preliminary partition layouts, recommendations for construction materials, the reflected ceiling plan, typical locations of furniture, recommendations for special area treatments, and recommendations for new furniture. Models and perspectives may also be presented.

All of these tools are composed in such a way to tell a story. It is important for the design team to know what concepts need to be stressed, and what critical issues must be addressed at the meeting. Integral to the development of the design concept is the project budget and schedule, which the team also prepares and reviews with the client at these two presentations.

BUDGET AND SCHEDULE

In our firm all design occurs with full knowledge of budget and schedule parameters. Our teams develop concepts with these factors in mind. We find that this knowledge actually opens opportunities for creative problem solving. Thus, the design concept presented to the client fully reflects the budget and schedule.

The project budget is separated into key areas: construction costs, furniture costs, operations expenses, consultant fees, and incidental expenses. In the schematic design phase, the budget is considered a preliminary estimate. Past experience, expertise, and current industry knowledge inform estimating the preliminary costs of the key components.

The design team provides a list of recommended options to the client. This allows the client to participate in the decision-making process. Decisions on the scope of the base costs must be agreed on, then other items can be selected that have estimated additional costs.

Furniture and construction budgets can either be prepared as an estimate or as a high/low range. High/low-range furniture budgets list the item, the quantity required, and the pieces' cost range. High/low construction budgets break out each of the individual construction trades line by line, with a range given for each of these line items. A client can use a high/low range to target its priorities at a more focused level.

Careful manipulation in the planning of spaces and volumes can produce an exceptional product, regardless of budget limitations. In refining the project budget and client goals, overall values and qualities help allocate additions or reductions in budget. Goals are prioritized. Yet, the high/low budget allows that the visual concept will be carried through even if an item is of low priority. For example, high contrast on feature walls may receive high or low priority: the low-range option might be dark paint on drywall, the high might be a dark veneer or stone. The visual concept stemming from the client's goals is met either way.

CONCLUSION

After the preliminary schematic design presentation, the design team comes back together and evaluates the initial client response in order to make revisions or secondary proposals. The design team explores plan revisions and alternate furniture and finish recommendations. The team then prepares for a final review meeting. The goal at the end of this meeting and the schematic design phase is to have an approved plan, finish direction, mutual agreement as to the overall aesthetic of the project, and approved preliminary cost estimate and schedule. Following the meeting, minutes are prepared that confirm the decisions reached. In addition, an end-of-phase client sign-off form is completed that acknowledges approvals and allows the design team to move on to the next phases of the project.

Bibliography

Ching, Francis D.K. *Architecture: Form, Space & Order.* New York: John Wiley & Sons, 1996.

30

Design Development: Designing the Project

STUART COHEN, AIA

Design development is the process of taking the work produced during the schematic design phase of a project, the conceptual design sketches and other forms of information or research, and continuing its development. This is usually done through the design decisions that go into greater detail with respect to the quantifiable aspects of a project such as size, materials, and methods of construction. Depending on the type of project and the role of the design professional, the work to be done may include a first attempt at generating dimensioned floor plans and wall elevations, the selection of materials and manufactured products, and the design of construction details showing how different materials and finishes come together. Because we are architects as well as interior designers, during this phase of our work, we are concerned with the development of both the exteriors and interiors of the buildings we do.

As architects we are often puzzled by the conceptual separation between the interior and the exterior of a building and the separation of professional services that characterizes the work of most architects. We believe that the same formal and compositional ideas that generate the exterior of a building should inform its interior. Our practice is primarily custom residential architecture. While most of our clients will work with an interior designer or a decorator on the selection of furnishings, we define the scope of the services we provide as extending to the design, selection, and specification of everything that is permanently attached to a building. Because we are designing both the building and its architectural interiors, we usually deal, during schematic design, with the building's basic planning rather than issues related to interior design. During this phase we are establishing basic plan organization and exterior massing in freehand sketches. Window locations are always considered from the inside as well as the outside, but the interiors are still thought of as spaces rather than being fully conceived. These spaces may have unique characteristics because of their configuration in plan or section but the materials, finishes, colors, details, and other features we associate with the work of interior design are rarely considered at this point. Occasionally, we will make thumbnail interior perspectives to examine a special feature of a space that we want our clients to understand in three dimensions. This usually happens when the space or element being sketched is integral to the floor-plan strategy we want to convince the client to accept. The real work of conceiving the interior features of the houses we design begins during the design development phase.

The computerization of the drawing process requires precise dimensional information to be entered into the computer to draw each line. Thus, early in the design development phase, the plans and exterior elevations of the building have been drawn and quite a lot of technical information has been established. Decisions about exterior wall construction, exterior materials, floor-to-ceiling heights, and window types and sizes have been established through the simple need to enter real dimensions into the computer. Design questions such as, do the windows go floor to ceiling or do they sit on top of base trim or an apron, can be addressed. If the windows go to the ceiling, is the top of the window held down from the ceiling by the dimension of any interior trim such as a head casing and crown molding? It becomes evident that something as simple as establishing the height for the tops of windows and interior doors may depend on selecting, designing, and detailing interior trim conditions. This is true whether these are profiled millwork or drywall and plaster corner beads. After these decisions have been made, the work of conceiving the interiors can really begin.

As with schematic design we conceive the interiors in freehand drawings. These are usually perspective drawings (Figure 30-1) that show the features of a space such as vaulted or angled ceilings, clerestory windows, interior windows and doorways connecting interior spaces, fireplaces, and built-in cabinetry. These freehand sketches will be made for all the principle spaces in a house. These sketches are never constructed perspectives. They are developed in the same manner as sketch plans, through successive layers of tracing paper on which alternatives and revisions are drawn over the original drawing.

FIGURE 30-1
Living Room Perspective
(Cohen & Hacker
Architects).

A sketch may be redrawn and revised to look at alternative ideas. The process continues until the drawing looks good. This may result in revisions being made to the floor plans. The perspective sketches are idiosyncratic in that they may have multiple vanishing points in an attempt to unfold or view the space as it might appear to us when we turn our heads to take in things that fall outside our normal field of view. In many cases the finished space is remarkably like the initial sketch. This can happen because the finishes and details suggested in the sketch are conditions that have been worked out before and are completely understood both architecturally and in terms of their detailed construction. We will then meet with our clients. Reactions are usually very positive and often a client will say, "Oh, now I understand what you were trying to describe."

With the main features of the interiors approved based on perspective sketches, development can proceed. On the computer, each interior elevation is laid out from the plan. The perspective sketches, plus information already established, are used as the basis for this step. Here, because each line drawn represents a corner, the edge of a surface, or a joint between materials, typical finishing details can be solved in a new layer within the floor plans which were already drawn on the computer. These are conditions that are unlikely to change, and this allows the interior elevations which are drawn and refined as a part of the work of design development to be converted directly into working drawings after any client-directed changes have been incorporated. For us the final step is to model the main spaces in three dimensions. These models, while they are great presentation tools for our clients, are also design tools for us. They allow us to see visual adjacencies and potential relationships between interior elements that cannot be imagined looking at plan or elevation drawings and which might be missed in 3-D computer models and in animated walk-throughs. For the time being we are biased toward the construction of real physical objects, although as more powerful 3-D programs become available this could change.

The models we make are constructed rapidly by printing floor plans and interior elevations from the computer at one-half-inch equals one-foot scale. These are glued down to foamcore board, cut out and quickly assembled. They can be rapidly modified based on client comments or visual problems with the design identified by studying the model. Like all the other materials prepared during the design process, they serve the purpose of showing us what our ideas will look like when constructed. They are interactive tools which we can alter, correct, and improve until the information they present to us convinces us that our designs will look good when actually built. At one-half-inch scale the models are doll-house-like in their ability to engage a client's attention. We encourage our clients to handle them, to hold them up to eye level, to look into them from different angles, and to use them the way we do, as aids to visualization.

The model then becomes the primary frame of reference in subsequent client meetings when materials are presented and chosen. These are referenced back to the appropriate surface or location in the model. While a client may not really understand issues of continuity between adjacent surfaces, these are easy to see and explain in a model. Often we will make sample boards; however, presenting materials is usually less formal. We will lay out wood, tile, and stone samples on our conference room table along with catalogue sheets for lighting fixtures, plumbing fixtures and fittings, and hardware. While we try to get our clients to make all of these decisions during design development, many may be put off into the working drawing phase. Although the difference between natural wood and painted cabinetry is enormous in its visual impact, rarely does a construction detail change when one is selected over the other. However, changing tile or stone thickness or tile size can necessitate the redrawing and redesign of detail conditions. So we are always uncomfortable when these decisions are put off until later in the project. We have redrawn and redimensioned entire residential kitchens when a client decided they wanted to use Delft picture tiles or some other patterned tile that cannot just be cut at any point along its dimension. I can still remember spending days as a young intern architect working out the tile layout and bonding for floor and wall tiles in the public toilets in Philip Johnson's IDS Center in Minneapolis. This was done so all the tile joints on the floors and walls would align. We now do this by computer, including scanning the patterns on picture tiles (Figure 30-2).

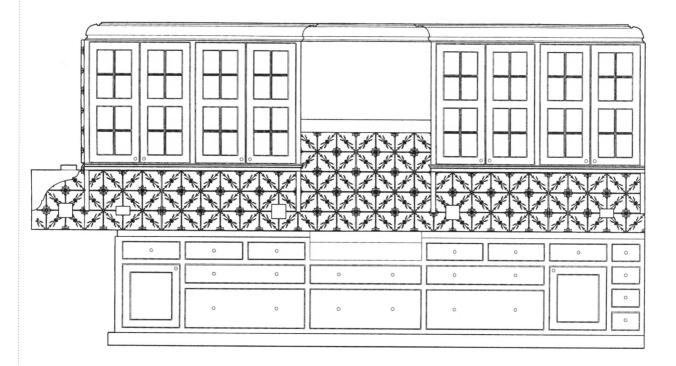

FIGURE 30-2
Kitchen Tile Layout
(Cohen & Hacker
Architects).

As fixtures and fittings are selected they are added into the elevation drawings. Drawing these elements to scale keeps us from making embarrassing mistakes, such as a medicine cabinet in a bathroom that won't open because the spout on the lavatory set the client selected was taller than the height allowed for the backsplash. Drawing all the elements to scale can save us from aesthetic mistakes as well as functional ones. A very talented interior designer we work with tore out and moved a pair of antique wall sconces three times. With antique fixtures or special items of furniture, working from a photo and some measurements, we will draw an object to judge its location and position against a wall or to judge its scale. Is the chandelier going to be too big or is it so small in a space that it will look silly? Drawing a light fixture in an interior elevation can help deciding at what height to hang it.

Drawing fixtures and fittings to scale has become easier to do as many manufacturers now supply graphic catalogues of their products on CD-ROM. These allow a drawing of the product to be imported directly into the design development drawing. As mentioned above we've found this very useful with wall- and ceiling-hung light fixtures, although few lighting manufacturers supply drawings of their fixtures on disc. We usually pinpoint other elements such as electrical switches, outlets, and HVAC wall registers during working drawings. This extra work can save unhappy moments in construction coordination.

In the history of design development there is a cachet afforded to drawing or modeling full-size details. Mies van der Rohe's office built full-size models of the details of exterior curtain walls. For the Ford Foundation building Kevin Roche had an entire conference room constructed and furnished. LeCorbusier, the great twentieth-century French architect, had a 12-foot-tall chalk board on the rear wall of his studio on which he sketched details and building wall sections full scale. During design development we often call in favors from cabinet shops and other suppliers we work with on a regular basis to make us sample cabinet doors or samples of custom-milled running and standing trim. Because the millwork and trim assemblies in our houses are a key factor in determining vertical heights, as well as plan dimensions at openings in walls and at inside and outside corners, it is important to us to determine these profiles and dimensions early in the design development phase. To do this we plot computer drawings of trimmed window and door

FIGURE 30-3
Photo of finished space illustrates the level of detail in millwork development.

openings full scale including base and crown moldings. These long scrolls of computer plots are taped up to the walls of our office or to the walls of a house we may be remodeling. Interior features such as cabinetry and fireplace mantels are printed and considered full size. This allows us to consider the contour and profile of details, but more importantly it allows our clients to determine how much of an upper kitchen cabinet they can reach without standing on a stool, or where the mantel of a fireplace should fall in relation to their eye level.

Throughout this process our objectives are to study all aspects of the design in greater detail, to flesh out areas of the project that have not yet been considered, and to guide our clients through the process of understanding what their building will look like and how it will function for them. With most of the design decisions made, we are ready to start the construction drawing phase. However, before we begin, we need to know if the project is still on budget. During schematic design, estimates of probable construction cost are based on cost information from comparable projects and on unit costs (cost per square foot allowances). In the schematic design phase we are primarily concerned that the scope of the work, the size of the project, is not out of line with our client's budget. Because of the detailed information now available on interior finishes, fixtures, fittings, millwork, and cabinetry, it is important to determine that preliminary assumptions and allowances haven't been exceeded. Because the choices made during this phase of the work can have such large financial ramifications, we usually ask our clients to pay for a detailed cost estimate. While we are capable of providing this service we usually prefer to employ a cost estimator or a general contractor. If the project is over budget we then must go through the often painful and difficult process of backtracking and reconsidering the decisions we have worked so hard to convince our clients are the right choices for their project.

Below is a list of the steps in the design development process.

1. Work out floor plans, equipment, furniture, and fixture layouts to scale from schematic or freehand sketches. Review any resulting changes in size or layout with client.

2. If you have not previously done so, conceive and communicate to the client your visual ideas for the interiors. What are their character, ambiance, etc.?

3. Draw to scale elevations of all interior surfaces and elements, including built-in cabinets and custom furniture.

4. Do research necessary to select all materials, fixtures, fittings, and furnishings.

5. Draw construction and finishing details for all typical and atypical conditions in the project.

6. Prepare or commission a sufficiently detailed cost estimate to determine if the cost of the project design, as you've developed it, exceeds the original cost estimate or the budget established by the client.

31

Design Development:
The Reality

TAMARA DINSMORE

So, what is design development? Very simply, it is the phase of a project in which already established and approved design concepts are turned into definitive design solutions. Sounds pretty straightforward, right? Well it can be, or should be, but it requires that the plan and spatial volumes remain as agreed on in earlier phases, approved and signed-off by the client, and strictly adhered to by everyone involved in the project—from the client side and the design side, both. Once this occurs, the team can concentrate on taking the approved concepts and developing them into actual design solutions. The design development phase will succeed only if earlier phases—programming and schematic designs—are smooth and complete, and if both the design team and the client adhere strictly to the parameters—that is, move the design forward, not revisit already approved concepts. The goal is to document ideas on paper so effectively that the participants in the project can, as a team, turn a design vision into a real space.

THE DESIGN DEVELOPMENT "MIND SET"

During the design development phase of the project, designers require a great amount discipline. They must remember that this is the point in the project where the ideas created in the conceptual design phase are executed—and not where new ideas should spring up. The "it's never too late for a good idea" approach can be very detrimental to the project schedule and the design fee, unless an adjustment to the schedule and or/fee is negotiated. No matter how good an idea may be, a late change should only be entertained with the full knowledge of the client and an extension in the schedule. Otherwise, what often happens is that the design team either donates personal hours or erodes the fee in order to revise drawings, get approvals, and play catch-up in order to keep a job on schedule.

Milestones are important, and increasingly more so, because they are often attached to payments that are attached to schedules that are attached, in turn, to agreements with authorities. Milestones can either be "percent of completion," requiring the design firm to issue drawings to the client and program manager when design development documents are 40 and 80 percent complete, or benchmark presentations. Design development is the phase of the project that is characterized by progress—moving the project to completion. Therefore, the design development phase has an important list of deliverables attached to it:

- *Floor plans annotated with general partition types and extent of finishes*

- *Visual representation of the spaces through models or perspectives*

- *Details reflective of general design/construction intent*

- *Telephone and electric layouts*

- *Reflected ceiling plans annotated with quantities and fixture types*

- *Design detail hierarchy clearly delineated*

THE REALITY OF DESIGN DEVELOPMENT REQUIRES SPECIAL PEOPLE

At Skidmore Owings & Merrill, during the design development phase the team that was originally assembled for the schematic design phase is supplemented with additional team members who have specific technical, financial, detailing, research, and coordination expertise. Through the integration of these people with specialties, the design team is enriched and design decision making is facilitated.

Because design development is the phase that articulates the design direction, the progress made in this phase becomes the foundation for the next phase, construction documentation. The proximity of design development to the construction document phase places immense pressure on the team, to continue to focus on solutions that meet the pre-established budgets and project schedule. However, the project team does need to remain flexible during this phase. Sometimes a client will have a new requirement that will necessitate having the team study a particular area "off line," or perhaps new information is discovered that affects previous decisions. When this occurs, the team may find itself investing additional time and resources not originally anticipated or budgeted. This investment can adversely affect the schedule and fee.

When new or unexpected items find their way into the project, such as adding an additional department on a floor that has already been designed and approved, it is all too easy to start redesigning. Proper management techniques help avoid this. These techniques include keeping all team members informed about the project's exact scope of services. It is also important to advise the client of any requests that are beyond the original project's scope so that an adjustment to the fee can be agreed on prior to moving forward on the changes.

DESIGN DEVELOPMENT PRESENTATION

Both designers and clients consider the completion of the design development phase to be a project milestone. The amount of progress that occurs during this phase is immense and the best way for the design team to communicate the progress to the client (and to get the client's approval to continue to move forward) is through a design development presentation. Comprehensive design development presentations are critical to the success of the project, are incredibly involved, and can take weeks to accomplish. It is very important to make the most of this opportunity. Presentations are beneficial not only for informing the client about the progress of the project but also for the project team, who work closely together and share ideas.

At SOM, a typical design development presentation will usually include:

- *Theme boards*

- *Related market analysis*

- *Major goals and project values*

- *Diagrams*

- *Plans*

- *Elevations*

- *3-D models*

- *Finish selections and mock-ups*

THE RESULTS ARE SPECTACULAR!

When the design team works within a single vision it becomes extremely effective at turning that vision into a design reality. A good example of this was when four designers from Skidmore Owings & Merrill's San Francisco office were completing the design development phase of a headquarters project. The team had designed the general office space, executive suites, and conference center, but there remained a small place of worship within the headquarters building that had not yet been designed. Because the team was scheduled to leave on a flight overseas that afternoon for the client presentation, we needed to have the design completely worked out before we left. As a first step, our team worked quickly together to establish the vision for the space. Once the vision was established, the team collaborated in order to design and detail the entire chapel—including a complicated system of different screening elements that were introduced to filter the daylight as the sun moved around the building. It was a very rewarding feeling to board the plane knowing that we had completed the entire design development package and, while time was short, our solution was in no way compromised—in fact, we thought it benefited.

THE DIFFERENCE BETWEEN MARGINAL AND MAGNIFICENT DESIGN

The anecdote in the previous subsection may give the impression that design development is magical or impressionistic. Far from it—it is a process that depends on a comprehensible relationship between many distinct parts and steps—a design hierarchy. Design hierarchy takes an idea to the next level. It is a sense of layering of ideas, materials, and detailing which can be understood and tracked. Although it may not be obvious to the visitor, who may see the design as one whole, a design is a conceptual arrangement of joints, lines, and overlaps to create a structure for which the design exits. In a sense, design hierarchy is a methodology for "making"—for creating the project itself and an understandable view of its design.

When a team has a clear direction of design intent or hierarchy, that team will move forward. If team members have a framework within which to develop the design, chances are much better that they can more easily tie all elements together. To create the team dynamic and keep communication open, which it must be to develop design hierarchy, it is important to touch base often, one on one with team members and as a group. In a team approach, each member often has a distinct role requiring collaboration with other team members. It is important that the team leader maintain a balance between everyone's contribution.

DESIGN DEVELOPMENT IS ABOUT PROBLEM SOLVING

During the design development phase designers should pretend that they are in a construction drawing phase, except for dimensioning, additional detailing, and final selection of colors. In essence, your drawings in the design development phase will be used for pricing. Accurate pricing is directly related to accurate and complete drawings. This ideal is, of course, easier said than done because in this phase the design team continues to solve problems.

Often, the biggest culprit stems from an inherent problem in the plan that requires the team to reorganize some of the basic planning requirements. Do you ever find that no matter what you do to fix the problem or how you reorganize the requirements, something just isn't working? For design development to run smoothly, the plan needs to be near perfection, to account for as many elements of the space and its projected use as can be anticipated. If your planning has a flaw it will quickly begin to curtail your development of the design. It is best to find a solution for a flawed plan; if it remains flawed, it may continue to undermine your development of other aspects of the project. A flawed plan usually goes back to an approach or decision which may have appeared like a good or workable idea at the time but, in fact, was not. Some common examples are:

- *Asking too much of a space—for example, insisting on fitting ten conference rooms into a space where it is clear that only eight will fit.*

- *Creating circulation confusion—for example, where public and private paths cross when they should in fact have a clear separation; circulation confusion places a burden on security and way finding.*

- *Assuming that functions can be shared—when in fact duplicating the function can greatly simplify cross-traffic and improve efficiency within the daily workday.*

Sometimes, a flawed plan may actually stem from a project directive. For example, consider a directive for flexibility in multifunctioning spaces: all conference rooms should be able to be opened up to permit "all-hands" meetings. The notion is that such a specification will give the space ultimate flexibility. Yet a conference room has a completely different set of requirements compared to an all-hands gathering, and the cost and aesthetic challenge of making an acoustically appropriate conference room and then transforming it into a party space requires attention to detail that is often beyond the goals set for the project. It is important that designers learning such a concept should not just be accepted as a given; it can be challenged, and since design development is the place where a design begins to become real, this is the phase where notions such as "multifunction" need to become reality— or to go away.

PULLING A DESIGN ALONG IN LAYERS: FOCUSED MEETINGS

To make problem solving easier in the design development phase, designers can employ a powerful organization tool, the weekly design team/consultant coordination meeting. This meeting is a time to coordinate the design work with lighting, electrical, and mechanical consultants. On a large, complicated job these meetings may be divided by discipline. If there is a particular area of difficulty, then a special meeting involving key participants is called to engage in a very focused discussion, related to a specific issue. The idea here is to have all parties buy into a direction and then move their respective team forward, discipline by discipline, and always together with a clear vision in mind.

The real work is to keep all of the layers of the design related and connected to each other; they must be brought along together. Earlier I mentioned that design development was about pulling the design together, but the layers of the design must also be brought along together. This "bringing along" process is a bit like painting a wall: when you paint, each coat of paint goes over the entire wall; you do not put all three coats on one area and then move onto another section of the wall. In design development, when the team manages layers of development, in equal percentages over all aspects of the project, the team will go a long way toward ensuring that each element of the design makes sense in its own area and as a component of the overall design hierarchy.

Treating design development as a project involving interacting layers can be difficult. Designers often find themselves trying to "buy time" for two reasons. Understandably, some elements of the design require more time than others to work out. In addition, not every aspect of the design is required at the same time. On a fast-track project, it is not uncommon during design development to issue early packages for construction. When this occurs, the "we still have time to work it out" attitude quickly vanishes. All of a sudden, the design becomes real—really soon, often too soon. The team needs time, or rather its ideas need time, to develop. In a longer-term project, if the overall schedule requires that the team issue long lead-item packages to allow advance purchasing while the project is still in the design development phase, the fast-track "it's happening now" approach will not work.

Designers need to know well in advance about early package issues in design development, and they need to plan for them in this phase and the previous phase. Common early packages are for long lead items such as specialty glass, stone pavers, and/or steel. Before advance development can take place, these items and everything related to them ideally needs to be "frozen." Consequently, the design development process for a complex project with early packages will require a gestation period. Otherwise, if, when these packages get issued, the drawings are rushed just to get them out the door, then the team may quickly see that the design is locked in. The result would then be that, instead of working with a space or an element of the design, the team must work around it, almost as though they were required to renovate an unbuilt space.

In fact, it can be said that, for any project, designers need concentrated quality time in the design development phase if they are to move a design forward. "Quality time" means that, before the design development phase begins, it is very important that earlier phases be fully completed. In this phase, the "oh, we'll pick it up in the next phase" attitude quickly forces designers to spend the short amount of time they do have just playing catch-up. Design development is the turning point in a project—it is the bridge between ideas and reality, not the time to do what should have been done before.

The Layered Approach to Design

The "layered" approach has consequences for the way designers should think about the quality of their design development phase. Designers should not measure the success of design development by the number of sheets produced or details recorded. Even so, the drawings you do send should be more than just toss-offs designed to solve an immediately pressing problem—they must be a real part of the design hierarchy. It is very important that, when drawings do get issued for review or pricing, only carefully thought-out drawings leave the office. All too often, a quick response to the request that you "just send me what you have, I realize it is only preliminary" locks you into a palette of finishes, design intent, or level of detail which has not been properly thought out. You should assume that you will be held to what is shown on even the most preliminary drawing. Draw quickly and thoughtfully, and bring all aspects of the job along at the same pace. It is better to issue ten drawings that are 30 percent developed than one sketch which has not been adequately considered or folded into the greater whole of the design.

CONCLUSION

Design development is a process—that of advancing the development of the design of an entire project at a similar pace—in which the design team fashions each piece or section or area with a strong design hierarchy that can be followed by the team and understood by the client. For, at the end of the design development phase, ideas must appear on paper, documented in such a way that the larger team client, contractor, and designer can move comfortably and confidently into the next phase, knowing that the design is ready to become a reality.

Bibliography

Britt, David. *Joseph Beuys*. New York: Abbeville Press, 1987.

De Franclieu, Francoise. *LeCorbusier Sketchbooks*, Volumes 1–4. Cambridge, MA: MIT Press, 1982.

Ford, Edward R. *The Details of Modern Architecture*. Cambridge, MA: MIT Press, 1990.

Hays, K. Michael, and Carol Burns, Editors. *Thinking in the Present: Recent American Architecture*. New York: Princeton Architectural Press, 1990.

Rilke, Rainer Maria. *Letters on Cezanne*. New York: Fromm International Publishing, 1985.

Zaknic, Ivan. *Journey to the East*. Cambridge, MA: MIT Press, 1987.

32

Contract Documentation: Integrating Interiors and Architecture

DARIA PIZZETTA, AIA

Hardy Holtzman Pfeiffer Architects (HHPA) is an architectural firm with an interiors department, but rarely do we work independently of each other. Creating complementary architectural and interior designs is essential to our work, and there is a fine line between where one stops and the other starts. While the interiors department is responsible for producing certain contract documents, such as furniture and finishes plans, we also significantly contribute to developing interior elevations, reflected ceiling plans, millwork drawings and details, and all material selections.

Our approach to contract documentation is straightforward: Provide only the pertinent information required to specify the scope of the work, materials to be used, and design intent. Means and methods are the contractor's responsibility. However, since HHPA's interiors feature unusual forms and original material applications, it is necessary for us to thoroughly detail unique design elements. Our goal at the end of this phase is to supply bidders with adequate information to correctly price the job, provide drawings and specifications from which to build, and insure that design elements and materials are in keeping with established budgets.

Contract documentation (CD) efforts start in schematic design (SD). Under the best of circumstances, the drawings that are developed through SD and design development (DD) evolve into CD. At the beginning of the SD phase, the project manager sets up a "blue book" that outlines all of the drawings we plan to produce during the course of the project and what information each will contain. Through the development of SD, DD, and CD the drawings progress from a sketchy outline to a complete novel, revealing the plot page by page.

HHPA's CD consists of both graphic drawings and a narrative specification book. These documents both complement and supplement each other. Drawings illustrate space configurations, dimensional aspects, material details, and the generic name of each building material (i.e., gypsum wall board, not Sheetrock; plastic laminate, not Formica). The specification manual and its supplemental schedules indicate the manufacturers, model numbers, colors, etc., for each product. Then, if a product changes, it is revised only in the specification or schedule, not throughout the drawing sheets.

There is rarely more than one interior designer assigned to the CD phase of any project. Collaboration among the architects and designer is necessary to determine the information required on each drawing, the details to be drawn, and the project schedule. Our designers typically coordinate drawings with the project electrical engineer and lighting designer as the location of furniture and the reflectance value of finishes greatly impact their work.

Over the past decade, the computer has had great impact on our methods of producing CDs. To start a drawing we use reference drawings as base plans with a structured layering system; specific layers are designated for interiors. When producing a furniture layout or a finish plan, we can insert coded furniture symbols or finish keys accessed from an electronic symbols library. These codes and keys are standard elements used repeatedly on each project. In one aspect, we violate our own rule by placing finish schedules, indicating manufacturers and model numbers, on the plan. There is a definite reason for this: Who has ever seen a painter on site with a specification manual? They refer only to the plan for paint or finishes locations.

CODE RESEARCH AND APPLICATION

HHPA keeps on hand the major codebooks such as the New York City Unified Building Code and Southern Standard Building Code, as well as the Americans with Disabilities Act handbook and many of the standards for the ASTM test procedures.

Before we start design or documentation, we research which codes apply to our project and who are the reviewing authorities. (They may have a particular vexation of which to be aware.) Because we work in many jurisdictions, many different codes have applied. For major projects we are fortunate to employ code experts who interpret local codes.

When it comes to applying codes to interior projects, two stand out in our mind, the Americans with Disabilities Act (ADA) and the flame-spread codes (mostly Cal. Bulletin 113 and 133). The ADA has made it easier to standardize layouts for toilets, elevator cabs, and door swings all throughout the United States. Once you have drawn a compliant toilet in your computer system, it is not too hard to apply it to the next project. However, these codes have an unfavorable effect on your net-to-gross building requirements. They are larger.

Our public projects require that we are familiar with the flame-spread codes as they apply to furniture. Furniture manufacturers are very helpful in determining which codes need to be met in which jurisdictions and in providing burn tests to demonstrate that the furniture and upholstery assembly meet code.

Another code constraint that we encounter is replacement cost. (This rule varies from state to state.) HHPA's work includes many renovation and restoration projects. When the cost of the renovation or restoration equals a certain percentage of the replacement cost (typically 50 percent) of an existing building, you are required to upgrade the entire building to meet all the codes (travel distance, fire alarm systems, emergency lighting, etc.) including ADA codes. This was the case with the restoration of Radio City Music Hall. HHPA's scope of work included the rectifying of a number of ADA code violations.

Our best advice regarding code application is to employ an expert to review your drawings and specifications. It can save you and your client from numerous problems and costly changes.

MATERIAL RESEARCH

A signature of HHPA designs is the innovative use of inexpensive materials. For us to preserve our signature, we are always searching for new materials or inventive ways of applying standard materials. On a weekly basis, HHPA's Interiors staff meets with numerous vendors to view and collect material samples which will be applicable to upcoming or specific projects. We look for

Our approach to contract documentation is straightforward: Provide only the pertinent information required to specify the scope of the work, materials to be used, and design intent. Means and methods are the contractor's responsibility.

materials that have the qualities of both visual appeal and durability when we are assessing value versus costs. When evaluating materials, we apply our imaginations. Can a flooring product be used on a wall or a tabletop? Can an inexpensive wood veneer be stained a beautiful color? What if the material was used backwards or upside-down? Is there merit to those applications?

If a material is deemed worthy due to its appeal, it then must be considered for its specific application. Will it meet the Fire Class Ratings, are they maintenance free, will they abrade, corrode, or rust? If fabrics are being evaluated, do they meet the upholster-ability test of the furniture manufacturer, are they the correct fiber content and weight to hold up against stains and double rubs?

Our materials research is not confined to our offices. We have subscriptions to all the major design magazines and frequently use them for inspiration. We attend trade shows, search the Internet, visit showrooms, and even explore Home Depot in search of materials. All of the Interiors staff is encouraged to become materials experts and share their knowledge. And, somehow all the acquired materials samples have to be kept current. Having a good materials librarian is key to keeping your research to a minimum.

There are downsides to using materials uniquely. Most of our work is publicly bid. It is sometimes problematic to receive competitive bids when you are doing something new. The designer feels guilty when the vendor who worked so hard to develop a new product or application is underbid by a competitor who did not participate in the development process.

While some contractors welcome the challenge of using unique materials or building interesting forms, others will charge a premium due to their inability to understand the use of the new material or an unwillingness to do anything out of the ordinary. One solution is to hold a "materials fair" prior to the bid opening so that the contractors can see the specified materials and their intended installation and can speak with the building products' manufacturers representatives.

By the start of CD, the material research process should be complete. Our next task is to apply our research by correctly drawing and specifying the selected materials.

SUSTAINABLE DESIGN PRACTICE SPECIFICATIONS

In a typical design practice, sustainability is unfortunately not always the overriding priority, and many times loses out to the bottom line. However, manufacturers in recent years have become more attuned to this issue, and, for many, creating sustainable products is almost second nature. For HHPA, sustainability is often hand-in-hand with our design philosophy of finding innovative, cost-conscious materials. When specifying for sustainable design, furniture and building products should be selected based on which leave the least chemical imprint on the building's indoor air quality. Products that produce low gas emissions from paints, stains, sealers, sealants, insulations, etc., should be carefully considered. With modern technology, it is possible to manufacture custom carpet without the use of artificial dyes. From the point of view of air quality, carpets can be specified with jute (versus synthetic) backing and either tacked or adhered, when necessary, with a water-based low-VOC adhesive. Decisions about wall paints, enamels, adhesives, and linoleum flooring should also take potential chemical impact into consideration.

FURNITURE AND FINISHES SPECIFICATIONS

While furniture selection begins during the DD phase, the specification of furniture is truly a contract document function. Furniture is selected to enhance the design, but also for function and durability and to meet a set budget. HHPA packages have included everything from statement pieces down to the trash receptacles. We also create custom furniture, especially for our library and restaurant projects.

Typically, a furniture specification manual will include front-end sections, including instructions to bidders and bid tally sheets, and a written specification outlining the scope of work, listing specified manufacturers and noting quality standards, materials, and warranties. Each coded furniture item is depicted in a specification sheet that shows the code, manufacturer, model number, dimensions, fabric and/or finish, and a sketch or scanned image of the furniture piece. Large projects may be assembled into packages so that similar furniture categories, or dealer-specific items, can be issued for separate bids. Our library projects, for example, typically include a package just for the shelving and then additional packages for library furniture and back-of-house items. Each specification manual is accompanied by a furniture layout. We consider it the bidder's responsibility to be accountable for the quantity takeoffs.

Our furniture drawings and specifications are united by a database. Customized for our needs, the database allows the department to track furniture by room and department locations or by type, as corresponding to our coding system, or by assigned package. The database further provides a running count of furniture items, assuming that they have been correctly inserted into the drawings.

Finishes specification starts during the SD phase with the creation of an outline specification. Historically, we have employed a specification writer who is familiar with HHPA's material use. This consultant meets with us during the various phases of the project to review the materials being specified, their application, and their approved equals. We provide all details with regards to the specifications and act as editors of the specification manual.

To conclude the furniture and finishes specifications, HHPA assembles furniture and finishes binders that document each furniture piece and its specification and finish. A separate binder documents all finish materials. These are extremely helpful for reference while processing shop drawings and for future reference should the client call back in five years and want to re-paint in the same colors.

FURNITURE PROCUREMENT

Once the furniture package has been awarded, it is up to the selected vendors or dealership to procure, deliver, and install the specified furniture. We participate in the process by reviewing shop drawings and creating a punch list, but the ordering, scheduling, and installation processes are left to the dealer. A relationship is established between the client and the dealer so that all contractual agreements, deposits, and payments are between them.

In many instances, we are working with facility departments or university procurement offices. Once they receive the specifications, they assume the responsibility for the bid award and monitoring of the furniture packages.

COMMUNICATION METHODOLOGY

Clients

During the CD phase, our clients are kept updated on the progress of the documents through frequent drawing reviews. Although the design is complete, final details and finishes selections are proceeding throughout the CD phase. It is important that our clients participate in the CD meetings so that they are fully aware of any adjustments that are a result of value engineering, found building conditions, or material modifications. These meetings usually consist of a pin-up of all drawings and finishes and a walk-through of each drawing.

Outside Consultants

With the advent of e-mail it is simple to keep the entire project team, including outside consultants, updated on the day-to-day progress of the contract documents. Broadcast e-mails and faxes are used to inform the entire project team, both in-house and consultants, of important drawing changes and meeting dates and to issue meeting minutes.

This is the most critical phase in which to have coordination meetings with the consultants to assure that they are working with the most current base plans and that the design concepts developed in previous phases are being correctly executed. We communicate drawing changes through meetings that result in red-line drawing sets that coordinate all our work. Outside consultants participate in the client drawing reviews and are responsible for presenting their work to the client.

Landlord/Builder

If a landlord is involved, we continue to issue progress documents for their review to assure them we are abiding by the building rules and regulations.

We keep the landlord informed with regards to the Building Department reviews and our schedule for document issuance and to ask for recommendations for qualified contractors to bid on the project. Usually, the contractor is not yet selected. We are communicating with potential bidders with regards to scope of work and schedule, but generally frequent communications with the contractors do not start until the drawings are issued.

33

Contract Documentation: Clarity of the Drawings

JAMES D. CARTER, AIA, IIDA, IFMA

Working drawings are the graphic portion of *construction documents*, a term that is commonly used to describe the overall family of documents prepared by the architect/designer for the bidding and constructing of a project. There are many non-graphic (text-only) documents such as specifications that come into play as well. For convenience, the non-graphic documents are frequently bound together into a book format known as a *project manual*.

Drawings produced for bidding and construction are traditionally referred to as *working drawings* because they communicate design intent in sufficient technical detail to enable the project to be constructed. They must be coordinated with specifications, so that together they depict the materials and systems from which the project is to be built and indicate their quantity and arrangement. Working drawings include architectural design drawings, as well as drawings of all the engineering and specialty consultants. Specifications contain the written descriptions of the construction materials, components, and systems to be used in the project overview.

The production of working drawings should be guided by these fundamental tenets:

- ***Drawings must reflect designs that comply with all applicable codes and regulations promulgated for the protection of public health, safety, and welfare.***

- ***Drawings must reflect the scope of services that the designer/architect has been contracted to provide the client.***

- ***Drawings must reflect the design intent established in the previous documents produced for the project.***

- ***Drawings must be created in accordance with the internal business goal of producing documents that convey the maximum of information with the minimum amount of effort.***

Drawing What the Governing Authorities Require for Granting Approvals

Prior to actual construction, the technical portions of construction documents are typically reviewed by governmental agencies charged with ensuring public health and safety. These may be municipal building departments, or a state agency such as the Bureau of Buildings and Construction at the local Department of Community Affairs. The submitted documents are reviewed for compliance with applicable building codes. Once approved, the documents are released for construction, and the party executing the construction can then obtain a building permit. Proceeding without valid approvals is *never* a good idea.

To facilitate expeditious review of the documents, they should include the type of information that is germane to a review of code issues. Very often codes specifically ask for such information to be included on the drawings rather than stashed away in the project manual. The items necessary for a review of code issues include:

- *Use group classification of the building*

- *Type of construction and fire resistance rating of building elements*

- *Height and area limitations for the type of construction selected*

- *Detailed requirements for fire resistance and fire protection systems*

- *Energy conservation compliance*

- *Interior environment, including accessibility, egress, and interior finishes*

It is useful to include much of the above information in one place in the set. For most buildings, it is possible to include annotated, reduced-scale floor plans and tabulated code compliance data on a single sheet. Special sheets or CADD should be set aside for code information.

Doing Only What We Owe Our Clients

It is very important throughout the design and documentation process to keep in mind the scope of services agreed on between the architect, the designer, and the client. The nature of the design and its complexity and extent must meet the client's expectations, without needlessly exceeding them. There is a direct correlation between the intricacy of design and the amount of time required to document it on the drawings. This is true for a design that has many special features and one that attempts to bring together materials and building systems in unusual and innovative ways. Frequently, fees agreed on cannot accommodate the added effort necessary to document such high design level. Everyone involved on the project team needs to be aware of this and exercise an appropriate level of self-discipline.

This is also true in relation to any alternate designs that the client would like to have the architect/designer document. Typically, alternates are included in the bidding documents primarily to allow the client to receive bids on several possible project scopes or levels of quality—and thus meet the client's budget. As such, they are there largely for the client's convenience, and generally, they are not included in the basic scope of services. Before including alternates in the working drawings, it should be ascertained by the project team whether this work is part of the services we are actually obligated to perform.

Drawing What the Contractors Need

Another guiding principle for working drawings is to provide *sufficient* information regarding design intent. "Sufficient" can be described as adequately depicting and describing *every* design aspect of the project *once*. It has been witnessed that construction problems (and, unfortunately in many cases as a direct consequence, litigation problems) arise when the drawings do not show enough, when they show too much, or when they are just plain incorrect.

Repetition within the drawings or the specifications goes beyond the requirements of the designer/owner agreement, and furthermore, creates the potential for conflict, error, inconsistency, and confusion. The ideal set of construction documents would show the full extent of every item and its interface on drawings only once, with clear cross-referencing and coordination with specifications. Thus, someone unfamiliar with the project would be able to find all the necessary information without the need for outside interpretation. While this ideal is just about impossible to achieve in real life, all project team members should strive to come as close to it as possible.

Another guiding principle for working drawings is to provide sufficient *information regarding design intent.* "Sufficient" *can be described as adequately depicting and describing* every *design aspect of the project* once.

There are certain things that *must* be on the drawings, regardless of the size and scope of the project:

- *Identification of all materials*

- *Dimensions allowing the constructors to correctly place all materials and assemblies*

- *Details showing intended relationships between the parts*

- *Clear indication of quantities of manufactured items (such as toilet accessories, equipment, and various fixtures)*

Remember that all drawings that may have been prepared as an aid to solving design problems need not be included in working drawings. For example:

- *Building sections (not wall sections), often prepared during the schematic design phase or the design development phase, usually convey little information actually needed for construction and can be omitted. They can be useful for showing relationships of multilevel spaces to other spaces (such as in the case of atria), and for keying-in interior "wall" sections for spaces with special design features (such as different floor level, stepped ceilings, coves, fascias, soffits, etc.).*

- *Locations of plumbing, mechanical, and electrical items, such as floor drains, electrical panels, and power and data receptacles may have been established as part of the design process. However, unless such locations are essential to achieving a specific architectural effect, they should be shown only on the consultants' drawings. The preceding guideline is not meant to suggest that the drawings of various disciplines should not be coordinated with each other.*

- *It may be necessary during design to draw a plan of a toilet room at a 1" = 1'-0" scale to determine the dimensions required to avoid cutting of ceramic tiles. Once the dimensions are ascertained, 1/4" = 1'-0" scale is probably adequate to provide construction information.*

USING THE POWER OF COMPUTER-AIDED DESIGN AND DRAFTING

Preparation of working drawings, like just about every other aspect of our professional lives, has been profoundly altered by the digital revolution. Computer-aided design and drafting (CADD) offers tools to the architect/ designer that permit many of the tedious and repetitive tasks involved in documenting a design to be accomplished with relative ease. The same is true for making minor and major changes to drawings.

Most importantly, CADD offers us a chance to have the drawings become graphic representations of nongraphic construction information. This information can be accessed and used to generate valuable reports about the project using computer applications other than CADD. Whether used for quantity take-offs, strategic facilities planning, or facilities management, the electronic project data can transcend being merely digital replication of manually produced drawings. On the other hand, it is also important to keep in mind that the power of CADD can be abused as well. The ease with which one can create and copy graphics may lead to repetition for repetition's sake: excessive rendering of materials designations being the most egregious example.

Graphic Standards

There are strategies and instructions for dealing with specific types of drawings, from planning to execution, but certain general principles and attitudes are universally applicable:

- *As much as possible, standard project prototype files should be used to set up all aspects of a project, including working drawings.*

- *As much as possible, proven detail standards should be used as sources of graphics components and assemblies.*

- *While CADD facilitates fairly painless process of revisions, that should not become an excuse to forego properly planning out a set of working drawings.*

- *As much as possible, an effort should be made to create a single graphic database for the project. This should be done to avoid several versions of a specific design to coexist on the drawings. For example:*

  ○ *Whenever possible and appropriate, plan details should be created using the main plans as "background." When such details are created separately, and without direct reference to the overall plan, they are less likely to be updated when revisions are instituted on main plans.*

  ○ *Whenever possible and appropriate, vertical section details should be created using corresponding wall sections as "background." In fact, an approach that relies on assembling wall sections from a series of section details may result in wall sections, which always reflect the design solutions at the "brass tacks" level.*

  ○ *Room names and numbers should be placed on appropriate layers and positioned on sheets so that they can be used for floor plans* and *any other plans for that level, such as reflected ceiling plans, interior finish plans, etc.*

Keeping some of the above general principles in mind will allow project team members to keep a focus on what needs to be achieved by working drawings.

LINE-WORK AND LINE-STYLES

To obtain clarity of line-work the principles of CADD drafting still rely on the foundations of hand drafting. The blackest, most opaque lines are still produced by ink. Plotters try to match this process and continually improve on obtaining an equivalent level of contrast between the ink and toner placed on the blank media. With CADD the simplest way to obtain contrast is by varying the line thickness. With so many different types of printers and plotters in our offices it is no longer suggested that one only rely on hardware/software-defined pen density settings to achieve contrast. With CADD one can define over 5,000 different line-styles, each with its own

Most importantly, CADD offers us a chance to have the drawings become graphic representations of nongraphic construction information. This information can be accessed and used to generate valuable reports about the project . . .

thickness and pattern. To achieve the three-level hierarchy of graphics for our working drawings, we typically only need to use a fraction of what is available.

WORKING DRAWINGS

It is important to remember that working drawings are not exclusively technical; they are the embodiment of both design intent and the technical means to achieve it.

Working drawings must meet the following criteria:

- *Physically endure for two or more years*

- *Be conducive to numerous revisions*

- *Remain clear through various printing, reproduction, publishing, and delivery techniques*

- *Hold up as reproductions under use in the field, including exposure to sunlight and dirt*

- *Be conclusive when viewed by individuals who might "guess" differently than their author*

OVERALL CLARITY OF DRAWINGS

Drawings, particularly floor plans, should be designed from the onset with a three-level hierarchy of graphics. The architectural graphics (i.e., walls, doors, windows, stairs) should occupy the *middle* level. Within this level the graphics should be appropriately assigned differential line weights and line styles to convey the design concepts and design intent. When viewing the drawing from a distance or when simply squinting your eyes, the dimensions and notes should not necessarily be clearly discernable, as these items are to

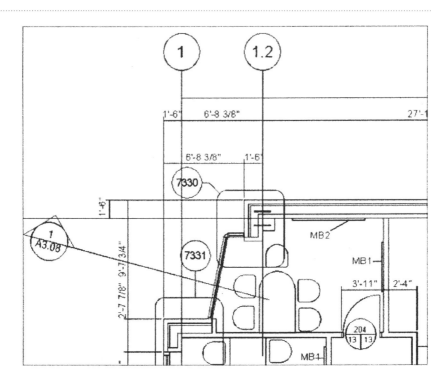

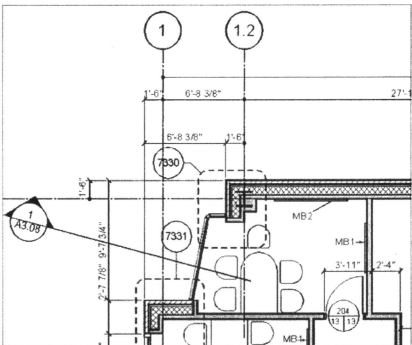

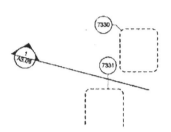

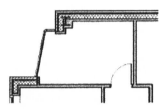

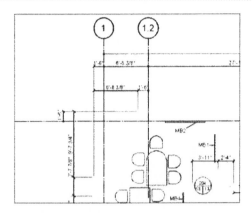

Highest Level
Includes symbols to designate enlarged plans, sections and details.

Middle Level
Includes exterior walls, doors, windows, partitions, stairs, etc.

Lowest Level
Includes general text, dimensions, general symbols for doors, partition types, equipment, furniture, etc.

FIGURE 33-3
Same Section of
Working Drawing with
Different Graphic
Content Levels.

be considered on the *lowest* level of the hierarchy. However, the architectural graphics of the middle level should remain clear. The *highest* level of the hierarchy should include references to larger-scale information, such as enlarged floor plans at $1/4'' = 1'-0''$ or wall sections at $3/4'' = 1'-0''$. Figure 33-1 is an example of a section of a working drawing with no hierarchy of graphic content. Compare this to Figure 33-2, which reflects the three-level hierarchy of graphic content. Figure 33-3 shows three illustrations of the same section of floor plan separated into the *lowest*, *middle*, and *highest* levels.

34

Contract Administration: The Different Solution

KEVIN WALZ

Clients of my design firm, Walzworkinc., frequently say that they choose to work with us because they have the sense that we will arrive at a different solution. I will approach the subject of contract administration from that perspective of the different solution. You may get the sense from textbooks and other professionals, big firms perhaps, that contract administration is all about steps in a rigid process; it is professionalized. But is it really professional to have a design phase followed by a separate document phase, and then a bidding phase, and then the administration of the contract? Or is it simply neater? Is better design produced under a rigid format, where activities are compartmentalized and separate? Take note: designers have a bad reputation in the world. Behind their backs the world has noticed their overly tidy demeanor: the matchy-matchy clothes, perfect hair, and the desire to control and contain life, rather than support it. I think professionalism in its formulaic procedures detaches relationships by putting the lid on interaction, and discourages creativity by encouraging us to serve up yet again what we know, rewarmed.

We are careful at Walzworkinc. to explain to our clients, and everyone involved with our projects, that to achieve the best design we can, we leave many decisions unresolved after the completion of the design phase. True, construction documents and specifications are binding and legal, but this does not mean they can't be descriptive of open, flexible ideas. They can speak of intent, goals, and concepts, like a flexible map. The construction documents are the route a design will travel in order to arrive at a completion. Yet we have found that the phase of contract administration can be another creative phase where ideas come together in a refining of themes, relationships, and visual dialogues. True, the designer is the representative of the client during contract administration and what is supposed to be going on during this period of time is construction, but there is not a designer alive who can imagine every element of the design during the design phase nor imagine the best way to realize them alone or ahead of time.

This open-endedness does not cause jobs to escalate in cost. This open-endedness does not make schedules expand. It is based on the idea that maybe the best idea is yet to come, with "best" meaning: more cost-effectively detailed; more structurally sound; using materials that are going to cost less and perhaps be available sooner than the ones first selected; elements assembled the way the selected fabricator does it best, not the way specified in the design drawings.

MY PERSPECTIVE ON DESIGN

I never studied design, but fine art. When one makes art one's mind stays aware throughout the process, and so I think that the same ought to be true in design. I like to keep my mind aware and active during all the phases of a project. Each step should be alive and fluid to me. Also, I like to treat each project as a great opportunity to learn and grow. If one has only one life to be a designer, each project should be seen as full of possibilities.

My path as a designer could be characterized as one that has moved from possibility to possibility. It is an accident that I took up designing at all. But after I designed a loft for my wife and myself I wanted to work with space again and the only way I could see having the opportunity to do that was to get some clients. I taught myself to draft. Friends who were designers slipped me the contracts their offices used, so I understood how a design firm worked, how it billed, and what its responsibilities were in relationship to the client and in the realization of the design. I never used the contracts, as the processes seemed wrong for how I wanted to work. From what I learned about the processes in standard contracts, and how I wished to develop designs for clients, I made up my own letter of agreement. Then, I got some clients.

We are a small and nimble interior design firm. We are four people. The very largest we ever were was eight people. This was too big for me. I became unhappy with my role in the company. Somebody had to be the boss, so I got to conceptualize the projects and pass the projects on to my staff. I did keep the product design for myself. What I enjoyed the most was doing the details, but I needed to give it up to have enough time to run the company, schmooze for new work to feed the machine. All the people working for me had great things on their desks that I wished I was doing.

One day I mailed in an application for the Rome Prize, a fellowship awarded every year to a designer to live and think at the American Academy in Rome. Upon my return from the post office, I began firing the staff until there was no one left. Now I have a very small office in New York, the city where I do not live anymore, but visit regularly. In Rome, where I now live and never left after winning the Rome Prize, I have a 400-year-old studio in the walled-in garden of a villa in Trastevere. This is where I now design and make art.

CONTRACT ADMINISTRATION AND THE ONGOING PROCESS OF DESIGN

I like to step back and rethink the nature of things: turn the structure of doors and walls inside out, use materials for purposes they have not been used before, run the traffic of an office around the window wall. This is a process full of effort for us, but when we work hard we are rewarded, and we do not ask more effort of our clients. It makes sense to me that if we are to realize any of our designs, we need to make the best use of all the wisdom and knowledge and experience of the design team, the client, the contractor, and the fabricators. And we can't possibly achieve this best use of all of our resources if we limit our learning and work solely to the initial design phase, a phase I find insular and narcissistic by nature. Design needs to be responsive to the clients and their needs; the designer doesn't have to live with his/her solutions, the clients do. The best way to design the most appropriate space is to engage the clients throughout the design phase. We never make a design presentation, a standard procedure in this industry, but have regular meetings during the design phase to continue to receive input from the clients. The effort of a formal design presentation is better spent responding to the clients' comments as ideas are developed. What is most important for our projects is to use the wisdom of the entire cast of characters of a project—the client, the contractor, and as many of the key fabricators as possible—and this needs to start as early as possible in the process. The designs all start in our office and studio, but the final designs with their details and full conviction spring up from somewhere between all of us.

Also, we never fill a set of plans with dimensions. We use dimensions only when this is the best way to describe our priority of requirements. Other things we say about a measurement are "line up," and "center" and "equal." This way the lines drawn in the plans can more easily be responsive to the realities of the space. It is a format with priorities and emphasis.

Specific Components of Contract Administration: Recommendations

In this context of flexibility, I can address some specifics of what is traditionally known as *contract administration.* The contract administration phase includes the following eight stages for the designer.

REVIEW SHOP DRAWINGS

Designers should see shop drawings not as strict limitations or controls over the project but rather as opportunities to solve problems they may encounter on the way to implementing their vision. For me, this is an opportunity to encourage the fabricators to bring their knowledge to the process, to use what they can do best and modify the details if necessary. But I will fight for a detail or a concept that is critical to my vision. Once I designed five-foot by ten-foot sliding doors in 1/4-inch aluminum sheets for the offices of a record company. I had simple tubing attached on one side running horizontally, and on the other side the tubing ran vertically. To me it was a hollow core door, but inside out. The contractor worried it wouldn't work. The fabricator said it would warp and rack. I asked them to send it to their engineer. He said it wouldn't work. To understand this structure better I lay my fingers of one hand horizontally across the vertical fingers of the other. I could see it would work. "Make one and if it doesn't work I'll pay for it." It worked and they made all four.

APPROVE SAMPLES

Designers should never try to match the sample of one material to another; this is a perverse idea. If they aren't the same material, then they won't have the same qualities. When designers develop custom samples they should offer "recipes" to fabricators for the direction they think might work best and ask for some variations, if necessary. For instance: "Take the fir plywood, stain it black and then sandblast it," and "Take the fir plywood, sandblast it and then stain it black." These are recipes. Every fabricator will give you different solutions, because every fabricator's hand is different. It is difficult enough matching a sample by another fabricator in the same material. Celebrate the difference of the materials, the processes, and the eye and hand of the fabricator. Never give the client the expectation of matchy-matchy, which looks OK on a computer screen but not in life.

SUBMIT MATERIALS, CUT SHEETS, AND PRODUCTS

Although we start this procedure way back in the initial design phases while we are developing ideas, some design elements require research or are dependent on other decisions and can't properly be selected until later. Many times a materials choice will require designers to use salesmanship and communication skills: The designer may need to sell a client on an idea that is difficult to imagine. When you present the material you wish to use, it makes it more difficult to imagine, like the sandpaper we have used as a wallcovering of a showroom. You need to explain how it will look different (better) in context. Also, never promise a performance from a material that is not possible. Everything wears. Some materials wear in and some wear out. Many times we pre-wear elements of our designs.

REVIEW PROGRESS AND QUALITY OF WORK

Being flexible in the process of design does not mean being sloppy. When it comes to making satisfactory progress and finishing a quality project, professionalism is critical, and from the get-go designers must establish procedures and methods for handling all questions and changes. Communication of expectations is critical and the first sign of not meeting these expectations (workmanship, schedule, attendance) should be identified sharply and clearly. Then, as necessary, the designer should grease the squeaky wheel. A client may wander onto a jobsite and question procedure with unauthorized personnel, like a worker on the job. When clients see elements appear out of order or out of the context of the rest of the design on a site, they frequently need reassurance that the right choices have been made, that the work is being carried out correctly. They may ask, "Why is this happening this way?" Similarly, they may ask a worker whether an item can be changed easily, whether the worker who is working on the site likes the design, why (seemingly) nothing is happening. A client must use proper channels to ask questions about the design and its implementation. A client must make all changes by approved methods and approve the cost to make those changes before the change is implemented.

EVALUATE APPLICATIONS FOR PAYMENT

We like to work with a construction management format with our contractors. This format is critical for our type of designing, because it allows us to leave allowances while working out details during this phase. You'll always, always get a better price from a painter when he sees the job near the time he is to do his work. In the construction management approach, when designers review progress and quality, they can isolate problematic work by withholding payment, without penalizing those who are doing their job well.

CLOSE OUT THE PROJECT (PUNCH LIST)

Be quick and consistent with objections and their resolution as a project is going on. Document all concerns and copy the information to everyone. Should the client have unrealistic expectations, you need to find the way to explain the difference.

VERIFY COMPLETION

Because add-ons or late changes occur during most construction projects, make sure the client does not pay the contractor until the work is complete and all such issues negotiated. Make sure you are satisfied, ditto the client. Then approve final payment.

COORDINATE CONTROLLED INSPECTIONS

Try never to file for permits more than necessary, especially where the building department is corrupt. Just do things to code and hire the best expeditor you can find.

COMMUNICATION AND CONTRACT ADMINISTRATION: PEOPLE SKILLS WHEN PERSPECTIVES DIFFER

During the contract administration phase one has the opportunity to keep on top of the budget when working with a construction management format. It makes sense to allow research into alternative processes that might keep the project in budget. This is best accomplished when there is an overall but flexible view of the project and when the actual cast has been selected to do the work. When a designer works with a fabricator with skill and experience, he or she might do well to listen to the fabricator's ideas about the best or most cost-effective methods for fabrication. The detail you might select is likely not to be the best or most cost-effective unless you understand the skills of the selected fabricators. But a warning is in order: Some contractors and fabricators consider thinking an extra. To make the flexible view of the project work, designers need to develop people skills and a real sense of how to understand others' perspectives and motivations.

Some people think that their job is only a job. With some contractors and some fabricators, budgets go out the window as soon as they are asked to think. I avoid fabricators like these. I will not make a design that does not require thinking. A designer needs to pull everyone to the same side of the fence, so there is a sense of a common goal. In Italy, where I live, people consider thinking an essential part of their workday, as essential as the good meal at lunch time. There is a joy when a solution is found to a problem during the construction administration phase. Construction documents are an essential element of the design, but the final design is scribbled on the wall. In Italy on a jobsite every element might need to be marked in the space on the wall with a stubby pencil for final location, proportion, and detail. Lawyers are not called upon, and everyone's word is the final contract. It is much easier to keep a design alive and responsive during the contract administration phase in an atmosphere of trust and common goals, such as I have found while working in Italy.

A few summers ago I was renovating a penthouse apartment in Manhattan and at the same time an apartment in Rome. While in New York I had a meeting with the contractors on the penthouse project. The contractor reported, "We can't possibly reuse this door hardware or the baseboard and door moldings. It will be easier and cheaper and better to simply replace it all."

It makes sense to me that if we are to realize any of our designs, we need to make the best use of all the wisdom and knowledge and experience of the design team, the client, the contractor, and the fabricators.

"But it is all original. I don't care if it looks old; that would be the good news," I said. "It's what the client wants and I want. And it's in the construction documents that way."

"No, the old hardware won't work and we can't be responsible," the contractor said, knowing that would make me responsible for the choice.

I returned to Rome later that week and, on the construction site there, I mentioned that the contractor was probably going to suggest we toss the hardware and the wood moldings. "Why would we do that?" he said incredulously, "This is all original to the apartment. It will be so easy to remove and scrape everything and rework the mechanisms. Look." The contractor took a brass door handle out on the balcony and ran a steel brush across it while another worker held the handle with pliers and another used a blow torch on it. "Look how easy this will be and much more beautiful than new ones."

Designers need to know that as important as it is to make nice space, working with people is just as important. Design professionals could benefit from a course in psychology or how to work with other people and how to communicate. These courses are as obviously missing from the design curriculum as nutrition and the understanding of the entire well-being of the patient are missing from the study of medicine. In the schools where I've taught, the study of making presentation drawings is rampant, but this material could be reduced to one lesson. Students could more productively spend that time learning how to present ideas to clients and contractors, how to work with difficult people, how to tell people bad news, and very important, how to get people to do things you need them to do to realize your ideas. Sometimes when a designer has a good idea and the fabricator says some part of the idea can't be done, then a tactic might be to ask the same question again and again and again with variations until the desired answer is heard: "Yes, it can be done." Maybe that is not psychology at all, but persistence.

With regard to the client, it is important to portray a real scenario of the construction process. The truth is that the process is a near-impossible orchestration of numerous procedures and elements. Your project may not be the only thing on their mind, so be brief, but do keep the client abreast of everything. Have everything copied to the client in writing, particularly if the client sends a representative, or if the client is a committee. There is a tendency among clients to remember what they wish to have heard.

A SCENARIO: CONVEYING INFORMATION THE CLIENT DOESN'T WANT TO HEAR

Lots of unexpected things can happen during the construction administration phase and it does take a skilled psychiatrist to know the best way of presenting all kinds of news. While renovating a waterfront farmhouse on Shelter Island, NY, I arrived on the construction site for my first meeting with the plumbing team, ahead of the contractor, who was always late. I saw several plumbers stick their heads out of a hole in the wood floor from the basement. "So how is the plumbing looking?" I asked.

"Plumbing's OK."

I tried to extract a more detailed response. "Anything we need to remove or replace that we weren't counting on?" I admit I may have actually dropped the "g" sound at the end of "counting" to reduce the distance between us in this first meetin'.

"Yup."

"Well, like what? Can you tell me what you have found?"

"Well, we got most of the asbestos out already."

"What? You did what?" I responded. "You found asbestos and then you took out the asbestos yourselves? That's dangerous and illegal. We need to bring people in to remove asbestos, don't you know that? People who are protected and licensed. It needs to be discarded safely and properly. Where's the contractor?"

"Lunch. Found something else, too."

"Another problem?"

"Might be."

"What?

"Bones. In the basement. And they ain't no deer bones. It's somebody. All cut up with a power saw, too."

Conveying news like this needs several people skills. Separating the messenger from the message for your own personal safety. Breaking each part of the message into resolvable units rather than one impossible situation. Putting yourself at the side of the client as someone who will work to resolve the issues. Allowing the client to see this small glitch in the scope of their entire life. One can tell the client almost anything if it is done in the right way.

CONCLUSION

Walzworkinc.'s contract administration process is certainly not considered standard in the industry. But our approach is extremely successful in encouraging and supporting responsive and intelligent design solutions. While our process is unique to our firm's personality, our success has to do our ability to be responsive, flexible, and able to effectively communicate to the many different players in the entire design process. This approach allows us to arrive at a different solution. And that is what our clients are looking for—a solution that is created just for them.

Bibliography

Stockebrand, Marianne. *Donald Judd: Architecktur* WestFälischen Kunstverein Münster, 1989.

35

Contract Administration: Getting Started

GREGORY SWITZER, AIA, NCARB
with **ROBERT T. SUTTER**, AIA, NCARB

Like contract documentation, the contract administration phase of a project requires a different set of competencies from the earlier phases of a project. The competencies required during this phase are less focused on the aesthetic of the project and more administratively focused and entail looking at issues of costs, schedules, and code compliance.

The administration phase is critical to the success or failure of the project. Contract adminsitration, the last phase of a project, is often one phase the client remembers. If this phase is successful in the client's mind, the client will likely consider the entire project successful. However, if this phase is unsuccessful, no matter how well the team performed in earlier phases, it is this failure that the client will likely remember.

THE PERMIT PROCESS

When it comes to the permitting process, most jurisdictions have different requirements. Before design professionals proceed with design or prepare documents, they should understand what is required and how long it will take to obtain approval for a permit application. If designers invest in some advance planning and develop a clear understanding of a particular jurisdiction's permit process, they may actually help speed permit applications along by knowing when to use resources provided by the jurisdiction and by ensuring that contractors plan for inspections.

Permit applications involve much detail, not only in terms of the information the applicant must provide, but also in terms of the administrative steps through which each application must pass. Be certain to consider the following elements:

- *Applicable codes, federal law (ADA), and local requirements*

- *Proposed "use" of the facility versus that for which it may be presently approved*

- *Applicable area calculations (gross, net) and identification of project area (key plan)*

- *Scope of work and legal description of project premises (lot, block)*

- *Obtaining building owner approval in the case of tenant fit-out projects*

- *Required reviews (planning board, building department, fire department, preservation commission)*

- *Time needed to process applications*

- *Cost of making the application (usually 1 percent of the cost of the work)*

- *Streamlining options that may be available (self certification, self inspections)*

- *Required information on the plans (occupancy group, construction type, applicant data, construction cost, egress and fire resistance data, critical dimensions)*

- *Required information on forms (owner, applicant, contractor, insurance requirements, notarization)*

In some ways, the time just before the application is submitted is as significant as the application process itself, because what happens in this period will do much to determine how quickly and smoothly the applications procedure will be. In general, if designers can arrange to have the local building official conduct a preliminary review of the application before it is formally submitted, the project is likely to be reviewed and approved more quickly. During this preapplication time, the jurisdiction can be petitioned as necessary to reconsider or grant exceptions to the codes. A planning or zoning review may be needed if the proposed "use" of the facility is changing. Designers should keep in mind that these types of reviews add time to the process, from as little as a few weeks to as much as a few months. Moreover, the time available just before the application is made is critical to making sure that the team carefully checks the completeness and accuracy of plan review submissions for approval prior to permit. Even a minor typographical error can lead to unnecessary delays.

Although it is generally helpful to take advantage of streamlining options that may be available to expedite plan approval and inspections, designers need to evaluate the consequences of these options. Consider the pros, cons, and liability of undertaking these options, which frequently transfer the responsibility of the jurisdiction to the responsibility of the design professional, contractor, or client. Sometimes, it may be desirable to use a third-party expediter to process the application on behalf of the client if time can be saved.

Even when the permit is issued, the permit process has not ended, and designer professionals must remain vigilant to make certain that the project is completed according to all conditions imposed by the permit. During construction, the design professional must compel the contractor to undertake the necessary steps leading to required inspections. If contractors continue to work past the point where an inspection is required, they may need to uncover a piece of completed construction, a step that can lead to unnecessary cost and delays. At project completion, design professionals should be aware of the approvals that are needed from the jurisdiction before occupancy can take place.

Professional trade organizations such as the AIA have published detailed methodologies on the permitting process in their *Handbook of Professional Practice*, 12th ed., Volume 2, section 3.72.

THE BIDDING PROCESS

The interactions of various codes and the complexity of a project involving multiple systems and many inspections complicate the permit process. The same complexity is a feature of the bidding process. In what follows, we detail some key considerations that can help designers control who is likely to bid and how they will respond, and identify potential problems with the project in advance.

Preparation of Bid Set

Part of the design professional's interaction with the client involves completing construction documents, even if they are only for bidding purposes (i.e., 75 percent completion to 100 percent). Designers should always review in great detail, and as a separate task, the construction drawings that are used for purposes of pricing. This pricing review must take into account the expectations of the other parties involved, namely the general contractors and their subcontractors, building or property owners, and managers. To generate the best results from the bidding process, designers must understand that they will need more than a comprehensive set of construction documents—they will need to provide more detailed information about various components. At first glance, the drawings will always illustrate the level of detail and information that the contractor needs to construct the project, but often the designer should include basic information that may not affect the architectural essence of the project but will provide for a more complete interpretation by the contractor of the designer's submission. The key is to leave as little as possible for interpretation. With this in mind, there are a few simple methods, that have proved to be ideal for projects of any size or type.

Projects involving a construction management process will require special consideration for bidding. In these projects, trades may be split apart from the overall job and one another. Without information from the design professionals, individual contractors will not have information about how the work they are bidding on may be affected by others' work. This type of bidding process requires unusually tight coordination since bids may be solicited at different time intervals.

Contractors find it useful when, in addition to the actual contract documents, they receive an itemized list of key items to be considered in their take off and costing exercises. Typically, this detailed list should be organized in accordance with the room or area numbers for interior finishes and requirements and general notations, which should reference the plan. An example of such would be:

ROOM 100
RECEPTION AREA

- Building standard carpet (Upgraded from Building standard/cost: $20.00 uninstalled) with marble surround
- 3-way switch for general lighting
- 2 core drills for power/data
- Electronic strike and release to reception desk. Programmable keypad for door release at public corridor side.

- Class E tie-in
- Fire strobe
- 4 outlets
- Emergency lighting with battery backup
- Paint all walls and door frames
- Drywall ceiling
- 12 down lights
- Millwork reception desk
- Herculite doors with accessible hardware and concealed closers
- Building standard hollow metal door to adjacent interior corridor

Your list can be as detailed or as simple as you like, but it should be synchronized with the level of detailed information in your construction documents. Other things to consider are fire extinguisher enclosures, egress signage, blinds or special treatments for windows, and ADA-compliant hardware and appliances. Remember that the more details you provide, the less room there is for oversight by the contractor. Similarly, know what contractors look for on drawings for cost and, even more important, where they look for certain information within a set of construction documents.

The next rule of thumb is quite simple: place notations or special requirements on the documents where they are most obvious—that is, a note about a special requirement should appear on the sheet to which it pertains. This is a good habit, especially for bid documents, and can help to eliminate the problems that arise when design professionals write catch-all general notes at the beginning of the set. These general notes can be overlooked, confusing, redundant, or irrelevant to the actual project. In contrast, page-specific notes allow contractors to bid realistically.

Professional trade organizations such as the AIA, ASID, and AGCA have published detailed methodologies on the bidding process in their respective handbooks of professional practice and by-laws.

Contractor Pre-Qualification

Before bids are taken, the design team should compile a long list of possible contractors for consideration. It may identify firms through advertisement, past experience, lists maintained by the building owner, or other means. In addition, the team should prepare a list of criteria that are important to them in selecting a contractor. Consider such things as financial stability, years in business, reputation, on-time and on-budget completions, assigned staff, quality of work, references and satisfaction, and any requirements for union labor. Once the team has evaluated each long-listed firm, it can then narrow the number of possible contractors to a reasonable number. Consider market conditions and size of the job in determining the number of contractors. We suggest a minimum of three and maximum of six for the typical interior fit-out project.

RFP Preparation

Request for Proposal (RFP) preparation is perhaps one of the most important items of the entire bidding process, and designers must follow a standard process with very little deviation if possible. The RFP will succeed only if the design team conscientiously prepares a form of request that is comprehensive and project specific. The form of request should include the following key elements:

1. *Project Description.* Briefly describe the project in terms of location and size. Include a general scope of the work to be performed by the contractor. Keep it simple. It is not very important to be very detailed here, just describe the essence of the work to be performed.

2. *List of Drawings.* The RFP should always incorporate a comprehensive list of drawings and their issue dates. It is important for the contractor to know that the set of drawings received is complete.

3. *Bid Form.* The RFP should include a bid response form. This form allows you to specify how you wish to receive the bid information back from the contractor. Typically, each trade is broken down into its constituent parts, with unit and or line-item costs for the project. The bid form is provided for the purpose of evaluating bids equally and to determine the appropriateness and completeness of each submission.

4. *Terms and Definitions.* Incorporate a list of definitions for terms used in the RFP, regardless of how rudimentary they may seem. Such a list leaves little room for interpretation.

5. *Scope of Services.* Provide a detailed scope of services indicating the responsibilities of the contractor.

6. *Project Schedule.* Indicate the project start date and any other critical project dates.

7. *General Provisions.* General provisions includes project guidelines for bid submission, requirement of site visits prior to bid submission, and contractor due diligence.

8. *Substitutions.* Provide a clear policy of how substitutions will be addressed.

9. *Insurance Requirements*

10. *Other Project Requirements.* Other requirements which should be considered as part of the RFP include an attachment of building, landlord, or property requirements, rules, and regulations.

11. *Other Attachments.* A particular project may require that the RFP include additional attachments. The standard form of contract between owner and contractor such as the AIA Document A101 or A107 should also be considered.

12. *Submission.* In the interest of competitiveness and discretion, sealed bids, delivered to the client at a time and place of mutual agreement, are essential. Submissions on municipal projects may require special procedures and they may also involve purchasing units or agents.

Again, the RFP preparation process will establish how contractors interpret project concerns, parameters, rules, guidelines, and form of contract. It is very important to follow a cohesive format and always provide parameters for submission.

The form of response as previously mentioned, is essential to the evaluation of bid responses. Typically, one of the most difficult tasks of the design professional during the bid phase is to evaluate what "is" and what "is not" included in the contractor's submission. If your submission guidelines are clear and include the above structure, this process becomes quite simple. Figure 35-1 is the culmination of a well-prepared Request for Proposal.

SAMPLE REQUEST FOR PROPOSAL

Mr. John Watson,
President
XYZ Contracting Company
123 New York Avenue
New York, New York 10022

Re: **Request for Proposal – General Contractor
Design Firm Project No.**

Dear Mr. Watson:

On behalf of the Owner, **Client Name; The Design Firm** Name is seeking to obtain bid proposals from a General Contractor, who shall be retained as a member of the project team, responsible for the completion of the project as described herein.

I.   <u>**PURPOSE:**</u>

    A. The services involved will be those of a General Contractor and it is intended that the contract between our client and the successful firm would be a modified AIA Standard Form of Agreement Between Owner and Contractor (AIA A101, Latest Edition) and will include the AIA General Conditions (A201, Latest Edition) as well as Supplemental Conditions, copies attached. The successful firm will become part of the project team consisting of The Design Firm the MEP engineering firm **XZY Mechanical Engineers** hereinafter (MEP Professional) and the expediting firm, **Expedite R-US**.

II.   <u>**PROJECT DESCRIPTION:**</u>

    A. Interior alteration for our client, **Project Name** as it pertains to space recently leased at **address**. **Project name** will be occupying approximately 10,000 rentable square feet of executive office space on the 2nd and 3rd floors.

    B. The contract documents are as follows.

        1.

a) Interiors		b) Engineering	
<u>No.</u>	<u>Description</u>	<u>No.</u>	<u>Description</u>
xx	Title Sheet	xx	Mechanical Plan
xx	Legend & General Notes	xx	Electrical Plan & Specifications
xx	General Notes/Specifications	xx	Electrical Specifications
xx	General Notes/Specifications	xx	Sprinkler Plan & Specifications
xx	Composite Plans	xx	Plumbing Plan & Specifications
xx	Partition Types; Elevations; Details, Etc.		
xx	Finish Plan & Details		

        2. <u>Documents</u>

          a) This RFP
          b) AIA A101 Owner-Contractor Agreement - Stipulated Sum
          c) AIA A201 General Conditions of the Contract for Construction
          d) Applicable terms of Lease between Building Landlord and Owner (Tenant)
          e) Building Rules and Regulations

FIGURE 35-1

Sample Request for Proposal (RFP).

III. **TRADES INVOLVED (BID FORM):**

The following form is provided for Owner's convenience in bid analysis. Omission of a line item or consolidation of items under multiple lines does NOT relieve the performance of work called for in the contract documents.

General conditions	$_____
Insurance	$_____
Filing	$_____
Permits	$_____
Demolition	$_____
Concrete	$_____
Masonry	$_____
Metalwork and structural steel	$_____
Millwork	$_____
Waterproofing	$_____
Fireproofing and fire stopping	$_____
Roofing	$_____
Hollow metal work	$_____
Storefronts	$_____
Hardware	$_____
Glass	$_____
Acoustical ceiling	$_____
Drywall and carpentry	$_____
Flash patching	$_____
Wall base	$_____
Tile and resilient flooring	$_____
Carpet	$_____
Painting and wall-covering	$_____
Toilet compartments and accessories	$_____
Raised access flooring	$_____
Specialties	$_____
Furniture	$_____
Signage	$_____
Equipment	$_____
Elevator work	$_____
HVAC	$_____
Plumbing	$_____
Sprinkler	$_____
Fire Alarm	$_____
Electrical	$_____
Communications cabling systems	$_____
Security systems	$_____
Audio/visual systems	$_____

SUBTOTAL	$_____
Overhead and Profit	$_____

TOTAL BID	$_____

Note: "NIC" denotes work, which may be separately contracted by Owner. General Contractor shall, however, include all coordination, supervision and general conditions for any "NIC" trades in the base proposal.

IV. SCOPE OF SERVICES

If you are the successful Bidder, the scope of services shall require execution of AIA A101-Owner\Contractor Agreement, Stipulated Sum. Work shall be in accordance with AIA Form A-201 General Conditions of the Contract for Construction attached hereto. Your scope of service shall also include the following items. The listing of these items as an omission or exclusion on your proposal shall NOT relieve the performance of the required services as a part of the stipulated sum base contract.

1. Full-time site supervision and construction management of day-to-day operations and schedules including but not limited to weekly project meetings, as well as establishing and coordinating meetings with subcontractors to expedite the construction process as required.

2. Project expediting and administration to assure proper scheduling of trades, materials and supplies. Identification of any long lead items and pre-purchasing of same as required to meet project schedules. Preparation of guarantees and operation documents and commissioning of all systems and components with the Owner prior to final completion.

3. Obtaining all necessary permits required of jurisdictions having approval over the project, including but not limited to environmental tests (asbestos), filing of all work types for approval (except in city where OT work type is filed by others), payment of all fees, pulling of all permits (including OT work type and equipment use permits in city), securing inspections (except in city where contractor shall retain RA/PE acceptable to Owner to conduct all controlled inspections for all work types and retain licensed tradespersons to self-certify applicable work) and approval of all work and securing final approval of the work by certificate of occupancy (except in city where a letter of completion issued by the Department of Buildings may suffice for Ateration Type II projects).

V. TIME

A. Time is of the essence, but shall not give rise to any claim for non-workmanlike performance or quality other than a "first-class" installation. Critical dates are as follows:

- Start construction no later than or about **DATE** with all major trades, long lead items, etc. and finish on accelerated schedule as soon as possible.

B. Completion of all punch list work, if any, must be performed no later than thirty (30) days after substantial completion. Failure to achieve final completion by this period may result in a forfeiture of retainage.

C. Provide Gantt schedule for entire project breakdown by all trades including required time for permit approvals, shop drawing turnaround, and all "NIC" trades.

VI. CONTRACT INFORMATION

A.   See Part IV Scope of Services.

B.   General Requirements:

B.1   By making and submitting a Bid Proposal, the Bidder represents:

a. That they have carefully examined and understands the Bidding Documents, and his Bid is made in accordance therewith.

b. That the Bidder has visited the site of the proposed Work, is fully familiar with local conditions and other conditions and regulations where the Work will be performed,

FIGURE 35-1 (Continued)

and has correlated his observations with the requirements of the proposed Contract Documents and has included such requirements in his Bid.

c. That the Bidder has utilized complete sets of Bidding Documents in preparing Bids; neither **Client** nor the Design Firm and its Consultants shall assume any responsibility for errors or misinterpretations resulting from the use of incomplete sets of Bidding Documents.

d. That the Bidder has included all sums to cover the cost of the Work and any portion thereof, including all fees, coordination fees, overtime, shipping, freight, delivery, and other added sums as required and specified within the Bidding and Contract Documents. After the execution of the Contract Agreement, no consideration will be given to any claim of misunderstanding of Bidding and Contract Documents.

The submission of a Bid will be construed as evidence that such examinations and stipulations in the Bidding Documents have been made and that all amounts/costs for performing the proposed Work or portions thereof are included. Any later claims for labor, equipment, materials, fees, or for any difficulties encountered on any item stipulated in the Bidding Documents shall not be recognized.

B.2 Bidders shall promptly notify The Design Firm, and **Client** of any ambiguities, inconsistencies, errors, or discrepancies in, or omissions from the Bidding and Contract Documents. Any clarifications or interpretations required shall be requested in writing at least five (5) calendar days prior to the date for receipt of Bid. In addition:

a. The Owner and The Design Firm along with their Consultants shall be the sole judges of the interpretations of the Bidding and Contract Documents.

b. Any interpretation, correction or change of the Bidding Documents will be made by Addendum. Interpretations, corrections, or changes in the Bidding Documents made in any other manner will not be binding, and Bidders shall not rely upon such interpretations, corrections and changes. Each Bidder shall ascertain prior to submitting his Bid that he has received all Addenda issued, and he will acknowledge their receipt in his Bid.

c. In all cases where a discrepancy between items, description and model number, assemblies, details, engineering vs. architectural coordination, and between drawings and specifications exist, the Contractor shall include in his bid price, the more expensive nature. This shall hold true of all work throughout the entire course of the work.

d. **Substitutions:**

1. The materials, products and equipment described in the Bidding Documents establish a standard of required function, dimension, appearance and quality to be met by any proposed substitution.

2. No substitution will be considered prior to receipt of Bids unless written request for approval has been received by The Design Firm at least five (5) days prior to the date for receipt of Bids.

3. Approval or disapproval of requested substitution is by The Design Firm, any decision will be final. If The Design Firm approves any proposed substitution prior to receipt of Bids, such approval will be set forth in an Addendum.

4. No substitutions will be considered after the Contract award unless specifically provided in the Contract Documents.

B.3   All other work shall be considered as occurring in normal working hours. Bidder shall identify any additional expected overtime costs as a separate line added cost in his Bid, stating the scope and nature of each such costs.

B.4   The Bidders will include in his Bid all costs (including overtime) for removal, new installation and reinstallation work for any plumbing, ceiling (take-down and reinstallation), electrical or telecommunication work, mechanical work, or other work under his Scope of Work included in the Bidding Documents that is required on the vacant, or occupied and operational floors above, below, or adjacent to the Demised Areas.

B.5   Bidders will include in his Bid a listing of all Insurance Certifications, Bonds, Release of Liens, or other requirements per the Owner's Lease Agreement with the Landlord/Building Owner. Procurement of same will be required by the time of Contract and Agreement. Costs of such items shall be included in the Base Bid sums of this Bid submittal.

B.6   The Bidders will include as part of his Bid any costs stipulated in the Bidding Documents that pertain to filing, controlled inspections, etc. as set forth in the drawings and section IV.3 of this RFP.

C.   The General Contractor shall conform with all Building Rules and Regulations.

D.   The General Contractor shall comply with all obligations from Tenant's Lease related to alteration as attached to this RFP. Proposals must include all costs reflecting insurance requirements, delivery hours, etc. as specified in lease or Rules and Regulations.

E.   No hazardous materials, as in the case if asbestos is present, will be utilized/installed in this work.

F.   All invoices shall be subject to retainage of ten percent (10%) to be released upon final completion of the work as provided for in the Contract Documents.

VII.   **INSURANCE**

Upon signing of the Construction Contract, the General Contractor shall furnish to **Client** and The Design Firm certificates evidencing the existence of the following:

A.   Workmen's compensation insurance covering all persons employed for such work and with respect to whom death or bodily injury claims could be asserted against Landlord, **Client** and The Design Firm, or the demised premises.

B.   General liability insurance naming Landlord, its designees, and **Client** and The Design Firm. as insured, with limits of not less than $3,000,000.00 in the event of bodily injury to any number of persons in any one occurrence, and with limits of not less than $500,000.00 for property damage. The General Contractor, at its sole cost and expense, shall cause all such insurance to be maintained at all times when the work to be performed for or by Owner is in progress. All such insurance shall be for company authorized to do business in New York, and all policies, or certificates therefore, issued by the insurer and bearing negotiations as evidencing the payment of premiums, shall be delivered to the Owner.

C.   Contractor's Insurance: The contractor shall secure, pay for and maintain until all work is completed, such insurance as will protect him and **Client** and The Design Firm. from claims under Workmen's Compensation Acts, Workmen's Occupational Diseases Act, and from any other claims from damages to property or for bodily injury, including death, which may arise from operations under this contract whether such operations be by this contractor or anyone directly employed by either of them. Such insurance shall cover all contractual obligations which the contractor has assumed including the "Indemnification of Owner" agreement.

FIGURE 35-1 (Continued)

D. Indemnification of **Client** and The Design Firm.: The contractor shall defend any and all suits brought against **Client** and The Design Firm, by any employee or other person (whether employed by the contractor or not) for damage or property and/or injury to persons (including death) alleged or claimed to have been caused by or through the performance by the contractor of the work, and shall indemnify and hold harmless **Client** and The Design Firm, Inc. from and against all claim or claims arising out of the work performed by the contractor; also, the contractor shall pay, liquidate and discharge any and all claims or demands for bodily injury (including death) and/or loss of or damage to any and all property caused by, growing out of or incidental to the performance of the work performed by the contractor, including damage to the building and other property of the owner and including all damages for the obstruction of private driveways, streets, alleys and all cost and expenses of suits and reasonable attorney's fees. In the event of any such injury (including death) loss or damage (or claim or claims therefore) the contractor shall give immediate notice thereof to **Client** and The Design Firm. Insurance required above, A., B., C., shall be maintained continuously during work. Certificates shall provide for notices of cancellation of not less then 90 days. Indemnification, above D., shall survive the completion of work.

VIII. **SUBMISSION OF PROPOSALS**

The following submission requirements shall strictly be adhered to. Due to time constraints., if proposals are not submitted <u>exactly</u> as indicated, proposal will be rejected. No exceptions will be made.

A. Proposals shall be submitted on company letterhead and signed by an authorized representative.

B. Proposals shall be submitted in the exact format per Article III of this RFP.

C. No telephone, telegraphic or unsealed proposals will be accepted.

D. Provide five (5) relevant projects completed within the past three (3) years including base contract value of approved change orders and client contacts (name, address, telephone).

E. List of Project Team Members and their qualifications to be included.

F. The Owner reserves the right to reject, with or without cause, any or all proposals submitted, to waive any formalities therein, or to accept any proposal where it may appear to be in the Owner's best interest to do so. The cost of Contractor's bid proposal submission is to be borne by Contractor regardless if the proposal is accepted, cancelled or rejected.

G. Delivery - Sealed proposal (Labeled Bid Enclosed) shall be delivered no later than **Date at 4:00 PM**.

Attention:
Client Contact,
Client Title
Client Name
Client Address
City, State, Zip Code

Provide a copy in sealed envelope (Labeled Bid Enclosed) at the same time to:

The Design Firm Name
Address
City, State, Zip Code

Late or incomplete proposals will be rejected. All proposals shall be binding for a ninety-day period after submission.

F. For all inquiries, information, clarifications and visits to the site, etc., contact **Name** at (phone number).

END OF RFP

Walk-Throughs and Clarifications

No project will succeed if the contractor cannot easily interpret what the design professional intends. Designers can greatly assist contractors to better understand the project and the work required to complete the project if they hold pre-bid conferences or walk-throughs (preferably at the proposed new project location). It is here that the design professional and the potential bidders meet and discuss issues or clarify questions pertaining to the project.

The design professional should be very conscious of the questions asked and provide not only oral replies but written ones as well. All questions and responses given during the walk-through should be forwarded in writing to all in attendance. This practice alleviates any misinterpretations about what was said during the site visits and again allows for written documentation of what is required for a comprehensive submission. The same should be done for all questions or clarifications asked pertaining to the project throughout the bid process.

Bid Opening/Compliance

The design professional should establish a formalized procedure for the receipt and opening of bid materials. Regardless of project type, bids should be opened in the presence of the owner or a designated owner's representative. Before the submissions are evaluated, the bids should be recorded and submitted to the project file as received for future reference.

Further, all submissions should be governed by simple guidelines for compliance, in an effort to ensure the timely receipt of bids, format of bid content, and how bids are received. Designers should consider the standard requirements:

- *Proposal cost information should be completed in the exact format provided in the RFP.*

- *Proposals should be submitted on company letterhead and signed by an authorized representative of the general contractor (GC).*

- *Telephone, telegraphic, electronic submissions, or unsealed proposals should not be accepted.*

- *Ask for key project staff (GCs) to be assigned to the project.*

- *Establish a deadline for submissions. Be detailed.*

Evaluation of Bids

Bid evaluation requires the time and expertise of someone familiar with the project and the construction process. It is important for this individual to have the authority to address the corresponding contractors with questions for the purpose of determining whether their bid submissions are complete. As a rule of thumb, the evaluation process requires that the responsible person prepare a spreadsheet to compare the line-item costs of each bidder.

Figure 35-2 is an example of the level of information such a spreadsheet may entail.

This process of bid review is also called "leveling" and is a critical step in understanding the contractor's view as to the value of the job. It allows the design team to see how the bidders have thought through what is really required to construct the project. Pay very close attention to any list of exclusions, alternates, and substitutions submitted in their response. The leveling process should address any exceptions to the RFP:

- *Omitted items*

- *Clarified items*

- *Missing items*

- *Conflicting terms and conditions*

In each case, the bid leveling review should result in removing the exceptional item, or placing an add/deduct cost next to the item. In this manner, all bids are equally compared.

Award of Contract

The design professional should always send a letter to the unsuccessful bidders to thank them for their interest in the project. Similarly, it is customary to provide the successful bidder some form of written notification to officially inform them that their bid has been accepted before the signed agreements are returned. This letter should also include any information regarding the project kick-off meeting, start dates, and any forms or additional information required before construction commences.

COMPANY XYZ

BID ANALYSIS
Leveling Spreadsheet

Design Firm Project #

NIC BIDDERS		
BIDDER	BID	REMARKS
MILLWORK		
Millworker #1	$ 160,000.00	* Cushions not included
Millworker #2	$ 149,900.00	
Millworker #3	$ 146,420.00	
Millworker #4	$ 220,300.00	* Cushions not included
CARPET		
Carpet Installer #1	$ 36,072.75	* Includes Sales Tax
Carpet Installer #2	$ 28,145.00	* Includes Sales Tax
Carpet Installer #3	$ 29,221.82	* Includes Sales Tax
Carpet Installer #4	$ 30,692.12	* Includes Sales Tax
SIGNAGE		
Signage Vendor #1	$ 2,485.00	
Signage Vendor #2	$ 2,300.00	
CARPET		
Addendum #4 (Stone to Carpet)		
Carpet Installer #1	$ 42,116	
MILLWORK (Painted Doors)		
Addendum #4		
Millworker #2	$ 148,400	
Millworker #3	$ 142,420	

FIGURE 35-2

COMPANY XYZ

BID ANALYSIS

Level Spreadsheet

Date:

Design Firm Project #

	CONTRACTOR #1	CONTRACTOR #2	REMARKS
1. Demolition	$ 750	N.I.C.	
2. Concrete & Masonry	N.I.C.	$ 900	
3. Fireproofing	N.I.C.	N.I.C.	
4. H.M. Doors & Frames	$ 2,100	$ 2,000	
5. Hardware	$ 6,500	$ 6,489	
6. Drywall & Carpentry	$ 47,000	$ 48,700	Includes blocking
7. Lath & Acoustics, Metal Clg.	$ 55,000	$ 53,000	
8. Metal Work & Steel	$ 20,000	$ 9,100	
9. Millwork			See Below
10. Paint/Wallcovering	$ 14,000	$ 11,918	
11. Carpet V.C.T. Base			See Below
12. Window Treatment	$ 2,000	Included in #17	
13. Stone Work, Ceramic	$ 20,000	$ 25,245	
14. Glazing/Glass	$ 58,000	$ 59,102	
15. Appliances	$ 600	Included in #17	
16. Convector Enclosure	$ 14,000	Included in #17	
17. Projection Screen, Specialties	$ 1,650	$ 35,270	
18. Fabric Panels	$ 2,750	Included	
19. Signage			See Below
20. HVAC	$ 60,000	$ 55,000	
21. Plumbing	$ 8,000	$ 8,875	
21A. Flash Patch	Included	Included	
22. Electrical	$ 300,000	$ 295,000	
23. Fire Alarm	Included	Included	
24. Roll Down Grill	$ 2,400	Included in #17	
25. Permits	Included *	Included	*No price submitted - Estimated Cost
26. Filing	Included *	Included	*No price submitted - Estimated Cost
27. Insurance	Included in #28	Included in #28	
28. General Conditions	$ 51,476	$ 70,000	
29. Overhead & Profit	$ 20,287	$ 19,646	
TOTAL BASE BID	**$ 686,513**	**$ 700,245**	

Millwork	$	165,000	$	156,497	
Carpet V.C.T. Base	$	30,000	$	32,500	
Signage	$	4,417	$	4,858	*No price submitted - Estimated Cost
N.I.C Totals	$	199,417	$	193,855	
Total including NIC Trades	$	885,930	$	894,100	

Alternates

1. Delete Glass Transom and Channel at Desk - Add Gyp-BD & Paint	$	(5,500)	$	(500)
2. Delete MDF Board & Base Beyond Door #27	$	(4,000)	$	(4,600)
3. Metal Convector Cover in Conference Room	$	(10,000)	$	(8,500)
4. Install Sub Zero	$	3,300	$	5,610
5. Skim Coat Elevator Walls - Mount Buttons	$	3,200	$	990
6. Delete Glass Above Soffit in Reception	$	(500)	$	320
7. Install Gyp Board Furring At All Walls, Ceilings & Beams	$	85,000	$	77,000

Schedule

EXCLUSIONS

* Elevator service, building charges. (Electrical Shutdowns)

* Overtime (Except for building Standards)

* Fire Watch

* Asbestos Removal

* Sales Tax (Submit copy of capital improvement)

* Controlled Wiring & BMS System Wiring

FIGURE 35-2 (Continued)

COMPANY XYZ

Bid Analysis
Addendum 4 & 5

Design Firm Project #

BIDDER	CONTRACTOR #1	CONTRACTOR #2
ADDENDUM #4		
ITEM #1		
Delete glass door #27 with sidelite (elevator lobby). Add hollow metal, gypsum board and paint.	$ (5,200.00)	$ (5,175.00)
ITEM #2		
Provide paint grade office doors in lieu of wood veneer	$ (3,200.00)	$ (2,150.00)
ITEM #3A		
Carpet and vinyl base in lieu of stone in Reception & Waiting	$ (12,300.00)	$ (16,000.00)
ITEM #4A		
Delete perimeter office soffits and Type 'E' lighting and delete	$ (7,500)	$ (4,700)
A' Sconces - Replace with 2x2 ceiling tile.		
Add to base bid		$ 3,500
Delete S/R at office slab & beams	$ (9,000)	$ (6,800)
ITEM #4B		
Substitute lighting in offices		$ (4,700)
Option 1	$ (4,000)	$ 22,000
Option 2	No Change	$ 28,531
Option 3	$ 10,000	$ 47,528
ITEM #5		
Delete sheetrock soffit and type J lights in Conference Room.	$ (1,500)	$ (1,500)
Extend 2x2 ceiling and install (4) type 'D' fixtures.		
ITEM #6		
Furnish & install 2x2 acoustical ceiling in lieu of 2x2 painted aluminum ceiling.	$ (5,500)	$ (1,000)
ITEM #7		
Substitute "Bretford" white board in offices to wall tackers 4'L x 50"W	No Change	$ 1,500

ITEM #8

Cleanup fire hose cabinet in leiu of replacement $ (2,500) $ (2,000)

ITEM #9

Type 'D' lighting change   No Change   See Item #12 for Add

ITEM #10

Delete price to cut glass around beams & slab at Reception - Install gypsum board $ (2,500) $ (1,600)

Add to base job ceiling $ 900

ITEM #11   No Change $ (5,000)

ITEM #12

Electrical Adds (for 4, 5, 9 & 11) $ 21,097

ADDENDUM #5

Delete various electrical & data outlets throughout $ (10,000) $ (13,800) *

* Contractor #2 has not given credit for any lighting substitutions

FIGURE 35-2 (Continued)

Summary: Bid Preparation and RFP

In short, the following should serve as a brief guide for design professionals during the bidding and negotiations portion of a project.

- *Review contract documents for bidding purposes*

- *Prequalify a long list of possible contractors*

- *Prepare the Invitation to Bid document*

- *Prepare Instructions to Bidders, Forms of Agreement, and solicitation of bids or negotiated proposals from reputable contractors and suppliers known to and deemed appropriate to the project*

- *Conduct prebid meetings with all trades*

- *Handle questions and clarifications through a formal process with all bidders*

- *Conduct formal bid opening with client*

- *Prepare a detailed spreadsheet-leveling of all trade bids and assessments of submission*

- *Confer with client on submissions/evaluation of bids*

- *Award the contract*

Selection of the Contractor

As important as the process of selecting a contractor is to the project, it is a tedious task. Still, the design professional should always be proactive in this process and become intimately involved with the client in establishing pertinent criteria for assessing contractor qualifications. The following are recommended criteria in evaluating the qualifications of a contractor: quality standards, construction and technical expertise, communication and service, experience and viability, references, and willingness to be responsible in terms of price, insurance, and dispute resolution.

CONSTRUCTION AND TECHNICAL EXPERTISE

The owner and design professional should make a conscious effort to look for a contractor who is familiar with or specializes in the proposed project type. It is important to understand that a contractor who is familiar with the project type understands important issues, such as the material specifications and scheduling required to finish the job within the proposed project schedule.

A reputable contractor will also have an in-depth knowledge of the permitting and safety processes of the local jurisdiction. The more familiar a contractor is with the project type, the better equipped the contractor is to deal with issues that may arise during the construction process. Further, a contractor who is familiar with the project type is most likely able to prepare reliable estimates for the overall project's scope.

Because of their vast knowledge of local construction practices and procedures, the qualified contractor should also assist the design professional and the owner with knowledge of products and materials that are readily available for the project and be capable of suggesting supporting information to the design professional and client when selecting products, materials, and techniques. This is extremely important where there can be a cost or time savings.

COMMUNICATION AND SERVICE

It is very important for a contractor to listen to the design professional and owner and understand what they need and want. During your initial conversation with contractors, look for a level of enthusiasm and interest in the overall project. Be particularly aware of their ability to interpret design ideas and their ability to suggest ways to make them work within the project budget. A good contractor should possess the ability to alleviate concerns about the project process. The owner and the design professional should always ask the potential contractor for examples of how similar projects were implemented and solved.

Communication is essential. Make certain that the contractor maintains a viable place of business and is readily accessible in an effort to foster maximum communication. There will always be questions and concerns during the project process that will often require an expeditious response. Communication of this sort is a key to the satisfaction of a successful relationship.

A contractor who prides himself or herself on customer services is a key to overall customer satisfaction. The general contractor and his or her employees should always be courteous, competent, professional, and attentive to details. Always check references and ask questions about the contractor's performance and the level of customer services provided.

When the construction documents are finalized, the bid process is over, and the design professionals have decided on a contractor, there are still several important factors that should be addressed before construction begins. For instance, the construction process may change the conditions of inhabitation for the duration of the project. Though in most cases these changes or inconveniences will be minor, the owner should be made aware of any such potential problems that may arise prior to the start of construction.

Let's face it, quality takes time and should be remembered throughout the process. This may constitute a wait for special-order materials, or waiting for a particular specialty trade contractor (such as a specialized wall finisher) known to be reliable. We know that delaying construction may have cost implications to the client and should be avoided.

The best way to educate your client to prepare for the construction process is to allow for communication within the entire project team, which includes the contractor. The contractor must be fully informed of the detailed activities that take place during the construction process.

EXPERIENCE AND VIABILITY

Before design professionals consider a contractor for a particular project, it is important that they confirm whether or not the contractor has an established presence. A general rule of thumb suggests that if a contractor has been in business five or more years and has been involved in projects of scope similar to the project under consideration, then the construction firm most likely maintains a solid practice and is capable of establishing a solid level of workmanship and providing warranties for work performed.

In addition to a presence, a contractor must be able to meet obligations if something goes wrong on the project. The design professional may be able to gather some information by talking with other experienced trade contractors such as subs who may have worked on previous jobs with the contractor in question. The design professional will want to know about factors that will provide a level of comfort about a contractor's business experience. Look for such things as licensing and insurance coverage.

REFERENCES

Design professionals should never hesitate to request a list of references from contractors. Believe it or not, references will almost always be the most reliable source in determining a contractor's level of experience and his or her

Clients and design professionals always approach a project with cost in mind. However, it is extremely important that the design professional and owner not engage a contractor by price alone.

ability to perform the work required. Take time to follow up on references, and try to visit one or more of the contractor's recently completed projects. Seeing a completed project may be very telling about the contractor's workmanship and ability to complete a project.

All references are not the same; there are various types of references to be considered in evaluating contractors. In requesting references, pay close attention to long-term relationships with clients. References can refer to:

1. Jobs in progress

2. Projects completed over the past year

3. Projects completed four or more years ago.

Also verify through local authorities whether a contractor has been named in any lawsuits or illegal activities.

LIST OF QUESTIONS TO ASK WHEN CHECKING CONTRACTOR REFERENCES

- Would you use the same contractor again on future projects?
- Did the project meet your scheduling requirements?
- Were you presented with change orders? If so, how were they justified?
- Were you pleased with the level of workmanship and quality?
- Did the project go over budget?
- How were the subcontractors on the job? Were they knowledgeable and reliable?
- Was the project site kept clean and safe throughout the construction process?
- Was the contractor principally involved on the project site? If so, how regularly? If not, who was involved on behalf of the contractor?

SELECTION BASED ON PRICE

Clients and design professionals always approach a project with cost in mind. However, it is extremely important that the design professional and owner not engage a contractor by price alone. Although the lowest price may be particularly accommodating, other issues should be factored into the decision-making process. The designer and owner should consider the ability of the contractor to perform the required work within the client's schedule, as well as his track record, workmanship, and references. In addition, the design professional should consider a detailed examination and breakdown of each bid to determine whether or not the bid includes all project requirements.

Mistakes have been known to happen. It is extremely important to check and double-check each submission to ascertain the accuracy of each submission. Remember, the lowest bid may initially appear to be the lowest price, but in practice it may involve serious cost increases. Only detailed bid analysis can determine whether an apparently low bid will translate into low costs in reality.

INSURANCE REQUIREMENTS

In the interest of protecting the client and the design professional, it is highly recommended that a contractor maintain proper insurance throughout the entire project process. The design professional should be aware of basic coverage that should be required for most projects. In addition, the design professional should also be aware of the requirements established by the property owner and require the contractor to request such requirements directly from the property owner to ensure that they are all met. Types of coverage typically required include:

- **Workman's Compensation Insurance.** *Protects the owner and design professional in case a worker is injured on the property.*

- **General Liability Insurance.** *Covers the owner and design professional in the event the contractor damages the owner's/building owner's property.*

- **Automobile Insurance.** *Protects the owner in the event that a contractor's vehicle damages another vehicle on the property under construction.*

The design professional must receive a contractor's certificate of insurance. Request that a certificate of insurance be provided by the contractor's insurer and delivered to you directly from the insurance provider. This practice protects both the design professional and the owner/property owner. Receipt of a certificate of insurance generally suggests that the insurance is valid and is in the form of an original. Further, all insurance should name the owner of the project, the building owner, and the directors and employees as additional insured to maximize the coverage umbrella.

LICENSING

Design professionals should always verify whether or not a license is required to perform the services being offered to their clients. Check governing authorities to confirm such requirements and to ascertain whether or not the contractor's license is valid and up to date. Where law does not require licenses, it is vitally important to investigate all references and business practices of the contractor in great detail.

DISPUTE RESOLUTION

Before a design professional engages a contractor, it is very important that all parties understand the rights of your clients concerning dispute resolution. This policy should be clearly established in writing as part of the contract between the owner and contractor. If you, as the design professional, are responsible for engaging the contractor on the client's behalf, you too should have a clear understanding of how disputes are to be resolved and how they may affect you. It is extremely important to have a legal professional review all such contracts to ensure that a reasonable means of dispute resolution is covered. Typically, clauses contained within the agreement between the design professional and the client, the agreement between the client and contractor, and the agreement between the design professional and the contractor provide for mediation or arbitration if a dispute occurs. Meditation and arbitration are generally less expensive than lawsuits as a means of resolving disputes.

CONTRACTOR SELECTION SUMMARY

The process of selecting a contractor is not an easy task and requires a great deal of diligence on behalf of the owner, design professional, and contractor. Keep in mind the following key components in establishing a process that is fair and reasonable in the selection process:

- *Quality standards of the contractor should be evaluated.*

- *Refer to industry standards from AIA, ASID, AGCA.*

- *Construction and technical expertise.*

- *Communication and service should always be explored in certifying contractor qualifications.*

- *Experience/viability are key factors in selection process.*

Make sure the service provided during the contract administration portion of a project is clearly defined in the proposal of services provided to the client.

- *References should always be checked.*

- *Selection based on price should not be the determining factor; track record and reliability should be considered as part of the selection process.*

- *Insurance requirements.*

- *If required by authorities having jurisdiction over the project, always verify the validation of licenses required of the contractor.*

- *Dispute resolution should be clearly defined in the form of the contract between the owner or design professional and the contractor.*

MANAGING THE BUILDOUT

Once the contractor is chosen, design professionals may have the contractual responsibility to manage the actual work done on the project. Make sure the service provided during the contract administration portion of a project is clearly defined in the proposal of services provided to the client. Further, it is important for the design professional to discuss these services with the client at the outset of the project. This is extremely important as a way to clarify issues of responsibility between the owner and the design professional. Design professionals typically provide the following sorts of oversight and communication responsibilities during contract administration.

- *A representative of the design firm should periodically visit the project premises to assess the progress and quality of the work performed by the contractor. During these visits, the design professional should visually inspect the premises and determine if the work is proceeding in accordance with the construction documents.*

- *Representatives of the design firm should at all times have access to the work and have a fiduciary responsibility to recommend to the client the rejection of any work which does not conform to the contract documents.*

- *A project representative of the design firm should attend regularly scheduled job meetings with the contractor to review overall project progress and assist with any required clarifications.*

- *The design professional should also prepare field reports, bulletins, and field orders if required.*

- *The design firm should always review and take appropriate (in a timely manner) action on contractors' submittals such as shop drawings, product data, and samples, for conformance with the design concept of the work as outlined in the construction documents.*

- *Based on field observations, the design firm should always review the contractor's application for payment to confirm the percentage of completion.*

- *Change orders for design and scope impact for uncovered conditions or approved revisions should be reviewed by the design professional and should always be discussed and agreed on with the client prior to providing approvals to proceed with the change request. However, it is important to stipulate that the design firm should have authority to order minor changes to the work scope that do not involve an adjustment in the contractor's contract cost or schedule.*

- *At the completion of the work, the design firm should always prepare a punch list of deficiencies for remedy by the contractor, and should, on completion of the punch list, attend a compliance walkthrough.*

The following services are usually recommended as an additional level of support during construction to oversee the activities of general contractor/subcontractors. Often these services provide the client with an extra level of accountability for a timely project delivery.

- *To act as the client's project representative with respect to management of the project during construction*

- *Receive, analyze, and process payments for all approved invoices*

- *Review and negotiate all change orders for necessity and time and cost impact*

- *Provide daily field presence as may be necessary during construction*

- *Maintain a spreadsheet of project costs*

- *Interface with the contractor, subs, and suppliers to a degree practical to assess project performance*

- *Monitor shop drawings, material orders, and deliveries by the contractor*

- *Monitor contractor's schedule for sub trades*

- *Source alternative suppliers for discontinued, late, or damaged material shipments*

- *Coordinate client vendors (e.g., datacom/telecom providers, movers, furniture installers) with contractor and arbitrate any back-charges or scheduling issues*

- *Provide item-by-item monitoring of contractor's punch-list completion*

- *Resolve all final payments and claims*

Professional trade organizations such as the AIA, ASID, and AGCA have published detailed methodologies on managing the build-out in their respective handbooks of professional practice and by-laws. These methods may govern the process based on the form of contract used to retain the design professional and contractor.

CONCLUSION

There are myriad tasks the design professional takes on to realize the efforts of the design phases of a project. Careful attention to detail will always be the key factor in the implementation and the successful completion of any project.

The preceding sections were written to illustrate the various components of the post-design process that design professionals should follow. The exact process may vary from firm to firm, but it is important to understand that a level of order and consistency should be maintained from project to project, regardless of the project size or scope. This allows the design professional a system of checks and balances and, thus, a level of comfort from the bidding and negotiations phase through the actual project build-out.

The sections of this chapter were written to illustrate various components of a thorough approach to the administrative portions of the project process. Of course, several processes may be modified to compensate for existing internal workings, but the end result is typically exemplified by strict adherence to a formalized process. The following should serve as a brief list of those things to which special attention should always be given.

1. Always review contract documents thoroughly before sending them out to bid. If possible, have a checklist in place to review the basics as far as format and critical filing information.

2. Know your jurisdiction as it pertains to codes that may impact your project.

3. Know the capabilities of those who are to perform the work for you, namely, contractors—always check references.

4. The owner and design professional should make a conscious effort to look for a contractor who is familiar with or specializes in the proposed project type.

5. Leave little room for interpretation. Bid documents should be clear and concise.

6. Know from whom you are soliciting bids. Prequalify your contractors at all times.

7. The format of proposal requests should be comprehensive and project specific.

8. Time and expertise of someone familiar with the project being designed and the construction process should be allocated to evaluate contractor proposals.

9. Written notification should be the only method of notification that a bid has been accepted.

10. Educate your client throughout the project process and allow communication within the entire project team.

11. The design professional should be very conscious of the questions asked and provide not only oral replies but written responses.

12. The design professional is always aware of the basic coverages required for projects.

13. Design professionals should always verify whether or not a license is required to perform the services being offered to their clients.

14. Before a design professional engages a contractor, it is very important that all parties understand the rights of the clients concerning dispute resolution.

15. Make sure the service provided during the contract administration portion of a project is clearly defined in the proposal of services provided to the client.

16. Document the entire process.

Mana

gement

36

Goals of Project Management

KATHY ROGERS

Design professionals see themselves as good managers. To succeed, designers must manage time, staff, their needs, and clients' expectations; they must allocate resources, motivate, guide, communicate, and learn. When designers are accomplished at managing a business, a professional life, and the complex bases of knowledge they must master, "project management" may seem to be business as usual, but on a larger scale. Yet this approach discounts the complexities of project management, and may lead design professionals to involve themselves in responsibilities that will ask too much of them if they are not prepared. Project management is the act of leading a group of people through a process to achieve a goal. Successful project management requires that the design professional employ leadership skills, management skills, professional and industry knowledge, and practical experience. It is also critical that the designer who acts as a project manager understand people and what motivates them. The project manager role is based on good communication and listening skills and good people skills, including respect, trust, and patience.

Project management is also a discipline that requires a special and broad skill set. Design professionals can benefit from understanding project management as a set of interrelated responsibilities. This chapter will first identify the key components of the project management task, then go on to detail the responsibilities that the project manager must undertake and the factors that contribute to (and detract from) successful project management.

THE KEY COMPONENTS OF PROJECT MANAGEMENT

The People

Ideally, the group involved in a project becomes a team working together. The team includes, at a minimum, in-house design firm staff and the client. It is also likely to include specialty consultants and, as the project progresses, contractors and vendors. The project manager must therefore understand the relationship of the work of each group to each other group and to the accomplishment of the total project. Everyone, directly or indirectly, looks to the project manager to guide the effort. A successful project manager has developed the skills to work with many different kinds of people, and to orchestrate those individuals into a strong, cohesive team working toward shared goals.

The in-house staff encompasses not only design professionals, such as programmers, interior designers, architects, and engineers, but firm management, administrative support, accounting staff, and technology (information systems) support staff. The client may include representatives from different levels of the client organization, or from different business units, departments, or agencies within the client organization.

It is most common for the team to include specialty consultants whose expertise does not reside within the design firm. Examples of such expertise include lighting, acoustic, audio-visual, security, food service, and information technology design. Depending on either the resources of the design firm or the way the team has been put together for a specific client project, another design or consulting firm may provide basic design services such as mechanical, electrical, plumbing, and fire protection engineering, and building code consulting. It is increasingly common for the team to include relocation consultants whose responsibility it is to plan and manage every aspect of the client's move to the new facility. Design firms frequently form associations or joint ventures for the purpose of providing all or most of the services required for a specific project.

Teams sometimes include the real estate brokers responsible for acquisition of space, either through lease or purchase. When a client engages a broker to provide oversight, the client relies on the broker to protect the client's interests. Brokers frequently offer oversight services such as selection of the design firm(s), project scheduling, and cost management. These oversight services are in addition to the traditional project management responsibilities in these areas provided by the design firm.

No matter what its size at the inception of the project, the team will expand over the course of the project. The team's size will depend largely on the size and complexity of the project. At a minimum the team will grow to include the general contractor and his subcontractors; furniture manufacturers and dealers; and information systems cabling and hardware vendors. It may also include vendors from specialty areas such as the audio-visual vendors; food service vendors; sound masking vendors; and security vendors.

Depending on the size of the project, the number of people in each of these groups can vary from a few to many. Each group is made up of individuals with differing experience, attitude, goals, approaches, and personalities. Some of the groups will be managed directly by the project manager in order to accomplish the work of the project. Even though the project manager will not manage the work of other groups directly, these groups will rely on the project manager as an interface between themselves and others. If each group is to perform well, the project manager must coordinate all efforts.

The Process

The project process encompasses the phases of the design effort, from pre-design services through contract administration. The project manager is responsible for leading the team through the process, by establishing that process and guiding team members through every step. As the project begins, the project manager must establish the infrastructure within which the team will execute each phase of work until the project is successfully completed. This infrastructure includes all of the supporting processes of establishing scopes of work, contracts, work plans, quality standards, communication protocols, documentation methods, fee budgets, project schedules, project budgets, etc.

Once this infrastructure has been created, the project manager must guide the team through the phases of work within the context of a defined scope of services, contractual agreements, staff hours and fee projections, quality standards, communication and documentation methodologies, and an approved project schedule and budget. While it is critical that the project manager continually monitor the progress of the project against this context, monitoring is not enough: effective project management is a proactive rather than a passive activity. The project manager must actively guide and coordinate the team effort if the team is to move successfully through each phase of work and meet quality, time, and cost objectives.

The Project Manager

The project manager is the team's orchestra leader, using his or her baton to direct the different groups of people at the right time, through many tasks and activities, to achieve the goals of the project. If project managers want individual team members' efforts to create a whole, they must make sure that these efforts occur within a framework that takes into account knowledge relevant to each component of work and how each component relates to the overall project. This coordination effort is key to the success of any project. In order to be successful, a project manager must have good technical knowledge and understand people.

The project manager's technical knowledge comes from experience. Experience begins with design education and expands when design professionals work in the profession, performing or participating in the execution of components of project work. A project manager would find it difficult to understand how a project is made up of individual components without the experience of performing those components and seeing first hand how they come together. This includes both the design and business components of work, such as scopes of work, contracts, fee projections, staff hour projections, etc.

The most successful project managers understand people not only as team members but as individuals. These project managers have learned not only that the whole of a team is greater than the sum of its individual parts, but that all individual team members must be valued if they are to contribute effectively to the team. In order to get a group of people to work as a team, the project manager must have developed good people skills and good communication skills. The project manager can best ensure the success of the individual, the team, and the project by creating an atmosphere of cooperation, teamwork, and individual responsibility through leadership and empowerment.

OBJECTIVES COMMON TO ALL DESIGN PROJECTS

The objectives of every project are as varied as the clients and design firms who come together to execute the project. At the most basic level, however, the objectives for every client and design firm are the following:

FOR THE CLIENT:

- *A project delivered within established time and cost parameters*

- *A project that meets organizational, functional, operational, and business goals*

- *A project that supports and enhances the lives and work of the clients' employees or residents*

- *A project delivered by a team that understands the client, that listens and responds to the client, and that uses its professional knowledge to guide the client through difficult and unfamiliar decisions*

- *A project that supports the professional goals of the individual client members*

FOR THE DESIGN FIRM:

- *A project that meets the financial goals of the design firm*

- *A project that utilizes the resources of the firm*

- *A project that challenges the staff and allows them to grow professionally*

- *A project the firm will be proud of—a good example of the firm's work*

- *A project that satisfies and hopefully delights the client*

- *A project that promotes a relationship between the client and the design firm*

The project manager is responsible for understanding the objectives of each group, for structuring a project process that supports these objectives, and

The most successful project managers understand people not only as team members but as individuals. These project managers have learned not only that the whole of a team is greater than the sum of its individual parts . . .

for guiding the team through the process. A project manager's success can be measured by whether the client is happy at the end of the project, whether the design team feels professionally fulfilled by the process and the project, and whether the project is a financial success for both the client and the design firm.

A Happy Client

A happy client is the best client. Every client deserves to feel good at the completion of his or her project. The design firm typically benefits too, from a satisfied client, either through additional work and a long relationship with the client, or via reference, with new clients. The project manager is the primary client contact and has the major responsibility for keeping the client happy. Successful project managers understand that happy clients believe that the project manager listens well, communicates clearly and regularly, and works to satisfy or exceed clients' expectations for the project.

A happy client believes that he or she is being heard. The project manager fosters this belief first and foremost with good listening and communication skills. It is imperative that the design firm, led by the project manager, hears and understands what the client is saying. The project manager must ask questions so that the design firm can understand the real concerns and issues being expressed by the client. The best way to do this is to develop good communication with the client. Good communication includes understanding the client's communication style, frequent communication, and the use of tools for documenting all communication. A happy client typically believes that he or she is being heard and directing the work of the design team.

In addition, a happy client feels that the project process, which may be unfamiliar, at least at the start of the project, is comprehensible and does not add additional stress to his or her life. Frequently, the client representative has been asked to take on the responsibility for the project in addition to normal job responsibilities. Whether the project is an additional task or the main job responsibility for the individual, projects are fraught with stress—deadlines, decisions, construction problems, etc. The project process should not in itself create additional stress. If the client can count on the project manager to lead him clearly and calmly through the myriad of decisions, issues, and problems, the client will indeed be a happy client.

Furthermore, a happy client feels that the work of the design firm is meeting the established expectations and objectives of the client. Very frequently, clients have not worked with a design firm and have not experienced the design process. For the design professional, each project offers new opportunities for the design firm to deliver a project that exceeds expectations and delights the client. For the client, it is critical that the process is working toward meeting his or her established objectives, on this project. Frequently, a client will not realize until the end of the process—typically when the space comes on line—that the work of the team truly exceeds the expectations and objectives.

Finally, a happy client believes that quality, as defined by each client, has been achieved. Quality may pertain to the overall design of a new facility, to the materials specified, to the building systems engineering, to practical details, to the absence of errors, to the perceived value of the facility against the cost—or to all of these. The project manager cannot achieve quality without establishing processes and procedures within the design firm and with the client/design firm team. The project manager is responsible for establishing and enforcing these processes and procedures. Even though this responsibility requires a rigor that may be difficult to deliver in the heat of a project, especially when project schedules are tight, that rigor costs the design firm little compared to what would happen if the processes were not monitored and enforced.

A Professionally Fulfilled Design Team

The project manager is responsible for providing opportunities for professional fulfillment for his or her staff. Project managers can easily become so focused on serving the client—sometimes at all costs—that they overlook the professional fulfillment of the design team. If the individuals on the design team are not challenged, given the opportunity to produce quality work and to grow professionally, the immediate project may suffer, but the design firm will suffer in the long term. It is increasingly difficult to find and retain staff due to the shortage of professional staff and the economic stability the country is experiencing. The work of a design firm is nothing more than the work of individuals. All of the firm's credentials, standards, and procedures are nothing if the corporate memory walks out the door. To retain valuable staff, the project manager must perform a difficult balancing act: balancing the client and project requirements with the individual requirements of his staff. The project manager must have an astuteness and attitude, borne of experience, about what motivates and inspires people. The client can only benefit from the leadership of a project manager who achieves this balance.

A Financially Successful Project—for the Client and the Design Firm

If a project is to succeed for the client, it must be a financial success: it must meet established budgets. It is equally important that the project be a financial success for the design firm. Design practices are businesses. No design practice can exist long term if its products—the services it sells—are not financially successful. The project manager, more than any other individual on the client/design team, holds the key to the financial success of the project for both the client and the design firm.

Competition is typically fierce for design projects, and as a result professional service fees remain highly competitive. Fee negotiations between clients and design firms are typically tough negotiations. Yet clients do want to work with firms that are financially sound. Most clients realize that it is reasonable to expect to pay a fair price for design services. Their problems grow exponentially when a design firm incurs financial difficulties while delivering their project.

Once a fee has been established, it takes a skilled project manager, utilizing a variety of tools, to guide a project through the entire process and achieve financial success. As will be discussed later, the process begins with planning the project and establishing expectations, and continues throughout the project with ongoing monitoring of hours spent against progress on the project. If every project proceeded according to the initial project plan, it would be relatively easy to monitor the expenditure of fee. Rarely does a project proceed that easily. A project manager must have the skill and flexibility to manage change over the course of the work and still achieve financial success.

For the client, he or she will develop budgets, and manage the delivery of design services and products to those budgets. For the design firm, he or she will establish the number of hours required for each component of work, and manage the design team to deliver the work for those hours. Change, whether due to scope or schedule change or any number of other variables, must be monitored because it impacts the financial success of the project for both the client and the design firm. Good planning, communications skills, an in-depth understanding of the total design process, and proactive management skills are the keys to financial success.

RESPONSIBILITIES OF THE PROJECT MANAGER

The project manager touches every aspect of the project, from marketing the project to closing out the last details of the project. Project managers are typically identified during the marketing of the project, when the design firm makes initial contact with the client, by responding to a Request for Proposal and/or presenting qualifications and a project approach to the client. The project manager is almost always a significant player in these preproject efforts. The project manager is also typically the last person from the design firm to have contact with the client. After the project is complete, the client has occupied its new facility, and the rest of the design team has moved on to other projects, the project manager will still represent the design firm to close out remaining contractual, financial, and administrative issues.

Project management responsibilities fall into eight broad categories:

1. *Understand the client*

2. *Document project goals*

3. *Develop a project work plan*

4. *Establish communication and documentation protocols*

5. *Establish project budgets*

6. *Maintain client relations*

7. *Lead the project*

8. *Manage change*

Understand the Client

In order to complete a successful project the design team must first understand their clients. They must understand their clients' objectives—as an organization and as the individuals they will work with daily on the project. The design team needs to understand their clients' expectations, perceptions, and biases about the project; how they make decisions; their organizational and individual values; and what will make the organization and individual successful. Projects are increasingly complex, and frequently involve multiple client groups. The project manager must implement procedures that enhance the team's capacity to understand fully the clients' and the firm's conflicting objectives, requirements, expectations, and values. These procedures must encourage listening, the exchange of information, and self-knowledge.

The project manager must lead the design team to recognize that they bring their own expectations, perceptions, biases, and individual and firm values to the project. It is important to sort through the differences and similarities between the client's values and the firm's and team members' values. Frequently this sorting happens during the process of selecting the design firm. It is very common for clients to select a design firm they perceive to share values and expectations about the project at hand. When this occurs it can create a very positive and comfortable working relationship from the start of the project, a natural "fit."

Whether this sort of "fit" occurs during the selection process or not, it is critical for the project manager, as the leader and integrator of the effort, to create the conditions of listening and responding in which the sense of "fit" can develop. The project manager must listen carefully to the client and help the design team understand their client. It is incumbent on the project manager to help the design team find ways to tailor their approach to the project to best serve their client. The success of the project depends on the ability of the client and design firm to work together.

Once a design firm has been selected, the best opportunity to begin to understand the client occurs during the dialogue associated with documenting project goals and developing or refining the scope of services and schedule for the project. At this stage, the design firm and the client must address many issues if they are to develop a clear scope of services and project schedule. This conversation offers a wonderful opportunity for the project manager and design team to get to know their client. The astute project manager asks questions, listens to, and observes the client throughout this process and shares his or her understanding with the design team.

Document Project Goals

It is easy for a design team or a client to get caught up in a project in such a way that the original goals are forgotten, and when this happens there is usually a day of reckoning when everyone is reminded of the original goals. However, such a situation can be avoided if the project manager focuses the team by involving them in documenting project goals. The client's goals for the project should be clearly documented before the design team begins work. The project manager should initiate this documentation, based on his or her understanding of the client, and share it with the design team.

The team will find that it is very worthwhile to discuss how they feel they can achieve the client's goals through their work on the project. The discussion should include project approach, budgetary and schedule parameters, and design objectives. This exercise provides an opportunity for the team to begin to work together, and typically results in parallel sets of goals for the effort—those of the design team and the individual. It is positive for the team and individuals to see each new project as an opportunity for growth. The client can only benefit from this attitude.

Once the team has documented the project goals (those of the client, the design team, and the individuals on the team), the project manager can use them as a benchmark to be referred to throughout the course of work on the project. The project manager should ask the team to review the goals at key points during the work on the project—typically at the beginning or end of a major phase of work. Such benchmarking will help reorient the team.

Just because project goals are documented does not mean that they cannot change during the course of a project. There are many reasons a client's goals for a project can change. Once the project manager senses that the goals are changing, it is critical to discuss the change with the client; assess the impact on the project; address any scope, schedule, and contractual issues; document the change; and share it with the design team. They cannot be held accountable to deliver a project which meets client goals if they are not made aware of those goals.

Develop a Project Work Plan

The most critical phase of any project is planning the work. The work plan establishes the scope of work, including detailed lists of tasks, activities, and deliverables; the schedule for the work; and the professional service fees associated with accomplishing the work. The work plan is the basis for all contracts with the client and with consultants. It establishes the baseline for monitoring the progress of the work—the completion of tasks, activities, and deliverables within a specific time frame and expenditure of staff hours. If a work plan is developed, the likelihood of having a successful project increases dramatically. Without a plan the team may get lucky, but as the number of complex issues associated with design projects has increased, it has become increasingly risky to work without a clear plan.

The work plan is a road map for everyone on the team to follow. If the project manager monitors it throughout the course of work on the project, any deviations from the work plan will be known immediately. The project manager then has the opportunity to make the necessary adjustments to get the project back on track, or make modifications to the work plan. Such modifications may be as simple as a fine-tuning of the work plan, without contractual, schedule, or budgetary adjustments. If significant changes have occurred, it may be necessary to reexamine the project scope, schedule and fees, which may mean contractual modifications.

As important as it is to develop the work plan as a tool, it is equally important to strike the right balance between an underdeveloped and an overdeveloped work plan. If the work plan is not fully developed, it will fall short of being a useful tool against which progress on the project can be monitored. If it is overdeveloped, it will become so cumbersome that it will either be ignored, or the project manager will spend so much time managing the work plan itself that there will be no time to lead the project.

A work plan is typically initiated during the marketing effort associated with the project—responding to a Request for Proposal or presenting the design firm's approach to the project during a marketing interview or presentation. Once the firm has been selected for a project, the project manager should begin to develop a detailed work plan, with participation from key project team members and in communication with the client. This process provides the opportunity for understanding and buy-in by both parties.

There are seven key components to a work plan, which the project manager must establish before the team starts substantive work on the project:

1. *Scope of work*

2. *Tasks, activities, and deliverables*

3. *Contracts with the client and consultants*

4. *Design team*

5. *Project schedule*

6. *Internal project budget*

7. *Administrative procedures*

SCOPE OF WORK

The scope of work must be clearly defined or refined by the client, project manager, key members of the design team, and consultants together. This process builds solid working relationships and provides the basis for the contract between the client and the design firm and consultant firms.

Essentially, the scope of work describes what is to be done—what is the project. All project parameters and requirements should be reviewed. Project parameters include the client's goals for the project, the design firm's project goals, the phases of work necessary to deliver the project, the deliverables associated with each phase of work, the overall project budget, and schedule expectations.

At the center of this discussion is the question of overall level of design for the project. While the broad phases of work may be the same for a relatively straightforward project and one that is more complex or "high end," the scope of work for the two projects will be quite different. This discussion should address aesthetics, level of design detail, material selections, maintenance requirements, and environmental concerns. It should also address issues such as the requirement for flexibility in the design to accommodate future change, start-up and long-term operating costs, and the impact of anticipated future business plans on the design of the facility. If all project parameters and requirements can be discussed, everyone can start on the same foot.

A client's availability and decision-making process may affect the project, either in time, money, or relations. It is important to discuss these topics so that everyone has the same expectations as the project moves forward. Some clients are unaware of the amount of their time a project may require, and their unavailability may slow down the project. Some clients are unable to devote time to the project except for key decisions and rely heavily on the experience of the design firm they have selected to produce the project. Some clients have lengthy review processes by multiple parties for decisions and approvals, which require time and extensive presentation materials.

TASKS, ACTIVITIES, AND DELIVERABLES

Once all of the project parameters and requirements have been discussed and documented, the next step is to develop a detailed list of the tasks, activities, and deliverables necessary to fulfill the scope of work.

At various points in the project, the tasks and activities result in products, or deliverables, that document a component of work. In order for the team to begin work on the project, it must be broken down into components of work that combine and build upon each other to produce the desired project. In order for the project manager to be able to build a project with detailed tasks and activities, some of which are sequential and some of which are parallel, the project manager must have the right kind of project experience. He or she must have been a part of similar efforts—either as a team member or as leader. The more detailed the list of tasks, activities, and deliverables, the easier it will be for the team to execute the project. The structure of their work is in place. The project manager has thought through each component of work and how it interfaces with other components of work. The team has their road map and is free to focus their creative energy on the work itself.

The list should be used to select or finalize the design team or consultants based on the skills required for each component of work, and to determine the number of staff hours required to produce the project—and thus the fees for the project. Even though normative data exist for fees per square foot for interior design services, the best way to calculate professional service fees and explain the fees to the client is to show how the fees are based on staff hours for each task, activity, and deliverable. It is a mistake to enter into a contract with a client until this step is complete.

If, when calculated, the fee is too high, the project manager can make reductions by adjusting the tasks, activities, and deliverables. Ultimately, it may be necessary for the project manager and client to review the list together if there

Design projects are a team effort. The best teams function like a well-oiled machine—each part working in the right way and at the right time with the other parts.

is a serious disparity between the number of staff hours required for the tasks, activities, and deliverables for the scope of work, and the fee the client has in mind. This is the time, before a contractual agreement has been signed, to come to agreement on the detailed work and the costs associated with it. Either the design firm may need to alter its approach to the project, or the client may need to rethink the fees it anticipated for the scope of work.

CONTRACTS WITH CLIENT AND CONSULTANTS

Once the client, design firm, and consultants are in agreement about the scope of work and detailed tasks, activities and deliverables, contractual agreements should be finalized so that all parties understand their baseline agreement. Contracts legally bind the client, design firm, and consultants together. The contract should document all agreements that address expectations, scope of work, and the plan for executing the work. The firmer the understanding and agreement on these issues among all parties, the less likelihood there is of misunderstandings during the course of the project. The contract is a legally binding document, but it should also be viewed as a tool, to be referred to over the course of the project when questions about scope or methodology arise. It is the baseline understanding among client, design firm, and consultant firms. If conditions or expectations change during the course of the project, the contract can and should be modified to reflect changes to the baseline.

DESIGN TEAM

Design projects are a team effort. The best teams function like a well-oiled machine—each part working in the right way and at the right time with the other parts. The project manager's role will be easier and the opportunity for a successful project greater if this level of performance can be achieved. It will also be a more rewarding project for all involved.

The first step in structuring the design team is to select the right number of individuals with the right skills and experience for the work. Ideally, the individuals will also have the right attitude and motivation for the project. The project manager will probably work with the management of the design firm or discipline leadership, depending on the organization of the firm, to establish the team. The size of the design team, and the number of hours of work required of each member of the team, is directly proportional to the magnitude of the overall effort and the time frame in which the work is to be completed. It will take a smaller team a longer period of time than a larger team to produce a large project.

Establishing the size of the design team is a balancing act. Too few people can extend the schedule, necessitate overtime work, and possibly affect the quality of the project. Too many people can cause inefficiencies, make it difficult to manage the project to an agreed-upon number of staff hours and fee, and possibly also affect the quality of the work.

Once the team is selected, it is the project manager's responsibility to document the organizational structure of the team, including team members from consultant firms. Everyone associated with the project should have a clear understanding of who the team members are and what their respective responsibilities are.

The individual team members, their role and responsibilities, and the organizational structure of the design team should be shared with the client. The design team, in turn, should understand the client's organizational structure and representatives for the project.

PROJECT SCHEDULE

Once the detailed tasks, activities, deliverables, and design team have been established, the project manager can develop a project schedule. The project schedule is a tool. At the beginning of the project it is used to show graphically how the work will be accomplished over time for both the client and the design team. It can be used to fine-tune the project approach in order to achieve the client's schedule parameters. It can also help determine staffing resources required for the project. As the project moves forward, progress on the project should be monitored regularly against the project schedule.

The project schedule simply overlays the tasks and activities on a calendar of days, weeks, or months, depending on the level of detail of task or activity. The tasks and activities are assigned a duration of time based on the amount of work and number of people producing the work. They are also laid out in the sequence that the work must be accomplished. The schedule will typically show deliverables and key decision points, meetings, or presentations as milestones.

Project managers must determine how detailed the schedule should be for each team and each project. Project schedules can be as simple as a schedule which shows the five or six major phases of work, or as complex as a schedule which is hundreds of lines long, showing many tasks and activities within each phase of work. A large, complex project typically requires a rather detailed project schedule that assists both the client and design team in managing the work and monitoring the progress on the project.

As changes occur, to the goals, the scope, the tasks, activities, and deliverables, or to the design team, the schedule should be revised to reflect these changes. Project schedules are essentially a diagram of the work. They show tasks that may be performed on parallel tracks of work and tasks which cannot start until all or part of another task is completed. Interdependent tasks form the critical path for the project. Before the project manager can change the completion date of the project, he or she must adjust the tasks that form the critical path in some way. For example, in order to complete the project earlier, the project manager may be able to apply additional staff resources to specific tasks on the critical path. Sometimes, the contract and negotiated fees can accommodate such changes. Other times, the contract and negotiated fees will also require adjustment.

INTERNAL PROJECT BUDGET

The contract between the client and the design firm may structure the design firm's compensation in a variety of ways: as a lump-sum fee; as a fee per project square foot; as a percentage of construction; as a not-to-exceed fee based on approved tasks, activities, and deliverables; or at hourly rates for professional services. No matter how the firm will be paid by the client, the project manager should establish an internal budget for the project based on number of staff hours per phase of work, task, or activity, at the appropriate salary costs. Once this budget is established it will provide a key tool for the project manager to measure progress on the project.

The approach and methodology for establishing internal project budgets varies widely from firm to firm. It is the most important tool for monitoring the progress of the work and, ultimately, the financial success of the project. Still, no matter what the firm, the internal project budget generally contains several components. It identifies all design firm labor costs, reimbursable direct project costs, nonreimbursable direct costs, overhead and profit, consultant costs, and costs associated with any special services.

Labor costs are simply the compilation of all salary costs for the staff assigned to the project. Labor costs are based on individual salaries plus direct personal expenses (DPE)—those costs associated with the employment of people, including benefits such as vacations, holidays, health insurance, pensions, etc. In order to preserve confidentiality, many firms address average labor costs by category or discipline.

Direct costs are those costs that are incurred in the execution of the work and include those costs associated with travel, reproduction, printing, photographs, postage, telephone and fax costs, etc. Some or all of these costs may be either reimbursable or nonreimbursable, depending on the contract with the client.

Firm overhead and profit are calculated in many different ways. The internal project budget must account for overhead and profit, however they are computed in the design firm.

Consultant costs fall into the same categories as those of the design firm. Fortunately, the project manager for the design firm typically need only manage and monitor the overall consultant fee. The project manager for the consultant firm has the same responsibilities as the design firm project manager to manage the consultant's internal project budget.

Most project managers have learned, and some design firms insist, that a portion of the design fee be set aside as a management reserve. This reserve is intended to be used to cover work which takes longer to produce than planned, and it is usually at the sole discretion of the project manager to use. Ten percent of the fee is a typical management reserve.

ADMINISTRATIVE PROCEDURES

In addition to establishing internal financial budgets, it falls to the project manager to set up all project procedures, files, and records for the project. It is important to the design firm that procedures are followed and records are maintained by the design team during the course of work on the project, to ensure that all contractual obligations are met. These records also become important historical data for future business decisions and marketing efforts.

Some firms require a project procedures manual as a part of starting every new project. The manual provides the team with project information such as client and team directories, organizational charts, and schedules. It also establishes the framework for all communication protocols and documentation procedures and formats for the project.

The project files should include the marketing materials for the project, the documented project goals, the project scope, the work plan, the schedule, the internal project budget, and all project contracts, amendments, and additional service documentation. All project correspondence, drawing files, reports, surveys, and other project documentation should be added to the files over the course of work on the project. It is important to organize both paper and electronic files.

As tedious as these housekeeping duties are, it is important that they be addressed at the beginning of the project. Once the project gets underway there will be no time to address these administrative responsibilities. The files and record keeping may be sloppy and the team will not enjoy the advantage of being able to move through the project work within a framework of established administrative rules and procedures.

Establish Communication and Documentation Protocols

Good communication is essential to the success of the project. The project manager is typically the primary contact between the client and the design team and consultants. In this capacity, the project manager establishes the way that information is transmitted among all parties. It is his or her responsibility to see that information is transmitted in a timely manner and that it is fully documented. Once a project is underway, this alone can be a full-time job. Even though other key members of the design team and consultant firms may develop communication channels with the client, it is essential that the project manager be the primary contact, so that he or she can remain directly connected to the project, constantly monitor the progress of the project, and ensure that all goals are being met.

A record of the many conversations that lead to decisions concerning the project, and the decisions themselves, is an essential part of the historical data of the project. Much of the communication on a project is verbal—telephone conversations, voice-mail messages, in-house design team meetings, project team meetings with the client, and formal client presentations. It is in these conversations and meetings that decisions are made which set the direction for the project. It is difficult for either the client or design team to look back and remember every decision, or the reason for the decision. A paper trail, which is produced throughout the course of work on the project,

Good communication is essential to the success of the project. The project manager is typically the primary contact between the client and the design team and consultants.... the project manager establishes the way that information is transmitted ...

can mitigate a lot of anxiety on the part of the client and the design team. This is especially true when questions about work based on earlier decisions arise. The best way to respond to such questions is to be able to refer to documentation of those decisions that is a part of the project record, and which was distributed to everyone on the team.

Most firms have standard formats for all project documentation. The documentation for conversations and meetings should include:

- **Telephone logs**, *which document conversations containing project data or decisions. E-mail is a good way to document telephone conversations.*

- **Meeting agendas**, *which are distributed in advance of a meeting and which notify participants of the topics to be discussed or presented at the meeting.*

- **Meeting notes**, *which document the discussion, decisions, and issues from the meeting.*

- **Action-item reports**, *which are frequently attached to meeting notes and which identify and track outstanding issues and the party responsible for addressing or resolving the issue.*

At the beginning of the project, the project manager should establish a distribution list for these documents. He or she will need to update the list throughout the course of work on the project as the number of parties involved increases. Documentation of conversations and meetings should be distributed in a timely manner. Telephone logs should be distributed immediately if information relevant to the immediate work has been addressed. Meeting notes and action-item reports should be distributed for review no later than a week after the meeting or presentation.

Other kinds of project documentation, which are important parts of the project data, include:

- **Letters**, *which are typically used for more formal communication.*

- **Memoranda**, *which are more commonly used to communicate project information.*

- Transmittals, *which should accompany every submission to the client or consultant firm as a record of the submittal.*

- E-mail, *which is commonly used to communicate a wide range of project information. It has become the preferred method of written communication with clients and consultant firms because of the speed at which information can be communicated.*

- Monthly status reports, *which summarize all activities and issues and update the project schedule for the client.*

The project manager will initiate much of this communication and documentation. It is his or her responsibility to see that all team members communicate and document in the same way. All project correspondence and documentation should be added to the project files.

Establish Project Budgets

The project manager is responsible for seeing that client budgets for the project are established and updated at agreed-upon points in the development of the project. The design firm typically has responsibility for establishing and maintaining budgets for construction and furnishings. It is increasingly common for the design firm to be asked to oversee as well the budgets for furniture inventories, audio-visual equipment, security systems, food service equipment, information systems, and relocation costs. The project manager must arrange for budgets to be developed, and he or she must also monitor and update them and communicate regularly to the client regarding them.

Some budgets are typically developed in-house, when the skills are available. Construction budgets are typically developed in-house by cost estimators. If these skills do not reside in-house, it is advisable to retain a cost-estimating firm as a consultant to the project. If a general contractor has been retained in the early phases of work, either through negotiation or as a part of a design-build process, the general contractor will be the best source for construction budget information. Furnishings budgets are also typically developed in-house. Interior designers or furnishings specialists can work with furniture manufacturers and dealers to develop furniture budgets.

Budgets for the furniture inventories, audio-visual equipment, security systems, food service equipment, information systems, and relocation costs are best developed by the consultant firms or vendors who specialize in these areas. Consultant services should be structured to include cost estimates. Vendors will provide cost estimates either for a fee or as a part of their services associated with selling the equipment.

The project manager is ultimately the keeper of all project budgets. It is his or her responsibility to establish the budgets and see that they are updated per the approved scope of work. If the project manager senses a change in the project or a decision that will affect costs, it is his or her responsibility to advise the client of this potential impact on costs immediately. The client may elect to add an additional budget update to the scope of work if the impact of the change or decision is serious enough.

The client's checkbook pays the project costs, and the client has every right to be fully informed about the costs of the project throughout the design of the project. The project manager must assume responsibility for making sure that the entire design team knows that when clients are presented with options, they should be informed of any cost differences associated with each option. No client likes to be surprised at the cost of a design that has been approved. Costs that are too high can cause difficulty for clients within their own organization. They certainly can cause bad feelings between clients and design firms. Costs that are low may be received very positively by the client. They may also be perceived to represent a missed opportunity for a better project. If clients feel that they have choices, are given cost information about each choice, and are given reliable budget information regularly through the course of the project, they will develop trust in the design firm. Without trust, the relationship between clients and design firms will be strained.

Maintain Client Relations

Everyone on the design team bears a responsibility to develop a good working relationship with the client, but the project manager is primarily responsible for tailoring the project's management to the client's needs, and for including the client in the design team.

Maintaining a good relationship with a client is a continuous effort that requires dedication, sensitivity, patience, and good listening and communication skills. It also takes understanding that it is necessary to modify project management style with every client. The project manager should make every effort to understand how the client likes to receive information, how decisions are made, the client's communication style, management style, time availability, and the level of formality the client wants to maintain in its relationship with the design firm. With this knowledge, the project manager can tailor the way the project is managed to the client.

It is also an important part of maintaining client relations to make sure the client understands his obligations in the development of the project. The client will be responsible for providing information, for arranging access to existing facilities, for setting up meetings, for making decisions, etc. The project manager can help the client fulfill these obligations by advising the client as early as possible of upcoming tasks or decisions. It is important to give clients time frames for all activities or decisions which require their time and/or coordination with other members of the client organization. Clients who have never participated in design projects are usually grateful to the project manager who guides them through the process. All clients like to feel that they are being treated respectfully and that the project manager recognizes the value of their time.

It is important for the project manager to be forthright in discussing problems with clients. Unfortunately, it is unlikely that everything will go smoothly on a project and that there will be no rough bumps along the way. Since people create projects, and people are not perfect, mistakes, misunderstandings, communication problems, documentation problems, and other challanges will be generated by the team doing the work. Clients should feel comfortable raising concerns about the project, the work, or the team with the project manager. These conversations should be handled in as professional and calm a way as possible. Clients should always feel that the project manager will be there to support them—in the good times and the rough times.

Lead the Project

Even though the project manager position includes plenty of behind-the-scenes responsibilities, the role is not a passive, behind-the-scenes role. The project manager must actively lead the project. He or she is the orchestra leader, the captain of the ship, the coach, the mentor, the negotiator, the moderator, the voice of reason, and the figure of authority.

Controlling the team's work and leading the team are two very different approaches. Certainly, in order to be successful in this role, the project manager must be knowledgeable about every aspect of the project and how the parts come together. The project manager must continually monitor the work. The team looks to the project manager to guide them. This does not mean, however, that the project manager does all of the work or makes every decision. It is the project manager's responsibility to support the team in the delivery of their work within the infrastructure, which he or she has established.

The client, too, looks to the project manager to be knowledgeable about every component of the project and also to delegate authority properly. To meet this expectation, the project manager must actively lead project meetings and communication with the client. Because client organizations are not dissimilar in structure to that of the design firm, most clients also expect the project manager to lead rather than do the work of the project team. Clients are astute in this area. They want to do business with leaders.

Manage Change

Change has become the norm during the delivery of nearly every design project. Even though project schedules are shorter than in the past, client organizations and businesses continue to change so fast that it is rare to complete a project without experiencing a change to the work. Change can occur at any point in the design process and frequently even during construction. The project manager must monitor requests for change and establish a dialogue with the client about how such changes may affect design fees.

Clients expect to pay for changes. The project manager must address the changes with the client as soon as they are known and work with the client to develop an agreement on how the cost of the changes will be addressed. It is almost impossible for everyone—the client and the design firm—to accurately and fairly address changes at the end of a project. No one will remember the details, and it will be difficult to reach agreement on costs. The design firm may not be able to recoup the cost of work already delivered. Clients may refuse to pay because they don't remember the details or because their resources have been expended. They may feel pressured to pay for work they no longer understand the depth and impact of. Not only may the design firm realize a financial loss on the work, but also a good client/design firm relationship may be affected.

The project manager should always look for ways to accommodate change to the project with the least impact on project budget, schedule, and fees. Work sequence may need to be altered or parts of the project moved ahead while the components of work affected by the change are revised. There are many creative ways to keep a project moving and mitigate the effects of change on the schedule and budget. Looking after the client's interests is one of the project manager's responsibilities. A proactive approach like this on behalf of the client will strengthen the relationship between the client and design firm and raise the level of trust the client holds for the project manager and the design firm.

CONCLUSION: VARIABLES AFFECTING SUCCESS

Many variables contribute to the success of a project manager. Other than performing the responsibilities as described above, a few particular variables, some within the project manger's control, others not, that can affect the success of the project manager, include:

Listening, hearing, communication skills.
- Listening and hearing are different. Understand the difference and practice each accordingly.

Personality conflicts.
- In dealing with people, personalities are a big factor and sometimes there are conflicts. Address the issue, and if it cannot be corrected, take action. This may include changing a member of the design team—even the project manager.

Client trust.
- Without client trust the project will be difficult for everyone—client, project manager, and design team. Work hard to earn client trust.

Design team experience.
- If the design team does not have the experience to do the project, it will be difficult to deliver the project the client expects and put a huge burden on the project manager. Structure design teams carefully to achieve a balance between experienced and inexperienced team members.

Design firm support.

- The design firm must support the project manager in the delivery of projects with staff resources, timely financial performance information, and appropriate technology. If the design firm has not put its own infrastructure in place, it cannot expect the project manager to be successful in his or her work.

Project management is a pivotal role in the business of design. It is as creative and challenging a role as the individual makes it. Project managers have tremendous opportunities not only to influence projects, but also to lead clients and design teams.

37
Managing the Internal Design Team

ERIC WAGNER

A project manager in a construction environment must be a good team leader or the project will not succeed. In this demanding environment, the project manager is either a member of the design team or, as described in this chapter, a separate entity, retained by the client to manage the entire process. In addition to establishing the construction budget and schedule, the project manager's scope of work involves assisting the client in lease negotiations, evaluating and retaining required consultants, establishing preliminary programming, and providing quality control. The project manager acquires a formal team leadership role and has been granted the authority and power to oversee the project team. Concomitant with this "macro" level of responsibility, the project manager is held accountable for the success or failure of a project. This macro level of management thus involves the potential for significant liability or for significant achievement. In some management contexts, design professionals may be able to rely to some extent on the personal management skills they have developed as members of in-house design teams. They know that an effective team leader must be influential in motivating the participants to achieve the project's objective. They should be comfortable with the tools of informal approach, trust, and credibility that project managers use most effectively to capture the interest and commitment of the team.

In the construction environment, however, interpersonal skills may be necessary, but they are not sufficient to integrate a team and allow its members to work as parts of a complex whole. Team leaders must have management and technical skills that will enable them to complete the project within the established criteria. Although the construction goal (build the required structure) of the project is often clearly understood by the project team, the project manager must give focus to the individual tasks distributed and closely monitor the coordination of this effort. This chapter sets out an approach to team leadership based on integration—understanding the connections between the underlying tasks that project managers must accomplish and procedures central to their work.

A team leader must not only monitor the cost and schedule of a project, he or she must also ensure that the team is working together in an efficient and productive manner. A project manager must establish formal standard procedures for the duration of the project, both to provide focus for the project and to foster cohesiveness. No amount of monitoring will hold team members to a standard of efficiency unless some organizational benchmark exists. This organizational procedure will create a structured project environment that will enable the team to work as a cohesive "unit" to create a sense of morale. In addition, these procedures provide a channel of communication which can clarify roles and responsibilities. During the course of a project, the team leader must communicate and create a collaborative environment. Collaboration is important not only for the final result—building the building—but also for the process. The team leader should measure the success of a project not only in terms of whether the building is completed but also in terms of whether the primary resources (people) have integrated their scope of work in a social and professional manner. Toward this end, the organizational processes should be designed not to be rigid but to provide structure; team members may adapt them, and if the processes allow for flexibility, the project manager can avoid conflicts that may arise. It is through the enforcement of these organizational procedures, systems, and methods that the project manager is perceived by the team as one who establishes order, direction, and focus in achieving the project's ultimate goal.

Perhaps the most important integrative task of project managers is their work to establish for the team the relationships between the "macro" understanding of the project and the "micro" level of scheduling. In the early stages of planning, the project manager in a construction environment must organize the implementation of the project at a macro level. Once team leaders comprehend the overall project requirements and specifications, they can determine the necessary work breakdown structure (WBS) required to complete the various tasks. The documentation of the WBS will delineate each of the tasks that need to be completed. The project manager can then delegate these tasks to the project team participants, with estimated milestone dates of completion. The milestone dates are the critical points within the project schedule that must be completed before the team can move to the next phase of the project. The schedule is an essential project management tool which will enable the project manager to understand clearly the magnitude of the project.

In addition to the overall project schedule, if a project extends over a long period of time, the prudent project manager will distribute a schedule at a micro level so that the team remains focused on the immediate deadlines. This document will outline the various tasks required to achieve the project goal. Similar to milestone dates, the critical path of the entire schedule is also illustrated, whereby tasks must be completed sequentially. In a construction project schedule, the critical path often includes the design, procurement, fabrication, and installation time frame required for a specific component, for example, an elevator or escalator. A team leader must be cognizant of the fact that project planning is a process by which he or she must integrate the project needs and specifications to achieve the desired goal. In addition, the project manager must have a clear understanding (at a macro level) of what needs to be done, by whom, and by what date.

Project managers must undertake two types of project planning: strategic and operational planning. In the strategic planning phase of a project, the team leader gathers the necessary information to carry out the ultimate goal. In the construction industry, these goals are typically long range and must be accomplished within a specific time frame. The long-range goal of constructing a building needs to be accomplished in a sequential manner that will coincide with the project schedule. For example, the concrete foundation of a building must be set in place before the walls, floors, and roof are erected. With this understanding, a project team participant can perform a series of tasks that will achieve the goal through the process of operational planning. In their book, *Management*, the authors, Patrick Montana and Bruce Charnov explain how long-range goals set through strategic planning are translated into activities that will ensure reaching the goal through operational planning.[1]

The operational plan delineates the "objectives" necessary to move toward the goal. The project manager in a construction environment may request that each participant on the design team (architect, mechanical engineer, structural engineer, audio-visual consultant, information technology consultant, etc.) complete the construction documents within a specific time frame so that construction activity can commence. It is through the strategic and operational planning process that a project manager can advocate control of the project's objective.

Project managers must undertake two types of project planning: strategic and operational planning. In the strategic planning phase of a project, the team leader gathers the necessary information to carry out the ultimate goal.

Once project managers have completed the planning necessary to provide structure to the project, to remain effective, they must control and monitor the day-to-day progress of a project and the individual performance of the members of the integrated team. For a project manager in a construction environment, control and monitoring happen best when the manager takes an active role in developing the construction documents and then visits the construction site regularly. This active role will track the daily activities of the project, which will ensure that objectives have been completed in a timely fashion. In addition, when project managers manage and control a project aggressively, they can develop individual standards of performance. These standards can be perceived as a motivating benchmark toward which the participant must work if the team is to progress to the next phase or objective of the project. This level of commitment by team participants is essential for the success of a project goal. As an "integrator" the project manager must be cognizant of the fact that he or she must be influential in motivating the project team. For this reason, part of the active role of the manager is to reward participants when responsibilities are fulfilled. To a project participant, a sense of belonging and appreciation for the project team adds a valuable dimension to a project environment and creates an enthusiastic approach to the work itself. When project managers make positive reinforcement a part of monitoring and controlling the project, they can develop the support and commitment from the participants needed to get the job done. The team participant is then given credibility in acting out his or her role in contributing to the project's success.

Controlling and monitoring day-to-day progress does not mean that the project manager must take on the role of the technical expert. Rather, the project manager's role and responsibility is that of a technical "generalist" who employs the managerial skills that will lead to the success of a project. For this reason, project managers must divorce themselves from the micro-management activities of a project. This restraint is especially necessary where the aspect of the project involves the project manager's own technical expertise: "There is a heavy temptation for Project Managers to practice their technical discipline (e.g., Hardware Engineer, Software Systems Analyst) throughout the project rather than manage the *process* of the project itself. This is a classic reason for project failure. In this case, not only are project planning and team building sorely neglected but the project also suffers from a 'myopic' or narrow technical view."[2] It becomes of ultimate importance that the project manager be perceived as the "controller" of the project without trying to micro-manage the expertise of the professionals and/or tradespeople. If project managers do ignore or override the technical expertise of other professionals, they may expose themselves to liability issues that could have been avoided if they had separated themselves from the micro-management aspects of the project.

The Importance of Technical Expertise

Even so, technical expertise is important for project managers, who are also integrated into the team and yet responsible for resolving its problems. In the construction industry, the project manager is often faced with having to solve various problems due to the multidisciplinary efforts of the various consultants. For this reason, it is important that project managers have technical experience so that they may contribute effectively to the resolution of problems. For example, an architect may be limited or delayed in the design of a space as a result of the engineers' mechanical and structural requirements. This limitation in effect may cause a construction delay that will have a monetary impact on the project budget. With this understanding, an experienced project manager can request that certain construction tasks be phased or increase the personnel when the construction documents are complete, in order to avoid delay. Although contingencies should always be considered in a construction schedule, it is through the interpersonal relationship with the team members that the project manager can address the problems at an early stage.

The project manager should possess another sort of technical expertise: understanding of management skills, in particular, management styles described in the social project management behavioral approach to team leadership. The project management industry identifies an effective leadership style as a critical skill. A successful project manager must develop various "styles" with which to interact with each project participant. The two most common behavioral approaches are the task and the employee orientation. The task-oriented approach is that of a project manager whose primary focus is to accomplish the required goal. This approach is achieved through the delegation of work tasks and responsibilities that must be completed within the requested time frame. This scope of work is closely monitored and supervised by the project manager to assure the fulfillment of the project's objectives. The employee-orientation approach is associated with the project manager who values relationships with the team participants. There is no one correct style or approach that has proven to be effective in every project team; the project manager must choose an appropriate style depending on the team participants and the environment.

Project managers must monitor the project budget and schedule, but to succeed, they must also use their managerial skills to motivate and influence the efforts of the project team. The project manager must posses a strategic desire to get the goal of the project accomplished. To achieve the desired goal, an effective team leader needs the support and commitment of the project team. In order to organize the implementation of the project plan the team leader must establish standard procedures, systems, and methods. It is through this methodical and consistent approach that a project manager can create an integrated project environment that can function as a single "unit" to achieve a common goal. In addition, the performance criteria derived from the procedural standard can act as a motivating factor for the participants in achieving the project objective. The project manager must be cognizant of rewarding the participant when these objectives are complete. Depending on the project environment and/or participants, a project manager must come to the realization that various leadership styles may be required for different projects. To manage an integrated project team, then, the project manager must integrate various complementary professional skills—technical, organizational, and interpersonal.

Notes

1
Montana, Patrick, and Bruce Charnov, *Management*, 3rd ed., Barron's Business Review Series, Barron's, Hauppauge, NY, 2000, p. 90.
2
Kezsbom, Deborah, Donald Schilling, and Katherine Edward, *Dynamic Project Management: A Practical Guide for Managers and Engineers,* John Wiley & Sons, New York, 1989, p. 183.

Bibliography

Kezbom, Deborah S., and Katherine A. Edward. *The New Dynamic Project Management: Winning Through Competitive Advantage.* New York: John Wiley & Sons, 2001.

Montana, Patrick J., and Bruce H. Charnov. *Management* (Barron's Business Review Series). Hauppauge, NY: Barron's Educational Series, 2000.

38

Managing the Consultant Relationship

RICHARD J. JANTZ

Among designers, project management is often characterized as a success or as a failure only in terms of the final outcome: a project is completed successfully if, when all of the contract obligations are met and the space is in use, the project is on time, on budget, and everyone is happy. In this view, the many different parts and pieces that make up the project as a whole are a problem, and project managers provide value because they have the skill and the knowledge that allows them to treat those parts and pieces as components of the whole project, to hold them all in place and make them work together. Of course, this view represents an important part of what design professionals need to understand about project management. However, in the eyes of the client, perception often dictates the success of a project, involving a complex set of expectations that needs to be expertly handled. Even so, it is just as important that designers who understand the big picture do not then forget the parts and pieces, and how the project manager must deal with them, sometimes in surprisingly personal ways. The view of the project manager as a monolith, or an ultimate authority, or as an expert in team dynamics, may in some cases cause more problems than it solves. How do project managers guide if they or the design team as a whole lacks expertise in a certain area?

The answer is "consultants": the project manager must find the right experts and include their skills in the design team in a productive way to provide what the project needs to succeed. To manage the consultant relationship effectively, the project manager must be able to assess not only what the project needs, and to communicate that clearly to all members of the team, but also assess what consultants need, and keep them focused on the project and motivated to do their best.

In order to truly manage a design and construction project, the project manager must identify all of the parts and pieces that make up a particular

The theory that a manager must understand the individual in order to grasp the collective is based heavily in psychology, and indeed project managers have a tremendous advantage ... when they have a solid grasp of personality types ...

project team—all of the contributing representatives, designers, and consultants—and understand not only what they contribute to the project but also what they need, in a business sense and as individuals. Project managers need to understand the team members fully as independent entities in their respective fields if they are to anticipate how the team members might react to the needs of the project from a business standpoint. Project managers also need to analyze team members in terms of how they fit together as part of the team, which defines the project's personality. Project managers can act effectively in the best interest of the project only after they truly understand the individual needs of each team member and the collective needs of the project as a whole. The theory that a manager must understand the individual in order to grasp the collective is based heavily in psychology, and indeed project managers have a tremendous advantage in building and managing teams when they have a solid grasp of personality types as defined by scholars in that field. It is imperative that project managers understand *people* in order to manage the complex relationships of the team effectively. The project manager must understand the goals of each consultant as he or she performs a professional service on the project.

COMMUNICATION AS MOTIVATOR

Once project managers have a sense of who the consultants are, what they need, and what they can provide, they can use communication skills to motivate consultants to become part of the team. They can maintain and strengthen the consultant relationship by clearly communicating goals and project objectives of both the client and the team members. For each project, the client will have a vision of what the project should ultimately encompass; project managers are responsible for ensuring that goals are communicated to and fully understood by all of the consultants. Too often, project managers believe that everyone is working toward the same goal, only to find that some team members interpreted a goal or task in a different manner. If the project manager communicates effectively and handles clients' and consultants' goals thoughtfully, the entire team will find it easier to view the project as a challenge they savor the opportunity to be a part of.

Clear communication to and between team members and consultants also contributes to keeping the team working on task and to keeping consultants working with the team, because it fosters the discipline necessary for any complex project. Project managers can strengthen the cohesiveness exhibited by great teams if they establish clear lines of communication; clearly define roles and responsibilities of all team components; set unfaltering project objectives; and act as dependable, solid project leaders. Project teams generally embrace the discipline that a good project manager will impose on a project. Discipline gives everyone around the table a defined purpose and goal for which to strive. Occasionally, a team component will not respond at all, or will respond poorly to the discipline necessary to achieve the goals of the team. In a case such as this, the project manager must make every effort to impose the discipline required by framing his or her intentions in a manner that will motivate that particular consultant. It would be easy for the project manager to remove the uncooperative entity from the team, but a true manager will circumvent the discipline problem by communicating project objectives in a way so that everyone will respond. A by-product of this approach will be the increased respect of all of the other team members, who will recognize the manager as a flexible and capable leader.

THE OBSTACLE OF PERCEPTION

So far, we have discussed what a project manager must communicate about the project, its goals, and the expectations the project manager has for every team member, including consultants. In addition to these significant tasks, project managers must also be able to communicate about their role and their style. To ensure that consultants do their best, they must make it easy for consultants to perceive that they listen, and that they are inclusive of all members of the team. The largest obstacle for any project manager to overcome is perception. A project can be executed to technical perfection, but if a consultant or other team member is left out of an exchange of information leading to a key decision, that consultant will begin to perceive that the project manager has isolated him or her, or plays favorites, and these perceptions will affect the team dynamic. It has been proven in the design field that when a consultant has a poor perception of the project manager, that consultant's productivity will be upset, and ultimately, so will be the team's. Unbeknown to the project manager, this perception can escalate to the crisis level with a single consultant, or among a group of consultants. Every manager who has led a project team has witnessed this theory of perception and its detrimental effect on the team, and knows as well that poor perception can also affect the project manager's firm: it has happened that a project is a success by all measures, yet a particular consultant denies a letter of reference. In essence, project managers must remember that for consultants who are on "the fringe" of the team, the power of perception will always overshadow any amount of effort expended.

Project managers must constantly extend themselves to all of the consultants on the team in a personal and individual manner, so that they can attempt to identify and resolve perception problems as they begin. If project managers initiate frequent, private conversations with individual team members, they can take important steps to identify and correct perception problems that can hinder a consultant's performance and future work.

Project managers can benefit from understanding what behaviors might cause consultants to form a negative impression, and how to manage themselves, as project managers, to allow consultants to perceive them positively. One aspect of project management that greatly affects consultants' perceptions is how the project manager handles the flow of information. Quite often, the project manager is privy to a large quantity of information provided by the client or user group surrounding a project. Some or all of that information needs to be disbursed to various team members to keep the team informed of the day-to-day decisions that will affect the project and the team. If the manager's judgment is wrong and too much or too little information is communicated, it could be detrimental to how the team and the consultants perceive the success of the project. Further, the project manager cannot assume that each person interprets disbursed information in the same manner. It is therefore of paramount importance that the project manager ensures that information is clear and its source is consistent (for instance, that it all comes from the PM as informer). It is just as important that the project manager follows up all written correspondence with personalized attention to ensure that all team members, including consultants, interpret it consistent with the project's needs.

Project managers must constantly extend themselves to all of the consultants on the team in a personal and individual manner, so that they can attempt to identify and resolve perception problems as they begin.

CONSISTENT APPROACH

Another aspect of project management that affects consultants' perceptions is how consistently the project manager truly treats all of the team members with equal respect. Even if a consultant is responsible for a relatively insignificant project deliverable, the project manager must allocate equal time and attention to that team member. Regardless of how small a consultant's scope of work is for the project, chances are that without the information he or she is providing, the project goals cannot be fully achieved. Further, the project manager must tap the consultants' expertise in their particular discipline to solidify the overall project goals. The manager should confer with all of the professionals on the team to corroborate overall schedule and budgetary constraints. The project leader should keep in mind that the inherent knowledge and experience that consultants bring to the table regarding their discipline is an invaluable resource, and respect the validity of information the consultant presents to the client. If the project manager issues information as important as the project schedule and costs without team approval, the team will develop a perception that their leader does not want a collaborative effort from the team. Similarly, to preserve collaboration and communicate respect, the project leader should never criticize the work of the professionals on the team in a public forum. Instead, he or she should set up a private conversation, in which it will be possible to express displeasure surrounding a task or deliverable constructively. This gesture of respect will go a long way toward rectifying the problem and avoids the animosity created when a work product is demeaned publicly. The amount of effort the project leader exhibits in response to each consultant will be returned exponentially to the project in those consultants' efforts to do good work as members of the team. Team members will always respond favorably to a project leader who exhibits respect and attention to the team.

TIMELY RESPONSE

Another component of respect requires that the project manager work not only to understand consultants' needs but to respond to them, particularly the very real needs for payment. Project managers go a long way toward strengthening the relationship with project consultants if they process contracts and requisitions for payment in a timely way. If they handle these business issues quickly and seamlessly, they clear the way for the team to focus on project goals and not the ramifications of performing work without a contract in place, or what the status of their 60-day-old invoice might be. In other words, if project managers pay particular attention to contracts and billing and communicating their status on a regular basis, they will enable the consultant to respond better and faster to the needs of the project, and their particular or special requests. For instance, if the project manager needs to expedite a project milestone, the well-paid and informed consultant will be much more willing to dedicate additional resources to the cause if no questions surrounding payment and contracts exist.

Yet another factor in consultants' perceptions that project managers respect them is the degree to which the manager avoids favoritism. Occasionally, a dispute may arise between two or more members of the consultant team. The project managers must rely on his understanding of the positions of each of the team members to resolve the issue in an amicable fashion acceptable to all of the parties involved, while never losing sight of the project goals. The project leader must be careful not to take sides before understanding all the issues, and must also complete a fair investigation of the dispute. Because most disputes have very personal components, the resolution rendered must be nonpartisan, and it must also be consistent with the overall goals of the project. The project manager should provide a full explanation of the decision to all of the parties involved in the dispute, which will go a long way toward dispelling any perception problems that the team members may harbor, depending on the resolution.

CONCLUSION

The only way that a project manager can manage the consultant relationship well is never to stop learning. Regardless of how many years of experience and hundreds of jobs he or she has completed, the project manager will learn something new that can be applied to the next team. Even within the scope of a single project, the management of the consultant relationship is also an evolving learning process, because team interactions are as divergent as the personalities that fuel them. A truly gifted project manager will learn to identify and evaluate the team dynamic, perception issues, project goals, and his or her own skills, to make the next project even better.

39

Managing the Client Relationship

FREDERICK J. SCHMIDT
JOSEPH T. CONNELL, IIDA
GINA A. BERNDT

Other chapters in this book focus in detail on the rationales and mechanics of professional practices—the day-to-day steps involved in managing a career in interior design, from making sound choices about education to specialization to business development to working on a project. In each of them, design professionals will find themselves reading often about a central character, "the client," and they will find it easy to imagine who clients might be, what they are like, what their needs might be. Designers think that they must know how to handle clients and their relationships with them; they do it every day, and firms have institutionalized, in varied ways, many aspects of relating to clients. Yet if client relationships are so easy and natural, why is it that bad client relationships develop, that clients do not return, and that often *good* client relationships may seem to depend on personality, "fit," or chance?

Designers may not think of themselves primarily as people who, like other professionals, are in the business of managing relationships. They manage ideas, vision, space, and their relationships with peoples' needs; in its best moments, their work is an art form. Yet relationship management is an art form as well, and one that designers would do well to study—and master. When designers know how to assess just who the client is, just what the client's needs are, and just how well they have been satisfied by design services, they will be designers who can sustain a business that delivers meaningful results for human beings. This chapter will look first at the "ideal" client relationship, from both the client's view and the designer's view, in terms of a feature important to both parties: total satisfaction. It will then go on to discuss how designers can manage the client relationship to best ensure that the client has a quality experience of total satisfaction. Finally, it will introduce a method designers can use to measure whether they have indeed provided total satisfaction, and how they can adjust to better provide it in future client relationships.

THE IDEAL RELATIONSHIP

The Client's View

From the client's perspective, what is the "ideal interior designer"? Each client has unique goals, constraints, and expectations, so there may be as many definitions of "ideal" as there are clients themselves. Yet there are at least three core attributes that define a client's aspirations for an effective service relationship:

- **Understanding.** *Clients are human beings who want to be heard and understood. They want to work with service providers–designers– who listen to what they say–receptively, empathetically, actively. They want designers to take their ideas into account and they want responsive answers to their questions.*

- Value. *At its most basic level, the relationship between client and designer represents a business transaction in which service is rendered and payment is made. As the buyer, the client is practically obligated to seek a fiscally responsible solution–a fair price, a good deal, an outcome that serves the organization's business needs within budget.*

- Success. *Ultimately, clients want results: not just a designer with a good reputation, an impressive client list and a host of awards, but a designer whose solution and behavior reflects a true understanding of this client's needs and motivations. Ultimately, clients want to know that the outcome the designer delivers is exactly what they need to achieve their business objectives. They want the designer to help them succeed.*

In all these areas, clients desire complete fulfillment. They want more than a little value, a bit of understanding, or a hint of success; they want *total satisfaction.* And they will reward the designer for it. For example, three Harvard Business School professors researched why certain service organizations excel. In their book, *The Service Profit Chain,* they revealed that customers who rated Xerox a five (on a five-point scale) on customer satisfaction surveys were six times more likely to repurchase a Xerox product than those who gave the company only a four. Thus, "it was quickly concluded that fours were relatively meaningless," and Xerox management set the company's sights on achieving total satisfaction as a means of sustaining and gaining business.[1]

In other words, "satisfied" is a minimum standard, and it makes no guarantee of the designer's continued success. Authors Benjamin Schneider and David E. Bowen, drawing on the Harvard research noted above, assert that "businesses must strive for 100 percent, or total, customer satisfaction and even *delight* to achieve the kind of loyalty they desire."[2] Knowing the importance of total customer satisfaction, service providers may view their customers in a new light (see Figure 39-1). Some customers are so satisfied they become "apostles" for the provider—spreading the word about the product or service to other potential customers. An effective cadre of apostles can generate tremendous value for an organization at virtually no cost. Thus, service providers are wise to invest in converting "near-apostles" to "apostles." The other end of the spectrum warrants attention as well. There we find the "terrorists," whose dissatisfaction is so great that they also spread the word, professing their bad experience with the service provider to as many listeners as possible.[3]

FIGURE 39-1
Service Profit Chain Diagram.

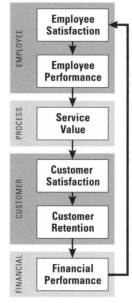

The Designer's View

To be confident that clients will come back again and again, an interior designer must ensure that clients are delighted with the services and solutions delivered. Such relationships are "ideal" for the designer because they contribute to the long-term viability of the designer's business through increased client retention and profitability. Satisfying the client is the designer's job, and achieving total satisfaction is largely within the designer's control as service provider. However, this is much more easily attained with clients who are more able and willing to "engage" the project process.

The truth is, not every organization needs or is prepared for the support of a professional designer. Organizations that *are* in the best position to engage design professionals have defined a specific business problem and are prepared to put forth the resources to reach a solution. These organizations recognize that the design of a workspace is a full-time job, even for the client, and they are ready and willing to apply their will, people, time, and resources to make decisions and advance the project process.

At an even grander scale, there are concepts embedded in the design process that go beyond the simple exchange of interior design services for payment. The interior designer's broader, altruistic mission is to create environments that meet human needs and support human activities. The most mutually gratifying relationships may be with clients who respect and share this mission and are willing to embrace the process of creating the built environment. And, as might be expected, the most rewarding relationships include an atmosphere of mutual respect. As the designer respects the client's business needs, the client respects the designer's potential to make a creative contribution to the client's business.

This is not to suggest that a designer cannot win new assignments unless both client and designer live up to "ideal" expectations. And interior designers sometimes accept work that does not fit their ideal client profile. These are the circumstances that require an intense commitment to client service and delivering total satisfaction. With proper attention and action, these less-than-perfect situations can become long-term relationships in which loyal clients return again and again for the designer's services and support.

THE PROJECT CIRCLE

The client/interior designer relationship is not a simple experience between two parties. Rather, it is an integral piece of a larger business collaboration involving a number of organizations represented by the Project Circle (see Fig. 39-2). The Project Circle depicts a key feature of design projects: inside

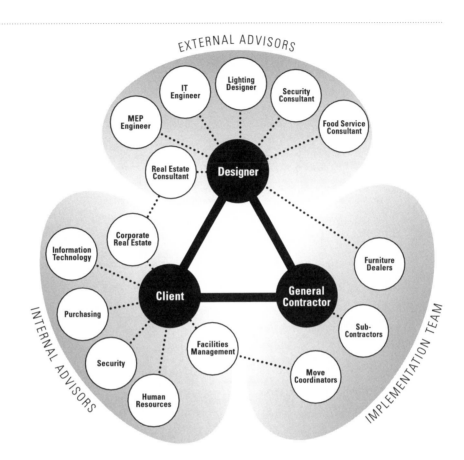

FIGURE 39-2
The Project Circle.

it is the client, a unit made up of competing interests, and surrounding the client is a web of players, all with their own professional interests and their own roles to play in providing a quality experience for the client.

Inside the Client

Within the client organization itself, several groups and individuals represent "interest groups" for which the designer must provide an integrated and workable quality experience.

• **Sponsor.** *The sponsor is "the client" personified. Generally speaking, he or she is the client's most senior person involved in the project and is a member of (or reports to) senior management. In turn, everyone working on the project—both within and outside the client organization—must satisfy the sponsor. The sponsor represents the client organization's business vision, builds the internal business case, and secures and manages funding for the project.*

- Client project manager. *Client project managers generally come from either a corporate real estate or a facilities management department. They are involved in the project's details and participate in ongoing work with the interior designer and other service providers. They are concerned with critical decisions and operational matters, such as space allocation, project scheduling, and adherence to fee and construction budgets. Client project managers also serve as a central point for communication within the client organization.*

- Human resources. *The client's human resources staff may be involved in a project from a communication standpoint. They may relay information to the design team, providing details about the organization's practices, structure, headcount projections, policies, culture, and employee behaviors—factors that define the client's needs and therefore the design response. They may also communicate with the workforce, helping the organization to manage change. For example, when a move is necessary, the human resources team often works closely with the facilities manager to facilitate the transition for employees and business groups, informing them of move schedules and particulars and fostering a cooperative environment.*

- Information systems and telecommunications. *The technology requirements are among the most critical challenges faced by the project team because they are very costly and integral to nearly all business today. Representatives from the client's technology departments can speak for current and anticipated requirements, enabling the project team to design an infrastructure that will support present and future plans.*

- Users. *The users are the people who ultimately will occupy or use the designed environment. Depending on the facility, the users may be internal or external to the client organization—employees, customers, recruits, vendors. In addition to their desires and preferences, these users depend (albeit unknowingly) on a design solution that allows for their personal safety and health.*

Each of these interest groups may claim to be entirely distinct from the rest, and each may assert that its priorities should take precedence over the rest. For example, an individual department may declare that its unique activities call for a deviation from the standard floor plan to achieve an efficient work process. The project manager, on the other hand, may hold fast to standardized space and/or amenity allocation to help reduce management costs, consolidate suppliers and buying power, maintain equity among various users, or other defensible strategies that may serve a larger objective.

Who resolves this conflict between efficiency and cost savings? Occasionally the client team is led by an authority figure who defines the priorities and makes such decisions. More often than not, however, projects are complicated by a variety of points of view, and the designer is left to reconcile the conflicts. The designer's challenge, then, is to:

- *Integrate all the interests to achieve a workable compromise. Each constituency must feel "embraced" and assured that the designer has made reasonable efforts to accommodate all points of view.*

- *Understand whose interests must be served for the project to meet the client's business objectives. Rarely can a design solution satisfy every desire of every individual or group. By identifying the client's larger business goals and realities, the designer can make fact-based decisions about the inevitable trade-offs.*

Outside the Client

As if the client's internal structure didn't hold enough challenge and complexity, an even more intricate organization develops outside the client's walls . . . a virtual team of service providers who are all part of the project delivery mechanism. The interior designer must operate effectively as a part of this team throughout the entire project process. A host of additional players around the Project Circle bring both support and challenges to the designer:

- **External project manager.** *The project manager, sometimes known as "program manager" or "owner's representative," is a third party hired by the client to ensure that all phases of the work proceed as planned. In this capacity, the project manager may be in a position to serve as advocate for or monitor of the interior designer and allied team members.*

- **Real estate consultant.** *From the interior designer's perspective, the real estate consultant is both customer and service partner*–customer, *because the consultant sometimes acts as advisor to the client, and* partner *because both designer and consultant attempt to develop and manage a solution that meets the client's business objectives. The designer's work reflects on the real estate consultant's success, and vice versa.*

- Manufacturers. *Manufacturers want designers to use their products (carpet, lighting, furniture, and the like) in the client's space. Generally, the client seeks product recommendations from the interior designer. Therefore, the manufacturer will feel compelled to make its most favorable impression on either the designer or the client. Yet manufacturers can provide a wealth of information to assist both the client and the designer.*

- Builder/contractor. *The builder/contractor uses the interior designer's plans as a framework for constructing the client's environment. Thus, the designer's input influences the builder/contractor's output. Conversely, the builder/contractor's execution may be seen as an indicator of the designer's effectiveness.*

- Other consultants. *The client or other project participants may enlist the support of other expert consultants for particular and usually highly technical areas such as mechanical, electrical, plumbing, acoustics, audio-visual systems, food service, lighting, security systems, fire protection, and structural engineering.*

If designers can collaborate effectively with everyone around the Project Circle, they can help build future business, because new assignments can come through any of these channels. Yet the designer's loyalties and focus must remain on the client and the project process. If the designer makes each decision with the client's interests in mind—not with an eye on pleasing other players—then the designer will gain a reputation for integrity. Members of the Project Circle who respect professional, responsible behavior likely will become future advocates for the designer.

Accepting Accountability for the Project Circle

Because the activities of all players in the Project Circle are so closely intertwined and contingent on one another, it can be difficult for the client to know where to assign responsibility for breakdowns or praise for accomplishments. From the client's perspective, all the players collectively hold accountability for attaining the project's goals. A wise strategy for the interior designer (and for all players, for that matter) is to think and act as the client's representative in all relationships. This can also be described as assuming a "stewardship" or "advocacy" role for the client.

Ideally, the designer will be on the "good side" of all the potential players in each of the service categories around the Project Circle–but none more than the others. Any appearance of preference could make the designer appear biased, calling the designer's recommendations into question. Was the designer really acting with the client's best interests in mind, or was the designer entering into an arrangement of "you scratch my back, I'll scratch yours" with another service provider? The designer is a professional, working to achieve the client's total satisfaction, not gain other service providers' approval. Certainly, no one wants to burn bridges with other service providers. But even a hint that a designer acts outside the client's interest can destroy the current relationship and put everlasting tarnish on the designer's reputation.

Handling the Complexity of the Project Circle

As the Project Circle illustrates, virtually any interior design project involves a complex web of players both inside and outside the client organization. And no single player–not even the client–can be completely responsible for the project experience, because so many factors are beyond one party's immediate control. Yet because anything that happens throughout the entire experience reflects on the designer, the interior designer is in a unique position of *perceived accountability*. For example, members of the interior design team do not physically build the space, hire subcontractors, order materials, or arrange for and monitor job-site safety, nor can they control unpredictable occurrences such as labor strikes or "acts of God." Yet the client's facility manager may look to the interior designer to provide guidance and delivery on the promise of a safe journey in the creation, construction and occupancy of a new space or facility.

The interior designer's challenge, then, is *to act responsibly without having total responsibility*. In the following ways, the designer must work to make accountability feasible and to influence the entire project experience without being truly liable for others in the Project Circle:

- **Be vigilant in reporting.** *Although the designer may not create the work schedule for all parties involved in a project, the designer likely will assemble a project timeline for the client by drawing upon input from many sources. The designer is not the author of the schedule, but rather the reporter. Yet if problems arise in the timeline, the designer may be implicated by mere association with any inaccuracies. The designer must be attentive and proactive in reviewing the details that come in from all parties, to make certain that the schedule represents the best estimates of those who are responsible for the activities.*

- Probe for details. *Particularly in the early stages of a project, the client (and to some extent even the designer) may be content to deal with vague information. Although the client may not want to be bothered with minutiae, engineers and contractors live in a world of facts, where details help them make safe judgments. The designer can influence a positive project experience for all parties by serving as a detail-minded strategist:*

  1. *Educating the client about the value of detailed specifications so all providers can make fact-based decisions.*

  2. *Alerting the client that the need for details will come—and when.*

  3. *Helping the client assemble details that are meaningful to the other players in the Project Circle.*

- Manage information. *Even the smallest projects involve volumes of information. Regardless of project size, the interior designer must exercise careful judgment in handling all specifications and data. The designer's task is to get the appropriate information at the appropriate time from the appropriate source. Then, he or she must deliver it in a suitable format to the appropriate users when and where they need it.*

In a now-famous interview with Charles Eames in 1972, interviewer Madame L. Amic asked if Eames had ever compromised. He replied, "No, but I have willingly accepted constraints." A thorough understanding of relevant constraints and details shapes the attributes of a design solution. Vigilance in understanding the need creates a more intelligent response—one that may solve more problems than are presented by the client or are apparent upon engagement or preliminary review.

This thorough understanding does not mean that designers step outside their field of expertise, just that they understand how their field works in connection with other fields contributing to the project. Speaking metaphorically, the interior designer is the conductor of a large orchestra working to ensure that all the players come in at the right time and play their parts with technical accuracy. None of the actions described above will take the designer outside the scope of the designer's responsibility, yet actions such as these will allow the designer to exert an appropriate measure of influence on the project process as a whole.

JUST DESIGNER AND CLIENT

It is difficult to conceive of the interior designer's relationship with a client in isolation from the rest of the Project Circle; the relationships are numerous and intertwined. However, if it is important to recognize the complex web of players involved in an overall project, it is just as important to understand the client/designer relationship. The interior designer may have limited control over the experience of the Project Circle as a whole, but the interior design team members have complete responsibility for the client's experience with their own service and outcomes. In fact, the way a designer manages a client relationship has a sizable impact on how the client will evaluate the designer's contribution to the business situation. This section of the chapter describes how interior designers can work to achieve total client satisfaction through effective business practices: building and supporting the core team, communicating effectively, and becoming a business consultant.

Build Support and the Core Team

Generally, the client expects to deal with a consistent team of a few talented, capable individuals who are attuned to the client's challenges, goals, and constraints. Typically, the design team might include a director, project manager,

In a now-famous interview with Charles Eames in 1972, interviewer Madame L. Amic asked if Eames had ever compromised. He replied, "No, but I have willingly accepted constraints."

senior designer, project designer, technical manager, and studio support staff. However, the client and design team members also need to know that appropriate extra resources and talent are available when needed. For example, the project may call for the knowledge of an expert in programming, lighting, or technical integration. The design team needs to know how and when to enlist support from such experts; and the client needs to know up front that this additional assistance may be required, as well as how specialized resources may affect project costs, if at all.

Communicate for Effectiveness

During both the predictable times of project routine and when unexpected or possibly difficult situations arise, effective communication is the strongest bridge between client and service provider. Successful communication occurs when both parties' messages are received and understood as intended. Good communication does not rule out the possibility of disagreements, but it does open the door to constructive discussion about the best course of action for meeting the client's business objectives. Designers can better ensure that clients will feel satisfied if they use the following strategies to encourage familiarity with procedures, clarity, and a heightened flow of information between individuals.

USE STANDARD COMMUNICATIONS TOOLS

Designers can accomplish some communications according to "formula," that is, where the designer follows a standardized, familiar format for project status reports, scheduled meetings, contracts, and so forth. For the designer, such tools simplify the work of preparing communications, and thus they preserve time in which the designer can develop thoughtful, creative content that will address the client's business needs. For the client, standard communications tools lend a helpful measure of predictability. Once clients are acclimated to a standard report format, for example, they will know exactly where to find the information they need—and the designer will have created a positive experience in which the client feels knowledgeable and in control.

SPEAK IN TERMS CLIENTS CAN UNDERSTAND

The process and profession of design often utilize a vocabulary that is unfamiliar to "outsiders." To communicate effectively, designers must avoid jargon or a professional lexicon hard for clients to understand. If this seems obvious, compare the following statements made by a client and design team to express the same process:

- **Client**: *"First select the architecture, then design the system, then program."*

- **Design team**: *"First develop the program, then design from the program, then build the architecture."*

In this case, the client is a multinational consulting firm with roots in information technology and systems development. Imagine how such transposition of terms and sequences could hinder a successful project launch.

In addition to creating confusion, "foreign language" can alienate the client from the designer and the design process. Moreover, a person's self-esteem can be bruised if he or she feels less knowledgeable about a subject—particularly if the subject is discussed in apparent code. Commonly, these subjects include:

- *Highly technical or detailed issues of electronics or machinery*

- *Detailed knowledge of the furniture industry*

- *Color*

- *Spatial attributes*

- *Elements and principles of design (rhythm, balance, proportion, mass, form, etc.).*

Designers provide a terrific service when they carefully guide clients and all project participants along the project path in areas where individuals may be uncomfortable or unable to express their views.

BUILD TRUST THROUGH ONE-TO-ONE RELATIONSHIPS

Despite the value of standardized communications, designers and clients share much knowledge and information in situations that are not necessarily prescribed by the project process: frequent phone calls, short conversations during meeting breaks, an exchange of thoughts during an elevator or cab ride. These unplanned encounters, when designers and client interact one on one, can be effective ways to learn from one another, and they may serve as the building blocks for interpersonal relationships that outlast a single project and result in a long-term association between client and interior designer.

Such one-to-one relationships need not arise solely for the sake of project efficiency, but also out of common interests or sheer interpersonal chemistry, so it is important to cultivate an atmosphere where rapport can build between individuals on both sides of the project. Primarily, this atmosphere requires that designers see team members unrestricted by job titles and work responsibilities. The designer must recognize where natural "fits" occur, and allow those relationships to form.

ASK GOOD QUESTIONS AT THE RIGHT TIME

One of the most important skills in client management is the ability to ask excellent questions. The designer must draw out the client's desires in terms that are specific enough for the designer to deliver a solution that does not merely meet expectations, but totally satisfies.

LISTEN

Reaching a true understanding of what the client wants can feel like an exercise in mind reading, but it is really an exercise in effective listening. The designer must be invested in listening for answers—both to the questions that have been asked (as described above), and to those that have not.

RESPOND

The designer's ultimate response to the client will be the end product: the designed environment. But the client must sense a designer's responsiveness long before the project is completed. In fact, some clients expect a response from the designer daily, or even more often during critical phases of the project. The following precepts demonstrate "responsiveness" in action.

- **Keep the client informed.** *The client has a right to know what is happening. Regular status reports and meetings may be sufficient under normal circumstances. If a special issue or problem arises, the designer may need to offer updates via phone or e-mail, or even an impromptu meeting.*

- **Be available.** *The client is paying to be able to talk with the designer, whenever he or she wants, during working hours. So the designer must be accessible. If the designer needs to be inaccessible* *for a short period, he or she should leave detailed information with the person who answers the phone, on voice mail and, if possible, as an automatic response to e-mail. This way, clients will know not to anticipate an immediate response and/or whom to contact in the designer's absence.*

- Be prompt. *The designer should deliver standardized communications according to schedule (such as the second day after weekly meetings or on the first of the month). If the client asks for information off-cycle, the designer must provide it promptly. A design firm may have standards for appropriate response times, such as returning phone calls and e-mail messages within one business day. Even if a designer does not have the answer, he or she should return the call to indicate that someone is working on it.*

- Keep promises. *If the designer promised a report or answer by Monday, the client must receive it by Monday. If the designer promised to get back to the client on a special issue, it must not be allowed to slip through the cracks.*

- Don't just react, anticipate. *Responding does not necessarily mean reacting to a client's request, question, or concern; in fact, some of the most responsive actions are those that anticipate the client's need.*

GET THE PICTURE

Much of the interior designer's work produces outcomes that are visual. The client pays the designer to create something that "looks right." Although the client defines "right," the interior design team must understand and translate that definition into a physical solution that lives up to the client's vision. To reach such an understanding, the designer must ask effective questions (as described above). Additionally, the designer and the client must share a "visual vocabulary" so that the design team understands the aesthetic perceptions the client puts behind such terms as "global," "first-class," "collegial," "warm," "modern," "high-tech," "nice but not too nice," and "colorful."

BE EFFICIENT

In years past, getting information to and from the client could add days and even weeks to the design process. The mere act of sending drawings for review, even with express delivery service, could take a day or more for a client cross-country. But current technology and alternative business practices allow clients and designers to use information immediately. For instance, electronic media technology allows both designers and clients to transmit information without delay. Internet or web-based tools allow designers to post drawings electronically for immediate review by a client who can offer quick feedback by e-mail or conference call. Designers who avail themselves of such technologies can trim time off the overall project schedule, or at least conserve time for more value-added activities.

Technology is not the only way to achieve greater efficiency in communication. Innovative changes in work process also can accelerate work routines. An alternative to the traditional "go-away-and-work" model is the *charrette* process. Charrettes are workshops that involve the client's decision makers and the designers working and collaborating directly to achieve immediate results.

Be a Business Consultant

Interior design for corporate and professional services clients is the strategic exercise of design principles to satisfy business objectives. As such, the people who work in corporate interior design must be not only creative but also business minded. Designers must understand the business problem as deeply as they understand the design problem. Thus, the members of an interior design team are business consultants in the eyes of their clients—and must live up to the rising expectations for this breed of service provider. This section continues to emphasize the drive for total client satisfaction, and describes several consulting tactics interior design professionals can use to advance their client relationships.

DEFINE GOALS AND CONSTRAINTS

Thinking like a business consultant means knowing what the client hopes to achieve, then developing a strategy for reaching that end. Thus, when meeting with a client regarding a new project, the designer's first order of business is to learn where the client wants to go. What will make the project a success in the client's eyes? This is the designer's first opportunity to ask effective questions, as described above. In particular, some of the most critical questions, as a new project begins, are about goals and constraints.

- Goals. *What does the client want? What is the organization's business mission? By what criteria does the client measure success? What does the client envision in terms of outcome? Who must the client satisfy? What message should this facility project? Learning about the client's goals will help the designer understand what the interior design solution needs to accomplish.*

- Constraints. *What are the client's limits? What potential "inhibitors" might stand in the way of achieving or framing the client's goals? The designer's questions should drive at customary constraints such as budget, time frame, and design standards, as well as less-expected issues such as density targets (square feet per person), national purchasing contracts, and reuse of existing assets.*

Doubtless, the client's goals and constraints may present numerous contradictions. The designer must reconcile these contradictions and define a solution that achieves the appropriate balance between considerations.

PROVIDE THE EXPERT OPINION

As insightful and educated as clients may be, they are not responsible for understanding the many interior design possibilities for the spaces they manage. Their time and attention are occupied by a host of other issues. So they hire interior designers to provide them with excellent ideas, solutions and service.

Notice that last word, *service*. It is not "servitude." Accepting an interior design assignment does not place the designer in bondage to the client's beliefs. As business consultants, designers have a professional obligation to educate and guide the client. Any proposed solutions must reflect the designer's best assessment of how to reach the client's business goals. Although designers should take the client's preferences into account, they need not propose a mere regurgitation of those preferences. The clients deserve educated advice, not just "yes."

Of course, the client is not obligated to take the designer's advice. In fact, it is the client's prerogative to make a decision that the designer deems "wrong." If the client insists on a direction different than the one the designer prefers, the designer must respect and support that decision (unless, of course, the direction violates local codes or the designer's code of ethics). The best the designer can do is educate the client on the benefits of investing in the proposed solution and make clear the consequences of the client's decision.

MAKE APPROPRIATE PROMISES

Because the designer is considered an "expert," the client will rely heavily on the designer's word. So the designer must be clear about what he or she can and cannot promise (recognizing once again that the complexity of the Project Circle leaves so many factors beyond the designer's immediate control). For example, a designer can promise a delivery date for drawings, but cannot guarantee a firm date for completion of construction. A designer can provide a statement of probable cost, but cannot define a precise budget without qualified bids from the marketplace.

AVOID AND RESOLVE CONFLICTS

Most conflicts in client relationships arise from "misses"–misunderstandings, miscommunications, miscalculations, missed deadlines. While these misses can occur on either side of the relationship, any problem can be construed as a negative reflection on the interior designer ("You should have warned us . . ."; "You should have anticipated this . . ."; "You should have known what I meant . . . "). Thus, the designer must take strategic and proactive steps to avoid conflict and resolve disputes should they arise. The designer must always remember to think of the relationship with the client as a business relationship, and to document it carefully.

For example, designers must ground their aesthetic recommendations on a business-based rationale. If clients are to believe in and support the designer's ideas, they need evidence that the recommendations are sound. Sufficient grounds for a client to spend thousands to millions of dollars to implement a design solution do not include gut instinct, intuition, or a sense of art. Therefore, when presenting ideas, the designer must provide more substantiation than a mere "trust me." For example, in making lighting recommendations, the designer can educate the client that 30 percent of electric costs are spent on lighting and show how a proposed lighting solution may actually save at the bottom line. This way, even if conflicts do arise, they likely can be discussed in terms of logic, reason, and business realities. When designers rely on such a business-based rationale, they can avoid arguments on subjective matters of taste, which are decidedly more difficult to reconcile.

Because the designer is considered an "expert," the client will rely heavily on the designer's word. So the designer must be clear about what he or she can and cannot promise . . .

Another useful strategy is to make documentation a discipline. By keeping a record of decisions and communication between interior design team and client, the designer creates an information source of value to both parties and the entire design team. Particularly when a discrepancy arises, the designer will have ready access to the facts needed to resolve the issue quickly and with minimal disruption to the project. In addition to the expected documentation such as contracts, proposals, drawings, correspondence, schedules, and cost estimates, designers' files should grow as they add e-mail messages and notes from meetings and phone conversations. If possible, designers should take advantage of electronic storage, whether on individual workstations, shared networks, or project websites, to make it easy for team members to locate, retrieve and share documentation.

TRANSFORM CLIENTS INTO APOSTLES

The interior designer is in business not just to satisfy clients' objectives, but also to accomplish his or her own business vision. Fortunately, one follows the other. In the best of relationships, designer and client become "patrons" for one another. A patron is a person chosen, named, or honored as a special guardian, protector, or supporter. As the designer guards, protects, and supports the client's business initiatives through design, the client will support and advance the designer and his or her reputation.

As we have seen, when clients are totally satisfied, they are far more likely to rehire the designer. The result is not a mere project relationship, but an enduring account-based relationship, in which the client becomes "apostle" and returns again and again for the designer's trusted expertise and support.

But there is more. As mentioned earlier in this chapter, apostles are not just loyal, but so satisfied they will recommend a service to others.[4] Thus, as satisfied customers become apostles, the designer gains not just long-lasting accounts, but new relationships as well.

RECOGNIZE HUMAN NEEDS

For all its bottom-line concerns, business is still a human endeavor. Designers may speak in terms of "clients," "organizations," and "enterprise," but they deal on a day-to-day basis with human individuals. And success, or total client satisfaction, depends on the general contentment (or even delight) of these human beings. Therefore, the interior designer as business consultant must take action to make personal connections with these people, treating them with the genuine respect and care they crave.

Schneider and Bowen suggest that human needs are so important that when a service provider fails to gratify them, customers can feel outrage, and conversely, when the service provider succeeds for customers, this success can generate exceptional delight. Borrowing concepts from psychology, philosophy, and personality theory, they maintain that businesses can make or break the client's experience according to three basic human needs: security, justice, and self-esteem.[5] The designer who violates trust in these areas faces great difficulty trying to "change the resulting outrage to satisfaction, much less delight." Threats to a person's physical or financial security are particularly difficult to overcome. A challenge to justice or fairness amounts to violation of trust—which also is hard to rise above.

Suffice it to say that designers must seek to understand the client's human concerns. One person may worry about making a safe journey from old to new space. Another may have anxieties about individual job security. Still another may experience stress under intense workloads that interfere with his or her quality of life. Although the designer may not be able to mitigate such issues through design work, a designer's willingness to hear and understand personal challenges may provide the client with a sense of relief. Also, the designer may build a friendship that not only strengthens the client relationship, but also enriches the designer personally.

MEASUREMENT

By and large, interior designers have measured quality by relying on intuition, or only the most basic of measurements to evaluate the success of their work. A designer might track the number of clients who answer "yes" to questions such as "Would you hire us again?" or "Would you give us a positive reference?" Perhaps the nearest the interior design industry has come to a method of scientific evaluation is the Post Occupancy Evaluation (POE). Typically, the POE is conducted six to twelve months after occupants move into a designed environment. The objective is to assess how people are functioning in the space. Ideally, the same population would have participated in a baseline evaluation to see how they measured the prior environment before the interior design project began. Such measures of quality can't help designers to ask whether their practices really do the job. Even with comparative data, so many factors may have changed during a move that survey respondents may be unable to isolate their feelings for the design of the facility; their opinions may be influenced by longer commutes, changes in child-care routine, difficulty finding a parking place, or new phone or computer systems —factors outside the interior designer's control. In addition, such measurements are purely historic: they define a level of acceptance at a moment in time—*how we have done.*

Most important, these measures do not convey *how we are doing.* They cannot help improve performance during the process. If these traditional attitudes toward measuring client satisfaction are ineffective, and total client satisfaction is the goal, then how will we know when we have achieved it? Is there a reliable way to track and measure the client's satisfaction? Yes. This section describes a system that designers can use to measure their success according to client-defined criteria.

Process/Outcome Measurement System

The alternative to traditional methods of measuring the client's satisfaction with the interior designer's work is a method for measuring the value of services in light of client requirements. In this client-based method, "quality" has a unique definition for each assignment, because every client has a range of goals that, in combination, make their project unlike any other. The interior designer's role is to understand those goals and deliver an appropriate solution in response to each client's objective. This method is notable because it separates the client's *encounter* with the designer from the ultimate *artifact* produced by the project. That is, the method evaluates client satisfaction in two distinct areas: the *process* of the interior designer's work and the *outcome* of that work.

Not coincidentally, we will discuss *process* first. Clients who express satisfaction with the process generally also express satisfaction with the outcome. A positive project experience predisposes the client to a positive feeling about the outcome, whereas a negative project experience will bias a client negatively toward the end result.

By and large, interior designers have measured quality by relying on intuition, or only the most basic of measurements to evaluate the success of their work.

Measuring Quality of Process—The Journey

The process is the experience of the client and others involved in the project as they move toward completion of the designed environment. If the current environment is Point A and the new environment is Point B, then process measures are the vector connecting the two points.

The process can be viewed in two categories: delivery and experience. *Delivery* measures are typical measures used as part of any project management process—variables such as fee compliance, schedule compliance, and resource allocation. *Experience* is more intangible and focuses on the client's relationship with the interior designer—the designer's communication, knowledge, empathy, timeliness, and so on.

EXPERIENCE

Customers expect good experiences, and they deserve them. The project team's responsibility is not only to solve problems but also to take the client through the journey of solving the problem, making it a collaborative exercise. An interior designer's future economic growth lies in the value of the experiences he or she provides to clients; goods and services are not enough. The journey is as important as the destination. A client's experience through the project process plays a pivotal role in the client's overall satisfaction with a project. Many experiences are characterized in "moments of truth"—such as when a consultant surprises the client with an immediate response or, conversely, fails to return a phone call. Experiences can play a negative role and decompose the client's perception of the interior designer in a very short time, regardless of how talented a project team is or how good the solution is.

DELIVERY

Given the complexity of the Project Circle—with its web of relationships, alliances, partners, contractors, and subcontractors—many extraneous factors contribute to and influence an interior designer's service delivery. Even with a designer's best intentions, sometimes projects cannot be completed on time or within budget. However, customers expect results, delivered on time, within or under budget. And the minimum expected from the interior designer is compliance with approved, well-communicated and formalized schedules, budgets, timelines, and deliverables. These delivery-focused aspects of the project process are understandably of concern to clients who want to achieve bottom-line results.

Measuring Quality of Outcome—The Destination

The outcome is the completion of the designed environment, and it can be seen from both a *physical* and a *behavioral* perspective. Naturally, an interior design project will change the physical space in functional and environmental terms. And such physical changes can profoundly influence the overall behavior of the organization and its culture, image, and effectiveness. While interior designers can make a clear and tangible impact on the physical outcome, the behavioral outcomes are, arguably, more critical to the client organization.

PHYSICAL OUTCOME

The physical elements of a space are perhaps the most beloved by interior designers because they are the elements designers can influence directly. Any interior design project includes a planning or programming phase in which the client's specific requirements are captured, quantified, and approved. The requirements may include headcount projections, cost information, spatial layout information, and equipment information.

BEHAVIORAL OUTCOME

Interior designers do not simply design a physical environment in a vacuum; they create a space within the context of the client and its business and behavioral objectives. Environments designed to reinforce business objectives are a strategic means of facilitating the achievement of business objectives. Whether the client aims to achieve worker collaboration or improve recruitment or raise employee satisfaction, the designed space plays a role—either as reinforcement or as detriment.

The System in Practice

Even when using a client-defined approach to measurement, in which the client defines "quality," the interior designer bears the responsibility of tracking, measuring, and acting on results. Implementing a measurement system may be a challenge for interior designers who have never used a formal evaluation method, yet the process is not difficult.

- **Expectations.** *Before the project begins, members of the client team meet to identify their expectations.*

- Qualifications. *During the project and often at completion of each project phase, the design team uses the expectations document (de-*

scribed above) to remain focused on meeting the client's explicit goals and objectives. The interior designer and client work together to make any mid-course corrections that may be necessary.

- Evaluation. *At the close of the project, members of the client team share their perceptions to evaluate how well their expectations were met.*

- Action. *After evaluation is complete, the interior designer disseminates the results of the client's assessment among design team members and prepares a plan for acting on the feedback.*

The measurement system outlined here is a framework, and interior designers or design groups will need to customize it to align with their own business objectives. No matter how the process is customized, designers must use the ultimate process with the following basic guidelines in mind:

- *Formalize the process consistently within the organization.*

- *Integrate measurement with the project process.*

- *Administer by a disinterested and unbiased party; project owners must not measure their own work.*

- *Communicate so all members of the firm can embrace and easily understand the process.*

- *Use the process to enrich the entire organization, not just a few individuals or even individual project teams; share knowledge gained from the process throughout the organization so all can learn from each project.*

The benefits of the process/outcome measurement system are at least threefold.

1. The mere fact that a designer measures satisfaction, as well as the scientific means the designer uses, will raise the client's perception of the designer's value. That is, the fact that a designer asks for feedback may be even more important than the suggestions the client makes. Moreover, any ongoing quality process is likely to improve ongoing client relationships.

2. The designer will be in a constant process of discovery to identify flaws in the work product and project process. This process will equip the designer to take immediate steps to solve problems in current projects. And, perhaps even more important, the designer will know where to make process improvements that will benefit projects and clients in the future.

3. The designer can substantiate his or her value with tangible measures of performance linked to business strategy, and can communicate these measures to clients, prospective clients, and counterparts.

CONCLUSION

If designers and clients carefully attend to and nurture client relationships, they both gain immediate and long-term benefits.

- *Diligent relationship management is likely to produce a positive experience for all parties involved in the project at hand. And there is great value in that intangible sense of pleasure and accomplishment. For design firms, for instance, an individual designer's sense of personal satisfaction adds value because a satisfied employee translates to low employee turnover.*

- *Experiences that not only satisfy but also delight the client engender a sense of loyalty that keeps the client coming back for more. Because it is easier and less costly to develop business with current clients than to find new ones, the designer benefits financially.*

- *In the ultimate client relationship, a delightful experience—or a series of them—converts the client to an apostle: an uninhibited, credible, no-cost marketer for the designer. In addition, apostles contribute to a firm's long-term viability because they bolster the designer's reputation and attract new customers, not to mention continued business from the apostle itself.*

Even though relationship management may not be the designer's craft, it certainly is an art form worthy of study—and mastery—by designers who are serious about creating a sustained, lucrative business that delivers meaningful results and meets human needs or, better yet, creates human delight.

Notes

1

Heskett, James L., W. Earl Sasser, and Leonard A. Schlesinger, *The Service Profit Chain*, The Free Press, New York, 1997, p. 81.

2

Schneider, Benjamin, and David E. Bowen, "Understanding Customer Delight and Outrage," *Sloan Management Review*, Fall 1999, p. 35.

3

Heskett et al., *The Service Profit Chain*, pp. 86–87.

4

Heskett et al., *The Service Profit Chain*, pp. 84–85.

5

Schneider and Bowen, "Understanding Customer Delight and Outrage," p. 38.

Bibliography

Barabba, Vincent P., and Gerald Zalman. *Hearing the Voice of the Market: Competitive Advantage through Creative Use of Market Information*. Cambridge, MA: Harvard Business School Press, 1991.

Brand, Stewart. *How Buildings Learn: What Happens After They are Built*. New York: The Penguin Group, 1995.

Drucker, Peter F. *The Effective Executive*. New York: HarperCollins, 1996.

Heskett, James L., W. Earl Sasser, and Leonard A. Schlesinger. *The Service Profit Chain*, by *Command Performance: The Art of Delivering Quality Service*, featuring articles from the *Harvard Business Review*, preface by John E. Martin; 1994 Harvard Business Review/New York: The Free Press, 1997.

Neuhart, John, Marilyn Neuhart, and the Estate of Ray Eames. *Eames Design: The Work of the Office of Charles and Ray Eames*. New York: Harry N. Abrams, 1989.

Sennett, Richard. *The Corrosion of Character*. New York: Norton, 1998.

40

Gauging a Successful Design

THE EDITORS AT INTERIOR DESIGN

Architect Guillermo Garita, of the firm Datum/0, recalls a client whose office he recently completed and who contacts Garita for approval prior to any adjustment greater than replacing a light bulb—such is their dedication to the integrity of his final design, their faith in his judgment, and their ultimate satisfaction with the results.

In conclusion, Kronick invokes the hackneyed but nonetheless appropriate adage: "You're only as good as your last project."

THE PROJECT REINFORCES THE CLIENT'S IDENTITY

The design should not only address the pragmatic aspects of the program—quotidian concerns such as adequate storage, ample daylight, and technological and acoustical requirements—but reflect and reinforce the client's identity. Whether the client is a huge corporate brand or a small business, interior design is both a means of self-expression and a potential marketing tool—one of the most concrete and lasting reasons for a company to present its values and ideologies to the public. Interior environments can function as a device to attract and retain clients, to generate a positive buzz about the company, and to support employee recruitment and retention efforts. The project should be sensitive to such possibilities of reinforcing corporate messages.

An interior design project may require working within a preestablished aesthetic, in the form of color, furniture, or materials standards (or a more ambiguous sense of corporate culture), to ensure continuity of an existing identity. More often than not, the design process provides an opportunity for clients to reinvent or revitalize their brand. And for less-established organizations, the design process itself can be a first step toward inventing and leveraging an identity.

Residential design projects require channeling the idiosyncrasies of a discrete individual, a couple, or a family. Todd Davis of Brown Davis Interiors considers a design successful if it projects "a beautiful look that may not be for everyone, but that suits the client's needs and reflects their personality." Visitors should recognize and appreciate the home's aesthetic merits, he says, regardless of whether it meshes with their particular taste.

Reflecting the client's identity involves a collaboration; designers should avoid imposing a predetermined "look" on a space in favor of working to manifest the client's particular creative vision.

The Space Is Functional, Not Just a Decorated Shed

A successful project is not only appealing to the eyes and to the senses but supports the movements, operations, circulation, and activities of its occupants. It is not a stage set, but a habitable space suited to the occupants' living and working patterns. It should be comfortable and functional, without contrivances. An open-plan office, for instance, may be a desirable concept in theory, but is inappropriate for a corporate client with strict privacy requirements. If the project at hand is a health-care facility, adequate room for equipment, medical maneuvers, and visitors should be accounted for. It is the designer's role to advocate for the specific functional needs of those who occupy the space—whether or not their input has been formally solicited.

The Environment Has Ambiance and Atmosphere

Looks, function, and contextual appropriateness are key deliverables. But positive user experience also involves creating a welcoming ambiance. Because spatial surroundings are perceived viscerally as well as visually, the psychology of a space is a fundamental attribute of the overall design.

The Project Is Delivered on Time and within the Designated Budget

Completing the project within the prescribed budget and time frame is paramount. Scheduling delays and escalating costs can offset the impact of an otherwise good design. Mastering this concept involves managing expectations—creating a realistic time frame and informing the client about what can and cannot be accomplished within the allotted budget.

Prioritizing aesthetics at the expense of timing and economics benefits neither the client nor the contractors and project managers whose livelihood depends on these deliverables. Contractors, of course, bear much of the burden when it comes to scheduling, and their merit is evaluated primarily by whether they can deliver the project on time. Jana Bailey, managing director of administration and facilities for the multinational bank HVB, has overseen numerous office renovations, upgrades, and relocations during her tenure. Having construction completed—and employees moved in—"is of utmost importance," she insists, "a crucial mark of success for upper management."

Planning and foresight, to say nothing of experience, are instrumental in creating realistic budgets and schedules. Bailey learned on the job; for a recent design of the corporation's New York headquarters, she scrutinized variables and standards from many previous HVB projects to create an ample budget that would nonetheless be mindful of financial resources. The result? "The budget was never an issue," remarks Richard Kronick, the project architect. "It was like hitting paydirt," he claims, to be given a budget and time frame that were based on realistic information.

The Design and Construction Processes Run Smoothly

After five successive and invasive renovations to a single residence over the course of 25 years, seasoned client Ginny Blair built her next home from the ground up. The overwhelming success of her latest endeavor, she claims, was less a matter of meeting schedule and budget (both were overshot), but of "things running smoothly. I am willing to overlook issues of budget and timing only if I think the project is going to be done the right way, and to my high standards." She is also more likely to embrace progressive ideas when she trusts the design team implicitly. And success, says Mark Oller, "is when a client trusts you." While delayed delivery assures a disgruntled client, an effortless process, in contrast, generates confidence in the designer's capabilities.

The Creative Process, and the Resultant Design, Stimulate the Intellect

Although all designers interviewed claimed that making money is a top priority in maintaining a business, profit alone cannot guarantee a project's success. Designing for the sake of a paycheck is neither rewarding nor conducive to inspired results. "As designers, we need a little more motivation," says Tony Chi, president of Tony Chi & Associates, who seeks opportunities to flex and engage his intellectual muscles, to implement creative strategies. Although any design effort involves some measure of compromise, even budgetary and scheduling constraints can inspire innovative solutions if the designer has the resources and inspiration to use such limitations to his or her advantage.

Good design can inspire and support productivity, creativity, social interaction, and a sense of community, as well as physical and psychological well-being. Individual, subjective taste obviously plays a role, but good design is more universal . . . .

Jerry Kugler, president of Kugler Tillotson Associates, a lighting design concern, actively seeks partnerships with clients and designers who offer "no restraints, who say 'let's do the best we can do,' who toss around ideas without a specific end point in mind." Engineer Thomas Polise also prefers to partner with designers seeking creative collaboration and challenging projects. Such efforts, he claims, "often lead to breakthrough design."

The Design Has a Long Shelf Life

Longevity, as well as anticipation of and adaptability to a client's future needs, is an important benchmark of success. Longevity entails not only a timeless design that transcends visual cliches and trends, but also one that performs adequately over time. Many corporate clients outgrow a site even before construction has been completed. How well the design anticipates such circumstances generally depends on the designer's foresight and an open-ended dialogue with the client. Withstanding the test of time requires a degree of prescience, but growth and change can be anticipated by asking the right questions, knowing the client, and being observant.

The Project Receives Recognition from the Critical Community, in the Form of Awards or Press Coverage

"It's important to subject yourself to peers and editors," says Kronick, who nonetheless insists that there are "only a handful of design magazines we care about being published in." Editorial coverage is "good to toss on a resume, to attract clients, and to keep clients happy," he says. Although Kronick does not gauge the success of a project by whether or not he receives an award or editorial coverage, he does believe peer review is a great means "of self-check, to ask how I am doing."

Other firms beg to differ, asserting that media opportunities are the best way to gain visibility, generate new business and larger clients, and even command higher fees. "It is so important for a young firm to get editorial coverage for exposure and validation," says Mark Oller, who finds that many clients keep tabs on industry hot-shots and newcomers by reading industry and consumer magazines. He cites a recent project that became one of his most successful business generators to date: a small rendering of an unbuilt project published in a design magazine. Thomas Polise agrees that magazine coverage constitutes success by fostering business-to-business activity; many designers, he says, have discovered and hired his firm as a direct result of published projects. Media exposure is a cost-effective marketing tool, particularly for practices and designers who cannot afford the high cost of advertising.

The Project Is Influential beyond the Borders of the Design Industry

Does the design (or the process of realizing it) hold some societal value, such as revitalizing a run-down neighborhood, providing a source of beauty or inspiration to visitors, or otherwise enriching the lives of a community of people? Tony Chi, for instance, exploits the didactic possibility of strategic design, and strives to educate developers about their power to favorably impact urban planning. Contributing to the fabric of a project's surrounding environs is one indicator of success. Another may be employing environmentally conscious design practices or educating a client about them.

The Design Has Artistic Integrity

For Todd Davis, "successful results are a combination of a professional relationship and creating a beautiful product." Budget, scheduling, functionality, client response—these are tangible, quantifiable elements of successful design. But artistry is the dividing line between successful design and good design. Judging a project's artistic merits takes into account aesthetics, innovation, ambiance, substance, and the design's underlying ideas and values. Good design can inspire and support productivity, creativity, social interaction, and a sense of community, as well as physical and psychological well-being. Individual, subjective taste obviously plays a role, but good design is more universal: a commingling of the senses and the intellect that transcends subjective taste.

FOSTERING SUCCESSFUL RESULTS

Given the aforementioned attributes and indicators of success, how does a designer work toward ensuring a successful outcome? What methodologies should be employed? Although there are no hard-and-fast rules, a little common sense will go a long way. To wit:

Know the Client, and Know Who Calls the Shots

The design team should determine not only the client's intent and expectations, but also who calls the shots and what internal politics may affect the project's outcome. Whether the client is a young married couple or a large multinational conglomerate, "there is one person in the position of authority who is willing to make things happen and to operate in a smart way," says Todd Davis. "In the beginning, we ask clients who all the decision makers are, and let them know that we need to have access to them." It is very difficult, he asserts, to address the concerns of someone who seemed peripheral to or absent from the planning stage and who suddenly emerges, five months into the project, with legitimate thoughts and concerns.

"We often have to sift through fifty layers of bureaucracy to get to the main people," says Mark Oller. Likewise, Tony Chi attests to the value of navigating bureaucracy to ensure partnership with "permanent, rather than transitory" employees, those who are committed to the project's success and who will see it through to completion. Be sure that designated in-house project managers have a direct conduit to upper management and are communicating from the top down, says Richard Kronick. Furthermore, communication breakdowns can also occur between a company's international headquarters and its regional offices, he cautions.

With respect to residential projects, a husband and wife may have divergent goals and expectations. Beware the couple who claim that only one will actually be involved in the project, says Todd Davis. Both are invariably involved and will want to voice their opinions.

Manage Information and Communicate

Designers should partner closely with the client, and with attendant members of the design team, to gather essential information up front. Communications lines should be open at all times to ensure that the designer can respond to evolving needs and shifting priorities. Kronick champions the importance of listening to what the client is saying, as well as to what they are holding back. For various reasons, "the client isn't always in a position to tell you what they want," he warns.

Jana Bailey advises design practitioners to ensure that information flows in both directions: from client to designer, and from designer to client. She insists, for instance, on informing everyone—from the CEO to the IT staff to the maintenance crew—about move-in dates and scheduling. "Moving can be a scary process," she says, but fear can be minimized by awareness and knowledge of what to expect and when to expect it.

Communicate not only about practical matters of timing, furniture delivery, and flooring installation, but about "ideas and concepts," says Todd Davis, who has found that such dialogue is a major contributor to a successful outcome. Unfortunately, "intelligent discussion back and forth is what's so often missing from the process," he says.

Be Flexible and Expect Surprises

The design process has a certain improvisational quality. Thus, serendipity and surprise are inherent aspects of the medium. With few exceptions, projects need to be planned up-front, off-site, and in the mind. Major financial and emotional resources are at stake. It is impossible to envision exactly how the final product will gel, despite renderings, models, and computer drawings approximating the results. Nor will mock-ups or prototypes capture the experience of walking through the completed space. There are no dress rehearsals in design; raw materials are gathered, and the process unfolds in waves of effort. Although any artistic process requires a gestation period to let ideas take hold, interior designers generally do not have the luxury of much more than refining an idea once the construction process moves forward; few clients have the budget (or the patience) to scrap a completed project and start over again when the desired outcome is not achieved. Successful design results from managing surprises and overcoming impediments along the way. Because of the amount and nature of anxiety this process breeds, gaining client trust is paramount.

Mutual Respect Is Key

Interior designers should respect their clients and their clients' needs and demands. But practitioners in the field should cultivate respect by upholding professional standards and ethical conduct. Clients should respect the designer's talent, experience, education, instincts, and vision, and the designer should likewise defer to the client as "the executive decision maker," says Todd Davis. "We tailor very much to the individual client. It's our job," he says, "to collaborate"—not dictate. The designer's *modus operandi* is one of interpretation, of translating the client's verbalized goals into a physical, three-dimensional result.

Interior design is a profession, not just an art form. A client who calls that into question hinders the design. Moreover, designers should know where to draw the line—when to challenge clients beyond their comfort range (and when not to), how to lead them to inspired, even progressive, results. The commitment and faith of the client is of utmost importance. But nurturing a successful relationship with a client entails upholding a measure of professional distance, says Davis, "not about becoming best friends with the client." He considers if a potential client is someone "we could work with from a professional standpoint. There are a lot of people who don't have the proper boundaries when it comes to their homes," who are too controlling, who take the job too personally. "We are public servants," says Tony Chi. Nonetheless, designers are hired for their strategic opinions, and should not compromise their professional integrity by bowing to the client's every whim.

Be Realistic, but Don't Let Pragmatism Inhibit Creative Thinking

Maintaining a logical outlook concerning practical matters and economic limitations is paramount. But when it comes to the ideation processes, designers should think outside the box, and should not be afraid to challenge the client in innovative directions, says Chi. "After all, what do you have to lose?" The worst thing that can happen, he says, is that a client vetoes an idea that requires too much of a leap of faith. Oller, however, tells a cautionary tale. He cites a presentation that he and his partner labored over on behalf of a client who initially expressed the desire to explore a bold new direction. After many brainstorming sessions, significant market research, and reviewing the final concepts with scores of peers, "we thought we nailed it. But when we presented the proposal, the client freaked out because it was such a departure," laments Oller, who realized that the client was not committed to moving forward, but was actually looking for reassurance that their current image and look sufficed. The proposal was shelved and the client opted for small gestures instead, drastically reducing the scope of the project. Oller demurs, however, that if he had read all the cues, he probably would have discerned the client's hesitancy from the very beginning.

Davis issues the following warning to clients: "I may present concepts that will stretch your mind." It is better to offer innovation up front, "even if it's a little unsettling," than after the window of opportunity closes, he believes. "One of the biggest compliments I can get," continues Davis, "is when a client comes up at the end of a project and says how they finally understood why I pushed them in a particular direction." Letting the client know what is possible within the allotted budget—and what is not possible—is a savvy move, says Ginny Blair: clients (herself included) have an interesting way of mobilizing resources for ideas that initially seem out of reach if they are sold on the design.

Assemble a Successful Team

"We are in the people business," says Tony Chi, "so chemistry is the back-bone" of a project. The design team—the contractor, the HVAC and lighting consultants, the client (to say nothing of the architect and the interior designer)—should mesh. Although many firms offer both architecture and interior design services, interior designers frequently interface with architects from outside practices. Kronick offers advice to that effect. He examines the team already involved in a project (with corporate clients, he has discovered that project managers, engineers, and real estate consultants are sometimes hired first) to evaluate whether or not he can collaborate happily over a period of six months to a year. "I ask who I can have a dialogue with, and who I like." Although fees and credentials are important, "comfort level" is more so. "By the end of a project, people often end up hating each other—it is easy to become antagonistic," exclaims Oller. Although this does not preclude a successful outcome, "when you end on good terms with a client, they are more likely to recommend you to others," and to give you repeat business.

Be Selective about Choosing Projects

It is generally evident from the beginning whether or not a project bears the earmarks of potential success. Are client expectations suitably realistic? Are there opportunities for creative expression? Is the design team "simpatico" with the client? By extracting as much information about the project, the client, and the target objectives up front, and weighing the pros against the cons, a designer can predict probable outcomes. A job may be lucrative, but will it involve hand-holding a high-maintenance client, compromising design integrity, or sacrificing sanity?

"From a visual and artistic standpoint, we ask ourselves if this is a project we are going to be proud of," says Davis. "We assess in the very beginning so that in the end the client is pleased and feels they have spent their money well."

Thomas Polise, who heads a small, family-owned engineering practice, says his firm "definitely picks and chooses who we work with," including both designers and clients. Although "clients who pay" are his number-one consideration, it is just as important, he says, to ascertain whether the team involved is likely to give total commitment to the project. "Can the client or designer allocate the time to give 100 percent?" he asks.

Oller looks for clients who are "unique, fun, and irreverent," but also "that I'm comfortable with. I don't ever want to feel like the client and I are on completely different pages." A comfortable dialogue and a "cool, casual, creative atmosphere," make the process enjoyable and worthwhile.

In the end, such insights are a result of the "gut instinct" that comes from maturity and experience, says Chi. If the project does not seem likely to lead to a successful outcome, it probably won't.

Bibliography

Bachelard, Gaston, Maria Jolas (Translator), and John R. Stilgoe. *The Poetics of Space*. Boston: Beacon Press, 1994.

Hodgins, Eric. *Mr. Blandings Builds His Dream House*. Chicago: Academy Chicago Publishers, 1999.

Huysmans, Joris-Karl. *A Rebours*. Mineola, NY: Dover Publishing, 1969.

Vidler, Anthony. *The Architectural Uncanny: Essays in the Modern Unhomely*. Cambridge, MA: MIT Press, 1994.

Wharton, Edith, and Ogden Codman Jr. *The Decoration of Houses*. New York: W.W. Norton & Company, 1997.

ACKNOWLEDGMENTS

My sincere appreciation and thanks to the contributors of this book and the editorial advisory members who so graciously shared their time, expertise and knowledge in support of this book and the interior design profession.

I thank *Interior Design* magazine's Mark Strauss, Publisher; Cindy Allen, Editor-in-Chief; and Yasmin Spiro for their endless dedication and commitment in making this book come to life.

My appreciation to McGraw-Hill's Scott Grillo, Elizabeth Schacht, Margaret Webster-Shapiro and Steven Melvin for their tireless assistance throughout this demanding undertaking and to Wendy Lochner whose original vision for this book got us all started.

I am grateful to Joseph Guglietti, Guglietti Design, for the clarity he possessed in creating the graphic design for the book and for his ardent efforts in producing a beautiful jacket design.

I appreciate the efforts of the University of Chicago's Writing Department, led by Kathryn Cochran, who brought heightened clarity to the manuscript.

My thanks to Harvey Sussman, Kate Scully, Tom Charlton, and Carlye Lay of Northeastern Graphic Services for their exceptional diligence in setting the type for the book and their skillful trafficking of all the material that came their way.

A very special heartfelt thanks to Judith Joseph of Joseph Publishing Services who single-handedly led and coordinated this team and the entire effort from inception to completion. Her wisdom, commitment, dedication to excellence and good humor made this project a truly wonderful experience.

And finally my love and thanks to my husband Neil and my daughter Emanuela for possessing a never-ending enthusiasm.

—Cindy Coleman

ADVISORY MEMBERS

Dr. Francis Duffy

Neil P. Frankel, FAIA, FIIDA

Edward C. Friedrichs, FAIA, FIIDA

Linda Keane

Eva Maddox, FIIDA

Mayer Rus

CONTRIBUTORS

Pamela Anderson-Brulé, AIA
Anderson-Brulé Architects

Gina A. Berndt
The Environments Group

Michael Byun
Gary Lee + Partners

James D. Carter, AIA, IIDA, IFMA
The Hillier Group

Travis Clifton
Gary Lee + Partners

Stuart Cohen, AIA
Stuart Cohen and Julie Hacker Architects

Cindy Coleman
Frankel + Coleman

Joseph T. Connell, IIDA
The Environments Group

James P. Cramer, Hon AIA, Hon. IIDA
Greenway Consulting

Orlando Diaz-Azcuy
Orlando Diaz-Azcuy Designs

Tamara Dinsmore
Skidmore Owings & Merrill

Paul Doherty, AIA
The Digit Group

Dr. Francis Duffy, RIBA
DEGW

Cheryl P. Duvall, FIIDA
avancé, LLC

Traci A. Entel
Katzenbach Partners, LLC

Neil P. Frankel, FAIA, FIIDA
Frankel + Coleman

Edward C. Friedrichs, FAIA, FIIDA
Gensler

David Grout
Gary Lee + Partners

Beth Harmon-Vaughan, FIIDA
HOK

Judith Heerwagen, Ph.D.
J. H. Heerwagen & Associates, Inc.

Jo Heinz, FIIDA
Staffelbach Design Associates

Richard J. Jantz
Quatararo & Associates

Jan Johnson, IIDA
Teknion

Jon R. Katzenbach
Katzenbach Partners, LLC

Linda Keane
SAIC and the University of Wisconsin/Milwaukee

Mark Keane
SAIC and the University of Wisconsin/Milwaukee

Debra Lehman-Smith, IIDA
Lehman-Smith + McLeish

Barry B. LePatner, Esq.
Barry B. LePatner & Associates, LLP

Jessica Lipnack
NetAge, Inc.

Eva Maddox, FIIDA
Eva Maddox Associates, Inc.

Karen Mahony
Katzenbach Partners, LLC

William J. Mitchell
Massachusetts Institute of Technology (MIT)

William Odell, AIA
Helmuth, Obata, Kassabaum

Derrell Parker, IIDA
Parker & Scaggiari, Inc.

David J. Pfeffer, Esq.
Barry B. LePatner & Associates, LLP

Daria Pizzetta, AIA
Hardy Holzman Pfeiffer Associates

Lisbeth Quebe, FSMPS
RTKL

Kathy Rogers
Jacobs Facility

Frederick J.Schmidt
The Environments Group

Andre Staffelbach, FIIDA, ASID
Staffelbach Design Associates

Jeffrey Stamps, Ph.D.
NetAge, Inc.

Karen Stephenson, Ph.D.
Net Form International

Robert T. Sutter, AIA, NCARB
The Switzer Group

Greg Switzer, AIA, NCARB
The Switzer Group

Sharon Turner
Swanke Hayden Connell Architects

Eric Wagner
Quartararo & Associates

Kevin Walz
Walzwork Inc.

Gary E. Wheeler, FASID, FIIDA, AIA
Perkins & Will

LIST OF CONTRIBUTORS WITH BIOGRAPHIES

PAMELA ANDERSON-BRULÉ, AIA
Anderson-Brulé Architects

Pamela Anderson-Brulé is a founder and the president of Anderson-Brulé Architects, Inc. Pamela has been visionary in her creation of a firm that serves clients with design excellence, as well as strategic planning for architectural design. The breadth of her experience over the last 21 years has been dedicated to public and institutional architecture. She is an expert in public process and facilitation and is able to carefully plan projects so that they can allow for appropriate public participation, which is meaningful and helpful in the development of the design.

GINA A. BERNDT
The Environments Group

As a founding Principal of The Environments Group, Gina serves in numerous capacities, from directing the firm's marketing strategy to leading selected client engagements, and serving on the firm's management committee and on the firm's board of directors. Gina has lead projects for such clients as PricewaterhouseCoopers, Chubb Group of Insurance Companies, and the law firm of Schiff Hardin & Waite.

MICHAEL BYUN
Gary Lee + Partners

Michael Byun received a Bachelor of Science from the College of Architecture and Environmental Design at Arizona State University in 1990. Since that time, Michael has been the lead designer on a number of award-winning commercial projects including American Guaranty Corporation/Chicago, Madison Dearborn Partners/Chicago, and McKinsey & Company/Chicago.

JAMES D. CARTER, AIA, IIDA, IFMA
The Hillier Group

James Carter has been with The Hillier Group since 1986 and is known for his strategic thinking, strong design talents, and his ability to interpret and satisfy clients' needs. Mr. Carter is devoted to the advancement of interior architecture, technically and aesthetically, and to the influence of spaces on the quality of life.

TRAVIS CLIFTON
Gary Lee + Partners

Travis Clifton received a Bachelor of Architecture from Cornell University in 1988. Travis has worked on a number of notable commercial projects including Madison Dearborn Partners/Chicago, Russell Reynolds Associates/Chicago, and Winston & Strawn/New York in addition to her vast experience in high-end residential work and participation in product design for Knoll Studio's Lee Lounge Collection.

STUART COHEN, AIA
Stuart Cohen and Julie Hacker Architects

Mr. Cohen is a partner in the firm of Stuart Cohen & Julie Hacker Architects, specializing in custom residential projects. He is a full professor of architecture at the

University of Illinois, Chicago where he teaches architectural design. Mr. Cohen has authored numerous articles on architecture and served as a corresponding editor for *Progressive Architecture* magazine.

CINDY COLEMAN
Frankel + Coleman

Editor-in-Chief Cindy Coleman is a graduate of the Art Institute of Chicago in Interior Architecture. She is a partner in the Chicago-based design and communications firm, Frankel + Coleman and the former executive editor of the International Interior Design Association's magazine *Perspective*. She is a frequent contributor to many of the nation's design-related magazines and newsletters, advocating the value of design.

JOSEPH T. CONNELL, IIDA
The Environments Group

As a Principal at The Environments Group, Joe is a senior client contact and leads a studio of design professionals. Joe has extensive experience with engagements centered around work process transformation, alternate space use strategies and scenarios, and environmental image and identity solutions. Having managed projects for such industry leaders as Herman Miller, Interface, and The Hull Group, Joe has been integral to redefining workplaces.

JAMES P. CRAMER, Hon. AIA, Hon. IIDA
Greenway Consulting

Founder and Chairman of Greenway Consulting, James P. Cramer works with some of the world's most innovative design firms and provides strategic consulting services for architecture, design and construction associations in Europe, North America, and Japan. Cramer is the author of *Design + Enterprise, Seeking a New Reality in Architecture* and edits the annual *Almanac of Architecture and Design* and the monthly *Design Intelligence*.

ORLANDO DIAZ-AZCUY
Orlando Diaz-Azcuy Designs

Cuban-born Orlando Diaz-Azcuy is one of America's most respected and awarded designers for elegant, disciplined, and intelligent work of innovative economy. He was among the first in his profession to be inducted into the industry's prestigious Hall of Fame, sponsored by *Interior Design* magazine and in 1993 he was recognized by the readers of *Interior Design* as one of the five most respected designers in the United States.

TAMARA DINSMORE
Skidmore Owings & Merrill

A graduate of Parsons School of Design in New York, Tamara joined Skidmore, Owings & Merrill (SOM) in 1984. Her tenure at SOM has taken her around the world several times, working in London and on projects in Dubai, Singapore, Beijing, and the Philippines. Today, Dinsmore heads up the SOM Interiors Group in San Francisco, California.

PAUL DOHERTY, AIA
Clearbuilt Technologies
Paul Doherty, a Registered Architect, and principal partner of Clearbuilt Technologies, a management consulting and information technology services firm based in Memphis with offices worldwide, is one of the industry's most sought-after lead consultants of information technology and the new economy. He is an author, educator, analyst, and consultant to Fortune 500 organizations and to the most prestigious architectural, engineering and contracting firms in the world.

Dr. FRANCIS DUFFY, RIBA
DEGW
Francis Duffy is an architect educated at the Architectural School in London, and at Berkeley and Princeton. He is a founder of the international architectural and consultancy practice DEGW. His specialty is improving the design of the working environment to respond to the changing needs of people and organizations. Duffy was President of the Royal Institute of British Architects (RIBA) from 1993 to 1995, and was awarded the CBE in 1996. Duffy's latest books, *The New Office* and *Architectural Knowledge*, reflect his commitment to DEGW and the RIBA.

CHERYL P. DUVALL, FIIDA
avancé, LLC
Cheryl P. Duvall, FIIDA is founder of avancé, LLC, a business and workplace consulting practice. Prior to forming avancé, she was a Senior Vice President with Griswold, Heckel & Kelly Associates, Inc. The focus of her practice has been leading project teams in the development and delivery of specialized services, such as innovative officing, change management, and post-occupancy evaluations.

TRACI A. ENTEL
Katzenbach Partners, LLC
Traci A. Entel is an Engagement Manager at Katzenbach Partners, LLC. In addition to her work in pharmaceuticals and information technology, she assisted in designing her firm's New York City office. Traci graduated from Dartmouth College with a degree in Economics.

NEIL FRANKEL, FAIA, FIIDA
Frankel + Coleman
Previous to accepting a position in the graduate faculty at the University of Wisconsin/Milwaukee, School of Architecture and Urban Planning, Neil Frankel was responsible for Skidmore, Owings & Merrill's Chicago architectural interiors practice. Frankel's professional career has been characterized by a commitment to excellence in design and client service. Elected into the *Interior Design* magazine Hall of Fame in 1994, Frankel served in 1998 as President of the International Interior Design Association (IIDA).

EDWARD C. FRIEDRICHS, FAIA, FIIDA
Gensler
Architect Edward C. Friedrichs is CEO and President of Gensler, the global architecture and design "giant." After graduating from the University of Pennsylvania, he

joined the firm in 1969. Ed is now based in San Francisco after directing the firm's Los Angeles office for 24 years.

DAVID GROUT
Gary Lee + Partners

David Grout received a Bachelor of Science from the College of Architecture and Environmental Design at Arizona State University in 1990. He has worked as the lead designer for the American College of Surgeons' Chicago Headquarters, Latham & Watkins/Chicago, and Winston & Strawn/Los Angeles in addition to participating in the Knoll Studio's Lee Lounge Collection and Holly Hunt's Indigo Collection.

BETH HARMON-VAUGHAN, FIIDA
HOK

Beth Harmon-Vaughan's distinguished practice spans 25 years and has produced an award-winning body of work. Now a practice leader with HOK Sport, Venue + Event Architecture in Kansas City, Missouri, she serves as the current chair of the Foundation for Interior Design Education Research (FIDER) Board of Directors and is a Fellow and the past international president of International Interior Design Association (IIDA).

JUDITH HEERWAGEN, Ph.D.
J. H. Heerwagen & Associates, Inc.

Judith Heerwagen is an environmental psychologist whose research and writing have focused on workplace ecology and the human factors of sustainable design. She has a B.S. in Communications from the University of Illinois/Champaign-Urbana and a Ph.D. in Psychology from the University of Washington. She currently has her own research and consulting business in Seattle.

RICHARD J. JANTZ
Quatararo & Associates

As Vice President, Mr. Jantz oversees and participates in all aspects of Quartararo & Associates project management activities. Proficient in the use of management information systems, Mr. Jantz is adept at applying the appropriate technology and methods to individual projects and clients.

JAN JOHNSON, IIDA
Teknion

Jan Johnson is the Director of Workplace Learning for Teknion, where she acts as a resource to clients and design organizations as they address workplace issues and focuses on the correlation between business strategies and the planning, design and management of work environments.

JON R. KATZENBACH
Katzenbach Partners, LLC

Jon Katzenbach is the Senior Partner of Katzenbach Partners, LLC, a consulting firm in New York City that specializes in leadership, team, and workforce performance. Mr. Katzenbach has written numerous articles and books on team and workforce performance, including *Peak Performance*, *Teams at the Top*, *Real Change Leaders*, and the best-selling *The Wisdom of Teams* and the recently released *The Discipline of Teams*, both of which he co-authored with Douglas K. Smith. In addition, he is editor of *The Work of Teams*, a *Harvard Business Review* compendium.

LINDA AND MARK KEANE
SAIC and the University of Wisconsin/Milwaukee
Mark and Linda Keane are partners in the architectural practice, STUDIO 1032. They currently teach at the University of Wisconsin/Milwaukee and the Art Institute of Chicago. Their production of "Animated Architecture: A Retrospective of the work of Mark and Linda Keane" earned them a PBS Emmy in 1996. Active in K–12 Design Education, the Keanes have published two CD-Roms titled *Architecture: An Interactive Introduction* and *WsRcIaGpHeT: The Geometry of Wright*.

DEBRA LEHMAN-SMITH, IIDA
Lehman-Smith + McLeish
Debra Lehman-Smith, co-founding partner and lead designer at Lehman-Smith + McLeish, PLLC, is noted within the business and design communities for her ability to merge her clients' business objectives and aesthetic preferences. Ms. Lehman-Smith is an internationally renowned interior designer with an extensive portfolio of projects for government agencies and Fortune 500 companies. She was voted *Interiors* magazine's Designer of the Year in 1995; that same year she was inducted into the *Interior Design* Hall of Fame.

BARRY B. LEPATNER, Esq.
Barry B. LePatner & Associates, LLP
Mr. LePatner is the founder of Barry B. LePatner & Associates, LLP, attorneys at law. For over two decades, his law firm has been prominent in addressing the business and legal issues affecting the design profession.

JESSICA LIPNACK AND JEFFREY STAMPS, Ph.D.
NetAge, Inc.
Jessica Lipnack, CEO, and Jeffrey Stamps, Ph.D., Chief Scientist, are co-founders of NetAge, developing software and services that help people work together. Their 20 years of research and experience have taken them around the world to work with companies and public sector organizations, including Apple Computer, AT&T Universal Card Services, General Electric, Hewlett-Packard, Intel, NCR, Shell Oil Company, Steelcase, and the United Nations. They have written six books, most recently the best-selling *Virtual Teams* (John Wiley & Sons, 2000).

EVA MADDOX, FIIDA
Eva Maddox Associates, Inc.
Eva Maddox is a Creative Strategist and creator of Branded Environments, a research-based design approach that identifies and integrates a client's DNA into tangible experiences through the use of proprietary tools such as Patterning and the Strategic Opportunity Matrix. Ms. Maddox is co-founder of Archeworks, an alternative design school in Chicago.

KAREN MAHONY
Katzenbach Partners, LLC

Karen Mahony is an independent consultant affiliated with Katzenbach Partners, LLC. Karen graduated from Oxford University with a degree in Chemistry and later received a Masters in Water Management from King's College, London University. Karen currently lives in London with her husband and daughter.

WILLIAM J. MITCHELL
Massachusetts Institute of Technology (MIT)

William J. Mitchell is Professor of Architecture and Media Arts and Sciences and Dean of the School of Architecture and Planning at MIT. Among his publications are: *E-Topia: Urban Life, Jim—But Not As We Know It* (MIT Press, 1999); *High Technology and Low-Income Communities*, with Donald A. Schön and Bish Sanyal (MIT Press, 1999); and *City of Bits: Space, Place, and the Infobahn* (MIT Press, 1995). Before coming to MIT, he was the G. Ware and Edythe M. Travelstead Professor of Architecture and Director of the Master in Design Studies Program at the Harvard Graduate School of Design.

WILLIAM ODELL, AIA
Helmuth, Obata, Kassabaum

William Odell is a design principal of HOK, St. Louis and co director of HOK's Sustainable Design Group. He recently co-authored, with HOK's Sandra Mendler, *The HOK Guidebook to Sustainable Design* (John Wiley & Sons, Inc., 2000).

DERRELL PARKER, IIDA
Parker & Scaggiari, Inc.

Derrell Parker is a partner in the contract/commercial interior design firm Parker Scaggiari. He is an Adjunct Instructor at the School of Architecture, Interior Design and Landscape Architecture at the University of Nevada/Las Vegas (UNLV). Derrell became involved with the Legislative Coalition of Interior Designers/Nevada (LCIDN) and currently serves on the "Model Legislation" Task Force for NCIDQ.

DAVID J. PFEFFER, Esq.
Barry B. LePatner & Associates, LLP

David Pfeffer specializes in design and construction law at Barry B. LePatner & Associates, LLP, where he represents corporate and institutional clients, design professionals, and real estate owners.

DARIA PIZZETTA, AIA
Hardy Holzman Pfeiffer Associates

Daria Pizzetta is a senior associate and administrative director of the Interiors department in the New York office of Hardy Holzman Pfeiffer Associates (HHPA). Ms. Pizzetta chairs the AIA/New York State Chapter Interiors Committee and is a member of the American Library Association and the Library Administration and Management Association.

LISBETH QUEBE, FSMPS
RTKL

Lisbeth Quebe has led firm-wide marketing for RTKL and Perkins & Will. Her contributions to the design industry were recognized in 1993 when she received a Fellowship in the Society of Marketing Professional Services and SMPS's highest accolade, the 1995 National Marketing Achievement Award.

JEN RENZI
Interior Design *Magazine*

Jen Renzi is a senior editor at *Interior Design*. Prior to joining the magazine in 2000, she was a business strategist for a web-based retailer of furniture and home accessories, and has more than seven years of communications experience in the fields of product design and fine art. Renzi holds a B.A. in Art History from Yale and received her M.A. in Cinema Studies from New York University.

KATHY ROGERS
Jacobs Facility

Kathy Rogers has 25 years of experience in the interior design profession. She has worked with The Stubbins Group in Boston, Gensler & Associates in Denver and Salt Lake City, HOK in St. Louis, and Jacobs Facilities in St. Louis and Washington, D.C. In addition to serving as project manager for large corporate and government projects, she headed Interiors Groups at HOK and Jacobs Facilities in St. Louis.

MAYER RUS

Former Editor-in-Chief Mayer Rus was the fourth person in *Interiror Design* magazine's 70-year history to hold this esteemed title. In 1990, Rus joined the staff of the magazine, having graduated from Yale University with a degree in Art History. Rus has written for *The New York Times*, *Vogue*, *Artforum*, and *Elle*. His book, *Loft*, was published by The Monacelli Press in 1998 and is now in its third printing. Rus is the current Design Editor at *House & Garden*.

FREDERICK J. SCHMIDT
The Environments Group

Fred Schmidt is the Managing Principal of The Environments Group. In this role, he serves as chair of the Management Committee, which guides the operational, marketing, financial and administrative functions of the firm. Prior to assuming his general management position, he founded the firm's facility programming practice.

ANDRE STAFFELBACH, FIIDA, ASID and JO HEINZ, FIIDA
Staffelbach Design Associates

Andre Staffelbach and Jo Staffelbach Heinz are Principals of Staffelbach Design Associates, a Dallas-based international interior architectural, planning and design firm founded in 1966. They have served in various leadership positions in industry design and qualification associations and worked to further design education.

KAREN STEPHENSON, Ph.D
Net Form International

Karen Stephenson, president of NetForm International, teaches at Harvard University, the University of London, MIT, and UCLA. Internationally recognized in network theory and practice, she has been featured in leading journals and presses (*The Economist*, *Forbes*, *WSJ*, *Fast Company*, *London Times*, *Washington Post*, the *FT*, and *The New Yorker*). She received her Ph.D. in Anthropology at Harvard University, an M.A. in

Anthropology at the University of Utah, and a B.A. in Art and Chemistry at Austin College in Texas.

ROBERT T. SUTTER, AIA, NCARB
The Switzer Group

Mr. Sutter is President of The Switzer Group and has been with the firm since 1983. He interfaces directly with the executive level team members to provide guidance and professional overview for the development of an effective and comprehensive project plan.

GREGORY SWITZER, AIA, NCARB
The Switzer Group

Gregory Switzer is a principal with The Switzer Group, Inc., and he is responsible for marketing and external communications as well as The Switzer Group's Atlanta operations. He works with clients and project teams to attract new projects and establish project direction.

SHARON TURNER
Swanke Hayden Connell Architects

Sharon has 18 years of experience as a strategic space planner working with major international corporations. Her expertise in understanding corporate culture and business objectives and their impact on workplace design has resulted in her being a regular contributor to the debate about workplace strategy in both the press and on the speaking circuit. Her understanding of highly specialized facilities with many components brings a strong foundation to her projects.

ERIC WAGNER
Quartarao & Associates

As project manager, Eric Wagner oversees and participates in all aspects of Quartararo & Associates' project management activities. Proficient in the use of management information systems, Mr. Wagner is adept at applying the appropriate technology and methods to individual projects and clients.

KEVIN WALZ
Walzwork Inc.

Kevin Walz designs space, products, and makes art from his studio in Rome and his office in New York, Walzworkinc. He is a partner in KorQinc, a company that makes products of virgin recycled cork in Sardinia.

GARY E. WHEELER, FASID, FIIDA, AIA
Perkins & Will

Gary Wheeler, Board Member and Managing Director of Perkins & Will's Chicago office, is an established leader in the interior design profession. As president of the American Society of Interior Designers from 1994 to 1995, he advocated enhanced education and greater understanding in the business world for the strategic power of good design.

INDEX